NetWare 3.12 CNA Tasks

Task	CNA Tool	Exercise	Page
NetWare Directory Structures			
Creating Directories	FILER—Directory Contents—Ins	Case I	464
Removing Directory Branches	FILER—Directory Contents—Del	Case I	464
Monitoring Directory Growth	LISTDIR /A		341
Building Drive Mappings	MAP U:=*path*—network	Case II	350
	MAP S1:=*path*—search	Case II	350
NetWare Security			
WorkGroup Managers	SYSCON—Supervisor Options	Case III	439
Assigning User Passwords	SYSCON—User Information	Case III	437
Granting User Rights	SYSCON—User Information	Case III	442
Restricting Directory Rights	FILER—Current Directory Info	Case III	443
Calculating Effective Rights	FILER—Current Directory Info	9.2	464
Defining Security Attributes	FILER—Current Directory Info	Case III	444

Task	CNA Tool	Exercise	Page
Network Management			
Building the NetWare Log	NetWare 3.14 Worksheets	Appendix C	731
Tracking Network Information	NDIR		343
Customizing Boot Files	INSTALL.NLM—System Options		504
Writing System Login Scripts	SYSCON—Supervisor Options	Case III	570
Writing User Login Scripts	SYSCON—User Information	Case III	570
Installing Network Applications	INSTALL		532
Building a NetWare Menu System	NMENU *menuname*	Case IV	572
Performing Network Backup	SBACKUP.NLM		555
Establishing Remote Management	RCONSOLE		564
Performance Management			
Monitoring Server Performance	MONITOR.NLM	Case V	684
Optimizing Server Performance	SET	Case V	684

TALK TO NOVELL PRESS AND SYBEX ONLINE.

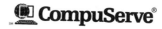

NOVELL'S ®
CNA CLM Study Guide

DAVID JAMES CLARKE, IV

Novell Press, San Jose

PUBLISHER: *Rosalie Kearsley*
EDITOR-IN-CHIEF: *Dr. R. S. Langer*
EXECUTIVE EDITOR, NOVELL PRESS: *David Kolodney*
ACQUISITIONS EDITOR: *Dianne King*
DEVELOPMENTAL EDITOR: *David Kolodney*
EDITOR: *Armin Brott*
PROJECT EDITOR: *Abby Azrael*
TECHNICAL EDITOR: *Mark D. Hall*
NOVELL TECHNICAL ADVISOR: *Kelley Lindberg*
BOOK DESIGNER: *Helen Bruno*
PRODUCTION ARTIST: *Charlotte Carter*
TECHNICAL ARTIST: *Cuong Le*
SCREEN GRAPHICS: *Cuong Le*
CARTOONIST: *Mike Kim*
DESKTOP PUBLISHING SPECIALIST: *Dina F Quan*
PROOFREADER/PRODUCTION COORDINATOR: *Janet K. Boone*
INDEXER: *Lynn Brown*
COVER DESIGNER: *Archer Design*
LOGO DESIGN: *Jennifer Gill*
COVER PHOTOGRAPHER: *Pierre Yves Goavec*

Screen reproductions produced with Collage Plus.

Collage Plus is a trademark of Inner Media Inc.

SYBEX is a registered trademark of SYBEX Inc.

Novell Press and the Novell Press logo are trademarks of Novell, Inc.

TRADEMARKS: SYBEX has attempted throughout this book to distinguish proprietary trademarks from descriptive terms by following the capitalization style used by the manufacturer.

Every effort has been made to supply complete and accurate information. However, SYBEX assumes no responsibility for its use, nor for any infringement of the intellectual property rights of third parties which would result from such use.

Library of Congress Card Number: 93-84947
ISBN: 0-7821-1139-4

Manufactured in the United States of America

Warranty and Disclaimer

WARRANTY

SYBEX warrants the enclosed disks to be free of physical defects for a period of ninety (90) days after purchase. If you discover a defect in the disks during this warranty period, you can obtain a replacement disk at no charge by sending the defective disk, postage prepaid, with proof of purchase to

SYBEX Inc.
Customer Service Department
2021 Challenger Drive
Alameda, CA 94501
(800) 227-2346
Fax: (510) 523-2373

After the 90-day period, you can obtain a replacement disk by sending us the defective disk, proof of purchase, and a check or money order for $10, payable to SYBEX.

DISCLAIMER

SYBEX and Novell, Inc. make no warranty or representation, either express or implied, with respect to this software, its quality, performance, merchantability, or fitness for a particular purpose. In no event will SYBEX or Novell, Inc., their distributors, or dealers be liable for direct, indirect, special, incidental, or consequential damages arising out of the use or inability to use the software, even if advised of the possibility of such damage.

The exclusion of implied warranties is not permitted by some states. Therefore, the above exclusion may not apply to you. This warranty provides you with specific legal rights; there may be other rights that you may have that vary from state to state.

I dedicate this book to the human race for never ceasing to amaze me.

Acknowledgments

So many people to thank, and so little time. What a cliché, but it's true. I believe we are all molded by our past and present experiences. With this in mind, I would like to take a moment to thank the sculptors of my personality. It all started with my family—literally. My wife, Mary, deserves the most credit for supporting my work and bringing a great deal of happiness to my life. Thanks! To Leia—my new daughter—this book pales in comparison to her grand arrival. Thanks for providing my life with much-needed perspective.

I owe a tremendous amount to my parents for their unending support and devotion. They were very active artists in molding my life. I couldn't have done any of this without their help. In addition, my sister, Athena, and her new family, Ralph and Taylor, deserve kudos for supporting me through the wild times—childhood. Thanks to my second family for opening their hearts to me. Don and Diane for their kindness, and Keith and Bob for their wisdom. Finally, I owe a great deal to Dr. James Buxbaum and Rene Mendoza—my mentors and extended family.

Speaking of virtual family, I would like to thank all of the frightfully talented students who have shared their dreams with me over the past five years. Talk about molding...thanks to the Wednesday night therapy crowd at Clarity, weekend Jack and the heart attacks, the beta classes from DVC, and all the curious night owls at Las Positas College. Let's not forget the Irvine Valley classes and their wonderful sense of humor. It's safe to say that my students have had a profound effect on my life. Draw your own conclusions.

In publishing this book, there are numerous friends to thank. Lori Jorgeson, for her relentless help and timely editing. We make a great team. Armin Brott, for his remarkable editing talent and creative abilities. Thanks for polishing the personality of my book. Mark Hall for his technical expertise and valuable input. Abby Azrael for spearheading the project, the SYBEX production team for putting the book together, and Lynn Brown for a wonderful index. And of course, Mike Kim for his magical cartoons and inspiring sense of humor. You are a genius. And

speaking of inspiration, thanks to Altima for an incredible notebook and Tears for Fears for musical therapy. Finally, thanks to David Foster and K.C. Sue at Novell Education for their support and contribution.

Probably the most important architects of *Novell's CNA Study Guide* are Rose Kearsley, Peter Jerram, and David Kolodney—they are Novell Press. Thanks Rose, for your friendship, enthusiasm, and support; Peter for your wisdom and ideas; and David for your exceptional guidance. I owe a great deal to all of you for banding around a common idea and bringing this book to life. What a great team.

I saved the best for last. Thanks to YOU for caring enough about your NetWare career to buy this book. You deserve a great deal of credit for your enthusiasm and dedication—this education can change your life. Good luck with NetWare, and enjoy the book!

QUOTE
Welcome to your life, there's no turning back!

Tears for Fears

CONTENTS AT A *Glance*

TABLE OF Contents

Appendices 691

Foreword

The goal of Novell Education is to help "accelerate the growth of network computing." Over the past ten years, we have developed a global network of Novell Authorized Education Centers and Certified NetWare Instructors. Together we provide state-of-the-art training to approximately 300,000 students each year. While we at Novell are very close to attaining our goal, many of you have a different goal in mind—"to accelerate the growth of your network computing career." That's fine, because your goals and ours work hand-in-hand through Novell's technical certification programs.

We began the NetWare certification program seven years ago with the introduction of the Certified NetWare Engineer (CNE) credential. A few years later we added the Enterprise CNE (ECNE)—an advanced degree of sorts. These programs are complex, time-consuming, and broad in scope. They are intended for experienced networking professionals who intend to design, install, and maintain large NetWare LANs.

What about system administrators? What about managers who aren't interested in the intricacies of Ethernet frame formats or routing algorithms? What about the managers who only have time to add users, fix the printer, and grab a quick lunch? For you, the CNE program is overwhelming and unnecessary. For you, we have created the Certified NetWare Administrator (CNA) program. The goal is to provide focused training which addresses the daily roles and responsibilities of the NetWare system administrator. The program is simple and straightforward.

In a continuing effort to provide the most complete education possible, we have worked together with Novell Press to create *Novell's CNA Study Guide*. This guide is an invaluable tool intended to accompany Novell course materials,

instructor-led courses, and computer-based training. It offers additional exercises, electronic simulations, and practice tests—all in an easy-to-understand format. *Novell's CNA Study Guide* is another tool which puts all of us closer to attaining our goals.

Good luck.

David Foster   Education Program Services Manager

Mitch Carter   CNA Program Manager

*I*ntroduction

The README.NOW File

So you want to be a Certified NetWare Administrator—a noble proposition!

Life as a CNA is both exciting and rigorous. It is an obstacle course of unpredictable network challenges—connectivity problems, user complaints, security violations, and so on. But just like any obstacle course, the goal is to finish in one piece. Don't worry, you'll do great.

In this book, we will walk through the pitfalls and triumphs of NetWare system management—together. You will acquire a NetWare "Utility Belt" filled with wondrous CNA tools, including Novell resources, advanced management techniques, security procedures, and sample login scripts. In addition, we will learn about NetWare directory structures, drive mapping, security, menu utilities, printing, network management, and LAN optimization. Wow!

To aid you on this noble journey, *Novell's CNA Study Guide* is filled with valuable learning tools: icon-oriented text, 3-D graphics, laboratory exercises, technical tips, simulations, crossword puzzles, and most importantly, a bank of new, original CNA test sample questions. The goal is to present a superset of Novell's CNA program in an effective, entertaining manner. I think you'll like it.

Before we get started, let's warm up with a brief preview of what's ahead. We'll start with an overview of the similarities and differences of NetWare 2.2 and NetWare 3.12. Then, we will explore the layout of the land—icons, exercises, diskettes, and that sort of thing. Finally, we'll finish with some HELP and, of course, the Bottom Line.

NetWare 2.2 vs. NetWare 3.12

QUOTE

Never invest in anything that eats or needs repairing!

Billy Rose

NetWare 2.2 and 3.12 represent Novell's seventh and eighth generations of their best-selling NetWare network operating system. NetWare 2.2 is a complete 16-bit solution that meets the needs of small businesses, professional offices, workgroups, and departments. It is a nonmodular "rock" of technology that provides excellent file and printing services, but no support for multiple protocols or interconnectivity. NetWare 3.12, on the other hand, is a fully modular 32-bit operating system that supports simultaneous access from DOS and non-DOS workstations. In addition, NetWare 3.12 takes full advantage of the 32-bit file server architecture by providing nearly unlimited access to shared disk storage, memory, and interconnected LANs.

NetWare 2.2 is Playdoh—rigid, and moderately useful. NetWare 3.12 is Legos—modular, robust, and fun. Let me explain. Playdoh is flexible at first. It can be easily molded into any shape. But once it dries, it becomes an inflexible rock—no changes. Similarly, NetWare 2.2 is flexible at first. But once the operating system has been installed and the NET$OS.EXE file has been configured, the system manager is pretty much stuck with the design.

Legos, on the other hand, can be easily assembled into a beautiful palace and then dismantled and reassembled into a race car. This level of modular versatility is evident through NetWare 3.12's NetWare Loadable Module (NLM) architecture. With this design, all LAN facilities can be loaded and unloaded at will. NetWare 3.12 consists of three components: the NetWare file system, the system executive, and NLM software bus. With the right imagination, the system manager can build any type of network—small, medium, or large.

In this book, we will focus on the strengths and weaknesses of NetWare 2.2 and 3.12 by splitting them into two distinct halves. The NetWare 2.2 CNA program focuses on the role of the CNA as the manager of an apartment building—with rooms, tenants, security, and a LAN laundry room. The NetWare 3.12 CNA program moves up in scope to a luxurious hotel resort. You will wear many management hats including architect, handyman, house detective, and interior decorator. These analogies will serve to highlight the key differences between NetWare 2.2 and 3.12. In addition, they will provide some common ground for understanding the roles and responsibilities of the NetWare system manager.

Two Books in One!

QUOTE

Some books are to be tasted, others swallowed, and some few to be chewed and digested.

Francis Bacon

Novell offers CNA 2.2 and CNA 3.12 certifications. In an effort to be both clear and complete, we have broken this book into two programs—the NetWare 2.2 CNA program and NetWare 3.12 CNA program. The 2.2 CNA program is designed for system managers who work primarily with NetWare 2.2 LANs. The 3.12 CNA program is slanted towards the more advanced NetWare 3.12 platform. The trick is to cover both programs completely without too much repetition. We chose to approach each version autonomously; that is, each program is covered completely in its own half of the book. We avoid repetition because NetWare 2.2 and 3.12 differ dramatically in their approach to system management. Each CNA program has its own unique focus. Think of it as getting two books in one—what a deal!

The first step towards becoming a Certified NetWare Administrator is a clear understanding of NetWare basics. It all begins with Part I: CNA Fundamentals. In Chapters 1 and 2, we will lay the foundation for the NetWare CNA program—Microcomputer/DOS Fundamentals and NetWare Basics. NetWare 2.2 system management is comprehensively detailed in Part II: The NetWare 2.2 CNA Program. Chapter 3 starts the NetWare 2.2 CNA program with a discussion of NetWare directory structures and drive mapping. Security is next, with an outline of NetWare 2.2's multilayered security model. Chapter 5, NetWare 2.2 Utilities, introduces you to some of NetWare's most useful and productive CNA tools.

Chapter 6, NetWare 2.2 Network Management, provides an in-depth discussion of the CNA's key system management responsibilities—login restrictions, login scripts, user interface, and backup. Finally, the NetWare 2.2 CNA program ends with a journey into the world of printing installation and management.

The exciting journeys of NetWare 3.12 CNAs are chronicled in Part III: The NetWare 3.12 CNA Program. Chapter 8 explains NetWare directory structures and drive mapping. Security, Chapter 9, delves deeply into the maze of login restrictions and access rights. In addition, the security chapter provides you with some easy-to-follow models for high and low levels of NetWare 3.12 security. Chapter 10, NetWare 3.12 Utilities, focuses on the tools available for NetWare 3.12 CNA system management—menu utilities, command line utilities, supervisor utilities, and console commands. Chapter 11, NetWare 3.12 Network Management, provides an in-depth discussion of the NetWare 3.12 CNA's key system management roles and responsibilities. It begins with a peek at system management strategies, and then dives into login scripts, user interface, multi-protocol management, backup, and the remote management facility. Chapter 12 focuses on NetWare 3.12 printing installation, management, customization, and troubleshooting. Finally, the NetWare 3.12 CNA program ends with a journey into the world of NetWare 3.12 performance management. This is a special chapter that explains NetWare's performance management components and provides a checklist of strategies for monitoring and customizing NetWare 3.12 server performance. What a way to end.

In addition to the two NetWare CNA programs, this book includes a variety of valuable appendices. Appendix A is a comprehensive overview of Novell's education strategy. Warning: information contained in this appendix could change your life. Appendices B and C include rare NetWare 2.2 and 3.12 installation and management worksheets. These forms lay the foundation for your all important NetWare Log. Appendix D is filled with detailed answers to all of the lab and case exercises, and Appendix E is a dictionary of the acronyms used throughout the book. Finally, Appendix F provides you with a step-by-step stroll through the NetWare 2.2 simulation exercise—included on diskette, and Appendix G gives you a more in-depth look at the contents of the two diskettes included at the back of the book. Don't ignore the appendices—they're full of valuable CNA resources.

Are We Having Fun Yet!?!!

QUOTE

All animals except man know that the principal business of life is to enjoy it.

Samuel Butler

I couldn't have said it any better myself—so I won't.

The main goal of this book is to take the reader through a magic carpet ride of CNA responsibilities, tools, and technologies—nobody said it couldn't be fun! To accomplish this monumental task and cover the enormous wealth of NetWare knowledge, I have incorporated a variety of different learning tools: text and graphics, exercises, icons, and diskettes. Let's take a quick look.

TEXT AND GRAPHICS

The majority of the information is in the text. The format is interesting and I have made every effort to provide you with an enjoyable level of readability. Learning doesn't have to be torture. In addition, I have included "pull quotes" to highlight key concepts and milestones. This provides a whole new level of speed reading. Also, there are over 100 graphics to illustrate major technical points. They are clear and concise.

EXERCISES

The exercises provide you with hands-on experience. Concepts are important, but the real test is in the doing. There are over 30 original exercises that fall into four different categories:

> **Lab Exercises**—some call for written answers, but most are hands-on. These exercises are designed to provide the reader with "real-life" experience in implementing important CNA responsibilities. In addition, they help you to practice the CNA tools you have learned. Note—most of the Lab Exercises assume that you have access to a NetWare LAN. If you don't, we have made an on-line lab available to you

through LAN*imation*—refer to the Help! section of this introduction for more details.

Case Exercises—this is as real as it gets. You will manage, maintain, and troubleshoot an existing NetWare 3.12 LAN for Snouzer, Inc.—a pseudo-fictional doggie fashions company.

Matching Exercises—test your skills against four different matching exercises—covering topics such as Microcomputer Fundamentals and Performance Management Components.

Crossword Puzzles—have fun with three challenging puzzles—covering Part I, Part II, and Part III.

The answers to all of the exercises are included in excruciating detail in Appendix D.

ICONS

The icons are my pride and joy. These quips provide instant information in the form of Quotes, Knowledge, and Tips. Here is what they look like—

QUOTE
The Quotes add flavor from people more dazzling than myself.

KNOWLEDGE
Knowledge icons point out critical theories, concepts, and/or delectable facts.

TIP
Tips highlight time-proven management techniques and action-oriented ideas.

Refer to the icons throughout the text for additional information and added value. This strategy provides another level of speed reading.

DISKETTES

Diskettes have been included with *Novell's CNA Study Guide* to enhance and support your NetWare education. There are two 3$\frac{1}{2}$-inch high-density diskettes with compression. Inside you will find three surprises:

NEW CNA Test Questions—with help from Novell Education, we have developed a *new* set of CNA test sample questions. In electronic form, these questions can serve as invaluable study tools for the Net-Ware 2.2 and NetWare 3.12 CNA certification tests. In addition, this information is also useful in studying for the CNE and CNI certification tests.

NetWare Buyer's Guide—a complete electronic version of the latest *NetWare Buyer's Guide*. This guide provides on-line access to NetWare information in a hypertext database format (folio). CNAs can use the folio database to search for valuable information concerning NetWare documentation, education, products, and services. This is a comprehensive CNA utility tool.

NetWare 2.2 Installation Simulation—with the help of Novell Education, we have included a NetWare 2.2 Installation Simulation. This interactive tutorial walks you through the entire process of installing and customizing NetWare 2.2 servers, workstations, and routers. It's almost real. Refer to Appendix E for instructions.

There really is no substitute for personal, live training. But we have done everything we can to make this study guide almost as interesting. Some say this book has a mind of its own!

Help!

QUOTE

An ounce of action is worth a ton of theory.

Friedrich Engels

Inevitably, you are going to want to apply this great NetWare knowledge to some physical structure—a LAN perhaps. One assumes you will ACT on this book's CNA concepts, theories, methods, and procedures. It would be very irresponsible of me to abandon you at the very point you need the most help—real life! So in an attempt to provide you with the most complete assistance possible, I have created an organization called LAN*imation*. LAN*imation* is a team of CNEs, students, authors, and networking professionals who have banded together to offer NetWare assistance to readers of this book. We currently use a variety of different resources, including CompuServe, Internet, and World Wire. If you are interested in joining LAN*imation* or just need some help, contact us at any of the following locations:

Electronic Mail	COMPUSERVE at David James Clarke, IV—71700,403
	INTERNET at DCIV@Garnet.Berkeley.EDU
Phone	LAN*imation* at (510) 254-7283
Physical Mail	LAN*imation* at 140 Stein Way, Orinda, CA 94563-3431
World Wire (see explanation below)	(510) 254-1193 or local access number

In addition to LAN tips and answers, LAN*imation* supports a remote on-line NetWare LAN for readers who don't have a network of their own. You can use the system to complete the lab exercises, SNOUZER case studies, or just practice what I preach. The system is called World Wire, and it requires a PC, modem (14.4 Baud supported), and any communications software (see Chapter 2). A graphical user interface can be downloaded for free. Give it a try.

Bottom Line

QUOTE

The longer the island of knowledge, the longer the shoreline of wonder.

Ralph W. Sockman

The bottom line is this: *Novell's CNA Study Guide* covers all of the CNA and most of the CNE/CNI system management objectives.

If you are interested in obtaining any of these three NetWare certifications, you should definitely attend Novell-authorized courses. This book is designed to supplement Novell's traditional education methods. But it can also be used to supplement your practical knowledge and NetWare LAN experience. The information provided in this book is comprehensive, accurate, and Novell-compatible. Certification is within your grasp. In this book, we will cover three certification versions: NetWare 2.2, 3.11, and 3.12. The NetWare 3.11 and 3.12 material is covered together in the NetWare 3.12 CNA section. This is because 3.11 and 3.12 are nearly identical. They differ only in workstation software, documentation, NCP packet signature, menu software, backup, electronic mail, and alloc short term memory. In each of these cases a TIP is used to point out the differences.

Have a great time and good luck with NetWare. Enjoy the book!

"Faster than a speedy microprocessor,
more powerful than a file server,
able to solve printing problems in the blink of an eye.
Look! By the workstation, it's the ..."

CNA Fundamentals

So you want to be a Certified NetWare Administrator. A noble proposition. Life as a CNA is both exciting and rigorous. It is an obstacle course of unpredictable network challenges: connectivity problems, user complaints, security violations, and so on. But just like any other obstacle course, the goal is to finish in one piece. Don't worry, you'll do great.

In this book, we'll walk through the pitfalls and triumphs of NetWare system management—together. You will acquire a NetWare utility belt filled with wondrous CNA tools, including Novell resources, advanced management techniques, security procedures, and sample login scripts. In addition, we'll learn about NetWare directory structures, drive mapping, security, menu utilities, printing, network management, and LAN optimization. Wow!

To aid you on your journey, *Novell's CNA Study Guide* is filled with valuable learning tools: icon-oriented text, 3-D graphics, laboratory exercises, sample computer-based training, simulations, Q & A, and—most importantly—a bank of NEW CNA test questions. The goal is to present a superset of Novell's CNA program in an effective, entertaining manner. I think you'll like it. You be the judge.

Novell offers three CNA certifications—2.2, 3.12, and 4.0. In an effort to be both clear and complete, we have broken this book into two programs—2.2 and 3.12. The 2.2 program is designed for system managers who work primarily with LANs running NetWare 2.2. The 3.12 program is slanted towards the more advanced 3.12 platform. Each program corresponds with the appropriate 2.2 or 3.12 CNA certification. The trick is to cover both programs completely without too much repetition. We chose to approach each version autonomously—with each program covered completely in its own half of the book. We avoid repetition because NetWare 2.2 and 3.12 differ dramatically in their approach to system management. Each CNA program has its own unique focus. Think of it as getting two books in one—what a deal.

Before we dive into the first CNA program, NetWare 2.2, we need to spend a few minutes reviewing LAN fundamentals. The first two chapters of this book cover the basics of microcomputers/DOS and NetWare. Chapter 1, Microcomputer/DOS Fundamentals, provides a quick system management review of microcomputer and DOS concepts. Chapter 2, NetWare Basics, focuses on the fundamentals of LAN management and Net-Ware hardware/software basics. These early fundamentals will provide you with a holster for your NetWare system management tools. Once you acquire your NetWare utility belt, you will be ready to fill it with valuable CNA tools.

Let's begin with Microcomputer/DOS fundamentals.

Microcomputer/DOS Fundamentals

Before we dive into the glamorous pool of NetWare system management, we must put on our swimming suit of microcomputer/DOS basics. A fundamental understanding of microcomputers and DOS (Disk Operating System) is necessary to make the transition from the shallow end of stand-alone computing to the deep waters of network management. After all, you don't want to be swallowed by the Ethernet whitewash or devoured by the mainframe sharks.

In this chapter we will explore the basics of microcomputer hardware and DOS software. We will focus on how these components affect LAN connectivity and NetWare system management. The most important thing to get out of this chapter is an appreciation for the complex relationship between file server hardware (Intel-based microcomputers) and workstation software (DOS). Let's begin with microcomputers.

> The most important thing to get out of this chapter is an appreciation for the complex relationship between file server hardware (Intel-based microcomputers) and workstation software (DOS).

Understanding Microcomputers

Since its introduction in 1977, no other electronic component has altered the course of humanity's future more than the microcomputer. Its presence is evident in every aspect of our lives—our homes, our schools, our jobs, and our books. The microcomputer is also the basis of our local area networks—workstations and file servers.

The microcomputer architecture follows the same fundamental concepts as earlier computers. The basic functions of any computer, whether it's a micro-, mini- or gigantic mainframe computer, can be summarized into four basic operations:

- input
- processing
- storage
- output

Figure 1.1 graphically displays the relationship of these basic computer operations. Input is the process of feeding a computer raw data. Input tools include keyboards, mice, trackballs, and scanners. Some microcomputers even have voice-recognition systems which will allow users to input data by simply talking to their machines. This opens a whole new arena for psychiatrists and counselors.

Once data has been fed into the system, it waits in a buffer until the microprocessor is ready to process it. Data processing is performed by a critical computer component called the Central Processing Unit (CPU). The CPU consists of two components—the control unit and arithmetic/logic unit (ALU). We will discuss the details of microcomputer processing later in the chapter.

FIGURE 1.1

The Computer Model

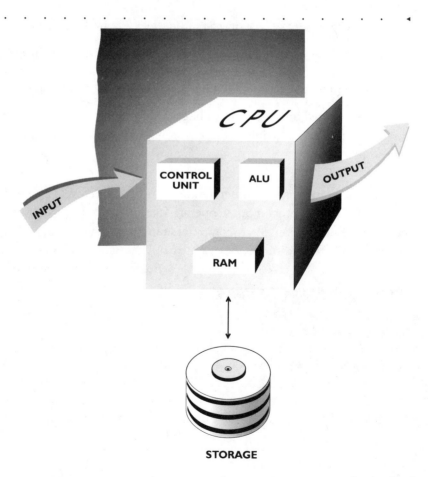

KNOWLEDGE

Processing includes a variety of different computer operations—classifying, sorting, calculating, recording, summarizing, combining, and separating. In reality, all of these complex operations are accomplished by seven simple arithmetic/logic tasks—addition, subtraction, multiplication, division, less than, greater than, and equal to. At the most elementary level, these seven tasks are the only things a computer can do!!

Once data has been input and processed, it becomes useful *information*. Information has three different places to go:

▶ It can be sent to an external output device—monitor, printer, plotter, etc.

▶ It can be written to a temporary or permanent storage location. Computer storage involves recording the information as electronic bits on a magnetic media such as a hard disk, floppy disk, or magnetic tape.

▶ Processed information can be returned to the microprocessor as input. In this case, the information becomes data for a secondary computer operation.

All of these internal computer gyrations are made possible by electronics. The electronics of a microcomputer operate like a light switch—on or off. This is called *binary* operation. Microcomputers represent binary data as digits of information. An ON condition is represented by the digit 1 and an OFF condition is a logical 0. The computer's binary digits—0s and 1s—are called *bits*. Bits are further organized into logical words called bytes—8 bits make a *byte*.

> All of these internal computer gyrations are made possible by electronics. The electronics of a microcomputer operate like a light switch—on or off.

Unfortunately, most humans don't understand bits and bytes. The real trick is to translate microcomputer electronics into something understandable—like characters of the alphabet, for example. One such translation code is called ASCII, or American Symbolic Code for Information Interchange. The ASCII code takes a combination of 8 bits and translates them into an ASCII character. Most of the ASCII characters are recognizable— letters, numbers, and so on—but some are reserved as graphic symbols. Standard ASCII consists of 128 characters of 7 bits per byte whereas the extended ASCII set has 256 characters in 8 bits per byte.

While all of this techno-babble is fascinating to some, it doesn't mean a hill of beans to many LAN users because it represents information as non-tangible components. It's very difficult to touch an electronic bit (but if you do, watch out— they've been known to cause some very serious hair). Our discussion of microcomputer fundamentals is not going to focus on the electronics of the computer. Instead, we will explore the microcomputer's relationship with NetWare and the components which create LAN workstations and file servers.

QUOTE

You can lead a boy to college, but you cannot make him think.

Elbert Hubbard

In this chapter, we will explore six fundamental microcomputer components:

- ▶ microprocessor
- ▶ disk
- ▶ data bus
- ▶ video display
- ▶ memory
- ▶ input/output

These components work together in synergy to bring form and function to NetWare LAN hardware. The first component is the microprocessor, or CPU. The CPU communicates with other internal components over the data bus pathway. Memory is required for the CPU to carry out its function and performs a temporary storage role for CPU instructions and software. Disks are permanent storage for NetWare files and workstation operating systems. Video display provides a colorful graphic output for users, and input/output components provide a facility for the integration of external peripherals and other hardware components.

Let's begin our discussion with the details of the microprocessor.

MICROPROCESSORS

As mentioned above, the microprocessor is the brains of the microcomputer. Microprocessors are miniature wafers of silicon with tiny integrated circuits and intelligent transistors. Silicon provides a semi-conductive surface for electronic communications and a semi-insulated surface for decreased friction. Silicon closely resembles carbon on the periodic table.

The world of microprocessors has united around two manufacturers—Intel and Motorola. The Intel-based microprocessors are powerful and arithmetic-oriented. The Motorola-based microprocessors are also powerful, but in a different way. They are designed to perform complex display operations for engineering, artificial intelligence, and advanced graphics.

As mentioned earlier, microprocessors are functionally organized into two primary components: a control unit and arithmetic/logic unit (ALU). The control unit handles internal operations and directs the software instructions to the proper elements of the ALU. The arithmetic/logic unit performs the real "computing"—add, subtract, multiply, divide, less than, greater than, and equal to.

KNOWLEDGE

The microcomputer brain is composed primarily of silicon, a versatile, durable element which closely resembles carbon. Many scientists have theorized that a computer made of carbon could literally think like a human being. Ironically, the human brain is made entirely out of carbon and water. It makes you think, doesn't it?

The world of microprocessors has united around two manufacturers—Intel and Motorola. The Intel-based microprocessors are powerful and arithmetic-oriented. They perform complex mathematic calculations and excel with spreadsheet and database software. Intel microprocessors are the foundation of IBM-compatible microcomputers. The Motorola-based microprocessors are also powerful, but in a different way. They are designed to perform complex display operations for engineering, artificial intelligence, and advanced graphics. The Motorola microprocessors are the foundation of Apple Macintosh, Silicon Graphics, and NeXT microcomputers. The following is a brief discussion of Intel and Motorola microprocessors.

Intel Microprocessors

Intel introduced its first microprocessor in 1978. Over the past fifteen years Intel has produced eight unique microchip generations and is currently working on numbers nine and ten. The Intel chip has been the mainstay of the microcomputer revolution as it spawned the IBM PC line of microcomputers and clones. It uses a relatively simple, yet effectively open architecture. Here are descriptions of each of Intel's eight microchip generations.

8086   The 8086 was Intel's first chip. It surprised everybody by using a 16-bit architecture because the standard at that time was 8-bit. Unfortunately for Intel, nobody could use the chip—it was simply too advanced. So they returned to the proverbial drawing board and created an 8-bit version of the 8086 which they called the 8088.

KNOWLEDGE

Data communications within the microcomputer is analogous to lanes on a freeway. The more lanes, the faster the traffic. Hence, the more bits allowed through the computer, the faster the data communications. For example, a 16-bit microprocessor can handle 16 bits of information simultaneously—a significant improvement over the earlier 8-bit architecture.

8088   The 8088 chip was Intel's compromise in 1979. The 8088 was basically the same as the 8086, except it used 8-bit data communications. This was necessary to support the 8-bit hardware of that era. The 8088 became the foundation of IBM's original IBM PC. In addition, this chip featured 20-bit memory addressing (up to 1MB RAM) and clock speeds of 4.77 to 10 megahertz (MHz). A MHz represents one million clock cycles per second. A clock cycle is required for each fundamental microprocessor task. The more MHz, the faster the microcomputer.

80286   In 1984, Intel introduced a revolutionary advancement beyond the 8086—the 80286. The 80286 chip's 16-bit architecture became the foundation of IBM's new AT class of microcomputers. The new 16-bit microprocessor boasted numerous enhancements over its predecessors. Here's a brief list:

▸ The 80286 could simulate a large amount of internal real memory as virtual memory. Virtual memory is disk space which appears as random access memory (RAM). The 80286 was capable of 1GB of virtual memory.

▸ The 80286 supported hardware multitasking. Multitasking allows the computer to entertain multiple programs simultaneously. Unfortunately, Intel didn't create any multitasking programs to take advantage of this feature. The multitasking capabilities laid dormant for years until Microsoft caught up and introduced the first multitasking program—Windows/286.

▸ The 80286 supported two modes of operation—real and protected mode. In real mode, the 80286 simulated an 8086/8088 for DOS compatibility. In protected mode, the 80286 supported multitasking and program protection against lockups and system failure. In addition, the 80286 supported 16MB of memory and clock speeds up to 20MHz.

80386   The 80386 is currently the most popular microprocessor in the world and it represents a significant advancement over the earlier chips. The 80386 uses 32-bit communication lines within the chip and on the external data bus. The 32-bit architecture provides enhanced flexibility and unparalleled speeds. Some of the most notable improvements are:

▸ The 80386 can switch between real and protected mode without resetting the system.

> ▸ In addition to real mode and protected mode, the 80386 offers *virtual real mode* which allows multiple real mode sessions simultaneously. This requires a software manager.

> ▸ The 80386 supports a variety of different clock speeds—16, 20, 25, and 33 MHz. Also, the new 32-bit architecture supports 4GB of real memory and 64TB (Tera-bytes—1,000 GB) of virtual memory. Wow!

The only problem with the 32-bit chip was compatibility with existing 16-bit expansion cards. While the 80386 supported the cards, many thought it was a waste of 32-bit resources. In response, Intel released a cheaper version of the 80386 chip which included a 32-bit internal chip and 16-bit external data bus. It was called the 80386SX. The original 80386 was then renamed 80386DX.

> The 80386 is currently the most popular microprocessor in the world and it represents a significant advancement over the earlier chips.

80486 The leap to the 80486 microprocessor wasn't nearly as big as from the 80286 to the 80386. The 80486 chip is simply a turbo-charged version of the 80386. In addition, the 80486 includes an internal memory cache controller. The 80486DX has a math coprocessor built-in (which provides additional functionality for complex mathematic calculations and computer-aided design operations.) Earlier chips required an extra math chip on the motherboard. Intel also offers a 80486SX which is a full 80486DX without the built-in math coprocessor. The 80486 also offers 8 KB of internal memory caching. This feature directs CPU operations through special high-speed memory which is part of the microchip. The end product is faster processing and better ALU throughput.

KNOWLEDGE

Intel has jumped on the coat tails of the 80386SX by offering a cheaper, less powerful version of the 80486 (also with an SX designation). The irony is that the chip is exactly the same as the 80486DX except the math coprocessor functionality has been turned off. When users upgrade to an 80486DX, Intel sends them another full

80486 chip with everything turned off *except* the math coprocessor functionality. The end product is a machine with two partially-functioning full 80486 microprocessors.

The 80486 uses the same 32-bit communications path as the 80386, so its specifications are identical. The 80486 clock speeds, however, are greatly enhanced over the 80386. This is due to a feature called "clock doubling". Clock doubling allows the chip to process two tasks for every clock cycle. This in effect doubles the processing throughput of the microprocessor. The clock doubling chip is referred to as the DX2. The 80486DX at 25MHz becomes an 80486DX2 at 50MHz. Amazing!

Pentium P5   The latest and greatest Intel chip is the Pentium P5, or 80586. The Pentium was so named to distinguish Intel's microprocessors from those of the increasing number of clone manufacturers. The Pentium represents a quantum leap ahead of earlier Intel chips. The Pentium P5 includes two 80486-type CPUs for true dual processing, independent access to multiple internal data cache (8KB each), backward compatibility to the 80386, over 120 MHz speeds, a 64-bit wide internal interface, and 3 million transistors. In addition, the Pentium features a super-scalar design which uses a mix of RISC (Reduced Instruction Set Computing) construction and CISC orientation. The redesigned FPU (Floating Point Unit) uses mathematical firmware to achieve a 300% improvement in geometric computations. Simply stated, this is one HOT microchip!

> The latest and greatest Intel chip is the Pentium P5, or 80586. The Pentium was so named to distinguish Intel's microprocessors from those of the increasing number of clone manufacturers. The Pentium represents a quantum leap ahead of earlier Intel chips.

KNOWLEDGE

Processing capabilities of Intel microchips has become so advanced that scientists are now using mainframe measurements to gauge performance. A typical mainframe processing benchmark is MIPS, or millions of instructions per second. Early Intel chips were capable of

less than one MIP, compared to minicomputers and mainframes which could process in the 50-100 MIP range. But Intel microprocessors quickly caught up, and now the Pentium surpasses most minicomputers and a good number of mainframes.

Here is a brief look at the evolution of microprocessor MIPS:

8086/8088	0.33 MIPS
80286	3 MIPS
80386	11 MIPS
80486	41 MIPS
Pentium P5	over 100 MIPS

Motorola Microprocessors

The first Motorola microprocessor was introduced in 1979. The chip was the MC68000 and it spawned the Apple line of personal computers. The Motorola architecture is more sophisticated than the Intel chip, but it lacks pure processing power and speed. The Motorola chip is better suited for advanced graphic operations and multitasking. Following are descriptions of Motorola's five microchip generations.

MC68000   The MC68000 was Motorola's first chip. It offered a startling 24-bit internal architecture and a 16-bit data bus. The MC68000 supported 16MB of internal memory and up to 16MHz clock speed. Motorola's first offering was comparable to Intel's 80286, but it lacked virtual memory addressing and protected mode. The MC68000 is the brains for the following Apple Macintosh computers:

- ▸ Macintosh 128K
- ▸ Macintosh 512K
- ▸ Macintosh 512Ke
- ▸ Macintosh Plus

- ▶ Macintosh SE

- ▶ Macintosh Classic

- ▶ Macintosh Portable (uses the MC68HC000, a low-powered version of the chip)

KNOWLEDGE

In the beginning, Motorola chips were regarded as highly superior to the Intel microprocessors. The MC68000 offered more flexibility and a highly specialized architecture. In fact, Novell used the MC68000 microchip as the brains of its first NetWare server. But Motorola signed agreements with other companies who favor closed-architectures—Apple and NeXT. Meanwhile, Intel opted for a more open approach and quickly gained the lion's share of the microprocessor market. Today, the debate continues—Intel or Motorola, IBM or Apple, Coke or Pepsi.

MC68020   The MC68020 was the first full 32-bit microprocessor. It offered 32-bit communications within the CPU and 32-bit communications throughout the data bus. In addition, the MC68020 supported 4GB of real memory, 16MHz clock speed, and an additional math coprocessor. The MC68020 is the brains for the following Apple Macintosh computers:

- ▶ Macintosh LC

- ▶ Macintosh II

MC68030   The MC68030 was the third generation of Motorola microprocessors and became the foundation for the NeXT computer revolution. It offered a unique approach to microcomputing—two buses. The MC68030 supported two independent 32-bit data buses which could service the microprocessor twice as fast. This revolutionary new chip represented the first attempt to multiprocess within a microcomputer. In addition, the MC68030 offered internal memory caching, a math coprocessor, and clock speeds up to

40MHz. The MC68030 is the brains for the following Apple Macintosh computers:

- Macintosh SE/30
- Macintosh IIx
- Macintosh IIcx
- Macintosh IIci
- Macintosh IIsi
- Macintosh IIfx

MC68040   The latest Motorola microprocessor is the MC68040. This evolutionary chip builds on the advancements of the MC68030. It offers 64-bit communications and faster multiprocessing capabilities. The MC68040 is the brains of the Apple Macintosh Quadra computer.

QUOTE

Every great advance in science has issued from a new audacity of imagination.

John Dewey

The microcomputer revolution is in full swing. As you can see from the previous pages, there have been some major technological advancements over the past 15 years. Table 1.1 below summarizes the differences between the different Intel and Motorola microprocessors. By the time you are finished reading the table, it will already be obsolete.

T A B L E 1.1					
Comparing the Capabilities of Intel and Motorola Microprocessors	MICRO-PROCESSOR	INTERNAL	DATA BUS	CACHE/MATH	MAX MHZ
	Intel 8086	16-bit	16-bit	No/No	8 or 10
	Intel 8088	16-bit	8-bit	No/No	8 or 10
	Intel 80286	16-bit	16-bit	No/No	20
	MC68000	24-bit	16-bit	No/No	16

T A B L E   I.I

Comparing the Capabilities

of Intel and Motorola

Microprocessors (continued)

MICRO-PROCESSOR	INTERNAL	DATA BUS	CACHE/MATH	MAX MHZ
Intel 80386SX	32-bit	16-bit	No/No	20
MC68020	32-bit	32-bit	No/Extra	16
Intel 80386DX	32-bit	32-bit	No/Extra	33
Intel 80486SX	32-bit	32-bit	Yes/Extra	33
MC68030	32-bit	32-bit	Yes/Yes	40
Intel 80486DX	32-bit	32-bit	Yes/Yes	66 (DX2)
MC68040	64-bit	64-bit	Yes/Yes	64
Pentium P5	64-bit	32-bit	Yes/Yes	120

THE DATA BUS

If the microprocessor is the microcomputer's brains, then the data bus is its nervous system. The microcomputer data bus provides a pathway for communications between the intelligent CPU and external system components—memory, disks, video and peripherals. This pathway exists as an internal electronic circuit which transfers tiny bits of data from one component to another. Figure 1.2 shows for an illustration of the internal microcomputer architecture.

> If the microprocessor is the microcomputer's brains, then the data bus is its nervous system. The microcomputer data bus provides a pathway for communications between the intelligent CPU and external system components—memory, disks, video and peripherals.

The data bus connects all of the system components. The speed and physical method which govern data transfer are dictated by the type of data bus you use. Earlier we talked about the 8-bit, 16-bit and 32-bit processors which use internal and external parallel channels. External processor channels define the microcomputer data bus. In this discussion, we will explore five different data bus architectures and learn how their electronic throughput affects the performance of microcomputer workstations and file servers.

FIGURE 1.2

Inside the Microcomputer

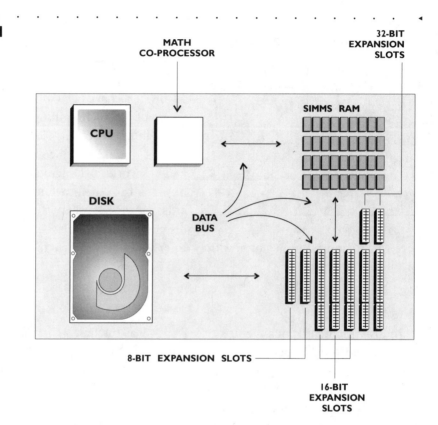

MATH
CO-PROCESSOR

32-BIT
EXPANSION
SLOTS

CPU

SIMMS RAM

DISK

DATA
BUS

8-BIT EXPANSION SLOTS

16-BIT
EXPANSION
SLOTS

Besides the microprocessor and memory, the most important component of the data bus architecture is expansion slots. These slots typically support 8-, 16- or 32-bit channels and communicate directly with the microprocessor and memory. Expansion slots allow the system to accommodate external peripherals and sub-components, including video, disk controllers, modems, parallel ports, sound cards, additional memory modules, and of course, one of the most important components to us, the network interface card. The expansion bus architecture of the original IBM PC used the simplest design and minimal support circuitry. In 1981, however, this was considered quite advanced. The IBM XT bus was 8 bits wide and it used an 8088 Intel microprocessor. The next generation, in 1984, was called the Advanced Technology, or AT Bus. It offered numerous improvements over the IBM XT—a 16-bit data bus, access directly to the 80286 microprocessor, and backward compatibility with earlier 8-bit expansion cards.

Recently, there has been a movement towards 32-bit bus channels. The 32-bit architecture offers a substantial improvement over earlier designs in performance of key components like memory, the CPU, and expansion cards. For example, new 32-bit cards have been introduced for all facets of microcomputing—32-bit network interface cards, 32-bit disk controllers, and 32-bit video.

> Recently, there has been a movement towards 32-bit bus channels. The 32-bit architecture offers a substantial improvement over earlier designs in performance of key components like memory, the CPU, and expansion cards.

The world of microcomputer data buses is broken into four main standards: ISA, EISA, VESA, and MCA. We'll discuss each of these in some depth and give you an understanding of how they differ and which is ideal in a workstation or file server format.

ISA

Industry Standard Architecture, or ISA bus, was the first standard introduced in 1979 and quickly became the mainstay of the IBM XT and AT microcomputers. With its 8-bit or 16-bit data/expansion bus, the ISA bus is the most common format. ISA bus communications are based on the same parallel model we discussed earlier—multiple paths working together to simultaneously transmit 8, 16, or 32-bits of data. The ISA bus is ideal for workstations and low-end file servers. Keep in mind that the 16-bit ISA bus doesn't take advantage of the 32-bit processing capabilities of the 80386 microprocessor. Incidentally, most of the standard clones—Compaq, AST, Dell, etc.—use the ISA bus.

EISA

The EISA bus, which stands for Extended Industry Standard Architecture, was developed to provide 32-bit throughput over the standard ISA architecture. EISA was developed in September, 1987 by a consortium of PC makers in response to the IBM dominance of that era. This particular organization, known as the Gang of Nine, included Compaq, AST, Epson, Hewlitt-Packard, NEC, Olivetti, Tandy, Wise, and Zenith. EISA did not replace the AT bus, it simply expanded on it. EISA offered backward compatibility, 32-bit throughput, and auto-configuration. The typical EISA motherboard includes two 32-bit EISA slots and six 16-bit ISA slots. The EISA architecture is ideal for NetWare file servers when it is combined with a 32-bit disk controller and 32-bit network interface card. This configuration optimizes server disk throughput and network communications.

VESA

The VESA standard is an enhanced EISA design which provides a dedicated 32-bit line directly from the VESA slot to the microprocessor. This technology is called *local bus* because it treats the VESA components as part of the native data bus. VESA throughput is dramatically improved over EISA and ISA. Some industry experts say that a VESA local bus system is in the neighborhood of 10 times faster than the ISA standard. NetWare file servers respond very favorably to the excellent throughput and performance of VESA disk controllers and NICs.

While EISA and VESA are expensive, they're not extravagant. The increase in speed and communications performance is justified for NetWare file servers. EISA and VESA for a workstation is harder to justify. Workstations don't process the multiple disk and communication requests that file servers do. They simply handle their own specific load.

MCA

MCA, Micro Channel Architecture, was developed by the IBM Corporation in 1987 to provide a proprietary, 32-bit alternative to ISA. MCA provided several improvements over the existing ISA architecture—32-bit throughput and auto-configuration. On the downside, MCA is truly proprietary (no compatibility with ISA or EISA). This becomes a really big problem with component swapping and file server upgrades. IBM's isolationist approach with Micro Channel has caused many system managers to shy away from the technology, no matter what they think of it.

The Micro Channel architecture is the basis of IBM's second generation microcomputer, the PS/2, or Personal System 2. While the PS/2 line became synonymous with Micro Channel, not all PS/2 models have the Micro Channel architecture. The model 25 and 30 machines are built around the ISA bus. Most machines with the 80386 microprocessor have the MCA bus—models 50, 60,

70, 80, and 90/95 (which are 80486s). The models 50 and 60 use a 16-bit version of the MCA bus while the models 70, 80, and 90/95 use 32-bit Micro Channel.

KNOWLEDGE

The term MCA was recently withdrawn by IBM after the Music Corporation of America, also known as MCA, filed a lawsuit. This architecture is now simply known as Micro Channel.

While 90% of the microcomputers made today use one of the four data bus standards described above, there are two other architectures that warrant some discussion here—Compaq's FLEX standard and the NuBus design of the Apple Macintosh.

The FLEX architecture, designed by Compaq Computer Corporation, was the first extension of the ISA design. It was intended to provide direct access from memory to the processor by packing megabytes of information across a dedicated line. This particular design was based on a solution called DMA, or Direct Memory Access. The FLEX architecture is no longer being designed in its original form, although variations of this design are built into EISA and VESA microcomputer architectures.

Apple Macintosh data bus designs differ dramatically from the IBM-compatible standards we are used to. Designed by Texas Instruments and adopted by Apple, they're built around what is called the NuBus architecture. NuBus relies on one proprietary processor slot called the Processor Direct Slot, or PDS. The PDS slot gives direct access to the processor from one expansion card. While PDS expansion has performance advantages, the card must be processor-specific. This means that a card from a Motorola 68030 Processor Direct Slot won't work in a new 68040 machine. In some cases, the NuBus data bus architecture and the Processor Direct Slot are mutually exclusive. That

> Apple Macintosh data bus designs differ dramatically from the IBM-compatible standards we are used to. Designed by Texas Instruments and adopted by Apple, they're built around what is called the NuBus architecture.

is to say, most Macintosh II computers are built around the NuBus design and do not use the Processor Direct Slot. The Mac SE, on the other hand, has no NuBus, but it uses the Processor Direct Slot architecture. The exceptions to this rule are the Mac 2FX and some of the new Quadra machines which use six NuBus slots and one Processor Direct Slot. I'm confused.

QUOTE

Perplexity is the beginning of knowledge.

Kahlil Gibran

Configurations

As you can see from our discussion of data bus standards, this is quite a complex system. High-speed communications between multiple expansion cards, memory, and the CPU can pose some interesting configuration problems. It is important to have an organized, effective method for controlling these communications. The key is to avoid component interference. The microcomputer industry has settled on three methods for controlling component configuration:

▸ interrupts

▸ memory addressing

▸ I/O addressing

The interrupt configuration method describes a dedicated pathway from microcomputer hardware to the central CPU. Each of the computer's internal components—disk controller, network interface card, keyboard, memory, printer card, and so on—use the interrupt configuration as a pathway and the I/O address as a door for microcomputer communications. The memory address reserves a special place in microcomputer RAM for buffering CPU requests.

Data bus configurations are defined using a variety of different elements. In this section, we will take a moment to review the three different configuration concepts and the five popular elements which define them.

Configuration Concepts Communications between microcomputer hardware and the CPU are based on the interrupt model. When a hardware device requests processing from the CPU, it sends a signal through the interrupt line to the CPU. The CPU will stop whatever it's doing and pay attention to that device for a fixed period of time. This interrupt line is called the IRQ, or Interrupt Request line. Each time the CPU receives a request from hardware to perform an operation, it goes to memory and recalls a hardware-specific routine of instructions called the Interrupt Service Routine. The CPU keeps track of the host hardware device by noting its IRQ. The IRQ number determines which interrupt service routine to perform. Another important function of the IRQ is that it allows each of the components to coexist without interrupting each other or stepping on each other's toes. Since each device must have its own dedicated IRQ line, it is imperative to configure the microcomputer hardware correctly. If two components share the same IRQ, one of them will not function—first come, first serve. See Table 1.2 for some sample microcomputer hardware interrupts.

The second configuration methodology for expansion board communication is memory addressing. The memory address is similar to the IRQ in that it provides a dedicated line to the CPU for data communications. The difference is that the IRQ is used for a device communication and memory is used for instruction set communications. Let me explain what this means. The primary function of memory is to provide a buffer for instructions to the CPU. When a device uses the IRQ line to interrupt the CPU for some service, the CPU uses the IRQ number to find a corresponding memory range in RAM. The CPU uses this range as the source for this particular device's operation instructions. It's very important to match a device's IRQ with the memory address it needs to store the instructions for that process.

The final, and third, configuration methodology is I/O address, or Input/Output addressing. The I/O address controls device handling by providing a hardware door to the CPU. In analogy, the IRQ is a dedicated hallway to the CPU. The I/O address is a door upon which the device knocks when it wants to enter and place a request.

KNOWLEDGE

Think of the microcomputer as a restaurant—McDonald's, for example. The CPU is the kitchen, servicing our request for a Big Mac. The IRQ is the line you stand in (each person is in a separate one).

The memory address is the cash register which marks down all of your requests and sends them back to the kitchen. The cashier itself would be the I/O address. Hungry yet?

Table 1.2 shows a list of basic hardware components and their default configurations. Now, if you understand the concepts of configurations and why interrupts, memory addressing, and I/O addressing are so important, let's move on to the actual hardware elements which define these different configurations.

TABLE 1.2

Common Microcomputer Hardware Configurations

DEVICE	IRQ	I/O
Serial Port 1	4	3F8
Serial Port 2	3	2F8
Parallel Port 1	7	378
Parallel Port 2	5	278
Default NIC*	3	300
Tape Controller	5	280
Mouse Card*	5	280
E.G.A. Adapter	2	3C0
Internal Modem*	3	2F8
Sound Card*	7	220

* = typical

Configuration Elements   Configuration elements are important because they provide us with a way of enforcing configuration concepts. Configuration elements consist of hardware and software devices which provide a methodology for defining specific configuration values. These hardware and software devices include dip switches, jumpers, terminating resistors, CMOS, and drivers. Here's a detailed description of the five most popular microcomputer configuration elements.

Dip switches (Dual In-line Package) are used to customize hardware device options on expansion boards or the motherboard itself. They are used on expansion boards—NICs for example—to define the existence of a PROM (Programmable Read Only Memory) chip or to configure the appropriate port for Ethernet connections. Dip switches are used on the motherboard to configure the status of internal hardware components—type of video, amount of memory, number of disk drives, and so on. There are two different types of dip switches: the rocker switch and the slide switch. Each switch has two states: on or off. You can use a bank of dip switches in combination to define multiple options. For example, a bank of eight dip switches would provide 2^8 or 256 possible options. This is quite common.

Jumpers are also used to configure microcomputer hardware devices. Jumpers are much more common in network interface cards for setting IRQ, memory addresses, and I/O addresses. Jumpers exist in two states: jumped or not jumped. The jumper consists of two pins that stick up out of the expansion board. A jumped state is achieved by attaching a metal jumper to both pins and creating an electronic contact between them. A not jumped state is achieved by leaving the contact open. Most jumpers work in banks. For example, a bank with 5 jumpers would provide a variety of different options—jumper 1 set, jumper 2 set, jumper 3 set, jumpers 2 and 5 set, and so on. One good application of this approach is used by the popular NE2000 NIC (Network Interface Card). The existence of jumpers on certain pin numbers defines IRQ and I/O address—IRQ 3 and I/O address 300H (default setting), for example.

Terminator Resistors, or terminators, are used to terminate the end of cable systems. This is important for two very popular types of cabling systems: SCSI disk drives and Ethernet coaxial trunks. SCSI stands for Small Computer System Interface. These large disk drives actually work in parallel of each other, daisy-chained together. Terminators are required at the end of the chain or else the signal will reflect back on itself and cause collisions. The same thing happens with Ethernet cabling trunks, which incidentally are used to connect network interface cards together on a LAN. Ethernet signals travel at very high speeds over the cable. When they reach the end of the cable, they must be terminated or else they will bounce back and collide with other signals. This can cause such serious problems as data loss, corruption, or hardware failure.

CMOS (Complementary Metal Oxide Semiconductor) is the most common setup program or setup configuration option on microcomputers. The CMOS firmware is built into the computer's BIOS, or Basic Input/ Output System. The BIOS is a chip on the motherboard which keeps track of critical system setups, including date, time, the amount of memory you have, the type of video adapter you're using, whether or not you have a math coprocessor, the type of disk drive you have for floppy A,

> CMOS (Complementary Metal Oxide Semiconductor) is the most common setup program or setup configuration option on microcomputers. The CMOS Firmware is built into the computer's BIOS, or Basic Input/Output System.

floppy B, or hard disk C, whether or not you want the memory test to continue upon boot up, the boot sequence, and so on. These global configurations are stored in the BIOS using the CMOS chip. The CMOS is configured using a special BIOS setup routine. This routine is typically activated by pressing the Del key during bootup.

Drivers are special software routines which communicate between the operating system and internal hardware devices. This is important because hardware must have a way of communicating what it's doing when the time comes for the user to request a service. LAN drivers, for example, provide a communications pathway between NetWare and internal network interface cards.

That completes our discussion of the data bus and its configurations. The next critical hardware component is memory. If you remember from our earlier discussion of the microprocessor and the data bus, the microprocessor needs to have instructions loaded in memory before it can process any instructions.

Memory provides data buffering services and acts as a holding cell for key CPU instructions.

MEMORY

Memory, busiest of the microcomputer components, is a key player in almost all operations. Figure 1.3 shows a basic microcomputer layout of the CPU, memory, and expansion bus. If you were to follow the steps of data as it traveled through the micro-computer forest, you would find that memory played a very important role. Let's say, for example, this particular figure shows a file server servicing a user's request for data.

> Memory, the busiest of the micro-computer components, is a key player in almost all operations.

There are 12 steps from the point the internal NIC receives the request until it sends the data back to the user. Let's follow these steps:

1 • The request is received by the network interface card. The NIC is not intelligent, so it says, "Gee, I don't know what to do with this." The first thing it does is send it to memory.

2 • Before anything can happen, the request is held in memory until the CPU can be interrupted.

3 • During step three, the request is sent from memory over a specific interrupt request line—the NIC IRQ—to the CPU where it enters a specific I/O door (the NIC I/O address). The CPU knows this is a NIC request because it monitors the IRQ and I/O address. The CPU assumes this is most likely a request from a user for a network resource. It processes the request and says, "Oh, this is a request for data." The processor goes to NetWare and says, "This is a request for data. What

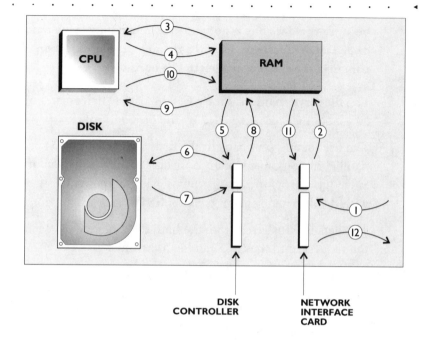

FIGURE 1.3

The Microcomputer Layout and 12 steps for Processing Data

should I do with it?" NetWare says, "Oh, well, here's the Directory Entry Table and the File Allocation Table." These two tables tell the system where on the hard disk to look for the data. The CPU takes that information and sends it back to the disk controller.

4 · The data request and disk addresses are sent back to memory where they wait to be shuffled off to the disk controller.

5 · The data request and disk addresses are shuffled over the expansion bus to the disk controller on a specific IRQ line—the disk controller's IRQ. The disk controller takes a look at the location on the disk where the data resides and goes to get the data.

KNOWLEDGE

All the steps to this point have taken place on the data bus. That's because we've been transferring requests and processing information. Steps six and seven involve the transferring of data to and from

the server disk. **This process does NOT take place on the data bus because the data bus is not capable of handling large amounts of data. Data transfer takes place through a special ribbon cable that connects the disk controller to the hard disk.**

6 · The file server hard disk retrieves the data which corresponds to the addresses that were provided by the disk controller.

7 · The user data is sent back to the disk controller over a specialized parallel ribbon cable which connects the disk controller and the disk. Since the disk controller is unintelligent, it doesn't know what to do with the data and sends it back to the CPU for instructions.

8 · The data is transferred from the hard disk to memory. Memory holds the request until the CPU can be interrupted.

9 · The request is sent from memory over a specific interrupt request line (the disk controller IRQ) to the CPU where it enters a specific I/O door (the disk controller I/O address). The CPU knows this is data because it monitors the IRQ and I/O address. The CPU says, "Oh yeah, I remember this data. What should I do with it?" The CPU asks NetWare, and NetWare says, "Send it back to user Q."

10 · The answer is sent back to memory where it rejoins the data and waits for a trip to the NIC.

11 · The data is shuffled off to the network interface card over the NIC's unique IRQ line.

12 · A reply packet is generated with user Q's address and the data is attached to it. The reply packet with the data attached is sent to the user over network cabling.

As you can see, there's a lot going on inside the file server when you make a simple request. Hopefully this scenario has given you a new appreciation for the complex relationship between memory, CPU, expansion cards, the data bus, and LAN cabling.

Memory played a very key role in the above scenario. Memory is the only component which touched the request every time it moved from one component to another. This is because RAM acts as a holding tank for the CPU. Also, memory stores the software instructions which the CPU needs for processing (NetWare, for example, was in memory).

Types of Memory

The file server memory from our example is called Random Access Memory, or RAM. RAM is volatile; when you turn off the power to your computer, the information stored in memory goes away. RAM is also very fast—100 times faster than disk access. That's a 10,000% increase in performance! In addition to RAM, there is Read Only Memory, or ROM. ROM is semi-permanent—it keeps information once power is lost, but doesn't store it in a permanent, disk-like format. ROM simply holds the information in a memory buffer which is fed by a very small trickle battery. ROM is much smaller than RAM. It stores special system configurations like BIOS information and remote booting instructions. The CMOS we spoke about earlier is a specialized type of ROM.

Let's spend a moment discussing the two types of memory, and then move on to a more detailed discussion of RAM and how it is used in a typical microcomputer workstation or file server.

RAM   RAM is the memory used by programs, the CPU, and special expansion cards. There are two different types of RAM in a microcomputer: Dynamic RAM (DRAM) and Static RAM (SRAM). The most popular and most common is DRAM. DRAM contains hundreds of tiny capacitors which store information in bit format—0s and 1s. A 1 is represented by an electrically charged capacitor. If the capacitor is discharged, it is a 0. On the downside, the amount of charge is so small that it dissipates very quickly. This means that DRAM needs to be continually refreshed.

SRAM differs from DRAM in that it's not actually electronic (instead, it's made of thousands of tiny switches and is more mechanical in nature). The switches are either set on (representing a 1) or off (representing a 0). SRAM is very fast, but it tends to be much more expensive than DRAM. SRAM is not very popular these days and is typically used for cache memory.

Both types of RAM are temporary and require power from the computer. They also need to exist in large amounts so programs and large computer software instructions can function properly. RAM performance is typically measured in nanoseconds. Some of today's most common memory has access times of 60 to 70 nanoseconds. Most microcomputer RAM exists in SIMMS modules, or Single In-line Memory Modules. The SIMMS module is a small card which stores 1-, 4-, 16-, or 32-megabyte chunks of RAM. The SIMMS card slides into a small SIMMS slot on the motherboard. There are typically 8 SIMMS slots—two banks of 4— which provide the capacity for 256 MB of DRAM on the motherboard.

ROM   ROM, on the other hand, stores programs permanently so they can be recalled during system boot up. ROM is reserved for global system-type configurations. You cannot add or subtract the amount of ROM a system has. Microcomputers are designed to have a certain amount of ROM on the motherboard and that's it! ROM BIOS, Basic Input/Output System, is the most common type of ROM. This is where the boot procedures and operating system instructions exist for activating the microcomputer environment. ROM memory is programmed at the factory and is virtually impossible to change. There are two types of ROM chips, however, that *can* be changed: PROM (Programmable Read Only Memory) and EPROM (Erasable Programmable Read Only Memory). But changing them is difficult and it's not a good idea to mess around with your system ROM.

KNOWLEDGE

Hardware is the type of computer component you can touch. Software, on the other hand, is typically made of electronic information which you can't touch. ROM is known as *firmware* because it's *soft*ware that's been programmed onto a *hard*ware chip. What will they think of next?

System Memory

The discussion so far has focused on the fundamentals of what RAM and ROM are. What does this really mean? How does it affect the user? Why do I care? In this section, we will discuss the fundamentals of system memory as it applies to the user. We will focus on how memory—primarily RAM—affects application programs and a user's ability to perform his/her duties.

When the first IBM PC was introduced, the 8088's ability to address 1MB of memory was very exciting. 640K of that memory was directly accessible as conventional memory. Figure 1.4 shows a breakdown of system memory into its

> The discussion so far has focused on the fundamentals of what RAM and ROM are. What does this really mean? How does it affect the user? Why do I care?

multiple components (conventional memory at the bottom, followed by 128K of video memory and 256K of ROM memory for a total of 1024K, or 1MB).

KNOWLEDGE

The 640K conventional RAM barrier was originally created because at that time, most microcomputers had a system memory limitation of 64K. The DOS designers figured that a 10-fold increase would be more RAM than anybody could ever use. Boy, do they have egg on

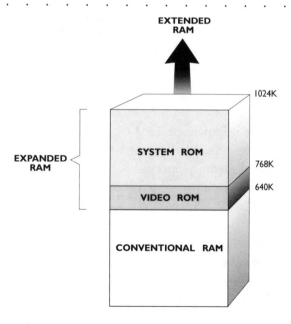

FIGURE 1.4

The Components of System Memory

> **their face! Just as an example, NetWare 4.0 or Windows NT re-**
> **quires in excess of 12MB of memory just to run the operating system.**

As more complex CPUs came along, they provided 16-bit addressing instead of 8-bit addressing and the amount of addressable memory rose dramatically. The 80286 supports 16MB of system memory while the 32-bit 80386 supports up to 4GB of addressable RAM. Besides conventional memory, there are two other memory categories: expanded and extended. Expanded memory uses the top 256K of 1MB as a temporary swapping pool for system programs—we'll talk about this in just a second. Extended memory is any RAM above 1MB. So if you had 16MB of memory, the first 640K would be conventional, the middle 384, including the video memory, would be expanded and the 15MB above the 1MB barrier would be extended memory.

Let's take a look at conventional, expanded and extended memory and see how NetWare and other operating systems use them.

Conventional Memory Conventional memory is the only memory DOS can directly address. NetWare can address all memory, but DOS can only address this 640K conventional RAM. If you're running Windows, for example, Windows will address expanded and extended memory, but it will first have to run your DOS programs in conventional memory. This poses a problem. You might have 100MB of memory, but only 640K can be used by your DOS programs. This is why some programs run out of memory even if you have plenty of expanded and extended RAM.

Expanded RAM Expanded RAM is memory that is not directly addressable by the CPU or DOS. Expanded memory requires a special software driver called EMS, or Expanded Memory Specification. If you use EMS in conjunction with expanded memory, it allows you to break the 640K barrier. The latest EMS software, LIM EMS 4.0, incorporates a technique called bank switching to swap different banks of expanded memory in and out of this reserved area. This is how it works: the 256K ROM area which we talked about earlier is reserved for PC memory addressing. It is addressable by the CPU. You can swap programs in and out of this area in 16K or 64K pages from extended RAM. In effect, although you're only addressing 256K of memory at one time, you can address 32MB by swapping it back and forth from the extended memory area. The problem with this is that it's very, very slow.

KNOWLEDGE

The LIM EMS and LIM XMS standards are named after the three companies which developed them—Lotus, Intel, and Microsoft. While it's hard to imagine cooperation between these three industry giants, it's amazing what can be accomplished with a little teamwork.

Extended Memory   Extended memory is memory beyond the 1MB barrier which is addressable to the CPU. But again, you must run a special software driver called XMS, or Extended Memory Specification. In the past, extended memory has gone primarily unused. Now there are new operating systems which can directly address extended memory—OS/2, UNIX, Windows NT, and NetWare. Microsoft Windows, for example, is probably the most popular memory management software. It's not an operating system, but a memory management software program. Windows allows you to directly address extended memory and will use the RAM for processing Windows-based programs. Other memory management software programs also allow you to activate extended memory in DOS—QEMM, for example. In addition, DOS has its own memory management drivers which provide support for applications which use extended memory.

> For the most part, the NetWare file server uses all the memory it can to load the network operating system, run programs, and perform internal file caching.

QUOTE

Experience is a comb that life gives you after you lose your hair.

Judith Stern

This completes our discussion of memory. It's important that you understand the difference between RAM and ROM. Also, be aware that RAM is the only memory we're concerned with in a network environment. For the most part, the

NetWare file server uses all the memory you can to load the network operating system, run programs, and perform internal file caching (explained in the next chapter).

If you're a workstation, you'll most likely be using DOS. If that's the case, you're going to need some memory management software to address memory above the 640K barrier. Windows has become the most popular. If you're using another workstation operating system like OS/2, UNIX, or Windows NT, you'll be able to address extended memory directly and not have to worry about using any memory management software.

DISKS

Earlier, we talked about the CPU and how it processes information using the data bus. We also described how the data bus shuffles requests from the CPU to other internal components. We talked about memory and how it's a holding cell for CPU requests. The last and most important component from a data storage standpoint is of course the disks—floppy and hard.

If you think about the file server and its primary purpose for a moment, you get an overwhelming feeling that the disk is pretty important. After all, the file server's main function is to *serve files*. Without a doubt, the most important resource on the LAN is the file server disk. Outside of the LAN, an argument can be made for floppy disks. Floppy disks are important because they provide a way of transporting files from one microcomputer to another—assuming, of course, that you don't have a network.

> Without a doubt, the most important resource on the LAN is the file server disk. After all, the file server's main function is to serve *files*.

Both floppy and hard disks use the same means of recording data—small electronic bits on a magnetized recording media. Incidentally, this technology is almost identical to the technology used by audio or video tape. Here's how it works: a recording head, or read-write head, magnetizes small particles of electronic information on some specially coated recording media—tape or disk. The magnetized spots represent 1s and the demagnetized spots represent 0s.

Again, this ties back to the way memory stores data. Before a disk can be used to store data, it must be formatted. Formatting a disk enables the computer to place data in a specific place and then be found again. Formatting entails logically dividing the disk into two small patterns: circles and slices. The circle divisions consist of concentric circles (called tracks) that encircle the disk. The slice divisions consist of pie slices (called sectors) throughout the circular disk. Each location on the disk is then represented as a cross section between a track and a sector (Figure 1.5.)

FIGURE 1.5

*The Layout of
Magnetic Disks*

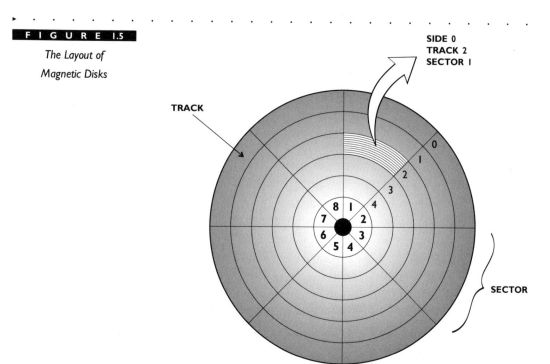

The more sectors and tracks you have, the more data you can store. There are 4 different types of floppy disks (5-1/4", 3-1/2", high density, and low density) and many different types of hard disks.

KNOWLEDGE

A new series of hard disks is emerging for notebook computers. They have the same storage capacities as the larger ones, but are housed in a 2" frame and can be balanced on the tip of your finger.

Let's take a closer look at floppy disks.

Floppy Disks

As we mentioned above, floppy disks come in two sizes: 5-¼"and 3-½". Most of today's microcomputers use the 3-½" floppy because its harder encasing provides a little more durability. Both sizes come in two flavors—low and high density. The 5-¼" floppy disk provides slightly less capacity (360K and 1.2MB respectively) than the 3-½" disk (720K and 1.44MB respectively). The floppy disk itself is enclosed in a vinyl or hard plastic cover. The protective cover keeps the disks from harmful exposure—sunlight, water, electronics, magnetic fields, and so on. Also, there's a metal slider at the bottom of the 3-½" disk which protects the write area from accidental exposure. It's not a good idea to get these disks near any magnetic fields because direct exposure to any magnetic field will completely remagnetize your disk—no data!

Disk drive compatibilities are very important for floppy disks. Make sure that when you're formatting a particular floppy disk you use the right density drive. Later in the DOS section of this chapter, we'll discuss the format command and how to specify which density you're formatting. Keep in mind that if you have a 5-¼" high density diskette, you must format it with a 5-¼" high density drive. A 5-¼" high density disk cannot be read by a low density drive. The reverse, however, is not true (a high density drive can in fact read a low density disk). The same goes for 3-½" disks.

KNOWLEDGE

A new floppy disk technology has emerged which combines the read/write flexibility of magnetic media with the storage capacity of optical media. These new floppy disks (called *flopticals*) can store 21MB on one 3-½" disk.

That just about does it for floppy disks. Now let's take a detailed look at hard disk technology.

Hard Disks

Hard disks are the foundation of the network—especially from the file server's point of view. Hard disks differ from floppy disks in many respects and are probably the most important resource on the LAN. The hard disk obviously has a much larger capacity than the floppy disk and is non-removable. It's also much faster than the floppy disk because it moves at much higher rpms (revolutions per minute).

The physical structure of the hard disk also differs from the floppy—it's not made of floppy mylar. Instead, the hard disk is made of aluminum and coated with a magnetic recording material. This disk itself is called a platter. Most hard disks are made of 5 platters, each with two sides. The platters are stacked inside a vacuum sealed container to keep out dust and other contaminant particles. The read-write head is also sealed inside the vacuum, and reads the data as it travels from the outside to the inside of the disk. The platters revolve clockwise at 3600 rpm to 7200 rpm for newer hard disks.

The hard disk is organized exactly the same way as the floppy disk—concentric circles (tracks) and pie slices (sectors). In addition to tracks and sectors, hard disks have *cylinders*, which are tracks that span parallel platters. Cylinders provide the capability of reading data from multiple platters as well as multiple sectors and tracks.

> The hard disk is organized exactly the same way as the floppy disk—concentric circles (tracks) and pie slices (sectors). In addition to tracks and sectors, hard disks have *cylinders*, which are tracks that span parallel platters.

Hard disk performance is measured by random access time. The random access time of a hard disk is a measurement of the amount of time required for the drive to deliver data after the computer sends a request to the disk controller. Most of today's quality disks have access times in the range of 10-20 milliseconds.

The hard disk has two components which the floppy disk will never have: partitions and interfaces. Hard disk partitioning is the process of dividing the disk into logical pieces for alternative operating systems and files. Interfaces define the mode of communications between the disk controller and the disk. The following is a brief discussion of hard disk partitioning and interfaces.

Hard Disk Partitioning   Hard disk partitioning refers to the process of preparing a hard disk for formatting. Hard disks are formatted in the same way as floppy disks except they're much larger, so they must be prepared or partitioned before they're formatted. Typically, partitioning takes place for a variety of different reasons. An operating system like DOS 3.3, for example, only allows a maximum partition of 32MB. This limitation is unacceptable for most microcomputer applications, so you are forced to create multiple 32MB partitions. Also, you can use multiple partitions to support multiple operating systems on one hard disk. For example, in NetWare 3.12, the file server is booted from a DOS partition. The server then moves to the NetWare partition and stores all data files there. NetWare 2.2, incidentally, requires the entire hard disk be partitioned for NetWare. In DOS, partitioning is performed using the FDISK utility. In NetWare, partitioning is performed using the INSTALL utility.

Hard Disk Interfaces   The hard disk interface describes a communications methodology for data transfer between the disk controller and hard disk. This is the language the disk controller uses for transferring data between the disk and the microcomputer data bus. It is essential that the hard disk interface be designed so that it's compatible not only with DOS but also with NetWare. There are four major hard disk interfaces which are currently accepted, each with its own advantages and disadvantages. Let's review them.

> **MFM/RLL** interfaces were developed by Seagate Technologies in the late '70s. Typically known as the ST506 interface, this particular technology describes a data transfer rate of 5 megabits per second and uses a data encoding method called Modified Frequency Modulation, or MFM. RLL was created a few years later as an enhancement to MFM and it used a data encoding method called Run Length Limited. RLL supports a data transfer rate of 7.5 megabits per second. On the downside, these encoding methods cannot be interchanged. This means that a disk controller created for an MFM disk cannot be used

with an RLL drive. MFM and RLL are common with older drives in the 20MB and 40MB range. These standards have been replaced by faster, more sophisticated technologies—namely, ESDI, SCSI, and IDE.

ESDI is an enhanced version of the ST506 interface which was developed by a consortium of disk drive manufacturers in the mid-1980s. It is now accepted as a standard by ANSI (American National Standards Institute). The data transfer rate for ESDI is around 10 megabits per second, but some faster controllers can operate as quickly as 15 megabits per second. ESDI is well understood and accepted as a reliable technology for mid-sized drives—100 to 340 MB. On the downside, ESDI has a tendency to break down in high load environments. This is because the technology is in the controller, not the drive.

SCSI (Small Computer System Interface—pronounced "scuzzy") is a very high speed interface which was developed as an enhancement to ESDI and ST506. The key difference is that SCSI uses parallel communications—the other interfaces use serial communications for data transfer (one bit after another). The parallel SCSI interface is much faster and more reliable than the other serial technologies. Also, SCSI controllers speak the same language as the data bus. This enhances microcomputer data transfer rates.

Another big difference between ESDI and SCSI technology is that SCSI is not just a drive interface, it's a *system* interface. As a general system interface, SCSI supports additional storage components beyond just disks—including CD-ROMs, tape backup drives, read-write optical, and so on. The SCSI technology allows you to daisy chain up to 7 devices from one controller. Just make sure to terminate the final device with a terminating resistor.

> Another big difference between ESDI and SCSI technology is that SCSI is not just a drive interface, it's a *system* interface. As a general system interface, SCSI supports additional storage components beyond just disks—including CD-ROMs, tape backup drives, read-write optical, and so on.

The SCSI standard provides a very fast data rate, reliability, and high storage capacity. It's an excellent choice for large file server disks in excess of 300MB.

IDE (intelligent drive electronics) was developed by Western Digital Corporation in the mid- to late 1980s. IDE is similar to SCSI in that the intelligence is on the drive itself, not on the controller board. IDE controllers are relatively inexpensive, but the drives are a little more expensive than ESDI. IDE differs from SCSI in that it's a drive interface, not a system interface. On the downside, IDE drives use RLL encoding which is an older type encoding that operates at 1 to 5 megabytes per second. IDE is extremely flexible and it has excellent capacity and reliability for smaller workstation drives—under 340MB.

KNOWLEDGE

There are many alternative technologies which enhance the hard disk environment. Caching controllers, for example, combine DRAM chips with the disk controller to provide memory buffering for hard disks. This combination can increase hard disk access time performance more than 10,000%. Another technology involves EISA motherboards and 32-bit disk controllers. In addition, some operating systems—NetWare 4.0 and MS-DOS v6.0 for example— provide built-in data compression which can effectively increase the storage capacity of a 340MB hard disk to almost 1GB!

VIDEO DISPLAY

The video display component is an important piece of the microcomputer puzzle because it defines a critical interface between the user and the computer. The two most important interface components for the user are input (keyboard) and output (display). Output is defined in two different ways: softcopy and hardcopy. Softcopy output includes the temporary pictures which appear on the screen. Hardcopy output, on the other hand, includes the permanent printed pages which create reports, memos, and books. In this section, we will focus on softcopy output and the display standards which define a user's environment.

QUOTE

Men are born with two eyes, but with one tongue, in order that they should see twice as much as they say.

Charles Caleb Colton

Although the terms *display* and *monitor* are often used interchangeably, they are not the same thing. The display is the device or the technology that produces the image on the screen. The monitor is the entire package which includes the display electronics as well as the display itself. Monitor operation is very similar to a television set, and uses CRT, or cathode ray tube technology. While this is common for most large monitors, laptops and notebook computers use a more advanced technology known as liquid crystal or gas plasma display. Some of the more advanced notebooks today use what's called an active matrix gas plasma display. This produces a very high resolution color signal over a thin small screen. CRT technology uses either a digital or analog signal in producing the video image. Digital signals are more similar to the other computer components, but they don't produce very vivid colors or high resolution. Remember, digital signals are limited to only two states—on or off. This is ideal for most computer operations. With display, however, you want as much variation as possible. Analog CRT monitors produce a much higher resolution image with a greater variety of colors, but they are typically more expensive.

> Although the terms *display* and *monitor* are often used interchangeably, they are not the same thing. The display is the device or the technology that produces the image on the screen. The monitor is the entire package which includes the display electronics as well as the display itself.

In this section, we will discuss the display elements which define video and the standards which have been adopted to define resolution, color, intensity, and so on. Let's start with display elements.

Video Display Elements

There are two basic modes of display operation: text and graphics. The text mode is used to display simple basic—ASCII—characters. The graphics mode, on the other hand, defines a much more complex signal which provides a variation of colors as well as three dimensional images. There are three basic display elements which define the graphics mode: quality, resolution, and color. Each of these elements work in synergy to define the interface that the user spends time staring at all day. It is important that these elements work together in creating a quality picture which can be viewed both accurately as well as without eyestrain.

Quality   Display quality is vital because the user is going to be spending the day staring at the computer screen. Also, quality dramatically affects productivity. A good, clear, quality display provides much more clarity and reduces eyestrain.

Resolution   Resolution is important because it affects the quality of the display. Also, poor resolution can affect the accuracy of softcopy and hardcopy output. Resolution is measured in pixels, or picture elements. Pixels are dots which combine to create images on the screen. One of the main differences between the various graphic systems available is the number of dots per square inch the screen supports. The more dots, the better the resolution and the clearer the picture.

Color   Multiple colors can provide more accurate softcopy output. This typically equates to better user productivity. There are two different types of display color: monochrome (one color) and color (a larger variety of colors). Monochrome displays come in a variety of different configurations: green on black, amber on black, or black on white. Green monochrome is the most popular, but amber is better for the eyes. Monochrome displays are common for applications which produce simple, text-based output. Color displays, on the other hand, are very useful for applications which produced complex, graphical output. Color also reduces eye stress and makes the screen easier to look at. If you have to stare at a screen all day, you might as well enjoy what you're looking at.

This concludes our discussion of video display elements. As you can tell, these different elements play a key role in the quality, resolution, and effectiveness of the video output. These display elements have been combined into a variety of different standards which define resolution, quality, color, and so on. In the next section, we will explore the five most popular display standards and describe the specifications of each.

Display Standards

The display monitor interfaces with the microcomputer through an expansion card called a *video adapter*. Most video adapters are specifically created to support a standard specification—resolution, color, and so on. Users purchase video adapters to match the capabilities of their monitor. There are five different standards which define the quality and effectiveness of video adapters and monitors:

- ► monochrome
- ► RGB
- ► CGA
- ► EGA
- ► VGA

Let's take a quick look at these five different display standards.

Monochrome   As you remember, we described monochrome as a single color on a black background. There are four different monochrome standards: TTL, Composite, VGA, and Multiscanning. TTL monochrome is the original display offered by IBM on its first PC computer. It was a digital signal generated by what's called transistor logic. This is a family of integrated circuits which creates a boxy, low-resolution, green-colored display on a black background. Composite monochrome is the lowest resolution of all monochrome monitors. It has the same resolution as CGA (Color Graphics Adapter), but without the color. Composite monochrome is very inexpensive and it can be plugged into any of the low-end video adapters. VGA is a very high resolution standard. It uses an analog signal to produce a high-quality image. VGA monochrome is not compatible with color VGA devices. Multiscanning monochrome describes a very flexible standard which can be incorporated into a general monochrome monitor. A multiscanning monitor will support all of the monochrome standards. Multiscanning means that the monitor itself will switch over to the correct frequency and the correct standard as specified by the adapter.

RGB   The RGB is the original color display for the IBM PC and is analogous to TTL monochrome. RGB stems from the additive primary colors: red, green, and blue. These were the only colors supported by this particular standard. It was a digital standard and for a very long time the only color adapter available. If you've ever seen an RGB, you know that it's very difficult to look at.

CGA   The CGA (Color Graphics Adapter) was the first *real* color graphics standard. Like RGB, CGA is a very low resolution standard. CGA only supports 16 colors—13 more than RGB—and provides a very low resolution display: approximately 320 horizontal pixels X 200 vertical pixels. CGA can cause serious eyestrain in both text and graphics modes.

EGA   The first serious quality color standard came along with some of the later IBM PS/2 models. It was EGA (Enhanced Graphics Adapter) and represented a dramatic enhancement of RGB. The industry moved away from CGA, and created a better RGB which supported 64 colors and higher resolution: approximately 640 x 350. EGA is a digital standard which supports many of the earlier monochrome screens.

> Keep in mind that display quality is extremely important because it describes the interface between the user and the microcomputer. A high-quality display can increase productivity while decreasing user stress. The minor investment is well worth it.

VGA   VGA (Video Graphics Array) is the most popular and highest resolution standard to date. It represents a dramatic improvement over EGA and supports more than just one mode. VGA can switch between high resolution/low colors and low resolution/high colors. It supports 640 x 480 resolution with 16 colors or 320 x 200 resolution with 256 colors. The balance is due in part because the standard is limited by a fixed communications throughput. A recent offshoot of VGA, called Super VGA, provides much better throughput and 800 x 600 resolution with 256 colors. This is probably the best of both worlds because you're getting the high number of colors as well as the high resolution.

QUOTE

The science of today is the technology of tomorrow.

Edward Teller

That completes our discussion of video display. Again, keep in mind that display quality is extremely important because it describes the interface between the user and the microcomputer. A high-quality display can increase productivity while decreasing user stress. The minor investment is well worth it.

INPUT/OUTPUT

Until now, we have discussed many different hardware components which work together to define the microcomputer. We have talked about the microprocessor, the data bus, memory, disks, and video. The final component they use we're going to discuss are the input/output components—serial and parallel lines.

The input/output components provide an interface between the microcomputer and other external devices—modems, printers, and so on. This discussion will focus on the technology as well as the productivity of serial and parallel input/output devices. We will also explore how they work in workstations and file servers throughout the network environment. Keep in mind that the microcomputer becomes most effective when it combines its internal operations with external hardware devices.

As I mentioned above, the input/output ports define a communications path between the inside components of the microcomputer and external peripherals. There are two types of ports: parallel and serial.

> Input/output ports define a communications path between the inside components of the microcomputer and external peripherals. There are two types of ports: parallel and serial.

pherals. There are two types of ports: parallel and serial. Parallel ports are primarily used for printers and operate as one-way communication devices. This means that when you send something out to the printer, it doesn't send anything back. Serial ports, on the other hand, operate as bi-directional devices which send and receive data at the same time. Serial ports are primarily used with data communication devices like modems.

Parallel and serial communications operate in two distinct ways. Parallel communication operates as 8 different communication lines sending 8 different bits simultaneously. Serial communications use one communications channel and send 8 bits of data one after another. Figure 1.6 provides an illustration of the difference between parallel and serial communications.

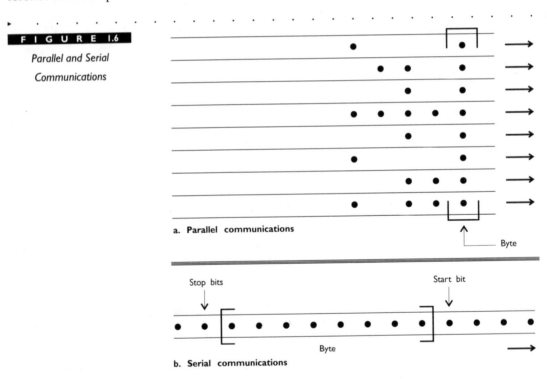

F I G U R E 1.6

Parallel and Serial

Communications

a. Parallel communications

Byte

Stop bits

Start bit

Byte

b. Serial communications

Parallel Ports

The parallel port is often called the printer port because it is almost exclusively used for printers. However, parallel ports can be used for high speed communications between internal microcomputer components and external tape drives, CD-ROMs, or add-on network interface cards. Configuration of the parallel port is extremely easy because it uses a "plug-and-play" connection—just plug it in and it works. There's no configuration. This is due in part to the fact that the parallel port speaks the same language as the internal data bus. The parallel port convention, which is used on most IBM-compatible machines, was developed by the Centronix company. It describes a 25-pin female connector on the microcomputer and a 36-pin edge connector on the printer. Parallel ports are typically defined as LPT1 for the first parallel port, LPT2 for the second parallel port, and LPT3 for the third parallel port (although it's rare to have more than one parallel port per microcomputer).

The main advantage of parallel ports is their speed. Parallel communications are extremely fast because they transmit 8 bits of information simultaneously. Another advantage is cost. The technology for building parallel port communications is extremely inexpensive since it uses the same communication scheme as the internal data bus.

Parallel communications is not without problems, however. Parallel communications, with their high speeds and parallel configurations, can only travel 10 or 25 feet. This is due primarily to cross talk. Cross talk is a phenomenon which occurs when parallel communications travel long distances and two different channels interfere with one another. Another disadvantage is that since parallel communications are designed for one-way communications, parallel devices are uni-directional. This negates any intelligence on the part of the external component. Intelligent bi-directional communications is reserved for serial ports.

Serial Ports

The serial port is also known as the asynchronous port or COM1. It operates according to the EIA (Electronics Industry Association) RS232C standard, and is also called the RS232 port. IBM connections call for up to four serial ports designated as COM1, COM2, COM3, and COM4. However, you can only use two serial devices at the same time because COM1 and COM3 use the same configuration and COM2 and COM4 are the same. Serial communications differ dramatically from parallel communications in that they use single channels. While this configuration is not nearly as fast as multiple channels, it is more reliable. Also, serial devices can transmit data over much longer distances.

There are two different methods for serial communications: synchronous and asynchronous. Synchronous communications describes a method where both devices on each end of the cable are said to be synchronized. That is, they each know what bits comprise a byte and how the information should be organized. Asynchronous communications, on the other hand, doesn't rely on expensive synchronizing machinery. It relies on fundamental procedures for recognizing bits and bytes. The most popular method for organizing asynchronous serial bits into bytes is the *data frame*. The data frame consists of 11 bits—8 bits of data, called a byte, 1 bit on the front end (start bit), and 2 bits on the back end (stop bits). This method is simple and reliable, but it's not very efficient.

Serial communication speeds are measured in bits per second, or bps. A device's bps rating is partially determined by its *baud* (a measurement of the device's changes of state per second). A change of state describes a movement from one frequency state to another. In a typical monobit system, each change of state transmits one bit of data. So a 2400-baud modem would transmit 2400 bits per second. Not all devices are monobit. Many of the new faster modems are di-bit or quadbit. In a di-bit environment, each baud transmits 2 bits of data—therefore, a 2400-baud modem would have an effective throughput of 4800 bits per second. Quadbit devices follow the same principle—4 bits are transmitted for each baud. Just to give you an example, your typical 2400-baud modem is really a 2400 bits per second modem which is di-bit running at 1200-baud. Your typical 9600-baud modem, which is actually 9600 bits per second, is a 2400-baud modem running at quadbit.

A typical 2400-baud modem is really a 2400 bits per second modem which is di-bit running at 1200-baud. A typical 9600-baud modem, which is actually 9600 bits per second, is a 2400-baud modem running at quadbit.

Serial ports are configured using a variety of different communications parameters: transmit rate, data bits per byte, parity, and stop bits. The transmit rate is typically measured in baud, although this is really a measure of bps. Most serial ports have range of 110 to 19,200 bits per second. The next serial parameter is data bits per byte. In most serial systems there are 8 bits per byte. But some communications prefer to use 7 bits for each character. In this case, the extra bit is used for parity. Parity is an error-checking algorithm. Serial ports use even parity, odd parity, or no parity.

Finally, serial ports are also configured according to stop bits. In most systems, the asynchronous serial port defines 2 stop bits, although it is possible to use just one.

The RS232 serial standard defines two different types of devices: the DTE (Data Terminal Equipment) and the DCE (Data Communication Equipment). The Data Terminal Equipment is the computer at the end of the serial line. The DCE describes the modem or the device which is actually performing the serial translation between the DTE and the phone line. Typically, the Data Terminal Equipment connects to the DCE through a serial connector. This connector can be 9-pin or 25-pin. The 25-pin port looks very similar to parallel except it uses a male connector.

KNOWLEDGE

The highest transmit rates are reserved for dedicated digital lines. Most telephone lines can only support relatively low rates—from 300 to 9600 bits per second.

In the first half of this chapter, we discussed the microcomputer and its many internal components. We have explored the CPU, data bus, memory, hard disk, video display, and the input/output ports. Now let's shift our focus from microcomputer hardware to the microcomputer operating system which controls the hardware. The operating system interfaces between the intelligent hardware devices and internal software to provide user productivity. The most popular microcomputer operating system is DOS, or the Disk Operating System. In our discussion of DOS, we'll focus on the fundamentals of DOS and the many internal and external DOS commands.

QUOTE

There is one thing stronger than all the armies in the world, and that is an idea whose time has come.

Victor Hugo

Understanding DOS

DOS is a very important piece of the microcomputer package because it provides an interface between the software programs which provide user productivity and the microcomputer components which provide processing and disk storage. DOS consists of a basic set of computer instructions which manage the flow of information in and out of the computer. It sits between the hard disk, memory, and the CPU. Controlling the display of information on the screen as well as the transfer of information in and out of I/O ports. DOS can be thought of as a messenger between the computer hardware and the application programs.

> DOS can be thought of as a messenger between the computer hardware and the application programs.

There are other operating systems that also perform similar messenger functions.

NetWare is a network operating system which provides file sharing and security on the file server.

Windows NT (New Technology) is a local operating system which runs on workstations and provides some basic file sharing functionality.

UNIX is similar to NT in that it provides some basic file sharing, but UNIX is more difficult to use.

OS/2 is the second-generation operating system which provides a friendlier interface and greater functionality than DOS. Unfortunately, OS/2 never gained the support it needed.

But to this day, DOS reigns over all other local operating systems and NetWare reigns over all other network operating systems. It is a natural marriage.

DOS controls 95% of the microcomputers currently on the market because it's simple, reliable, and has been around for 10 years. The two most popular types of DOS are manufactured by Microsoft (MS-DOS) and Novell (DR-DOS and

Novell DOS). Both versions currently offer much more functionality than any other local operating system, including virus protection, memory management, and file compression. In the remainder of this chapter, we will explore the basic operations of DOS and review the internal and external commands which provide the user with local resource management. Before you can begin your journey into the NetWare jungle, you must understand the fundamentals of the local operating system—DOS. Look out for crocodiles.

BASIC DOS OPERATIONS

To better understand DOS, it's important to have an appreciation for its basic parts. DOS has two main components: the operating system itself and the auxiliary utility programs which go with it. The operating system itself is made up of 3 files:

>   **IBMBIO.COM**, also known as IO.SYS, provides the basic facilities for handling the microcomputer's input and output devices—keyboard and video display. This file is hidden and stored in the root directory of the C: drive.

>   **IBMDOS.COM**, also known as MSDOS.SYS, is the central DOS program which controls communications between the internal microcomputer components. It is also a hidden file in the root of the C: drive.

>   **COMMAND.COM** is the command interpreter. It reads commands from the keyboard and decides how to carry out the request. COMMAND.COM directs user requests to appropriate internal components— CPU, memory, disk, and so on. It actually executes or interprets all commands which are entered at the keyboard.

The second part of DOS is its many utility programs which are broken into two groups: internal and external. Internal commands are part of the operating system; that is to say they aren't comprised of separate files. Internal utilities are actually part of the COMMAND.COM file. External DOS commands are separate files with .EXE or .COM extensions. These utilities are executed from a DOS directory on the hard disk. We will discuss most of the common DOS commands later in the chapter.

DOS is activated when you turn on your computer. The three system parts of DOS—IBMBIO.COM, IBMDOS.COM, and COMMAND.COM—are executed automatically during the start-up or *boot* process.

> DOS is activated when you turn on your computer. The three system parts of DOS—IBMBIO.COM, IBMDOS.COM, and COMMAND.COM—are executed automatically through the start-up or *boot* process.

Boot is a general computer term which comes from the *bootstrap* program (a series of basic microcomputer start-up instructions which load from the ROM BIOS (Read Only Memory Basic Input/Output System)). There are two different ways to begin the boot process. You can perform a cold boot (the power is turned off and then back on from a cold state), or a warm boot (by pressing the Control-Alt-Delete keys simultaneously to restart a running system). Either way the computer is re-initialized and the three following bootstrap steps are executed:

Initial Power Up—During the initial power up stage, the CPU performs two basic functions—circuitry check and ROM execution. First, the CPU checks its own circuitry to make sure that everything is functional. Second, it looks for ROM memory and performs any instructions it might find there, including the bootstrap instructions. Nothing at this point has been affected by the operating system. This is just an internal microcomputer check for component failures.

KNOWLEDGE

During the initial power-up stage, the CPU performs an internal circuitry check. If any of the components fail, the system will emit "x" number of beeps. This is a BIOS error-checking feature. The number of beeps correspond to a particular component. Six beeps, for example, points to the internal video adapter. Consult your microcomputer documentation for a list of the error beeps and corresponding hardware components.

DOS Search—Once the bootstrap instructions have loaded, they say, "Let's go find the local operating system and load it into memory." The first thing the bootstrap program loads is IBMBIO.COM and IBMDOS.COM. The first place it looks is the A—or first bootable—drive. Then it looks at B, and finally C—the hard disk. This order can be changed in the CMOS. If the bootable disk is found and the DOS components are hidden there, the system loads them into memory and goes onto the third step—DOS configuration.

DOS Configuration—After the two hidden files are loaded, the CPU looks for a configuration file called CONFIG.SYS. If the file is present, the system uses it to define certain operating system parameters—including device drivers, memory configuration, and so on. Next, the system looks for COMMAND.COM—the command interpreter. Once it loads COMMAND.COM, the computer is ready to perform its duties—DOS and otherwise. The very first thing the computer does once it loads COMMAND.COM is execute a file called AUTO-EXEC.BAT. This file is an auto-executing batch file which contains preliminary configuration instructions. Incidentally, both CON-FIG.SYS and AUTOEXEC.BAT are workstation-specific user-editable files. They can quickly become the system manager's nemesis.

So that's how DOS does it. Besides the built-in bootstrap instructions, DOS has some basic operational components which allow it to understand the microcomputer software environment. First there's COMMAND.COM execution during the last step of the booting procedure. Then there's file maintenance (understanding how to set up files and organize them into directories). There's directory maintenance and batch files which allow you to execute large numbers of commands very easily. Finally, there's DOS configuration—CONFIG.SYS and AUTOEXEC.BAT. In the remainder of this chapter, we will explore these different DOS operations and gain an understanding of their relationship with microcomputer hardware and software. Finally, we will learn the most popular internal and external DOS commands. Let's begin with command execution.

Command Execution

Once COMMAND.COM has been executed, the system is prepared to process any valid user request. These requests are made at the DOS command line. The command line is called the *DOS prompt*. The DOS prompt is an operating system fixture on the screen which says, "I'm ready, prepared, and at your service." The DOS prompt is typically displayed as a drive letter, A or C, and a greater than (>) sign—followed by a blinking line, called the cursor. The blinking cursor represents the input point for user requests and looks like this:

C>_

Information is not processed until the Enter key is pressed. The PROMPT command allows you to customize the way the DOS prompt looks. You can add other information, including current directory, date and time information, text, and so on. Users can customize the DOS prompt to provide information as well as look appealing. The options are almost limitless.

DOS commands are entered at the DOS prompt using proper syntax. This means you must enter commands in upper or lower case (DOS is not case sensitive), spell commands correctly, no spaces, and always press the Enter key at the end. Also, whenever specifying a drive letter, always follow it with a colon (C:). As we talked about earlier, DOS supports floppy drives A and B, and hard disks C, D and E. These are the different drive designations you can specify when you go looking for your files. If you need to abort a command or break out of a DOS program, press Control-C or Control-Break simultaneously.

> The DOS prompt is an operating system fixture on the screen which says, "I'm ready, prepared, and at your service."

Another way of customizing command execution is to use a switch, or command parameter. The switch is a way of telling DOS that you would like to execute a particular command with a specific type of environment. Switches typically follow the command and are preceded by a forward slash.

Let's use the DIR command (which lists the files in a given directory) as an example. If the file list exceeds the length of the screen, the system will continue to scroll, and will chop off the top of the list. This is bad. Executing the DIR command with a /P switch instructs DOS to list the files one page at a time. If you would like a complete list of all the switches for a given command, type the command followed by /?. Switches can be very useful in customizing the more complex DOS commands.

File Maintenance

Think of the hard disk as a filing cabinet. The drawers are disk drives, inside of which are folders (directories). The folders contain electronic files with file names and DOS attributes. It would be difficult to find your files without folder and file labels. Directory and file names are extremely important to the electronic filing cabinet. In the next two sections, we will explore the electronic filing cabinet through file and directory maintenance. File maintenance deals specifically with the rules and regulations of creating and maintaining DOS files, while directory maintenance deals with DOS directories.

As a file is created in DOS, the system makes note of it in the File Allocation Table (FAT). The DOS FAT keeps track of file names, extensions, and the file's physical location on the disk by track, sector, and cylinder. The DOS filename consists of two parts: an 8-character name and a 3-character extension. The file name and extension are separated by a period. Other FAT information includes file size, creation date, modified date, and file attributes. There are a few conventions which must be followed when naming DOS files:

▸ Use a maximum of 8 characters, followed by a period and a 3-character extension

▸ Use no spaces

▸ Use any keyboard character except special characters

▸ DOS reserves the following special characters:

   ▸ Asterisk (*) and question mark (?), which are reserved for wild cards

   ▸ Period (.) which is used to separate a file name and extension

   ▸ Colon (:) which is used to identify drives and other types of devices like LPT1 and COM1

‣ Forward slash (/) which is used to identify switches

‣ Backward slash (\) which is used to identify directories

‣ Less than (<) and greater than (>) symbols which are used for redirecting data

Once you create a file name using the proper convention, DOS will attach an appropriate extension. Extensions are used to identify file types and functionality. Many times the application defines the extension, not the user. The following is a list of standard DOS extensions and what they mean. Understanding this list will help you identify specific files and their function in the DOS environment.

.EXE is used for executable program files. These files contain instructions which are processed by the CPU. They are usually created by some compatible programming language.

.COM indicates a command file. These files are typically executed at the DOS prompt and normally cannot be changed. Typically a COM file is an external utility which is part of the DOS operating system.

.BAT identifies DOS batch files. Batch files are text files, programmed with valid DOS commands, that allow users to execute multiple commands from a single file.

.SYS indicates a system file. System files are used to interface between the operating system and hardware. Typically, .SYS files are drivers. MOUSE.SYS, for example, interfaces between DOS and the mouse hardware device.

.OVL are overlay files. Some DOS programs are so big that they cannot reside in the 640K of conventional memory. Overlay files allow programs to divide themselves into smaller pieces which can be swapped in and out of conventional RAM.

.DAT indicates a data file. Some programs create their own data files while they are running. These temporary files use the .DAT extension to distinguish themselves. Most permanent data files use a program-specific extension, including .XLS for Excel, .DOC for Word, and so on. Other program-specific data files, such as WordPerfect, use no extension.

.**BAK** indicates a backup file. Backup files are typically created by programs which store important data. Word processing, spreadsheet, database applications, for example, create automatic backup copies of the file you're working on with a .BAK extension. These .BAK files can be lifesavers in cases of data loss, corruption, or disk crash.

.**BAS** indicates a source code file from the BASIC programming language.

.**C** indicates a source code file from the C programming language.

DOS also provides two wildcard characters: the asterisk (*) and question mark (?). These wildcards can be used for file searching, copying, and deleting. The asterisk represents any group of characters—in the file name, extension, or both. For example, *.BAK defines any file name with the .BAK extension; DAVID.* would define the file DAVID with any extension; and *.* defines any file name with any extension—i.e. all files.

The question mark is a little different in that it represents a single character. For example, ?.BAK defines any one character file name with the .BAK extension. Also, DAVID.B? would define the file DAVID with any 2 character extension that starts with B.

> While files are the mainstay of the DOS data filing system, directories provide a higher level of organization. They are the folders in which the files are stored.

While files are the mainstay of the DOS data filing system, directories provide a higher level of organization. They are the folders in which the files are stored. And like files, directories follow a few simple DOS conventions.

Directory Maintenance

DOS directories are organized into a tree structure which, not surprisingly, has its basis in what's called the *root* directory. The root directory is the highest level of the tree—all other directories branch from the root. (You can think of it as the electronic drawer in which all other folders are organized.) Subdirectories provide further organization by branching from parent directories. Directories and subdirectories are denoted with the backslash (\). For example, a directory on the C: drive named 123 would have the designation—C:\123. C: is the volume and \123 is the directory name. Directories use the same naming conventions as files—8 characters, a 3-character extension, with a period separating the two.

The route from the root directory to a particular file is called the path. The path denotes the subdirectory structure that one travels from the root directory to any given file. For example, if the file DAVID.BAT was in the DATA subdirectory under DAVID under 123, the path would be C:\123\DAVID\DATA\DAVID.BAT. DOS uses paths to create a *search list*. The DOS search list is a table of subdirectories which are searched when users request specific files—.BAT, .COM, or .EXE. Users can use the PATH command to build a search list with a particular search order. We will discuss the PATH command later in the chapter.

Directory maintenance is extremely important because it provides a tool for organizing user data. Some programs provide graphical representations of the DOS directory format. Microsoft Windows, for example, specifies the directory tree in a format that is very easy to follow. Directory maintenance is an essential part of the system manager's job.

Batch Files

Speaking of productivity and ease of use, DOS includes a programming feature called which allows users to create simple text file with multiple DOS commands. These are called *batch files*. They make command execution extremely easy and provide a nice facility for autoloading specific programs or commands.

Batch files are text files with a .BAT file name extension. They contain a series of DOS commands that, when performed in sequence, execute a specific task. To invoke a batch file, simply type the name of the batch file without the extension and press Enter. DOS executes each of the batch commands in order. Creating batch files is as simple as creating a text file. Just make sure to follow proper batch file syntax. Batch files support any and all DOS commands and even a few non-DOS commands. The following three batch file commands are not supported at the DOS command line.

REM is the remark command which enhances batch file processing by providing a way of inserting documentation into the file. Here's an example:

REM This line copies all files from A to B.
Copy A:*.* B:*.*

ECHO, when placed at the beginning of a batch file, will echo all commands to the screen so you can follow the batch file execution—line by line. If you do not want to confuse users and would prefer not having the commands echoed to the screen, use ECHO OFF (this makes all execution appear transparent (invisible) to the user).

PAUSE is used to suspend the operation of the batch file until another key is pressed. If you put a PAUSE command anywhere in the batch file, execution will stop and the message, **Press any key to continue** or **Strike a key when ready** will appear on the screen. As soon as the user strikes a key, the batch file execution will continue.

DOS Configuration

DOS configuration is important because it provides a way of customizing each user's workstation environment. There are two specific configuration files which work in the DOS environment: CONFIG.SYS and AUTOEXEC.BAT. Both of these configuration files are automatically loaded during the microcomputer boot process. Let's take a closer look.

CONFIG.SYS   CONFIG.SYS is a system configuration file which automatically loads during the second stage of the boot process. CONFIG.SYS instructs DOS how to communicate with new and existing hardware. It provides some memory management functionality. There are four commands which are commonly used in the CONFIG.SYS file:

BUFFERS tells DOS how much memory to set aside for local disk buffers. This is an area in memory which the computer will use for temporary data storage. Data buffering speeds up the processing and movement of files from disk to memory. The BUFFER = 40 command is optimal. DOS will support any number from 3 to 99. Each buffer consists of 512 bytes of information and will make that particular area of memory directly and instantly available to the CPU.

FILES controls how many disk files DOS will allow to be open at the same time. Many of the popular software programs—Microsoft Windows, for example—require multiple open files and this command can be used to accommodate them. FILES = 40 is optimal. DOS supports as many as 255 open files simultaneously.

LASTDRIVE is especially important for network users because it reserves the local DOS drives. As you remember, DOS reserves the drive letters A and B for floppy drives, C, D, and E for hard disks. If you have the LAST DRIVE = D command, for example, the last drive that DOS is capable of addressing is D. You can also go further and have other drives available to DOS—G and H, for example. In this case, you would use the LAST DRIVE = H command and your first available network drive would be I.

DEVICE is the most important CONFIG.SYS command. DEVICE tells DOS how to handle the microcomputer's internal hardware devices. Earlier we learned that device drivers are software programs which interface between microcomputer hardware and the operating system. The DEVICE command in CONFIG.SYS provides the interface for device drivers, DOS, and internal hardware. Some of the most popular device drivers are ANSI.SYS, MOUSE.SYS, and VDISK.SYS. ANSI.SYS interfaces between DOS and the input/output systems. MOUSE.SYS provides mouse support in DOS. VDISK.SYS creates a virtual disk and provides communications between the hard disk and memory.

AUTOEXEC.BAT   The AUTOEXEC.BAT file is another DOS configuration file which helps to customize user environments. AUTOEXEC is the last file that DOS executes once the boot up process is completed. The AUTOEXEC name means that it is automatically executed when COMMAND.COM is loaded. Some common AUTOEXEC.BAT commands include PROMPT, ECHO OFF, CLS, and

PATH. We will discuss these internal and external commands next.

This concludes the fundamentals of DOS operation. We talked about command execution, file maintenance, directory maintenance, batch files, and DOS configurations. In the fleeting moments of this chapter, we will explore the variety of DOS internal and external commands and learn how they work together to customize the operating system environment. These are the commands which make the computer useful.

QUOTE

The mode by which the inevitable comes to pass is effort.

Oliver Wendell Holmes

COMMON INTERNAL COMMANDS

Internal DOS commands, as we learned earlier, are not composed of actual .EXE or .COM files. Instead, they are part of the COMMAND.COM program. Internal DOS commands can be executed from any location, as long as you have a DOS prompt. These commands are used for file maintenance, directory movement, DOS configuration, and workstation setup. Following is a brief description of the most common internal DOS commands.

> Internal DOS commands are not composed of actual .EXE or .COM files. Instead, they are part of the COMMAND.COM program.

CD

CD stands for Change Directory. This command allows you to change your current directory. DOS keeps track of where you are and the directory you're working in through the DOS prompt. You can move to another directory by typing **CD [name of directory]**. There are a few conventions to remember when using the CD command:

CD specifies the root

CD\123 specifies the 123 directory under the root

CD 123 specifies the 123 directory under the current directory

KNOWLEDGE

DOS includes two reserved directory names: ".". and "..". The "."
alone represents your current directory. The ".." represents the pre-
vious parent directory. For a shortcut to move to the parent direc-
tory, try typing CD..

CLS

CLS is the clear screen command. This command will clear the screen and
move the prompt in the top left-hand corner. Clear screen is very effective in
batch files for clearing garbage from the screen.

COPY

The COPY command is a very useful DOS command which allows users to
copy files from one location in the directory structure to another. The COPY
command creates a copy of the file and moves it to another location, keeping the
original file intact. The COPY command can be used to copy files within the same
disk—from one level of the directory structure to another—or from one disk to
another—from the C: drive to A: for example. The COPY command syntax reads
COPY [source drive and file name] [target drive and file name].

TIP

An interesting variation on the COPY command is COPYCON.
COPYCON is an internal DOS command which creates text files by
copying the contents of the screen to a file. This is ideal for DOS con-
figuration files such as CONFIG.SYS and AUTOEXEC.BAT. Type in
COPYCON and then the name of the file, press Enter. You will
receive a blinking cursor. Input text by typing and pressing Enter at
the end of each line. To finish, type Control-Z on a line by itself. As
soon as you press Enter, the system responds with 1 file copied.
All done.

DEL

The DEL (delete) command is used to delete or erase DOS files. DEL (or ERASE) can be used to delete large numbers of files when used in combination with wildcard characters. Be very careful when using the DEL command with wildcard characters; you can accidentally delete large numbers of files. DEL *.*, for example, will delete everything in the current directory.

> **TIP**
>
> When a user types DEL *.*, **DOS responds with** Are you sure? Yes or No. **This is a built-in, fail-safe feature which gives the user the option to back out of a perilous situation.**

DIR

The DIR command provides a listing of the files and directories within the current directory or disk. A typical directory listing provides the file name, extension, size, and last update time/date. At the bottom of the file/directory listing, DOS will display the number of files in the directory and the amount of free space which is available. DIR is particularly useful in locating specific files and directories. The directory listing

> A typical directory listing provides the file name, extension, size, and last update time/date.

scrolls extremely quickly on the screen, so you can use Control-S (pressing Control and S simultaneously) to pause the scrolling at any point. Use Control-S again to continue the scrolling.

There are a few DOS switches which can be used with the DIR command:

/p causes the command to pause after a screen is filled, typically 23 lines.

/w presents the listing in 5 columns across the screen. This parameter only displays the file names and extensions.

MD

MD is Make Directory. MD is identical to CD in convention and syntax, except in this case we are making directories, not changing them.

MORE

The MORE command causes softcopy output to be displayed one screenful at a time. This is very similar to the /P switch for DIR, except MORE works with any command. You can type the command and send it to MORE by typing the command followed by ¦ **MORE**. The "¦" symbol is called a pipe, and it is one of the three DOS redirection symbols. "<" and ">" are the other two.

PATH

The PATH command is extremely important because it builds a search list for DOS program files. The PATH command, when put in the AUTOEXEC.BAT, will specify a list of directories for DOS to search, in order, when a user requests a specific program file. For example, if you attempt to execute a particular .COM, .EXE, or .BAT program file from a directory where the file doesn't exist, the system will respond with **Bad Command or Filename**. The PATH command builds a search list which DOS will use to try and find your file. If DOS finds your program in any of the PATH directories, it executes the file.

The PATH command is a variable which is be retained in memory until you either execute another PATH command or until the computer is rebooted. The DOS syntax for the PATH command is pretty simple. The PATH command alone displays the current path; PATH followed by an equal (=) sign builds a search list of DOS directories. Subdirectories are separated by semicolons (;). Keep in mind that the order that subdirectories appear (from left to right) specifies the order in which the system searches for DOS commands and program files. Here's an example:

PATH = C:\;C:\DOS;C:\WINDOWS

PROMPT

The PROMPT command is important in that it specifies or customizes the DOS prompt. This is useful for users who require more information than just the drive letter and a ">". DOS provides a variety of different parameters which can be used with the prompt command. Here's a brief list of some of the more common PROMPT parameters:

- **pg**—the drive letter and the full path of your current directory.
- **$t**—the time.
- **$d**—the date.
- **$v**—the version number of DOS.
- **$n**—the default dive.
- **$q**—an = sign.
- **$$**—the $ (weird?!)
- **$1**—a "<".
- **$b**—a pipe, or vertical line.
- **$_**—a carriage return, or line feed.

The PROMPT command also supports text. For example, you could type PROMPT Today is $d and the DOS prompt would display Today is May 3, 1994. The PROMPT command alone returns the DOS prompt back to its default state—C>.

REN

REN is an internal DOS command which allows you to rename a file without copying it. REN creates a copy of a file, gives it a new name, and deletes the original. The rename command will rename the file and store it in the default directory. You can always rename a file to another directory but you have to copy the file there first.

RD

RD (Remove Directory) is identical to CD and MD except it removes directories instead of changing or making them. The same conventions apply.

TIP

You cannot remove a directory containing files or subdirectories—they must be deleted first.

SET

The SET command is a complex internal DOS command which provides a great deal of flexibility and DOS customization. The SET command inserts a variable string into the command processor's environment. This allows any program to recall the string from DOS whenever a user asks for it.

TYPE

The TYPE command displays the contents of a file on the screen. Users can also type a file to the printer or redirect it to a file. Text files are displayed in alphanumeric characters. Program files are not as simple—they contain all sorts of programming notations. These control characters are displayed as strange little ASCII characters (smiley faces, for example) and loud beeping noises. To redirect files to a printer, use the following notation: TYPE > LPT1:.

VER

VER is a DOS internal command which displays the version number of DOS. DOS version information is important for certain programs which are sensitive to particular versions.

COMMON EXTERNAL DOS COMMANDS

External commands differ from internal commands in that they exist as external files, with .COM or .EXE extensions. .COM files are command utilities while .EXE files are add-on DOS applications. External DOS commands are not part of COMMAND.COM. They are typically stored in the C:\DOS subdirectory. Most external DOS commands are specialized tools and are not part of the microcomputer's everyday operation. The following is a brief description of DOS's most popular external commands.

ATTRIB

The attribute command, or ATTRIB, displays and changes file attributes. An attribute controls access to a file and provides a very simple level of DOS security.

There are two attributes which are specifically useful in DOS: read-only and archive. The read-only attribute says, "This file can only be read, it cannot be written to." Read-only files cannot be copied or deleted. The Archive attribute says, "This particular file needs to be backed up. It's been modified since the last backup." The ATTRIB command allows you to add or subtract either of these two file attributes. To add an attribute, type **ATTRIB** followed by +r. To subtract an attribute, type **ATTRIB** followed by -r. In the case where the read-only attribute has been disabled, the file is said to be read-write—this means it can be read from and written to simultaneously. Typing the **ATTRIB** *.* command displays the current attribute status of all files in the default directory.

> External commands differ from internal commands in that they exist as external files, with .COM or .EXE extensions. .COM files are command utilities while .EXE files are add-on DOS applications.

BACKUP

BACKUP is a useful DOS utility which allows users to make backup copies of files, directories, disks, and diskettes. This is the main DOS fault tolerance feature. BACKUP will make an archive of all files and all subdirectories on the disk and save the archive in a specific backup format. The DOS BACKUP format can only be restored using the RESTORE command. Also, BACKUP only works on hard disk or diskette—so imagine backing up a 40MB or 80MB hard disk to 80 high-density diskettes. Talk about boring.

TIP

**The DOS BACKUP command is misleading and unreliable. It
creates a proprietary archive diskette which cannot be copied or
deleted. If you want to restore one file, you have to restore the
entire backup set.**

CHKDSK

CHKDSK (CHecKDiSK) is a DOS external program which checks the integrity
of data on your disk. It can also make corrections. CHKDSK, when performed
alone, will check the default drive. Otherwise, you can specify a drive by typing
CHKDSK [drive]. CHKDSK will tell you the size of the drive, the capacity of the
drive, and how much disk space is available. It will also tell you if there are any
lost clusters, lost sectors, or corrupted data. **CHKDSK /F** performs low-level disk
maintenance and fixes any notable errors.

COMMAND.COM

COMMAND.COM is the most important DOS command—it loads the DOS
command processor. COMMAND.COM is one of the three main portions of
DOS. It is also the second-to-last program which is executed during the boot-up
process. If you type **COMMAND** at the DOS prompt, it will load a second copy
of the command processor. This is only used in specialized cases. Don't try this
at home!

DISKCOPY

The DISKCOPY command provides a method of duplicating DOS diskettes.
To use DISKCOPY, the source and destination disks need to be exactly the same.
For example, if the source disk is a 1.2MB high density 5-¼" floppy, then the tar-
get disk must also be a 1.2MB high density 5-¼" floppy. DISKCOPY makes a low-
level copy of all tracks and sectors—so it will also copy any hidden protection.
If the target disk is not formatted before the DISKCOPY is performed, DISK-
COPY will automatically format the disk for you.

To perform DISKCOPY, you simply type **DISKCOPY [source drive letter]** **[target drive letter]**. For example: **DISKCOPY A: B:**. If you would like to copy two diskettes from the same drive, type **DISKCOPY A: A:**—in this case, the system will prompt you for the source disk and the target disk. Keep in mind that since you have limited conventional memory in DOS, DISKCOPY will require multiple swappings—often 5 or 10 times per DISKCOPY session.

FDISK

FDISK allows you to break a hard disk into multiple partitions or define the entire disk as one large partition. FDISK will also allow you to delete existing partitions. Once you run FDISK, the hard disk is ready to be formatted. Formatting downloads the operating system and formats the disk into sectors, tracks, and cylinders. FDISK allows you to create primary DOS partitions, secondary extended DOS partitions, or non-DOS partitions. Incidentally, when you use FDISK to create a DOS partition in NetWare 3.12, you leave a large portion of the disk unformatted. NetWare 3.12 will create a non-DOS partition for itself.

KNOWLEDGE

DOS 3.30 and below allow a maximum of 32MB for each partition. DOS 4.0 and above allow unlimited partition sizes.

FORMAT

Once the disk has been FDISKed and partitioned, it is ready to be formatted. Formatting breaks up the disk platter into logical tracks, pie-shaped sectors, and parallel cylinders. The FORMAT command can be used to format a hard disk or floppy diskette. Keep in mind that a disk must be formatted and prepared before it can store any data. There are a variety of switches which can be used with the FORMAT command:

/s—to transfer the system files, namely IBMBIO.COM, IBMDOS.COM, and COMMAND.COM.

/v—specifies a volume label for this disk. During the format procedure, it will ask you for an 11-character volume name.

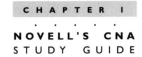
/x—required to format hard disks in DR DOS.

In addition to the above switches, FORMAT supports a variety of drive compatibility switches. This is to ensure that FORMAT understands the type of diskette you are using and the corresponding drive type:

FORMAT A: /F:720 formats a low-density 3-$\frac{1}{2}$" diskette in a high-density drive. (This only works with DOS 5.0 and above.)

FORMAT A: /4 formats a low-density 5-$\frac{1}{4}$" diskette in a high-density drive.

LABEL

The LABEL command makes it possible to create, change, or delete a volume label. This is important because many users like to have specific names or volume labels for their hard or floppy disks. This is an electronic filing system.

MEM

The MEM command is an external DOS (but only v5.0 and above) utility which allows you to display information about the way memory is currently being used. This command is very useful in troubleshooting and optimizing workstation RAM. After all, memory has become a central issue as more and more programs compete for limited memory resources. The MEM command, when executed alone, will display the currently available RAM as compared to the total amount installed. MEM /C provides a lot more information—it breaks up the memory into conventional, expanded, and extended. **MEM /C** displays the programs which are currently using RAM and how much they are using.

PRINT

The PRINT command is a simple printing utility in DOS. It allows you to print text files to a LPT1 printer. Simply type **PRINT** followed by the name of the text file and the system will print the file to the first default printer.

SHARE

SHARE is a DOS command which allows multiple access to otherwise stand-alone files. File sharing is something new in a DOS environment because typically you have one user accessing one file at a time. If you have programs that are capable of multitasking, like Microsoft Windows, and they want to access the same file simultaneously, you should have SHARE loaded. SHARE allocates DOS environment space for file sharing and locking instructions.

KNOWLEDGE

File sharing is quite common in a network environment. File attributes mark files as sharable, non-sharable, and so on. But with sharable data files, the question is "Which user's changes get saved?" The answer? "Whoever saves last, wins!"

SYS

The SYS command allows you to transfer the system files from a hard or floppy disk to another drive. SYS copies the system files—IBMBIO.COM, IBMDOS.COM, and COMMAND.COM—from the source disk to a target drive. For example, if you format a floppy drive and forget to use the /S parameter, the **SYS A:** command will transfer the system files to the floppy disk A and make it bootable.

UNDELETE

UNDELETE is an extremely useful fault tolerance feature which is only available in the newer versions of MS-DOS and DR/Novell DOS. UNDELETE allows users to recover deleted files if the files haven't been written over yet. When you run UNDELETE, the system will give you a list of files which are available for undeletion. This list is directory-specific. UNDELETE has saved many users from the proverbial firing line.

XCOPY

XCOPY was developed primarily to aid in working with hard disks and large groups of files. The XCOPY command expands on the functionality of COPY by providing the ability to copy files and subdirectories together. XCOPY supports four main switches:

/s tells XCOPY to copy a directory including all subdirectories under it. This is found to be extremely useful moving entire branches from one part of the tree to another.

/e copies all empty subdirectories and may only be used with the /s switch.

/v verifies the integrity of the data copied. DOS performs a read-after-write verification while it copies the data from one area of the disk to another.

/w causes XCOPY to wait before it starts copying files. This is important in copying files to a floppy-based system because it gives the user more time to switch the DOS disk from the source to the target destination.

This completes our discussion of DOS. In this chapter, we have explored the fundamentals of the microcomputer through the eyes of internal hardware and DOS. As a CNA, it is important that you gain an appreciation for the complexities of microcomputer hardware. In addition, you should understand the purpose of an operating system and feel comfortable with the basic operations of DOS. As we continue throughout the book, we will refer back to these components and discuss ways of optimizing

As we continue throughout the book, we will refer back to these components and discuss ways of optimizing the microcomputer hardware/software in a networking environment.

the microcomputer hardware/software in a networking environment. In the next chapter, we will use these microcomputer/DOS fundamentals as a springboard for NetWare basics. Remember, it all starts with that first step. Before you know it, you will be running the NetWare marathon.

QUOTE

A journey of a thousand miles must begin with a single step.

Chinese Proverb

EXERCISE 1.1: MATCHING MICROCOMPUTER CONCEPTS

1. Extended ASCII

2. Motorola

3. ISA

4. Serial

5. CGA

6. 80486

7. VGA

8. 80386SX

9. Extended RAM

10. CMOS

11. Keyboard

12. Pixels

13. SCSI

14. Intel

15. Floptical

16. MCA

17. RAM

18. CPU

A. Bus architecture of IBM AT class computer

B. Part of the computer's input system

C. Bus architecture of IBM's PS/2 class

D. Houses the control unit and ALU

E. A set of 256 characters in 8 bits per byte

F. Chip of choice for Macintosh computers

G. 16-bit data bus and 32-bit CPU internal bus

H. Chip of choice for IBM computers

I. Brains of the Macintosh iiFX

J. Includes a math co-processor and internal cache controller

K. Volatile storage

L. Keeps track of system configurations

M. Optical floppies

N. Memory used by Microsoft Windows to break the 1MB barrier

O. Best interface for NetWare servers

P. 16 colors in low resolution

Q. Picture elements

R. Most popular disk interface for smaller disks

19. Motorola 68030   S. 16 colors in very high resolution

20. IDE   T. RS232C standard

See Appendix D for answers.

EXERCISE 1.2: USING DOS COMMANDS

In this chapter, we learned about how the DOS workstation operating system interfaces between the microcomputer hardware and NetWare user. We learned about basic DOS operations, including command execution, file and directory maintenance, batch files and DOS configuration files. The bulk of the DOS discussion focused on 14 common internal and 14 common external DOS commands. In this exercise, we will practice using some of the most common DOS commands and gain a comprehensive understanding of how they can be used to work productively in a DOS environment.

Common Internal Commands

CD The CD command allows the user to change directories from the current directory to another one in the directory structure.

▸ Type CD\ and press Enter to change to the root directory. The system will return with a prompt indicating that you are currently in the root directory.

▸ Type CD\DOS and press Enter to move to a specified directory on the hard drive. This moves to the DOS subdirectory. Remember the backslash indicates that this directory resides directly off of the root.

CLS The CLS command can be used to clear the screen.

▸ Type CLS and press Enter.

COPY The DOS COPY command provides an effective strategy for copying files within a hard disk or between disk drives and floppy disks. To copy a file, you must either specify the source and target drive, or move to the source directory and specify the file from there.

▸ Type **CD** and press Enter to move to the source directory.

▸ Once at the root directory, type **COPY AUTOEXEC.BAT \DOS** and press Enter. This command will copy the AUTOEXEC.BAT file from the root to the DOS subdirectory.

DEL The delete command works similarly to the COPY command except it deletes files instead.

▸ Type **DEL \DOS\AUTOEXEC.BAT** and press Enter to delete the file we just copied.

DIR Use the DIR command to verify that the DEL, in fact, worked.

▸ Type **DIR \DOS\AUTOEXEC.BAT** and press Enter. The system will return with **File not found**. This is because we deleted the file from the DOS subdirectory.

▸ Now type **DIR AUTOEXEC.BAT** and press Enter. The system will respond with information about the AUTOEXEC.BAT file which resides in the root directory.

▸ Type **DIR/p** to gain information about more than one file. This will give us all information of files and directories in the current directory and give us one page at a time.

TYPE To see the contents of the AUTOEXEC.BAT file, use the TYPE command.

▸ Type **AUTOEXEC.BAT** and press Enter. This gives us the contents of the AUTOEXEC.BAT text file. If the text file is larger than one screen, you can use the MORE redirection command to view one screen at a time.

▸ Type **AUTOEXEC.BAT | MORE**.

PATH The PATH command allows users to search certain directories for files.

‣ Type **PATH** and press enter. This will show the current path. In order to customize the path, follow the path command with any specific set of directories separated by semicolons.

PROMPT The PROMPT command customizes the directory display so that users can view more information than just the directory they're in and the drive they're using.

‣ Type **PROMPT $d** and press Enter. The system will respond by changing the directory pointer so that it displays the date.

‣ Type **PROMPT vg** and press Enter. This will display the current version of DOS you are running followed by a greater than (>) sign. You can also use text in your DOS prompt.

‣ Type **PROMPT HI, HOW ARE YOU TODAY** and press Enter. The system will respond with **HI, HOW ARE YOU TODAY** at every screen. The text can be combined with variables to provide valuable information for the user.

‣ Type **PROMPT TODAY IS $d** and press Enter. This responds with **TODAY IS** and the date.

‣ Type **PROMPT pg** and press Enter to return to the prompt you're most used to. This prompt provides you with the drive and path plus a greater-than sign.

VER Finally the VER command allows users to gain information about the version of DOS they're using.

‣ Type **VER** and press Enter.

That completes our discussion of the use of some of the common internal DOS commands. These commands are stored in the COMMAND.COM file which automatically loads during computer startup.

Common External Commands

While the DOS internal commands reside in the one COMMAND.COM file, the DOS external command all reside in the DOS subdirectory. These are utilities which exist as .EXE or .COM files and they provide additional functionality beyond the internal DOS commands. Let's explore some of the more common external DOS commands.

CHKDSK—The CHKDSK command allows users to keep track of the use of disk space on floppy or hard disks as well as the health of their disks. In addition, CHKDSK displays the number of hidden files found on the disk.

▸ Type **CHKDSK** and press Enter. The system will respond with a group of information. If the hard disk has some problems and there are lost clusters or sectors, the system will respond with a warning message.

▸ Type **CHKDSK** /f and press Enter to repair any existing problems on the disk. If problems do not exist, it will ignore the /f switch.

MEM Another valuable utility for gaining information is MEM. The MEM command provides detailed information about internal workstation RAM.

▸ Type **MEM** and press Enter. The system will respond with a few lines of information about existing and available workstation RAM. More detailed information about which programs are loaded into memory can be accessed by using the /c parameter.

▸ Type **MEM** /c and press ENTER.

LABEL—The LABEL command allows users to electronically label their local and floppy disks.

▸ Type **LABEL** and press Enter to label the hard disk. The system will respond with an input box asking for any label up to 11 characters.

▸ Type in a name for your hard disk and press Enter.

DIR—Now that you've labeled your hard disk you can view the label.

▸ Type **DIR** and press Enter. The system will respond with a list of files in the root directory and the label of the hard disk.

XCOPY—Beyond COPY, DOS provides two other utilities which can be used in DISKCOPY special copy situations: XCOPY and DISKCOPY. XCOPY allows for copying of subdirectories and files and DISKCOPY allows for the duplication of entire floppy disks.

▸ Try them out on your hard disk and use them to copy floppy disks of the same type.

Be aware that DOS provides the facility for not only file and directory management but disk management as well. There are two utilities, FDISK and FORMAT, which perform dangerous disk-level operations. Be very careful when toying with these two utilities.

CHAPTER 2

NetWare
Basics

"A...is for Applications.
B...is for Backups.
C...is for Cabling... "

The first step towards becoming a Certified NetWare Administrator is a clear understanding of NetWare basics. In this chapter we will lay the foundation for the majority of the NetWare CNA program. We will learn about system management, hardware basics, and the fundamentals of network software. Novell education often likens the LAN to a large apartment building. Users are well-behaved tenants, workstations are appliances, and the system manager is the "LAN"-lord. Directory structures are rooms, network security is locks, and printing is performed in the laundry room. You get the idea.

> Novell education often likens the LAN to a large apartment building. Users are well-behaved tenants, workstations are appliances, and the system manager is the "LAN"-lord. Directory structures are rooms, network security is locks, and printing is performed in the laundry room. You get the idea.

In the context of this analogy, NetWare basics is the cement foundation upon which the apartments are built. You must have a firm grasp of the LAN fundamentals before you can effectively manage the network resources. There are many challenges and responsibilities which face the system manager each day. The difference between success and failure is a good utility belt with reliable hardware, transparent software, and technical know-how. Let's begin our discussion of NetWare basics with a look at the responsibilities and resources of the NetWare system manager.

QUOTE

My precept to all who build is, that the owner should be an ornament to the house, and not the house to the owner.

Cicero

The NetWare System Manager

The NetWare system manager is responsible for network design, implementation, and daily network management. In addition, he/she is required to perform preventative maintenance and timely network troubleshooting. Although this is not a job for the faint-of-heart, the rewards are plentiful—fame, fortune, and continued connectivity. In this section, we will explore the detailed responsibilities of the NetWare system manager and offer some valuable network resources for your utility belt. The remainder of this chapter focuses on the hardware and software basics which comprise NetWare LANs. Pay close attention to this chapter, because you never know when you will need a special torque-head screwdriver.

RESPONSIBILITIES OF A SYSTEM MANAGER

The NetWare system manager is a brave soul whose single task is to keep peace in the NetWare castle. System management is typically three full-time jobs smashed into one part-time person. In the past, the NetWare system manager was chosen by default—a dubious distinction. Nobody fully understood the time and effort it required to manage a NetWare LAN and the job was often given to the first employee who showed proficiency in using the copy machine or office microwave. Fortunately we have left the dark ages. Employers are beginning to appreciate the knowledge and skill it takes to correctly manage a LAN. The CNE and CNA certifications are gaining respect and—in many cases—are becoming a requirement.

Let's review the top ten responsibilities of a NetWare system manager:

1 • **Understand NetWare**—(Covered in Chapter 2). The first order
   of business for a NetWare system manager is a strong foundation of
   NetWare basics. After all, it is hard to manage something you don't
   understand.

2 • **Maintain Trustees & Security**—(Covered in Chapters 3, 4, 8 and 9).
   The most time-consuming responsibility a system manager has is
   maintaining network trustees and security. First, the users are created
   and organized into functional workgroups. Then their data and applications are installed and configured into an existing file structure.
   This step involves network directory structures and drive mapping.
   Next, the users are granted specific security privileges to various LAN
   directories. This step involves configuring user types and NetWare
   trustee assignments.

3 · **Monitor the File Server**—(Covered in Chapters 5 and 10). The file server is at the heart of the system manager's life. It houses the NetWare operating system and provides network users with applications, data, and shared resources. NetWare provides a variety of supervisor utilities for routine monitoring and maintenance of the file server.

4 · **Maintain the Network**—(Covered in Chapters 5, 6, 10, and 11). Once the NetWare LAN has been created and the users are defined, it is time to turn your system management attention to maintaining the network. Network maintenance has two faces—preventative maintenance and troubleshooting. Preventative maintenance is typically proactive, while troubleshooting is reactive. The former reduces the latter and ensures job stability and a relatively high quality of life.

5 · **Manage Printing**—(Covered in Chapters 7 and 12). The most mysterious and misunderstood facet of system management is printing. Printing represents 50% of LAN functionality and 10% of the system manager's time. Very little is written or said about managing network printing. In Chapter 9 we will begin with a discussion of the *Essence of Printing*. A critical topic that few people pay attention to.

6 · **Manage Network Applications**—(Covered in Chapters 6 and 11). Network applications are the functional workhorses of any NetWare LAN. They provide a purpose to the file system and give users something to do with their time. The system manager must optimize network applications by providing secure configurations and shared data directories.

7 · **Establish a User Environment**—(Covered in Chapters 6 and 11). Image is everything—well almost. In many cases the life or death of the network hangs in the balance of user interface. The LAN is only useful if the users are comfortable and productive with it. Involve the users in planning the network environment, but make sure they don't get in the way.

8 · **Maintain a System Backup**—(Covered in Chapters 6 and 11). All unemployed system managers have one thing in common: they didn't maintain a reliable system backup. System backup is the most important line of defense against unexpected network faults. Most employed system managers spend 15% of their time maintaining a reliable network backup system.

9 · **The NetWare Log Book**—(Covered in Chapter 11). Most system managers ignore this network documentation—and regret the decision later. A complete log of network details can save hours of guesswork during network maintenance and troubleshooting. The NetWare Log is at the heart of network documentation.

10 · **Staying up to date of Changing Technology**—(Covered in Other Novell Press Publications). The final system manager responsibility never ends. In addition to the previous nine responsibilities, the NetWare system manager must stay on top of changing technology. He/she must periodically re-evaluate the LAN in light of new advancements. The network is dynamic; it must evolve or else it will die. As new technologies arise, the system manager must be willing to incorporate them into the existing LAN. Other Novell Press publications provide an excellent library of alternative LAN technologies.

The system manager's diary is the NetWare Log. The log details valuable information about the LAN's hardware, software, and various configurations. Refer to Appendix B and C for a series of NetWare 2.2 and NetWare 3.12 worksheets which should be included in your diary. The NetWare Log consists of:

Identification—company name, system manager, and date

Version of NetWare—serial number and number of users

File Server Information—physical location and hardware

Volume Information—locations, types, and size

Workstation Information—users, node address, and hardware

Network Applications—location and configurations

Technical Support—names, phone numbers, hardware, and software

System Fault Tolerance—UPS, mirroring, and TTS

Recent Activity—a daily log of LAN configuration changes.

Addiction to network documentation can be a good thing and entering information into the NetWare Log should become a habit. In addition to the NetWare Log there are many other resources which aid the NetWare system manager in accomplishing his/her responsibilities: product documentation, NetWire, NetWare Express, NetWare Buyer's Guide, Network Support Encyclopedia, on-line help, and other Novell Press publications. Let's take a moment to explore each of these system manager resources. Get your utility belt ready.

SYSTEM MANAGER RESOURCES

The responsibilities of a NetWare system manager can be overwhelming at times. Fortunately, you have the comprehensive training of Novell's CNA program to guide you. This book and its affiliated courses will prepare you for 95% of the pitfalls of system management. Unfortunately, it's the other 5% which always seem to jump up and bite you. The good news is that you don't have to do it alone. Novell provides a variety of different tools which augment your impressive NetWare utility belt. Following is a brief discussion of the seven most popular Novell resources:

> This book and its affiliated courses will prepare you for 95% of the pitfalls of system management. Unfortunately, it's the other 5% which always seem to jump up and bite you.

Product Documentation

The NetWare 2.2 and 3.12 product documentation has been dramatically improved over the years. It contains a variety of resumes, including:

Concepts includes an alphabetical listing of NetWare terms. It also includes examples of critical NetWare topics such as directory structure, login scripts, and security.

Installing and Maintaining the Network offers an introduction to Net-Ware installation and network management methodologies. It is a cookbook of system management tasks including advanced installation, preventive maintenance, upgrade, and troubleshooting.

Print Server guides the system manager through the steps of designing, installing, configuring, and maintaining NetWare print services.

These are only a few of the many books available in NetWare's product documentation. There are 20 books in the NetWare 3.12 set! Keep in mind though, that while NetWare 2.2 includes all hard-copy books, NetWare 3.12 offers them only on-line.

QUOTE

The books that help you the most are those which make you think the most.

Theodore Parker

NetWire

NetWire is Novell's on-line information service. It provides access to Novell product information, press releases, network services, technical support, a calendar of events, forums, and downloadable files—patches, upgrades, and shareware utilities. NetWire is available 24 hours a day through the CompuServe Information Service (CIS). It is structured into eighteen forums and multiple software libraries, including electronic round tables for CNEs, version-specific details, an end-user area, and thousands of downloadable files. NetWire currently services over 100,000 network end users and professionals.

NetWire is an invaluable resource for CNEs. It requires a personal computer, a modem, communications software, and an account with CompuServe Information Service (CIS). CIS offers local access numbers with an on-line connect charge of $5—$12/hr., depending on speed. Contact CompuServe at (800) 848-8199 in the U.S. and Canada, or at (614) 457-0802 internationally.

World Wire

World Wire is a NEW global on-line information service that provides technical support and on-line LAN experience specifically for networking professionals. It extends beyond NetWire in providing a variety of on-line NetWare LANs, "real-time" technical support, classes, technical databases, and Internet access. World Wire is a personal, virtual city with many different "Rooms," a "Library" of files, and "Doorways" to network-related services, including a shopping mall, on-line books, articles, NetWare LANs, and on-line testing.

World Wire uses the Information Superhighway to provide local access from anywhere in the world, 24-hours a day. It is an invaluable resource for CNEs and requires a PC, modem, and any communications software. World Wire connect times are very low, ranging from $2 to $4/hr. Contact World Wire at (510) 254-7283 or ride the superhighway to (510) 254-1193.

TIP

Navigation through the on-line forest can be a losing proposition—the interface is very cryptic. Fortunately, there are two semi-free aids that automate much of the navigation lexicon: CIM and WIRERIP. CompuServe Information Manager (CIM) is a text-based or Windows-based (WinCIM) interface that provides menu choices for many of the cryptic CompuServe commands (it costs money). WIRERIP is a faster, graphical interface that personalizes navigation through the World Wire city (it's free). Either of these tools can triple your on-line productivity.

NetWare Buyer's Guide

The NetWare Buyer's Guide provides a comprehensive catalog of Novell's concepts, strategies, and products. It includes solutions for NetWare LANs, desktop computing systems, implementing wide area networks (WANs), connectivity to larger machines, and multiple workstation environments. The NetWare Buyer's Guide is a complete product catalog with four sections: Novell Corporate & Strategic Overview, Novell Product Overview, Novell Products, and Novell Support & Education. System managers can receive the guide for free by calling (800) LANKIND. The guide ships twice a year (April and October) and is currently available in paper or electronic form.

Network Support Encyclopedia

The Network Support Encyclopedia (NSE) is an electronic information database available on CD-ROM. It contains a comprehensive list of technical support questions, bulletins, patches, application notes, and on-line documentation. NSE is available in two different volumes: the Standard Volume and Professional Volume. The Standard NSE includes Technotes, Novell Labs bulletins, product documentation, a library listing of all NetWire files, and additional product information including press releases and the NetWare Buyer's Guide. The Professional NSE contains all the information from the standard volume plus all NetWire files, troubleshooting decision trees, NetWare application notes, and additional product manuals. Both NSE volumes are available on CD-ROM and are updated 4–12 times per year. Incidentally, one of the benefits of becoming a Certified NetWare Engineer is a free introductory copy of the Professional Network Support Encyclopedia.

On-Line Help

NetWare has an extensive HELP facility built into its products. The NetWare 2.2 help program is a hyper-text infobase from a company called *Folio*. The Folio Infobase provides on-line access to NetWare utility syntax, system messages, and NetWare concepts. The NetWare 3.12 help program is a Windows-based hyper-text bookshelf called *ElectroText*. ElectroText provides on-line access to all 20 books of product documentation. It is a dramatic improvement over Folio.

KNOWLEDGE

NetWare's on-line HELP facility has dramatically improved. The latest version, called *ElectroText*, was recently introduced with NetWare 3.12 and 4.0. ElectroText is fully Windows-based, indexed, context sensitive, and fuzzy logical. The most dramatic improvement is in the search engine. It supports multiple fuzzy searches with a huge variety of criteria. The cost for this technical evolution is hard disk space. The NetWare 2.2 infobase occupies roughly 1MB of server disk space, while ElectroText hogs almost 30MB of space—four times the size of the entire 2.2 product!

Other Novell Press Publications

In order to help you stay in touch with rapidly changing network technologies, Novell has developed a library of valuable LAN publications. At the heart of the Novell technical library is *Novell Press*—which has a direct line to the who's who in networking. Novell Press has access to top networking experts who work in conjunction with Novell's own technical, marketing, and management staff. Novell Press publishes an incredibly diverse collection of networking books, ranging from *Novell's Encyclopedia of Networking* to *Novell's CNA Study Guide*. A few more titles designed for the NetWare system manager include *Novell's Guide to Managing Small Networks*, *Novell's Problem Solving Guide for NetWare Systems*, and *Novell's Guide to NetWare LAN Analysis*. To order Novell Press books call Sybex, Inc. at (800) 227-2346.

QUOTE

Some books are to be tasted; others swallowed; and some few to be chewed and digested.

Francis Bacon

This completes our discussion of system management responsibilities and resources. Can you feel the weight of your NetWare utility belt?

To begin the transition from conceptual job responsibilities to meat and potatoes, we will spend the next few pages exploring NetWare's hardware and software basics. Then, we will dig in with Chapter 3—NetWare Directory Structure.

Hardware Basics

The term *network* has a variety of different meanings:

- ▶ An openwork structure of twine with periodic intersections
- ▶ An exceedingly average collection of television broadcast stations
- ▶ A system of electronic components which share a common function.

None of these definitions, however, captures the essence of NetWare. The type of network we are concerned with is:

> ▶ *A collection of distributed, intelligent machines which share data and information though interconnected lines of communication.*

Our network is a combination of hardware and software components. The hardware components control processing and communications. They include file servers, workstations, cabling components, and printing. On the other hand, the software components control productivity and intelligence. They include network operating systems, workstation shells, and network applications. In order for your NetWare LAN to operate at peak efficiency, you must balance hardware and software components with user needs and LAN synergy. In the remainder of this chapter, we will explore our definition of the network by introducing the basic concepts of LAN hardware, software, and synergy.

> In order for your NetWare LAN to operate at peak efficiency, you must balance hardware and software components with user needs and LAN synergy.

KNOWLEDGE

Synergy is defined as: *The whole is greater than the sum of its parts.*

When applied to NetWare LANs, synergy defines an environment where user interface, distributed processing, and topology components work together in harmony. To achieve NetWare synergy, the system manager must spend equal time with hardware, software, and user components. LAN synergy is highly recommended for NetWare system managers who value their peace of mind.

NETWORK TYPES

Just as a television network absorbs the minds of our young, a computer network gathers data and information. Small networks include 2–5 machines and one central file server. They are typically designed to share word processing documents or printers. Medium-sized systems share hundreds of machines with multiple file servers over a variety of different platforms—PCs, Macintoshes, and minicomputers. These networks are designed for large businesses with a variety of different computing needs. They share databases, electronic mail, and custom applications. Large internetworks are common in university settings, government institutions, or large corporations. These expansive internetworks include thousands of machines over large geographic areas. They incorporate a variety of different machines speaking a diverse collection of electronic languages.

QUOTE

We are all fellow passengers on a dot of earth. And each of us, in the span of time, has really only a moment among our companions.

Lyndon Baines Johnson

These three network scenarios provide only a snapshot of the amazing network community. Today's networks are so incredibly versatile that they touch every aspect of our lives—shopping, banking, working, and entertainment. The assumption is that networks improve our general quality of life, but the jury is still out on that one. Regardless of their philosophical value, networks make our lives easier and they are definitely here to stay.

> Regardless of their philosphical value, networks make our lives easier and they are definitely here to stay.

Computer networks are categorized according to size. Here's a brief peek at the three most popular LAN classifications.

LAN (Local Area Network) is a small collection of workstations in a local geographic area. LANs typically serve small to medium-sized offices on a single floor. LANs never extend beyond one mile.

WAN (Wide Area Network) is a large collection of LANs—kind of a LAN of LANs. WANs extend the local network over large geographic or technical boundaries. Geographic expansion is achieved through worldwide communication lines and advanced routers. Technical expansion is achieved through the integration of dissimilar machines speaking dissimilar languages.

MAN (Metropolitan Area Network) is a restricted WAN confined to a specific metropolitan area. MANs share a common goal—municipal integration. MANs provide electronic communications between a variety of different municipal entities, including banking, industry, broadcast cable, home computers, shopping, utilities, and entertainment. MANs are currently being developed in a small collection of pilot cities.

All of these different network classifications share one common thread—connectivity. Connectivity is the underlying theme of all computer networks. After all, their purpose is to share electronic resources through a collection of *interconnected* lines. Network connectivity is achieved in three different ways: Peer-to-Peer, Client/Server, and Interconnectivity. The following is a brief description of these three network connectivity fundamentals.

Peer-to-Peer Networks

The first connectivity option is peer-to-peer networks. These systems are unique in that they share computer resources without the aid of one central file server or network operating system. Peer-to-peer LANs rely on the workstations to control network operations. There is no one point of control or failure. In order to achieve this distributed control, the peer-to-peer network operating system is present on all workstations. The distributed workstations can share hard disks and printers directly with other workstations. Figure 2.1 illustrates a typical peer-to-peer network with multiple workstations and direct lines of communication. The figure shows each workstation with shared resources and two operating systems: the required workstation operating system (WOS) and a peer-to-peer network operating system (NOS). Notice how the lines of communication point from each workstation directly to all the others.

FIGURE 2.1

A typical Peer-to-Peer
network layout

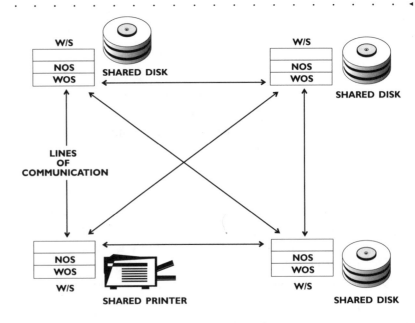

ADVANTAGES	DISADVANTAGES
low cost	slow
no central point of failure	difficult to maintain security
easy to use	limited number of workstations

Some of the most common peer-to-peer operating systems include NetWare Lite, LANtastic, Windows NT, and Windows for Workgroups. In addition, Net-Ware 3.12 and 4.0 will soon have some peer-to-peer functionality built into the new workstation shells.

Client/Server Networks

The second type of network connectivity requires a central file server and dedicated network operating system. The file server houses all shared resources and provides connectivity to the workstation clients. The client/server model relies on the central PC for network control, shared resources, security, and connectivity to other systems—interconnectivity. NetWare uses the client/server model because it provides a dedicated processor for complex network operations. The clients connect to the central NetWare server through a special workstation program called the *shell*. The NetWare shell interfaces between the workstation operating system and NetWare. Figure 2.2 illustrates a typical client/server system with the central file server attending to multiple client workstations. Notice that the lines of communication point from each workstation directly to the central server. Also, the shared disk and printer are attached to the server, not the workstations. In a client/server system, the local workstation resources are not available to other network clients.

ADVANTAGES	DISADVANTAGES
increased speed	expensive hardware
enhanced security	expensive NOS
expansion	difficult to install
excellent management tools	

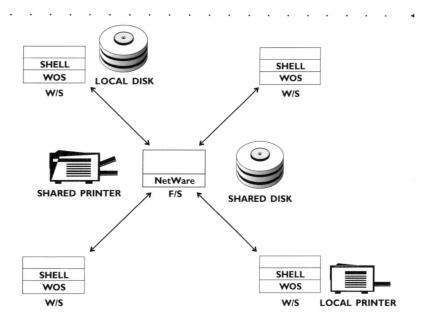

F I G U R E 2.2

A typical Client/Server network layout

Besides NetWare, there are a few other client server operating systems which provide similar network connectivity: Banyan VINES, Microsoft LAN Manager, and AppleShare, to name a few.

Interconnectivity

Another approach to network connectivity involves the extension of network resources beyond the local boundaries of a LAN. WANs and MANs require connectivity expansion beyond workstations and servers. This expansion is known as *interconnectivity*. Interconnectivity provides the capability of connecting multiple like or unlike LANs. Interconnectivity is achieved through one of two devices:

> **Routers** allow network expandability by interconnecting multiple file servers or LAN topologies. (A topology is a geographic arrangement of network nodes and cabling components.) A NetWare router can connect up to 4 like or unlike topologies from within the server (internal routing) or in an external workstation (external routing). NetWare allows an external router to run in dedicated real mode, dedicated protected mode, or nondedicated protected mode. Figure 2.3 illustrates internal routing between two unlike LAN topoligies: Ethernet and ARCNet.

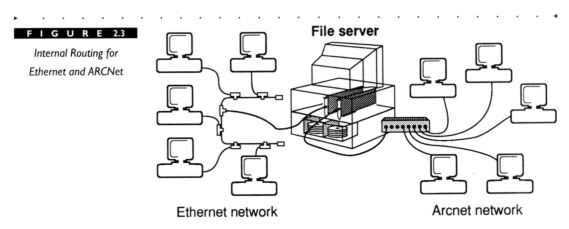

File server

Ethernet network   Arcnet network

Internal router

Gateways provide additional expansion and functionality by allowing connectivity between NetWare LANs and other unlike computer systems, including mainframes, minicomputers, SNA, TCP/IP, or X.25. Another form of gateway allows NetWare LANs to communicate with remote workstations. These systems rely on modems and dedicated PCs as asynchronous communication gateways.

KNOWLEDGE

When a NetWare workstation needs to access the services of a mainframe or minicomputer, the workstation requests a session from the gateway machine. If a session is available, the gateway grants the workstation a direct connection to the host computer and acts as a messenger between the two unlike systems. Novell provides gateway services through a variety of additional NetWare products. Refer to the NetWare Buyer's Guide for a complete list.

Connectivity is the true purpose of a NetWare LAN. So how is it achieved? Let's take a closer look at the hardware components.

NETWORK COMPONENTS

Earlier we talked about synergy and wholes and parts. So what about these network parts. What are they? How do they work together? Who killed Laura Palmer? Network hardware is organized into four different categories:

- ► File Servers and Workstations
- ► Topology Components
- ► File Server Memory and Disk Storage
- ► Network Printers

File servers and workstations are the real workhorses of the LAN. They provide distributed processing, network control, and a platform for network

> File servers and workstations are the real workhorses of the LAN. They provide distributed processing, network control, and a platform for network operating systems and applications.

operating systems and applications. Topology components provide network connectivity. They are the glue which binds the file servers and workstations together. Topology components include network interface cards (NICs), cabling, and hubs. Other components, namely file server memory and disk storage, increase network performance and provide the capacity for shared applications and data. Finally, network printers provide quality output for network users.

Let's take a closer look at the four categories of network hardware:

File Servers and Workstations

NetWare supports a variety of different workstations, but only one type of server—an Intel-based PC. NetWare 2.2 is designed for the 80286 Intel architecture and it supports 16-bit processing and 16-bit internal bus channels. The server must be at least an 80286 machine, but NetWare 2.2 will support an 80386, 80486, or Pentium processor. The two key bottlenecks for a NetWare server are the NIC channel and disk channel. NetWare 2.2 can slow down in heavy loads because it only supports 16-bit channels. NetWare 3.12, on the other hand, provides much better performance over a 32-bit 80386 architecture.

NetWare is much more accommodating from the workstation viewpoint. It inherently supports ISA, MCA, and Macintosh architectures, as well as DOS, Windows and OS/2 workstation environments. Additional support for Macintosh and UNIX is provided through special NetWare products. The greatest asset of NetWare is transparent connectivity. Transparent connectivity applies to NetWare's ability to simultaneously support diverse workstations while maintaining a consistent interface for all users.

Topology Components

Topology components provide network connectivity. They create a communications path between distributed workstations and the central NetWare file server. Topology components fall into three categories:

NICs (network interface cards) are internal components which communicate with the file server/workstation CPU and the network topology. The topology is the organizational standard for network communications. NetWare supports a variety of different topologies, including Ethernet BUS, Ethernet 10BaseT, ARCNet, Token Ring, and LocalTalk. The NIC card plugs into the file server/workstation expansion slot and connects directly to network cabling. NetWare and the workstation shells must be specially configured to communicate with the internal NIC.

Cabling provides the pathway for network communications. The topology standard and NIC determine which cabling type should be used. Table 2.1 provides a simple look at the relationships between topology, NIC, and network cabling. The most popular types of LAN cabling include coaxial, unshielded twisted pair, shielded twisted pair, and fiber optics.

Hubs provide a control point for signal routing or packet broadcasts. All hubs perform basically the same function, although they come in many different names—Ethernet 10BaseT calls them concentrators, ARCNet has active and passive hubs, and Token Ring uses MSAUs, or MultiStation Access Units.

T A B L E 2.1

The Relationship between Topology, NIC, and Network Cabling

TOPOLOGY	NIC	NETWORK CABLING
Ethernet BUS	BNC	0.2 inch Coaxial—50 ohm / Fiber Optics
	DIX	0.4 inch Coaxial—50 ohm / Fiber Optics
Ethernet 10BaseT	RJ-45	Unshielded Twisted Pair
ARCNet	BNC	Coaxial—93ohm
	RJ-45	Unshielded Twisted Pair
Token Ring	AUI	Shielded Twisted Pair / Fiber Optics
Local Talk	RJ-11	Unshielded Twisted Pair

QUOTE

What's in a name? That which we call a rose by any other name would smell as sweet.

William Shakespeare

KNOWLEDGE

The nemesis of network cabling is EMI, or ElectroMagnetic Interference. EMI distorts electronic signals and damages network communications. Some cabling is more susceptible to EMI than others. From worst to best, they are: unshielded twisted pair, shielded twisted pair, coaxial cabling, and fiber optics. The most common sources of EMI include elevator motors, fluorescent lighting, electrical wiring, and large generators.

File Server Memory and Disk Storage

NetWare LANs are heavily dependent on file server RAM (Random Access Memory). The server RAM is used to process network requests, speed up shared data requests, and buffer incoming messages. Disk storage is important for many different reasons. Although it doesn't help process requests or increase LAN performance, server disk storage is the single most important asset on the LAN. The server disk houses NetWare, network applications, and shared data. It is the permanent filing cabinet for network productivity.

> The server disk houses NetWare, network applications, and shared data. It is the permanent filing cabinet for network productivity.

NetWare RAM and disk storage work hand in hand. As requests are made for shared data, NetWare accesses the disk and moves the data into server RAM (this process occurs relatively slowly). When subsequent requests are made for the same data, NetWare can process the request from RAM (a much faster proposition). This phenomenon is known as *file caching* and it increases network performance while decreasing disk wear. File caching is described later in the chapter. Refer to Table 2.2 for a summary of NetWare features and storage capacities.

KNOWLEDGE

The difference between file server RAM and disk storage is clarified by asking two simple questions: "What is your home phone number?" and "What is the Kremlin's phone number?"

The first number should appear in your mind almost instantly (since you accessed it from RAM), while the second number might require a little more time and research (since you had to refer to permanent storage—a Russian phone book. If I asked the same two questions five minutes from now, file caching would be invoked.)

T A B L E 2.2		
NetWare Features Summary for NetWare 2.2 and 3.12		

MAJOR NETWARE FEATURES	NETWARE 2.2	NETWARE 3.12
DOS/Windows support	Yes	Yes
OS/2 support	Yes	Yes
Macintosh support	Yes	Additional
NFS UNIX support	No	Additional
AppleTalk support	Yes	Additional
File Server Bus	ISA, MCA	ISA, MCA, EISA
User Configurations	5, 10, 50, 100	5, 10, 25, 50, 100, 250
Maximum Disk Storage	2 GB	32 TB
Maximum Volume Size	255 MB	32 TB
Minimum RAM	2.5 MB	4 MB
Maximum RAM	12 MB	4 GB
Maximum Number of Open Files	1,000	100,000

Network Printers

The second most popular NetWare resource is shared printing. And since all productive network data must eventually be represented in printed form, network printers ultimately become very important. NetWare supports the following printing configurations:

> **Core Printing** refers to network printers attached directly to the file server. Core printing is established during the NetWare installation process and it provides the capacity for up to 5 network printers.

> **Print Servers** build on core printing by expanding the number of supported printers to 16. A NetWare print server can be installed on the file server or on a dedicated workstation (as PSERVER.EXE). Any print server can support users from a maximum of eight different file servers.

> **Remote Printing** was invented because print servers can support up to 16 printers throughout the LAN, but only 5 on one machine. Remote printing allows you to grant network access to local printers attached to distributed workstations. The workstation runs a small TSR (Terminate, Stay Resident) program called RPRINTER.EXE and all network users can instantly access that workstation's printer.

We will explore network printing in much more depth later in Chapter 9—Printing.

Software Basics

Our discussion of hardware basics focused on the network components which control processing and LAN communications. We discussed network classifications and the hardware parts which contribute to LAN synergy. Now we will delve into the network components which control productivity and LAN intelligence. Software basics involve distributed processing, file server software, and workstation shells. In this section, we will explore what makes NetWare so great and try to understand its processes, specifications, and support for diverse workstation environments. In addition, we will describe the many built-in system fault tolerance features which provide stability and peace-of-mind to LANs running critical network applications. Let's start at the beginning.

DISTRIBUTED PROCESSING

The primary difference between a network and any other computer system is where the processing occurs. In mainframe or minicomputer systems, the central machine does all of the work. The "slave"-like clients simply sit there and act dumb. Hence the name *dumb terminal*. A network is different for one very important reason—the *clients* do all of the work. In a NetWare LAN, all of the data is stored on the central file server. When a user wants to access the data, he/she attaches to the file server and downloads a copy of the data to local workstation RAM. The workstation runs the application and manipulates the network data—completely in workstation RAM. This is known as *distributed processing*. Once the user is finished with the data, he/she uploads a copy of the new data to the file server where it is stored for future use.

> The primary difference between a network and any other computer system is where the processing occurs. In mainframe or minicomputer systems, the central machine does all of the work. In a NetWare LAN, the clients do all the work!

The exciting part about distributed processing is that each user has access to an entire computer system. In a centralized system, the client terminals utilize only a fraction of the central processor. Also, the overall processing power of distributed systems increase as workstations are attached. The benefits of distributed processing also include enhanced security, concurrent data sharing, and system fault tolerance.

KNOWLEDGE

A harmful myth has permeated the network community—probably started by a mainframe person. It goes like this: every great network needs a really powerful file server—workstations don't matter. Even worse, people believe that all the available bells and whistles should

go onto the file server, not the workstations. I have seen many instal-
lations with $10,000 file servers and $500 workstations. This thinking
is absolutely wrong. The concept of distributed processing states that
95% of the LAN's work is performed by the workstations. File servers
are important, but workstations are the key to NetWare nirvana.

FILE SERVER SOFTWARE

The file server software is at the heart of the LAN. It provides network control,
security, file management, and transparent connectivity. Novell is the leading
manufacturer of file server software—nine generations of NetWare. The purpose of file server software is resource management. The network operating
system must be capable of managing internal RAM, network applications, user
requests, printing, and network directory structures. This is not a simple
proposition. In order to achieve this level of sophistication, NetWare has
evolved tremendously over the past 10 years. Its ninth generation, NetWare 4.0,
is over 70MB in size and offers a completely new perspective to networking—
logical directory services.

> The file server software is at the heart of the LAN. It provides network control, security, file management, and transparent connectivity. Novell is the leading manufacturer of file server software—nine generations of NetWare.

In this book, we are focusing on NetWare 2.2 and 3.12. The following few
pages provide some insight into NetWare's features, benefits, and specifications.
Follow this section carefully because it offers some very valuable ammunition for
your NetWare utility belt.

NetWare Specifications

As with any other software package, NetWare has some built-in limitations.
Although these limitations are logical in nature, they are controlled by the file
server hardware architecture. The fundamental difference between NetWare 2.2
and 3.12 specifications is in the 80286 vs. 80386 hardware. The 80286 processor
uses a 16-bit architecture, whereas the 80386 system includes a 32-bit processor and expansion bus. The 32-bit design provides a great deal more flexibility

and exponential improvements in RAM and disk capacity. Table 2.2 summarizes NetWare's major features and provides a comparison of the NetWare specifications for NetWare 2.2 and 3.12. For a complete list of NetWare specifications refer to the most current NetWare Buyer's Guide (included on disk at the back of this book).

The two most compelling improvements in NetWare 3.12 are *Maximum Volume Size* and *Maximum RAM*. With today's advanced machines and gigabyte capacities, NetWare 2.2's limitations are pretty severe. Again, this is due in part to the restrictive 16-bit file server architecture.

NetWare Performance Features

NetWare utilizes myriad advanced performance algorithms which improve network processing up to 10,000%! These features are built into the NetWare operating system core and automatically implemented each time the file server boots. The following NetWare performance features are included with NetWare 2.2, 3.12, and 4.0:

- ▸ Directory Caching

- ▸ Directory Hashing

- ▸ File Caching

- ▸ Elevator Seeking

Let's take a closer look.

Directory Caching   NetWare uses two different directory tables to keep track of network data: directory entry table (DET) and file allocation table (FAT). The DET stores basic information about NetWare file names, directories, file locations, and file/directory properties. The DET's file location parameter points to entries in the corresponding FAT. The FAT lists all files on the NetWare volume and the specific disk blocks they occupy. Whenever a user requests access to a NetWare file, the system must refer to the DET and FAT tables for basic file information. Directory caching speeds up this process by storing the DET and FAT tables in file server RAM. Each reference to the DET or FAT is performed

100 times faster from within memory. This allows the file server to locate the tables much more quickly and efficiently than if it had to read the information from disk.

Directory Hashing   Directory hashing further enhances DET access by indexing the table. This features allows NetWare to find the correct directory entry much more quickly, and reduces the response time of disk I/O by 30 percent.

File Caching   File caching has the largest impact on file server performance. As we learned earlier, data access from file server RAM is 100 times faster than data access from disk. Imagine how fast the system would be if all network data was stored in file server RAM. Unfortunately, this isn't feasible. But NetWare's file caching feature does provide users with the next best thing: all the most-recently-used files are stored in file server RAM.

Here's how it works: when a file is first requested, it is brought from the disk across the network topology to workstation RAM. At the same time, the system copies a duplicate of the file into file server RAM. All subsequent requests for the file are serviced from file server RAM. Once file server RAM fills up, NetWare replaces cached files in least-used order. The system will automatically use all available RAM for file caching. This performance feature also reduces disk wear and tear.

Elevator Seeking   Elevator seeking is an interesting animal. It is a disk management process which borrows ideas from elevator traffic movements. Elevator seeking prioritizes file requests according to their location on the server disk. It re-shuffles the order of user requests and creates the most efficient path for the disk's read/write heads. Figure 2.4 illustrates elevator seeking for four NetWare files: 1, 2, 3, and 4. Notice how the retrieval order has been reshuffled to minimize disk wear. Elevator seeking is a mind-boggling operation.

NetWare System Fault Tolerance

NetWare has seven built-in features which protect network data from harmful system faults. These features are grouped into a data integrity benefit called

Prioritizing disk requests
with Elevator Seeking

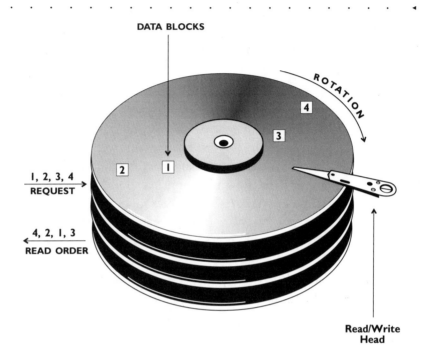

DATA BLOCKS

ROTATION

1, 2, 3, 4
REQUEST

4, 2, 1, 3
READ ORDER

Read/Write
Head

System Fault Tolerance (SFT). One possible definition of SFT is:

> ▶ *SFT is the measure of a system's tolerance to faults.*

In this case, the name says it all. A high level of system fault tolerance provides data protection against a variety of possible system faults, including power outages or disk crashes. A low level of SFT means that your LAN is susceptible to many different network faults: power spikes, brown-outs, data corruption, and so on. The seven features which make up NetWare SFT are included in all current versions of NetWare—NetWare 2.2, 3.12, and 4.0. Let's take a peek.

KNOWLEDGE

In the past, Novell organized the seven NetWare SFT features into two categories: SFT I (Read-After-Write verification, duplicate DETs and FATs, Hot Fix) and SFT II (Disk Mirroring, Disk Duplexing, TTS, UPS Monitoring). Today, these features are all bundled into one SFT

benefit. In addition, Novell has introduced another reliability feature known as **SFT III**. **SFT III is full server duplexing and it is only available in NetWare 3.12 and 4.0.**

Read-After-Write Verification   This feature assures that data written to the network disk matches the original data in file server RAM. Each time the server writes a file to the internal disk, it verifies the integrity of the data by reading it back and comparing it to the original file in memory. If the disk file matches the memory file, the server releases the data from memory and continues with the next disk operation. If the disk file doesn't match the memory file, the server retries. After a number of retries, the server gives up and marks the disk area unusable. At this point, NetWare reverts to another system fault tolerance feature called *Hot Fix*.

Hot Fix   Hot fix takes over when the read-after-write verification process discovers a bad disk block. Hot fix marks the bad block as unusable and redirects the data to a reserved portion of the disk called the *hot fix redirection area*. Figure 2.5 shows a typical bad block being remapped to the hot fix redirection area. Hot fix is sometimes called Dynamic Bad Block Remapping because it works on the fly. The hot fix redirection area occupies 2% of the server disk by default.

TIP

When network data is written to the hot fix redirection area it is never returned to the main portion of the disk. As a result, the hot fix redirection area quickly fills up. This is done to provide a red flag to the network manager. As a general rule of thumb, the hot fix redirection area should never reach 70% occupancy. If this occurs, it is a sure sign that the server disk is near failure.

Duplicate DETs and FATs   As we discussed earlier, DETs and FATs contain basic information for network directories, and files. NetWare automatically

*A bad block being
remapped to the Hot Fix
Redirection Area*

NETWORK
DATA AREA

HOT FIX
REDIRECTION AREA
(2%)

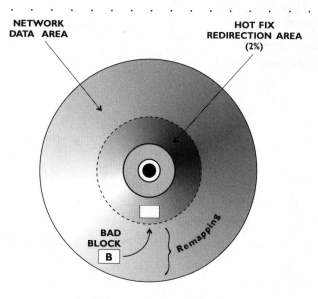

BAD
BLOCK

B

Remapping

duplicates the DETs and FATs on alternative portions of the server disk. This increases system fault tolerance by reducing the possibility of DET/FAT corruption or failure.

Disk Mirroring   Disk mirroring and disk duplexing are two SFT strategies for disk crash protection. Disk mirroring duplicates the entire contents of the server disk on a second "mirrored" disk. If the first disk fails, the second disk automatically takes over. No questions asked. Disk mirroring is accomplished by attaching both drives to the same disk controller. This strategy is cheaper, but it creates a single point of SFT vulnerability—the controller.

Disk Duplexing   Disk duplexing provides an additional level of data SFT by duplicating the controller as well as the disk. In addition, duplexing mirrors the external disk power supply and the controller cable. All disk components are duplicated. This level of SFT is very expensive, but it offers the greatest protection against disk crashes and network data loss. Refer to Figure 2.6 for an illustration of disk mirroring versus disk duplexing.

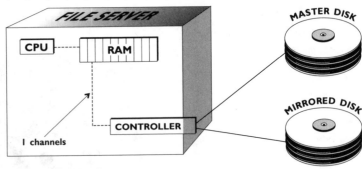

F I G U R E 2.6

Disk Mirroring versus
Disk Duplexing

DISK MIRRORING

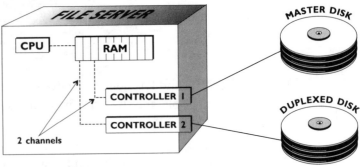

DISK DUPLEXING

KNOWLEDGE

**Disk duplexing also offers a performance feature that isn't possible
with disk mirroring. Since disk duplexing mirrors the entire disk
channel—disk, disk controller, cable, and so on—it can read and write
data to both disks at the same time. While this feature doesn't help
with disk writes (it has to write to both disks anyway), it dramatically
improves the response time of disk reads. This performance feature
is known as split seeking.**

Transaction Tracking System   NetWare's transaction tracking system
(TTS) provides data protection for selected network database applications. TTS
tracks database transactions from beginning to end. If a system fault interrupts a

transaction before it is completed, TTS will abort the transaction's updates and rollback the database to the last point of consistency. TTS protects large database files from data corruption, data loss, or transaction mismatch. In order to activate NetWare TTS, the system manager must specify it at installation and flag the network database as a TTS file. The database application must also be TTS-compatible. Ask your dealer or check with NetWire, NSE, or the most current NetWare Buyer's Guide.

UPS Monitoring   The final NetWare SFT feature is UPS monitoring. This feature protects NetWare file servers from sudden, unexpected power failures. An Uninterruptible Power Supply (UPS) is a stable energy source which provides power to network machines in the event of electrical brownouts or blackouts. Basically, it is a large, intelligent battery. Without a server UPS, power failures can cause irreparable damage to network hard disks, data, and topology components. UPS monitoring is a combination of hardware and software which *downs* the server gracefully in the event of an electrical brownout or blackout. (It first sends a message to NetWare users encouraging them to logout and downs the file server 15 minutes later.) UPS monitoring is available for NetWare 2.2, 3.12, and 4.0.

This completes our discussion of file server software. But you ain't seen nothin' yet. If you think NetWare is amazing, wait until you see what the workstations can do.

WORKSTATION SOFTWARE

If file server software is the heart of the LAN, workstation software is the brains. In a distributed processing environment, 95% of the work occurs at the network workstation. The real brains behind NetWare is in the workstation operating system (WOS). Without the WOS, NetWare would be useless. In addition, the workstation environment provides transparent connectivity to network users and a point of entrance to shared LAN resources.

> If file server software is the heart of the LAN, workstation software is the brains. In a distributed processing environment, 95% of the work occurs at the network workstation. The real brains behind NetWare is in the workstation operating system (WOS).

Novell understands these concepts very well. In fact, they have spent a great deal of time optimizing NetWare's workstation interface. NetWare's built-in interoperability allows many different users from a variety of different workstations to share the same network data. This level of interoperability is not achieved easily. It relies on a complex structure of workstation shells and network protocol stacks. After all, NetWare was originally written for DOS!

In our discussion of workstation software, we will focus on NetWare's support for DOS—namely IPX and NETx. We will, however, take a brief look at multi-protocol support (ODI) and the NEW NetWare DOS Requester (VLM). We will discuss workstation software in more depth in Chapter 11.

IPX

IPX stands for internetwork packet exchange. It is the NetWare protocol which handles communications between network interface cards and workstation shells. The workstation shells handle communications between IPX and the workstation operating system. At the server, IPX is built into NetWare. At the workstation, IPX runs from workstation memory as the file IPX.COM. IPX.COM is the union of IPX.OBJ and a NIC-specific LAN driver. IPX.COM is created with the WSGEN utility.

NETx

When IPX receives a network message which is destined for the workstation operating system, NETx handles the transfer. NETx is called a *shell* because it screens all workstation requests and decides whether they belong to the WOS or to IPX. It protects the WOS from the LAN just as a clam shell protects the clam. The NETx shell exists in workstation RAM as one of three different files:

 ▸ NETx.COM—the standard shell resides in conventional workstation RAM—the first 640K. NETx.COM requires about 47K or workstation RAM.

TIP

The best solution is to *load high* NETx.COM. This feature is available in DOS 5.0 and above.

▸ EMSNETx.EXE—the expanded shell resides in expanded workstation RAM—the reserved memory between 640K and 1MB. EMSNETx.COM requires the LIM 4.0 expanded memory manager and works with all versions of NetWare. It frees 34K of conventional RAM by loading primarily in expanded memory. Note: expanded memory is generally slower than conventional RAM.

▸ XMSNETx.EXE—the extended shell resides in extended workstation RAM—memory above the 1MB barrier. XMSNETx.COM requires the LIM 4.0 extended memory manager and also works with all versions of NetWare. It frees 34K of conventional RAM. Note: XMSNETx.COM must load in the High Memory Area (HMA)—or first 64K of extended memory. Unfortunately, this is the same area where DOS 5.0 loads high. Therefore, the extended memory shell is not compatible with DOS 5.0 or greater if DOS is loaded high.

KNOWLEDGE

NETx uses the "x" denotion because it recently became WOS version-independent. In earlier times, NETx was NET2, NET3, NET4, or NET5. Each of the NET# shells corresponded to a specific version of DOS. Today, NETx will work with any version of DOS from v2.1 to v6.0.

ODI

Open Data-link Interface (ODI) is not a shell. It is a protocol interface which replaces IPX in cases where multiple protocols are required. ODI speaks many languages and translates any ODI-compatible protocol into something the NetWare workstation can understand. It also provides support for multiple protocols within the same workstation NIC. For example, ODI allows NetWare workstations to communicate with NetWare servers using IPX and UNIX servers using TCP/IP—all through the same NIC. ODI is quickly becoming the workstation wave of the future.

NetWare DOS Requester

The NetWare DOS Requester is another new workstation technology that works in conjunction with ODI drivers to define NetWare 3.12's new workstation environment. The Requester is a set of Virtual Loadable Modules (VLMs) that provide communications between DOS and IPXODI. These VLMs are loaded automatically using the VLM Manager (VLM.EXE) and they replace the earlier NETX.COM files. The modular VLMs can be loaded and unloaded at will, therefore reducing workstation overhead while providing a development platform for third-party programmers.

Support for Non-DOS Workstations

As we mentioned earlier, NetWare supports a variety of different workstation environments. NetWare supports four additional workstation operating systems (WOSs) beyond DOS—Windows, OS/2, Macintosh, and UNIX. Windows support is built in but OS/2 workstations require special client drivers—the OS/2 Requester. Macintosh and UNIX workstations, on the other hand, have built-in network drivers. They don't require any special client software. Support for Macintosh and UNIX workstations is provided by special server software—namely, NetWare for Macintosh and NetWare for NFS, respectively.

QUOTE

It takes all sorts to make a world.

English Proverb

Well that does it for the NetWare basics. We have discussed system manager responsibilities, available resources, and the basics of network hardware and software. In addition, we have explored the purpose of the system manager's utility belt and provided some great tools to get it started. The rest of this book is all about how to build your repertoire of NetWare knowledge so that you can be the best CNA in the world. So sit up straight and pay attention. This is going to be fun.

EXERCISE 2.1: UNDERSTANDING NETWARE BASICS

1. A system manager responsibility	A. Dynamic bad block remapping
2. Concepts	B. Includes tech notes and online documentation
3. Interconnectivity	C. 32-bit operating system
4. NetWare 3.12	D. 32 terrabytes
5. NetWare 3.12 disk maximum	E. Decreases disk thrashing
6. Hot fix	F. Two disks, one controller
7. NSE	G. Maintain a system backup
8. Elevator seeking	H. Server duplexing
9. Disk mirroring	I. Uses 50-ohm coaxial
10. NetWare 2.2	J. 16-bit operating system
11. NetWare 2.2 RAM maximum	K. Routers and gateways
12. Network	L. A collection of distributed intelligent machines
13. WAN	M. Alphabetic listing of terms
14. Coaxial	N. A type of LAN cabling
15. Ethernet	O. A LAN of LANs
16. File caching	P. 12 megabytes
17. SFT III	Q. Increases disk I/O by 10,000%

See Appendix D for answers.

EXERCISE 2.2: USING NETWARE 3.12 ELECTROTEXT

NetWare 3.12 is equipped with a powerful new Windows-based documentation tool called "ElectroText." ElectroText is an on-line, electronic version of NetWare 3.12 documentation—all 20 books! Let's take a closer look.

1 · Begin Microsoft Windows.

2 · Enter ElectroText by choosing File ➤ Run from Program Manager and executing ET.EXE from the SYS:PUBLIC (network) or E:\PUBLIC (CD-ROM) subdirectory.

3 · This is the main library screen. Enter the NetWare 3.12 Manuals bookshelf.

4 · Notice the many electronic books that appear. Each book represents one of the 20 different NetWare 3.12 manuals. The extra book is a Novell Press catalog. Enter the Novell Press Catalog and type **CNA** in the Search For: box at the bottom of the screen. Click on "Next." How many instances of the word CNA appear in the catalog?

5 · Close the Novell Press Catalog and return to the NetWare 3.12 Manuals. Open the Concepts manual and find NETWIRE using the outline. Click on the "+" preceeding NNN. Find "NetWire" and click on it. Find "UPS Monitoring" and "MIRRORING."

6 · Search for information concerning the Supervisor. How many times does this topic appear in the Concepts manual? How many times does it appear in the entire NetWare 3.12 library? (Hint: to search the entire library, close the Concepts manual and begin the search from the main screen.)

7 · Experiment with the appearance of the outline screen. Open the Overview manual. Choose File ➤ Preferences. Notice the choices for positioning the outline screen. Highlight Top and Choose OK.

8 · Explore the NEW Features of NetWare 3.12. Review Novell ElectroText. What subtopics appear under Novell ElectroText? Which NetWare 3.12 manual is not available on-line?

9 · ElectroText includes hyper-text references within and between books. Notice the green-colored topic "Installing and Using Novell Electro-Text." This refers to a topic in Appendix B of another book—Installation and Upgrade. Jump to the hyper-text reference by clicking on the green-colored sentence.

10 · Exit the Installation and Upgrade manual. Let's explore the Printing features of ElectroText. Open the System Administration book. Find the reference to Printing in the Using Novell ElectroText section. Review the Procedure for printing from within ElectroText. What happens when you double-click on the green camera icon?

11 · Follow the printing procedures. First, select File ➤ Print from the title bar. Choose "Sections you choose from outline below." Which book appears in the outline?

12 · Let's print something. Click on the "+" preceeding How to Use this Manual. Select User Comments and choose OK.

Send a note to Novell Technical Publications telling them what you think of ElectroText.

Finish the exercise by exploring many of the other features of Novell Electro-Text. As you can see, this is a superior way of accessing critical NetWare documentation information. It's not the most natural way to read a book, but on-line documentation makes searching for details a lot easier.

> **TIP**
>
> **You can install Novell ElectroText on the network or a local hard disk. In addition, users can access the ElectroText database directly from the NetWare 3.12 system CD-ROM. For more information on installing ElectroText, refer to ElectroText itself.**

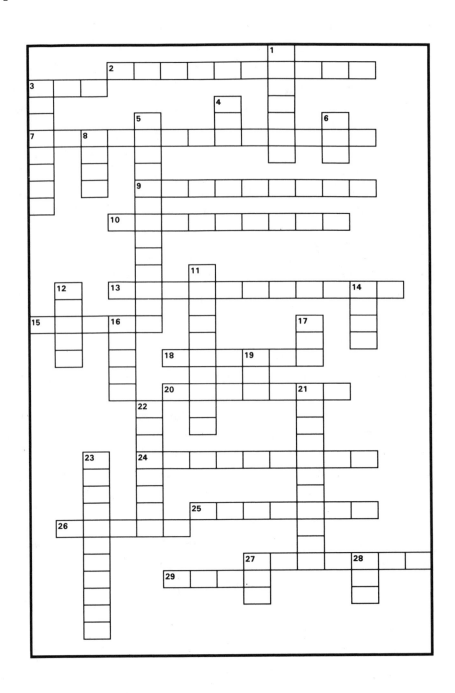

Part I—Fundamentals

ACROSS

2 16-bit NetWare for workgroups

3 Hot fix, mirroring, etc.

7 Protect against power outages

9 The home of the Motorola CPU

10 A dedicated line to the CPU

13 Increases file access 10,000%

15 Initial NetWare access tool

18 Dynamic bad block re-mapping

20 Intel's new 80586 microchip

24 Protect against disk crashes

25 Internal microcomputer freeway

26 Create a DOS volume name

27 Distributed data communications

29 Semi-permanent PC configurations

DOWN

1 Novell's on-line public service

3 Keep the bad guys out

4 A binary digit

5 The CNA must organize his/her stuff

6 The goal!

8 The ideal file server disk interface

11 Workstations talking to workstations

12 Copy DOS files and directories

14 The most current NetWare shell

16 The chip of choice for NetWare

17 NetWare's built-in protocol

19 Keeping track of DOS files

21 The CNA's secret weapon

22 Not hardware, not software

23 32-bit NetWare for large LANs

ACROSS

DOWN

27 A complete technical database

28 The new NetWare protocol drivers

See Appendix D for answers.

The NetWare 2.2 CNA Program

NetWare 2.2 is a complete, 16-bit network operating system designed to meet the needs of small businesses, professional offices, workgroups, and departments. It offers a reliable, versatile operating system that is easy to install, use, and administer. The most important goal in designing Net-Ware 2.2 was to build a single, versatile product that would meet the diverse needs of Novell's ever-changing client base.

NetWare 2.2 is actually more similar to NetWare 3.12 than to 2.15. Net-Ware 2.2 was designed as an intermediate upgrade path from existing NetWare 2.15 LANs to NetWare 3.12. The features, utilities, security, and printing components of NetWare 2.2 are dramatic improvements over its 80286-based predecessor. On the downside, 2.2 relies on a non-modular operating system file—NET$OS.EXE—which substantially restricts the system manager's ability to customize NetWare parameters. In addition, NetWare 2.2's 16-bit architecture severely affects its ability to support multiple protocols or alternative non-DOS workstation platforms.

Overall, NetWare 2.2 is a good investment and it gives you a great deal of network functionality for a relatively low price. Enjoy the show!

NetWare 2.2
Directory Structure

"Hey, Honey!
Instead of Disneyworld,
wanna go to Z:\Public for our vacation?"

As the NetWare system manager, you will inherit the LAN in the last of three construction phases—network management. The first two phases are analysis & design and Installation. During the analysis & design phase, the systems analyst and network designer evaluate the existing LAN resources and determine the system's needs. They work together to develop a solid LAN design which balances user needs with network performance and cost. Once the LAN design has been completed, the installation team takes over. They purchase the LAN materials and materialize the network design. The result is an empty shell of interconnected workstations and a central NetWare file server. No applications, no users, no life. It is the system manager's responsibility to breathe life into the empty NetWare shell.

Unfortunately, the NetWare system manager is rarely included in the first two phases of building a NetWare LAN. The manager is asked to breathe life into a system he/she had nothing to do with. He/she inherits a minimum base system—distributed workstations, connected topology components, a functioning file server, and NetWare. The minimum NetWare setup includes four system-created directories, two users, one group, and a few system/public files. This is where your job begins. It is your responsibility to hitch up the NetWare utility belt and get busy—creating a directory structure, installing applications, developing security, and adding users and groups. The process of NetWare system management begins with the creation of an efficient, secure network directory structure.

> The process of NetWare system management begins with the creation of an efficient, secure network directory structure.

Directory Types

In the previous chapter, we likened network directories to the rooms of an apartment building. These rooms take on a variety of different functions. Some rooms include apartment facilities—laundry room, garage, game room—while others house apartment staff—the LANlord and his/her family. Most apartment rooms are a home for apartment families, but a few double as business offices—for lawyers, self-employed, and so on.

NetWare directory types follow this same approach. The facility rooms are system-created directories which serve the Supervisor and daily LAN operations. The homes are user directories while the application/data directories are businesses for NetWare families. NetWare's directory structure is organized and efficient. It provides flexibility and security, while maintaining user autonomy. They are based on a vertical tree structure. Figure 3.1 illustrates a typical NetWare directory structure with the volume acting as the trunk (root) of the tree.

NetWare directories create functional groupings from the volume root. They house NetWare files or functionally-similar subdirectories. Figure 3.2 shows this directory structure as a filing cabinet with drawers (volumes), folders (directories/subdirectories), and documents (NetWare files). The filing cabinet analogy is particularly accurate.

FIGURE 3.1

A typical NetWare
directory structure

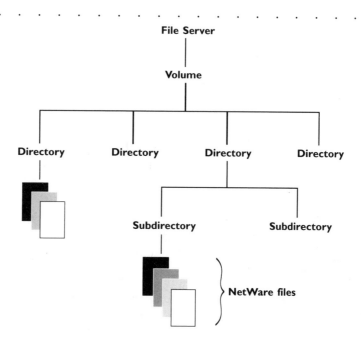

► . . . . ◄

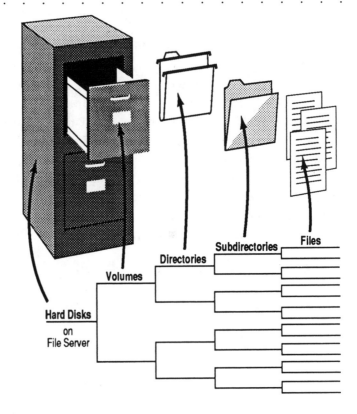

FIGURE 3.2

NetWare directories as a filing cabinet

Before we begin our discussion of NetWare's four main directory types, we need to explore the rules which govern the creation of our tree. Here's a brief list of NetWare's directory rules:

File Server	Name length is limited to 2-45 characters
	First character cannot be a period
	Name cannot contain special characters—* ? \ /
Volume	Name length is limited to 2-15 characters
	Name must end with a colon
	First volume on first disk must be SYS: Maximum of 32 volumes per server (up to 2GB)
	Maximum volume size is 255MB

Directory	Name length is limited to 11 characters (8 + 3)
	A period separates the first 8 and last 3 characters
	Directories should be limited to functional groups
Subdirectory	Name length is limited to 11 characters (8 + 3)
	A period separates the first 8 and last 3 characters
	Subdirectories share common functionality
	The number of subdirectories is limited by disk size

TIP

The rule of thumb for NetWare directory structures is KISS:

Keep It Safely Shallow

A hierarchical tree is easiest to maintain when it is not too tall and not too wide.

In our discussion of NetWare's directory structure, we will focus on the four main directory types:

- ▸ System-created directories
- ▸ DOS directories
- ▸ Application/Data directories
- ▸ User directories

> NetWare's directory structure includes system-created directories, DOS directories, application/data, and user directories.

Let's start with the system-created directories.

SYSTEM-CREATED DIRECTORIES

During the installation procedure, NetWare creates four system directories:

- ▸ LOGIN
- ▸ PUBLIC

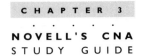

> ▸ SYSTEM

> ▸ MAIL

These four directories perform vital NetWare functions and house critical system/public files. Refer to Figure 3.3 for an illustration of NetWare's four system-created directories. All of these directories contain necessary NetWare files and should *not* be deleted. The following is a description of each of NetWare's system-created directories and their functions.

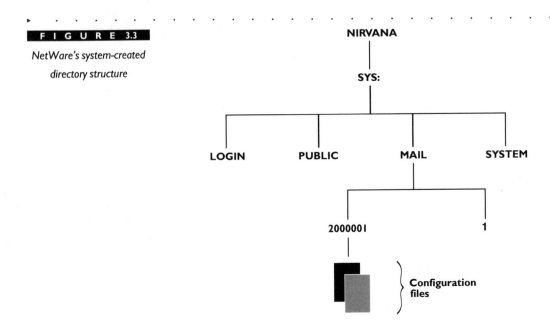

FIGURE 3.3

NetWare's system-created directory structure

LOGIN

The LOGIN directory is NetWare's welcome mat. It represents the first point of contact for attached NetWare users. Once a user attaches to the central file server, he/she has access to the LOGIN directory. But before the user can enter the rest of the apartment building (server), he/she must ring the doorbell (login) and provide the secret password. The process of logging-in is performed from the LOGIN directory.

The process of logging into a NetWare server consists of two main steps: workstation initialization and login procedures. Here's how it goes:

Workstation Initialization

1 · Boot the workstation with a supported WOS (workstation operating system)—DOS, OS/2, etc.

2 · Type IPX ↵ to load the NIC-specific NetWare protocol stack

3 · Type NETX ↵ to load the generic NetWare shell

Login Procedures

4 · Attach to the NetWare welcome mat by typing F: ↵

5 · Type LOGIN ↵

6 · Enter a valid username

7 · Enter the correct password if needed

The NetWare welcome mat contains two system files: LOGIN.EXE and SLIST.EXE. LOGIN.EXE is the executable file which allows users to log into the NetWare server. SLIST.EXE provides a list of available file servers. Notice that the available disk space in the LOGIN directory is zero. This restriction is lifted once you properly login.

SYSTEM

The SYSTEM directory is the second most important system-created directory next to LOGIN. SYSTEM houses critical NetWare files including the operating system file (NET$OS.EXE), supervisor utilities, and value added processes (VAPs). The SYSTEM directory is off limits to everybody except the Supervisor.

Novell uses a curious naming scheme to designate important system files—the "$" sign. Every critical system file in NetWare contains a $ in its name. Here are some examples:

▶ NET$OS.EXE—the NetWare 2.2 operating system file

▶ NET$LOG.DAT—the system login script file

▶ NET$BIND.SYS—one of the NetWare 2.2 bindery files

It's safe to say that Novell recognizes the monetary value of these critical system files.

PUBLIC

The PUBLIC directory is every user's playground. This is where the public Net-Ware programs are stored—commands, menu utilities, and other fun stuff. The PUBLIC directory is accessible to all network users and it provides a central shared area for frequently used network programs and system-oriented commands. Third-party utilities, for example, could be stored in the PUBLIC directory.

> The PUBLIC directory is every user's playground. This is where the public Net-Ware programs are stored—commands, menu utilities, and other fun stuff.

We will explore these public commands and utilities later in Chapter 5—NetWare 2.2 Utilities.

MAIL

The MAIL directory is left over from earlier days when NetWare included an electronic mail facility. Although E-mail is no longer included with NetWare, the MAIL directory does continue to be useful. MAIL is the parent directory for a collection of system-created user directories which correspond to each user's randomly-assigned user ID number. The user ID is a 7-8 digit, hexadecimal number which identifies each user to the NetWare operating system. For example, the Supervisor is number 1 and Guest is number 2000001. The user ID subdirectory under MAIL is used to store two very important user-specific configuration files: the user login script (LOGIN.) and printer configuration file (PRINTCON.DAT). The NetWare system manager will have to delete these user-specific subdirectories when users are deleted. This procedure is outlined in Chapter 5.

SUGGESTED DIRECTORIES

NetWare provides the system manager with a big head-start by building the four required system-created directories. The next step is to add some productive user/application directories on top of the existing directory structure. Novell suggests a variety of different approaches to creating custom directories: multiple volumes, applications sorted by user, group directories, and shared data directories. No matter how you slice it, Novell's custom approach seems to boil down to four directories. Let's take a closer look.

The DOS Directory

The DOS directory is important because it provides support for the most common workstation operating system—DOS. One of the most critical DOS files is COMMAND.COM—the workstation boot file. COMMAND.COM is loaded into workstation RAM whenever the workstation is turned on. During normal LAN operations, the COMMAND.COM file can be harshly removed from workstation RAM. If this happens, the workstation must be told where to find the file. The server's DOS directory and subsequent subdirectories provide the workstation with a simple path back to COMMAND.COM. In addition, the DOS subdirectories allow network users to access common DOS utilities from a centrally-shared directory. For this reason, the DOS directory is typically stored under PUBLIC.

In order to provide optimal workstation support, the DOS directory structure must follow a very strict pattern. Refer to Figure 3.4 for an illustration of the strict design of NetWare's DOS directories. We will explain this pattern in more depth later in Chapter 6.

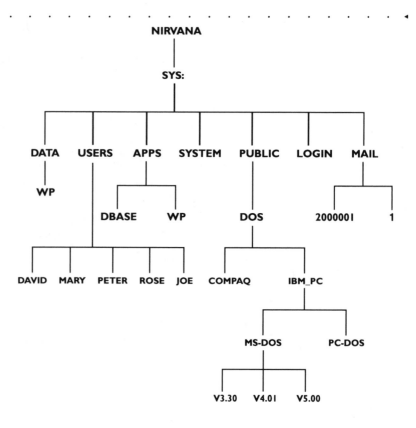

FIGURE 3.4

The Suggested NetWare
Directory Structure

QUOTE

A man travels the world over in search of what he needs, and returns
home to find it.

George Moore

User Directories

User directories provide NetWare users with their own little home and provide
them with a private subdirectory in which to begin their own personal directory
structure. User subdirectories serve two functions: security and organization.
From a security viewpoint, user subdirectories provide a secure place for private
user files or personal correspondence. From an organizational viewpoint, user subdirectories can become the parent directory of a complex user-specific directory

structure. User subdirectories should match usernames and be stored under the USERS root directory.

QUOTE

Home interprets heaven. Home is heaven for beginners.

Charles H. Parkhurst

> User directories provide NetWare users with their own little home and provide them with a private subdirectory in which to begin their own personal directory structure.

Application/Data Directories

Proper organization of application and data directories strongly impacts user productivity. If application directories are scattered, it makes it difficult for users to find network applications. Furthermore, disorganized data directories can confuse users who are trying to store network files. Application subdirectories should be created for each network application and stored under the APPS root directory. This makes application access easy for network users and security management more straightforward for the NetWare system manager. Data, on the other hand, can be stored in a variety of different directories:

- ▸ **personal data** should be stored in user directories

- ▸ **application-specific data** should be stored in DATA subdirectories under each network application

- ▸ **shared network data** should be stored directly in DATA

Refer to Figure 3.4 for a schematic of how application and data directories should be organized.

DIRECTORY PATH NAMES

All of this crazy organization can seem a bit overwhelming at first. But once you have had an opportunity to work with NetWare directories for a while, you will find them very efficient and useful. The following is an example of the syntax for NetWare directory path names:

file server/volume:directory\subdirectory

The forward slash separates the file server name and volume. The colon distinguishes the root of the volume, and the backslash separates the directories and subdirectories. Keep in mind that this format is very similar to DOS, except NetWare supports both the forward and backslash. Here's an example of a typical NetWare directory path:

CNA/SYS:USERS\DAVID

Path names are used to define file locations, drive mapping, and utility searches. It is important to use the correct syntax when establishing NetWare directory structures.

QUOTE

Sticks and stones will break my bones, but names will never hurt me.

English Proverb

Directory Structure Commands

Throughout this book, we will be adding many new system manager command tools to our NetWare utility belt. NetWare command tools are organized into three different categories:

Command-Line Utilities (CLUs) are used to manage the LAN environment. CLUs (NetWare has over 100 different ones) reside in the SYS:PUBLIC directory and are executed at the NetWare prompt—Z:\PUBLIC>. We will explore NetWare's CLUs in appropriate sections throughout the book. In this section, we will have our first discussion of NetWare command-line utilities as they apply to directory structures.

Menu Utilities provide a consolidated interface for frequently-used system management tools. We will explore NetWare 2.2 menu utilities in Chapter 5 and NetWare 3.12 menu utilities in Chapter 10.

> NetWare command tools are organized into three different categories: command-line utilities, menu utilities, and file server console utilities.

File Server Console Utilities allow supervisors to manage NetWare file servers. We will discuss NetWare 2.2's console utilities in Chapter 5.

Let's begin our discussion of NetWare command utilities with an exploration of DOS and NetWare directory commands.

DOS COMMANDS

NetWare works in conjunction with many different workstation operating systems. But it was primarily designed for DOS. Following is a description of some internal DOS commands which also work on NetWare directory structures.

PROMPT

Sets a new DOS prompt. There are myriad different prompt parameters (see Chapter 2 for a brief list). NetWare requires PROMPT PG to display current directory path names.

MD

Creates a NetWare directory or subdirectory. MKDIR also works.

CD

Changes the default DOS or NetWare directory. This command is particularly dangerous in NetWare if it is combined with search drive mappings. This is discussed later in the chapter. CHDIR also works.

COPY CON

Captures data from the screen and creates a text file. A very useful command for creating simple NetWare configuration files. Remember to use **F6** to exit the program and save your file.

DIR

Shows a listing of files and subdirectories of a given NetWare or DOS directory. DIR also displays information about directories and files, including creation date, creation time, and size.

TYPE

Displays the contents of a text file on the screen. The results of the TYPE command can be redirected to a printer or file by using the > sign:

- ▸ PRINTER—TYPE filename > PRN

- ▸ FILE—TYPE filename > FILE

RD

Removes an empty DOS or NetWare subdirectory. **RMDIR** also works.

NETWARE COMMANDS

NetWare directory structure commands build on the existing DOS commands by providing additional network functionality. NetWare offers network versions of most DOS utilities (but keep in mind that the NetWare utilities are designed to work on LAN drives only). Below is a discussion of the four most popular NetWare directory commands.

NDIR

The NDIR command is a versatile NetWare utility which allows you to search through NetWare volumes for data, applications, and utilities. NDIR is the NetWare version of DIR. In addition to the basic information—creation date, creation time, and file size—NDIR displays a plethora of network statistics, including owner, directory rights, last modified date, and file attributes. NDIR can be used to search one directory or a directory and all its subdirectories with the /SUB parameter.

Typing NDIR *.* /SUB display all information about all files in this directory and all its subdirectories.

RENDIR

The RENDIR command is a useful NetWare tool which isn't available in the DOS world. It allows you to rename an existing NetWare directory. I can't count the number of times I could have used this command in DOS.

LISTDIR

LISTDIR displays an enhanced graphic of the NetWare directory structure in a pseudo-tree layout. LISTDIR displays more security statistics than NDIR and allows you to specify which information you would like to view. Here's a description of LISTDIR syntax and its parameters:

LISTDIR /A displays all information for each specified directory

LISTDIR /D displays the creation date and time

LISTDIR /S displays all subdirectories below this directory

LISTDIR /R displays the directory rights for each specified directory

VOLINFO

VOLINFO is a graphic display of NetWare volume information and statistics. It lists volume sizes, total directory entries, free space, and available directory entries.

The NetWare directory structure is complex and sophisticated. It allows you to properly organize many different kinds of network information. A well-designed directory structure can increase user effectiveness and productivity. A related strategy for increasing user effectiveness is drive mapping. Drive mapping allows you to represent complex directory structures as simple alphabet letters. Let's take a look.

Drive Mapping

In the DOS world, we are comfortable with the idea of using letters to represent physical disk drives. In this world, the letter A represents the first floppy drive and B represents the second. Furthermore, C represents the first hard disk, while D and E indicate secondary disks. This scheme is simple and straightforward. It allows us to find data easily without having to bother with volume labels or physical mappings.

> DOS drives point to *physical* storage devices. NetWare drives point to *logical* areas on the same physical disk.

In the NetWare world, we use the same approach—kind of. NetWare also uses letters as drive pointers, but the letters point to *logical* drives not physical ones. The letter F, for example, points to a network directory (LOGIN), not a physical drive. In this case, F would represent the LOGIN directory—i.e. F:\LOGIN>. NetWare drive letters point to different directories on the same disk. This scheme is also simple and straightforward, but it takes some getting used to.

KNOWLEDGE

NetWare drive mappings can be user-specific, temporary environment variables. Each user can have a different set of drive mappings in their own workstation RAM. They are created each time the user logs in. When users logout or turn off their machines, drive mappings are lost. Fortunately, NetWare provides an automatic login script which establishes user mappings at each login.

NetWare uses two different types of drive pointers: regular and search. Regular drive pointers provide a convenient way of representing complex network path names with a single letter. Search drive pointers provide an additional level of functionality by building a search list for network applications. In this section, we will explore the details of these two NetWare drive pointers and learn how to implement them by using the MAP command. First, let's briefly review DOS pointers.

KNOWLEDGE

In this section the terms *drive pointer* and *drive mapping* will be used interchangeably. According to Novell, they are the same thing. Technically, it can be argued that the drive pointer is the alphabet letter and drive mapping is the process of assigning it to a network directory. But let's keep it simple: *Drive Pointer = Drive Mapping*.

DOS POINTERS

DOS pointers represent physical storage devices as alphabetic letters. These DOS storage devices are typically floppy drives, hard disks, or CD-ROMs. By default, DOS reserves the letters A-E for local devices. This number can be extended by using the LASTDRIVE = <letter> command in the workstation's CONFIG.SYS file. To move from one drive letter to another, you would simply type the drive letter followed by a colon and press Enter—i.e. A: ↵. Once you have moved to the correct physical drive, you can use the CD command to move between subdirectories of that drive.

TIP

It is possible to reassign a DOS pointer as a NetWare pointer. In this case, the local drive becomes unavailable to the network user. This is an effective strategy for restricting access to local floppy drives while users are attached to NetWare servers. The DOS pointer is returned to the user when he/she disconnects from the LAN.

NETWARE POINTERS

NetWare pointers are similar to DOS pointers in a few respects, but for the most part, they are two different animals. Table 3.1 provides a comparison of DOS and NetWare drive pointers. NetWare pointers use alphabetic letters to represent logical network directories—not physical disks. NetWare pointers use the same syntax as DOS pointers, but they begin where the DOS pointers ended—the

TABLE 3.1	FUNCTION	DOS POINTERS	NETWARE POINTERS
The Similarities and Differences between DOS and NetWare Drive Pointers	Drive Letters	alphabetic	alphabetic
	Syntax	<letter>:	<letter>:
	Alphabetic Range	A-E	F-Z
	Drive Type	physical drive	logical directory
	Destination	local workstation	network file server

letter F. This means that NetWare pointers have 21 possible choices—F-Z. Figure 3.5 shows a typical NetWare directory structure with the drive letter F pointing to the SYS:USERS\DAVID directory. NetWare uses two different types of drive pointers: regular pointers and search pointers.

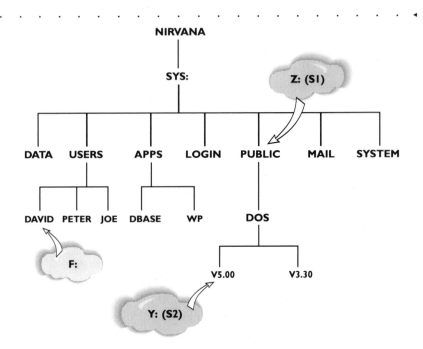

FIGURE 3.5

NetWare drive pointers and logical network directories

Regular Drive Pointers

Regular drive mappings point to user-defined data directories. These drive pointers are typically used for convenience and directory movement. Without drive mappings, movement throughout the directory tree would consist of long path names and the CD command. This is cumbersome and time-consuming. With drive mappings, movement is consolidated into one simple step—F: ↵. Regular drive pointers represent complex directory paths as simple alphabet letters. Figure 3.5 represents the path SYS:USERS\DAVID as the letter F:. Simple.

NetWare reserves the final 21 letters of the alphabet for network drive mappings. Regular drive pointers are assigned by NetWare users with the MAP command. They begin with F: and move forward. Note: if the workstation CONFIG.SYS file contains the **LASTDRIVE =** <letter> command, the first available

> NetWare reserves the final 21 letters of the alphabet for network drive mappings.

drive pointer will be the next letter. For example, **LASTDRIVE = G** will reserve A-G for DOS and the first NetWare pointer will be H.

TIP

You can actually assign 26 network drive mappings (A-Z) by overwriting all existing local drives.

Search Drive Pointers

Search drive mappings extend one step beyond regular drive mappings by providing the user with the ability to search for network application files. When a user executes a particular network application, the system searches the current directory for the application file—.EXE, .COM, or .BAT. If the file isn't there, the system looks for a search list. If a search list doesn't exist, the system will return the message: **bad command or file name**. If a search list does exist, the system will move through the list in order until it finds the application. This method is very similar to the DOS "path" command. Search drive pointers build NetWare search lists. The maximum number of search drives in a NetWare search list is 16.

QUOTE

The mind has its own logic but does not often let others in on it.

Bernard de Voto

Since search drive pointers are primarily used to build search lists, network users are more concerned with the order of the list than the letter which is assigned to the search pointer. For this reason, search drive mappings are assigned in search order by using the letter S and a number. For example, the first search drive would be assigned S1 and placed at the top of the search list. The second drive is S2 and so on. As a matter of convenience, NetWare also assigns an alphabet letter to each search pointer. This letter can be used to move around the directory structure just like a regular drive pointer.

This strategy poses an interesting question—How do you tell the difference between a regular drive letter and a search drive letter? The answer is simple: you don't! There is no way of distinguishing one from the other by simply looking at it. So as a matter of convention, NetWare assigns search drive letters from Z and moves backwards. Therefore, S1 becomes Z:, S2 becomes Y:, and so on. Figure 3.5 shows the first two NetWare search drives as Z (S1) = SYS:PUBLIC and Y (S2) = SYS:PUBLIC\DOS\V5.00. With this in mind, you can assume that the early alphabet letters are regular pointers and the later alphabet letters are search drives. Keep in mind, this is only an assumption—and you know what they say about assumptions. Table 3.2 shows a comparison of regular and search drive pointers.

> Network drives point to data directories while search drives provide service to NetWare applications.

T A B L E 3.2	FUNCTION	REGULAR	SEARCH
Comparing the Functions of Regular and Search Drive Pointers	Purpose	movement	searching
	Assignment Method	as the letter	in search order (S1, S2, etc.)
	Letter Assignment	by the user	by the system
	First Letter	F:	Z: (S1)
	Directory Types	data	applications

TIP

In the course of assigning search pointers, NetWare will skip any drive letter which is already defined as a regular drive pointer.

TIP

The CD command is off-limits to NetWare users. If the CD command is used on a NetWare pointer, it reassigns the pointer to a different directory. This can be fatal for search drives which point to critical applications or utility directories. But if you must use the command, switch to the J: drive before doing so. The J: drive holds no special significance except that it is typically used as a JUNK pointer. (You can use another letter if J: is already in use.)

USING THE MAP COMMAND

Now that we understand the fundamentals of NetWare drive mapping, we must learn how to implement it. The MAP command is one of the most versatile NetWare utilities. Below is a discussion of the many different MAP commands which allow system managers to implement NetWare drive mappings. Keep in mind that drive mappings are user- and/or group-specific and temporary. You'll have to do this all over again tomorrow.

MAP

The MAP command without any parameters will display a list of the current drive mappings. It will list the alphabet pointers in order beginning with the local drives (A-E), the regular drives, and then the search drives. Here's an example of how the MAP display is organized:

```
Z:\PUBLIC>map

Drive A:  maps to a local disk.
Drive B:  maps to a local disk.
Drive C:  maps to a local disk.
Drive D:  maps to a local disk.
Drive E:  maps to a local disk.
```

```
Drive F: = NIRVANA\SYS: \LOGIN
  -----
SEARCH1: = Z:. [NIRVANA\SYS: \PUBLIC
SEARCH2: = Y:. [NIRVANA\SYS: \PUBLIC\DOS\V5.00
```

MAP F:=SYS:LOGIN

MAP followed by a specific drive letter specifies a *regular* NetWare drive pointer. The above command would map the LOGIN directory to the drive letter F:.

MAP SI:=SYS:PUBLIC

MAP followed by an S# specifies a *search* drive pointer. The # represents the pointer's place in the search list. NetWare assigns an appropriate letter beginning from Z: and moving backwards. In this example, the PUBLIC directory will be inserted at the top of the search list and receive letter Z:.

MAP INSERT S2:=SYS:APPS\WP

The MAP INSERT command inserts a new search drive into the search list. The new pointer is inserted into the search list as the number specified. All search drives below the new pointer are bumped down one level in the list. The quirky thing about MAP INSERT is that the letter assignments are unaffected. All of the previous drives retain their original drive letter and the new pointer is assigned the next available drive. For example, if the above command was executed in Figure 3.5, the DOS drive (S2) would become S3 but still retain the drive letter Y:. The new directory, SYS:APPS\WP, would become S2 and inherit the drive letter X:.

TIP

Search drive mappings occupy the same environment space as the DOS PATH command. For this reason, NetWare search mappings eliminate DOS PATH commands. The only way to retain the DOS path in a NetWare environment is to add the path directories to the NetWare search list. This can be accomplished by always using the

MAP INSERT command. The DOS path directories are added to the end of the search list. Don't worry, the DOS path directories don't occupy any of your 16 available search slots.

MAP DEL G:

MAP DEL deletes an existing NetWare drive mapping. It works with either regular or search drive pointers. MAP REM (remove) performs the same function as MAP DEL.

MAP ROOT H:=SYS:USERS\DAVID

MAP ROOT is an intriguing command. It establishes a regular drive mapping as a false root. The user sees the drive as if it is the root directory. In the above example, the SYS:USERS\DAVID directory will be mapped to the drive letter H:. In addition, the H: drive will appear to be the root of the volume even though it is actually the SYS:USERS\DAVID subdirectory. It will appear as H:\>. False root mappings are dangerous because they limit users to specific branches of the network directory tree. In this example, no other directories would be available to the user David.

MAP NEXT SYS:DATA

The MAP NEXT command assigns the next available drive letter as a regular drive pointer. This command doesn't work with search drive mappings. In Figure 3.5, the above MAP NEXT command would assign the letter G: to the SYS:DATA directory. MAP NEXT is useful to system managers because it keeps track of the alphabetic letters for you.

TIP

Although MAP NEXT doesn't work with search pointers, there is a way to achieve the same effect. Simply use MAP S16. NetWare will not allow you to assign search drive mappings out of order. So if you specify S16, NetWare will automatically assign the directory to the next available spot in the search list.

That's it for NetWare directory structure. In this chapter, we explored logical trees, system-created and suggested directories, path names, and drive mapping. I'd say we got a pretty good head-start on network management and LAN configuration. The next step in building our vital NetWare LAN is security. Security configuration establishes integrity and protection for network users and shared data files. In the next chapter, we will install locks for rooms in our network apartment building, and pass out user keys.

QUOTE

Security is mostly a superstition. It does not exist in nature, nor do the children of men as a whole experience it. Avoiding danger is no safer in the long run than outright exposure. Life is either a daring adventure, or nothing.

Helen Keller

EXERCISE 3.1: USING THE MAP COMMAND

Use the directory structure illustrated in Figure 3.1A to provide the appropriate syntax for mapping logical drive letters to the directories indicated.

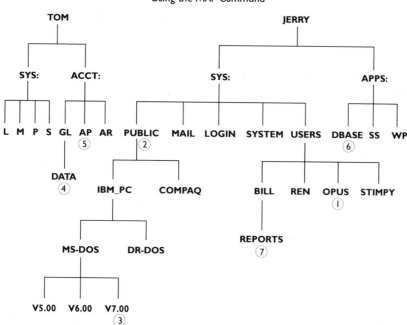

FIGURE 3.1A

Using the MAP Command

1 · Give Opus a drive mapping to his home directory.

_____

2 · Map the first search drive to PUBLIC.

_____

3 · Map the next search drive to the appropriate DOS subdirectory.

_____

4 · Map the next available network drive mapping to the data subdirectory.

_____

5 · Map an appropriate search or network drive mapping to the accounts payable application.

_____

6 · Insert the third search drive mapping to the database subdirectory.

_____

7 · Map a pseudo-root to Bill's report subdirectory.

See Appendix D for answers.

EXERCISE 3.2: THE EFFECTS OF CD ON MAP

This exercise provides an illustration of the effects of the change directory command on search drive mappings. Carefully follow these steps:

1 · Login to the network.

2 · Type **Z:** and press Enter. This should move you to the PUBLIC subdirectory.

3 · Type **MAP** and press Enter. The system will respond with a list of all logical mappings and their appropriate directories.

4 · Type **CD ..** at the prompt and press Enter. This should move you from the PUBLIC subdirectory to the root.

5 · Type **MAP** and press Enter. What happened and why?

_____

_____

6 · Once you have pondered this factoid, type **CD PUBLIC** and press Enter. This will move you back to the PUBLIC subdirectory.

7 · Now that your Z: drive has been remapped to the PUBLIC subdirectory, type **MAP** and press Enter. What happens and why?

_____

_____

8 · Now let's view the effects of CD on mapping search drives from other drive pointers. Once again, from the PUBLIC subdirectory Z: drive, type **F:** and press Enter. This should move you to the F drive.

9 · At this point, type **MAP** and press Enter. Notice the system responds with a list of current drive mappings. This occurs because the Z: drive at PUBLIC is a search drive and the system finds the MAP command in that directory.

10 · Move to the PUBLIC subdirectory once again by typing **Z:** and pressing Enter.

11 · Remap the Z drive by typing **CD ..** and pressing Enter. This will remap the search drive Z: to the root subdirectory.

12 · Now move back to the F drive by typing **F:** and pressing Enter.

13 · Type **MAP** and press Enter. What happened and why?

_____

_____

14 · Return to the Z: drive by typing **Z:** and pressing Enter. Now remap the Z: drive back to PUBLIC by typing **CD PUBLIC** and pressing Enter.

15 · Return to the F: drive, type **F:** and press Enter.

16 · Now type **MAP** and press Enter. What happened and why?

_____

_____

17 · Now let's view the effects of creating search drive and network drive mappings of our own. Return to the Z: drive by typing **Z:** and pressing Enter.

18 · Remap the Z: drive by typing **CD ..** and pressing Enter.

19 · Return to the F: drive. Type **F:** and press Enter.

20 · Type **MAP** and press Enter. Notice the MAP command does not work.

21 · Create your own network drive mapping by typing **MAP NEXT SYS:PUBLIC** and press Enter. The system will respond with the next available drive mapping which in most cases will be G.

22 · Now type **MAP** and press Enter. What happened and why?

_____

_____

23 · Let's attempt the same exercise but create a search drive mapping instead. Type **MAP S16:=SYS:PUBLIC** and press Enter. This will create a search drive mapping with the next available search letter to the PUBLIC subdirectory.

24 · Now type **MAP** and press Enter. What happened and why?

_____

_____

25 · Now to complete the exercise, be sure to return to the Z: drive and remap it to PUBLIC. Type **Z:** and press Enter.

26 · Type **CD PUBLIC** and press Enter.

When you're through, refer to Appendix D to verify your answers.

CHAPTER 4

NetWare 2.2
Security

"Meet the Netware Security Guard."

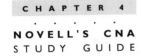
Have you ever wanted to be a locksmith? Just imagine the things you could do:

► Build unbreakable locks

► Design reliable keys

► Protect countless valuable treasures

► Provide peace of mind and security for your clients.

But the locksmith has a difficult job. He/she is burdened with the responsibility of protecting the world's assets. The goal is to create a reliable security system which locks out the bad guys but welcomes everybody else in. While the job is not easy, locksmithing typically pays very well.

Clients generally come to locksmiths for unbreakable locks, reliable keys and peace of mind. As the NetWare system manager, you are the locksmith of your LAN. Users come to you for application security, data organization, and general peace of mind. Your LAN locksmith duties are some of the most important responsibilities you will have and you must take them very seriously.

> The goal is to create a reliable security system which locks out the bad guy but welcomes everybody else in.

In this chapter, we will learn about NetWare security from the locksmith's point of view. We will discover NetWare's multilayered security model and explore each layer in depth. In addition, we will discuss some of the command line and menu utilities which NetWare provides to help manage LAN security. Keep in mind, this is a very important tool in your NetWare utility belt—LAN locksmithing is somewhat of a lost art.

The NetWare Security Model

The multilayered NetWare security model provides a level of protection for entrance to the LAN. Since the data on a network is typically shared, it is important to secure the data in directories where only authorized users have access. In a stand-alone environment, security isn't as critical. The only way to access stand-alone data is to physically walk over to another user's workstation. However, in a network environment, you can let your fingers do the walking. Without security on the central LAN hard disk, it would be easy for users to access each other's data. This is bad.

The NetWare security model provides a level of data protection by forcing users through a specific series of security events on their way towards shared data. NetWare security consists of access restrictions, privileges, and file conditions. This way you can store data in certain directories on the server disk without having to worry about anybody accessing that data.

The NetWare security model consists of three layers (see Figure 4.1 for an illustration).

▸ Login/password security

▸ Access rights

▸ File attributes.

FIGURE 4.1

*The NetWare
Security Model*

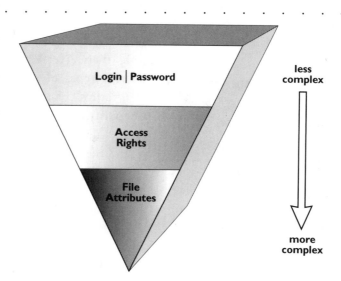

Login/password security governs initial access to the file server and provides a system for user authentication. In addition, NetWare's login/password security level includes a variety of login restrictions which prevent users from accessing the system during unauthorized time periods, from unauthorized workstations, or with unauthorized configurations. Access rights define a complex set of privileges which can be assigned to directories and to users. When in combination, they create what is called *effective rights*. Effective rights define a user's actual privileges in a given directory on the disk. NetWare 2.2 provides seven different access rights. As the LAN locksmith, it is imperative that you understand each of these rights intimately and have a firm handle on how they are combined, both at the directory level and at the user level, to create effective rights. Access rights are the most common form of NetWare security and provide a very versatile system for controlling who has what privileges to which files.

> The NetWare security model consists of three layers: login/password security, access rights, and file attributes.

The final layer of NetWare security is attribute security. File attributes are conditional privileges which control file sharing, reading, writing, executing, hiding, tracking, and archiving. Access rights define which users can have access to a file, while file attribute security controls what the users can do with the file once they are there. NetWare provides two different types of file attributes: security attributes and feature attributes. Security attributes affect how users access files and feature attributes affect how the system accesses files. File attribute security is a very complex level of NetWare security, and it is never implemented by most system managers. The first two layers of the NetWare security model provide more than enough security for 95% of the NetWare 2.2 LANs. File attributes are the infrared motion detectors of LAN security.

> The first two layers of the NetWare security model provide more than enough security for 95% of the NetWare 2.2 LANs.

Let's being our discussion of the NetWare security model with an exploration of login/password security.

QUOTE

Spoken language is merely a series of squeaks.

Alfred North Whitehead

Login/Password Security

Login/password security is the first layer of the NetWare security model. This level controls LAN access at the first point of entrance—login name and password. Login/password security is effective because it requires two pieces of information—an authorized login name and valid password. Keep in mind that the password and login name must match the system exactly. Any discrepancy is grounds for LOGOUT!

Once the login name has been entered and the password has been matched, the user is granted conditional access to the system. Permanent access is contingent on the user passing through a supplemental level of login/password security called *login restrictions*. Login restrictions further scrutinize LAN access by matching the login name with a variety of other qualifications: is this user authorized to login during this time period? is this user authorized to login from this particular machine? is this user authorized to login on this date? and so on. In addition, NetWare login restrictions incorporate an access tracking feature called Intruder Detection/Lockout. This security feature tracks unauthorized login attempts and automatically locks accounts which exceed a given bad login threshold count. The user account can only be unlocked by the NetWare supervisor.

To review, here's the login process:

1 • Load IPX.

2 • Load NETx.

3 • Move to F:\LOGIN>.

Once a user accesses the F:\LOGIN> directory, he/she is on the doorstep of the LAN. At this point, the user has limited access to only two NetWare files—LOGIN.EXE (to login) and SLIST.EXE (for a list of available servers). The user is ready to exercise his/her login security. The user logs into the network by specifying the file server name and a login name. Once the system verifies the login name, it will respond with Password: If the user enters the correct password for this login name, he/she will be granted conditional access to the LAN. Next, the system will match the user's login name with a collection of login restrictions and apply another level of security at that point. Once the user passes the scrutiny of login restrictions, he/she will be greeted with a NetWare prompt.

Upon receipt of the long-awaited NetWare prompt, the user has completed level one of the NetWare security model. The next level—access rights security—controls the user's movements throughout the directory structure and provides limited access to only authorized areas of the disk.

NetWare responds curiously to a variety of different login conditions:

▸ If the username is valid and there is no password, the system grants immediate access.

▸ If the username is valid and there is a password, the system prompts the user for a password. If the password is entered correctly, the user is granted access.

▸ If the username is not valid, the system prompts the user for a password anyway. This is to fool would-be hackers into thinking this is a valid username.

NetWare is designed on the principle of "What you don't know can't hurt us!"

There are numerous command line utilities that allow the supervisor to customize login password security and login restrictions. We will discuss a few of these commands at the end of the chapter. Also, login restrictions are covered in greater depth in Chapter 6—Network Management.

Access Rights

Once the user has passed login/password security and login restrictions, he or she is greeted with a NetWare prompt. Users cannot freely access all files and directories in the system—this would be entirely too 1960s. Instead, users are limited to only those files and directories in which they have been given specific privileges.

Access to shared network data is controlled at two different levels: the user level—Trustee Assignments—and the directory level—directory rights, or the maximum rights mask (MRM). We will discuss each of these two levels of security and talk about how they combine to create effective rights. But before we dive into trustee assignments and directory rights, we must take a moment to understand the access privileges themselves and appreciate how they are used to limit specific user actions in NetWare directory structures.

> Movement throughout the network directory structure is controlled by access rights.

UNDERSTANDING ACCESS RIGHTS

In understanding access rights, you need to ask one simple question: "What are the types of things users do in a network directory?" Ready for the answer?

- ▸ Read from files
- ▸ Write to files
- ▸ Copy files
- ▸ Change the names of files
- ▸ Access applications
- ▸ Erase files
- ▸ Create directories

Wow, users are extremely active. Fortunately, NetWare provides a simple facility for controlling their actions. Each of these user activities corresponds with a specific NetWare access right. In NetWare 2.2, there are seven different access privileges.

W—Write	write to an existing file
R—Read	read an existing file
M—Modify	modify file names and attributes
F—File Scan	search the directory or subdirectory
A—Access Control	determine access rights
C—Create	create and write to new files or subdirectories
E—Erase	delete existing file or subdirectories

TIP

Notice that the NetWare 2.2 rights spell a word—WoRMFACE. (The "o" is silent.) Ironically, the "o" (open) is a NetWare 2.15 right which has been incorporated into W and R. Funny how it falls into place so nicely—almost as if we planned it that way.

Each of these seven access rights corresponds with a particular user function. Five of them correspond with common functions—writing, reading, creating, erasing, and searching. The other two are a little more quirky—modify and access control. These rights pertain to the process of assigning and modifying NetWare security. Modify provides the ability to customize file attributes and Access Control allows users to change their access privileges—this is dangerous.

TIP

These rights evolve as you move from one version of NetWare to another. Access rights in NetWare 2.2 are different from 2.15 and also change as you move forward to NetWare 3.12. Pay attention to the version of NetWare you are using and understand the differences—however subtle they may be.

The key to access rights is understanding which rights it takes to perform common NetWare activities. Table 4.1 provides a list of some common NetWare activities and the rights which are required to perform those activities. As the LAN locksmith, it is your responsibility to go through the directory structure and assign specific access rights to specific directories for specific users based on the types of activities they perform in those directories. Sounds simple, right?

TABLE 4.1

Rights Requirements for Common NetWare Activities

ACTION	RIGHTS REQUIREMENT
Read from a closed file	R
Write to a closed file	W
Create and Write to a file	C
Make a new directory	C
Delete a file	E
Search a directory	F
Change file attributes	F M
Rename a file	M or C W
Change directory rights	A
Change trustee assignments	A

If we return for a moment to our earlier analogy of the system manager as a locksmith, you can think of the LAN locksmith as having two major responsibilities—keys and locks. The first responsibility is to create the keys which unlock all doors in the building. The other locksmith responsibility is to install the locks in appropriate network directories. Once the keys have been created and the locks are in place, each user is given an appropriate set of keys—the NetWare key ring. This analogy is actually very close to what happens in the NetWare security model—the keys are analogous to trustee assignments and the locks are analogous to directory rights. If a lock exists and the user has the correct

> Think of the LAN locksmith as having two major responsibilities—keys and locks.

key, that user is said to have the effective right or privilege to unlock the directory. Remember, users can only perform the privileges which match the notches on their key.

TRUSTEE ASSIGNMENTS

When a user or group is given a trustee assignment to a given directory, he/she is said to be a trustee of that directory. In addition, trustee assignments flow from parent directories to their children. So when an access right is granted to a trustee for a given directory, the privilege is inherited by all subdirectories. Figure 4.2 shows an example of flowing trustee assignments. Access rights do not flow up, however, and so it would be impossible to grant user trustee assignments to a parent directory unless you went to that directory and assigned them specifically at that point. You can, however, assign large sweeping sets of privileges by granting trustee assignments to global parent directories—like APPS, for example.

Another interesting side effect of trustee assignments is that when access privileges are given in a subdirectory, all other keys are taken away. It's not an additive effect. On the other hand, trustee assignments are additive from the viewpoint of users and groups. In other words, a user's trustee assignment in a given directory is the combination of his/her user assignment and the assignment of

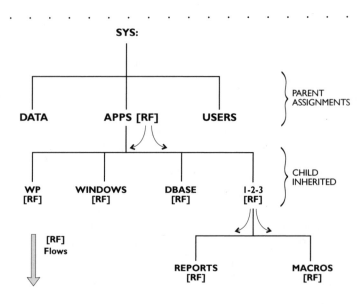

FIGURE 4.2

The flow of trustee assignments from parent to child

groups to which he/she belongs. Here's an example: Bob is granted the read and write privileges in the APPS\WP directory as a user. In addition, he is a member of the ADMIN group which is assigned file scan, access control, and modify. So Bob's actual trustee assignment in APPS\WP is read, write, file scan, access control, and modify. See Figure 4.3 for an illustration.

This strategy is particularly useful because it allows the LAN locksmith to assign keys to large groups of individuals—all in one swoop. It might seem trivial at this point but as soon as you begin assigning trustee assignment and directory rights throughout the system, you'll find that it can become quite a monumental task. An intelligent approach to trustee assignments would involve group assignments for global directories—PUBLIC, APPS, DATA, and so on—and user assignments for user-specific directories—USERS\BOB. Also, keep track of how the rights flow. Use inherited rights for multiple subdirectories of global parents—APPS\WP, APPS\DBASE, and APPS\WINDOWS for example.

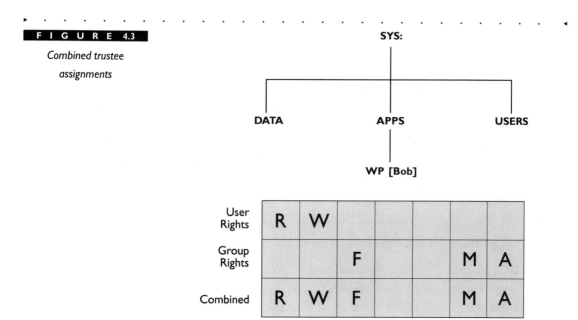

FIGURE 4.3

Combined trustee assignments

In order to create a trustee assignment for users and groups, NetWare needs three pieces of information:

1 · The name of the trustee

2 · The trustee rights to be assigned

3 · The path to the directory where the assignment begins.

Trustee assignments can be granted in two ways: SYSCON or GRANT. Assignments can be made in the SYSCON utility using the User Information or Group Information screens. (We will explore this utility in great depth later in Chapter 5—Menu Utilities.) Assignments can also be made using the GRANT command (which we will explore later in this chapter).

There are a few users and groups which automatically exist when you first take over the LAN. These system-generated users and groups include the GUEST user which has basically no rights, the SUPERVISOR user which has unlimited rights, and the group EVERYONE which has specialized default rights. These system-generated users and groups have default trustee assignments which are also created by the system. Here's a brief description of the default user/group trustee assignments:

 ▸ **EVERYONE** includes all users who currently exist and all users who will eventually exist. Most global assignments are granted to EVERYONE because it provides an effective strategy for assigning sweeping trustee privileges. EVERYONE is assigned the read and file scan privileges to SYS:PUBLIC and the create right to SYS:MAIL.

 ▸ **SUPERVISOR** inherits all rights to everything. Also, these rights cannot be removed and the SUPERVISOR account cannot be deleted.

 ▸ **GUEST** provides the bare minimum NetWare security. GUEST assumes the trustee privileges of EVERYONE, plus all rights except access control to his/her own SYS:MAIL\userid directory.

In addition, each user is given a default trustee assignment of create, erase, file scan, modify, read, and write to their own specific user SYS:MAIL\userid directory. Also, users are given the same rights to their own specific SYS:USERS\username directory (assuming, of course, that the directory has been created).

Let's return for a moment to the locksmith analogy. If the trustee assignments are keys, then the keys are only effective in directories which have locks. If there are no locks, the key can't work.

> If the trustee assignments are keys, then the keys are only effective in directories which have locks. If there are no locks, the key can't work.

The absence of a lock in the NetWare analogy does not mean you have all access. In fact, it means the opposite—you have *no* access. In order for a user to have effective rights in a given directory, the user must be granted both the key and the lock to that directory. Let's see how directory rights fit into this puzzle.

QUOTE

Some problems are so complex that you have to be highly intelligent and well informed just to be undecided about them.

Laurence J. Peter

DIRECTORY RIGHTS

Directory locks, or directory rights, are directory-specific, *not* user/group specific. Directory rights are assigned to directories, and do not flow down. In addition, the existence of a directory lock is independent from the existence of a user key. If the locksmith decides to put a lock on a given directory, that lock is susceptible to any user key that matches (see Figure 4.4). This level of NetWare security can get out of hand very quickly.

Fortunately, the directory rights in NetWare 2.2, by default, include all locks on all directories—which means every directory in the entire system has all locks available. This is useful because it eliminates the directory rights facility and makes NetWare 2.2 security dependent only on trustee assignments. This

FIGURE 4.4

The Flow of Keys and Locks

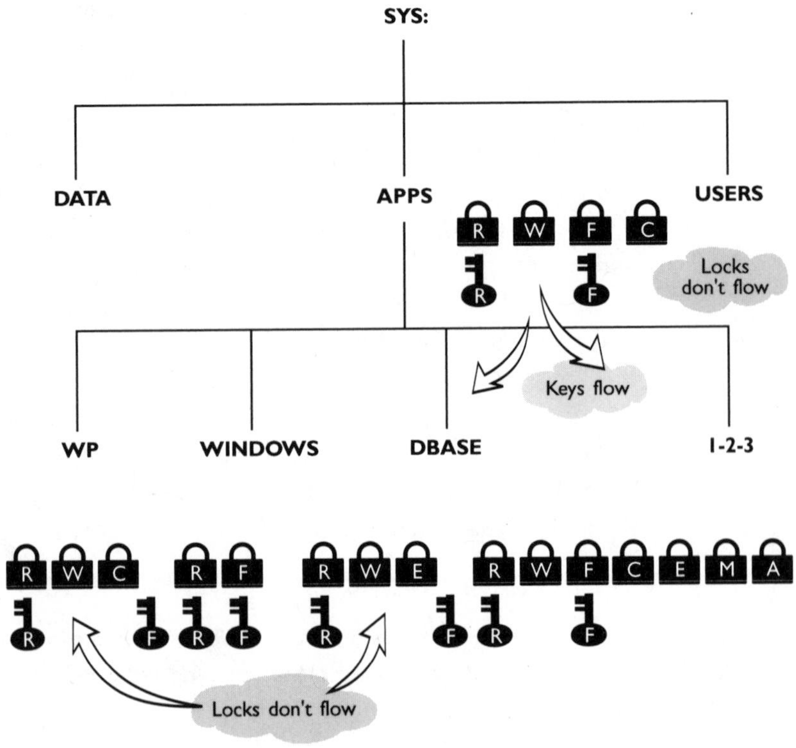

dramatically simplifies the locksmith's job. If the LAN locksmith is specifically concerned about a given directory, the locksmith can remove the lock from that directory. Otherwise, he/she can leave it alone.

Directory locks are only necessary in sensitive directories —like applications, users, or the SYSTEM directory. NetWare directory rights are called the Maximum Rights Mask, or MRM. The MRM is based on the following assumption— "Here are the maximum rights you can have in this directory." For example, if the SYS:APPS\WP subdirectory has sensitive application files that shouldn't be deleted, you can remove the erase lock from that directory. This way, no matter who has access—even if they have the erase key—users will not be able to exercise the erase right in the SYS:APPS\WP directory. Remember, the maximum rights mask is only useful in very specialized circumstances and can become quite confusing in calculating effective rights. An effective way to implement

NetWare security is to leave all directory locks in their default state and rely 100% on trustee assignments—user keys.

CALCULATING EFFECTIVE RIGHTS

So what does all this really mean? The bottom line is this: A user's actual privileges in a given directory is calculated as the intersection of the user's trustee assignments and the directory's MRM. These are defined as effective rights.

If you look at it in a global sense, a user's trustee assignments and a directory's maximum rights mask are meaningless until you put them together and calculate what the user's real effective rights are. After all, the effective rights are the only rights which a user can exercise in a given directory.

Effective rights is defined as the combination of a privilege key and the existence of that privilege lock. For example, in the APPS\WP subdirectory, all locks exist—by default. In addition, the user has been granted the read, write, and file scan keys. Therefore, the user's effective rights are read, write, and file scan (see Figure 4.5). If, for some reason, the LAN locksmith or system manager decided that this person should not have the write privilege in the directory, the system manager has two choices: remove the user's write key or remove the write lock. The first choice would affect the one user only, while the second choice would restrict the write privilege for ALL users in the LAN.

> Effective rights is defined as the combination of a privilege key and the existence of that privilege lock. If either is absent, the privilege is revoked.

If all of this is a little confusing and overwhelming, don't be concerned. When we get into the Network Management section in Chapter 6, we'll talk a little bit more about implementing security. Also, there are some exercises at the end of this chapter which will help you understand effective rights for certain cases. As the LAN locksmith, you must fill your NetWare utility belt with a strong understanding of NetWare security and some efficient methods for implementing trustee assignments (keys) and directory rights (locks).

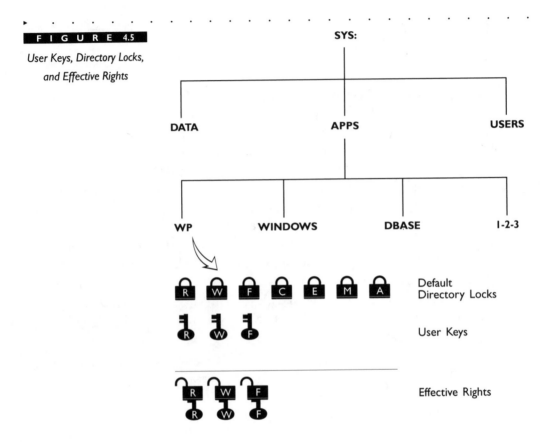

FIGURE 4.5

User Keys, Directory Locks, and Effective Rights

File Attributes

File attributes provide a very complex level of security which allow you, as the LAN locksmith, to specifically affect what users do with files once they have access to them. File attributes are global security elements which affect all users regardless of their rights. Attributes can be used to override all previous levels of security. For example, let's say your effective rights are read, file scan, and write privileges to the SYS:APPS\WP directory. The system manager can still restrict you from writing to a specific file by assigning the READ-ONLY file attribute. This level of NetWare security overrides all previous security.

The true effective rights to a given file in a given directory is determined by the combination of trustee assignments, directory rights, *and* file attributes.

NetWare 2.2 supports two different types of file attributes: security and feature. Security attributes affect each user's security access. Features attributes affect how the system interacts with files—whether or not the files can be archived or whether or not transactional tracking has been activated. In this section, we will describe NetWare 2.2's different security and feature attributes and then move on to the many command line utilities which allow the LAN locksmith to implement NetWare's three-layered security model.

SECURITY ATTRIBUTES

The first set of file attributes in NetWare 2.2 are security attributes. Security file attributes protect information at the file level within directories by controlling two kinds of file access: file sharing and file alteration. File access security controls not so much who has access to the files but what kind of access people have. Once a user has been given the proper trustee assignments to a given directory, that user then has the ability to access any of the files within that system. File attributes tell that person what they can do with the files once they have access. The file alteration attributes not only tell you what you can do with them but limit file access to execute only or hidden. If a file has the hidden attribute, users cannot see, use, delete or copy over the file.

Here's a list of the filing sharing and filing alteration attributes.

NS—Non-Sharable	Access is limited to one user at a time
S—Sharable	Simultaneous access by multiple users
RW—Read/Write	Users may see the file and alter its content
RO—Read/Only	Users may only see the file; no changes
X—Execute Only	Execution only; users cannot copy or delete
H—Hidden	Users cannot see, use, delete, or copy over

The non-sharable and sharable attributes limit access to files to either one user at a time or provide simultaneous access by multiple users. When multiple users have access to a directory and the files are flagged sharable, you run into a problem where multiple users are accessing the same data and trying to save their version of the file. If the file is flagged sharable, the last person who saves the file will win the race. This is where the non-sharable attribute comes in handy. If you want only one person to access a file at a time, you can assign the non-sharable attribute to a file—the system will keep track of who gets to save and who doesn't.

The read/write and read/only attributes also affect file access but in a different way. These attributes affect what the user can do once he/she has the file open. The read/write attribute allows users to see the file and alter its contents whereas read/only means they can open the file but cannot make any changes. The read/only attribute is useful for application files which you want users to be able to access—but not change the contents of—in a shared environment.

The execute only attribute is extremely sensitive and provides the highest level of NetWare security. The execute only attribute can only be assigned by the supervisor to an executable file or .COM file. Execute only files cannot be copied or deleted—just executed. Also, once the execute only attribute has been set, it cannot be removed.

> The execute only attribute is extremely sensitive and provides the highest level of NetWare security.

The hidden attribute is reserved for special files which cannot be seen, used, deleted, or copied over. The hidden attribute is for archived files. In order to access a file which has been flagged hidden, the supervisor must remove the hidden attribute.

FEATURE ATTRIBUTES

The next set of file attributes are feature attributes. Feature attributes provide access to special NetWare functions or features including backup, indexing, and transactional tracking. The feature attributes are listed below.

TTS—Activate TTS	Identifies this file for transactional tracking
I—Indexed	Identifies this file for turbo FAT indexing
SY—System	Identifies this file as system-owned
A—Not yet Archived	This file has been modified since last backup

The one that warrants the most attention is the system (SY) attribute which is assigned by the system. The system attribute identifies the file as being system owned and can only be used for system functions. The NetWare 2.2 operating system file—NET$OS.EXE—is flagged as system so that nobody can delete, copy or write to that file. The archive (A) attribute is interesting. It allows the system to keep track of which files have been modified since the last backup. The indexed (I) allows turbo FAT indexing. This feature speeds access to very large data files (over 64 FAT entries). The TTS attribute is assigned to files which need to be transactional tracked by NetWare's internal transactional tracking system (for a review, see Chapter 2).

These file attributes, in combination, can create very effective security tools in controlling who has access to do what with very specialized NetWare files. The default attribute combination for all files on the system is non-shareable read/write (NSRW). This is fine for most applications and most data files. There are specialized instances, however, where you can justify customizing these attributes. Here's a brief list:

▸ Stand alone applications which are not to be shared should be flagged non-sharable read/only.

▸ Data files which are shared but should not be written to simultaneously, should be non-sharable read/write.

▸ Data files which are part of larger multi-user applications that provide specialized record locking and other advanced features and can keep track of file sharing, data sharing on their own, should be flagged sharable read/write.

▸ Application files which are accessed by simultaneous users should be flagged sharable read/only.

▸ Large database files which are important to the system should be flagged with the transactional tracking attribute.

▸ Very sensitive archive files—records which are rarely accessed, payroll records or general ledge which are accessed once a month—should be hidden.

▶ All system files which are owned in the most part from the system are flagged system. But again, this is an attribute assigned by the system, not by the user.

▶ Sensitive application files which cost lots of money and are shared on the system should be flagged executable so that the supervisor is not liable should piracy occur.

TIP

Recently, a very popular software manufacturer sued a company for piracy when it was found that many of the company's network users had taken copies of the application home with them. The manufacturer won the case based on *system manager negligence*. Evidently, the LAN administrator had not flagged the executable application file execute only. Doing so is not only a good idea, it can probably save your job.

This completes our discussion of the NetWare security model and the concepts which combine to create the complex level of NetWare security which is necessary in this type of shared environment. We're going to have a chance to practice these concepts as we go along. You should feel much more comfortable with NetWare security once you get an opportunity to get your locksmith feet wet. In the remainder of this chapter, we will learn about many valuable LAN locksmith tools and begin to build the security portion of our NetWare utility belt. Don't let it weigh you down.

Security Command Line Utilities

Have you ever watched a locksmith make a key? This amazing process involves a very complex set of specialized tools and fine precision. The process of building locks is also an amazing one. The intricate machinery inside combines to create not only the strength of the unbreakable locks, but also their reliability. Imagine what's required to make the lock match only one key.

This process in analogous to what the LAN locksmith must go though in implementing access right keys and directory locks. The process of building keys and building locks is not easy—it's time-consuming, complex, and grand in scope. The LAN locksmith must be aware of the many ramifications of assigning NetWare security. NetWare security tools, or command line utilities, are broken into three different categories—login/password security, access rights, and file attributes. The command line utility tools with respect to access rights are further broken down into trustee assignment tools and directory rights tools.

These tools are augmented by the menu utilities which we'll discuss in the next chapter. Most of the login/password security and access rights tools can be found in the SYSCON menu utility. While the directory rights and file attribute tools can be implemented in the FILER menu utility. The menu utilities provide a great deal more functionality and a much friendlier format than command line utilities—but the Command Line Utilities (CLUs) are fast and to the point.

LOGIN/PASSWORD SECURITY—CLUs

The first level of security tool is login/password security. As we mentioned above, login/password security deals with initial user access to the system. It incorporates a login name, a password, and specific login restrictions. There are five login/password security tools which can be used by the LAN locksmith to set passwords and get information about who is logged in. Also, these tools provide a list of servers and allow users to attach to other file servers. Login/password CLUs are not only used by the LAN locksmith, but can also be used by any user to gain general login information.

SETPASS

The first login/password security tool is SETPASS. SETPASS is a command line utility which allows users to set their own password. At any NetWare prompt, type **SETPASS**. The system takes a look at who you're logged in as and goes out and gathers information about your authorized password. If a password already exists, the system will then ask you to enter your password followed by a new one if you pass the first test. The reason for this security is so that not just anybody could login as a different user and change their password.

ATTACH

ATTACH allows user and supervisor access to other file servers. Within Net-Ware, a user can login to only one file server because the key component of the login is the execution of what is called a login script. The login script contains many specific variables for a file server and loads specific variables into workstation memory. While it is possible to attach to multiple servers, you can only login to one server because if you logged into multiple servers, each server's login script would overwrite the other. The main difference between logging in and ATTACH is the execution of the login script. If you login to a server, it does execute the system login script. ATTACHing to a server performs exactly the same thing except it does not execute the system login script.

Keep in mind, in order to map drives or to access directories on other file servers, you must be physically attached to those file servers through the ATTACH command. The ATTACH command will ask for a user name and a password and you will be subject to the same login restrictions as if you had logged in. The only difference is, again, that ATTACH does not execute the file server's host login script. The syntax of ATTACH is the same as LOGIN: type **ATTACH [name of filer server]\[name of user]**. The system will then prompt you for a password if there is one. Keep in mind that NetWare lets you attach only up to 8 file servers at one time.

SLIST

Another login/password security tool which works in conjunction with ATTACH is SLIST. SLIST allows the user to view a list of all available servers that they are currently physically attached to so that they can decide whether or not they would like to logically login or attach to those multiple servers. In large complex internetworks, the SLIST command is extremely useful because it provides a simple list of all servers which are currently available. The SLIST does not tell you whether or not you have a valid login account on any of those servers; it simply gives you a list of all servers which are physically recognized by your internal network interface card.

USERLIST

Another listing command login/password tool which is useful for users as well as LAN administrators is USERLIST. USERLIST does not provide a list of servers but instead provides a list of *users*. USERLIST is useful because it will only give you a list of the users who are currently logged in to the file server you're specifying and displays login information about those users and what they're currently doing on the system. There are some command switches which work with USERLIST, specifically /e which lists network and node addresses and tells you where these users are logged in. Also you can specify as a switch the specific user name and gain valuable information about specific users. For example, if you type **USERLIST GUEST**, the system will respond with relevant information specifically for the user GUEST. That only works again if the user is logged in.

> **TIP**
>
> One possible use of **USERLIST** for the network supervisor is **USER-LIST /e** for all network and node addresses. Then use that information to restrict users to locking in only from their authorized workstations. This type of login restriction is extremely useful for users who have a tendency to migrate through the **LAN** and login from multiple workstations.

WHOAMI

The final login/password security tool is WHOAMI which at first sight has an existentialist tone to it. The WHOAMI utility displays information about user name, file servers you're currently attached to, your connection number and the date and time of your last login. WHOAMI can be a very useful tool for users who find it difficult to come to grips with their purpose in life, and also provides valuable information about users and their current network environment.

> WHOAMI provides a dual purpose: to display user information and to help out during an identity crisis.

There are four WHOAMI switches which provide more focus for the WHOAMI command. They allow you to focus in on only specific types of information.

WHOAMI /G lists the groups you belong to.

WHOAMI /E lists your security equivalences. Again it's possible for you to be equivalent to another user in your security.

WHOAMI /R lists the effective rights in the network directory structure.

WHOAMI /A lists the groups, security equivalences and your effective rights so /a would be for all.

Again, WHOAMI is useful only for the user who is logged in because it takes a look at who you're logged in as and grabs information about you from the NetWare bindery.

TRUSTEE ASSIGNMENTS—CLUs

The next set of NetWare security tools refer to access rights—specifically trustee assignments and directory rights. We'll break it out according to those two different categories so that we'll discuss the tools first which apply to trustee assignments and then move onto directory rights.

Trustee assignment security tools apply almost exclusively to the LAN locksmith. These tools are very powerful and are easily abused. Keep in mind that in order to assign trustee rights or directory rights, the user in question must be granted the access control right to that particular directory. Again, the only person who has global access rights to assign all rights or privileges to the system is the supervisor or somebody who is granted what is called *supervisor equivalents*.

TLIST

The first trustee assignment tool is TLIST. The TLIST command line utility displays the trustees and their effective rights in a specific directory. TLIST is generally for information only and can only be applied to a specific directory or drive letter in the mapping environment. TLIST is useful because it provides information about all the different trustees which are assigned access to a directory and their effective rights in that directory. It calculates the combination of trustee assignments and directory rights to display the effective rights. This could be very useful for the LAN locksmith who is trying to figure what security should be granted to whom in a given directory. They can first type **TLIST** and get information about what already exists.

The next three trustee assignment tools apply to the actual implementation of trustee assignments.

GRANT

The GRANT CLU is the most effective for trustee assignment. GRANT allows this supervisor to assign or grant specific privileges to specific users within specific directories. The syntax for GRANT is **GRANT [rights] for [directory or drive name] to [user or group]**. For example, if I wanted to assign the R and F rights to user DAVID in the SYS:APPS\WP directory, the syntax would be **GRANT R F for SYS:APPS\WP to DAVID**.

This is a particularly useful and efficient CLU because it allows very quick access to the security system and quick implementation of trustee assignments. GRANT is hard to use, though, in that it doesn't provide a list of existing trustee assignments for given users or groups and it provides a very specific syntax so that if you do not follow it exactly, you can get into trouble. The SYSCON menu utility is a lot more friendly in the assignment of trustee privileges.

REVOKE

REVOKE is exactly the opposite of GRANT. The REVOKE syntax is exactly the same as GRANT, but remember that instead of granting rights to a user, you are revoking rights from a user. Again, REVOKE is very specific in its syntax and does not provide a simple way of viewing all trustee assignments for given users.

REMOVE

REMOVE is dramatic in its scope in that it removes all rights for a given trustee in a directory and completely removes that user as a trustee so that user from this point has no rights whatsoever to that given directory.

TIP

Use **GRANT** if you want to grant any rights for a given user to a directory, **REVOKE** to revoke partial rights, or **REMOVE** to revoke all rights.

DIRECTORY RIGHTS—CLUs

There are two security access right tools which work in conjunction with the trustee assignment CLUs and they are the directory rights command line utilities, namely RIGHTS and LISTDIR. These command line utilities are specifically used in the directory situations and do not apply to users, groups or trustee assignments. RIGHTS and LISTDIR are used to allow you to view not only the directory rights of a given directory but the trustees and the effective rights of a given directory. All the previous access right tools allow you to view information about trustees. These particular tools allow you to view information about directories and effective rights.

Again, RIGHTS and LISTDIR, which are the directory rights tools, are not only used by LAN administrators but by users as well. The RIGHTS and LISTDIR utilities provide valuable information not only for system administrators but for users to have access to information such as what their effective rights are, and what the directory structure is.

RIGHTS

RIGHTS is similar to TLIST in that it displays effective rights in a specific directory. It does not, however, display all the trustees of that directory. RIGHTS displays your trustee rights and effective rights for a particular directory. The RIGHTS command takes a look as who you're logged in as and reads your trustee assignment from the bindery. It uses the directory rights to calculate effective rights.

LISTDIR

LISTDIR is a lot more effective at providing information about directory rights than the RIGHTS command. LISTDIR displays the effective and directory rights and all information pertaining to the directory including all subdirectories of a parent directory. There are six switches which are relevant here and which work in conjunction with the LISTDIR command.

> **LISTDIR /e** shows the effective rights you have in the directory and subdirectories of a parent directory.

> **LISTDIR /r** shows the directory rights for this directory and all subdirectories of the directory.

> **LISTDIR /a** shows the maximum rights mask, the effective rights and all of the other date and time information.

> **LISTDIR /d and /t** show the creation date and time of the directory and subdirectories.

> **LISTDIR /s** shows the subdirectory information in an entire tree structure of all subdirectories of a given parent directory.

Again, LISTDIR is a useful utility which provides subdirectory information and a directory tree structure including effective rights, maximum rights mask and creation date and time of directory structures.

FILE ATTRIBUTES

There are two file attribute command line utilities: FLAG and NCOPY. These two command line utilities are designed to provide the LAN locksmith with the ability to view and assign file attributes as well as copy files with their attributes attached. Let's take a closer look.

FLAG

The FLAG command line utility allows supervisors and users with the modify access right to view or change the file attributes of a given file. The syntax with the FLAG command is **FLAG [file name]**. The flags consist of the first few letters of the attribute name. If you refer to the earlier bullet list of security/feature file attributes, the bolded letter corresponds to the flag switch which would be used with this command. One switch which is not included on that list is the N switch which allows the supervisor to assign the normal series of attributes to files and thus return the file attributes to the default state—non-sharable read/write.

NCOPY

The NCOPY command is extremely useful for a variety of different reasons. It is included at this point because it does retain the file attributes for files which are copied using the NCOPY command. This is not the case for files which are copied using the DOS COPY command. NCOPY works exactly the same way as the COPY command. The syntax is similar. Type **NCOPY [file name] to [file name]**. Again, you can also leave out the "to" and insert a space between the two file names in which case NCOPY would assume a "to" in between.

KNOWLEDGE

Since NCOPY is a NetWare utility, it accesses the NetWare file allocation table and directory entry table with a great deal more efficiency than DOS COPY does. Because NCOPY works within the memory of the file server, NCOPY provides a much safer, much faster means of copying files across the network. If files are copied from one directory on the file server to another, NCOPY does not copy the files down to workstation memory and back up (thereby creating a load on the network). Instead, it copies the files in file server RAM, which is much faster and does not create a load on the network. It's safer because NCOPY utilizes the read-after-write verification fault tolerance feature which is incorporated into NetWare. This read-after-write verification is not performed if you use the DOS COPY command.

It's important also to note that the NCOPY command supports all wildcard characters, including the ? which is supported with the DOS COPY command.

That completes our discussion of the NetWare security tools and our discussion of NetWare 2.2 security. Keep in mind that the responsibilities of the LAN locksmith are to make sure that all the user data is safe and that sufficient access and data integrity security has been implemented. That way unauthorized users are left out, but the system is still efficient and transparent enough so that it doesn't get in the way of normal operations for authorized users. Many times the

LAN locksmith gets caught up in the whole complex security model of NetWare and creates such a secure system that it's impossible to use. Keep in mind that security and productivity must be balanced. NetWare's security functionality is extensive, and supports a great many options. But remember the KISS principle: Keep It Safe and Simple.

NCOPY offers a much safer and faster way of copying files across the network.

In the next chapter we'll talk a little bit more about directory structures, drive mapping and security from the menu utilities standpoint. Throughout these first two chapters, we have discussed the command line utilities tools which have helped bolster your NetWare utility belt. Now what we'd like to do is spend some time discussing the menu utilities which can only augment or enhance your NetWare utility belt. In the chapters that follow, we'll go into much more depth on network management and printing. The NetWare menu utilities will provide a springboard for that discussion.

Without any further ado, let's get on with shew.

EXERCISE 4.1: CALCULATING EFFECTIVE RIGHTS

In this exercise, we will calculate the effective rights for a number of different security cases. In each case, you will be provided with the user rights and the maximum rights mask and you will be asked to calculate the effective rights using the worksheets provided. Remember that in all cases, the maximum rights mask limits the user rights which can be exercised in a given directory.

Use one of the forms in Figure 4.1A for each of the scenarios below. Check your answers in Appendix D.

▶ · ◀

F I G U R E   4.1A

Calculating Effective Rights

①   R   W   C   E   M   F   A

USER RIGHTS						
MRM						
EFFECTIVE RIGHTS						

②   R   W   C   E   M   F   A

USER RIGHTS						
MRM						
EFFECTIVE RIGHTS						

FIGURE 4.1A

Calculating Effective Rights (continued)

③
R W C E M F A

USER
RIGHTS

MRM

**EFFECTIVE
RIGHTS**

④
R W C E M F A

USER
RIGHTS

MRM

**EFFECTIVE
RIGHTS**

⑤
R W C E M F A

USER
RIGHTS

MRM

**EFFECTIVE
RIGHTS**

1 · As a user, you are granted the R, W, C, and F privileges. The maximum rights mask is set at the default. What are your effective rights?

_____

2 · This directory is a subdirectory of the one from Case #1. The maximum rights mask has been set to R and F. What are your effective rights?

_____

3 · Your user rights in a given directory are R, C, E, and F. The maximum rights mask has been set to W, M, A. What are your effective rights?

_____

4 · As a user, you are granted R and F rights to a given directory. As a member of the group EVERYONE, you inherit the W and C rights. What are your combined rights? In the same directory, the maximum rights mask is set to R, F, W, and E. What are your effective rights?

_____

_____

5 · As a system manager, you want to restrict a particular user from having any rights in the PUBLIC subdirectory. Using their default user rights, how would you configure the maximum rights mask so that this particular user would have no rights in the PUBLIC subdirectory?

_____

_____

NetWare 2.2
Utilities

In Chapter 2, we defined the NetWare system manager as "a brave soul whose single task is to keep peace in the NetWare castle." The system manager is the LANlord of his/her network apartment—managing workstation appliances, directory rooms, and user tenants. It's definitely a challenging, rewarding, and exciting life.

In order to accomplish his/her many LAN management duties, the NetWare system manager relies on a variety of CNA resources, including Product Documentation, Netwire, NetWare Express, the NetWare Buyer's Guide, Network Support Encyclopedia, On-Line Help, and valuable Novell Press Publications. But the most important system manager resource of all is the magic NetWare utility belt—Batman for the LAN.

The NetWare utility belt is comprised of a variety of different tools—command line utilities (CLUs), menu utilities, supervisor utilities, and console commands. Command line utilities are productive management tools which provide NetWare customization from the workstation command line. CLUs are the mainstay of the NetWare arsenal. These utilities are primarily designed for system managers, but there are a few tools which appeal to NetWare users as well. Menu utilities provide the same functionality as CLUs, but with a friendly menu interface. In addition, some menu utilities provide extended functionality beyond what the CLUs offer. Menu utilities are more popular than CLUs and comprise 85% of most system manager utility belts. Supervisor utilities are specialized CLUs and menu tools which have been designed for supervisor use only. Most supervisor utility tools come equipped with a warning label—"WARNING : This tool contains explicit supervisor functionality. Keep out of the reach of children and NetWare users." Finally, console commands are NetWare tools which provide customization of the network operating system environment. Console commands are advanced utilities and must be executed at the file server console. These tools can be very hazardous if not handled correctly.

> The most important system manager resource of all is the magic NetWare utility belt—Batman for the LAN.

QUOTE

There is no knowledge that is not power.

Ralph Waldo Emerson

In many cases, a good NetWare utility belt can be the difference between system management success and failure. In Chapters 1 and 2, we started our NetWare utility belt with a holster of microcomputer/DOS fundamentals and NetWare basics. In this chapter, we will fill the holster with valuable NetWare tools—menu utilities, supervisor utilities, and console commands. In addition, we will examine practical applications for these tools and even practice them with some lab exercises and NetWare simulations.

Let's begin with NetWare menu utilities.

KNOWLEDGE

In this chapter, you may have noticed that the command line utilities are missing. Since there are so many CLUs and they represent the mainstay of your utility belt, we have opted to cover them in detail throughout the chapters as they apply to CNA objectives. This is a much more effective strategy for learning the many CLUs and gaining practical experience using them in a "real world" environment.

Menu Utilities

NetWare menu utilities are the most productive and friendly of the NetWare system management tools. Menu utilities provide all the same functionality as command line utilities plus some additional features all wrapped up in a friendly user interface. These tools can be broken down into two basic categories—user menus and supervisor menus. Some user menus double as supervisor menus and allow supervisors to perform additional administrative tasks, including user creation, directory maintenance, security and login password configurations.

In this section, we will discuss the three most popular NetWare menu utilities: SYSCON, FILER, and SESSION. These utilities are for users and system managers. The next section focuses on supervisor-only menu utilities. But before we begin, let's take a moment to discuss the look-and-feel of NetWare menu utilities.

NetWare menu utilities are a progression of screens which provide additive levels in an easy-to-use format. Each menu screen consists of a border—either single-lined or double-lined. The single-lined border denotes an information-only box which means that the contents of this box cannot be edited—it is for viewing only. On the other hand, a double-lined border denotes a box which contains information which can either be viewed or edited. All NetWare menu utilities are displayed in a blue and gold color format which is the default color palette.

> In this section, we will discuss the three most popular NetWare menu utilities: SYSCON, FILER, and SESSION.

TIP

The color palettes for NetWare's menu utilities are configurable using the COLORPAL menu utility. The default menu colors are defined as Palette 0.

FUNCTION KEYS

Learning to use a menu is not something I think you're going to have a lot of trouble with. These menus are designed to be simple, straightforward, and provide basic system management facilities—all in an easy-to-use framework. Most of the menu functions are self explanatory, but there are a few function keys you should be aware of that will help you navigate through NetWare's menu utilities:

RETURN key or ENTER moves you to the next level

ESCAPE key returns to the previous level

INSERT adds an entry in a particular double-bordered box

DELETE will remove an entry

F1 provides help.

F1 F1 (two in a row) identifies the function keys which we're talking about now.

The last three function keys are NetWare-specific and provide specialized functionality within only NetWare menu utilities.

F3 modifies the highlighted choice and allows you, for example, to rename users and directories as well as modify security rights.

F5 is a toggle switch that marks and unmarks multiple options. Marking multiple options with F5 is particularly useful in environments where you're configuring multiple options.

Alt-F10 combination will quickly exit a NetWare menu utility without saving. Alt-F10 is very useful if you want to jump out of a menu from within multiple nested screens without saving any of the work you've accomplished.

TIP

When you come across a list screen with a double border, NetWare allows you to highlight particular options within that list and continue. If the double-bordered list is empty, it is a perfect opportunity for using the INSERT key to insert a choice into the list. This is particularly evident when assigning rights and user names.

NetWare menu utility navigation is a little quirky at first but you'll soon get the hang of it and find yourself buzzing through windows like a pro. Now we will move onto the three most popular NetWare menu utilities in a little more detail.

SYSCON

SYSCON is the mother of all utilities. SYSCON stands for SYStem CONfiguration and it is used for most of the system management tasks. It is used to configure trustees, trustee assignments, account restrictions, login restrictions, accounting, login scripts, users and group information. During

> SYSCON is the mother of all utilities.

our discussion of menu utilities, we will focus on both the command line utilities which are integrated into the menu utility and the extended functionality that the menu utility provides.

SYSCON incorporates the seven command line utilities we've introduced so far.

- ▸ GRANT

- ▸ REMOVE

- ▸ REVOKE

- ▸ RIGHTS

- ▸ SETPASS

- ▸ SLIST

- ▸ TLIST

The SYSCON menu and its submenus can be viewed in Figure 5.1. The standard NetWare menu utility format calls for the name of the menu utility across the top header with the date and time. In addition, it provides the next line with user information and the filer server that you're currently attached to. The available topics menu in SYSCON contains six choices:

- ▸ Accounting

- ▸ Change Current Server

- ▸ File Server Information

- ▸ Group Information

- ▸ Supervisor Options

- ▸ User Information

Now let's take a moment to go into each of these available topic menus in a little more depth.

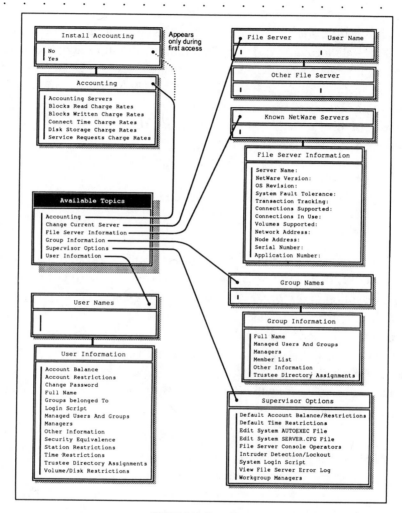

FIGURE 5.1

The SYSCON Menu Utility

SYSCON Overview

Accounting

The Accounting submenu of SYSCON is where the system manager installs and manages NetWare accounting. NetWare accounting is a feature which allows system managers to monitor and charge customers for using specific file server resources. Another strategy for using NetWare accounting is to track network usage and resource utilization by charging specific prices for particular network resources such as disk blocks read, disk blocks written, file server attach time and processor utilization. NetWare 2.2 includes an elaborate reporting system.

To install accounting, simply highlight the accounting option from the available topics menu in SYSCON and press Enter. The system will ask you whether or not you would like to install accounting. Highlight YES and it will install accounting on the default server. It's possible to install accounting on multiple servers from this SYSCON menu by inserting multiple file servers in the accounting servers window.

QUOTE

Either I will find a way, or I will make one.

Phillip Sidney

The accounting submenu provides six choices: Accounting Servers—where you would add the servers which are going to support NetWare accounting and the five different resource accounting features—blocks read, charge rates, blocks written, connect time, disk storage and service requests. Network accounting supports two other command line utilities which provide reporting functionality. They are ATOTAL which provides a summary of weekly accounting charges and PAUDIT which provides a detailed tracking of all user logins, logouts and accounting charges. We will discuss accounting in more detail in Chapter 6—Network Management.

Change Current Server

The next choice in the available topics menu is Change Current Server. This choice simply allows the user or the system administrator to change the server upon which they are using SYSCON. This changes their default server from the current server to any server which is currently attached to the internetwork. Change Current Server displays a menu with the current default file servers on the left-hand side and the user names that are used to login on the right-hand side. To add a server to this list, attach to another server, or change current servers, you can press INSERT at the Change Current Server menu screen and the system responds with a list of available servers. Highlight a server from the Other File Server screen and the system will ask for a user name and password. Keep in mind you are attaching to another file server so it is important that you follow the same login security levels as you would if you were logging in.

KNOWLEDGE

The only difference between attaching and logging in is that when you attach, you do not execute the login scripts.

File Server Information

The File Server Information screen is a single-bordered box which displays relevant details about the current default file server. These details include server name, NetWare version, operating system revision, level of system fault tolerance, network address, serial number and the number of connections supported and in use.

TIP

A connection is not a user but a physical workstation connection to the server. It is also a print server, a router, or any other device which requires communication with the NetWare file server. If, for example, you buy a 100-user version of NetWare, you are actually buying 100 connections for this server. Since you're buying a 100-connection license and the print servers and routers cut into these connections, NetWare supports 16 additional connections beyond the 100—to support print servers and routers. If you have more than 16 print servers and routers, you will start to lose user connections. The moral of the story is a 100-connection version of NetWare will support 116 connections but only 100 user connections because NetWare discerns between user connections and print server and router connections.

Group Information

The Group Information submenu provides information and configuration options for NetWare groups. The Group Information submenu is similar to the user information submenu in functionality but provides fewer choices. The Group

Information submenu of SYSCON provides seven choices:

- ▶ Full name
- ▶ Managed users and groups
- ▶ Managers
- ▶ User list
- ▶ Other information
- ▶ Trustee directory assignments
- ▶ Trustee file assignments

Before you can enter the Group Information screen, you must identify which group you would like to view. This is done with an intermediate menu called the Group Names menu which is a double-bordered box. At this point, you are allowed to either insert, delete, or choose a specific existing NetWare group. The Group Information box in SYSCON is particularly useful for assigning group specific or group-wide security options. Trustee assignments can be made for large groups of users by using the group information window to assign trustee assignments to a group and then using the member list option to assign users to this group. This is a very effective way to cure baldness in system managers who worry too much about user-specific security.

Supervisor Options

Supervisor Options is the submenu in which the system manager spends most of his or her time and which provides the most system administrative functionality. In NetWare 2.2, the Supervisor Options menu provides eight different choices and can only be accessed by a supervisor or supervisor equivalent:

- ▶ Default account balance restrictions
- ▶ Default time restrictions
- ▶ Edit system AUTOEXEC file
- ▶ File server console operators

- ▸ Intruder detection/lockout
- ▸ System login script
- ▸ View file server error log
- ▸ Work group managers

> The Supervisor Option submenu of SYSCON is where the NetWare system manager will spend most of his/her time.

All these choices will be explored in greater depth in Chapter 6, Network Management, when we discuss the intricacies of advanced system management. If the NetWare system manager can spend most of his or her time in the Supervisor Options screen and stay away from customizing group information and user information, he or she will be much better off with respect to file server maintenance—and general quality of life.

User Information

The User Information option in SYSCON is the largest and most useful of the SYSCON submenus. In NetWare 2.2, the User Information submenu provides 14 different options including full name, password, login script, security equivalences, time restrictions, trustee directory assignments and volume disk restrictions. See Figure 5.1 for a complete list. The User Information configuration follows the same format as Group Information in that the intermediate user names lists all known users of the system and users at this point can be deleted, inserted or highlighted.

> The User Information option in SYSCON is the largest and most useful of the SYSCON submenus. In NetWare 2.2, the User Information submenu provides 14 different options.

TIP

NetWare provides a hidden facility for configuring small, select groups of users. The system manager can use F5 to mark multiple users in the User Names window of SYSCON. Pressing Enter provides a limited configuration window for setting specific parameters for the marked users. The window is called Set User Information and it consists of four choices—Account Balance, Account

Restrictions, Station Restrictions, and Time Restrictions. This is as close as you are going to get to configuring global login restrictions.

The User Information submenu is used to specifically configure security and environmental variables. The system manager can use the User Information submenu of SYSCON to fine tune group-wide and system-wide security down to the user level. This is done through the user login script, user-specific passwords, trustee assignments and account restrictions. The less time system managers spend in the user information screen, the better off they are because each time a configuration is performed in the user information screen, it must be performed not only for this user but for all other users as well. This can be quite overwhelming in an environment where 500 or 1,000 users exist on one server or on one LAN.

KNOWLEDGE

The User Information submenu in SYSCON can also be used by users to customize their environment; or to change their login scripts, passwords, or full name. The user information screen will appear with all 14 options as long as a specific user is accessing his or her own user information options. A severely abbreviated version of this User Information menu will appear if a user tries to access the configurations of any other user. The User Information menu will appear for other users except that it will have a two options: full name and groups belonged to. The idea here is to provide information about users to anyone in the LAN without allowing just anybody to come along and change other user configurations.

As you can see, the SYSCON menu utility is quite extensive and provides a great deal of functionality for NetWare system managers. It is very important that you become well aware of the many features of the SYSCON menu utility and become familiar with its use. The next menu utility we'll talk about is not so much for the administration of users and groups but instead involves the configuration of the NetWare directory structure.

QUOTE

Great thoughts reduced to practice become great acts.

William Hazlitt

FILER

The FILER NetWare menu utility is designed to control volume, directory, file and subdirectory information. FILER is just as extensive as SYSCON in its approach but instead of configuring users and groups, FILER specifically configures files, directories, volumes and subdirectories. The associated command line utilities which are incorporated into the FILER menu utility are:

► FLAG

► LISTDIR

► NCOPY

► NDIR

► RENDIR

► DOS XCOPY command

> The FILER menu utility is extremely refreshing for users who are used to using the DOS interface or the DOS command line for directory management.

The FILER menu utility is extremely refreshing for users who are used to using the DOS interface or the DOS command line for directory management. FILER provides exceptional functionality beyond DOS by allowing you to rename directories, delete entire branches of the tree, and change file security from within one menu. These functionalities are very similar to some of the third-party utilities such as Norton Utilities and XTree which have been incorporated into the DOS environment.

The FILER Available Topics menu can be viewed in Figure 5.2 and includes these five choices:

► Current Directory Information

► Directory Contents

► Select Current Directory

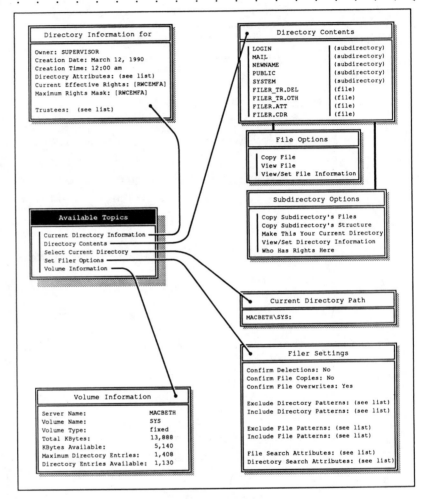

FILER Overview

FIGURE 5.2

The FILER Menu Utility

- ▶ Set FILER options
- ▶ Volume Information

FILER provides a consistent interface with SYSCON and the other menu utilities by using double-bordered and single-bordered boxes. It uses the same blue and gold format and the same header across the top. The header in FILER's case, instead of describing the user and the file server you're attached to, describes your current default directory. While FILER can be used by both users and system administrators, it does limit the functionality to directories and files with which users have rights. The system administrator has full functionality within the FILER utility. Let's take a moment to explore the five submenus under the FILER available topics menu.

Current Directory Information

Current Directory Information provides detailed information about the current default directory. It provides information such as the owner, the creation date and time, the directory attributes and other security information. Some of the most valuable information in the current directory information box is security related. It provides a detailed list of directory and file attributes, maximum rights mask, trustees and their trustee assignments, and the calculated effective rights. This is the only menu utility which provides calculated effective rights because it incorporates both trustee assignments and the maximum rights mask.

TIP

The trustee assignments and maximum rights mask boxes within the directory information screen of FILER are double-bordered, which means this information can be edited by the system administrator or anybody with access control rights in this directory. This FILER screen provides an effective strategy for calculating and managing NetWare security at the directory level.

Directory Contents

The Directory Contents menu provides a listing of all files and directories within and underneath the current default directory. The directory contents menu is where the system administrator can perform file and subdirectory creation, deletions, pruning, and general maintenance. Besides subdirectories and files, the directory contents menu includes two other components: the double dot (..) which represents the parent directory, and the backslash (\) which represents the root directory.

System administrators and users can highlight subdirectories/files and press Enter to receive a third submenu which provides additional functionality—subdirectory options and file options. The subdirectory options screen includes functionality for copying subdirectories, making this your current directory, viewing directory information or getting a list of who has rights to this subdirectory. The file options submenu provides information about copying, moving and viewing files. You can also get information about viewing and editing file information and again who has rights to this file.

The directory contents option within FILER is probably one of the most versatile menu utilities provided by NetWare. The system administrator can insert or create directories at this point by pressing the INSERT key, or delete directories by using the DELETE key. Another interesting feature provided by the directory contents screen is pruning. When the system manager highlights a directory and presses DEL, the system responds with two choices—delete only a subdirectory's files or delete the entire subdirectory structure. In the latter case, you would prune the directory tree at the branch level. This is a very effective strategy for deleting entire portions of the subdirectory structure without having to delete each of the files first and then remove the directories.

Select Current Directory

The Select Current Directory option simply allows you to move throughout the directory structure and change your default directory. This is useful when moving back and forth between current directory information and the Select Current Directory options box.

Set FILER Options

The Set FILER Options choice allows you to set the parameters which are currently used by the FILER utility for accessing, editing and viewing NetWare directories/files. Numerous parameters can be configured in the Set FILER Options, including confirm deletions, confirm file copies, preserve file attributes, include and exclude patterns, and search attributes. The last choice is particularly useful when searching for hidden and system files which are not normally displayed in the directory contents box of FILER.

Volume Information

Volume information is similar to SYSCON's file server information in that it is a single-bordered box which provides information only about the default volume. Volume Information includes the file server name, the volume name, the type of volume, the total size, the kilobytes available, and information about directory entries.

SYSCON and FILER comprise 95% of the system manager's utility needs. They are both extensive in functionality and easy to use. The final of the three most popular NetWare menu utilities is SESSION, not because of its system manager functionality, but because it provides a simple user interface for some common user tasks. These tasks include drive mappings, user lists, and so on. Let's take a closer look at the SESSION user tool.

SESSION

The SESSION menu utility is extremely useful because it provides a single central point for accessing NetWare's user-specific configurations and features. The SESSION menu controls file servers, default drive mappings, search drive mappings, messages, and lists of users and groups. There are four associated command line utilities which work in conjunction with the SESSION menu utility.

▶ MAP

▶ SEND

▶ USERLIST

▶ WHOAMI

> The SESSION menu controls file servers, default drive mappings, search drive mappings, messages, and lists of users and groups.

The SESSION menu (Figure 5.3) includes six different available topic options:

▶ Change Current Server

▶ Drive Mappings

▶ Group Lists

▶ Search Mappings

FIGURE 5.3

The SESSION Menu Utility

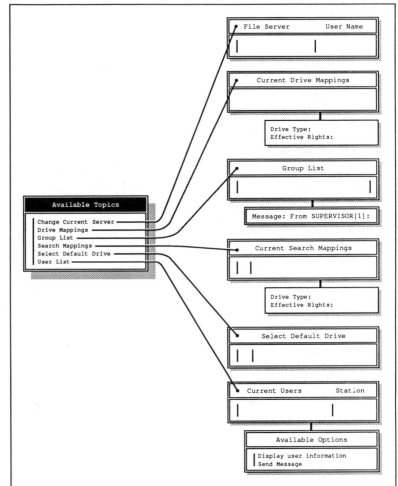

SESSION Overview

▸ Select Default Drive

▸ Userlist

SESSION uses the same NetWare menu interface with the blue and gold colors and the header across the top describing the SESSION manager utility.

The Change Current Server option works the same way as it does in SYSCON. In addition, the Select Default Drive option in SESSION is similar to the Change Current Directory option from FILER. The remainder of the SESSION functionality is grouped into two categories—user group lists and drive mappings. Let's spend a moment discussing each of these different categories and learn how they can be used in a productive NetWare environment.

User List/Group List

The User and Group List option in SESSION provides a quick and simple way to access or view a list of who is logged in and which groups exist on the system. The User List option provides only a list of users who are currently logged in, and allows users to view connections which are currently open. A not-logged-in user would appear in cases where users have logged out but not turned off their machine (this doesn't clear the connection). Both the Group List and the User List allow users to send messages to other users. Simply by highlighting a user from the User List, or a group from the Group List and pressing Enter, the system displays a message input screen. The message input screen can include any message of 40 characters or fewer which will then be sent to the bottom console session of each person's screen. This functionality is identical to the SEND command.

TIP

The down side of the SEND and the User List and Group List message options is that they lock up the destination computer until the combination Control-Enter is input. For example, the computer is unattended and a message is sent to that computer. The process will halt and the message will not be cleared until a user comes up to that machine and presses Control-Enter. To avoid having messages lock up unattended machines use CASTOFF and CASTON. CAST-OFF blocks the display of broadcast messages on any machine. CASTON reopens the machines.

Drive Mappings

The Drive Mappings options in SESSION provide users with a simple user menu interface for deleting, inserting and changing drive mappings. The drive mappings option from the available topics within SESSION provides a double-bordered list of all network drive mappings, while the search mappings option provides a double-bordered list of all search drive mappings. Within the double-bordered list of mappings the user can press INSERT to insert a mapping and DELETE to remove a mapping. In addition, users can use the F3 key when highlighting a directory to change an existing drive mapping.

TIP

While selecting a directory to either insert or change for a given drive mapping within SESSION, the user can press INSERT during the Select Directory prompt box and the system will respond with a list of available directories and subdirectories within that structure. This very useful feature allows users to quickly navigate the system.

SESSION is a nice utility which provides simple message and list functionality as well as drive mapping for network users who are not savvy in the ways of Net-Ware management. Incidentally, Microsoft Windows provides a utility called NetWare Tools for Windows which is in effect the SESSION utility in a graphical user environment. This has been a very successful tool for users who are comfortable in the Windows environment and would like the same functionality that SESSION provides.

That finishes our discussion of NetWare menu utilities from the system manager and user view-point. The next set of NetWare tools for the system manager's utility belt is Supervisor Utilities. These utilities are designed specifically for the supervisor and are not to be used by general users.

QUOTE

To be absolutely certain about something, one must know everything or nothing about it.

Olin Miller

Supervisor Utilities

Supervisor Utilities are Batman tools designed especially for NetWare system managers and which allow them to customize and configure dangerous NetWare environments. Supervisor utilities come in two flavors: command line utilities and menu utilities. Some of the most hazardous supervisor utilities are tucked away in the SYS:SYSTEM directory. Other harmless user utilities reside in PUBLIC. By placing supervisor utilities in the SYSTEM subdirectory, NetWare is restricting access to only those users with rights to SYSTEM. By default, nobody has rights to SYSTEM except the super-visor and supervisor equivalents. This is an effective strategy for limiting the use of supervisor utilities to system man-agers and users with appropriate rights.

In this section we will discuss the most popular supervisor command line utilities and the most effective NetWare menu utilities. Once we have a firm

> Supervisor Utilities are Batman tools designed especially for NetWare system managers. They allow them to custom-ize and configure dangerous NetWare environments.

grasp on the purpose and functionality of supervisor utilities, we will move on to the console commands which provide customization at the file server console itself.

SUPERVISOR COMMAND LINE UTILITIES

NetWare provides eight supervisor command line utilities. Their functions range from accounting to bindery restoration to workstation shell updates. As system manager, it is important to get a firm grasp on the use of these utilities because they will provide a very specialized and powerful set of tools for your NetWare utility belt. Here's a detailed look.

ATOTAL

The ATOTAL utility provides a daily and weekly summary of NetWare ac-counting services. NetWare accounting is a very useful tool, not only for charging back against shared network resources, but also for system managers to track resource utilization and user logins/logouts. ATOTAL does not provide a breakdown of user resource utilization but does provide a weekly and daily summary.

BINDFIX

BINDFIX is an extremely important supervisor utility which allows for corruption recovery and restoration of the NetWare bindery. Earlier we spoke about the NetWare bindery as being the flat file database which keeps track of all NetWare objects, properties, and their values. The NetWare bindery is the most important system file within NetWare besides the operating system file itself (NET$OS.EXE). The NetWare bindery keeps track of users, groups, file servers, print servers, routers and anything else with a name. It stores their rights, connections, configurations, and so on. All objects which use the network, all properties, and all values which define the NetWare LAN are tracked in the NetWare bindery. The NetWare 2.2 bindery consists of two files: NET$BIND.SYS and NET$BVAL.SYS.

The system manager can run BINDFIX from the SYSTEM subdirectory in cases where he or she suspects foul play (somehow the bindery has been corrupted or objects and values are not tracking correctly). BINDFIX has the ability to run consistency checks on the bindery and track relationships between objects, properties, and values. If an error is found, BINDFIX will restore the error and de-corrupt the bindery. Two other functionalities which are built into BINDFIX include deleting rights and trustees for users who no longer exist and deleting MAIL\userid subdirectories for users who no longer exist. BINDFIX, while fixing the bindery, creates a backup of the original bindery in the names of NET$BIND.OLD and NET$BVAL.OLD. These .OLD files are text files which can be copied from the network and kept on a diskette.

TIP

It's always a good idea to run a BINDFIX on a new network so the pristine bindery can be saved as the .OLD files and kept on a diskette—just in case corruption occurs and BINDFIX does not solve the problem in the future. Also, run BINDFIX twice before making backups—once for de-corruption and once for backup.

BINDREST

BINDREST is a related utility which restores .OLD files—files which have been created during a BINDFIX session. BINDREST can restore .OLD files from previous or new BINDFIX sessions. BINDREST can also be used to restore old copies of the bindery which were backed up onto a floppy diskette from earlier bindery sessions. Using BINDFIX and BINDREST on a daily basis or routine basis, such as once a month, is a good strategy for saving thousands of hours of work in creating users over again and reconfiguring NetWare security. Remember, when running BINDFIX and creating a backup copy of the bindery, it's a good idea to run BINDFIX twice.

DCONFIG

DCONFIG is a very useful utility in NetWare 2.2 which changes the configuration information of routers, IPX files, and the NET$OS.EXE NetWare operating system file. DCONFIG is important in NetWare 2.2 because the LAN driver configuration options, network address, node address, disk controller type and configuration, are built into the NET$OS.EXE file. This information is defined during the NetWare 2.2 installation process and cannot be changed once the file has been installed. The only way to change this information without having to reinstall the entire operating system is to run DCONFIG. This is particularly useful in file servers which gain hardware conflicts later in their lives and the configuration options of the LAN drivers or disk drivers need to be changed. Incidentally, DCONFIG is not automatically copied to the SYSTEM subdirectory during the install procedure and should be copied from the SYSTEM-2 diskette manually.

DOSGEN

DOSGEN is an extremely useful supervisor utility which creates a remote boot image for files that can be used for logging in from *diskless workstations*. Diskless workstations—or remote booting—define an environment where users are logging in from workstations with no floppy or hard disks. In these cases, the user will boot from a boot PROM (Programmable Read Only Memory) chip which is located on the network interface card. The boot PROM redirects the user to the file server F:\LOGIN directory for a boot image. The boot image is downloaded to the workstation RAM and the AUTOEXEC.BAT, CONFIG.SYS, and COMMAND.COM are executed from there. The creation of a boot image is performed using the DOSGEN utility. Remote booting in diskless workstations is effective in protecting against theft from the network or from viruses being entered into shared disks.

PAUDIT

PAUDIT is another accounting supervisor utility which provides reporting functionality for system managers. PAUDIT provides a lot more detail in user resource utilization, specifically a full track of all user logins and logouts as well as user access of network resources. PAUDIT creates a very large and detailed file which can be imported into a database package and configured into a meaningful report. PAUDIT also provides information with respect to security violations and intruder detection/lockout.

SECURITY

The SECURITY supervisor utility is excellent for identifying weaknesses in file server security. The SECURITY command, when entered at the command line from the SYSTEM subdirectory, will analyze the NetWare bindery and report any instances of security weakness or violations. NetWare identifies a variety of different security conditions as violations including passwords which are less than five characters; users who have security equivalents to supervisor, who have been assigned as work group managers, who are not required to enter a password, who have no full name attached, and so on.

> The SECURITY supervisor utility is excellent for identifying weaknesses in NetWare security.

QUOTE

Too many people are thinking of security instead of opportunity. They seem more afraid of life than death.

James F. Byrnes

WSUPDATE

The WSUPDATE supervisor utility can be used to update workstation shells and configuration files from one central location. The WSUPDATE utility compares the date and time of all destination workstation configuration files with a central source file and will copy or replace existing workstation shell files with the source file if the source file is found to be newer than the workstation originals. The WSUPDATE utility is not limited to NetWare shell files. This utility can update any file including application and program files. The command syntax for WSUPDATE is

WSUPDATE [source file name] [destination file name] /[switch].

There are a variety of different switches in WSUPDATE:

/f=[**file name**] allows the system manager to set a variety of different WSUPDATE files in one text file and then specify that text file for reading in source and destination information.

/i (the default option) forces the utility to prompt you for an action each times it finds an outdated file.

/c automatically copies a new file over an existing file without prompting.

/r copies the new file over the old file and renames the old file with a .OLD extension.

/s instructs the utility to search not only the destination, path and drive name but also all subdirectories of the destination path.

/l=[**path and file name**] creates a detailed log of all activity, all searches, all finds and all copies.

/o copies over and updates Read/Only files. Since many of the NetWare shell files on the workstation are flagged Read/Only for protection, the /o parameter is required to update Read/Only files. This parameter will instruct the utility to change the attribute of the file to Read/Write, copy over it, update it and then change the attribute back to Read/Only.

That takes care of our discussion of supervisor command line utilities. As you can see, they provide you with a variety of different system manager tasks and tools. Now let's focus on supervisor menu utilities which will further enhance the NetWare utility belt.

SUPERVISOR MENU UTILITIES

While the supervisor command line utilities provide direct functionality from the command line, the supervisor menu utilities provide greater functionality within a friendly user interface. The supervisor menu utilities are also stored in the SYS:SYSTEM subdirectory and restricted to only supervisor, supervisor equivalents, or users with Read and File Scan rights to that directory. These 10 menu utilities provide a variety of features—from printing and disk management to user setup and even downing the server. The following is a detailed description of each of the 10 different supervisor menu utilities and the features they provide for the NetWare system manager.

DSPACE

DSPACE is a utility which is used to limit a user's disk space on all volumes of the file server (Figure 5.4). DSPACE provides the same functionality as the disk restriction option in SYSCON except here you can choose users and volumes from a central location. The available options menu of DSPACE includes three choices: change file server, user restrictions, and directory restrictions. While in 3.12 DSPACE allows system administrators to limit users' disk space within directories, NetWare 2.2 does not support this feature. The user disk space limitation information screen provides the system manager with a central place to specify the user, the amount of space to restrict and the amount of space which is available for this particular user. The DSPACE utility is one of the rare supervisor menu utilities which is placed in the PUBLIC directory during installation.

FCONSOLE

The FCONSOLE utility is NetWare 2.2's version of the MONITOR NLM which is provided in 3.12. FCONSOLE (Figure 5.5) is the mother of all supervisor menu utilities and provides a great deal of functionality both in monitoring and

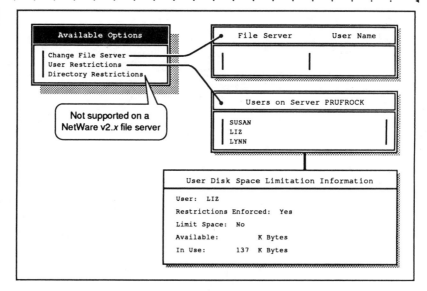

FIGURE 5.4

The DSPACE Supervisor
Menu Utility

configuring file server performance. In addition, experienced network programmers can use FCONSOLE to obtain information for writing, testing and debugging their multiuser programs and advanced system administrators can use FCONSOLE to finetune server performance. The available options menu in FCONSOLE provides the following features:

- ▶ Broadcast Console Message

- ▶ Change Current File Server

- ▶ Connection Information

- ▶ Down File Server

- ▶ File Log Activity

- ▶ LAN Driver Information

- ▶ Purge All Salvageable Files

- ▶ Statistics

> FCONSOLE is the mother of all supervisor menu utilities. It provides a great deal of functionality both in monitoring and configuring file server performance.

FIGURE 5.5

*The FCONSOLE Supervisor
Menu Utility*

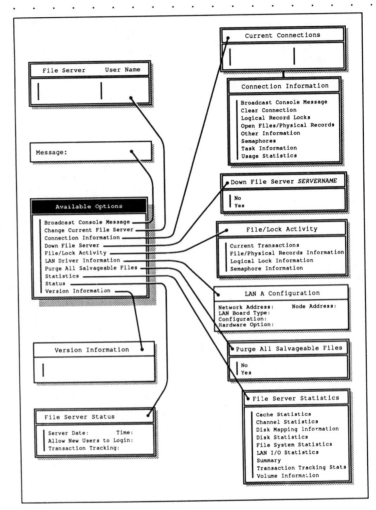

FCONSOLE Overview

- Status

- Version Information

The most useful feature in FCONSOLE is the File Server Statistics screen. This screen provides information on cache statistics, channel disk mapping, file system I/O statistics and a summary statistic screen which provides invaluable information about the performance of the file server. FCONSOLE should be restricted only to supervisors because it allows remote downing of the file server.

FILER

The FILER menu utility, which we talked about earlier, is the file structure's version of SYSCON. SYSCON is a utility used to manage users, groups and security where FILER is used to manage files, directories and security. The FILER utility can also be used by the supervisor to customize the trustee assignments, the maximum rights mask, and to view effective rights. Since FILER is also used by users, it is another one of the rare supervisor menu utilities that is stored in the PUBLIC directory.

MAKEUSER

The MAKEUSER menu utility provides the ability to design large user scripts which can be used to create or delete multiple users. The MAKEUSER functionality is based on a text script file with the .USR extension. This is used by the MAKEUSER program to create and delete large numbers of users, set security, define users and groups, define home directories and login scripts.

The MAKEUSER syntax is similar to login scripts in that it requires specific key commands and syntax. Below is a list of the 19 MAKEUSER key words which—as you can see—provide a wide range of functionality as far as creating users, groups and establishing security. Each of these key words must be preceded by a pound (#) sign:

> **ACCOUNT_EXPIRATION** followed by the month, the day and the year when the account expires.
>
> **ACCOUNTING** followed by a balance and a low limit.
>
> **CLEAR/RESET** which clears the processing of the script from this point on.
>
> **CONNECTIONS** number which specifies the maximum concurrent connections.

CREATE followed by a user name and a variety of different options. This command creates users with specific full names, passwords, group membership and directory rights.

DELETE followed by user name.

GROUPS followed by a group name. This assigns users to specific groups.

HOME_DIRECTORY followed by a path which creates a home directory for this user.

NO_HOME_DIRECTORY which overrides the creation of a default home directory.

LOGIN_SCRIPT followed by a path which points to a specific text file written in login script syntax.

MAX_DISK_SPACE and a number which establishes a maximum disk space for this user.

PASSWORD_LENGTH specifies a minimum password length between 1 and 20.

PASSWORD_PERIOD followed by days specifies the number of days before the password will expire.

PASSWORD_REQUIRED

PURGE_USER_DIRECTORY will delete subdirectories owned by the user when the user is deleted.

REM (for Remark) for documentation.

RESTRICTED_TIME day, start and end specifies which days and hours the users cannot login in.

STATIONS followed by the network number and the station address for station restrictions for this user.

UNIQUE_PASSWORD requires new passwords that are unique.

Once a MAKEUSER script has been created, it can be used over and over again to establish new or existing user environments. This is particularly useful in situations where the system is recreated every semester in school environments or where there's been a failed disk and you need to restore the bindery.

QUOTE

Only the educated are free.

Epictetus

NWSETUP

NWSETUP is a NetWare 2.2 phenomenon which provides the beginning system manager with a headstart. NWSETUP is a simple menu template interface which creates users, login scripts and home directories with default settings. If your network has a small number of users and you're just getting started, NWSETUP is for you.

PCONSOLE

PCONSOLE (Figure 5.6) is the mother of all printing utilities. It provides a wide range of configuration options for printing, print servers, print queues and printers. The three components which establish the printing environment in NetWare are the print server, the print queue and the printer. In order to set up NetWare printing, the print queue must first be created, the print server created, and finally the printers defined. These steps are all accomplished using the PCONSOLE utility. The available options menu in PCONSOLE includes Change Current Server, Print Queue Information and Print Server Information. The Print Queue Information allows for the creation and management of print queues. Print server information allows for the creation and management of print servers and printers. We will discuss PCONSOLE and printing in a greater depth later in Chapter 7. Incidentally, the PCONSOLE utility is stored in PUBLIC because it is available to users as well as system managers.

FIGURE 5.6

The PCONSOLE
Menu Utility

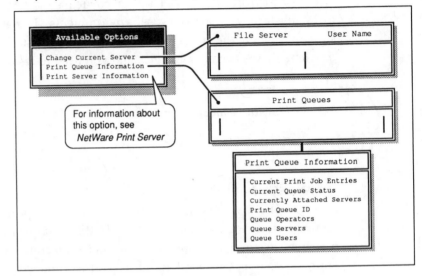

PCONSOLE Overview

PRINTCON

The PRINTCON supervisor menu (Figure 5.7) utility allows for the configuration of print jobs. Once a printing system has been established using the PCONSOLE utility, the system administrator has two options with respect to printing customization. He or she can either customize the print jobs which are the actual printed tasks, or customize the printers themselves. The print job configuration is accomplished through the PRINTCON utility. Printer configuration and definition is established through the PRINTDEF utility. Within PRINTCON, the supervisor can configure or customize specific print job parameters such as number of copies, file contents, tab size, banner, form name, auto endcap and default print queue. PRINTCON will also be discussed briefly in Chapter 7.

FIGURE 5.7

The PRINTCON
Menu Utility

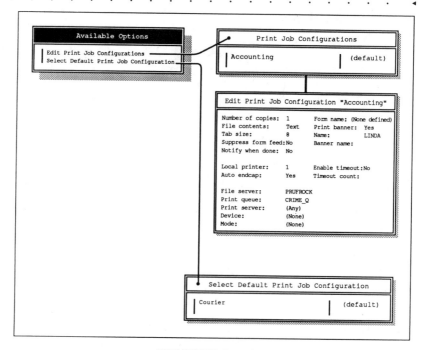

PRINTCON Overview

PRINTDEF

The PRINTDEF options menu in Figure 5.8 has two choices: print devices and forms. Print devices are specific printer definitions which include escape sequences for defining customized printing orientations such as compressed print, landscape print or specific fonts. Print devices can be imported from existing PDF or printer definition files or edited using the PRINTDEF utility. The forms option specifies the length and width of different forms which are used in the printing environment with these printers. Some example form definitions include checks, legal, greenbar or simple 8.5x11. We will also discuss the PRINTDEF utility and its functionality briefly in Chapter7.

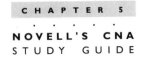

FIGURE 5.8

The PRINTDEF Menu Utility

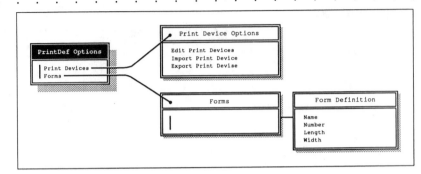

PRINTDEF Overview

SYSCON

SYSCON is the mother of all utilities. SYSCON provides not only user and group information but supervisor options as well. These include default account balance restrictions, time restrictions, editing of the AUTOEXEC file or SERVER.CFG file, file server console operators, the system login script, establishment of intruder detection/lockout, the file server error log or the creation of work group managers. Refer to the menu utilities section at the beginning of the chapter for an in-depth discussion of SYSCON and its many options.

USERDEF

USERDEF provides the same functionality as MAKEUSER in that it allows you to create large numbers of users from one simple menu utility. The difference between USERDEF and MAKEUSER is that MAKEUSER uses a script format and allows the supervisor to create *and* delete users while USERDEF is a template which only allows the supervisor to create users. The USERDEF template (Figure 5.9) provides a more user friendly and graphic environment for the system manager to create user parameters of customization. However, it doesn't provide nearly the flexibility or versatility of options that MAKEUSER does. The USERDEF template includes user parameters such as default directory, groups belonged to, account balance, concurrent connections, require password, password changes and unique passwords. See Figure 5.10 for an illustration of the USERDEF menus.

FIGURE 5.9

The USERDEF Template

```
┌─────────────────────────────────────────────┐
│        Parameters for Template CLERK          │
├─────────────────────────────────────────────┤
│ Default Directory:   SYS:                     │
│ Copy PrintCon From:  (see list)               │
│ Groups Belonged To:  (see list)               │
│ Account Balance:                      1000    │
│ Limit Account Balance:                No      │
│     Low Limit:                                │
│ Limit Concurrent Connections:         No      │
│     Maximum Connections:                      │
│                                               │
│ Require Password:                     Yes     │
│     Minimum Password Length:          5       │
│ Force Periodic Password Changes:      Yes     │
│     Days Between Forced Changes:      90      │
│ Require Unique Passwords:             Yes     │
└─────────────────────────────────────────────┘
```

USERDEF limits the system manager to creating large groups of files using one template at a time, which means the system manager can only create similar groups of users at the same time. MAKEUSER, on the other hand, provides the facility for changing configurations in mid-stream and creating all users from one script.

FIGURE 5.10

The USERDEF Supervisor Menu Utility

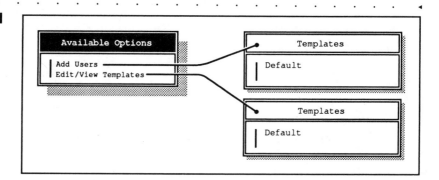

Console Commands

At the beginning of this chapter, we defined console commands as advanced NetWare tools which provide customization of the network operating system. Console commands are advanced utilities which must be executed at the file server console. These tools can be very hazardous if not handled correctly, so please make sure to keep these console commands out of the reach of children and NetWare users.

> Console commands allow the system manager to perform a variety of system administration tasks including controlling file servers, printers, and disk drives, sending messages, setting the server clock, and performing general control tasks.

Console commands allow the system manager to perform a variety of system administration tasks including controlling the file servers, printers, and disk drives, sending messages, setting the server clock, and performing general control tasks. Some of the more popular console commands include MONITOR, BROADCAST, TIME, WATCHDOG, VAP, SPOOL and, of course, DOWN. The syntax of console commands is relatively straightforward. The command itself is entered at the console prompt—a colon (:)—and various switches are displayed. Keep in mind that anybody can execute a console command as long as they have access to the file server console. This is a very good reason to limit access to the file server console and possibly to keep the file server itself under lock and key.

QUOTE

Hesitancy in judgement is the only true mark of the thinker.

Dagobert D. Runes

Console commands have a direct line to the operating system itself so they can perform customization of the file server code. For this reason (and the inherent lack of security) console commands are the most dangerous supervisor utilities. Let's begin with a detailed discussion of the 22 most popular NetWare 2.2 console commands.

BROADCAST

BROADCAST is a console command that is used to send a message of 40 or fewer characters to all users who are currently logged in or attached to the file server. The BROADCAST console command syntax is **BROADCAST [message in " "]**. The messages users receive with the BROADCAST command are exactly the same as messages users receive with the SEND command—40 characters at the bottom of the screen with the prompt **Press Control-Enter to clear**. These messages will lock up the workstation until the user intervenes. Only users or workstations who are actually logged into the system will receive the BROAD-CAST command. Any user who is attached to the file server's login directory will not receive that file server's BROADCAST message. Again, BROADCAST is used to send a simple message to all users in the network simultaneously.

All these console commands are internal operating system commands very similar to the DOS internal commands, and are built into the network operating system. The console commands are inherent to the operating system and therefore can only be executed at the console prompt.

CLEAR MESSAGE

The CLEAR MESSAGE console command clears the messages from the message display area at the bottom of the file server console screen from within MONITOR. This command allows system administrators to clear the message area without clearing the entire screen and this can be useful in certain troubleshooting situations. The syntax is **CLEAR MESSAGE**.

CLEAR STATION

The CLEAR STATION console command is a dramatic utility which allows the system administrator (or anybody from the file server console) to abruptly clear a connection for a particular workstation. This command removes all file server resources from the workstation and can cause file corruption or data loss if executed while the workstation is processing transactions. This command is only useful in environments where workstations have crashed or users have turned off their machines without logging out. In each of these particular instances, the connection would stay open even though the files are not currently being used.

The syntax for the CLEAR STATION command is CLEAR STATION [number]. The connection number for a specific workstation can be viewed from either the MONITOR console command or from FCONSOLE. This number is randomly allocated as workstations attach and is not the same from one session to another.

CONFIG

The CONFIG console command is used to display the operating system's hardware configure information for all known internal components. CONFIG is useful not only for the NetWare file server but also for external dedicated routers. The type of information which is displayed using the CONFIG command includes the file server or router name, the number of service processes which have been defined, LAN network interface card configuration information and disk channel configuration information. The network interface card information includes the network address, the type of the card, the version of the shell, and the configuration settings including IRQ, I/O and memory address. The disk channel information includes the hardware type with the shell version information and the hardware settings including the I/O and the interrupt.

DISABLE/ENABLE LOGIN

The DISABLE LOGIN and ENABLE LOGIN commands provide a feature for the NetWare system manager to use when troubleshooting or maintaining critical NetWare components. DISABLE LOGIN prevents anyone from logging into the system from that point forward until login has been re-enabled. DISABLE LOGIN is particularly useful when system managers are working on the bindery, backing up files, loading software or dismounting or repairing volumes. Keep in mind that DISABLE LOGIN does not affect users that are currently logged in until they log out. This command should only be used in situations where it's absolutely necessary. The ENABLE LOGIN command enables logins for users which have been disabled. It also provides one other facility, the supervisor account can be reactivated in the case where intruder detection/lockout has locked it. ENABLE LOGIN can only be used by supervisors to activate locked accounts.

The syntax for DISABLE LOGIN and ENABLE LOGIN are simply DISABLE LOGIN or ENABLE LOGIN.

DISABLE/ENABLE TRANSACTIONS

DISABLE TRANSACTIONS and ENABLE TRANSACTIONS function similarly to DISABLE LOGIN and ENABLE LOGIN—except that instead of working on the user login, they work on NetWare's internal transactional tracking system. DISABLE TRANSACTIONS manually turns off the transactional tracking system until ENABLE TRANSACTIONS has been invoked. This command is particularly useful for application developers who are testing the performance or system fault tolerance functionality of transactional tracking where the tracking has been turned on and off.

DISK

The DISK console command is used to monitor the status of internal file server disk drives. DISK provides a variety of different information about the status of particular drives, channels, controllers and the hot fix redirection area. The DISK console command provides a matrix of drives and their particular interrupt values as well as the amount of hot fix redirection space which has been used. The following list shows all the information provided in the DISK table:

- ▶ The drive number assigned to NetWare

- ▶ The channel number which the disk controller is using

- ▶ The address set on the controller for the disk

- ▶ The disk address itself

- ▶ The status, which can be either OKAY (which means hot fix is running fine), NO HF (which means hot fix has been shut off), DOWN (which means the drive is not operating), M (for Mirrored), or D (for Duplexed but is not working)

- ▶ List of I/O errors (the number of input/output errors that have occurred on the drive

- ▶ A list of the blocks free for the disk's redirection area

- ▶ A list of the number of blocks which have been used in the hot fix redirection area

The redirection information is particularly useful because as the number of used blocks increases, an indication is given that the drive is performing poorly. The DISK console command can also be followed by a volume name which provides information about specific volumes.

DISPLAY NETWORKS

DISPLAY NETWORKS is a particularly useful console command which provides data about all of the networks that the file server or router is currently aware of. A network consists of a unique network address cabling trunk which is further interconnected to this particular file server or router as a network. The listing for DISPLAY NETWORKS can be seen in Figure 5.11 and provides three pieces of information. First, the network address (an 8-character hexadecimal number), followed by a number and slash (/), then another number. The first number preceding the slash is the number of hops or the number of networks which must be crossed to get from this particular file server to that network. The number following the slash is the estimated time in ticks which it would take for a packet to reach that particular network address from this server. (A tick is 1/18th of a second.)

> DISPLAY NETWORKS is a particularly useful console command which provides data about all of the networks that the file server or router is currently aware of.

FIGURE 5.11

The Layout of DISPLAY NETWORKS

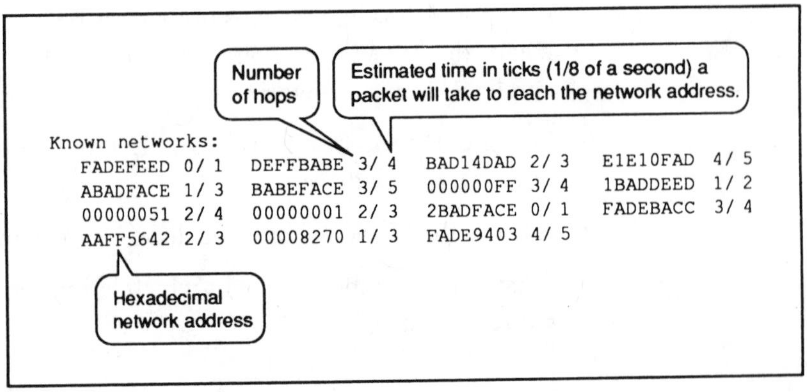

```
                                    Number          Estimated time in ticks (1/8 of a second) a
                                    of hops         packet will take to reach the network address.

Known networks:
    FADEFEED  0/ 1    DEFFBABE  3/ 4    BAD14DAD  2/ 3    E1E10FAD  4/ 5
    ABADFACE  1/ 3    BABEFACE  3/ 5    000000FF  3/ 4    1BADDEED  1/ 2
    00000051  2/ 4    00000001  2/ 3    2BADFACE  0/ 1    FADEBACC  3/ 4
    AAFF5642  2/ 3    00008270  1/ 3    FADE9403  4/ 5

    Hexadecimal
    network address
```

QUOTE

No brain is stronger than its weakest think.

Thomas L. Masson

DISPLAY SERVERS

DISPLAY SERVERS is similar to DISPLAY NETWORKS except that instead of displaying all of the networks a particular server or router knows of, it displays all of the *file servers*. DISPLAY SERVERS consists of two pieces of information: the file server name and the number of hops. The file server name is limited to the first 12 characters of the name in this particular utility. Keep in mind that a file server can have 45 characters in its name. The output for DISPLAY SERVERS can be seen on Figure 5.12.

FIGURE 5.12

The Layout of DISPLAY SERVERS

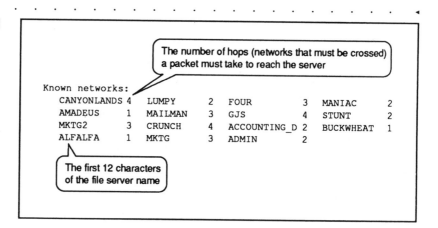

DOWN

The DOWN command is the most dramatic and harmful NetWare console command. It completely shuts down the file server activity and closes all open files. DOWN can be performed only from the console command, but keep in mind that the FCONSOLE supervisor utility provides its own internal downing feature. DOWN performs a variety of different activities before it shuts down the operating system. First it clears all the cache buffers and writes them to disk, then it closes all open files. It then updates the appropriate directory and file allocation tables with the particular files which have been written to disk, dismounts all volumes, clears all connections, and finally shuts down the operating system. Once DOWN has been entered at the file server console prompt, the system responds with a command to turn off the system and turn it back on to reboot.

DOWN is particularly harmful because of its effect on maintenance background statistics. FCONSOLE relies heavily on background information and averages for providing information about statistics and file server fine tuning and performance. Once the system has been DOWNed, all these statistics are flushed and brought back to a default state. Obviously, the statistics are more meaningful the longer they're being measured.

> The DOWN command is the most dramatic and harmful NetWare console command.

MONITOR

MONITOR is the most popular console command because it provides a central screen for tracking file server activity, workstation connections, and who is logged in. The default monitor screen displays information on six blocks at one time although it can support many more than that. In order to continue beyond the first six blocks, the system manager must type in **MONITOR [number]**. MONITOR also displays the operating system version, the percentage of file server utilization (updated every second), and the number of cache buffers that have been changed in memory but have not yet been written to disk. These are called *dirty cache buffers*.

Every time a workstation requests a transaction, MONITOR displays the file status message and up to five files which are being accessed. The file status message includes the following:

PERS, which indicates the file is logged but not locked, LOCK which indicates the file is locked

A, which means the file server is running dedicated NetWare

T, which indicates that the file is flagged as transactional and is open

H, which indicates that the transactional file is on hold until the transaction is completed

This information is extremely useful for NetWare system managers who continually monitor file server performance for proactive maintenance strategies. Incidentally, the MONITOR console command in NetWare 3.12 is much more useful (and integrates both MONITOR and FCONSOLE) than NetWare 2.2.

NAME

The NAME console command simply displays the name of the file server. It uses an underscore (_) to represent a space in the name. Remember, space is not a valid character. The file server name may range from 2 to 45 characters.

OFF

The OFF console command simply clears the file server console screen and conserves the file server monitor. The OFF command is not particularly useful when trying to monitor network activity but it does provide a way of uncluttering the screen before you enter subsequent commands.

PURGE

The PURGE utility is used to remove or completely erase all *salvageable* deleted files. In NetWare, when a user deletes a file, the system keeps track of the file and allows the user to recover it through the SALVAGE utility. These salvageable files take up space on the file server and create inefficiencies in disk access. The PURGE command, when entered at the console prompt, deletes all salvageable files from all volumes on the system and clears directory entry and file allocation tables. PURGE can be an effective strategy when file server disks become sluggish. Remember, the PURGE command is not selective—it purges everything or nothing.

RESET ROUTER

The RESET ROUTER console command resets the file server or router table if it becomes inaccurate or corrupted. The router table is used by the filer server or router to recognize other servers and other networks and to send or receive packets between them. If any other servers, networks or routers go down on the network, the packets will be lost and the router table will become inaccurate. In normal situations, the router table is updated every two minutes, but this time period could provide a window of errors. When the RESET ROUTER command is issued, the server (or router) sends out a service advertising packet (SAP) which advertises itself to all nearby file servers and networks. The networks then respond with information about their network address, their name, their location, hops and ticks which are then used to build a new router table. The syntax for RESET ROUTERS is **RESET ROUTER**.

SET TIME

The SET TIME console command is used to set the time and the date that is kept by the file server. The syntax is **SET TIME [month, day, year] [hour:minute:second]**. You can enter the time in either standard or military format. If you use standard format, you may follow the time with AM or PM. The file server always displays the time in standard format. Date can be entered not only in month, day, year but also with numbers as well as letters in the format day, month, year. You can set the date and time separately using two commands or you can use them together by putting a space between them. To view the current file server date and time, simply enter the set time command without any parameters.

This console command is particularly useful for daylight savings time or when the file server clock slows down. Keep in mind, though, this can be a security risk for users who have access to the file server console since many of the login restrictions are tied to the date. It's quite common for users whose accounts have expired to gain access to the file server console and change the filer server date, thereby granting themselves access to the system.

SPOOL

The SPOOL command is used in NetWare 2.2 to list or change spooler assignments. A spooler assignment is necessary for the proper execution of NPRINT and CAPTURE printing utilities as well as compatibility with earlier versions of NetWare 2.x. Spooling will automatically redirect jobs from NetWare 2.0a file servers to the appropriate queue and printer. The SPOOL command by itself will list the current spooler assignments as well as the syntax for those assignments. To assign a specific printer to a specific queue, type **SPOOL [printer number] to queue [queue name]**. Spooler assignments are not required in NetWare 2.2. They are only recommended in situations where the system exists with earlier versions of NetWare.

TIME

The TIME command simply displays the file server's date and time. This command is the same as SET TIME, but without any parameters. TIME will not allow the system manager to alter the system date and time—it will simply allow him or her to display it.

TRACK OFF/ON

The TRACK ON and TRACK OFF commands are used to display network service advertising packets as they are sent or received both from the file server and the router. The information is formatted according to whether the file server is receiving the information (in which it would be an IN), or broadcasting the information out to other networks. Figure 5.13 shows the format of the TRACK ON screen and provides information about the many different components which provide valuable information. These components include the sending file server's network address, node address, name, hops from that file server to this one, network addresses known by the sending file server and the number of tics that a packet would take this network from the sending file server or router. Issuing a TRACK ON command will open an auxiliary window or screen on the file server console which is known as the file server tracking screen which will constantly display the information until the TRACK OFF command is issued. The TRACK ON command is particularly useful for system managers who are

▶ • • • • • • • • • • • • • • • • • • • ◀

FIGURE 5.13

The Format of TRACK ON

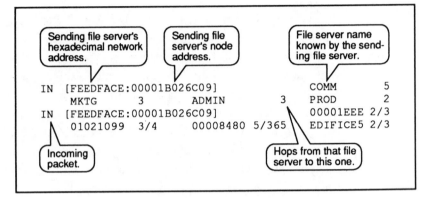

Server Information

troubleshooting network connections or simply interested in what other networks or file servers exist out there.

UPS

The UPS command is used to indicate the status of a connected uninterruptible power supply. This utility does not provide any functionality for editing the parameters of the UPS, it simply displays the status. Other uninterruptible power supply manufacturers provide software which works in conjunction with NetWare to provide what is called UPS monitoring. UPS monitoring sends a message to the file server when power falls below a particular threshold. The file server responds by sending a message to users, closing all open files and downing the file server. This is done to avoid data corruption (which occurs when the file server's power is abruptly turned off or lost).

VAP

System managers can use the VAP command to display a list of all value added processes which are currently loaded on the NetWare server. In addition, the VAP console command provides information about the VAP's parameters and customized commands. A value added process is a specialized network application which runs on the server (but not within the normal confines of the disk subsystem). VAP processes include printers, MacIntosh connectivity, and UPS monitoring.

WATCHDOG

The WATCHDOG console command monitors file server connections for inactivity and lost connections. The syntax for WATCHDOG is **WATCHDOG START=[number] INTERVAL=[number] COUNT=[number]**. The START value defines how long the file server will wait to check a user's new connection. The default is 300 seconds (5 minutes). This value is specified in seconds with a minimum of 15 and a maximum of 1,200 or 20 minutes. The INTERVAL value is also specified in seconds with a minimum of 1 and a maximum of 600. The INTERVAL value specifies how often the system will monitor this particular connection. The default is 60 seconds. The COUNT value specifies the number of intervals after the start before it will clear an inactive connection. The minimum interval count value is 5; the maximum is 100. If all defaults are set and the WATCHDOG command is simply executed without any parameters, the system will wait 5 minutes after a new connection has arrived then check the connection every 1 minute for inactivity. If it finds inactivity of the connection, it will wait 10 intervals or 10 minutes before clearing the connection.

> The WATCHDOG console command monitors file server connections for inactivity and lost connections.

The WATCHDOG feature is important in NetWare 2.2 because it allows the system manager to automatically clear inactive connections which are reserving valuable NetWare licensing connections. Since NetWare is licensed for X number of connections, if users are turning off their machines without logging out, it is locking up valuable connections which others cannot use. In addition to users, there are other NetWare device components which use connections including file servers, routers and print servers.

That's it for NetWare console commands. These commands are part of the NetWare operating system and provide functionality for configuring or customizing the internal workings of NetWare. Console commands are entered at the file server console with no security and can therefore be quite dangerous. The only security against console commands is locking up the file server.

At the beginning of the chapter, we defined the NetWare system manager as a brave soul whose single task it is to keep peace in the NetWare castle. As the NetWare LANlord of his or her own apartment, the system manager's NetWare utility belt is his/her only defense against problems and user uprisings. The utility belt is comprised of a variety of different tools including command line utilities, menu utilities, supervisor utilities and console commands. In this chapter, we have explored the many different NetWare utilities and provided enough functionalities so that the system manager can fill his or her belt with the best tools available. Think of this chapter as an open tool chest providing everything you need to succeed in network management.

> Think of this chapter as an open tool chest providing everything you need to succeed in network management.

QUOTE

My interest is in the future because I am going to spend the rest of my life there.

Charles F. Kettering

In the next chapter, we will explore network management in greater detail, discussing the specific tasks which the system manager must perform to fine tune and optimize the user environment. Beyond creating users, directory structures and drive mappings, the system manager must define login restrictions, create login scripts, install network applications, user interface, workstation software and perform routine NetWare backups. We will learn about all of these concepts in the next chapter. Get ready for the ultimate NetWare puzzle.

NetWare 2.2
Network Management

The Ultimate Netware Puzzle

In previous chapters, we mentioned that the NetWare system manager inherits the LAN in the third of three construction phases: network management. The network management phase breathes life into an otherwise limp and lifeless LAN. The network designer and installation team leave you with wires, workstations, a file server, and some barely-functional software. As the system manager, it is your responsibility to take this empty frame and fill it out with users, groups, applications, menu systems, security, login scripts, and SFT. Network management is the most challenging, exciting, and rewarding aspect of LAN construction. You can't imagine how lucky you are.

> The network management phase breathes life into an otherwise limp and lifeless LAN.

QUOTE

It does not take much strength to do things, but it requires great strength to decide on what to do.

Elbert Hubbard

The world of NetWare network management is one big puzzle. At first, the NetWare components are scattered randomly throughout the LAN—users, workstations, software, and rights. None of it makes sense. But with a cool head and the right tools, the NetWare system manager can begin to arrange these puzzle pieces into a meaningful LAN picture.

- ▸ The directory structure is formed and drive mappings are created
- ▸ Login names and passwords are assigned
- ▸ Access rights take shape
- ▸ Login restrictions are established
- ▸ Numerous login scripts are written
- ▸ Workstation software is installed
- ▸ Application software is installed

▸ The menu system is created

▸ A tape backup system is established

▸ The NetWare printing system is defined

Just like any large puzzle, the organization of these many NetWare components can be overwhelming at first. But with a little patience and the right guidance, you will quickly get the hang of it. NetWare network management can really be a piece of cake. In this chapter, we will explore the network management puzzle pieces and learn how to organize them into a meaningful NetWare picture. The first three pieces from the list above were discussed in Chapter 3 and 4. The final piece, NetWare printing, is covered in Chapter 7. *This* chapter focuses on the grunt work of NetWare network management—login restrictions, login scripts, user interface, and NetWare backup.

QUOTE

All wish to possess knowledge, but few, comparatively speaking, are willing to pay the price.

Juvenal

Clear off the table, this is going to be a BIG picture.

NetWare Login Restrictions

In Chapter 4, we discussed the three different layers of the NetWare security model. We learned that when a user logs into the system, his or her username is matched against a list of valid login names. If the username matches, the system asks for a valid password. If the password matches, the user is granted preliminary access to the LAN. He/she is not yet at the NetWare prompt. There is one more door to pass through—login restrictions. Login restrictions provide a final level of login/password security which allows the LAN locksmith to restrict user access according to four different categories:

▸ Account Restrictions

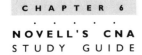
- ▸ Time Restrictions

- ▸ Station Restrictions

- ▸ Intruder Detection/Lockout

Account restrictions apply to user accounts and password/data restrictions. Time restrictions and station restrictions apply to login times and workstation locations. Intruder detection/lockout is a NetWare v2.2 feature which tracks invalid login attempts and locks out unauthorized users. Each of these puzzle pieces is an important component in the overall security picture. It is important to take time and care in designing NetWare login restrictions. Let's begin with Account Restrictions.

ACCOUNT RESTRICTIONS

NetWare account restrictions provide a method for controlling and restricting user access to the NetWare file server. They are established in two different ways:

- ▸ *Default Account Balance/Restrictions* in Supervisor Options of SYSCON

- ▸ *Account Balance/Restrictions* in User Information of SYSCON

Default account restrictions establish configurations for all new users and are defined in the Supervisor Options screen of SYSCON. User-specific account restrictions establish configurations for individual users and are defined in the user's specific User Information window of SYSCON. Default restrictions only take effect for users created from this point on—they do not affect current users. For this reason, you should define the default account restrictions *before* you create any users.

KNOWLEDGE

Default account restrictions take effect for all users who are created after the restrictions are put in place. This means that these restrictions will not take effect for any users who currently exist.

TIP

Good news. There's a little trick which can save you hours of work if you get caught in the trap described above. In order to configure login restrictions for large numbers of users, simply highlight those users with the F5 key in the User Information window of SYSCON. Press Enter. The Set User Information screen will appear with four choices—Account Balance, Account Restrictions, Station Restrictions, and Time Restrictions. Simply define the appropriate restrictions and they will take effect for all highlighted users. Whew, that saved a ton of time. Good thing you read this tip.

NetWare's account restrictions screen (Figure 6.1) provides a variety of different options for NetWare system managers. Below is a brief discussion of each of these options.

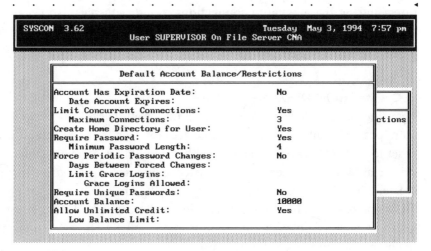

FIGURE 6.1

Suggested Default Account Restrictions in SYSCON

```
SYSCON  3.62                                    Tuesday  May 3, 1994  7:57 pm
                    User SUPERVISOR On File Server CNA

                    ┌─────────────────────────────────────────┐
                    │     Default Account Balance/Restrictions  │
                    ├───────────────────────────────────────────┤
                    │ Account Has Expiration Date:        No     │
                    │    Date Account Expires:                   │
                    │ Limit Concurrent Connections:       Yes    │
                    │    Maximum Connections:             3      │
                    │ Create Home Directory for User:     Yes    │
                    │ Require Password:                   Yes    │
                    │    Minimum Password Length:         4      │
                    │ Force Periodic Password Changes:    No     │
                    │    Days Between Forced Changes:            │
                    │    Limit Grace Logins:                     │
                    │       Grace Logins Allowed:                │
                    │ Require Unique Passwords:           No     │
                    │ Account Balance:                    10000  │
                    │ Allow Unlimited Credit:             Yes    │
                    │    Low Balance Limit:                      │
                    └───────────────────────────────────────────┘
```

Account Expiration Date

Account Expiration Date is a useful tool for temporary employees or students in an academic environment. It allows the system manager to lock an account after a specific date. By default, the Account Expiration Date is set to NO. If you change the value to YES, today's date will appear as the default Date the Account

Expires. You can change the date at any time; keep in mind that the account locks at midnight.

Limit Concurrent Connections

Limiting concurrent connections is useful against users who like to migrate throughout the LAN or login from multiple different workstations. The system manager can limit a user's concurrent connections by changing the default from NO to YES (by default, Limit Current Connections is set to NO), then configuring "Maximum Connections" for 3. Three concurrent connections means that this user can login from only three workstations simultaneously. This particular account restriction works in conjunction with station restrictions. You can enhance a user's concurrent connection limitation by combining it with a specific physical workstation limitation—station restrictions (We'll discuss station restrictions a little later.) A good average setting is YES, limit current connections, and set the maximum connections to 3. If you set this in the default account restrictions, it will take effect for all users who are created beyond this point.

Create Home Directory for User

Create Home Directory for User is an important part of the network management puzzle because it defines a home area for each user (by default this option is set to YES). This home area is used by many other configurations, including drive mappings, login scripts, and trustee assignments. User drive mappings are created in the system login script with an identifier variable called %LOGIN_NAME. This identifier variable will create a home directory mapping for all users based on what their unique login name is. However, this only works if a home directory exists for each user.

Require Password

Password restrictions are applied using the Require Password and other related restrictions. By default, the system does not require a password. This is a huge oversight. It is recommended that you require a password for all users and that you set the minimum password length to something in excess of five characters.

TIP

There is a password-hacking routine which is circulating that can guess any five-character password in less than 20 minutes. The program connects directly to the NetWare

It is recommended that you require a password for all users and that you set the minimum password length to something in excess of five characters.

bindery and matches random character combinations with existing password information. So if your minimum password length is four characters or less, this program can break into the system very, very quickly.

Force Periodic Password Changes

Once a password has been required and a suggested minimum password length of seven characters has been set, you should explore using the Force Periodic Password Changes account restriction. This restriction forces users to change their password at periodic intervals. If you set Force Periodic Password Changes to YES, the system will ask you to input the days between forced changes. The default is 45 days—this is a little short and can become a nuisance very quickly. A periodic password interval of 90 days is optimal.

Once a password interval has expired, the user is required to change his/her password. If the user does not change his/her password at the point of login, the system will lock the account. This is where *grace logins* come in. Grace logins allow the user to login even without changing the password. Keep in mind this is a temporary situation, because even grace logins expire. Seven grace logins is ideal for most users. Once a user logs in for the seventh time and chooses not to change his/her password, the account is locked. Locked accounts can only be unlocked by the supervisor. So who unlocks the supervisor's account? Stay tuned for the answer.

TIP

When the periodic password interval has expired, the system will respond with Your password has expired. Would you like to change it now? **This gives users an opportunity to change their password**

**right away. Otherwise, users can use SETPASS or SYSCON to
change their password at any time.**

Require Unique Passwords

Require unique passwords works in conjunction with forcing periodic
password changes. When the periodic password interval expires and the user is
required to change his/her password, Unique Passwords forces him/her to enter
a new, *different* password. If the system manager takes the time and effort to make
the users change their passwords periodically, it makes sense that those
passwords should be unique each time. It does not make sense for the user to
continually use the same password.

KNOWLEDGE

**Requiring unique passwords relies on an internal NetWare password
table. The table keeps track of the last 10 passwords. Once the tenth
different password has been used, the user can in fact use a previous
password.**

Account Balance

Account balance restrictions apply to NetWare's internal accounting feature.
NetWare has a built-in accounting feature that tracks user logins, logouts, and
access to network resources. The system manager can install accounting through
the SYSCON menu utility. In addition, he/she can use SYSCON to define network
resources and establish charge rates for access to those resources. Account
balance is a dynamic measure of each user's accounting usage.

By default, the account balance is set to 0 and unlimited credit is set to NO.
This is a problem because once the system manager installs accounting, users
begin accumulating resource charges—the account balance is immediately negative. If the low balance limit is set to 0, users are instantly in violation of NetWare
accounting. Once a user's account balance becomes negative, the system locks
their account—they can no longer login. So it is very important to set the account
balance to at least 1,000 when you decide to install accounting. Low balance limit
refers to the number which needs to be reached in order for the user to be locked
out. Typically, an account balance of 1,000 (depending on the charge rates) and

a low balance limit of 0 is optimal. It's not a good idea to set unlimited credit because that defeats the whole purpose of charging for resources.

Another interesting use of NetWare accounting in NetWare 2.2 is resource tracking. Instead of charging users for their specific resource usage, you can use accounting to track how uses are accessing resources—by setting the allow unlimited credit to YES and setting the account balance to 0 and the low balance limit to 0. Then you charge each user a rate of 1 unit per usage on each of the five different resources. The five different resources which can be tracked are:

▶ Time usage

▶ Blocks written

▶ Disk space

▶ Blocks read

▶ Processor utilization

By setting each of these resource charge rates at 1, you can receive a comparative view of how users are using your LAN resources (you can match their time utilization with processor utilization to see if they are really working, for example). By setting the Allow Unlimited Credit to YES, you are allowing the number to go well below 0 and users will quickly accumulate a negative balance. The number that appears in their negative account balance under User Information exactly correlates with their use of NetWare resources. While NetWare does not inherently support any kind of auditing feature or resource tracking feature, a clever and creative use of NetWare accounting can provide the same functionality.

Limit Server Disk Space

Users can be restricted to specific amounts of disk space on the shared server disk. NetWare tracks disk space by who owns (created) what. Also, if you copy a file, ownership is transferred to the destination user. If Limit Server Disk Space is set to YES, the system will ask for a maximum server disk space parameter—in kilobytes. Typically, this parameter works in deterring disk abuse. Also, in academic environments, it's a good idea to limit students so that they don't clutter the disk with games and miscellaneous utilities. Unless, of course, they give you a copy of the game. A good value for limiting server disk space is 1,000 kilobytes, or 1 megabyte.

> Users can be restricted to specific amounts of disk space on the shared server disk.

The next three login restrictions are Time Restrictions, Station Restrictions, and Intruder Detection Lockout. They provide a certain level of login security but not near the flexibility or versatility of Account Balance Restrictions. Let's take a quick look at them.

QUOTE

The wisest man has something yet to learn.

George Santayana

TIME RESTRICTIONS

Time restrictions are useful because they allow you to control how much time users have access to the system. As with Account Restrictions, Time Restrictions can be applied as a default at the user level. Remember that default time restrictions only take effect for users who are created from this point forward. Time restrictions are valuable when they are configured intelligently. But when configured carelessly, they can dramatically hinder user performance and productivity.

The default time restriction screen (Figure 6.2) is a matrix of days and time periods. The days of the week, Sunday through Saturday, are displayed on the left-hand side of the matrix and a 24-hour clock, in half an hour increments, is listed across the top. Each asterisk in the system indicates a time period when this particular user or all users can login. By default, the time restriction screen has all asterisks—all users can login at any time. To restrict users, simply move the cursor to a particular point in time and press the space bar. This blanks the time period and makes it unavailable for user access.

FIGURE 6.2

Default Time Restrictions in
SYSCON

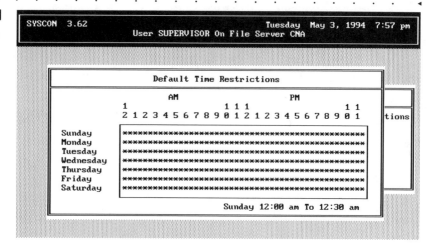

Some common time restrictions include:

Restrict entire days—weekends, for example

Restrict evenings—10:00 PM to 5:00 AM

Restrict backup time periods—11:00 PM to midnight

These are effective strategies for protection against mild-mannered janitors who turn into superhackers at midnight, or users who spend too much time in front of the computer. Keep in mind that time restrictions are dynamic—once the user enters a blank time period, the system clears your connection. Don't worry, there is a five-minute warning before the connection is cleared.

> Time restrictions are effective in protecting against mild-mannered janitors who turn into superhackers at midnight, or users who spend too much time in front of the computer.

TIP

When a time restriction is encountered and a user connection is cleared, the system does not perform a proper logout—it simply clears the workstation connection. But watch out—files are not saved. When the system

prompts you with a five minute message, it's a good idea to pay attention and logout.

The F5 key is very useful with time restrictions in that it allows you to highlight blocks of time and press the asterisk key to insert an available time slot or the space key to restrict that time slot. Remember, intelligent time restrictions increase network security, while careless ones significantly hinder user productivity.

STATION RESTRICTIONS

Station restrictions are another effective way to control user access. But this time, you're not restricting user access with passwords, disk restrictions, or time slots. Instead, you're restricting the physical workstation users login from.

Here's how it works: each workstation is equipped with an internal network interface card. The card has a 12-digit hexadecimal node address that is programmed at the factory. This node address is unique for all network interface cards in the world and is used by the cabling media to identify this network interface card from all others on the LAN. The node address can also be used to identify which users can login from which machines. In a certain sense, it can be said that the user is logically attached to a specific network interface card.

Since station restrictions are linked so closely to the user and node address, there is no such thing as default station restrictions. It wouldn't make sense to restrict all users on the network to a particular node address. If you did, all users in the network would have to login from the same workstation. Massive gridlock!

Station restrictions are configured for specific users in the user information screen of SYSCON. In order to define a station restriction for a given user, the system manager must provide two pieces of information: network address and node address. The network address defines the cabling scheme upon which the workstation is attached. The node address is a 12-digit hexadecimal number which identifies the workstation network interface card. Unfortunately, this information is not readily available to NetWare system managers. The only easy way to access this information is with the USERLIST utility. USERLIST provides a list of all users who are currently logged in and the station addresses of the machines they are using. The best strategy is to print out a list of each user's USERLIST and use the information in SYSCON to establish station restrictions.

Station restrictions are another example of how login restrictions can be used to enhance access security but—if abused or mishandled—can significantly impede user productivity. If station restrictions are set to only one workstation and that workstation is down or busy, he or she cannot login from any other workstation. While this is a useful security tool, it can be detrimental to user relationships.

INTRUDER DETECTION/LOCKOUT

Intruder Detection/Lockout is not so much a restriction as it is a security tracking feature. Intruder Detection/Lockout tracks invalid login attempts by monitoring users who try to login without correct passwords. The Intruder Detection/Lockout feature keeps track of invalid password attempts and locks a user account once the threshold number of attempts has been exceeded—usually three. Intruder Detection/Lockout is a system-wide configuration—it is either activated for all users or none.

> Intruder Detection/Lockout tracks invalid login attempts by monitoring users who try to login without correct passwords.

By default, Intruder Detection/Lockout (Figure 6.3) is set to NO. You can choose Intruder Detection/Lockout from the Supervisor Option screen of SYSCON. Intruder Detection/Lockout has two components: intruder detection and account lockout. Let's look at each one in detail.

Intruder Detection

Intruder detection is activated as soon as a valid user logs in with an incorrect password. The Incorrect Login Attempt Threshold is a number which continues to increment as invalid passwords are entered for the same user. As soon as the incrementing number exceeds the Incorrect Login Attempt Threshold, the system activates account lockout. The Bad Login Count Retention Time is a window

FIGURE 6.3

Intruder Detection/Lockout

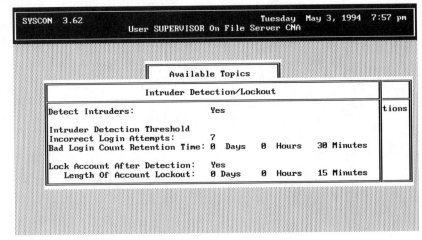

of opportunity, so to speak, that the system uses to increment the incorrect login attempts. Here's how it works:

> ► Assume the Incorrect Login Attempts is set to 7 and Bad Login Account Retention Time is set to 24-hours. The system will track all incorrect login activity and lock the user account if the following condition occurs—the number of incorrect login attempts exceeds 7 in a 24-hour window.

Account Lockout

Account lockout is activated when the intruder detection threshold is exceeded and account lockout is set to YES. It doesn't make much sense to activate Intruder Detection/Lockout without initiating a user lockout once the intruder detection threshold is exceeded. By setting the lock account after detection to YES, the system asks for a length of account lockout. The Length of Account Lockout is the time period that the account is locked once account lockout is activated. By default, this value is set to 15 minutes (this doesn't make much sense, does it?) This value invites the hacker to come back 15 minutes later and try all over again. Typically a value equal to or exceeding the bad login account retention time is adequate.

TIP

The most common target for NetWare hackers is the Supervisor. If Intruder Detection/Lockout is activated and users try to access the Supervisor account more than 7 times with an incorrect password, the system will lock the supervisor account. This is particularly disconcerting—especially since the Supervisor is the only user who can unlock NetWare accounts. Fortunately, NetWare has incorporated a console command (called **ENABLE LOGIN**) which resets the Supervisor account.

TIP

When the Supervisor unlocks a user account, he/she performs this function in the User Information screen of **SYSCON**. At the Intruder/Detection Lockout screen, it displays the node ID of the last station which attempted an incorrect login. This is useful information if you have a problem with particular users who are accessing other users' accounts.

That's it for login restrictions. In this section, we learned about the various account restrictions, time restrictions, station restrictions, and NetWare's Intruder Detection/Lockout feature. These restrictions, when used in coordination with login/password security and access rights, can create a very effective security strategy for the NetWare LAN locksmith.

The next piece of our network management puzzle is login scripts.

Login Scripts

Login scripts are executed once a user passes through the many layers of NetWare security and becomes an active player in the LAN. Login scripts are very useful tools in customizing user environments. If you think back for a moment to our discussion of drive mappings, you'll remember that they are temporary user mappings which point to specific

> Login scripts are batch files for the network.

areas of the shared disk. Drive mappings are activated (defined) each time a user logs in. Login scripts allow the system to establish and define custom user configurations and are transparent to the user.

Login scripts are batch files for the network. As the NetWare LANlord, it is your responsibility to create login scripts which are both productive and easy to maintain. NetWare provides three different types of login scripts:

The system login script provides user configurations and system-wide drive mappings for everybody who logs into the network.

The user login script is a user-specific script which provides user customized configurations (each user executes his/her own script).

The default login script executes in cases where there is no user script. The default login script contains minimum drive mappings and system configurations.

TIP

A well-designed and well-written login script can save the system manager literally hours of individual configuration. It is highly recommended that you make use of this particular NetWare tool for decreasing your maintenance load and increasing your general quality of life.

QUOTE

Ability is of little account without opportunity.

Napoleon Bonaparte

LOGIN SCRIPT TYPES

All three login scripts work together to provide system-wide drive mappings and user-specific customization. In this section, we will explore the details of the three login script types. In addition, we'll bolster our NetWare holster with a comprehensive understanding of NetWare login script commands and their syntax. Let's take a closer look.

System Login Script

The system login script provides a facility for system-wide drive mappings. The system login script is executed by all users as soon as they login. This script can only be created and edited by the supervisor—under the supervisor options menu of SYSCON. The system login script is a special text file—NET$LOG.DAT. It is stored in the SYS:PUBLIC directory so all users can have access to it. The system login script file must consist of valid login script commands and be organized according to NetWare login script syntax and conventions.

User Login Script

The user login script is a user-specific script. It provides customization at the user level. The supervisor can use this script to further customize user parameters beyond the system login script. The user login script typically contains user-definable drive mappings and commands that are customized for particular individuals. While the user script is a nice feature, it can quickly become a maintenance nightmare. Imagine hundreds and hundreds of user login scripts to constantly maintain. The user login script is the text file LOGIN. in each user's unique SYS:MAIL\userid directory. In our discussion of directory structures, we talked about a system-generated series of user directories under SYS:MAIL. This subdirectory is used to store user-specific configuration files like the user login script.

TIP

The intelligent system manager can create an effective system login script which makes user login scripts obsolete. This is ideal because it provides the flexibility of user-customization while retaining the ease of maintenance and centralization of one system script. Try as hard as you can to fit all of your login script commands into one system login script.

Default Login Script

The default login script is activated only when a user login script doesn't exist. The default login script contains some basic mappings for the system and a COMSPEC command which points to the appropriate network DOS directory.

The default login script cannot be edited because it exists as part of the LOGIN.EXE system file. The default login script was created and is maintained by the NetWare system and therefore cannot be edited, modified, or deleted.

> The default login script contains some basic mappings for the system and a COMSPEC command which points to the appropriate network DOS directory.

Earlier we learned that the ideal scenario is to have a system login script with no user login script. In this particular case, the default login script would execute after the system login script. The downside to this is that the default login script contains specific system-wide mappings which stomp all over the already-created system login script mappings. This is not good.

There are a variety of different ways to remedy this situation. One of which is to create a user login script with just one line. While this is an effective strategy, it doesn't make sense because it defeats the purpose of having one centrally located login script. The best strategy, however, is to employ the EXIT command and bypass the default login script. We will discuss this scenario later in the section.

Login Script Execution

Login script execution plays a critical role in the effectiveness of NetWare login scripts. It's important to have a firm understanding of how the different login scripts relate to one another and how they are executed. The system login script executes first and contains system-wide configurations. If a user login script exists, the user login script will execute after the system login script. Once the user login script has been executed, the system will return to the NetWare prompt, at which point the user has control of the system. If a user login script does not exist, the system will automatically execute the default login script (which is part of the LOGIN.EXE file). The default login script will also execute in situations where no system or user login script exists. This is typically the case when the system is first created.

Again, the ideal scenario is one system login script, and no user or default script. We'll talk about how to do this in just a moment.

LOGIN SCRIPT COMMANDS

Login scripts consist of commands and identifiers—just like any other program or batch file. A NetWare login script—whether it's a system, user, or default script—must be comprised of valid login script commands and recognizable identifier variables. In addition, the script must follow valid syntax and conventions. The syntax for login script programming is quite simple—each line begins with a login script command and must contain either an identifier variable or a fixed value. For example, consider the following line:

MAP F:=SYS:\USERS\%LOGIN_NAME

This follows login script syntax because it contains the login script command MAP and the login script identifier variable %LOGIN_NAME. Identifier variables are extremely useful login script components which provide diverse customization. The idea is to establish one login script command which serves a variety of different users. For example, the %LOGIN_NAME identifier variable will return the value of each user's login name, depending on who logs in. This is particularly useful for mapping user directories in a system login script. Remember, the ideal scenario is to have one login script which customizes both system-wide and user-specific environment variables. This is made possible through the use of identifier variables. Figure 6.4 shows a detailed list of all of the NetWare 2.2 identifier variables. Some of the more useful login script identifier variables include the following:

- ▸ MEMBER_OF_GROUP
- ▸ DAY
- ▸ DAY_OF_WEEK
- ▸ YEAR
- ▸ GREETING_TIME
- ▸ FULL_NAME
- ▸ LOGIN_NAME
- ▸ USER_ID

► MACHINE_OS

► OS_VERSION

Identifier variables are preceded by a % sign and must be capitalized. In order to be an effective system manager and create productive NetWare login scripts, you must have a firm understanding of all of the login script commands and how they are used in system, and user and default login scripts. In the remainder of this section we will focus on the 14 most recognizable NetWare 2.2 login script commands. In addition, we will discuss how they are used to optimize the system and user environment. Remember, our focus in this section is to create one system login script which can satisfy both our system-wide and user-specific needs.

> Identifier variables are extremely useful login script components which provide diverse customization. The idea is to establish one login script command which serves a variety of different users.

COMSPEC

COMSPEC (COMmand SPECifier) is a very, very important login script command. It redirects the DOS COMMAND.COM file to the appropriate NetWare DOS directory. This is required because as applications load into workstation memory, they have a tendency to knock the COMMAND.COM file out of RAM. If an application loads itself and unloads the COMMAND.COM file, the system has to know where to go to find the COMMAND.COM file. That's where COMSPEC comes in; it tells NetWare where to find COMMAND.COM. Without it, users will receive the message **Invalid COMMAND.COM** or **COMMAND.COM cannot be found** or **Insert boot disk in drive A**. This can be quite disruptive to users in a network environment.

COMSPEC is important because it tells the system where to look for the appropriate COMMAND.COM. Keep in mind that each version of DOS on each of your workstations supports a different type of COMMAND.COM. You must use the DOS directory structure we discussed earlier to store the different COMMAND.COM files. In addition, use a drive mapping—typically S2—to make them easier to find. There are three identifier variables which allow us to map the

FIGURE 6.4

NetWare 2.2 Identifier Variables

	Identifier variable	Description
Conditional	ACCESS_SERVER	Returns TRUE if Access Server is Functional, otherwise FALSE
	ERROR_LEVEL	An Error Number, 0=No Errors
	MEMBER OF *"group"*	Returns TRUE if member of group, otherwise FALSE
Date	DAY	Day number (01-31)
	DAY_OF_WEEK	Day of week (Monday, Tuesday, etc.)
	MONTH	Month number (01-12)
	MONTH_NAME	Month name (January, June, etc.)
	NDAY_OF_WEEK	Weekday number (1-7, Sunday=1)
	SHORT_YEAR	Year in short format (88, 89, etc.)
	YEAR	Year in full format (1988, 1989)
DOS Environment	< >	Use any DOS environment variable as a string
Network	NETWORK_ADDRESS	Network number of the cabling system (8 hex digits)
	FILE_SERVER	Name of the file server
Time	AM_PM	Day or night (am or pm)
	GREETING_TIME	Morning, afternoon, or evening
	HOUR	Hour of day or night (1-12)
	HOUR24	Hour (00-23, midnight = 00)
	MINUTE	Minute (00-59)
	SECOND	Second (00-59)
User	FULL_NAME	User's full name (from SYSCON files)
	LOGIN_NAME	User's unique login name
	USER_ID	Number assigned to each user
Workstation	MACHINE	The machine the shell was written for, e.g., IBMPC
	OS	The workstation's operating system, e.g., MSDOS
	OS_VERSION	The version of the workstation's DOS
	P_STATION	Station number or node address (12 hex digits)
	SMACHINE	Short machine name, e.g., IBM
	STATION	Connection number

appropriate search drive to the appropriate DOS subdirectory based on which machine was used. This is a very effective strategy when used in combination with the COMSPEC command. We will talk about these identifier variables and mapping DOS directories later when we get to the MAP command. At this point, it is important to note that COMSPEC is an important login script command which provides support for COMMAND.COM redirection. The syntax for COMSPEC is **COMSPEC S2:COMMAND.COM**.

Remember COMMAND.COM must follow the appropriate drive pointer—S2 in most cases. Refer to the MAP command later in this section for a discussion of S2, COMSPEC, and DOS.

DISPLAY/FDISPLAY

The DISPLAY and FDISPLAY login script commands allow the system manager to display a text file as soon as users reach a certain point in the login process. The text file is displayed on the screen in its most simple format, without any control codes or formatting characters. If a text file contains control codes and formatting characters, the DISPLAY command will display those characters as ASCII bullets. This can be quite distracting for users who see garbage all over the screen. The FDISPLAY command will filter these types of text files and won't display control codes—the characters are filtered out and only the text is displayed. The syntax of DISPLAY and FDISPLAY are identical:

DISPLAY textfile

When the login script execution comes to this particular line, it goes out and finds the selected text file. Then it displays it on the screen. This particular command is especially useful when used in combination with the PAUSE command— which allows the system to pause execution until a key is pressed. This allows users to see the text file as it is displayed on the screen. Without the PAUSE command, the text display will go by on the screen very quickly.

DRIVE

The DRIVE command is a useful login script command which allows the system manager to specify where NetWare should leave the user once login script execution has finished. By default, the system will leave the user at the first available network drive—typically F. In some cases, this can be confusing because F is usually mapped to LOGIN and the users will think, "Wow, I've already logged in. Why am I back here?" The DRIVE command is an effective strategy for system managers who want to leave users in their own home area—this is accomplished by typing DRIVE U:. Again, this strategy assumes that you've set up a home directory for each user and it specifies the U: drive.

DRIVE can also be useful if you are going to use the EXIT command to exit to a menu program at the end of login script execution. The menu program typically will be stored either in a public place—Z:—or in each user's own subdirectory—U:. The DRIVE command can be used preceding the EXIT command. This will dump the user in the directory where the menu command is to be executed.

EXIT

The EXIT command is a very useful login script command which provides a number of functions. EXIT terminates the login script and executes a specific network program. The network program can be any .EXE, .COM or .BAT file and must reside in the default drive. When used in combination with the DRIVE command, EXIT can be an effective strategy for creating a transparent turnkey system whereby users log in and are left within a menu system. The syntax for the EXIT command is relatively simple: EXIT [name of program file].

It is important to note that the program which is inside of the quotes can only be a maximum of 14 characters long. Some system managers find this to be a harsh limitation because they might want to execute a particular program name with many switches. To remedy this situation, you can exit to a batch file which then performs the appropriate program commands and switches.

> When used in combination with the DRIVE command, EXIT can be an effective strategy for creating a transparent turnkey system whereby users log in and are left within a menu system.

KNOWLEDGE
If the EXIT command is included in the system login script, it will skip the user and default login script. While this is an effective strategy, it is also very dangerous. Keep in mind that the EXIT statement in the system login script will bypass any user login scripts which have been created—past, present, or future.

FIRE PHASERS

FIRE PHASERS is a fun command which emits an ear-piercing Star Trek-like phaser sound from the workstation. FIRE PHASERS is a useful strategy in cases where text is displayed on screen and you want to draw users' attention to the screen. FIRE PHASERS can also be used in cases where you feel there is a breach in security. The syntax for FIRE PHASERS is simply FIRE [number].

The maximum number of phasers which can be fired in one command is 9—a 1-digit number limitation. For instance, FIRE 39 would fire 3 times because 3 is the first character found. If you would like to fire phasers more than 9 times, you can simply nest multiple fire commands—one after another. There is no limit to the number of FIRE PHASERS commands you can have in a row, although it can get quite annoying.

QUOTE

Big shots are only little shots who keep shooting.

Christopher Morley

IF...THEN

The IF...THEN command is probably the most versatile login script command and provides for script programming logic. IF...THEN checks a given condition and executes your command only if the condition is met. Otherwise, the IF...THEN skips the conditional command. For example, if you would like the system to display a message and fire phasers on each person's birthday, you can use the date identifier variables and the IF...THEN command to search for a specific date. This is also useful in displaying text messages on Fridays or Tuesdays, whenever there are staff meetings, or if a report is due at the end of the week.

IF...THEN is also useful in customizing group login scripts. Since there is no facility for group login scripts, the IF...THEN command can be used with the MEMBER_OF_GROUP identifier variable to configure specific drive mappings and configurations for groups of users. The IF...THEN command in combination with all of the many different identifier variables makes it possible for the intelligent system manager to create one system login script which satisfies all user-specific customization needs.

If multiple activities are dependent upon a condition, NetWare provides the BEGIN and END commands in conjunction with IF...THEN. This allows the system manager to create groups of conditional commands. For example:

```
IF DAY_OF_WEEK = "FRIDAY" THEN BEGIN
    WRITE "Welcome to Friday. Glad you could make it"
    DISPLAY Friday.txt
    MAP R:=SYS:DATA\REPORTS
END
```

This is effective in adding complexity to the login script programming. Keep in mind that NetWare 2.2 does not support any nested IF ... THEN statements.

INCLUDE

The INCLUDE login script command is provided for cases where one login script isn't enough. The INCLUDE statement branches to a DOS text file which is written using proper login script conventions. INCLUDE will execute the text file as if it were a login script. Once the INCLUDE statement is finished, the original login script continues from the point of the INCLUDE statement. This is useful, particularly when used in combination with IF ... THEN to provide customization for specific users and groups.

MAP

MAP is the most widely used user-specific configuration. Mapping is a very important part of NetWare navigation and provides a facility for representing large directory paths as drive letters. The problem with mapping is that it's both session-specific (meaning drive pointers disappear when users logout), and user-specific (meaning they're unique for each user). The temporary nature of drive mappings makes them particularly annoying—the complex map commands must be entered each time a user logs in. Fortunately, NetWare provides a facility for mapping automation: the system login script.

MAP commands are entered at the very top of the system login. Also, network mappings are typically activated before search drive mappings—search mappings are a lot more friendly in their acquisition of drive letters. All MAP commands work in login scripts except the MAP NEXT command, which can only be used at the NetWare prompt. The default login script includes two MAP commands:

```
MAP S1:=SYS:PUBLIC
MAP S2:=SYS:PUBLIC\%MACHINE\%OS\%OS_VERSION
```

Earlier we mentioned the importance of having different DOS versions in the network directory structure. This is to provide workstation access to the appropriate COMMAND.COM. The MAP S2 command, in conjunction with three identifier variables, allows us to intelligently MAP the appropriate DOS directory for the appropriate version of workstation DOS. The above S2 command uses three different identifier variables:

%MACHINE identifies the machine type. IBM_PC for example

%OS identifies the operating system. MS-DOS for example

%OS_VERSION identifies the DOS version. V5.00 for example

This one command in the system login script satisfies the COMSPEC requirement for all users on all workstations using all versions of DOS. Remember to put the correct COMMAND.COM file in each %OS_VERSION directory. Also, be very precise about the directory structure which you created—it must match the parameters exactly.

PASSWORD_EXPIRES

NetWare 2.2 introduces a new login script parameter called PASSWORD_EXPIRES, which is not really a command but more like an identifier variable (proceeded by a %). PASSWORD_EXPIRES is used in coordination with the IF…THEN command to provide a facility for letting users know when their password is on the verge of expiration. This is particularly useful when the Periodic Password restriction is set and users are forced to enter a unique password. The syntax for PASSWORD_EXPIRES is

```
IF PASSWORD_EXPIRES = VALUE "4" THEN BEGIN
    WRITE "Your password expires in 4 days"
```

WRITE "You better run SETPASS sometime soon"
END

or

WRITE "Your password expires in %PASSWORD_EXPIRES days."

This provides a proactive strategy for system managers who are having problems with grace login abuse. A friendly reminder never hurts.

PAUSE

The PAUSE command pauses execution of the login script at a certain point and asks the workstation user to **Press a key to continue**. This is useful in combination with the DISPLAY and FDISPLAY commands so that large messages can be displayed one screenful at a time.

REMARK

REMARK allows comments and documentation to be placed in the login script—without generating an error. Besides the word REMARK, NetWare 2.2 supports three other uses of the REMARK command: REM, an asterisk (*), and a semicolon (;). Any text preceded by REMARK is ignored by the system. This is an effective way to track script editing when you have multiple supervisors maintaining the system login script. This is also useful for documenting large login scripts for system managers who follow you.

TIP

When these system login scripts get quite large and complex, it is very hard to follow exactly what is going on. Novell, for example, in their international headquarters, has a login script that supports the whole organization—it exceeds 17 pages. This system login script must be highly documented so that people can follow exactly what's going on and how it's being implemented.

WRITE

The WRITE command allows you to display any message on the screen. Any comment enclosed in quotes following the WRITE command is displayed during the appropriate point in login script execution. WRITE can display information not only in a text nature but can also display identifier variable type information. For example, WRITE can display:

- ▶ WRITE "Your username is %LOGIN_NAME"

- ▶ WRITE "Your workstation number is %STATION"

- ▶ WRITE "You DOS version is %OS_VERSION"

- ▶ WRITE "Today is %DAY_OF_WEEK"

Another interesting identifier variable which is used with WRITE is GREETING_TIME. GREETING_TIME will return a value of "Morning", "Afternoon", or "Evening" depending on the time of day. The following WRITE command provides a nice greeting to all users:

WRITE "Good %GREETING_TIME, %LOGIN_NAME"

QUOTE

Personality is to a man what perfume is to a flower.

Charles M. Schwab

(DOS Executable)

The DOS executable (# sign) command is extremely detrimental in ANY login script. It has been included by Novell in a last ditch effort to support other commands outside the login script. But watch out—it can cause more harm than good. Any non-login script command preceded by the # can be executed from within a login script. The problem is that while the command is running, the entire login script is stored in workstation RAM. Once the # command is finished,

NetWare reloads the login script from memory. The problem is many workstations do not completely free up the workstation RAM which was occupied by the login script temporarily. In many cases, as much as 70 to 100K of workstation RAM can be lost when using the #.

A more effective way of executing non-login script commands is the EXIT command. It is a good idea to use the EXIT command and execute a batch file at the end of the login script. This will

> The DOS executable (# sign) command is extremely detrimental in ANY login script. It has been included by Novell in a last ditch effort to support other commands outside the login script. But watch out—it can cause more harm than good.

remove the login script from memory and execute any list of non-login script commands from within a batch file.

TIP

The CAPTURE command is a critical component in NetWare printing and needs to be executed at start-up.

That completes our discussion of NetWare login scripts. Keep in mind, login scripts are very effective tools for customizing user workstation environments and providing system-wide drive mappings. A well-designed system login script can save hours of maintenance for the NetWare LANdlord. Once you have the login script puzzle piece in place, the picture should start to take form. At this point, you have established a NetWare directory structure, drive mappings, access rights, login/password security, login restrictions, and a login script. All that remains is the user interface.

User Interface

User interface involves workstation software, application software, and menu systems. One of the most important jobs the NetWare system manager has is to make users feel comfortable with the network. There is nothing worse than users who are apprehensive, intimidated and threatened by the idea of logging in to a large network. There has been a lot of hyperactivity lately surrounding the Big

Brother syndrome and many people are becoming LANphobic. They feel that becoming part of a larger electronic system will cause them to lose their individuality. One of the most important cures for LANphobia is to provide customization and individuality for each user. That way, even though they are part of a larger whole, they can feel as if they are a very important part of the system alone.

Another important aspect of user interface is productivity. It is the system manager's responsibility to set up a productive software environment for each user so that they can perform their tasks in synergy with the other LAN users while at the same time maintaining some unique job specialization. This strategy is accomplished by intelligently loading application software so that it is both shared by everyone on the LAN and yet customized for each specific user's needs.

> One of the most important jobs for the NetWare system manager is to make users feel comfortable with the LAN.

In this section, we will explore the user interface responsibilities of the NetWare system manager by focusing on the intelligent installation of application software for specific user productivity and the alleviation of LANphobia by installing an intelligent and friendly custom menu environment. Before we begin, let's take a look at workstation software and the many different shells which connect the user with the NetWare LAN.

WORKSTATION SOFTWARE

As we learned in Chapter 2, the NetWare workstation software consists of IPX.COM and NETx.COM. IPX is the protocol utility which controls communications between NETx.COM and the internal network interface card. IPX is generated using the WSGEN utility and requires approximately 32K of workstation RAM. NETx.COM is the NetWare shell which handles the communications between DOS and the IPX.COM protocol. NetWare provides three versions of the NETx shell (Figure 6.5) which accommodate different workstation environments.

FIGURE 6.5

NetWare Shells and
Workstation RAM

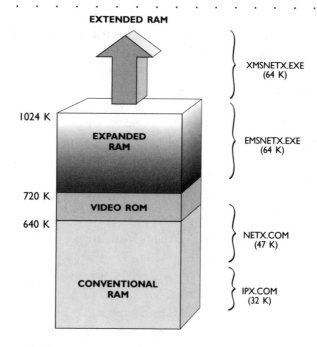

NETx.COM—the basic NETx shell which loads in conventional memory. It supports any version of DOS from v2.1 to v6.00.

EMSNETx.EXE—the EMS (Expanded Memory Specification) version of NETx. EMSNETx.EXE runs in expanded memory and frees approximately 34K of conventional RAM. On the downside, EMSNETx.EXE is very slow.

XMSNETx.EXE—the XMS (Extended Memory Specification) version of NETx. XMSNETx.EXE runs in extended memory and also frees approximately 34K of conventional RAM. On the downside, XMSNETx.EXE occupies the same 64K high memory as DOS v5.00 and v6.00. Therefore, DOS HIGH and XMSNETx can't operate together—the user must choose one or the other.

TIP

The workstation memory requirements for NetWare 2.2 differ depending on the user activities. Normal workstations require 512K of RAM, while workstations running WSGEN require the maximum conventional RAM of 640K.

NetWare provides a variety of other solutions for non-DOS workstations, including:

OS/2—the OS/2 Requester which comes with NetWare 2.2. It loads on the OS/2 workstation and control communications between the workstation operating system and NetWare.

Macintosh—the NetWare for Macintosh product which contains two components: VAP and DA. The NetWare for Macintosh VAP loads on the NetWare 2.2 server and provides translation tables between NetWare and AppleTalk (the Macintosh protocol). The NetWare for Macintosh DA is a group of Desk Accessories which load on the Macintosh workstation and provide elementary NetWare tools in the native Macintosh interface.

It is important to choose the correct NetWare workstation software. Keep in mind, the workstation is the user's link to the LAN. In many cases, it can make or break user productivity.

APPLICATION SOFTWARE

As mentioned earlier, one of the user interface responsibilities of the system manager is to provide synergistic LAN productivity through application software while at the same time customizing it for individual user needs. This is accomplished through a seven-step approach to installing application software. In this section, we're going to explore in detail the seven different steps and how they optimize application software in a NetWare environment. It is important to note that this is a general discussion and most application software has specific exceptions with respect to the installation process and certain configurations.

For the most part, though, these seven steps will help in creating a synergy between user pro-ductivity and shared application software.

QUOTE

Example is not the main thing in life—it is the only thing.

Albert Schweitzer

Step 1: NetWare Compatibility

The first step is determining NetWare compatibility. It is very important to determine whether or not the application software is NetWare compatible before it is purchased. There are 4,000 or more software packages which are compatible and registered with Novell. This compatibility information is important because NetWare makes demands on application software which in some cases can cause it to corrupt data or, at the very least, provide a non-productive work environment. NetWare compatibility information can be accessed on Netwire which is Novell's electronic bulletin board or from your local Novell sales and operations center. In addition, you can contact the software vendor for NetWare compatibility information.

> NetWare compatibility information can be accessed on Netwire—Novell's electronic bulletin board—or from your local Novell sales and operations center.

Step 2: Multi-user

Once you have established that the application software is NetWare compatible, it is important to establish whether or not it is a multi-user software program. For the best results and best user productivity in a NetWare environment, it is critical that the application software support multiple users simultaneously. A large number of application software programs are designed only to be used by one user, one at a time in a stand-alone environment. Most of your large software manufacturers with common and popular software packages are, however, creating multi-user versions of their software which provide file sharing and multi-user access. Again, to assure yourself of the most productive user environment, it is important to determine multi-user compatibility with the software before you purchase it.

Single user software can be used in a NetWare environment. NetWare supports any DOS applications, however they aren't as effective as those which provide not only data sharing but application sharing as well.

Step 3: Directory Structure

Before you can install the software or configure any of its components, it's extremely important to have an intelligent organization directory structure which supports not only the application software but the data it will generate as well. Each application program should have a specific subdirectory under the directory heading of APPS so as not to clutter the root directory. This also organizes application software for easy and efficient security design. Some software applications will create their own directory structure during the installation process. Unfortunately, this directory structure is typically created off of the root directory. This works fine in a local hard disk environment, but it doesn't work in a NetWare shared environment because we have many more people accessing the shared disk. You can map root the F: drive to SYS:APPS in which case the system will be fooled into thinking that the APPS subdirectory is in fact the root and it will create its directory structure under APPS instead of the real NetWare root.

Step 4: Installation

The fourth step in customizing network application software is installation. The installation process is typically left up to the application itself. Most applications require you to run a setup or install program so they can customize some configurations for your environment as well as unpack or decompress the files from the disk. It is not a good idea to just copy the programs off the install disks. Instead use the INSTALL program. If you must copy the disks to the NetWare drive, make sure not to use the DOS copy command but to use NCOPY because it both retains security and is a much more efficient command line utility for file copying.

Once the network application software has been installed, there are three very important configurations which need to be taken care of before the users can access or run the application software. These three configurations comprise steps 5, 6 and 7.

Step 5: File Attributes

It is very important that application software has the correct file attributes so it can be shared without being destroyed. Application files are normally flagged Sharable-Read Only, whereas data files are typically flagged Sharable-Read/Write. Most multi-user and NetWare compatible application software will provide some information about specific file attributes and the flagging of files for their applications specifically.

Step 6: User Rights

It is very important to grant user access or access rights to these applications. By default, users have no rights to the new directory structure you've created. If you were to install the application software and walk away, the users would have no access to the applications and would not be able to run them.

Typically, if everyone is going to use the same applications, use the group EVERYONE to assign the access rights, and assign them to the APPS directory. As you remember from our earlier discussion in Chapter 4, access rights do flow down to all subdirectories of the parent directory. Typically, the RF (Read and File Scan rights) are sufficient for all files in an applications directory. But all rights (except modify and access control) are typically needed in data directories. Application data can be stored in a variety of different places depending on the type of data. User-specific data should be stored in the user's own home directory. Group-specific data should be stored in a group subdirectory off of the root while data shared by all users on the system should be stored in a data directory from the root.

> If everyone is going to use the same applications, use the group EVERYONE to assign access rights, and assign them to the APPS directory.

Step 7: Workstation Configuration

Many programs require some DOS configuration at the workstation level for them to run properly. The most notable is the CONFIG.SYS file. In addition, there are device drivers which must be loaded for programs which use a mouse. And for large programs, environment space can be increased using the SHELL command in the CONFIG.SYS of the workstation. The actual command is **SHELL = COMMAND.COM /p /e:[number]** where number corresponds to the amount of environment space the application needs. Typically a number like 1024 provides enough environment space not only for NetWare but for all shared applications.

Once the application software has been installed and users have access to it, a friendly productive menu environment must be created to guide users from one application to another. Besides making it easy to access applications, a menu environment helps to alleviate LANphobia.

QUOTE

Many a man never fails because he never tries.

Norman MacEwan

MENU SOFTWARE

NetWare has a built-in menu system which provides a consistent Novell-looking or NetWare-looking menu system as well as a very simple script file for system managers to create a batch file-oriented menu system. This custom menu environment allows you to have large groups of users share the same menu file, or provide each user with his or her own specific individual file. In addition, NetWare supports a customized color palette which allows each menu or

> NetWare's menu system uses exactly the same function keys, and has the same look-and-feel as all other menus in the system such as SYSCON, FILER, SESSION, etc.

each submenu of the menu to have different colors and different characteristics which distinguish it from previous menus.

The most appealing thing about NetWare's menu system is that it uses exactly the same function keys and has the same look-and-feel as all other menus in the system such as SYSCON, FILER, SESSION, etc. It is therefore very easy for users to use and for the system manager to understand and maintain.

NetWare's menu facility has specific syntax and rules for execution. Before we review those, let's spend a moment talking about a custom menu environment and creating what's called a turnkey system.

Custom Menu Environment

A turnkey custom menu environment provides transparent use access from the point of turning on the computer to the point of bringing up applications. The idea is to perform as many of the configuration functions and access activities in the background so that the entire system is transparent to the user. The term "turnkey" comes from the notion that you can turn the key and everything takes care of itself. While this is a very nice environment and simple to use, it is somewhat complex for the system manager to set up and maintain. The turnkey system consists of four components:

1 · **The workstation boot disk** should contain the hidden system files COMMAND.COM, an IPX file for accessing the NetWare protocol, and a NETx file for attaching to the server. Finally, the workstation boot disk should include an AUTOEXEC.BAT batch file which not only loads IPX and NETx but also moves to the F: prompt and logs in the user.

2 · **The system login script** and user login script should be maintained so that they include an EXIT command which exits the user to a specific menu format. Whether or not that menu is user-specific or system-wide is not as important as the fact that the login script itself executes the menu.

3 · **The menu** must be easily executed and customized to the user needs. The menu can be executed either from a user-specific directory where a customized menu resides or from a shared directory where all users are accessing the same menu file.

4 · **The menu execution options** give users access to all of the applications, functions and utilities they need. They should all originate from within one central menu program.

Menu Syntax

NetWare's menu facility was designed using the KISS principle (Keep It Syntax Simple). The NetWare menu syntax is extremely easy to use and in many ways resembles DOS batch files. The NetWare menu file is a text file with the extension .MNU and must follow a few simple rules. The NetWare menu file consists of three different components: the title, the option and an executable. The title defines the menu title, its location, and color. The option is the choice which appears in the menu as the user sees it, while the executable is the actual program which is executed once the user highlights and chooses that particular option.

The title must be left justified and preceded by a "%." The location of the menu box is dictated by x-y coordinate. X is the number of rows from 0 to 23 on the screen and Y is the number of columns across the top from 0 to 79. For example, a value of 12, 40 would appear in the middle of the screen. The X and Y coordinates are followed by one last number indicating the color palette of the menu. (This is any number from 0 to 4 and it describes any of the five different color palettes which can be defined using the NetWare color palette utility.) Color palette 0 is the default palette which can be seen in all NetWare menu utilities, the blue and gold (GO CAL BEARS).

Options are also left justified but are *not* preceded by a "%." They can be any combination of characters and numbers and denote the particular option the user is choosing. The options are alphabetized automatically by the system—a feature that cannot be changed. If there is a particular order you would like your options to appear in (and it's not alphabetic), you can precede the option with a "1" or an "a" and it will alphabetize according to that format.

Finally, an executable must be indented underneath its appropriate option. Submenus are denoted by an executable with the same name as another title and preceded by a "%". For example, an executable with a submenu would say "%SUBMENU" and would branch off to the next point which would be a left justified title preceded by a "%" with the X-Y coordinates and the palette color number.

This simple syntax produces very flexible and nice-looking menus which again utilize the same function keys and the same conventions as Novell's own menu systems.

Menu Execution

NetWare menu execution is also straightforward. As you recall, the menu file itself by convention has a .MNU extension. To execute a file, you simply type **MENU [menu file name without the .MNU extension]**. The menu program is stored in the PUBLIC directory so that it can be accessed anywhere. Keep in mind, there are some security concerns which affect the execution of NetWare menus:

▸ The user must have the Read and File Scan rights to the directory that holds the .MNU file—typically their own directory or a shared directory like PUBLIC.

▸ The users must have all rights except Modify and Access Control in the directory in which they are currently logged in when they execute the menu command. This is because the menu command creates temporary batch files in the current directory. You should have users accessing or running menus from their own directory whether or not they are executing a menu file which exists there.

▸ If a menu file is going to be used by multiple users, it should be flagged as sharable.

That's it for menu systems and user interface in general. Keep in mind that menus, application programs and user configurations can be a very useful strategy in warding off LANphobia but I think the most effective strategy is a warm touch and a kind heart.

QUOTE

Consider the postage stamp, my son. It secures success through its ability to stick to one thing till it gets there.

Josh Billings

NetWare Backup

Nowhere is the old adage more true than here: "You never miss anything until it's gone." This holds just as true for NetWare data as anything else. NetWare backup is often overlooked because it is not needed on a day-to-day basis but only as soon as the data is lost, NetWare backup is the first responsibility which the NetWare manager is reminded of. In many cases, NetWare backup can be the difference between a successful and prosperous career as a NetWare system manager and the unemployment line. Make sure *never* to neglect your NetWare backup duties.

> Nowhere is the old adage more true than here: "You never miss anything until it's gone." This holds just as true for Net-Ware data as anything else.

NetWare backup is not as simple as inserting a diskette and copying files. This complex process involves the bindery, NetWare compatibility, reliability of backed up data, maintenance and efficient restore procedures. In this section, we will discuss briefly the NetWare backup considerations and talk a little bit about NetWare's own backup utility (called NBACKUP). Remember, the NetWare backup functionality or responsibility is probably one of the network manager's most volatile tasks.

NETWARE BACKUP CONSIDERATIONS

NetWare backup is different from local backup in that there are many more auxiliary components to back up. In a stand-alone environment, a backup consists primarily of the data and directories. In a network environment, the backup consists not only of data and directories but also security, file attributes, the NetWare bindery, users, and groups. This is why one of the most important considerations when choosing a NetWare backup system is NetWare compatibility. Many backup systems say that they work well with NetWare or that they're NetWare comfortable. But that does not mean that they're NetWare compatible. The key component in NetWare compatibility is whether or not the system can recognize the bindery. Backing up the bindery is a very serious task because it requires that the bindery be closed and re-opened (you cannot backup a file that is currently open).

Few backup systems know how to access the NetWare bindery and close and open it without bringing down the network. Most major name brands are, however, NetWare compatible and provide facilities for backing up the NetWare bindery. Keep in mind that not only is it important for the product to be NetWare compatible but it must be easy to use. Another consideration is who you're logged in as while you're performing the backup. In order to do a full NetWare backup including the bindery, the user must be a supervisor or supervisor equivalent. Also, it's a good idea to perform the back up when no other users are logged into the system. This is because the closing and opening of the bindery can cause very serious problems if any users are accessing the bindery at that moment. And if users are currently logged in, using data files or application programs, those files will not be backed up. This brings up another consideration—unattended backup. It seems contrary to want to login as a supervisor and run an unattended backup. This scenario opens the supervisor account to anyone, and leaves it vulnerable during non-working hours. The best strategy is to create a supervisor equivalent who logs in at a particular time and whose time restrictions lock the account after, let's say, 3:00 a.m., so that the system only stays logged on for a limited period of time.

The final consideration with respect to NetWare backup is reliability. It is very important to implement an intelligent schedule which provides complete data security while avoiding having to produce 365 tapes per year. The grandfather method is a good method which utilizes 24 tapes and provides at least four or five years worth of data integrity while recycling tapes every day, week, month and year. Reliability is maintained by performing periodic restores to non-active disks so you can verify that the backup is truly good and that the restore functionality of the backup system works.

One of the biggest problems with backup systems these days is that you spend your days, weeks, months and years backing up data without ever restoring any of it. It could be rather disconcerting to find out that after you have years worth of backup tapes, the system does not restore properly.

NBACKUP

The most NetWare-compatible backup system available is NetWare's own NBACKUP. While not the most feature-rich backup utility, NBACKUP provides the facility for backing up the bindery. It is reliable and it performs unattended backups. On the down side, though, NBACKUP only backs up to DOS devices—floppy disks, hard disks or read/write optical. Also, you must restore exactly to the system type you backed up from and NBACKUP only supports DOS and Macintosh file types.

NBACKUP backs up and restores 3.12 and 2.2 file servers. But you have to run NBACKUP from a workstation in order to back up the entire system. You also must be logged in as supervisor. If you back up a NetWare 2.2 server using NBACKUP, you must restore to a NetWare 2.2 server and the same with NetWare 3.12.

While the DOS device list dramatically limits the number of devices you can use for backup, Novell does supply the facility for manufacturers writing drivers which support the NBACKUP. These drivers must be loaded in the PUBLIC directory called DIBI$DVR.DAT. Unfortunately, not many manufacturers have found it necessary to write drivers for the NBACKUP utility since most manufacturers have written their own NetWare compatible software to run with the backup system. NBACKUP exists in the PUBLIC directory so it can be accessed by any user. In order for users to back up their own areas, they must have Read and File Scan rights in the directories they want to back up and they must have Write, Create, File Scan, Erase and Modify rights in the directories they want to restore to.

While NBACKUP is not the cream of the crop as far as NetWare backup is concerned, it provides adequate functionality and NetWare compatibility at the right price.

That's it for our discussion of NetWare backup and network management. Keep in mind network management is an extremely volatile portion of your job. It is quite a puzzle with respect to the many different activities and different responsibilities of the network manager. But once you get all of the puzzle pieces in place, the Novell picture is quite beautiful.

QUOTE

I feel that the greatest reward for doing is the opportunity to do more.

Jonas Salk

The final component of NetWare network management is NetWare printing. It's a dirty business, but fortunately, there's a LAN laundry room. We will learn about it next—just keep turning the pages.

EXERCISE 6.1: CONFIGURING NETWARE RESTRICTIONS

In this exercise, we will use each of the restriction options that have been discussed in this chapter. This exercise requires that you have access to an existing NetWare LAN and that you have supervisor equivalence. You will be asked to create three users and toy with their security restrictions. Be very careful to follow the steps precisely so that you do not get lost in the maze of NetWare restrictions. Let's begin by creating three users.

1 · Login as a user with supervisor equivalence and move to the NetWare prompt. Type Z: to move to PUBLIC. Type SYSCON and press Enter. Choose user information from the available topics menu in SYSCON. At the User Information menu, press Insert. Create the following three users: FRED, WILMA, and DINO. Don't be concerned with creating home directories or any security restrictions at this point. We will do that later in the exercise.

2 · Once you've returned to the User Names window, choose DINO and press Enter. Choose the second option, Account Restrictions.

3 · Disable the account. Notice that all other options have disappeared. By disabling DINO's account, DINO no longer has the ability to login and therefore security is not required.

4 · Press Escape until you reach the User's Name list and choose FRED. Press Enter.

5 · Under Account Restrictions, set the Expiration Date for today's date and Limit Concurrent Connections to 1.

6 · Press Escape until the exit confirmation window appears and exit SYSCON. At the NetWare prompt, type LOGIN FRED. Notice that by logging in as somebody else, it automatically logs you out from your supervisor equivalent account. Notice that it allows you to login FRED even though today is the expiration date. (The actual expiration date is one day after the "official" expiration date.) Go to another

workstation and attempt to login as FRED from there. Notice you will be denied because FRED has limited concurrent connections to 1. Return to your own workstation.

7 · Login as your supervisor equivalent account once again and change FRED's Expiration Date to yesterday's date. Exit SYSCON once again and attempt to login as FRED. Explain what happened.

_____

_____

_____

_____

8 · Login as your supervisor account and enter SYSCON once again. Highlight User Information from the available topics menu and press Enter. Highlight FRED and press Enter. From the User Information window, choose Account Restrictions. Notice that FRED's account has been disabled. This is because the account expiration date had been exceeded. Enable FRED and set the password requirements as follows:

A · Require Password: **Yes.**

B · Minimum Password Length: **7.**

C · Force Periodic Password Changes: **Yes.**

D · Days Between Forced Changes: **1.**

E · Date Password Expires: **today's date.**

F · Limit Grace Logins: **Yes.**

G · Grace Logins Allowed: **1.**

H · Remaining Grace Logins: **1.**

I · Require Unique Passwords: **Yes.**

Exit SYSCON and login as FRED once again. Test the above requirements to see if they have been implemented. Record the results below.

_____

_____

_____

9 · Login as your supervisor equivalent account and enter FRED's account restrictions once again. Change the date the password expires to yesterday's date. Login in once again as FRED and note the changes below.

_____

_____

_____

10 · Login as your supervisor equivalent account and highlight User Information from available topics. Press Enter. Choose WILMA from the Users Name window and press Enter. In the User Information window for WILMA, highlight Volume Disk Restrictions and press Enter. Limit WILMA's server disk space to 1KB.

11 · Login as WILMA and check her Maximum Disk Space and Disk Space in Use options from SYSCON. Note that the minimum is set to 4K. This is the lowest number NetWare 2.2 will accept so it automatically updates your entry from 1KB to 4KB. This is because the smallest unit of measurement on a NetWare disk is 4KB. This is called the default block size.

12 · Let's test the disk space restriction by creating a very small file and then expanding it. Exit SYSCON and return to the NetWare prompt. Create a very small file by typing **COPY CON WILMA.TXT** and press Enter. Type **Yabba dabba do** and press Enter. Press F6 and Enter. This will save the file.

13 · Enlarge the file by typing COPY WILMA.TXT + Z:MAIN.MENU NEW.TXT and press Enter. Note what happens below and check the limitations in SYSCON once again for WILMA.

_____

_____

14 · In the next portion of the exercise, we will restrict the station from which FRED can login. Before we enter SYSCON to configure station restrictions for FRED, we must find out what the node address is for this particular workstation. Login as your supervisor equivalent user.

At the NetWare prompt, type **USERLIST /e**. This will give you a list of all connections and appropriate node addresses. Pay particular attention to the user name with the asterisk next to it. This is your particular workstation. There are two pieces of information which are required for station restrictions. They are network number and node address. Write down the network number and the node address as they appear for your workstation.

15 · Enter SYSCON and choose FRED from the User Name window. In FRED's user information box, select Station Restrictions. Restrict FRED to the network number and node address that you wrote down for your workstation. Exit SYSCON and move to another workstation. Attempt to login as FRED. Make note of what happens.

Now attempt to login as FRED from your own workstation.

16 · Login as the supervisor equivalent and choose WILMA from the User Names window in SYSCON. Choose Time Restrictions from her User Information window and press Enter. Make note of what time it is. Restrict WILMA from logging in for the next few half-hours by using F5 to highlight those time periods and pressing the space bar. This will block out the asterisks for these times. Exit SYSCON and return to the NetWare prompt. Login as WILMA and notice that you are allowed to login because the restriction has not taken effect yet. Keep WILMA logged in until the half hour period approaches. Make note below of what happens as the system approaches the half hour which is restricted.

17 · Finally we will experience Intruder Detection/Lockout firsthand. Login as the supervisor account and highlight DINO from the Users Name list. Enter Account Restrictions from DINO's User Information

window and enable his account. Next, return to the available topics menu of SYSCON. Choose Supervisor Options and press Enter. Highlight Intruder Detection/Lockout and press Enter. Set the options to the following parameters:

A • Detect Intruders: **Yes**.

B • Incorrect Login Attempts: **2**.

C • Bad Login Count Retention Time: **30 minutes**.

D • Lock Account After Detection: **Yes**.

E • Length of Account Lockout: **15 minutes**.

Notice that these are close to the NetWare defaults.

18 • Enter DINO's User Information window and create a password for him. Exit SYSCON and login as DINO twice, using the wrong password. Finally, the third time, note what happens.

_____

_____

19 • Login as supervisor equivalent and highlight DINO from the Users Name window. Highlight Intruder Lockout status from DINO's User Information window. Notice that the account has been locked. In addition, the system indicates the last intruder address which was used for an incorrect login attempt. This address should match the network and node address of your workstation. Unlock DINO's account by changing Account Locked from Yes to No.

That completes our exercise for NetWare restrictions. Keep in mind that there's an incredible amount of flexibility and complexity in this level of NetWare security. This exercise has introduced you to some of the login restriction concepts. You can expand your knowledge by working with it further.

EXERCISE 6.2: WRITING LOGIN SCRIPTS

In this exercise, you will write a system login script for a fictitious NetWare LAN. This login script will contain required and optional components. In the second half of the exercise, you will have an opportunity to implement your login script for an existing NetWare LAN.

Let's begin by writing a login script.

1 · Create a login script which satisfies the following drive mapping considerations:

 A · MAP root to each user's home subdirectory.

 B · MAP drive G: to a data subdirectory from the root.

 C · MAP the next available network drive mapping to the login subdirectory.

 D · MAP the first search drive to SYS:PUBLIC.

 E · MAP the second search drive to the appropriate DOS subdirectory using proper syntax.

 F · MAP the third search drive to SYS\APPS\WP.

 G · MAP the next available search drive mapping to SYS:\APPS\DBASE.

 H · Insert the third search drive mapping to SYS:ACCT.

2 · Establish a comspec for COMMAND.COM in the DOS search directory.

3 · Satisfy the following WRITE conditions:

 A · Create a line which greets each user with their login name and the appropriate time of day.

 B · It's Friday, so write the following message: Congratulations, you made it through the week! Welcome to your Friday.

 C · It's May 3, the boss's birthday. To create a command which will fire phasers 27 times, write the following message: Happy birthday to you, happy birthday to you, you live in a zoo.

4 · Information.

    A · Show the date and time for each user.

    B · Show the DOS version each user is running on their particular workstation.

    C · If a user is a member of the group SALES, display the SALES.TXT file.

5 · Ending. Switch to each user's personal user directory and exit to a batch file called START.BAT.

6 · START.BAT should contain the following three components:

    A · A clear screen.

    B · A CAPTURE command to the laser queue with no banner, no form feed and a timeout of 10.

    C · The execution of a NetWare menu file called BOB.MNU.

7 · Finally, use the remark login script command to document each of these previous components.

In the second half of the login script exercise, you will have the opportunity to implement your system script. If you have access to a NetWare LAN, use SYS-CON to alter the system login script in accordance with the script you have created here. If the LAN you have access to is a productive working LAN, avoid using the system login script and create a login script for a fictional user. Then login as that user to view the changes which have been made.

To edit the system login script, choose Supervisor Options from the SYSCON available topics menu and press Enter. Choose System Login Script and press Enter. To edit a user's own login script, choose User Information from the available topics menu in SYSCON and press Enter. Highlight the user and press Enter. Choose login script from the user information window.

NOTE: Error messages will appear if drive mappings and user configurations are defined for directories which don't exist on your LAN. Remember, this is only a learning exercise.

EXERCISE 6.3: BUILDING MENUS

In this exercise, we will continue with the user interface lab from Exercise 6.2 and create a menu system for a fictitious user BOB. This menu system will be executed from the system login script so that BOB can simply login and have access to all of his user configurations and the menu system as a whole.

In the first half of this exercise, you will be asked to write a menu script which satisfies a series of given conditions and uses proper menu syntax. Once the script has been written on paper, you can have the opportunity to implement the script by inputting it into a text file and executing the NetWare menu program. The second half of this exercise requires that you have access to an existing NetWare LAN.

Using proper menu syntax, let's begin by writing a menu script for BOB which satisfies the following conditions:

1 · **The title** will be "Bob's Personal Menu." In addition, the main menu will appear exactly in the middle of the screen and use color palette 1.

2 · **The options** for Bob's personal menu are as follows:

   A · *Applications*, a submenu.

   B · *Utilities*, a submenu.

   C · *System configuration* which will execute the Z: SYSCON utility.

   D · *File management* which will execute the Z: FILER utility.

   E · *Logout*. The logout option will close the menu file, all open programs and log the user out. This can be accomplished by issuing the !LOGOUT command.

3 · **The Applications submenu** will appear on the top left corner of the screen and use color palette 2. This submenu will include the following options (all of which are under APPS):

   A · Word processing, a submenu.

   B · Spreadsheet which will execute 1-2-3 from the LOTUS subdirectory.

C • Windows which will execute WIN : from the Windows subdirectory under APPS.

D • Dbase which will execute Paradox from APPS\PARADOX.

4 • **The word processing submenu** will appear in the top right of the screen and use color palette 3. It includes the following three options:

   A • WordPerfect, executed as WP from the APPS\WP51 subdirectory.

   B • Microsoft Word, executed as WORD from the APPS\WORD subdirectory.

   C • WordStar, executed as WS from the APPS\WORDSTAR subdirectory.

5 • **The utilities submenu** will appear in the bottom righthand corner of the screen using the color palette 4. It contains the following options:

   A • SESSION management which executes SESSION from the PUBLIC subdirectory.

   B • Norton Utilities, which executes as NU from the APPS\UTILS subdirectory.

   C • Print Management, which executes as PCONSOLE from the PUBLIC subdirectory.

In the second half of this menu exercise, you will have the opportunity to implement Bob's menu. In order to implement Bob's menu, you must create a text file which follows exactly along with the script you have created. The text file will have the file name BOB.MNU. Bob's menu can then be executed using the menu command from the PUBLIC subdirectory of an existing NetWare Lan. Simply type **MENU BOB** and it will implement your menu.

Extracurricular Exercise

Try to add a level of complexity to Bob's menu so that when users press escape from the main menu, it doesn't exit the menu system. Instead, the Escape key brings them back to the main menu screen. Check Appendix D for an answer to this puzzling addition.

NetWare 2.2 Printing

"I was only speaking figuratively about Network printing
being the **LAN** laundry room."

Why do you use a LAN? A recent survey of CNA students revealed some interesting answers:

- ► To save money

- ► Because they're popular

- ► Because I have to

- ► I don't know

- ► What's a LAN?

While there is no wrong or right answer, the most popular answer is—"to share network resources." One of the most important shared resources is the network printer. Printers produce quality hard-copy output for brochures, reports, memos, and general bureaucratic paperwork. Network printing is one of the most productive and useful functions of a NetWare LAN.

> Why do you use a LAN? A recent survey of CNA students revealed some interesting answers.

As the NetWare system manager, it is your responsibility to make sure that the network printing system meets or exceeds the needs of your users. Think of it as the LAN's laundry room. In this chapter, we will explore network printing from the system manager's point of view. We will discuss the two major approaches towards NetWare 2.2 printing and provide some tools for effective printing management. In addition, we will practice printing setup with some simple lab exercises. But before we begin, let's take a quick look at the fundamentals of NetWare printing.

The Fundamentals of NetWare Printing

On the surface, NetWare printing may appear easy, but don't be fooled—it is probably the most troubling and mysterious management issue in the NetWare LAN. The fundamentals are relatively straightforward but it's the demands of the users which can quickly frazzle the system manager. NetWare 2.2 printing is designed around three different components:

The NetWare print queue is a shared area on the file server which stores print jobs in the order in which they are received. The print queue lines up the print jobs and sends them to the printer in an organized and efficient manner.

The print server is responsible for directing the print jobs as they move from the queue to the network printer.

The printer is the output device in a NetWare printing system and it typically receives the jobs and prints them appropriately.

Figure 7.1 illustrates the fundamental structure of the NetWare printing system. Keep in mind that the network printer is one of the most important shared resources on a NetWare LAN.

In a transparent NetWare printing environment, users print directly from their network applications and the output magically appears in the printer down the hall. This type of sophistication, while it might seem trivial to the user, is the result of great effort for the system manager.

QUOTE

High aims from high characters, and great objects bring out great minds.

Tryon Edwards

FIGURE 7.1

The NetWare Printing System

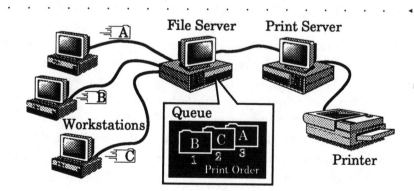

In this section we'll discuss the three different printing components and make an in-depth study of how they affect the NetWare printing system. Remember, the system manager must keep on top of these components and have a firm understanding of how they relate to each other.

> In a transparent NetWare printing environment, users print directly from their network applications and the output magically appears in the printer down the hall.

The word *queue* means "to stand in line." British citizens, for example, are often found queuing-up—waiting for tickets to cricket matches. In a printing environment, print jobs stand in line—a queue—and wait to be sent off to the network printer. Since print jobs are simply data being translated by the printer, print queues must exist as directories on the NetWare file server. Print queues are stored as subdirectories under the SYS:SYSTEM directory and are given random eight-digit hexadecimal names. As print jobs are sent from network workstations to the print queue, they are stored in the corresponding directory as files on the hard disk. The files are ordered by the print server and are tracked on their way from the file server off to the network printer. The print server never stores the print job information, it only directs and controls it.

Print jobs are sent directly to print queues in one of two ways: CAPTURE or network application printing. The CAPTURE command is a NetWare 2.2 command which literally captures the local workstation's parallel port and redirects any print jobs destined for that port off to the NetWare queue. Printing from NetWare applications, on the other hand, is a little more sophisticated because those applications recognize NetWare print queues and print directly to them. In either case, the workstation NETx shell formats the print job so that the network can recognize it and place it in the correct queue on the correct file server disk. When print queues are created, the system assigns print queue operators and print queue users which are special NetWare managers that control and use NetWare print queues. The print queue operator has the ability to add, delete or reorder the print jobs in a given print queue. By default, the user supervisor is assigned as the print queue operator on all NetWare print queues. Print queue users have the ability to insert print jobs into NetWare queues. By default, the group EVERYONE is assigned as a queue user for all new print queues.

The NetWare print server is not so much a physical device as it is a logical process. The print server can exist as a dedicated workstation or as a process running on top of a NetWare file server or router. As a dedicated workstation, the print server process runs through a file called PSERVER.EXE which is included with NetWare 2.2. As a non-dedicated process running on top of a NetWare file server or router, the print server exists as PSERVER.VAP or value added process.

In either case, the print server's purpose is to control and redirect print jobs as they travel from NetWare workstations to file server print queues and ultimately to network printers. The print server constantly monitors the print queues and network printers and makes logical attachments from one to the other. When a job is inserted into the print queue, it moves to the top of the line and the print server redirects it to the appropriate network printer. In addition, print servers monitor printers to make sure they're not out of paper, off line or jammed. If any of these situations occurs with network printers, the print server will notify the print server operator or supervisor.

> The NetWare print server is not so much a physical device as it is a logical process. The print server can exist as a dedicated workstation or as a process running on top of a NetWare file server or router.

There are certain specifications which restrict the functionality of the NetWare print server. The print server itself can only have up to five printers attached directly to it: LPT1, LPT2, LPT3, COM1 and COM2. The print server can service print jobs from print queues on up to 8 different file servers. In addition, NetWare has provided an auxiliary functionality which expands the five-printer limitation. It's called *remote printing*. Remote printing allows workstations with local printers attached to designate those printers as network devices. We will discuss remote printing in just a moment.

The real star of this show is the network printer. The network printer is the shared device which provides hard copy output to multiple NetWare users. Shared printers can be either attached to the print server, attached to the file server or attached to local workstations using the remote printing facility. Printers attached directly to the file server use NetWare 2.2's internal printing functionality, which is called *core printing*. Core printing describes the facility for controlling network printing inside the file server itself without the use of a print server. We'll discuss core printing in just a moment.

Printers attached directly to print servers are controlled by the print server and can service users on up to eight different file servers. Printers attached directly to local workstations and shared as network devices must use the remote printing facility. Remote printing is made possible through a terminate-stay-resident (TSR) program called RPRINTER.EXE which runs in workstation RAM. RPRINTER communicates directly with the print server and makes the printer available through the workstation NetWare shell.

In addition to these traditional printing configurations, the industry is providing some new, exciting, intelligent printers which are capable of communicating directly with the print server. Intelligent printers have internal network interface cards which allow them to attach directly to the LAN trunk. These printers act as workstations with remote printers attached. Some examples of intelligent printers include the new Hewlett-Packard Laserjet IIIsi and the Laserjet IV.

QUOTE

They are able because they think they are.

Vergil

In this chapter, we will explore the two different approaches to NetWare printing: print servers and core printing. We'll begin with core printing because it provides the basics of a standard printing configuration and then we will move onto the print server approach which provides a great deal more functionality, flexibility and enhanced performance.

NetWare Core Printing

During the NetWare 2.2 standard configuration and installation procedure, you'll be asked to specify whether you want to assign various parallel or serial ports on the file server to network printers. If you choose yes at this point, you will inadvertently install NetWare core printing. Installing network printers through core printing is the simplest way to go but it does not offer much flexibility. Core printing supports up to five printers attached directly to the file server and does not rely on an external print server process.

Core printing uses print queues just as print serving does and it relies on the same intervention from the NetWare shell NETx. Once core printing has been installed, it cannot be uninstalled without reconfiguring the NetWare operating system. Core printing and print servers can coexist in the same NetWare printing system but not within the same file server. If you choose to install core printing during NetWare configuration, you will be restricted from installing the print server PSERVER.VAP on this file server. In this section we will discuss when to use core printing and then evaluate the three steps which comprise the installation of NetWare core printing.

WHEN TO USE CORE PRINTING

Core printing is not installed as the default in NetWare 2.2 so it is an intentional choice during NetWare installation. Core printing should be installed in very small networks which require a maximum of five shared printers. Another factor in choosing core printing is whether or not the users should have physical access to the NetWare file server. Remember, core printing defines which printers are attached directly to the file server. Users who have access to printers also have access to the file server itself. Core printing is a good option if the file server is readily accessible to all NetWare users.

Another limitation of core printing is that it does not allow for the distribution of printers throughout the LAN. Print servers have the functionality of remote printing which allows the system administrators to distribute printers on local workstations. Core printing centralizes all printers at the file server so that they cannot physically be more than 15 to 25 feet (parallel) or 100 feet (serial) from the file server.

> Core printing should be installed in very small networks which require a maximum of five shared printers.

CORE PRINTING INSTALLATION

Installing core printing is not significantly easier than installing print servers and it severely restricts the functionality of NetWare printing. Core printing may seem simple on the surface, but there can be some hidden traps.

QUOTE

The only thing to do with good advice is to pass it on. It is never of any use to oneself.

Oscar Wilde

Core printing installation occurs initially at the first step of configuring the network operating system. The system will ask if you would like to install or define any ports for NetWare printing. If you choose YES to define the local parallel and serial ports on the file server, you have inadvertently installed core printing. Once core printing has been installed during the configuration stage, the system administrators must set up the core printing system and activate it, using three simple steps:

1 · Create the print queues

2 · Defining the printers

3 · Assign the queues to printers.

During the first step, the system manager creates the print queues and the system assigns a random eight-digit directory name. The print queue is stored on the same file server that is using core printing. During the second step, the system manager defines the printers and tells the system which port will be using which printers. The system administrators also name the printers so that they can be easily tracked through core printing. During the third step, the system manager closes the loop by assigning the queues to the printers. Assigning queues to printers is necessary so that print jobs which are sent from workstations to print queues can ultimately find their way to the appropriate network printer.

These three setup processes are very similar to the setup processes which the print server requires. The main difference is in how they are implemented. Core printing setup is implemented entirely at the file server console while print server setup is implemented through the PCONSOLE menu utility. Here's a detailed description of the process just described.

Creating Print Queues

Creating print queues is the first step in core printing setup. Print queues are necessary because they provide a buffering holding area for print jobs while they are waiting for available network printers. Queue creation in core printing is accomplished through the queue console command using the following syntax: **QUEUE [queue name] CREATE** and then Enter. For example: **QUEUE LASER-JET III CREATE** would create a print queue named LASERJET III.

There are a variety of other parameters which can be used with the queue console command in creating and managing core printing queues. They are:

QUEUE by itself which lists all print queues

QUEUE NAME CHANGE JOB NUMBER 2 PRIORITY X changes the job priority in a queue

QUEUE NAME DELETE JOB N deletes a given job from the print queue

QUEUE NAME DESTROY deletes the entire print queue

QUEUE NAME JOB lists all jobs which are currently in the print queue

To view these options and get a full listing of the queue console parameters, simply type **QUEUE HELP** or **QUEUE ?** at the file server console. There are a few things to remember while creating and managing NetWare print queues. One, queue name should be easily recognizable and somehow linked in name to their appropriate printer. Queue names cannot be more than 47 characters, but for easy management, should probably be less than 10. Remember, queues are subdirectories under the system directory. Print jobs are printed on a first in, first out basis in NetWare queues. This order, however, can be changed using PCONSOLE or the QUEUE NAME CHANGE PRIORITY console command. Queues should be assigned to their own printer although it is possible to have a queue assigned to multiple printers or to have multiple queues assigned to one printer.

Defining Printers

The next step in setting up core printing is defining the printers. Core printing does not allow the system manager to name his or her file server printers. The system manager is required to manage printers by number. Since there are only five printers available in core printing, the supervisor is limited to the numbers 0 through 4.

Defining the printer accomplishes three tasks:

1 · Selecting a printer number

2 · Specifying the port type

3 · Configuring serial ports if the port type is serial

Printer definition in core printing is accomplished through the printer console command using the following syntax: **PRINTER [number] CREATE PORT**. For example, **PRINTER 0 CREATE LPT1** will create Printer 0 and attach it to the LPT1 parallel port. If the port which is defined using the printer console command is a COM1, COM2, COM3 or COM4 port, the system manager must complete a third step: serial port configuration.

Configuring serial ports in core printing is accomplished through the PRINTER CONFIG console command. The PRINTER CONFIG console command provides a facility for viewing or changing serial printer configurations. The syntax is **PRINTER [number] CONFIG** which presents a list of the different printing configuration options. To change the serial printer configuration options, type **PRINTER [number] CONFIG [any of the 5 different serial configuration options]**. These include:

▸ BAUD

▸ WORD SIZE

▸ STOP BITS

▸ PARITY

▸ XON/XOFF

An example would be **PRINTER 4 CONFIG BAUD=2400 WORDSIZE=8 STOP-BITS=1 PARITY=0 XOFF/ON=YES**. While printer definitions in core printing are obviously extremely important, they are not very easy to grasp. One consolation is that parallel printers do not require any configuration.

Assigning Queues to Printers

The final step in core printing installation is the assignment of the queue to the printer. Once the print queue has been defined and the printer has been installed, the system manager must assign a queue to a printer. Queue assignments tell NetWare user print jobs where to go once they leave the queue. Keep in mind, with NetWare core printing, there is no print server to help control or manage the movement from queue to printer. This is accomplished through the operating system.

The assignments of queues to printers in NetWare 2.2 core printing is accomplished through the PRINTER ADD console command. The syntax is **PRINTER [number] ADD QUEUE [queue name] AT PRIORITY [number]**. For example, to add the Laserjet III queue to printer 0 at priority 1, the following command would have to be issued at the console prompt: **PRINTER 0 ADD LASERJET III AT PRIORITY 1**. Incidentally, the default priority in core printing is 1, which means that a particular print queue will have first crack at the printer in case there are multiple queues attached to the same printer. If there are 3 or 4 queues attached to the same printer and they each have different priorities, all jobs will be printed from queue with priority 1 before any jobs are printed from other, lower-priority queues.

Once the print queue has been created, the printer has been defined, and the queue has been assigned to the appropriate printer, NetWare core printing has been accomplished. From this point on, NetWare users can send print jobs to the specific queue which was created, and those jobs will be redirected to the appropriate network printer. NetWare core printing does not provide much flexibility with respect to multiple configurations, alternative resources, or distributing printer locations.

To build on the fundamentals of core printing, the system manager has the option of installing the print server system. The print server system is much more flexible and provides a greater amount of printing functionality.

TIP

Since core printing is installed at the file server console and since most of these configurations are not built into the operating system, all of the work which was accomplished by the system manager in setting up and installing core printing is lost once the server is down. In an effort to retain the system manager's sanity, it is recommended that you insert the previous core printing installation commands into the AUTOEXEC.SYS system configuration file. AUTOEXEC.SYS is executed whenever NetWare 2.2 file servers are booted. A sample AUTOEXEC.SYS would include a printer, a printer definition and an assignment of the queue to the printer. Print queues are permanent directories which exist on the file server. They do not go away.

QUOTE

Every action of our lives touches on some chord that will vibrate in eternity.

Edwin Hubbel Chapin

NetWare Print Server

Earlier we mentioned that 95% of all printing needs are satisfied using NetWare print servers. In the NetWare printing laundro-mat, print server would be the washer and dryer, while core printing is the sink. Print servers are more complex than core printing but provide the PCONSOLE utility for simple user interface and friendly printing management.

KNOWLEDGE

With print servers, complexity and sophistication outweigh simplicity.

WHEN TO USE PRINT SERVERS

Print servers are required when the number of printers exceeds the file server's limit of five, or when the physical layout of the LAN is so large that centralization of printer location is not feasible. Print servers are also required when users are utilizing specialized intelligent printers which are not attached to print servers or workstations. In NetWare 2.2, the print server functionality supports 16 printers and queues from up to 8 file servers. Print servers in NetWare 2.2 can be installed on two different devices: dedicated workstations or the file server. The creation of a dedicated print server on a workstation is made possible through the PSERVER.EXE file. In this particular case, the system manager should create a special configuration file called SHELL.CFG on the workstation which defines the command SPX CONNECTIONS = 60. This command is required so that communications can be maintained with multiple users, queues and file servers.

> Print servers are required when the number of printers exceeds the file server's limit of five, or when the physical layout of the LAN is so large that centralization of printer location is not feasible.

The non-dedicated or internal print server is defined as PSERVER.VAP which runs on the NetWare 2.2 server or router. The VAP (value added process) runs in parallel to the operating system. While VAPs take up considerable file server resources, they are well designed and coexist peacefully with the operating system or router functions. In addition to NetWare's print server functionality, there are some third party products which provide more tasks and detailed print job accounting. One of the most popular is Bitstream's Mosaic print server software.

PRINT SERVER TYPES

Regardless of which print server system you choose, print serving setup is accomplished with four simple steps. In a nutshell, they are:

1 · Create the print queues.

2 · Create the print servers.

3 · Define printers.

4 · Assign queues to printers.

In this section we will discuss the three different print server types and when to use them. Then we will go on to evaluate the four steps in installing NetWare print servers.

To review, print servers are required for a variety of reasons:

- ▶ When the number of printers exceeds five
- ▶ When printers must be distributed throughout the LAN for location reasons
- ▶ When the system manager would like to support intelligent printing devices
- ▶ When this printing system supports other file servers from newer versions of NetWare including 3.12 and 4.01

Available file servers processes determine when print servers should be used. File servers processes are internal operating system routines which are responsible for processing user requests. When the NetWare 2.2 file server is under a heavy load, file server processes can become busy and unavailable. In these instances, running core printing can severely diminish network file server performance. Running a print server offloads the file server's processes from the operating system itself—even if the print server is running on the file server. Keep in mind, the print server runs as a separate process from the file server.

While core printing limits the system manager to attaching printers directly to the file server, print server provides a great deal more functionality. The print server can exist as a separate process on the file server or router, or can exist as a dedicated process on a workstation. In either case, the print server functionality is identical.

Each of these three different print server types has its own advantages and disadvantages. The advantage of a non-dedicated print server is that it doesn't require additional hardware. It does, however, require you to share the print serving processes with an existing file server or router. The dedicated print server, on the other hand, operates exclusively as a print server—no sharing. Unfortunately, though, it does require additional hardware. The good news is a computer door stop will work fine (an 8088 CPU, 1MB RAM, and a 20MB hard disk.)

File Server

As mentioned above, running the print server process separately on a file server requires a value added process. The value added process runs in parallel to the network operating system and shares the same 286-based processor. The value added process also shares file server RAM.

NetWare 2.2 loads all value added processes it finds in the system directory during startup. It will prompt the system manager as to whether he or she would like to load available VAPs. At that point the system manager has one of two choices: YES to load all VAPs, and NO to load no VAPs. It's an all or nothing proposition. By default, the print server VAP is not loaded on the NetWare server. This is because NetWare makes no assumptions about printing configuration during installation. In order to activate the print SERVER.VAP, the system manager must copy the appropriate file from the appropriate NetWare diskette. The file name is PSERVER.VAP and it is stored on the PRINT 1 disk in the following subdirectory: A:\SYSTEM\VAP. Once the file has been copied from the PRINT 1 diskette to the SYSTEM directory on the file server, the file server must be downed and brought back up. Once the file server is brought back up, the system will prompt the system manager as to whether he or she would like to install all known VAPs. If the system manager chooses YES, the print server has been installed.

Workstation

The process of installing the print server on a dedicated workstation is much simpler. The dedicated print server file exists as PSERVER.EXE. This file runs as any other application program and completely takes over the processor and memory of the workstation. Before PSERVER.EXE can be run, the system manager must attach the workstation to the network cabling. This is accomplished by running IPX and NETx. The system manager does not have to log in this workstation in order for the dedicated print server facility to operate. The facility only requires an attachment so the system manager could run IPX, NETx and PSERVER.EXE followed by a name for the print server.

PSERVER.EXE is not a large file and can be stored in the root directory of the workstation or on a diskette. Keep in mind that if you are going to run PSER-VER.EXE on a dedicated workstation, you must include the SHELL.CFG file with one line: SPX CONNECTION = 60. This will open up enough connections so that the print server can communicate with multiple users, print servers and file servers.

> The dedicated print server file exists as PSERVER.EXE. This file runs as an application over DOS and completely takes over the processor and memory of the workstation.

Router

Loading the print server functionality on a router provides two advantages over the other print server types: efficiency and connectivity. Print serving efficiency is accomplished because the router does not have nearly the overhead that the file server does. Loading a PSERVER.VAP process on a dedicated router does not hinder the network nearly as much as it does running on a file server. In addition, router functionality provides a variety of different operations including dedicated and non-dedicated routers. In order to run PSERVER.VAP, the system manager must define a dedicated protected mode router—the highest level of NetWare 2.2 routing.

The second advantage is connectivity. The purpose of a router is to connect two distinct LAN topologies. Since the print server is running on a router, the print server functionality then becomes available not just to one but to both of the LAN topologies. This is a simple way of combining the efficiency of running the router on an existing machine with the connectivity of providing print services to more than one network at a time. A router can include up to four network interface cards which means it can connect up to four different LANs. In this scenario, the print server then would support print queues on four different file servers from four different networks.

PRINT SERVER INSTALLATION

The process of installing a print server on a router is similar to the file server except there is no SYSTEM subdirectory. Instead, the system manager defines a ROUTER.CFG file with the PSERVER.VAP included. Once the router is booted, the ROUTER.CFG file defines the print server function and loads the auxiliary process. From that point on, PSERVER can be used to manage and maintain the router print server.

Once you have chosen your print server type, it is time for the system manager to get down and dirty by installing the three different components of a NetWare printing system: the print queues, print server and printer.

Print server installation mirrors core printing installation in theory but that's where the similarities end. Print server installation is much more versatile and provides a workstation-based menu interface. There are no console commands included in print server installation. The installation process involves four steps:

1 • Creating print queues

2 • Creating print servers

3 • Defining printers

4 • Assigning queues to printers

During step 1, the system manager creates the print queues on the system and assigns print queue operators and users. During step 2, the system manager creates the print server and gives the print server a unique name and password. In step 3, the system manager continues with print server definition by defining the printers, assigning names to the printers, and configuring their internal parameters. These parameters include among other things, port type, interrupt and serial configurations.

> The installation process consists of four steps: creating print queues; creating print servers; defining printers; assigning queues to Printers.

The final step in print server installation is assigning the queues to printers which is performed in exactly the same way as it is in core printing. This is required so that print jobs can find their way from specific queues to appropriate printers. In this section, we will discuss each of these four steps in some depth and provide some tips for optimizing NetWare print server installation.

Creating Print Queues

Print queues are the central component in NetWare printing because they provide the link between NetWare workstations and shared printers. Print queues are created using the PCONSOLE menu utility which is stored in the PUBLIC directory.

To create a print queue in PCONSOLE, simply choose Print Queue Information from the available topics menu of PCONSOLE and press Insert at the Queue Name box. Next, type in a queue name up to 47 characters and press Enter. At this point, the print queue name will appear in the queue names box.

Once a print queue has been created, the system will assign it an eight-digit hexadecimal number and a subdirectory under the system-generated directory. Using PCONSOLE, the system manager can define other parameters with respect to print queues, including:

▶ **The Current Print Job Entries** screen provides a list of all print jobs which are currently held in this queue. This screen is a central point for queue management and job reordering.

▶ **Current Queue Status** displays the status of the queue with respect to number of entries in the queue, number of servers being serviced by this queue and operator flags.

▶ **Currently Attached Servers** is a list of print servers that can service this queue. Those print servers keep track of which network printers are also servicing this queue.

▶ **Print Queue ID** is the eight-digit random number which is assigned to this particular print queue and it matches the subdirectory under SYSTEM.

▶ **Queue Operators** is a list of users who have been assigned queue operator status. By default the supervisor is the only queue operator.

> ► **Queue Servers** is a list of print servers which can service this queue. It does not mean they are currently attached. The system manager can add or delete print servers from this list.

> ► **Queue Users** includes a list of all users who can add jobs to this queue. By default, the group EVERYONE is assigned as a queue user for all new print queues.

Once the print queue has been created, the system manager can move onto defining and creating the print server and attaching a link between the two.

Creating Print Servers

Print server creation consists of two steps: installation and setup. The print server installation step involves choosing a print server type and appropriate activation of print server files. For the print server on the file server, this includes the PSERVER.VAP. For a print server on a dedicated workstation, it's PSERVER.EXE and for a print server on a dedicated router, it's PSERVER.VAP and ROUTER.CFG.

Once the print server has been activated, the system manager is ready to set up the print server information. Print server setup is accomplished through the PCONSOLE utility using the printer server information menu from available options. The system manager simply presses Insert at the print server's menu screen and enters a print server name. We recommend that the system manager use the file server name followed by _PS to show the relationship between print servers and file servers they are servicing.

Once a print server has been created, the system manager can customize the print server configurations through the printer server information screen which includes the following information:

> ► **The Change Password** option allows the system manager to assign a password to the print server so that not just anybody can activate it.

> ► **The full name** provides more information about this particular print server and what queues and file servers it services.

> **Print server configuration** is used for steps 3 and 4 in print server installation.

> **Print server ID** defines the object ID of the print server. This is not particularly useful information because it is not used by any other NetWare configuration.

> **Print server operators** displays the list of the users and groups who have been assigned as operators for the print server.

> **Print server users** is a list of users or groups who can send print jobs to printers which are defined using this print server.

By default, the supervisor is assigned as a print server operator and the group EVERYONE is defined as print server users for all newly-created print servers.

Once the print server has been activated and configured, a seventh choice will appear in the print server information menu and that is print server status control. Print server status control option lets you view the status of the print server and provides valuable information about print servers which are currently running. This particular choice will not be available to system managers if the print server in question is not activated. Once the print server has been created, the system manager must define the printers which are going to be serviced by this particular print server.

QUOTE

The wind and the waves are always on the side of the ablest navigators.

Edward Gibbon

Defining Printers

Printer definition is accomplished through the PCONSOLE utility under Print Server Information. The print server configuration menu provides four choices:

> File Servers to be Serviced

> Notify List for Printer

> Printer Configuration

► Queues Served by Printer

The printer definition choice is Printer Configuration. This option allows the system manager to define up to 16 printers for this print server and customize their ports and configurations. By default, the 16 print server printers are assigned numbers 0 through 15 in order. Unlike core printing, the print server also has the flexibility of assigning a name to printers so that they can be tracked for management as well as queue assignment.

To define a particular printer, choose the printer number from the top of the list (typically 0 for the first printer) and press enter. The printer 0 configuration option appears which gives a variety of different options for defining, naming and configuring NetWare printers. The first option is Name which will define it for printing management as well as for queue assignment. The Type parameter is particularly useful in that it allows the system manager to define not only serial or parallel, but whether or not this printer is going to be attached to a local workstation. The printer types option appears with 19 different choices. The first seven are parallel and are used by printers which are attached directly to the print server: LPT1, LPT2, LPT3, COM1, COM2, COM3 and COM4.

The next seven are assigned to printers which are attached to local workstations running remote printing. These include remote parallel and remote serial. The final two are remote other unknown which is used for intelligent printers and defined elsewhere. They are used for printers which are being serviced by other file servers.

Once the printer type parameter has been set, the system manager can choose interrupts for parallel or BAUD rate, data bit, stop bits, parity and XON/XOFF for serial printing.

Assigning Queues to Printers

This particular step is important because it provides a path from the NetWare file server queue to the appropriate printer. If the system manager forgets this step, users will become quite miffed. The symptom is that print jobs are sent off to the NetWare queue and they sit there forever waiting to be serviced by the print server. It is typical for up to 100 or so print jobs to gather in the print queue without any of them being serviced by the printer. If this is the case, the first place to check would be the assignment from the queue to the printer.

Queue assignments are accomplished using the print server configuration menu and the queues serviced by printer option. Choose this option and the system responds with a list of defined printers. Choose the printer which is going to be assigned a particular queue, and press Enter. The system responds with the queue list. If this is the first queue to be assigned to this printer, the queue list will be empty. The system manager will press Insert and the system responds with a list of available queues. Choose the appropriate queue and assign a priority number which establishes the queue assignments with the printer.

Once a print queue has been assigned to the appropriate printer and all other steps have been activated, users can now print directly to the queue and that information will be forwarded to the appropriate printer.

> Once the print queues have been created, the printers have been defined, and the queue has been assigned to the printer, users are ready to print.

This completes the printer installation process. Once the print queues have been created, the printers have been defined, and the queue has been assigned to the printer, users are ready to print. While print server at first glance seems more complex, it really isn't—it's just sophisticated. NetWare print servers provide much more versatility than core printing. In addition, NetWare print server functionality is compatible with NetWare 3.12 and 4.01. Core printing was abandoned in later versions of NetWare.

QUOTE

Let us not be content to wait and see what will happen, but give us the determination to make the right things happen.

Peter Marshall

Printing Utilities

To better understand the process of installation and management of NetWare printing, it is important to have a firm grasp on the variety of different tools which are available to the system manager. NetWare 2.2 provides eight different utilities which enhance the printing system. These utilities range from capturing workstation data to configuring the print jobs. This also includes managing them once they're in the queue, assigning them to appropriate printers, defining the printer escape sequences, and controlling what time of day the print jobs are printed.

In the remainder of this chapter, we will discuss these eight printing utilities and see how they are analogous to the soap of our NetWare laundry room.

CAPTURE

The CAPTURE command is a printing utility which provides flexibility for the workstation so that printing can be done from non-NetWare applications. CAPTURE literally hijacks the local printer port and redirects all print jobs destined for that port off to a NetWare queue. The syntax of the CAPTURE command is **CAPTURE QUEUE=[name of queue] /[switch]**.

There is a huge variety of additional parameters which can be used with the CAPTURE command to customize the way print jobs are printed. Some of the more interesting CAPTURE parameters include:

/b for banner name

/c for copies

/ff for form feed

/j for job (which is a PRINTCON utility)

/l=[number] for the local port which needs to be CAPTUREd by default. Without the /l=[number] CAPTURE will capture the LPT1 parallel port.

/nff for no form feed

/nt for no tabs

/sh for show which will display the current status of the CAPTURE command

/t for tabs=[number] to replace all tab characters with spaces if you specify

/ti for timeout which is a timeout feature that is important for certain misbehaving non-network applications.

TIP

Here's an example CAPTURE command which is useful in most environments: CAPTURE QUEUE=[queuename] /nb /nt /ti=10 /nff.

ENDCAP

ENDCAP is a command line utility which ends the CAPTURE session. Once CAPTURE has been loaded into memory, it cannot be unloaded or stopped unless you issue an ENDCAP command. ENDCAP is particularly useful because it allows you the flexibility to capture to specific queues for specific applications and end that capture session, then recapture the local port for another queue in another application. Incidentally, all of this can be accomplished using batch files.

NPRINT

NPRINT is a workstation command line utility that sends a text file directly to a NetWare queue. The syntax of NPRINT is **NPRINT [queue name]** and it uses the same parameters as CAPTURE. But in this case, instead of capturing from a local port, NPRINT prints a text file from the command line directly to a NetWare queue. There's no port involved.

PCONSOLE

PCONSOLE is the printing management installation utility that we discussed earlier. PCONSOLE is responsible for all steps in print server installation and also for the management and maintenance of print servers, print queues and printers once NetWare printing has been installed.

> PCONSOLE is responsible for all steps in print server setup and installation.

PRINTCON

PRINTCON is an advanced NetWare system management printing utility which is used to customize print job configurations. Using PRINTCON, the system manager can define a specific set of configurations for a user and then attach those configurations to a print job using the CAPTURE /j parameter. The print job parameters are identical to the switches from CAPTURE except PRINTCON provides a facility for permanently storing these parameters in a menu format.

PRINTDEF

PRINTDEF is another advanced printing definition utility used in NetWare which provides the system manager with the facility to define or customize Net-Ware printers. PRINTDEF provides two facilities: form management and modes. Form management allows the system manager to define specific types of forms which are used by specific printers. These forms can include 8.5x11, 11x8.5, legal size paper, checks, etc. Forms are defined in PRINTDEF using the width and length parameters. Modes define specialized printing functions such as compressed, landscaped, bold, italic, etc. Modes can be defined using PRINTDEF for specific printers so that when print jobs are sent to NetWare queues, they can be configured using a special set of printer definition functions.

PSC

The PSC command is a very useful printer and print server control utility which system managers use to manage and maintain NetWare print servers. PSC provides similar functionality to PCONSOLE except it performs its operations from the command line. PSC issues commands directly to the printer or print server. With PSC, you can perform the following PCONSOLE tasks:

- View the Status of Printers
- Pause the Printer Temporarily
- Stop Printing the Current Job
- Start the Printer
- Mark the Top of Form
- Advance Printer to Top of Next Page
- Mount a New Form

TIP

You can use the DOS SET command to set a default print server and printer number for PSC so you don't have to specify this information at the command line every time.

The syntax for PSC is PSC=printserver P=printer.

RPRINTER

The RPRINTER command is the workstation utility which provides the remote printing facility. RPRINTER is a terminate-stay-resident (TSR) program which runs in workstation RAM and controls the movement of print jobs from queues to the local workstation. The RPRINTER syntax includes RPRINTER and Enter which will bring up the RPRINTER menu utility. Otherwise, RPRINTER parameters can be issued at the command line by typing RPRINTER PS=PRINTERSERVER and P=PRINTER. This particular command in an AUTO-EXEC.BAT file will activate the RPRINTER facility. Keep in mind that RPRINTER takes up some workstation RAM and communicates directly with local printer ports. RPRINTER can be removed from memory by using the -r switch.

KNOWLEDGE

RPRINTER does not require that the user actually be logged into the network—simply attached. An RPRINTER attachment can be accomplished by issuing an IPX and NETx. Once the workstation has been attached to the network, RPRINTER can be issued.

Congratulations! You have successfully completed the NetWare 2.2 CNA program. We learned about NetWare directory structures, drive mapping, security, menu utilities, supervisor utilities, console commands, login scripts, user interface, backup, and printing. This has been quite a journey.

In addition, we explored the NetWare apartment building, laundry room, locksmith duties, and LANlord status.

> Congratulations! You have successfully completed the NetWare 2.2 CNA program. Don't forget your utility belt!

Now you should feel amply prepared for the challenges which await you. But the NetWare 2.2 world can be a jungle, so don't forget your NetWare utility belt!

EXERCISE 7.1: USING THE CAPTURE COMMAND

As we learned in this chapter, the CAPTURE command provides a facility for redirecting print jobs from local workstation ports to NetWare queues. This facility is required for applications which are not aware of the NetWare printing system. In this written exercise, we will explore some common scenarios and generate appropriate CAPTURE statements. Refer to the discussion of CAPTURE flags to choose the appropriate switches.

For each question, write the appropriate CAPTURE command.

1 · Print jobs need to go to a queue named REPORTS with a timeout of 7 and four copies with no form feed. Your name and the file name should be on the banner.

2 · Print jobs need to go to the SALES file server to use their graphics queue. The jobs should be a Bytestream file and have no banner. All jobs sent to the graphics should be captured from LPT2 and have a form feed following the job.

3 · Print jobs captured from LPT3 should create a print file in the SYS:PLOTTER directory and should not print a hard copy.

4 · Someone's print jobs aren't getting to the queue. How can I see if the file server knows to pick up their jobs and redirect them?

5 · The accountant has a month-end report which will take 2 hours to print and would like to print it during off hours. The system manager has designed a print job configuration for this user under the name ACCOUNT. The ACCOUNT configuration defines a deferred print job to 10:00 p.m. that evening. What CAPTURE command does the accountant use to send this particular print job off to the network printer and have it deferred until 10:00 p.m. that evening?

6 · The sales department is using a non-network aware application which is acting quite finicky. You would like it to print with no banner, no form feed, a timeout of 10 and with no tabs.

7 · The system manager's machine has a local printer attached to LPT2 but typically uses a system login script which captures both LPT1 and LPT2. He or she would like to override the redirection of print jobs from LPT2 so he or she can use the local printer. What command would he or she use?

Check your answers in Appendix D.

Part II—NetWare 2.2

ACROSS

1 Displays routing info at console

4 Remote printing

8 Door-step of the LAN

9 Next available drive mapping

10 Trustee assignment minus MRM

13 Primary drive mapping tool

16 Printing setup utility

17 Shared user tools directory

21 Folders of the NetWare filing cabinet

23 Redirects local ports to queues

25 Unwanted user

27 NetWare's built-in backup utility

DOWN

2 Built-in NetWare 2.2 printing

3 Search the directory structure

5 Transparent user interface

6 To rename a file

7 To view effective rights in a menu

11 Assigning file attributes

12 Load the correct COMMAND.COM

14 A NetWare 2.2 menu file

15 The directory right analogy

18 Fix a corrupt NetWare OS

19 The user right analogy

20 A user with privileges

21 The mother of all NetWare utilities

22 The waiting room for print jobs

24 Assigning user rights

26 To find an application with MAP

See Appendix D for answers.

"A rose or a network operating system
by any other name would not be as sweet."

▶ • • • • • • • • • • • • • ◀

The NetWare 3.12 CNA Program

NetWare 3.12 is a complete network operating system designed for medium-to-large-sized LANs. It provides high performance, modularity, and flexible workstation connectivity. NetWare 3.12 is a substantial improvement over all previous versions of NetWare. NetWare 3.12's most notable improvements are in the 32-bit architecture, which provides greater memory management, performance, modularity, storage capacity, and connectivity.

NetWare 3.12 is the first truly modular network operating system. The core operating system consists of three components: the NetWare file system, the system executive, and NLM software bus. These components are integrated into one operating system file, SERVER.EXE. All other network services are attached to the NLM bus as modular components. These components are called NetWare Loadable Modules. They can be loaded and unloaded without disrupting the LAN. A variety of server applications has been written as both NLMs and operating system components. The operating system NLMs include disk drivers, LAN drivers, and name space modules. In addition, application NLMs consists of system fault tolerance, mail services, gateways, printing, multiprotocol support, and so on. Because of this modularity, NetWare 3.12 can provide a true open architecture solution. It is designed to provide file sharing, security, printing, system fault tolerance, and network management to many diverse platforms. NetWare 3.12 supports IPX/SPX, TCP/IP, AppleTalk, and OSI protocols from simultaneous workstations. These workstations can be running DOS, Windows, OS/2, System 7, or UNIX operating systems.

NetWare 3.12 takes full advantage of the 32-bit file server architecture by providing almost unlimited support for disk storage, memory, and concurrently open files. NetWare's built-in high capacity file system and universal file system allow 100,000 concurrently opened files and a maximum of 2,097,152 directory entries per volume.

In addition, NetWare 3.12 supports 64 volumes and 32 disks per volume for a total of 2,048 server disks. The maximum storage capacity is well beyond current technology—4GB file size, 32TB addressable storage—that's 32 trillion (32,000,000,000,000) bytes. Fortunately, NetWare 3.12 provides a host of system fault tolerance features to protect all of this connectivity and data storage. NetWare 3.12 supports fault tolerance levels I, II, and III. SFT Level III, server duplexing, is an additional product that requires two identical servers which are connected with a 100 Mb/s (Megabits-per-second) fibre optic line. SFT Levels I and II support read-after-write verification, hot fix, elevator seeking, disk duplexing, disk mirroring, and UPS monitoring.

NetWare 3.12's security is based on the same multilayered security model as NetWare 2.2. However, 3.12 provides some additional security enhancements—the supervisory trustee assignment, more directory and file attributes, and the concept of an inherited rights mask.

The most notable improvement in the NetWare 3.12 operating system is better performance. The 32-bit architecture has led to considerable improvements in file server throughput and response time. In addition, file service processes have been refined and the earlier dynamic memory pools have been expanded. NetWare 3.12's performance enhancements are optimized using two performance management utilities: SET and MONITOR. SET is a console command that offers immediate network operating system configuration. MONITOR, as an NLM, provides performance management and monitoring capabilities.

All of these features and enhancements have combined to make NetWare 3.12 the best selling network operating system in history. It's Novell's eighth generation of NetWare and provides an ideal solution for almost any networking environment.

NetWare 3.12 Directory Structure

The NetWare Architect

As the NetWare system manager, it is your responsibility to understand the many flexible functions and features of NetWare 3.12. In addition, it is your job to wear the many hats which are required for building, managing and maintaining such a complex system. Fortunately, NetWare provides you with all the tools you will need—including a NetWare utility belt. And this book provides you with a handy hat rack on which to hang your system manager hats.

> NetWare 3.12 can be thought of as a big luxurious hotel. Park Place, for example. As the NetWare system manager, it is your responsibility to make sure that all the users pass GO and collect $200.

NetWare 3.12 can be thought of as a big luxurious hotel. Park Place, for example. As the NetWare system manager, it is your responsibility to make sure that all the users pass Go and collect $200. Your system manager hats are analogous to the many different people who are required to manage and maintain a luxury hotel. The following is a brief example:

▶ **NetWare directory structures**—In working with NetWare directory structures, you are the architect of the LAN. The architect of a hotel designs the rooms, the lobby, the restaurants, builds the structure, and fills the structure with furniture and amenities. It is the architect's responsibility to create a comfortable, functional environment which is both practical and pleasing to look at.

▶ **NetWare security**—In managing security, you are the house detective of the LAN. The house detective builds the locks and keys for all of the rooms. In addition, he/she installs the infrared motion detection system and hires the lobby guards. The house detective makes sure that the hotel guests stay where they belong and are safe and secure.

▶ **NetWare utilities**—In working with your NetWare utility belt, you are the handyman of the LAN. You wear your NetWare utility belt with all of the different tools which are required to perform hotel maintenance. These tasks include fixer-upper projects, plumbing, electrical, heating, air-conditioning, and minor equipment repairs. Whenever anything goes down in the NetWare hotel, it is your responsibility to fix it—using your NetWare utility belt.

▸ **Network management**—The NetWare manager makes sure everything runs smoothly on a day-to-day basis. Park Place is under the guidance of the hotel manager who oversees the maids, the custodians, bellhops, reception desk and all other hotel staff. The hotel manager hat is one of the most challenging and rewarding of the system manager responsibilities.

▸ **Printing**—In managing and maintaining NetWare printing, you are the chef of the LAN, in charge of preparing fine cuisine for the hotel, including the restaurants and room service. Restaurant printing is analogous to centralized printing—the printers are attached directly to the print server. Room service is analogous to remote printing—the printers are distributed throughout the LAN.

▸ **Performance management**—The final and most exciting of your NetWare hotel hats is the interior decorator. The interior decorator is responsible for upgrading the quality of the rooms and the lobby. Daily operations include painting, purchasing fine furniture, hanging art-work and installing various amenities. A good interior decorator can make the difference between a mediocre hotel and a 5-star resort.

In our Park Place analogy, the rooms are workstations, the lobby and the restaurants are the file server and guests are users. The hallways and elevators are cabling which connects the rooms and the hotel lobby.

QUOTE

A wonderful discovery—psychoanalysis. It makes quite simple people feel they're complex.

Samuel N. Behrman

Novell's NetWare 3.12 CNA program is designed to provide you with the expertise and guidance you need to wear the many hats of the NetWare system manager. In the next six chapters, we will discuss the roles and responsibilities of the NetWare architect, house detective, handy man, hotel manager, chef and interior decorator. The discussion will focus on the responsibilities of each of these individuals and provide the system manager with a variety of tools for performing his or her duties. Keep in mind that "all work and no play makes Johnny/Jane a dull child." So, while we move through these chapters, let's take time here and there to discuss the positive aspects of this job and maybe rest and relax a little. After all, life as a NetWare manager is no vacation.

> Novell's NetWare 3.12 CNA program is designed to provide you with the expertise and guidance you need to wear the many different hats of the NetWare system manager.

QUOTE

The only way the magic works is by hard work. But hard work can be fun!

Jim Henson

The NetWare architect is responsible for building the directory structure, installing the applications and files, and establishing NetWare drive mappings. Once the architect has completed his or her job, the system is ready for security and user logins.

> The NetWare architect is responsible for building the directory structure, installing the applications and files, and establishing NetWare drive mappings.

At this point, Park Place is only a dream. It consists of an empty lot with concrete foundations and lots of empty frames. The network architect will design the rooms, the lobby, and the structure of the hotel so that it will be both luxurious and practical. The architect will follow up his or her design with intense construction which will include the building of rooms, a large foyer, garage, driveways, furniture, restaurants, and so on. Once the structure has been built and the interior has been decorated, the Park Place resort will be open for guests and business conventions.

In the same manner, the NetWare system manager is responsible for building the NetWare directory structure and drive mappings so that they are both easy to use and practical. NetWare directories create functional groupings from the volume root. They house NetWare files or functionally similar subdirectories. Figure 8.1 shows this directory structure as a filing cabinet with drawers, folders and documents. In this analogy, the drawers are volumes, the folders are directories and subdirectories, and the documents are NetWare files.

In our discussion of NetWare directory structures, we will focus on the four different directory types and their contents. Tools for managing the directory structure will be provided. In addition, we will explore drive mappings to understand how network and search drive mappings provide a tool for navigating through the directory tree.

FIGURE 8.1

NetWare Directory Structure as a Filing Cabinet

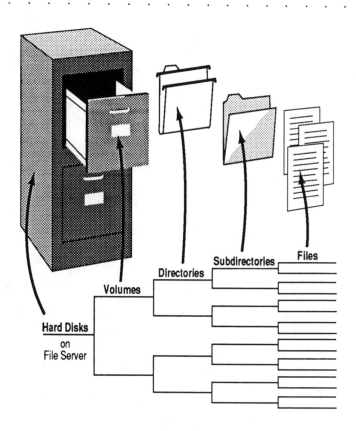

Files

Subdirectories

Directories

Volumes

Hard Disks
on
File Server

Directory Types

The NetWare system manager inherits a minimum base system; that is, distributed workstations, connected topology components, a functional file server, and NetWare. The minimum NetWare setup includes four system-created directories, two users, one group, and a few SYSTEM and PUBLIC files. This is where your job begins as the NetWare architect. It is your responsibility to hitch up the NetWare utility belt and get busy creating a directory structure, installing applications, developing security, and adding users and groups.

> The NetWare system manager inherits a minimum base system; that is, distributed workstations, connected topology components, a functional file server, and NetWare. The process of NetWare system management begins with the creation of an efficient, secure network directory structure.

The process of NetWare system management begins with the creation of an efficient, secure network directory structure. Earlier we likened the network directory structure to a filing cabinet with drawers, folders, and documents. The NetWare directory structure in this analogy relies on the file server, volume, directory and file components. These components are organized into a tree structure. The tree design of NetWare's directory structure is governed by a few rules. Here's a brief list of NetWare's directory rules:

File Server
- ▸ Name length is limited to 2-45 characters
- ▸ First character cannot be a period
- ▸ Name cannot contain special characters—* ? \ /

Volume
- ▸ Name length is limited to 2-15 characters
- ▸ Name must end with a colon
- ▸ First volume on first disk must be SYS:
- ▸ Maximum of 64 volumes per server
- ▸ Maximum volume size is 32TB

Directory   ► Name length is limited to 11 characters (8.3)

               ► A period separates the first 8 and last 3 characters

               ► Directories should be limited to functional groups

Subdirectory   ► Name length is limited to 11 characters (8.3)

               ► A period separates the first 8 and last 3 characters

               ► Subdirectories share common functionality

               ► The number of subdirectories is limited by
                  disk size

TIP

The rule of thumb for NetWare directory structures is KISS: *Keep It Safely Shallow.* **A hierarchical tree is easiest to maintain when it is not too tall and not too wide.**

In our discussion of NetWare's directory structure, we will focus on the four main directory types.

    ► System-created directories

    ► DOS directories

    ► Application/Data directories

    ► User directories

The system-created directories store valuable SYSTEM and PUBLIC files which are responsible for daily LAN operations. System-created directories are broken into two major categories: supervisor directories and user directories. Supervisor directories contain utilities and system files which are designed for supervisor access only. User directories contain global user management utilities which can be accessed by anybody on the network, including the guests.

DOS directories provide support for common workstation operating systems. Each version of workstation DOS should be supported by a corresponding DOS directory. Application data directories are the work horses of the LAN directory structure. The application data directories include both user applications and user- or group-specific data. Finally, user directories are designed to provide a home work space for each user on the LAN. Let's start with the system-created directories.

SYSTEM-CREATED DIRECTORIES AND THEIR CONTENTS

During the installation procedure, NetWare creates four system directories:

- ▸ LOGIN
- ▸ SYSTEM
- ▸ PUBLIC
- ▸ MAIL

These four system-created directories perform vital NetWare functions and house critical system/public files. See Figure 8.2 for an illustration of NetWare's

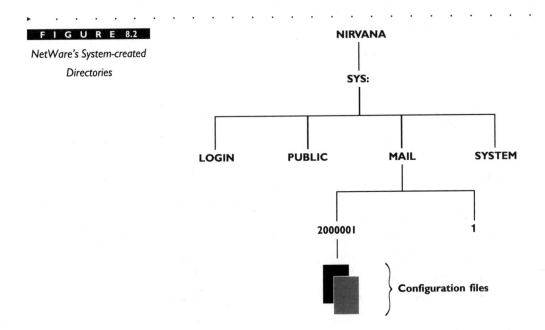

FIGURE 8.2

NetWare's System-created Directories

four system-created directories. All of these directories contain necessary Net-Ware files and should NOT be deleted. Following is a description of each of NetWare's system-created directories and their function.

LOGIN

The LOGIN directory is NetWare's welcome mat. It represents the first point of contact for attached NetWare users. Once a user attaches to the central file server, he/she has access to the LOGIN directory. Before the user can enter the Park Place hotel, he/she must ring the doorbell (login) and prove he or she has a reservation (password). The process of logging in is performed from the LOGIN directory.

The process of logging into a NetWare 3.12 server consists of two main steps: workstation initialization and login procedures.

- ▶ Workstation Initialization

    1 · Boot the workstation with a supported WOS—DOS, OS/2, etc.

    2 · Type LSL, NE2000 (or other), and IPXODI to load the protocol stacks.

    3 · Type **VLM** and press Enter to load the NetWare DOS Requester

- ▶ Login Procedures

    4 · Attach to the NetWare welcome mat by typing **F:** and pressing Enter

    5 · Type **LOGIN** and press Enter

    6 · Enter a valid username

    7 · Enter the correct password—if needed.

The NetWare welcome mat contains two system files: LOGIN.EXE and SLIST.EXE. LOGIN.EXE is the executable file which allows users to log into the NetWare server. SLIST.EXE provides a list of available file servers. Notice that the available disk space in the LOGIN directory is zero. This restriction is lifted once you properly log in.

QUOTE

Only the educated are free.

Epictetus

The LOGIN directory is the only network directory available to a user before he or she logs in, besides local DOS. The LOGIN directory is automatically mapped to the first available NetWare drive once the user attaches, using NETx. The first available NetWare drive by default is F:. If the system manager needs to make a file available to users before they log in, that file should be placed in the LOGIN directory. One case where this is useful is with remote booting where the workstation boot image is available to users before they log in. This boot image, incidentally, is placed in the LOGIN subdirectory.

SYSTEM

The SYSTEM directory is the second most important system-created directory next to LOGIN. SYSTEM houses critical NetWare files including the operating system bindery files, supervisor utilities, and NetWare loadable modules (NLMs). By default, all server NLMs are loaded from the SYSTEM directory. SYSTEM is off limits to everyone except the Supervisor.

Novell uses a curious naming scheme to designate important system files—the "$" sign. Every critical system file in NetWare contains a $ in its name. Here are some examples:

- ▸ VOL$LOG.ERR—the NetWare 3.12 error file

- ▸ NET$LOG.DAT—the system login script file

- ▸ NET$OBJ.SYS—one of the NetWare 3.12 bindery files

I guess it is safe to say that Novell recognizes the monetary value of these critical system files.

PUBLIC

The PUBLIC directory is every user's playground. This is where the public NetWare programs, commands, menu utilities, and other fun stuff are stored. The

PUBLIC directory is accessible to all network users. It provides a central shared area for frequently used network programs and system-oriented commands. Third-party utilities, for example, could be stored in the PUBLIC directory. We will explore these public commands and utilities later in Chapter 10—NetWare Utilities.

> The PUBLIC directory is every user's playground. This is where the public NetWare programs, commands, menu utilities, and other fun stuff are stored. The PUBLIC directory is accessible to all network users.

In addition, the PUBLIC directory is a good central storage area for global applications and utility files. The DOS directories, for example, are typically stored under the PUBLIC directory.

MAIL

The final system-created directory is MAIL. The MAIL directory is left over from the old days when NetWare included an electronic mail facility. Although the E-mail facility is no longer included with NetWare, the MAIL directory does continue to be useful. MAIL is the parent directory for a collection of system-created user directories which correspond to each user's randomly-assigned user ID number. The user ID is a 7-8 digit, hexadecimal number which identifies each user to the NetWare operating system. For example, the Supervisor is number 1 and Guest is number 2000001. The user ID subdirectory under MAIL is used to store two very important user-specific configuration files: the user login script (LOGIN.) and printer configuration file (PRINTCON.DAT). The NetWare system manager will never have to bother with these user-specific subdirectories under MAIL.

KNOWLEDGE

NetWare 3.12 includes three other auxiliary system-created directories: ETC, DELETED.SAV, and DOC. The ETC directory supports TCP/IP, DELETED.SAV contains salvageable files from deleted directories, and DOC includes ElectroText files.

That completes our discussion of the system-generated directories. Keep in mind, these directories are created by NetWare during installation and include all necessary NetWare system files and utilities. All other directories beyond this point are the responsibility of the NetWare architect. The three remaining directory types are suggested directories.

KNOWLEDGE

While the following three directory types are "suggested", NetWare doesn't operate properly without them. Also, directory design is a very personal issue. There are no right or wrong answers—only shades of efficiency.

SUGGESTED DIRECTORIES

NetWare provides the system manager with a big head start by building the four required system-created directories. The next step is to add some productive user/application directories on top of the existing directory structure. Novell suggests a variety of different approaches to creating custom directories: multiple volumes, applications sorted by user, group directories, and shared data directories. No matter how you slice it, Novell's custom approach seems to boil down to the following four directories: DOS, USERS, APPS, and DATA. Let's take a closer look.

> Novell's custom approach to suggested directories boils down to the following four directories: DOS, USERS, APPS, and DATA.

The DOS Directory

The DOS directory is important because it provides support for the most common workstation operating system: DOS. One of the most critical DOS files is COMMAND.COM, the workstation boot file. COMMAND.COM is loaded into workstation RAM whenever the workstation computer is turned on. During normal LAN operations, the COMMAND.COM file can be harshly removed from workstation RAM. If this happens, the workstation must be told where to find the file. The server's DOS directory and subsequent subdirectories provide the workstation with a simple path back to COMMAND.COM. In addition, the DOS subdirectories allow network users to access common DOS utilities from a centrally-shared directory. For this reason, the DOS directory is typically stored under PUBLIC.

In order to provide optimal workstation support, the DOS directory structure must follow a very strict pattern. Figure 8.3 shows an illustration of the strict design of NetWare's DOS directories. We will explain this pattern in more depth later in Chapter 11.

The Suggested NetWare Directory Structure

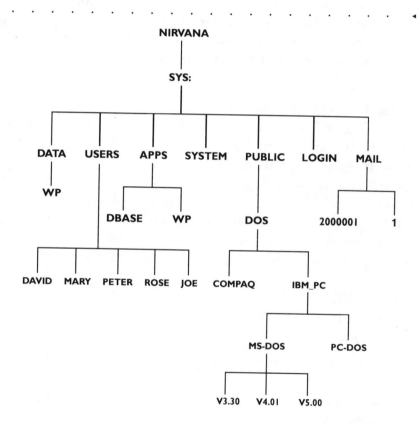

User Directories

User directories provide NetWare users with their own little home, giving them a private and secure subdirectory to begin their own personal directory structure. User subdirectories serve two functions: security and organization.

From a security viewpoint, user subdirectories provide a secure place for private user files or personal correspondence. From an organizational viewpoint, user subdirectories can become the parent directory of a complex user-specific directory structure. User subdirectories should match usernames and be stored under the USERS root directory. See Figure 8.3.

TIP

NetWare 3.12 provides a utility for specifying the parent directory for all users. The utility, SYSCON, allows the system manager to specify USERS as the parent directory. NetWare does the rest—it creates a home directory for each user at the point of their creation, under USERS with their unique username!

Application/Data Directories

Proper organization of application and data directories strongly impacts user productivity. If application directories are scattered, it is difficult for users to find network applications. Furthermore, disorganized data directories can be confusing for users who are trying to store network files. Application subdirectories should be created for each network application and stored under the APPS root directory. This makes application access easy for network users and security management more straightforward for the NetWare system manager. Data, on the other hand, can be stored in a variety of different directories:

- Personal data should be stored in user directories

- Application-specific data should be stored in application subdirectories under the DATA root directory

- Shared network data should be stored directly in DATA

Figure 8.3 provides a schematic of how application and data directories should be organized.

That's it for the NetWare system-generated and suggested directory types. While creating directories can be a very personal experience, there are a few rules to follow for optimal functionality. First, keep the number of subdirectories limited off of the root volume. Second, organize directories and subdirectories according to common functionality. Third, try to stay within the confines of the one SYS volume. This will help avoid the problem of running out of disk space on a volume even though the disk has plenty of space. And, finally, break data into three different areas so that it can be easily found by users, groups or everyone on the network.

QUOTE

Perhaps the reward of the spirit who tries is not the goal but the exercise.

E.V. Cooke

Try this: the next three Figures (8.4, 8.5, 8.6) provide some *wrong* ways of approaching NetWare directory creation. This would be similar to building a hotel on the edge of a cliff. Try to determine what is wrong with these three sample structures.

Figure 8.4 illustrates an unorganized directory structure with all directory types defined at the root. This design has serious ramifications. Figure 8.5 structures network data according to functional groups. While the design seems to make sense at first, it doesn't work well in "real-world" situations. This design makes it difficult to find users and track network information. Figure 8.6 organizes network directories within functionally separate volumes. This approach is inefficient because NetWare volume restrictions are written in stone. Once the volume size is defined, it cannot be changed without destroying the volume. Multiple volumes poses the problem of running out of disk space on the DATA volume even though there is plenty of room left in the APPS volume.

FIGURE 8.4

The Root of all Bad Directory Designs

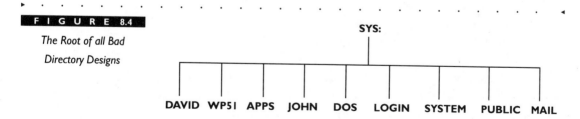

SYS:

DAVID   WP51   APPS   JOHN   DOS   LOGIN   SYSTEM   PUBLIC   MAIL

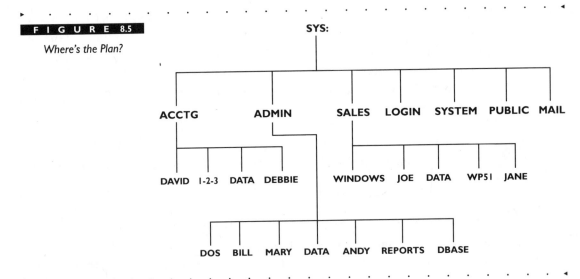

FIGURE 8.5

Where's the Plan?

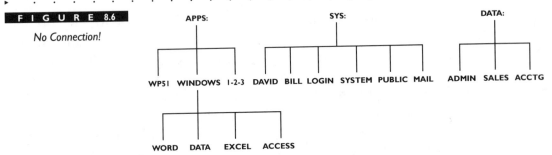

FIGURE 8.6

No Connection!

DIRECTORY PATH NAMES

All of this crazy organization can seem a bit overwhelming at first. But once you have had an opportunity to work with NetWare directories for a while, you will find them very efficient and useful. The syntax for NetWare directory path names is file server/volume:directory\subdirectory.

The forward slash separates the file server name and volume. The colon distinguishes the root of the volume, and the backslash separates the directories and subdirectories. Keep in mind, this format is very similar to DOS, except NetWare supports both the forward and backslash. A typical NetWare directory path looks like this: CNA/SYS:USERS\DAVID.

Path names are used to define file locations, drive mapping, and utility searches. It is important to use the correct syntax when establishing NetWare directory structures.

Directory Structure Command Line Utilities

Throughout this book, we have been bolstering your NetWare utility belt with a variety of commands. NetWare command tools are organized into three different categories:

Command-Line Utilities (CLUs) reside in the SYS:PUBLIC directory and are executed at the NetWare prompt—Z:\PUBLIC>. We will explore NetWare's CLUs (NetWare has over one hundred different ones) in appropriate sections throughout the book.

Menu Utilities provide a consolidated interface for frequently-used system management tools. We will learn about NetWare 3.12 menu utilities in Chapter 10.

File Server Console Utilities allow system managers to directly manage NetWare file servers. We will discuss NetWare 3.12's console commands in Chapter 10.

Let's begin our discussion of NetWare command utilities with an exploration of DOS and NetWare directory commands. These commands are the paper, pens, and drafting table of the NetWare architect. He/she wields them to design and create the organizational structure of Park Place's directories. Let's take a look.

> NetWare command tools are organized into three different categories: Command Line Utilities, Menu Utilities, and File Server Console Utilities.

DOS COMMANDS

NetWare 3.12 works in conjunction with many different workstation operating systems—DOS, OS/2, System 7, NT, and UNIX—but was primarily designed for DOS. In Chapter 1, we explored a variety of DOS commands and utilities. The following is a description of some internal DOS commands which have limited use in the NetWare directory structures.

PROMPT   Sets a new DOS prompt. There are myriad different prompt parameters—too many to mention here. NetWare requires PROMPT PG to display current directory path names.

MD   Creates a NetWare directory or subdirectory. MKDIR also works.

CD   Changes the default DOS or NetWare directory. This command is particularly dangerous in NetWare if it is combined with search drive mappings. This is discussed later in the chapter. CHDIR also works.

COPY CON   Captures data from the screen and creates a text file. A very useful command for creating simple NetWare configuration files. Use F6 to exit the program and save your file.

DIR   Shows a listing of files and subdirectories of a given NetWare or DOS directory. DIR also displays information about directories and files, including creation date, creation time, and size.

TYPE   Displays the contents of a text file on the screen. The results of the TYPE command can be redirected to a printer or file by using the ">" sign:

PRINTER—TYPE filename > PRN

FILE—TYPE filename > FILE

RD   Removes an empty DOS or NetWare subdirectory.
                      RMDIR also works.

NETWARE COMMANDS

NetWare directory structure commands build on the existing DOS commands by providing specific network functionality. NetWare offers network versions of most DOS utilities. The following is a discussion of the seven most popular NetWare directory structure commands.

CHKDIR

The CHKDIR command is used in NetWare to view information about a directory and a volume. The CHKDIR command displays the directory space limitation for the file server and volume. It also displays maximum volume capacity in kilobytes and directory restriction information. CHKDIR displays the number of kilobytes currently in use on the volume or in the specified directory. The system manager can use CHKDIR to check the volume by simply typing **CHKDIR** followed by Enter or can use CHKDIR to specify information about a given directory. The syntax for CHKDIR is **CHKDIR [directory]**.

CHKVOL

CHKVOL is used to view more information about a specific volume. CHKVOL provides the same information as CHKDIR. However, it expands to include the name of the file server, the volume name, the total volume space, the space used by files, the space in use by deleted files, space available from deleted files, the space remaining on the volume, and the space available to the user. CHKVOL also supports wild card characters. Incidentally, the user can only view disk space for directories for which they have sufficient rights.

LISTDIR

LISTDIR displays an enhanced graphic of the NetWare directory structure in a pseudo-tree layout. LISTDIR displays more security statistics than NDIR and allows you to specify which information you would like to view. Here's a description of LISTDIR syntax and its parameters:

LISTDIR /A displays all information for each specified directory

LISTDIR /D displays the creation date and time

LISTDIR /S displays all subdirectories below this directory

LISTDIR /R displays the directory rights for each specified directory.

NCOPY

NCOPY is a NetWare version of the DOS XCOPY command and provides much more reliability and greater functionality than XCOPY. The SYNTAX for NCOPY is NCOPY [source] [destination] /switch. A variety of different switches which are available to NCOPY that are not available in the DOS COPY environment. These include:

/s for subdirectories

/e for empty subdirectories

/c to copy files without preserving file attributes and name space

/v for a verify—a read-after-write verification on the original file

/a for all files which have the Archive bit set

TIP

NCOPY is particularly useful because it operates from within memory. This is useful in a NetWare environment because it does not create any network traffic on the LAN cabling. A DOS COPY command, on the other hand, copies the file into workstation RAM over the LAN cabling and back up to the file server.

QUOTE

The mind is like the stomach. It is not how much you put into it that counts, but how much it digests.

Albert Jay Nock

NDIR

The NDIR command is a versatile NetWare utility which allows you to search through NetWare volumes for data, applications, and utilities. NDIR is the NetWare version of DIR. In addition to the basic information—creation date, creation time, and file size—NDIR displays a plethora of network statistics. These include owner, directory rights, last modified date, and file attributes. NDIR can be used to search one directory or a directory and all of its subdirectories with the /SUB parameter: For example, type NDIR *.* /SUB to display all information about all files in this directory and all of its subdirectories.

> NCOPY is particularly useful because it operates from within memory. This is useful in a NetWare environment because it does not create any network traffic on the LAN cabling.

RENDIR

The RENDIR command is a useful NetWare tool which isn't available in the DOS world. It allows you to rename an existing NetWare directory. I can't count the number of times I could have used this command in DOS.

VOLINFO

VOLINFO is a graphic display of volume information and statistics. It lists volume sizes, total directory entries, free space, and available directory entries.

The NetWare directory structure is complex and sophisticated. It allows you to properly organize many different kinds of network information. A well-designed directory structure can increase user effectiveness and productivity. A related strategy for increasing user effectiveness is drive mapping. Drive mapping allows you to represent complex directory structures as simple alphabet letters. Let's take a look.

Drive Mapping

In the DOS world, we are comfortable with the idea of using letters to represent physical disk drives. In this world, the letter A: represents the first floppy drive and B: represents the second. Furthermore, C: represents the first hard disk, while D: and E: indicate secondary disks. This scheme is simple and straightforward. It allows us to find data easily without having to bother with volume labels or physical mappings.

> In the DOS world, we are comfortable with the idea of using letters to represent physical disk drives. NetWare also uses letters as drive pointers, but they point to LOGICAL drives not physical ones.

In the NetWare world, we use the same approach—kind of. NetWare also uses letters as drive pointers, but they point to LOGICAL drives not physical ones. The letter F, for example, points to a network directory (LOGIN), not a physical drive. In this case, F: would represent the LOGIN directory—i.e. F:\LOGIN>. NetWare drive letters point to different directories on the same disk. This scheme is also simple and straightforward, but it takes some getting used to.

KNOWLEDGE

NetWare drive mappings are user-specific, temporary environment variables. Each user has a different set of drive mappings in their own workstation RAM. They are created each time the user logs in. When users logout or turn off their machines, drive mappings are lost. Fortunately, NetWare provides an automatic login script which establishes user mappings at each login.

NetWare uses two different types of drive pointers: regular and search. Regular drive pointers provide a convenient way of representing complex network path names with a single letter. Search drive pointers provide an additional level of functionality by building a search list for network applications. In this section, we will explore the details of these two NetWare drive pointers and learn how to implement them by using the MAP command. But first, let's briefly review DOS pointers.

KNOWLEDGE

In this section the terms *drive pointer* and *drive mapping* will be used interchangeably. Technically, it can be argued that the drive pointer is the alphabet letter and drive mapping is the process of assigning it to a network directory. But let's keep it simple: *Drive Pointer = Drive Mapping.*

DOS POINTERS

DOS pointers represent physical storage devices as alphabetic letters. These DOS storage devices are typically floppy drives, hard disks, or CD-ROMs. By default, DOS reserves the letters A-E for local devices. This number can be extended by using the LASTDRIVE = <letter> command in the workstation's CONFIG.SYS file. To move from one drive letter to another, you would simply type the drive letter followed by a colon—i.e. A:—and press Enter. Once you have moved to the correct physical drive, you can use the CD command to move between subdirectories of that drive.

TIP

It is possible to reassign a **DOS** pointer as a NetWare pointer. In this case, the local drive becomes unavailable to the network user. This is an effective strategy for restricting access to local floppy drives while users are attached to NetWare servers. The DOS pointer is returned to the user when he/she disconnects from the LAN.

NETWORK DRIVE MAPPINGS

NetWare pointers come in two varieties: network drive mappings and search drive mappings. Network drive mappings are used for directory navigation and accessing data files. Search drive mappings, on the other hand, provide an additional functionality—the NetWare search list. The search list provides easy access to distributed network applications. In this section, we will learn how to implement network and search drive mappings.

Network drive mappings are similar to DOS pointers in a few respects, but for the most part, they are two different animals. Refer to Table 8.1 for a comparison of DOS and Network drive mappings. NetWare pointers use alphabetic letters to represent logical network directories—not physical disks. Network drive mappings use the same syntax as DOS pointers, but they begin where the DOS pointers end—the letter F. This means that Network drives have 21 possible choices—F-Z. Figure 8.7 shows a typical NetWare directory structure with the drive letter F pointing to the SYS:USERS\DAVID directory.

> Network drive mappings are used for directory navigation and accessing data files. Search drive mappings, on the other hand, provide an additional functionality—the NetWare search list.

Purpose

Network drive mappings point to user-defined data directories. These drive pointers are typically used for convenience and directory movement. Without drive mappings, movement throughout the directory tree would consist of long path names and the CD command. This is cumbersome and time-consuming. With drive mappings, movement is consolidated into one simple step: type F: and press Enter. Regular drive pointers represent complex directory paths as simple alphabet letters. Figure 8.7 represents the path SYS:USERS\DAVID as the letter F:. Simple.

	FUNCTION	DOS POINTERS	NETWARE POINTERS
TABLE 8.1 *The Similarities and Differences of DOS and NetWare Drive Pointers*	Drive Letters	alphabetic	alphabetic
	Syntax	<letter>:	<letter>:
	Alphabetic Range	A-E	F-Z
	Drive Type	physical drive	logical directory
	Destination	local workstation	network file server

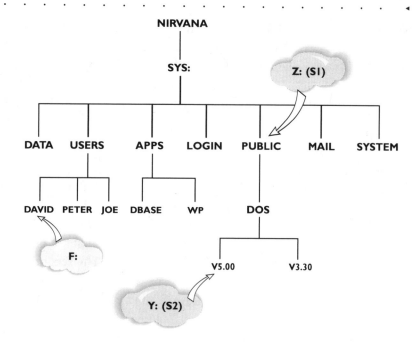

FIGURE 8.7

NetWare Drive Pointers and Logical Network Directories

MAP Assignments

NetWare reserves the final 21 letters of the alphabet for network drive mappings. Regular drive pointers are assigned by NetWare users with the MAP command. They begin with F: and move forward. Note: if the workstation CONFIG.SYS file contains the LASTDRIVE = <letter> command, the first available drive pointer will be the next letter. For example, LASTDRIVE = G will reserve A-G for DOS and the first NetWare pointer will be H.

TIP

You can actually assign 26 network drive mappings (A-Z) by overwriting all existing local drives.

SEARCH DRIVE MAPPINGS

Search drive mappings extend one step beyond network drive mappings by providing the user with the ability to search for network application files. When a user executes a particular network application, the system searches the current directory for the application file—.EXE, .COM, or .BAT. If the file isn't there, the system looks for a search list. If a search list doesn't exist, the system will return with the message bad command or file name. If a search list does exist, the system will move through the list in order until it finds the application. This method is very similar to the DOS PATH command. Search drive pointers build NetWare search lists. The maximum number of search drives in a NetWare search list is 16.

MAP Assignments

Since search drive pointers are primarily used to build search lists, network users are more concerned with the order of the list rather than the letter which is assigned. For this reason, search drive mappings are assigned in search order by using the letter S and a number. For example, the first search drive would be assigned S1 and placed at the top of the search list. The second drive is S2 and so on. As a matter of convenience, NetWare also assigns a letter to each search pointer. This letter can be used to move around the directory structure just like a regular drive pointer.

Available Drive Letters

This strategy poses an interesting question: How do you tell the difference between a regular drive letter and a search drive letter? The answer is simple: you don't! There is no way of distinguishing one from the other by simply looking at it. So as a matter of convention, NetWare assigns search drive letters from Z and moves backwards. Therefore, S1 becomes Z, S2 becomes Y, and so on. Figure 8.7 shows the first two NetWare search drives as Z: (S1) = SYS:PUBLIC and Y: (S2) = SYS:PUBLIC\DOS\V5.00. With this in mind, you can assume that the early letters are regular pointers and the later letters are search drives. Keep in mind, this is only an assumption—and you know what they say about assumptions. Refer to Table 8.2 for a comparison of regular and search drive pointers.

> The CD command is off-limits to NetWare users. If the CD command is used on a NetWare pointer, it reassigns the pointer to a different directory. This can be fatal for search drives which point to critical applications or utility directories.

TABLE 8.2

Comparing the Functions of Regular and Search Drive Pointers

FUNCTION	REGULAR	SEARCH
Purpose	movement	searching
Assignment Method	as the letter	in search order (S1, S2, etc.)
Letter Assignment	by the user	by the system
First Letter	F:	Z: (S1)
Directory Types	data	applications

TIP

In the course of assigning search pointers, NetWare will skip any drive letter which is already defined as a regular drive pointer.

The CD command is off-limits to NetWare users. If the CD command is used on a NetWare pointer, it reassigns the pointer to a different directory. This can be fatal for search drives which point to critical applications or utility directories. If you must use the command, switch to the J: drive before doing so (assuming, of course, that the system manager has created one). The J: drive holds no special significance except that it is typically used as a JUNK pointer. Using the CD command on the J: drive doesn't harm the system.

USING THE MAP COMMAND

Now that we understand the fundamentals of NetWare drive mapping, we must learn how to implement them. The MAP command is one of the most versatile NetWare utilities. Think of it as an architect's drafting board. The following is a discussion of the many different MAP commands which allow system managers to implement NetWare drive mappings. Keep in mind that drive mappings are user-specific and temporary. You will have to do this all over again tomorrow.

MAP

The MAP command without any parameters will display a list of the current drive mappings. It will list the alphabet pointers in order, beginning with the local drives (A-E), the regular drives, and then the search drives. Here's an example of how the MAP display is organized:

```
Z:\PUBLIC>map
Drive A:  maps to a local disk.
Drive B:  maps to a local disk.
Drive C:  maps to a local disk.
Drive D:  maps to a local disk.
Drive E:  maps to a local disk.
Drive F: = NIRVANA\SYS: \LOGIN
    -----
SEARCH1: = Z:. [NIRVANA\SYS: \PUBLIC
SEARCH2: = Y:. [NIRVANA\SYS: \PUBLIC\DOS\V5.00
```

MAP F:=SYS:LOGIN

MAP followed by a specific drive letter specifies a *regular* NetWare drive pointer. The above command would map the LOGIN directory to the drive letter F.

MAP SI:=SYS:PUBLIC

MAP followed by an S# specifies a *search* drive pointer. The # represents the pointer's place in the search list. NetWare assigns an appropriate alphabet letter beginning with Z and moving backwards. In this example, the PUBLIC directory will be inserted at the top of the search list and receive the alphabet letter Z.

MAP INSERT S2:=SYS:APPS\WP

The MAP INSERT command inserts a new search drive into the search list. The new pointer is inserted into the search list as the number specified. All search drives below the new pointer are bumped down one level in the list. The quirky thing about MAP INSERT is that the letter assignments are unaffected. All the previous drives retain their original drive letter and the new pointer is assigned the next available drive. For example, if the above command was executed in

Figure 8.7, the DOS drive (S2) would become S3 but retain the drive letter Y. The new directory, SYS:APPS\WP, would become S2 and inherit the drive letter X.

TIP

Search drive mappings occupy the same environment space as the DOS PATH command. For this reason, NetWare search mappings eliminate DOS PATH commands. The only way to retain the DOS path in a NetWare environment is to add the path directories to the NetWare search list. This can be accomplished by always using the MAP INSERT command. The DOS path directories are added to the end of the search list. Don't worry, the DOS path directories don't occupy any of your 16 available search slots.

MAP DEL G:

MAP DEL deletes an existing NetWare drive mapping. It works with either regular or search drive pointers. MAP REM performs the same function as MAP DEL.

MAP ROOT H:=SYS:USERS\DAVID

MAP ROOT is an intriguing command. It establishes a regular drive mapping as a false root. The user sees the drive as if it is the root directory. In the above example, the SYS:USERS\DAVID directory will be mapped to the drive letter H. In addition, the H drive will appear to be the root of the volume even though it is actually the SYS:USERS\DAVID subdirectory. It will appear as H:\>. False root mappings are dangerous because they limit users to specific branches of

> MAP ROOT is an intriguing command. It establishes a regular drive mapping as a false root. The user sees the drive as if it were the root directory.

the network directory tree. In this example, no other directories would be available to the user David.

MAP NEXT SYS:DATA

The MAP NEXT command assigns the next available drive letter as a regular drive pointer. This command doesn't work with search drive mappings. In Figure 8.7, the above MAP NEXT command would assign the letter G to the SYS:DATA directory. MAP NEXT is useful to system managers because it keeps track of the alphabetic letters for you.

TIP

Although MAP NEXT doesn't work with search pointers, there is a way to achieve the same effect. Simply use MAP S16. NetWare will not allow you to assign search drive mappings out of order. So, if you specify S16, NetWare will automatically assign the directory to the next available spot in the search list.

That completes our discussion of the NetWare directory structure. In this chapter, we explored logical trees, system-created and suggested directories, path names, and drive mapping. I'd say we got a pretty good head start on network management and LAN configuration. The next step in hotel management is security. Security configuration establishes integrity and protection for network users and shared data files. In the next chapter, we will put on our house detective trench coats and install locks for the hotel rooms, pass out guest keys, install an infra-red motion-detection system, and hire some guard dogs. I can barely wait.

QUOTE

The brighter you are the more you have to learn.

Don Herold

EXERCISE 8.1: UNDERSTANDING DIRECTORY STRUCTURE

In this exercise, we will explore a fictitious directory structure for two servers: Tom and Jerry. Use Figure 8.1A to help you answer the following questions:

1 · How many volumes have been defined in this directory structure?

_____

2 · Assuming that this is a NetWare 3.12 directory structure, which default system directories are missing?

_____

3 · How is the volume structure organized in the accompanying graphic? What are the benefits of this structure? What are the possible pitfalls of this structure?

_____

_____

F I G U R E   8.1A

Understanding Directory Structure

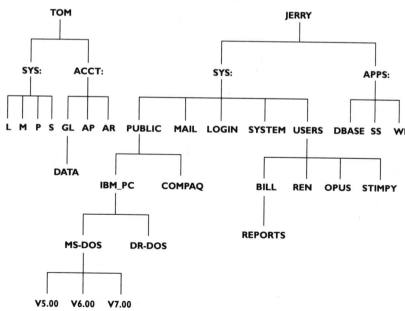

4 · Draw the path to each of the following directories:

    A · The REPORTS directory under BILL.

_____

    B · MS-DOS v7.00.

_____

    C · The user directory for OPUS.

_____

    D · The data directory for GL.

_____

5 · How would you communicate or copy files from one subdirectory to another? Indicate the NetWare command you would use to copy a file from STIMPY's user directory to the data directory under GL.

_____

_____

6 · What NetWare command would you use to view a graphical tree of the JERRY/SYS directory structure?

_____

_____

7 · What NetWare directory command would you use to view the space available on the TOM/ACCT volume?

SNOUZER, INC.—A CASE STUDY

Welcome to Snouzer, Inc., world renowned designer of doggie fashions. This year, Snouzer, Inc. is celebrating its silver anniversary. (Snouzer was formed 25 years ago in San Francisco, California to satisfy the need for canine fashions.) At that time, nobody was giving the dog its due, so to speak, but today doggie fashions are a multibillion dollar industry with 32 companies operating world wide. Snouzer, Inc., the founder of the doggie fashion industry, is the leader of the pack.

Snouzer, Inc. is best known for its top-of-the-line doggie accessories, including:

- ▸ Classy collars—a line of top notch dog necklaces including diamonds or cubic zirconia

- ▸ Bowser booties—a collection of all-leather high tops for canines

- ▸ Eel skin leashes for the discerning owner

- ▸ Doggie doos, a collection of fine hair pieces for dogs (their best selling product)

Snouzer, Inc. is a family owned business. It operates out of a large factory facility in San Francisco. Management consists of seven brothers and sisters. They operate all administration, design, and production departments. Figure 8.2A shows Snouzer, Inc's organizational chart. After many years operating with pen and pencil, Sophy Snouzer has decided that Snouzer, Inc. will move into the 21st Century. She hired the LANimation group in San Francisco to purchase her networking equipment and install the NetWare LAN. They did a tremendous job installing seven workstations and one 486 file server. In addition, the LANimation group installed NetWare 3.12 and all the workstation shells. Sophy is now coming to you to complete her dream. Your responsibility is to design, install, and manage the directory structure, users, groups, and applications. In addition, you will develop a security model and implement performance management facilities.

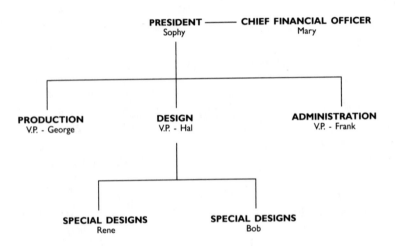

FIGURE 8.2A

Snouzer Inc.'s organizational chart

SNOUZER, INC.
Organizational Chart

In the case studies that follow, we will walk through the requirements of Snouzer, Inc. and discuss some possible solutions in the areas of:

- ▸ Directory structure
- ▸ Drive mappings
- ▸ Security
- ▸ Login scripts
- ▸ User interface
- ▸ Performance management

You will be asked to follow through from beginning to end the development of a productive and friendly NetWare LAN. Make sure to refer to the accompanying organizational chart throughout these case study exercises. It will provide you with the background information you need to make the right decisions concerning user-specific and group-specific configurations. Remember, Sophy and all of her brothers and sisters at Snouzer, Inc. are counting on *you* to make their dream come true and bring them into the 21st Century. Let's start with the development of a NetWare directory structure.

CASE STUDY I: CREATING A DIRECTORY STRUCTURE

In each of these case exercises, you will be given a description of Snouzer, Inc.'s environment and NetWare requirements. In the first half of the exercise, you will use pen and paper to draw a design of directory structures, drive mappings, security, login scripts, and so on. In the second half, you will get experience using the appropriate NetWare menu utility to implement your written design. These exercises have been written to maximize reality and fun. Have a good time!

As you can see from their organizational chart, Snouzer, Inc. is composed of three main departments and those are:

▸ Administration

▸ Production

▸ Design

These three departments are managed by seven different employees:

▸ Sophy, President

▸ Frank, Vice President of Administration

▸ Hal, Vice President of Design

▸ George, Vice President of Production

▸ Rene and Bob, Special Designers

▸ Mary, Chief Financial Officer

When you first begin your journey at Snouzer, Inc., the LANimation group has left you with functioning workstations, an active NetWare 3.12 file server and some system-generated users, groups, and directories. Figure 8.3A illustrates a skeleton directory structure for Snouzer, Inc. with the following four system-generated directories.

▸ SYSTEM

▸ MAIL

- ▶ PUBLIC
- ▶ LOGIN

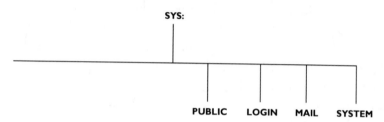

FIGURE 8.3A

A Skeleton Directory Structure for SNOUZER, INC.

   As the Snouzer system manager, it is your responsibility to build a productive and efficient network directory structure which satisfies their application and data needs. Let's review those needs for just a moment. Beyond the four system-generated directories, Snouzer has requirements for three more suggested directory structures:

- ▶ DOS directories
- ▶ Users directories
- ▶ Application data directories

Let's explore each of these in a little more detail.

DOS Directory

   LAN*imation* felt that Snouzer, Inc.'s production and application requirements could best be satisfied by a variety of workstation operating systems. They installed four different types and versions of DOS:

- ▶ Compaq DOS v5.00

> ▸ Compaq DOS v3.30

> ▸ MS-DOS v5.00

> ▸ MS-DOS v6.00

In addition, they've installed two different types of workstations: Compaq and IBM clone workstations. As the system manager, it is your responsibility to develop a DOS directory structure which satisfies the need for these four different types of DOS COMMAND.COM files. Incidentally, this structure should be designed off of the PUBLIC directory.

Each of the seven Snouzer management employees should have their own user subdirectory off of the USERS directory from the root. In addition, there are three groups which should be defined within the NetWare format: ADMIN, PROD, and DESIGN. Each of these groups should also have their own subdirectories under a GROUPS directory for storing group-specific data.

Application Data Directories

Snouzer, Inc. uses five main applications:

> ▸ DESIGN

> ▸ WP

> ▸ ACCT

> ▸ DBASE

> ▸ 123

The WP, DBASE and 123 applications are generic off-the-shelf network applications. The DESIGN application is a special doggy fashion design program which is actively utilized by Snouzer's design group. In addition, the design program writes special macros and data files within the same directory. The ACCT program relies on three subcomponents:

- GL

- A/R

- A/P

These three components are integrated into the application but require separate subdirectories under the application for the storage of specific data and macros. User-specific data will be stored in each of the users subdirectories. Group-specific data will be stored in group-specific subdirectories. Application data is stored within the directory of the special application. Finally, there should be a global data subdirectory where all users on the LAN can store public files.

That completes the requirements for the Snouzer, Inc. network directory structure. After you have completed your design on Figure 8.3A, use the common NetWare tools to implement and build the network directory structure on the shared 3.12 disk. The tools which are available are:

- FILER Menu utility

- CD to change directories

- MD to make directories

- RD to remove directories

Once you have finished designing and implementing the Snouzer, Inc. directory structure, you can move onto Case Study II, Drive Mappings for Snouzer, Inc.

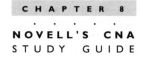

EXERCISE 8.2: USING THE MAP COMMAND

In this exercise, you will get an opportunity to work with drive mappings on an existing NetWare LAN. Using the MD command, create a directory structure which matches the one shown in Figure 8.4A. Follow the steps listed below.

FIGURE 8.4A
Using the MAP Command

```
                            SYS:
                             |
        _____
        |                                  |        |
       APPS                             USERS      DATA
        |                                  |
   _____                    _____
   |      |      |                    |         |
   WP   DBASE  WINDOWS               JACK      JILL
```

1 · MAP the G: drive as a root to the data subdirectory.

2 · MAP the U: drive to JACK's user directory.

3 · MAP the next two search drives to APPS, WP, DBASE in that order.

4 · Verify that the maps were created by typing MAP and pressing Enter. How does the system indicate a map root drive?

5 · Remove the U: drive which was mapped to JACK and remap it to JILL.

6 · Insert a search drive mapping at search drive 3 for APPS WINDOWS.

7 · Move to the G: drive. Now type **CD** to return to the SYS volume root. What happens?

_____

_____

_____

8 · Return to the U: drive. Map the next available network drive mapping to SYS:DATA.

9 · Type **MAP** and press Enter to verify that your changes have taken effect.

10 · How does the system execute the MAP command from the U: drive?

_____

_____

_____

11 · To view the effects of the CD command on search drive mappings, type **Z:** and press Enter. This will move you to the PUBLIC subdirectory. The PUBLIC subdirectory is mapped as the first search drive because it contains all the NetWare utilities including MAP.

12 · Type **CD ..** at the prompt and press Enter. This will remap the Z: drive, the first search drive, to the root.

13 · Go to the U: drive and press Enter.

14 · Type **MAP** once again to verify your drive mappings. What happened and why?

_____

_____

_____

15 · Go back to the Z: drive by typing **Z:** and pressing Enter. Type **CD PUBLIC**. This will remap the first search drive back to PUBLIC.

16 · Go back to the U: drive by typing **U:** and pressing Enter. Now type MAP and notice what happens.

Keep in mind that it is extremely dangerous to use the CD command on search drives especially search drives as important as S1. That's the end of the show. Good work!

CASE STUDY II: DRIVE MAPPINGS FOR SNOUZER, INC.

Regular and search drive mappings provide a navigation tool for moving around the Snouzer, Inc. directory structure. These tools are particularly important for running network applications and storing user-specific and group-specific shared data. Snouzer has pretty standard drive mapping requirements. They require a regular drive mapping to each user subdirectory, a group-specific drive mapping for the letter G to each group and a global network drive mapping of H to the shared data subdirectory.

The search drive mapping requirements are a little more complex. The first search drive mappings should be to the PUBLIC subdirectory and the second search drive mapping to DOS. These two search drive mappings are standard for all NetWare LANs. The next five search drive mappings should be mapped to each of the five different applications. It is important in mapping search drive mappings that you assign them in priority order. The Snouzer, Inc. managers have a tendency to use the WP application more than any other, then the DESIGN team and ACCT applications in that order. Finally, DBASE and 123 are used the least often.

Once you have completed your design, it is time to implement Snouzer, Inc.'s drive mapping structure. The following NetWare tools can be very useful in assigning NetWare drive mappings:

> **MAP**, the command line utility with all of its variations that provide drive mapping creation from the command line

> **SESSION**, a menu utility which can be used to assign regular and search drive mappings.

Remember that drive mappings you create here are only temporary. They will disappear once the user exits the system. The design you created will be used during the login case study as a template for creating drive mappings in the system login script.

NetWare 3.12
Security

"Looks suspicious to me."

Park Place is a beautiful hotel. It has water fountains, ice sculptures, atriums, and an indoor golf course. And as with any popular resort, Park Place needs security.

▶ To protect the guests

▶ To protect the staff

▶ To guard the ice sculptures

▶ To lock away valuable treasures

The king of Park Place security is the hotel's house detective. He/she oversees registration, guards the lobby, builds room keys, installs door locks, and locks away valuable treasures. He/she is burdened with the responsibility of protecting the hotel's assets. The goal is to create a reliable security system which locks out the bad guy and welcomes everybody else in. In order to perform these duties, the house detective has four main responsibilities:

> Park Place is a beautiful hotel. It has water fountains, ice sculptures, atriums, and an indoor golf course. As with any popular resort, Park Place needs security.

▶ Overseeing registration

▶ Guarding the lobby

▶ Locksmithing

▶ Locking away valuable treasures

In overseeing hotel registration, the house detective makes sure that all guests are registered and have an appropriate form of payment: credit card, cash, check, and so on. If guests are not registered, they cannot go beyond the confines of the hotel lobby. The passageway from the lobby to the rest of Park Place is guarded by two very large gold-plated gates which separate the small lobby from the rest of the hotel's rooms and amenities. The house detective is responsible for guarding these gates and making sure that only appropriate registered guests (who have paid) can pass through at appropriate times. Once guests have passed through the gates, they can roam freely throughout the resort, sampling the restaurants, enjoying the pools, ogling the ice sculptures, and resting in their rooms.

The house detective is responsible for making sure that each guest is granted a user key which gives them access to appropriate rooms in the hotel. The house detective is not only responsible for building the user keys, but for installing the door locks for each of the rooms. These functions are described as hotel locksmithing.

Finally, the house detective is responsible for locking away guests' valuable treasures in the hotel safe. These treasures can only be accessed—at appropriate times—by special guests with special privileges. Once the guests leave the hotel, they must take the valuable treasures with them.

As the NetWare security manager, you are the house detective of your LAN. Users come to you for application security, data organization and general peace of mind. Your LAN security duties are some of the most important responsibilities you will have and you must take them very seriously. Your duties include:

- ▶ Overseeing user registration

- ▶ Guarding access to the LAN

- ▶ LAN locksmithing

- ▶ Locking away valuable directories and files with attribute security.

QUOTE

The weakest link in a chain is the strongest because it can break it.

Stanislaw J. Lec

The goal is to create a reliable security system which locks out the bad guys and welcomes everybody else in. Sound familiar? With NetWare security, organization is the key. You must fully understand the ramifications of each of these different responsibilities so that you can navigate through the complex layers of the NetWare security model.

In this chapter, we will learn about NetWare security from the house detective's point of view. We will discover NetWare's multilayered security model and explore each layer in depth. We'll also meet the house detective's deputies: distributed security managers. In addition, we will discuss some of the command line and menu utilities which NetWare provides to help manage LAN security. Keep in mind, this is a very important tool in your NetWare utility belt. Good LAN security is becoming a lost art.

QUOTE

Happiness has many roots, but none more important than security.

E.R. Stettinius, Jr.

The NetWare Security Model

The multilayered NetWare security model provides a level of protection for entrance to the LAN. Since the data on a network is typically shared, it is important to secure it in directories where only authorized users have access. In a stand-alone environment, security isn't as critical. The only way to access stand-alone data is to physically walk over to another user's workstation. However, in a network environment, you can let your fingers do the walking. Without security on the central LAN hard disk, it would be too easy for users to access each other's data. This is bad.

The NetWare security model provides a level of data protection by forcing users through a specific series of security events on their way towards shared data. NetWare security consists of access restrictions, privileges, and file conditions. This way you can store data in certain directories on the server disk without having to worry about anybody accessing that data.

> The king of Park Place security is the hotel House detective. He/she oversees registration, guards the lobby, builds room keys, installs door locks, and locks away valuable treasures.

The NetWare security model consists of four layers:

1 · Login/password security

2 · Login Restrictions

3 · Access rights

4 · Attributes

As the NetWare house detective it is your responsibility to oversee registration (login/password), guard the lobby (login restrictions), build keys and locks (access rights), and finally hide the guest's special treasures (attributes). Following is an overview of these four security levels, and a discussion of how they incrementally increase file and directory protection (Figure 9.1). Let's begin with login/password security.

FIGURE 9.1

The Multi-layered NetWare
Security Model

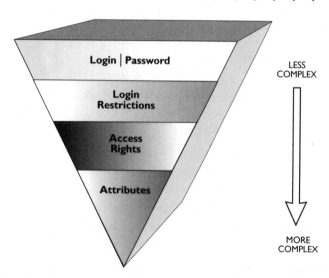

LOGIN/PASSWORD SECURITY

As mentioned above, login/password security governs initial access to the file server and provides a system for user authentication. In the Park Place analogy, login/password security would involve the duties of the registration desk. When guests register at a hotel, they provide a valid username. In NetWare 3.12, the username is authenticated once the user issues the LOGIN command. Furthermore, if the username is valid, the system must match it against an appropriate password—the Park Place guests' form of payment.

LOGIN RESTRICTIONS

Login restrictions is an additional level of login security which monitors a variety of different security conditions. Login restrictions define the second layer of the NetWare security model. They provide the security manager with a way of further filtering out users according to a variety of security conditions. These security conditions include:

▶ Account restrictions

▶ Time restrictions

▶ Station restrictions

▶ Intruder/detection lockout

▶ NCP Packet Signature

In our Park Place analogy, login restrictions involve having the house detective guard the hotel gates. Beyond payment, the house detective can make decisions about guests as they travel from the lobby into the hotel proper by asking questions or searching their belongings. This level of security can be as simple as saying "hello" or as complex as an x-ray search for weapons.

Once guests have passed through the gates into the hotel proper, their movements throughout the hotel and its many facilities are restricted by their collection of room keys. This level of hotel security is known as locksmithing.

ACCESS RIGHTS

The third layer of network security is governed by access rights. Access rights define a complex set of privileges which can be assigned to users or to directories. A user's rights are analogous to room keys. Directory rights are analogous to door locks. If a guest has a valid user key and the appropriate lock, he or she is granted access to the room. In the same manner, if a NetWare user has a user key and the appropriate directory lock, he or she is granted access to the directory. This combination of user and directory security is known as *effective rights* and defines a user's actual privileges in a given directory on the disk. NetWare 3.12 provides eight different access rights. As part of your LAN locksmith duties, it is imperative that you understand each of these rights intimately and have a firm handle on how they are combined both at the user level and the directory level to create effective rights. Access rights are the most common form of NetWare security and provide a very versatile system for controlling who has what privileges to which files. Park Place relies on this level of security. User's keys and directory locks limit guests to appropriate areas of the hotel. You can imagine how chaotic life in the resort would be if there was no room security.

> Access rights define a complex set of privileges which can be assigned to users or to directories. A user's rights are analogous to room keys. Directory rights are analogous to door locks.

ATTRIBUTES

The final level of NetWare security is attribute security. Attributes are conditional privileges which control file sharing, reading, writing, executing, hiding, tracking and archiving. While access rights define which users can have access to a file or directory, file attributes control what the users can do with the files once they are there. Attribute security is analogous to locking away a guest's treasures. Some guests do not wish to rely on the user keys and directory lock security, so they ask the hotel house detective to secure their valuable treasures away in the hotel safe. In the same way, NetWare attributes provide a higher level of security for very special files and directories. NetWare provides two different types of NetWare attributes: security and feature.

Security attributes affect how *users* access files while feature attributes affect how the *system* accesses files. Attribute security in general is a very complex level of NetWare security and is rarely implemented by most security managers. The first three layers of the NetWare security model provide more than enough security for 95% of the NetWare 3.12 LANs.

QUOTE

The only fence against the world is a thorough knowledge of it.

John Locke

THE NETWARE 3.12 BINDERY

The multilayered NetWare security model is implemented through a flat file database called the NetWare bindery. The bindery is an object-oriented database that contains definitions for users, groups and other objects on the network. The NetWare house detective uses the bindery to organize the user structure and define NetWare security. Before we begin our in-depth discussion of the four layers of NetWare security, let's take a moment to explore the three components of the NetWare bindery:

▸ Objects

▸ Properties

▸ Values

A NetWare bindery object defines any LAN component with a name—such as file servers, users, groups, print servers and so on. The NetWare bindery tracks LAN objects and defines a variety of their characteristics known as *properties*. Properties are object characteristics. These characteristics differ for each type of object. For example, user objects have characteristics or properties such as passwords, account restrictions, account balances, security, and login restrictions. File server objects, on the other hand, have a different set of properties such as file server name, NetWare version number, network address, and node address. The NetWare bindery tracks objects and their properties and includes a database of values for those characteristics.

Bindery values are the actual data sets that correspond to object properties. For example, a bindery object USER would have a property of NAME and a value of DAVID. NetWare 3.12 bindery objects, properties and data sets are tracked through three hidden system files: NET$OBJ.SYS for objects, NET$PROP.SYS for properties, and NET$VAL.SYS for values. These three files are hidden and system owned in the SYSTEM subdirectory.

TIP

The NetWare 3.12 bindery is an extremely sensitive database and must be guarded very closely. If the file server crashes, or power goes out in the middle of a user upgrade or configuration, the bindery can become corrupted quite easily. In this case, the security manager must use the BINDFIX or BINDREST utilities to decorrupt these files.

That's it for our overview of the NetWare security model. We will spend the majority of the chapter learning how it works and what steps can be taken to ensure the highest level of NetWare security. Before we begin, let's take a quick look at how the NetWare house detective can distribute the security load through distributed security managers.

Special User Accounts

Unfortunately, the Park Place house detective cannot be everywhere at once. Every day, he/she has a variety of different responsibilities in a variety of different locations. To aid the hotel house detective in his security responsibilities, the hotel manager has agreed to provide a security staff. The security staff which includes registration clerks, lobby guards, locksmiths and safe monitors.

In NetWare, the NetWare house detective's assistants include:

NetWare supervisor equivalents—distributed users who have all the same rights as the Supervisor.

Managers—used to create, manage and delete users and groups. Managers are designed to help with organizing user activities and login restrictions.

Operators—designed to provide specialized assistance. NetWare 3.12 supports three different types of operators: console operators, print queue operators and print server operators.

Supervisor equivalents, managers and operators are an effective way to lighten the NetWare house detective's load. Let's take a closer look at NetWare special user accounts.

THE SUPERVISOR

The supervisor is the all-knowing, all wise guru of the LAN—NetWare Yoda. He/she has all rights everywhere, but is still subject to the password and attribute levels of security. When NetWare is first installed, two users are created by default:

▸ SUPERVISOR

▸ GUEST

Both accounts are created during NetWare 3.12 installation. During initial login, the SUPERVISOR account has no password but still has all rights and access to all server configurations. Clearly, then, it is extremely important to give the SUPERVISOR a password immediately. The GUEST account, on the other hand, has severely limited security. The GUEST account is initially created so guest users can log in to the NetWare server and access the following fundamental shared resources:

> The supervisor is the all-knowing, all wise guru of the LAN—NetWare Yoda.

▸ Printing

▸ Public utilities

▸ Simple NetWare applications

In addition to SUPERVISOR and GUEST, the NetWare installation creates one other bindery object: the group EVERYONE. EVERYONE is created to provide global configuration and security access for the NetWare house detective. The EVERYONE group contains all users on the system, present and future. By default, the EVERYONE group has limited security and default login restrictions.

Beyond these default bindery objects, the system manager can create a staff of distributed security managers. The most skilled of the staff members includes the supervisor equivalent.

QUOTE

Some people blow their own horn, while others play a symphony.

Anonymous

SUPERVISOR EQUIVALENT

The supervisor can create a supervisor equivalent by entering the User Information window of SYSCON and assigning the Supervisor security equivalence to a specific user. We will learn more about them in the next chapter. With the following three exceptions, the supervisor equivalent user is identical to the supervisor.

1 · The supervisor equivalent can be deleted whereas the Supervisor cannot.

2 · The supervisor equivalent can only be created by the supervisor.

3 · The Supervisor account has a special User ID—1.

The supervisor equivalent special user provides an effective way to maintain the LAN. It is not a good idea to consistently login as the user Supervisor because some known network viruses search and piggyback this particular username. It is more secure to login as a regular network user who has been given supervisor equivalence.

TIP

You can use supervisor equivalence to create a back door. The system manager can create a fictitious user with an unpredictable username and make that user equivalent to the supervisor. In cases where the supervisor account has been locked or destroyed, the system manager can access the LAN and recreate the Supervisor password from the supervisor equivalent account.

MANAGERS

The NetWare house detective staff also consists of distributed managers who have limited capabilities over workgroups or guest members. NetWare 3.12 provides two different levels of manager staff:

▶ Workgroup manager

▶ User account manager

Workgroup managers are assistant supervisors which have been given special rights to create, manage, and delete users and groups. The Supervisor or supervisor equivalent creates workgroup managers and assigns them specific users and groups to manage. The workgroup manager can create further users under his/her group, or delete existing users from the group. The work group manager is restricted to deleting only users he/she created or users who are under his/her workgroup.

The user account manager provides the facility for managing and deleting users but not creating them. The main difference is user account managers can only manage users. They cannot create bindery objects. Workgroup managers can create user account managers for overseeing specific subsets of their workgroup. Workgroup managers and user account managers are both created using the SYSCON utility. We will discuss the steps for creating distributed management in the next chapter.

QUOTE

As knowledge increases, wonder deepens.

Charles Morgan

OPERATORS

Operators are distributed staff who oversee specific network functions. The Supervisor or supervisor equivalent can assign users as operators of the file server console, print server, or print queue functions. File server console operators have full access to the FCONSOLE utility except for the facility for downing the server or disconnecting other users.

KNOWLEDGE

FCONSOLE facilities have been dramatically limited in NetWare 3.12. Most of the useful functions from NetWare 2.2 have been incorporated into a more wondrous 3.12 utility called MONITOR.NLM.

Print server operators are special user accounts which are given rights to manage the print server. Print server operators can specify notify lists for printers, issue commands to the printers, change forms, change the queue serviced by a print server, change queue priority, or down the print server. Print server operators cannot create new print servers or assign other users as print server operators. By default, the Supervisor is a print server operator on all print servers which are created. Only the Supervisor or supervisor equivalent can assign print server operator status.

Print queue operators are special user accounts with rights to create, manage, disable and enable print queues. A print queue operator can also authorize a print server to service a queue. By default, the Supervisor is print queue operator of all print queues which are created. Only the Supervisor or supervisor equivalent can assign print queue operator status. In order to establish the proper connection between a print queue and print server, the user must be both a print server operator and print queue operator. Otherwise, the print server operator and print queue operator would have to work together in performing this valuable printing function.

That completes our discussion of special user accounts. Please refer to Table 9.1 for a summary of the "cans" and "can'ts" of NetWare Supervisors, Managers, and Operators.

CANS	CAN'TS
Supervisor/Supervisor Equivalent	
Can assign all other special user accounts, automatically acquire all rights to each volume, and change the supervisor password.	

TABLE 9.1

Cans and Can'ts for Special User Accounts

	CANS	CAN'TS
TABLE 9.1 *Cans and Can'ts for Special* *User Accounts (continued)*	*Workgroup Manager*	
	Manages users and groups, creates users and groups, delete users they've created, delete users they have been assigned, create user account managers.	No special file rights, cannot create a workgroup manager, cannot delete other than their own users, cannot assign rights they have not been granted.
	User Account Managers	
	Manage users, delete users they have been assigned, create other user account managers.	Create users or groups, manage groups, create workgroup managers, assign rights they have not been granted.
	Print Server Operators	
	Create notify list for printers, change forms, change queue priority, down the print server.	Create print servers, assign print server operators, assign queues to printers.
	Print Queue Operators	
	Manage print queues.	Create print queues, delete print queues, assign print queue operators.

TIP

The workgroup manager or user account manager are not given any rights to the directory structure. In order to adequately manage their own users and groups, the distributed managers should be given supervisor rights to particular branches of the directory tree.

Distributed security staff is a very valuable tool for the NetWare house detective. It makes his/her life a lot easier and provides a more secure system for the hotel guests. It is important before assigning this status to distributed staff, to assess the user's ability on the network and his/her comprehension of NetWare security. There is nothing more dangerous than a workgroup manager run amuck.

In the remainder of this chapter, we will discuss the house detective's approach to NetWare security and discuss the four layers of the NetWare security model in detail. We will begin with login/password security.

Login/Password Security

Login/password security is the first layer of the NetWare security model. It controls LAN access at the first point of entrance—login name and password.

Login/password security is effective because it requires two pieces of information—an authorized login name and valid password. The password and login name must match the system exactly.

Login/password security is the registration desk responsibilities of the NetWare house detective. When guests

> Login/password security is the first layer of the NetWare security model. It controls LAN access at the first point of entrance—login name and password.

first enter the preliminary hotel lobby, they are required to go to the registration desk and provide a valid form of identification for their reservation and a form of payment. The username is the ID that the NetWare user uses to validate access to the LAN. The password is their form of payment. Without an appropriate password, users are not allowed to continue to the second layer of LAN access.

TIP

In NetWare 3.12, usernames are required whereas passwords are optional.

Let's discuss the NetWare usernames and passwords, and explore the process of logging in.

USERNAMES

Usernames provide the first point of access to the LAN. Only network supervisors, supervisor equivalents, and workgroup managers can create usernames. In order to access the NetWare LAN, the user must log into the network by specifying the file server name and an appropriate username. Usernames can be anywhere from 2 to 47 characters in length. Usernames are objects in the file server bindery and are assigned specific properties. As you assign properties to usernames, you are in effect granting the user sufficient security clearance to do their jobs. By default, all users are automatically assigned a password property and membership to the group EVERYONE. Usernames can be assigned using the SYSCON menu utility or one of the two user creation utilities: MAKEUSER or USERDEF.

PASSWORDS

Once the user has provided a form of ID at the registration desk, he/she is required to make payment. In NetWare, payment is in the form of optional (though highly recommended) passwords. Passwords provide an effective strategy for filtering out unwanted users. NetWare provides a number of restrictions which may be used at the password level of security. Password protection may be enhanced by making passwords mandatory, defining minimum password lengths, or causing passwords to expire after a limited length of time. These password restrictions will be discussed in the next section.

Passwords can be changed by NetWare Supervisors, supervisor equivalents, workgroup managers, user account managers, or the users themselves. It is a good idea to immediately assign a password upon initial creation of a particular user. Users can then be allowed to choose and change their own passwords. As the NetWare house detective you do have the choice of not allowing users to change their own passwords.

KNOWLEDGE

A password's confidentiality has been a point of concern for many system managers. In NetWare 2.2 and below, the password was broadcast across the LAN cabling in text form. This meant that any user with the appropriate equipment could siphon the password and read it easily. NetWare 3.12 protects passwords with a feature called *password encryption* which means that user passwords are encrypted at the workstation and sent along the cabling in a format only the file server can decode.

LOGGING IN

Let's review the process of logging in:

1 · Load IPX

2 · Load NETx

3 · Move to F:\LOGIN>

Once a user accesses the F:\LOGIN> directory, he/she is on the doorstep of the LAN. At this point, the user has limited access to only two NetWare files: LOGIN.EXE (to login) and SLIST.EXE (for a list of available servers). The user is ready to exercise his/her login security. Login security consists of the following four steps:

1 · The user logs into the network by specifying the file server name and a username. The system verifies the username by matching it against an object in the NET$OBJ.SYS bindery file. Whether or not the username exists, NetWare prompts for a Password. This is done to fool would-be hackers into thinking this is a valid username. NetWare is built on the premise of "What you don't know, can't hurt us!"

2 · If the system verifies the username, it searches the NET$PROP.SYS file for a password property. If one exists, it responds with **Password:** If a password doesn't exist, the system jumps to step 4.

3 · The user enters a password. If the username is valid, NetWare compares this input to the value in NET$VAL.SYS. If the username is not valid, the system bypasses the search and responds with Access Denied.

TIP
Experienced hackers will eventually notice that invalid usernames respond much more quickly with Access Denied. This is because NetWare doesn't search the bindery for invalid username passwords. In the case of valid usernames, like GUEST, NetWare takes noticeably longer while it searches the NET$VAL.SYS bindery database.

4 · If the user enters the correct password for this username, he/she will be granted conditional access to the LAN. If not, the system responds with Access Denied. The user is left at the NetWare door-step. Next, the system matches the username with a variety of additional bindery values—login restrictions.

KNOWLEDGE

Upon receipt of the long-awaited NetWare prompt, the user has completed levels one and two of the NetWare security model. The third level, access rights security, controls the user's movements throughout the directory structure and provides limited access to authorized areas of the disk.

There are numerous command line utilities which allow the Supervisor to customize login/password security. We will discuss all of these commands at the end of the chapter.

Login Restrictions

Once the guests check in at the registration desk and provide proper payment, they must complete their access to Park Place by passing through the golden gates. The golden gates offer a final level of access security where the lobby guards can inspect the guests for firearms, contraband, and other security violations. In much the same way, login restrictions provide a final level of access security which allows the LAN house detective to restrict user access according to a variety of login conditions including time, workstation location, date

> The golden gates offer a final level of access security where the lobby guards can inspect the guests for firearms, contraband, and other security violations. NetWare provides a similar form of access security through login restrictions.

and so on. Let's take a quick look at how it works.

Once the username has been entered and the password has been matched, the user is granted conditional access to the system. Permanent access is contingent on a supplemental level of login/password security called *login restrictions*. Login restrictions further scrutinize LAN access by matching the login name with a variety of other qualifications; is this user authorized to login during this time period? is this user authorized to login from this particular machine? is this user authorized to login on this date? is this user really who he/she claims to be? and so on. In addition, NetWare login restrictions incorporate an access tracking feature called Intruder Detection/Lockout. This security feature tracks un-authorized login attempts and automatically locks accounts which exceed a given bad login threshold count. The user account can only be unlocked by the NetWare supervisor.

NetWare login restrictions fall into five different categories:

- ► Account Restrictions
- ► Time Restrictions
- ► Station Restrictions
- ► Intruder Detection/Lockout
- ► NCP Packet Signature

Account restrictions apply to user accounts and password/data restrictions. Time restrictions and station restrictions apply to login times and workstation locations. Intruder detection/lockout is a NetWare 3.12 feature which tracks in-valid login attempts and locks out unauthorized users. NCP Packet Signatures validate client/server communications. Each of these puzzle pieces is an impor-tant component in the overall security picture. It is important to take time and care in designing NetWare login restrictions. Let's discuss each one in detail.

ACCOUNT RESTRICTIONS

NetWare account restrictions provide a method for controlling and restricting user access to the NetWare file server. Account restrictions are established in two different ways:

Default Account Balance/Restrictions in Supervisor Options of SYSCON

Account Balance/Restrictions in User Information of SYSCON

Default account restrictions establish configurations for all new users and are defined in the Supervisor Options screen of SYSCON. User-specific account restrictions establish configurations for individual users and are defined in the user's specific User Information window of SYSCON.

TIP

Default account restrictions take effect for all users who are created from this point on. This means that these restrictions will not take effect for any users who currently exist. Let's say you have 100 users and you decide you want to restrict everybody from logging in on the weekend. You waltz over the default time restrictions and restrict the weekend time periods. What's wrong with this picture? The default time restrictions only affect new users created from this point on. These changes will not affect your current 100 users. The only option is to change each user's time restriction individually—all 100 of them! The moral of the story is "set your default restrictions before you create your users."

> Default account restrictions take effect for all users who are created from this point on. This means that these restrictions will not take effect for any users who currently exist.

TIP

Good news. There is a little trick which can save you hours of work if you get caught in the trap described above. In order to configure login restrictions for large numbers of users, simply highlight those users with F5 in the User Information window of **SYSCON** and press Enter. The Set User Information screen will appear with four choices: Account Balance, Account Restrictions, Station Restrictions, and Time Restrictions. Simply define the appropriate restrictions and they will take effect for all highlighted users. Whew, that saved a ton of time. Good thing you read this tip.

NetWare's account restrictions screen provides a variety of different options for NetWare system managers. Refer to Figure 9.2 for an illustration of NetWare 3.12's default account restrictions screen. Here's a brief discussion of each of these options.

FIGURE 9.2

Default Account Restrictions in SYSCON

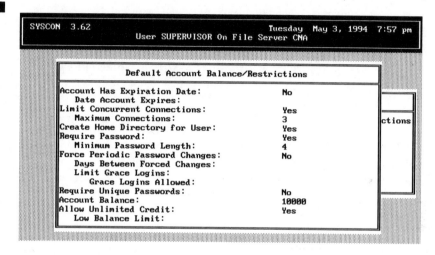

```
SYSCON   3.62                              Tuesday  May 3, 1994  7:57 pm
                      User SUPERUISOR On File Server CNA

                    ┌─────────────────────────────────────────┐
                    │      Default Account Balance/Restrictions │
                    │                                           │
                    │Account Has Expiration Date:        No     │
                    │   Date Account Expires:                   │
                    │Limit Concurrent Connections:       Yes    │
                    │   Maximum Connections:             3      │
                    │Create Home Directory for User:     Yes    │   ctions
                    │Require Password:                   Yes    │
                    │   Minimum Password Length:         4      │
                    │Force Periodic Password Changes:    No     │
                    │   Days Between Forced Changes:            │
                    │   Limit Grace Logins:                     │
                    │      Grace Logins Allowed:                │
                    │Require Unique Passwords:           No     │
                    │Account Balance:                    10000  │
                    │Allow Unlimited Credit:             Yes    │
                    │   Low Balance Limit:                      │
                    └─────────────────────────────────────────┘
```

Account Expiration Date

Account Expiration Date is a useful tool for temporary employees or students in an academic environment. It allows the system manager to lock an account after a specific date. By default, the Account Expiration Date is set to NO. If you change the value to YES, today's date will appear as the default Date the Account Expires. You can change the date at any time—the account locks at midnight.

Limit Concurrent Connections

Limiting concurrent connections is useful against users who like to migrate throughout the LAN or login from multiple workstations. The system manager can limit a user's concurrent connections by changing the default from NO to YES. An ideal setting is three concurrent connections, which means that this user can login from only three workstations simultaneously. This particular account restriction works in conjunction with station restrictions. You can enhance a user's concurrent connection limitation by combining it with a specific physical workstation limitations—station restrictions. By default, Limit Current Connections is set to NO. A good average setting is YES—limit current connections—with maximum connections set to three. If you set this in the default account restrictions, it will take effect for all users who are created beyond this point.

Create Home Directory for User

Create Home Directory for User is an account configuration which instructs the system to create a home directory for each user under the USERS subdirectory. By default, this option is set to YES. Create Home Directory for User is an important part of the overall security picture because it defines a home area for each user. This home area is used by many other configurations, including drive mappings, login scripts, and trustee assignments. User drive mappings are created in the system login script with an identifier variable called %LOGIN_NAME. This identifier variable will create a home directory mapping for all users based on what their unique login name is. But this only works if a home directory exists for each user.

Require Password

Password restrictions are applied using the Require Password and other related restrictions. By default, the system does not require a password. This is a huge oversight. It is recommended that you require a password for all users and that you set the minimum password length to something in excess of five characters.

TIP

There is a password-hacking routine that can guess any five-character password in less than 20 minutes. The program connects directly to the NetWare bindery and matches random character combinations with existing password information. So if your minimum password length is four characters or fewer, this program can break into the system very, very quickly.

QUOTE

You can't depend on your judgement when your imagination is out of focus.

John F. Kennedy

Force Periodic Password Changes

Once a password has been required and a minimum password length of seven characters has been set, you should explore using the Force Periodic Password Changes account restriction. This restriction forces users to change their password at periodic intervals. If you set Force Periodic Password Changes to YES, the system will ask you to input the days between forced changes. The default is 45 days. This is a little short and can become a nuisance very quickly. A periodic password interval of 90 days seems to be optimal.

Once a password interval has expired, the user is required to change his/her password. If the user does not change his/her password at the point of login, the system will lock the account. This is where *grace logins* come in. Grace logins allow the user to login without changing the password. Keep in mind this is a temporary situation, because even grace logins can expire. Seven grace logins is ideal for most users. Once a user logs in for the seventh time and chooses not to change his/her password, the account is locked and can only be unlocked by the Supervisor. So who unlocks the supervisor's account? Stay tuned.

TIP

When the periodic password interval has expired, the system will respond once they login with Your password has expired. Would you like to change it now? This provides an opportunity to change a password right away. Otherwise, users can use SETPASS or SYS-CON to change their password at any time.

Require Unique Passwords

Require unique passwords works in conjunction with forcing periodic password changes. When the periodic password interval expires and the user is required to change his/her password, Unique Passwords forces him/her to enter a new, *different* password. This is an effective strategy when combined with forcing periodic password changes and requiring passwords. If the system manager takes the time and effort to make the users change their passwords periodically, he or she should make sure those passwords are unique each time. It does not make sense for the user to continually use the same password.

TIP

Requiring unique passwords relies on an internal NetWare table which keeps track of the last 10 passwords. After the tenth different password has been used, the user can then use a previous password.

Account Balance

NetWare has a built-in accounting feature which tracks user logins, logouts, and access to network resources. The system manager can install accounting through the SYSCON menu utility. In addition, he/she can use SYSCON to define network resources and establish charge rates for access to those resources. Account balance is a dynamic measure of each user's accounting usage.

> NetWare has a built-in accounting feature which tracks user logins, logouts, and access to network resources.

By default, the account balance is set to 0 and unlimited credit is set to NO. This is a problem because once the system manager installs accounting, users begin accumulating resource charges, so the account balance is immediately negative. If the low balance limit is set to 0, users are instantly in violation of NetWare accounting. Once a user's account balance becomes negative, the system locks the account—he or she can no longer login. So it is very important to set the account balance to at least 1,000 when you decide to install accounting. Low balance limit refers to the number which needs to be reached in order for the user to be locked out. Typically, an account balance of 1,000, depending on the charge rates, and a low balance limit of 0 is optimal. It's not a good idea to set unlimited credit because that defeats the whole purpose of charging for resources.

Another interesting use of NetWare accounting in NetWare 3.12 is resource tracking. Instead of charging users for their specific resource usage, you can use accounting to track how users are accessing resources. This is done by setting the Allow Unlimited Credit to YES, the account balance to 0, and the low balance limit to 0. Then, you charge each user a rate of 1 unit per usage on each of the following five resources:

- ▶ Time usage
- ▶ Blocks written
- ▶ Disk space
- ▶ Blocks read
- ▶ Processor utilization

By setting each of these resource charge rates at one, you can receive a comparative view of how users are using your LAN resources. For example, match their time utilization with processor utilization to see if they are really working. By setting the Allow Unlimited Credit to YES, you are allowing the number to go well below 0 and users will quickly accumulate a negative balance. The number that appears in their negative account balance under User Information exactly correlates with their use of NetWare resources. While NetWare 3.12 does not inherently support any kind of auditing or resource tracking feature, clever and creative use of NetWare accounting can provide the same functionality.

Limit Server Disk Space

Users can be restricted to specific amounts of disk space on the shared server disk. NetWare tracks disk space by who owns (created) what file. Also, if you copy a file using a NetWare utilty, ownership is transferred to the destination user. If Limit Server Disk Space is set to YES, the system will ask for a maximum server disk space parameter (in kilobytes). Typically, this parameter works in deterring disk abuse. Also, in academic environments, it is a good idea to limit students so that they don't clutter the disk with games and miscellaneous utilities. Unless, of course, they give you a copy of the game. A good value for limiting server disk space is 1,000 kilobytes, or 1 megabyte.

The next three login restrictions are supplemental in their support of account restrictions. They provide a certain level of login security but not nearly the flexibility or versatility of Account Balance Restrictions. Let's take a quick look at them.

QUOTE

Adventure is the champagne of life.

G.K. Chesterton

TIME RESTRICTIONS

Time restrictions are useful because they allow you to control how much time users have access to the system. Time restrictions can be applied as a default at the user level just as with Account Restrictions. Keep in mind that default time restrictions only take effect for users who are created from this point forward. When they are configured intelligently, time restrictions help increase the security of the system. But when configured carelessly, they can dramatically hinder user performance and productivity.

The default time restriction screen, as seen in Figure 9.3, is a matrix of days and time periods. The days of the week, Sunday through Saturday, are displayed

► · ◄

F I G U R E 9.3

Default Time Restrictions in SYSCON

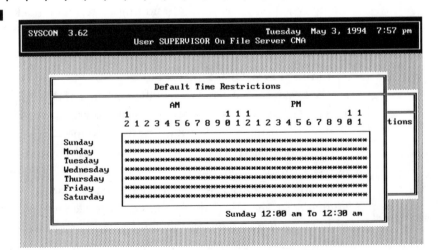

on the left-hand side of the matrix and a 24-hour clock (in half an hour increments) is listed across the top. Each asterisk in the system indicates a time period when this particular user or all users can login. By default, the time restriction screen has all asterisks meaning all users can login at any time. To restrict users, simply move the cursor to a particular point in time and press the space bar. This blanks the time period and makes it unavailable for user access.

Some common time restrictions include:

Restrict entire days—weekends, for example

Restrict evenings—10:00 PM to 5:00 AM

Restrict backup time periods—11:00 PM to midnight

These are effective strategies for protection against mild-mannered janitors who turn into superhackers at midnight, or users who spend too much time in front of the computer. Keep in mind that time restrictions are dynamic—once you come across a blank time period, the system clears your connection. But don't worry, there is a five-minute warning before the connection is cleared.

TIP

When a time restriction is encountered and a user connection is cleared, the system does not perform a proper logout, it simply clears the workstation—*without* saving the file. When the system prompts you with a five minute message, it's a good idea to pay attention and logout.

The F5 key is very useful with time restrictions because it allows you to highlight blocks of time and press the asterisk key to insert an available time slot, or the space key to restrict that time slot. Remember, intelligent time restrictions increase network security, while careless time restrictions significantly hinder user productivity.

STATION RESTRICTIONS

Station restrictions are another way to control user access. But instead of restricting user access with passwords, disk restrictions, or time slots, you're restricting the physical workstation users login from. Here's how it works—each workstation is equipped with an internal network interface card. The card has a 12-digit hexadecimal node address that is programmed at the factory. This node address is unique for all network interface cards in the world and is used by the cabling media to identify this network interface card from all others on the LAN. The node address can also be used to identify which users can login from which machines. In a certain sense, it can be said that the user is logically attached to a specific network interface card.

TIP

Since station restrictions are linked so closely to the user and node address, there is no such thing as default station restrictions. It wouldn't make sense to restrict all users on the network to a particular node address. If you did, all users in the network would have to login from the same workstation. Massive gridlock!

Station restrictions are configured for specific users in the user information screen of SYSCON. In order to define a station restriction for a given user, the system manager must provide two pieces of information: network address and node address. The network address defines the cabling scheme upon which the workstation is attached. The node address is a 12-digit hexadecimal number which identifies the workstation network interface card. Unfortunately, this information is not readily available to NetWare system managers. The only easy way to access this information is the USERLIST utility. USERLIST provides a list of all users who are currently logged in and the station addresses of the machines they are using. The best strategy is to print out a list of each user's USERLIST and use the information in SYSCON to establish station restrictions.

Station restrictions, like other login restrictions, can be used to enhance access security. If they are abused or mishandled, they can significantly impede user productivity. If station restrictions are set to only one workstation and a user's workstation is down or a user's workstation is busy, he or she cannot login from any other workstation. While this is a useful security tool, it can be detrimental to user relationships.

INTRUDER DETECTION/LOCKOUT

The final login restriction is Intruder Detection/Lockout. Intruder Detection/Lockout is not so much a restriction as it is a security tracking feature. Intruder Detection/Lockout tracks invalid login attempts by monitoring users who try to login without correct passwords. The Intruder Detection/Lockout feature keeps track of invalid password attempts and locks a user account once the threshold number of attempts has been exceeded—usually three. Intruder Detection/Lockout is a system-wide configuration—it is either activated for all users or none.

> Intruder Detection/Lockout tracks invalid login attempts by monitoring users who try to login without correct passwords.

By default, Intruder Detection/Lockout is set to NO. You can choose Intruder Detection/Lockout from the Supervisor Option screen of SYSCON (Figure 9.4). Intruder Detection/Lockout consists of two components: intruder detection and account lockout. The following is a brief discussion of each.

FIGURE 9.4

Intruder Detection/Lockout

```
SYSCON  3.62                                Tuesday  May 3, 1994  7:57 pm
                        User SUPERVISOR On File Server CNA

                            Available Topics
                       Intruder Detection/Lockout
  Detect Intruders:                  Yes                              tions
  Intruder Detection Threshold
  Incorrect Login Attempts:          7
  Bad Login Count Retention Time: 0  Days     0  Hours    30 Minutes

  Lock Account After Detection:      Yes
     Length Of Account Lockout:   0  Days     0  Hours    15 Minutes
```

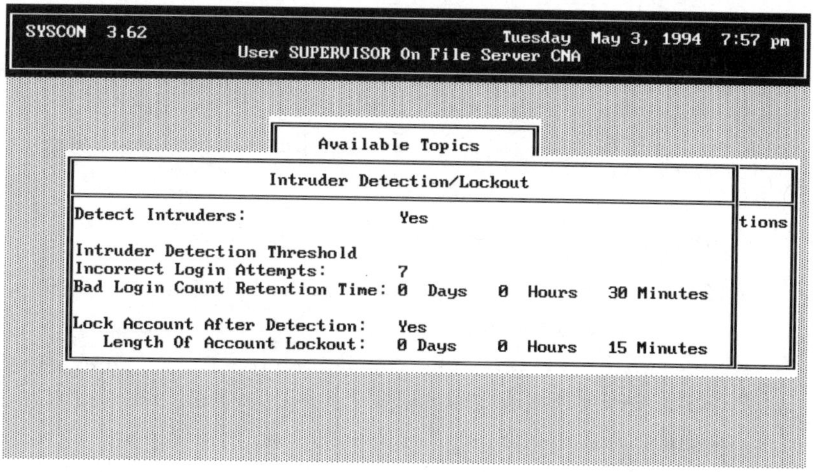

Intruder Detection

Intruder detection is activated as soon as a valid user logs in with an incorrect password. The Incorrect Login Attempt Threshold is a number which continues to increment as invalid passwords are entered—for the same user. As soon as the incrementing number exceeds the Incorrect Login Attempt Threshold, the system activates account lockout. The Bad Login Count Retention Time is a window of opportunity, so to speak, that the system uses to increment the incorrect login attempts.

Here's how it works: Assume the Incorrect Login Attempts is set to 7 and Bad Login Account Retention Time is set to 24-hours. The system will track all incorrect login activity and lock the user account if the following condition occurs—the number of incorrect login attempts exceeds 7 in a 24-hour window.

Account Lockout

Account lockout is activated when the intruder detection threshold is exceeded and account lockout is set to YES. It doesn't make much sense to activate Intruder Detection/Lockout without initiating a user lockout once the intruder detection threshold is exceeded. By setting the lock account after detection to YES, the system asks for a length of account lockout. The Length of Account Lockout is the time period that the account is locked once account lockout is activated. By default, this value is set to 15 minutes (doesn't make much sense, does it?). This value invites the hacker to come back 15 minutes later and try all over again. Typically, a value equal to or exceeding the bad login account retention time is adequate.

TIP

The most common target for NetWare hackers is the Supervisor. If Intruder Detection/Lockout is activated and users try to access the Supervisor account more than seven times with an incorrect password, the system will lock the supervisor account. This is particularly disconcerting—especially since the Supervisor is the only user who can unlock NetWare accounts. Fortunately, NetWare has incorporated a console command called ENABLE LOGIN which resets the Supervisor account.

TIP

When the Supervisor unlocks a user account, he/she performs this function in the User Information screen of SYSCON. The Intruder/Detection Lockout screen displays the node ID of the last station which attempted an incorrect login. This is useful information if you have a problem with particular users who are accessing other users' accounts. This information becomes especially valuable when it is combined with station restrictions—an open-and-shut case.

NCP PACKET SIGNATURE

The new NetWare 3.12 NCP Packet Signature feature is designed to protect the LAN from experienced hackers who forge data packets or pose as unauthenticated clients—NetWare Incognito. The best way to understand NCP Packet Signature is to review the steps that occur between a workstation and a server during normal LAN operations:

I · When a workstation client logs into a NetWare 3.12 server, the server and the client establish a shared key referred to as the *session key*. This key is unique for each client logged into the server and for each unique session.

2 · When the client requests services from the server, the client appends a unique signature to the data packet.

3 · The server validates the signature as soon as it receives the packet. If it is correct, the NetWare 3.12 server processes the request and attaches a new signature to the reply. If the client's signature is incorrect, the packet is discarded and an alert message is sent to the server console and error log.

TIP

The NCP Packet Signature feature causes a slight decrease in server performance. To aleviate this problem, consider enabling packet bursting or Large Internet Packets (LIP).

KNOWLEDGE

NCP Packet Signatures recently became necessary because of the overzealous activities of a group of students at Liedan University in the Netherlands. These mischievous students are credited with discovering a simple "piggy back" intrusion mechanism for NetWare 2.2 and 3.11 servers. The NCP Packet Signature feature slams the door on such would-be hackers.

NCP Packet Signing occurs at both the workstation and the server. NetWare 3.12 contains a default level of packet signing. By default, the client signs only if the server requests it and the server signs if the client is capable. Therefore, signing always occurs. The system manager can customize NCP Packet Signing by using the SET server command and NET.CFG workstation file:

> *At the Server (SET):*
> SET NCP PACKET SIGNATURE OPTION =
>
> *At the WORKSTATION (NET.CFG):*
> SIGNATURE LEVEL =

NCP Packet Signature can be set at varying levels for clients and servers depending on the security needs of the network. Table 9.2 illustrates the available otions for NCP Packet Signing:

That's it for login restrictions. In this section, we covered the various account restrictions, time restrictions, station restrictions, and NetWare's Intruder Detection/Lockout feature, and NCP Packet Signature. These restrictions, when used in coordination with login/password security, can create a very effective security strategy for the NetWare LAN house detective.

T A B L E 9.2

NCP Packet Signature Levels

Server Level	**0** Server does not sign packets	**1** Server signs only if client requests it	**2** (DEFAULT) Server signs if client is capable of signing	**3** Server always signs and requires *all* clients to sign (or login will fail)
Client level				
0 Client does not sign packets	No packet signature	No packet signature	No packet signature	No logging in
1 (DEFAULT) Client signs only if server requests it	No packet signature	No packet signature	PACKET SIGNATURE	PACKET SIGNATURE
2 Client signs if server is capable of signing	No packet signature	PACKET SIGNATURE	PACKET SIGNATURE	PACKET SIGNATURE
3 Client always signs and requires server to sign (or login will fail)	No logging in	PACKET SIGNATURE	PACKET SIGNATURE	PACKET SIGNATURE (maximum protection)

Access Rights

Welcome to Park Place. Once you have checked in at the registration desk and provided a valid form of payment, the lobby guards inspect your belongings. If you pass the lobby guard check, you are allowed through the Park Place gates.

Once inside the hotel proper, you will find that Park Place fountains, atriums and golf courses are quite overwhelming. The grandness of the hotel can cause your mind to spin. Fortunately, tour guides and drive mappings provide an effective strategy for finding your way around. Movement throughout the hotel grounds is generally unrestricted.

> Once the user has passed login/password security and login restrictions, he/she is greeted with a NetWare prompt. Movement throughout the network directory structure is controlled by access rights.

Access to certain areas of the grounds, however, are restricted to guests with specific user keys and door locks. In this section, we will discuss the responsibilities of the house detective in using locksmith tools for enhanced hotel security.

Access Rights define the third level of the NetWare security model. Once the user has passed login/password security and login restrictions, he/she is greeted with a NetWare prompt. Movement throughout the network directory structure is controlled by access rights. Users cannot freely access all files and directories in the system—this would be entirely too 1960s. Instead, users are limited to only those files and directories in which they have been given specific privileges.

Access to shared network data is controlled at two different levels: the user level (trustee assignments) and the directory level (directory rights, or the inherited rights mask (IRM)). We will discuss each of these two levels of security and talk about how they combine to create *effective rights*. But before we dive into trustee assignments and directory rights, let's take a moment to understand the access privileges themselves and appreciate how they are used to limit specific user actions in NetWare directory structures.

QUOTE

This is no time for ease and comfort. It is the time to dare and endure.

Winston Churchill

UNDERSTANDING ACCESS RIGHTS

In understanding access rights, you need to ask one simple question: "What are the types of things users do in a network directory?" Ready for the answer?

▸ Read from files

▸ Write to files

▸ Copy files

▸ Change the names of files

▸ Access applications

▸ Erase files

▸ Create directories

Wow, users are extremely active. Fortunately, NetWare provides a simple facility for controlling user actions. Each of these user activities corresponds with a specific NetWare access right. In NetWare 3.12, there are eight different access privileges. They are:

W—**Write** to write to an existing file

R—**Read** to read an existing file

M—**Modify** to modify file names and attributes

F—**File Scan** to search the directory or subdirectory

A—**Access Control** to determine access rights

C—**Create** to create and write to new files or subdirectories

E—**Erase** to delete existing file or subdirectories

S—**Supervisor** for all rights in directory and all subdirectories

TIP

Notice that the NetWare 3.12 rights spell a word—WoRMFACES. The "o" is silent. Ironically, the "o" (open) is a NetWare 2.15 right which has been incorporated into W and R. Funny how the "o" falls into place so nicely. It's almost like we planned it that way.

Each of these eight access rights corresponds with a particular user function. Five of them correspond with common functions—writing, reading, creating, erasing, and searching. The other three are a little more quirky—modify, access control, and supervisory. These rights pertain to the process of assigning and modifying NetWare security. Modify provides the ability to customize file attributes and Access Control allows users to change their access privileges—this is dangerous.

TIP

These rights evolve as you move from one version of NetWare to another. Access rights in NetWare 3.12 are different from 2.15. They also change as you move forward to NetWare 4.01. Pay attention to the version of NetWare you are using and understand the differences—however subtle they may be. In this book, we will explore the differences between NetWare 2.2 and 3.12 access rights.

The key to using access rights is understanding which rights are necessary to perform common NetWare activities. Table 9.3 provides a list of some common NetWare activities and the rights which are required to perform those activities. As the LAN locksmith, it is your responsibility to go through the directory structure and assign specific access rights to specific directories for specific users based on the types of activities they perform in those directories. Sounds simple, right?

> The key to using access rights is understanding which rights are necessary to perform common NetWare activities.

TABLE 9.3

Rights Requirements for Common NetWare Activities

ACTION	RIGHTS REQUIREMENT
Read from a closed file	R
See a Filename or Directory	F
Write to a closed file	W, C, E, M
Execute an EXE File	R, F
See the Root Directory	Any of the 8 rights
Create and Write to a file	C
Make a new directory	C
Delete a file	E
Change attributes	M
Rename a file	M
Copy files into a Directory	W, C, F
Copy files from a Directory	R, F
Modify disk space restrictions	A
Change directory rights	A
Change trustee assignments	A
Salvage Deleted Files	R, F, C

One of the LAN house detective's security responsibilities is locksmithing which includes two major responsibilities: keys and locks. The first responsibility is to create the keys which unlock specific doors in the hotel. The other locksmith responsibility is to install the locks in appropriate network directories. Once the keys have been created and the locks are in place, each user is given an appropriate set of keys—the NetWare key ring. This analogy is actually very close to what happens in the NetWare security model—the keys are analogous to trustee assignments and the locks are analogous to directory rights. If a lock exists and the user has the correct key, that user is said to have the effective right or privilege to unlock the directory. Remember, users can only perform the privileges which match the notches on their key.

KNOWLEDGE

NetWare 3.12 access rights apply to both files and directories. Most system managers apply access rights at the directory level, because most files in a directory share a common purpose. Keep in mind, though, you can apply access rights security to a single file within a directory.

TRUSTEE ASSIGNMENTS

Trustee assignments—access right keys—are assigned to users and groups. When a user or group is given a trustee assignment to a particular directory, he/she is said to be a *trustee* of that directory. In addition, trustee assignments flow from parent directories to their children. So when an access right is granted to a trustee for a given directory, the privilege is inherited by all subdirectories. See Figure 9.5 for an example of flowing trustee keys. Access rights do not flow up, however, and so it would be impossible to grant user trustee assignments to a parent directory unless you went to that directory and assigned them specifically at that point. You can, however, assign large sweeping sets of privileges by granting trustee assignments to global parent directories such as APPS, for example.

> When a user or group is given rights assignment to a particular directory, he/she is said to be a *trustee* of that directory.

This strategy for assigning user keys defines two different types of trustee assignments: explicit and inherited. Explicit trustee assignments are the rights explicitly granted to a user in a specific NetWare directory. Inherited trustee assignments are the rights which flow down from parent directories. See Figure 9.6 for an illustration of how explicit assignments in a parent directory become inherited rights for the children subdirectories. This is important, because NetWare 3.12 responds differently to explicit and inherited rights. We will learn how in a moment.

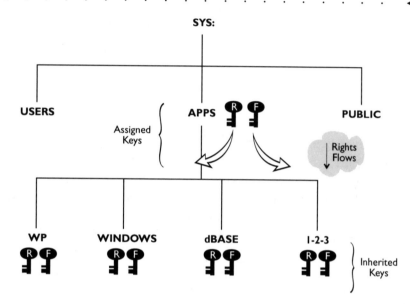

FIGURE 9.5

The Flow of Trustee Keys

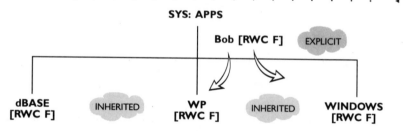

FIGURE 9.6

The Flow of Trustee Assignments from Parent to Child

Another interesting side effect of trustee assignments is that they can be both additive and non-additive. Let me explain.

Additive means that a user's trustee assignment in a given directory is the combination of his/her user assignment and the assignment of groups to which he/she belongs. Here's an example: Bob is granted the read and write privileges in the APPS\WP directory as a user. In addition, he is a member of the ADMIN group which is assigned file scan, access control, and modify. So Bob's actual trustee assignment in APPS\WP is read, write, file scan, access control, and modify.

Non-additive means that when a user is granted explicit assignments in a given directory, all other keys are taken away. That is, explicit assignments override inherited rights.

This strategy is particularly useful because it allows the LAN locksmith to assign keys not just to individuals but to large groups of individuals—all in one swoop. It might seem trivial at this point but as soon as you begin assigning trustee assignment and directory rights throughout the system, you'll find that it can become quite a monumental task. An intelligent approach to trustee assignments would involve group assignments for global directories—PUBLIC, APPS, DATA, and so on—and user assignments for user-specific directories—USERS\BOB. Also, keep track of how the rights flow. Use inherited rights for multiple subdirectories of global parents—APPS\WP, APPS\DBASE, and APPS\WINDOWS for example.

In order to create a trustee assignment for users and groups, NetWare needs three pieces of information:

- ▸ The name of the trustee

- ▸ The trustee rights to be assigned

- ▸ The path to the directory where the assignment begins—the parent directory name.

Trustee assignments can be granted in two ways: SYSCON or GRANT. Assignments can be made in the SYSCON utility using the User Information or Group Information screens. We will explore this utility in great depth later in Chapter 10—NetWare Utilities. Assignments can also be made using the GRANT command. We will explore the GRANT utility later in this chapter.

There are a few users and groups which automatically exist when you first take over the LAN. These system-generated users and groups include the GUEST user which has basically no rights, the SUPERVISOR user which has unlimited rights, and the group EVERYONE which has specialized default rights. These system-generated users and groups have default trustee assignments which are also created by the system. The following is a brief description of the default user/group trustee assignments.

EVERYONE includes all users who currently exist and all users who will eventually exist. Most global assignments are granted to EVERYONE because it provides an effective strategy for assigning sweeping trustee privileges. EVERYONE is assigned the read and file scan privileges to SYS:PUBLIC and the create right to SYS:MAIL.

SUPERVISOR grants all rights to everything. These rights cannot be removed and the SUPERVISOR account cannot be deleted.

GUEST provides the bare minimum NetWare security. GUEST assumes the trustee privileges of EVERYONE, plus all rights except access control to his/her own SYS:MAIL\userid directory.

Each user is given a default trustee assignment of create, erase, file scan, modify, read, and write to their own specific user SYS:MAIL\userid directory. Also, users are given the same rights to their own specific SYS:USERS\username directory.

QUOTE

Too many people are thinking of security instead of opportunity. They seem more afraid of life than death.

James F. Byrnes

Returning for a moment to the locksmith analogy: if the trustee assignments are keys, then the keys are only effective in directories which have locks. If there are no locks, the key can't work. The absence of a lock in the NetWare analogy does not mean you have total access. In fact, it means the opposite: you have *no* access. In order for a user to have effective rights in a given directory, the user must be granted both the key and the lock to that directory. Let's see how directory rights fit into this security puzzle.

INHERITED RIGHTS MASK

Directory locks, or directory rights, are *directory specific*—not *user/group specific*. Directory rights are assigned to directories. And they do not flow down. In addition, the existence of a directory lock is independent from the existence of a user key. If the locksmith decides to put a lock on a given directory, that lock is susceptible to any user key that matches. This level of NetWare security can get out of hand very quickly. See Figure 9.7 for an illustration of directory locks.

▶ · ◀

FIGURE 9.7

Directory Locks in
NetWare 3.12

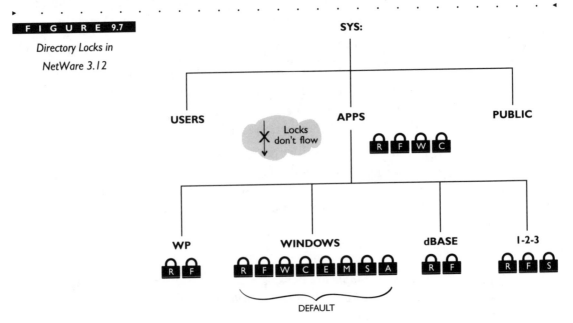

Fortunately the directory rights in NetWare 3.12, by default, include all locks on all directories. This means that every directory in the entire system has all locks available. This is useful because it eliminates the directory rights facility and makes NetWare 3.12 security dependent only on trustee assignments. This dramatically simplifies the locksmith's job. If the LAN house detective is specifically concerned about a given directory, he/she can remove the lock from that directory. Otherwise, he/she can leave it alone.

▶ · · · · · · · · · · ◀

> Directory locks, or directory rights, are *directory specific*—not *user/group specific.* Directory rights are assigned to directories. In addition, the existence of a directory lock is independent from the existence of a user key.

Directory locks are only necessary in sensitive directories—like applications, users, or the SYSTEM directory. NetWare 3.12 directory rights are called the

Inherited Rights Mask, or IRM. The IRM is based on the following assumption: "Here are the maximum rights you can inherit in this directory."

For example, if the SYS:APPS\WP subdirectory has sensitive application files that shouldn't be deleted, you can remove the erase lock from that directory (Figure 9.8). Without the erase lock, it doesn't matter who has access, or possession of the erase key. They will not be able to exercise the erase right in the SYS:APPS \WP directory. The user must be granted explicit rights in the SYS:APPS\WP subdirectory. Remember, the IRM only applies to INHERITED rights. Explicit rights override it.

The Inherited Rights Mask is only useful in very specialized circumstances and can become quite confusing in calculating effective rights. An effective way to implement NetWare security is to leave all directory locks in their default state and rely 100% on trustee assignments—user keys.

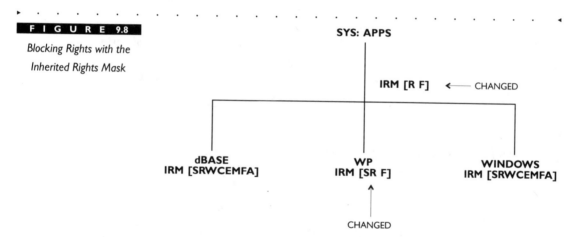

FIGURE 9.8

Blocking Rights with the Inherited Rights Mask

CALCULATING EFFECTIVE RIGHTS

So what does all this really mean? The bottom line is this: "A user's actual privileges in a given directory is calculated as the intersection of the user's trustee assignments and the directory's IRM. These are defined as effective rights."

If you look at it in a global sense, a user's trustee assignments and a directory's inherited rights mask are meaningless until you put them together and calculate what the user's real effective rights are. After all, the effective rights are the only rights which a user can exercise in a given directory.

Effective rights is defined as the combination of a privilege key and the existence of that privilege lock. Let's refer to Figure 9.9. Assume that all locks exist, by default, in the APPS\WP subdirectory. In addition, Bob has inherited the read, write, create, and file scan keys from SYS:APPS. Therefore, Bob's effective rights are read, write, create, and file scan. If, for some reason, the LAN locksmith decided that Bob shouldn't have the write or create privileges in APPS\WP, he/she could use one of two strategies: remove Bob's W and C keys, or remove the W and C locks. The first choice would affect Bob only, whereas the second choice would restrict the write and create privileges for ALL users in the LAN. The system manager opted for a more global strategy, and restricted the W and C locks with the IRM. Bob's effective rights become read and file scan. This also works for application subdirectories.

> A user's actual privileges in a given directory is calculated as the intersection of the user's trustee assignments and the directory's IRM. These are defined as effective rights.

The process of calculating effective rights is not always this straightforward. In many cases, effective rights are subject to NetWare 3.12 exceptions:

> ▸ The supervisory right is immune to any effect from the inherited rights mask. In addition, inheritance of the S privilege cannot be

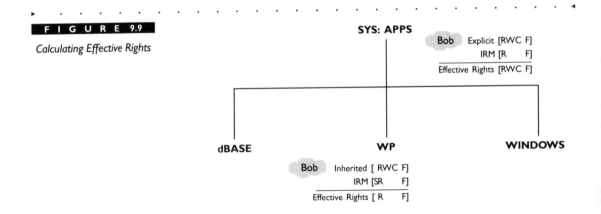

FIGURE 9.9

Calculating Effective Rights

revoked from subdirectories below the parent directory where it is explicitly granted. Explicit trustee assignments override the effects of IRM. IRM is only effective against inherited rights. Trustee assignments granted by users are affected separately from trustee assignments assigned by groups. For example, in a given directory, Bob's trustee assignments are the combination of his user rights and group rights. If his user rights are inherited and his group rights are explicit, his user rights will be affected by the IRM while his group rights will not.

▸ Inherited trustee assignments are actually the effective rights from the parent directory.

To illustrate the complexity of calculating effective rights, let's review the figures from this section. First, Figure 9.6, shows Bob's explicit assignments of Read, Write, Create and File Scan assigned to the APPS parent directory. These assignments become inherited rights in the three subdirectories of APPS: DBASE, WP and WINDOWS.

In Figure 9.8, the directory locks or inherited rights mask of APPS are R and F (which is different from the default of all rights). As the graphic shows, the inherited rights mask is not inherited by subdirectories of APPS. The DBASE and WINDOWS subdirectories maintain the default of all rights while the WP subdirectory has an IRM of S, R and F.

A simple calculation of Bob's effective rights is shown in Figure 9.9. Bob's explicit assignments of R, W, C, and F in the APPS directory combined with the IRM of R and F give him an effective rights of R, W, C and F. This is because explicit rights override the IRM.

In contrast, the WP subdirectory which has an IRM of S, R and F does, in fact, block rights from Bob's inherited trustee assignments. His inherited trustee assignments in WP are R, W, C and F and you can see that his effective rights are calculated as R and F in the WP subdirectory.

To further complicate the issue, Bob is a member of the WP group which is assigned a group explicit assignment of E and M in the WP subdirectory of APPS. Figure 9.10 shows that the IRM blocks W, C, E and M from Bob's inherited assignments but does not block the explicit assignment of E and M. Therefore, Bob's effective rights become R, E, M and F.

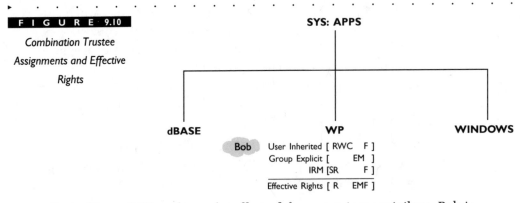

FIGURE 9.10

Combination Trustee Assignments and Effective Rights

Finally, in Figure 9.11 we learn the effect of the supervisory privilege. Bob is also a member of the ADMIN group which is assigned the explicit trustee assignment of supervisory at the APPS parent directory. This supervisory assignment overrides the IRM and gives Bob effective rights of S, R, W, C, E, M, F and A in the parent directory of APPS and all subdirectories below.

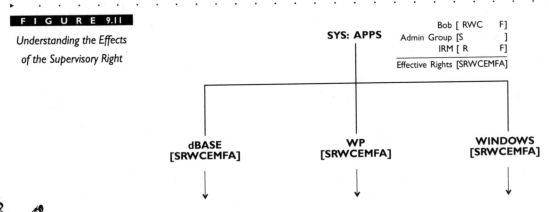

FIGURE 9.11

Understanding the Effects of the Supervisory Right

TIP

The supervisory right cannot be revoked by the IRM.

If all of this is confusing and a little overwhelming, don't be concerned. LAN security this extreme is rarely justified. Most NetWare LANs can easily afford a less complex security system—group trustee assignments and no IRMs. See Table 9.4 for a simple summary of calculating effective rights. In addition, there are some exercises at the end of the chapter which will help you to understand effective rights for certain cases. It is important, however, that you understand the full scope of effective rights ramifications. After all, LAN locksmithing is one of your most important responsibilities as the NetWare house detective. You must fill your NetWare utility belt with a strong understanding of how to implement trustee assignments (keys) and directory rights (locks).

TABLE 9.4

A Summrary of Calculating Effective Rights

"Is the Supervisory (S) right granted in this or the parent directory?"	YES ▸ Effective Rights = All Rights NO ▸ Move to next question
"Has the user been granted explicit rights in this directory?"	YES ▸ Effective Rights = Explicit Trustee Assignment NO ▸ Move to next question
"Is the IRM set to default (allowing all rights)?"	YES ▸ Effective Rights = Inherited Rights or Effective Rights of Parent Directory NO ▸ Effective Rights = Inherited Rights – IRM

QUOTE

A man, to carry on a successful business, must have imagination. He must see things as in a vision, a dream of the whole thing.

Charles M. Schwab

Attributes

The final layer of the NetWare security model is attribute security. Attributes are special assignments or properties which are assigned to individual directories or files. Attribute security overrides all previous trustee assignments and effective rights. Attribute security can be used to prevent deleting a file, copying a file, viewing a file, or writing to a specific file. Attributes are also used to control whether files can be shared, marking files as modified since the last backup, or protecting files from data corruption by ensuring that they are transactionally tracked.

> The final layer of the NetWare security model is attribute security. Attributes are special assignments or properties which are assigned to individual directories or files. Attribute security overrides all previous trustee assignments and effective rights.

Attribute security is analogous to the Park Place vault. When specific guests are concerned about particular belongings, they can go beyond existing door lock security and have them locked into a safety deposit box which can never be opened—except by the user or the house detective.

Attributes provide a very complex level of security which allows you, as the LAN locksmith, to specifically affect what users do with files once they access them. Attributes are global security elements which affect all users regardless of their rights. Attributes can be used to override all previous levels of security. For example, let's say you have the read, file scan, and write privileges to the SYS:APPS\WP directory. The system manager can still restrict you from writing to a specific file by assigning the READ-ONLY file attribute. This level of NetWare security overrides all previous security.

The true effective rights to a given file in a given directory is determined by the combination of trustee assignments, directory rights, *and* file attributes. NetWare 3.12 supports two different types of attributes: security and feature. Security attributes affect each users' security access (what they can do with specific files). Feature attributes affect how the system interacts with files (whether or not the files can be archived or whether or not transactional tracking has been activated). In this section, we will describe NetWare 3.12's different security and feature attributes and then move on to the many command line utilities which allow the LAN locksmith to implement NetWare's four-layered security model.

SECURITY ATTRIBUTES

Security attributes protect information at the file and directory level by controlling two kinds of file access: file sharing and file alteration. File access security controls not so much *who* has access to the files, but *what kind of access* they have. Once a user has been given the proper trustee assignments to a given directory, that user then has the ability to access any of the files within that system. Security attributes tell that person what he or she can do with the files once they have access. The file alteration attributes not only tell you what you can do with them but limit file access to execute only or hidden. If a file has the hidden attribute, users cannot see, use, delete or copy over the file.

> Security attributes protect information at the file and directory level by controlling two kinds of file access: file sharing and file alteration.

Here's a list of the filing sharing and filing alteration attributes. The asterisk (*) indicates attributes which affect both directories and files.

NS—Non-Sharable: Access is limited to one user at a time

S—Sharable: Simultaneous access by multiple users

RW—Read/Write: Users may see the file and alter its content

RO—Read/Only: Users may only see the file; no changes

X—Execute Only: Execution only; users cannot copy or delete

H (*)—Hidden: Users cannot see, use, delete, or copy over

D (*)—Delete Inhibit: Users cannot delete the file or directory

R (*)—Rename Inhibit: Users cannot rename the file or directory

C—Copy Inhibit: Macintosh users cannot copy the file

The non-sharable and sharable attributes limit access to files either one user at a time or provide simultaneous access by multiple users. When multiple users have access to a directory and the files are flagged sharable, you run into a problem where multiple users are accessing the same data and trying to save their version of the file. If the file is flagged sharable, the last person who saves the file will win the race. This is where the non-sharable attribute comes in handy. If you want only one person to access a file at a time, you can assign the non-sharable attribute to the file—the system will keep track of who gets to save and who doesn't.

The read/write and read/only attributes also affect file access, but in a different way. These attributes affect what the user can do once he/she has the file open. The read/write attribute allows users to see the file and alter its contents. Read/only means they can open the file but cannot make any changes. The read/only attribute is useful for application files which you want users to be able to access (but not change the contents of) in a shared environment.

The execute only attribute is extremely sensitive and provides the highest level of NetWare security. The execute only attribute can only be assigned by the supervisor to an executable file or .COM file. Execute only files cannot be copied or backed-up—just executed or deleted. Also, once the execute only attribute has been set, it cannot be removed. Hidden is reserved for special files or directories which cannot be seen, used, deleted, or copied over. The hidden attribute is for archived files or directories. In order to access a file that has this flag, the supervisor must remove the hidden attribute.

Inhibit attributes are new to NetWare 3.12 and they restrict user's access to delete, copy and rename files and directories. Delete inhibit attribute prevents users from erasing directories or files even if they have been granted the erase access right. If users have been granted the modify right, they can remove the delete inhibit attribute. Rename inhibit restricts users from renaming directories and files even if they have the modify right. If they have the modify right, they must remove the rename inhibit attribute before renaming the file or directory. The modify right thus eradicates the function of rename inhibit which then becomes a useless attribute.

Copy inhibit attribute restricts only the copy rights of users logged in from Macintosh workstations. If these users have been granted read and file scan rights, they still cannot copy the specific file. Macintosh users can, however, remove the copy inhibit attribute if they have been granted the modify access right. That completes our discussion of security attributes. Now let's take a closer look at NetWare 3.12's feature attributes.

FEATURE ATTRIBUTES

Feature attributes provide access to special NetWare functions or features including backup, indexing, and transactional tracking. The feature attributes are listed below.

T—Activate TTS: Identifies this file for transactional tracking

I—Indexed: Identifies this file for turbo FAT indexing

SY (*)—System: Identifies this file/dir as system-owned

A—Not yet Archived: This file has been modified since last backup

P (*)—Purge: This file/dir will be purged when it is deleted

Ra—Read Audit: Performs NO function

Wa—Write Audit: Performs NO function

The feature attribute that warrants the most attention is system (SY) which is assigned by the system. The system attribute identifies the file or directory as being system owned and can only be used for system functions. The NetWare bindery files, for example, are flagged as system so that nobody can delete, copy or write to that file. The archive (A) attribute is interesting. It allows the system to keep track of which files have been modified since the last backup. The indexed (I) allows turbo FAT indexing. The T attribute is assigned to files

> Feature attributes provide access to special NetWare functions or features including backup, indexing, and transactional tracking.

which need to be transactional tracked by NetWare's internal transactional tracking system. Finally, the Purge (P) attribute is assigned to files and directories which should be completely deleted and not available for salvage. This attribute is an effective strategy for wiping away any trace of sensitive files.

TIP

SALVAGE is a useful NetWare tool which allows users to recover files after they have been deleted. It is also a hacker's tool for covertly stealing valuable information. Keep in mind, that once a file has been deleted it is still available to any user with appropriate access rights (R, W, C, and F). The Purge attribute wipes away any trace of the file.

These files attributes, in combination, can create very effective security tools in controlling who has access to do what with very specialized NetWare files. The default attribute combination for all files on the system is non-sharable read/write (NSRW)—this has a tendency to be fine for most applications and most data files. There are specialized instances, however, where you can justify customizing these attributes. Here's a brief list:

▸ Stand alone applications which are not to be shared should be flagged non-sharable read/only.

▸ Data files which are shared but should not be written to simultaneously, should be non-sharable read/write.

▸ Data files which are part of larger multi-user applications that provide specialized record locking and other advanced features and can keep track of file sharing or data sharing on their own, should be flagged sharable read/write.

▸ Application files which are accessed by simultaneous users should be flagged sharable read/only.

▸ Large database files which are important to the system should be flagged with the transactional tracking attribute.

▸ Very sensitive archive files—records which are only accessed once a month, such as payroll records or general ledger—should be hidden.

▸ All system files owned by the system should be flagged system. This is an attribute assigned by the system, not by the user.

▸ Sensitive application files which cost lots of money and are shared on the system should be flagged executable so that the supervisor is not liable should piracy occur.

TIP

Recently, a very popular software manufacturer sued a company for piracy when it was found that many of the users had taken copies of the application home with them. The software manufacturer won the case based on *system manager negligence*. Evidently, the LAN administrator had not flagged the executable application file execute only. Doing so is not only a good idea, it can probably save your job.

That's it for our discussion of the NetWare security model and the concepts which combine to create the complex level of NetWare security which is necessary in this type of shared environment. We're going to have a chance to practice these concepts as we go along. You should feel much more comfortable with NetWare security once you get an opportunity to get your locksmith feet wet. In the remainder of this chapter, we will learn about many valuable LAN locksmith tools and begin to build the security portion of our NetWare utility belt. Don't let it weigh you down.

QUOTE

Few enterprises of great labor or hazard would be undertaken if we had not the power of magnifying the advantages we expect from them.

Samuel Johnson

Security Command Line Utilities

Have you ever watched a locksmith make a key? It's quite an amazing process involving a very complex set of specialized tools and fine precision on behalf of the locksmith. The process of building locks is also an amazing one to watch. The intricate machinery inside combines to create not only the strength of the unbreakable locks but their reliability as well. Imagine what's required to make the lock match only one key.

This process is analogous to what the LAN locksmith must go though in implementing access right keys and directory locks. The process of building keys and building locks is not easy—it's time-consuming, complex, and grand in scope. The LAN locksmith must be aware of the many ramifications of assigning NetWare security. NetWare security tools, or command line utilities, are broken into three different categories—login/password security, access rights, and file attributes. The command line utility tools with respect to access rights are further broken down into trustee assignment tools and directory rights tools.

> The process of building keys and building locks is not easy—it's time-consuming, complex, and grand in scope.

These tools are augmented by the menu utilities which we'll discuss in the next chapter. Most of the login/password security and access rights tools can be found in the SYSCON menu utility, while the directory rights and file attribute tools are implemented in FILER. The menu utilities provide a great deal more functionality and a much friendlier format than command line utilities—but the Command Line Utilities are fast and to the point.

LOGIN/PASSWORD SECURITY—CLUs

The first level of security tool is login/password security. As we mentioned above, login/password security deals with initial user access to the system. It incorporates a login name, a password, and specific login restrictions. There are five login/password security tools which can be used by the LAN locksmith to set passwords and get information about who is logged in. Also, these tools provide a list of servers and allow users to attach to other file servers. Login/password CLUs are not only used by the LAN locksmith, but can also be used by any user to gain general login information.

SETPASS

The first login/password security tool is SETPASS. SETPASS is a command line utility which allows users to set their own password. At any NetWare prompt, type **SETPASS** and the system takes a look at who you're logged in as and goes out and gathers information about your authorized password. If a password already exists, the system will then ask you to enter your password and then enter a new one if you pass the first test. The reason for this security is so that not just anybody could login as a different user and change their passwords.

ATTACH

ATTACH allows user and supervisor access to other file servers. Within NetWare, a user can login to only one file server because the key component of the login is the execution of what is called a login script. The login script contains many specific variables for that file server and loads these variables into workstation memory. While it is possible to attach to multiple servers, you can only login to one server because if you logged into multiple servers, each server's login script would overwrite the other. The main difference between logging in and ATTACH is the execution of the login script. If you login to a server, it does execute the login script. ATTACHing to a server performs exactly the same thing except it does not execute the login script.

Keep in mind, in order to map drives or to access directories on other file servers, you must be physically attached to those file servers through the ATTACH command. The ATTACH command will ask for a user name and a password and you will be subject to the same login restrictions as if you had logged in. The only difference is, again, that ATTACH does not execute the file server's host login script. The syntax of ATTACH is the same as LOGIN: **ATTACH server/username**. The system will then prompt you for a password if there is one. Keep in mind that NetWare only lets you attach up to 8 file servers at one time.

SLIST

Another login/password security tool which works in conjunction with ATTACH is SLIST. SLIST allows the user to view a list of all available servers that they are currently physically attached to. They can then decide whether or not they would like to logically login or attach to those multiple servers. In large complex internetworks, the SLIST command is extremely useful because it provides a simple list of all servers which are currently available. The SLIST does not tell you whether or not you have a valid login account on any of those servers;

it simply gives you a list of all servers which are physically recognized by your internal network interface card.

USERLIST

USERLIST does not provide a list of servers but instead, provides a list of users. USERLIST is useful because it will only give you a list of the users who are currently logged in to the file server you're specifying and displays login information about those users and what they're currently doing on the system. There are some command switches which work with USERLIST, specifically /a which lists network and node addresses and tells you where these users are logged in. Also, you can specify as a switch the specific user name and gain valuable information about specific users. For example, if you type **USERLIST GUEST**, the system will respond with relevant information specifically for the user GUEST. Again, that only works if the user is logged in.

TIP

One possible use of USERLIST for the network supervisor is to type USERLIST /a for all network and node addresses and then use that information to restrict users to logging in only from their authorized workstation. This type of login restriction is extremely useful for users who have a tendency to migrate through the LAN and login from multiple workstations.

WHOAMI can be a very useful tool for users who find it difficult to come to grips with their purpose in life. It also provides valuable information about users and their current network environment.

WHOAMI

The final login/password security tool is WHOAMI which at first sight has an existentialist tone to it. The WHOAMI utility displays information about user name, file servers you're currently attached to, your connection number and the date and time of your last login. WHOAMI can be a very useful tool for users who find it difficult to come to grips with their purpose in life and also provides valuable information about users and their current network environment.

There are four WHOAMI switches that allow you to focus in on only specific types of information.

WHOAMI /G lists the groups you belong to.

WHOAMI /E lists your security equivalences. Again it's possible for you to be equivalent to another user in your security.

WHOAMI /R lists the effective rights in the network directory structure.

WHOAMI /A lists the groups, security equivalences and your effective rights so /a would be for all.

WHOAMI, again, is useful only for the user who is logged in because it takes a look at who you're logged in as and grabs information about you from the Net-Ware bindery.

TRUSTEE ASSIGNMENTS—CLUs

The next set of NetWare security tools refer to access rights—specifically trustee assignments and directory rights. We'll break it out according to those two different categories so that we'll discuss the tools first which apply to trustee assignments and then move on to directory rights.

Trustee assignment security tools apply almost exclusively to the LAN locksmith. These tools are very powerful and can be abused quite easily. Keep in mind that in order to assign trustee rights or directory rights, the user in question must be granted the access control right to that particular directory. Again, the only person who has global access rights to assign all rights or privileges to the system is the supervisor or somebody who is granted what is called *supervisor equivalence*.

TLIST

The first trustee assignment tool is TLIST. The TLIST command line utility displays the trustees and their effective rights in a specific directory. TLIST is generally for information only and can only be applied to a specific directory or drive letter in the mapping environment. TLIST is useful because it provides information about all the different trustees which are assigned access to a directory and their effective rights in that directory. It calculates the combination of trustee assignments and directory rights to display the effective rights. This could be very useful for the LAN locksmith who is trying to figure what security should be granted to whom in a given directory. They can first type **TLIST** and get information about what already exists.

The next three trustee assignment tools apply to the actual implementation of trustee assignments.

GRANT

The GRANT CLU is the most effective for trustee assignment. GRANT allows this supervisor to assign or grant specific privileges to specific users within specific directories. The syntax for GRANT is **GRANT [rights] FOR [directory or drive name] TO [user or group]**. For example, if I wanted to assign the R and F rights to user DAVID in the SYS:APPS\WP directory, the syntax would be **GRANT R F FOR SYS:APPS\WP TO DAVID**.

The ALLOW security is related to GRANT. ALLOW uses the same syntax and performs the same general function as GRANT, but it manages the Inherited Rights Mask (IRM) instead of trustee assignments. Remember, the IRM is *directory-*specific, so any changes you make with ALLOW affect everyone. If you are concerned about using ALLOW, check your user's effective rights with LISTDIR or FILER.

REVOKE

REVOKE is exactly the opposite of GRANT. The REVOKE syntax is exactly the same as GRANT, but remember that instead of granting rights **TO** a user, you are revoking rights **FROM** a user. Again, REVOKE is very specific in its syntax and does not provide a simple way of viewing all trustee assignments for given users.

REMOVE

REMOVE is used not to revoke specific rights but to remove a trustee and all their rights from a directory. REMOVE is dramatic in its scope in that it removes all rights for a given trustee in a directory and completely removes that user as a trustee, Therefore, that user from this point has no rights whatsoever to that given directory.

TIP

Use GRANT if you want to grant any rights for a given user to a directory, REVOKE to revoke partial rights, or REMOVE to revoke all rights.

INHERITED RIGHTS MASK—CLUs

There are two security access right tools which work in conjunction with the trustee assignment CLUs: the directory rights command line utilities RIGHTS and LISTDIR. These CLUs are specifically used in directory situations and do not apply to users, groups or trustee assignments. RIGHTS and LISTDIR allow you to view not only the directory rights of a given directory, but the trustee as well as the effective rights of a given directory. All the previous access right tools allow you to view information about trustees. These particular tools allow you to view information about directories and effective rights.

QUOTE

Computers are useless. They can only give you answers.

Pablo Picasso

Again, RIGHTS and LISTDIR, which are the directory rights tools, are not only used by LAN administrators but by users as well. The RIGHTS and LISTDIR utilities provide valuable information not only for system administrators but for users as well. They provide access to information such as effective rights and directory formats.

RIGHTS

RIGHTS is similar to TLIST in that it displays effective rights in a specific directory but it does not display all the trustees of that directory. It only displays your trustee rights and effective rights for a particular directory. The RIGHTS command takes a look at who you're logged in as and reads the information from the bindery as to what your trustee assignments are. It takes a look at the directory rights for that given directory and then calculates your effective rights.

> The RIGHTS command analyzes your trustee assignment and the current directory's IRM. It uses this information to calculate effective rights.

LISTDIR

LISTDIR is a lot more effective at providing information about directory rights than the RIGHTS command. LISTDIR displays the effective and directory rights and all information pertaining to the directory including all subdirectories of a parent directory. There are six switches which work in conjunction with the LISTDIR command which are relevant here:

LISTDIR /e shows the effective rights you have in the directory and subdirectories of a parent directory.

LISTDIR /r shows the directory rights for this directory and all subdirectories of the directory.

LISTDIR /a shows the inherited rights mask, the effective rights and all of the other date and time information.

LISTDIR /d shows the date of creation of the directory and subdirectories.

LISTDIR /t shows the time of creation of the directory and subdirectories.

LISTDIR /s shows the subdirectory information in a tree structure.

Again, LISTDIR is a useful utility which provides subdirectory information and a directory tree structure including effective rights, maximum rights mask and creation date and time of directory structures.

ATTRIBUTES—CLUs

There are two file attribute command line utilities: FLAG and NCOPY. These two command line utilities are designed to provide the LAN locksmith with the ability to view and assign file attributes as well as copy files with their attributes attached. Let's take a closer look.

FLAG

The FLAG command line utility allows supervisors and users with the modify access right to view or change the file attributes of a given file. The syntax with the FLAG command is **FLAG [file name] [flags which are to be assigned to that file]**. The flag consists of the first few letters of the attribute name. If you refer to the earlier bullet list of the security in feature file attributes, the bolded letter corresponds to the flag switch which would be used with this command. One switch not included on that list is the N switch which allows the supervisor to assign the normal series of attributes to files. This returns the file attributes of that file to the default state—non-sharable read/write.

NCOPY

The NCOPY command is extremely useful for a variety of different reasons. It is included at this point because it does retain the file attributes for files which are copied using the NCOPY command. This is not the case for files which are copied using the DOS XCOPY command. NCOPY works exactly the same way as the XCOPY command. The syntax is similar. You type **NCOPY [file name]** to **[file name]**. Again, you can also leave out the "to" and insert a space between the two file names in which case NCOPY would assume a "to" in between.

KNOWLEDGE

Since NCOPY is a NetWare utility, it accesses the NetWare file allocation table and directory entry table with a great deal more efficiency than DOS COPY does. This means that it's a much safer and much faster means of copying files across the network. It's faster because NCOPY works within the memory of the file server. If files are copied from one directory on the file server to another, NCOPY does not copy them down to workstation memory and back up, thereby creating a load on the network. Instead, it copies the files in file server RAM, which is much faster and does not create a load on the network. It's safer because NCOPY utilizes the read-after-write verification fault tolerance feature which is incorporated into NetWare. This read-after-write verification is not performed if you use the DOS COPY command.

It's important also to note that the NCOPY command supports all wildcard characters that are also supported with the DOS COPY command.

That's it for NetWare security tools and for our discussion of NetWare 3.12 security. Keep in mind that the house detective's responsibilities are to make sure that all the user data is safe and that sufficient access and data integrity security has been implemented. The reasons for security are not only to ensure that unauthorized users are left out, but also to be efficient and transparent enough to not get in the way of normal operations for authorized users. Many times the house detective gets caught up in the whole complex security model of NetWare and creates such a secure system that it's impossible to use. Keep in mind that security and productivity must be balanced. NetWare's security functionality is extensive and supports a great many options. But keep in mind the KISS principle: Keep It Safe and Simple.

> Keep in mind that security and productivity must be balanced. NetWare's security functionality is extensive and supports a great many options.

In the next chapter we'll talk a little bit more about directory structures, drive mapping and security from the menu utilities standpoint. Throughout these first chapters we have discussed the command line utilities tools which have helped bolster your NetWare utility belt. Now let's spend some time discussing the menu utilities which can only augment or enhance your NetWare utility belt. Also, in the following chapters, we'll go into much more depth on network management and printing. The NetWare menu utilities will provide a springboard for that discussion.

Without any further ado, let's get on with shew!

T A B L E   9.1A

Understanding Special User Accounts

	S	SE	WGM	UAM	CO	PQO	PSO
Grant Supervisor Equivalence							
Automatically acquire all rights to dir/file							
Create other users/groups							
Manage all user accounts							
Manage special users accounts							
Manager/operator type can be user or group							
Create WGM							
Assign managed users as UAMs							
Delete any user account							
Delete special user accounts							
User supervisor functions of FCONSOLE							
Create print queues							
Manipulate print queues							
Delete print queue entries							
Create print servers							
Manage print server							

EXERCISE 9.2: CALCULATING EFFECTIVE RIGHTS

In this exercise, you will get some experience calculating effective rights for a variety of different scenarios. In each scenario, you will be given enough information to calculate the appropriate effective rights. The information is provided according to the following components: explicit user rights, inherited user rights, explicit group rights, IRM. Use the accompanying worksheets to follow the flow of rights and the effect of the inherited rights mask.

As the scenario study provides you with the appropriate information, put the right letter in the appropriate box (from the matrices in Figure 9.1A) and use the effective rights rules we learned in this chapter to calculate the appropriate privileges. You better put on your thinking cap for this one!

FIGURE 9.1A

Calculating Effective Rights

①

	S	R	W	C	E	M	F	A
EXPLICIT TRUSTEE RIGHTS								
IRM								
EFFECTIVE RIGHTS								

②

	S	R	W	C	E	M	F	A
EXPLICIT TRUSTEE RIGHTS								
IRM								
EFFECTIVE RIGHTS								

FIGURE 9.1A

Calculating Effective Rights (continued)

③

	S	R	W	C	E	M	F	A
EXPLICIT TRUSTEE RIGHTS								
INHERITED TRUSTEE RIGHTS								
IRM								
EFFECTIVE RIGHTS								

④

	S	R	W	C	E	M	F	A
EXPLICIT TRUSTEE RIGHTS								
INHERITED TRUSTEE RIGHTS								
IRM								
EFFECTIVE RIGHTS								

FIGURE 9.1A

Calculating Effective Rights (continued)

⑤

	S	R	W	C	E	M	F	A
EXPLICIT TRUSTEE RIGHTS								
INHERITED TRUSTEE RIGHTS								
IRM								
EFFECTIVE RIGHTS								

⑥

	S	R	W	C	E	M	F	A
EXPLICIT GROUP RIGHTS								
EXPLICIT USER RIGHTS								
COMBINED								
IRM								
EFFECTIVE RIGHTS (Public\DOS)								

FIGURE 9.1A

Calculating Effective Rights (continued)

⑦ S R W C E M F A

EXPLICIT GROUP RIGHTS
INHERITED USER RIGHTS
COMBINED
IRM
EFFECTIVE RIGHTS

1 · As a user, you are granted the R, W, C, and F privileges to a given directory. The inherited rights mask for the same directory is S, R, and F. Calculate the effective rights.

2 · In a different subdirectory, you are granted explicit user rights in reverse order; that is, the trustee assignments are S, R, and F and the inherited rights mask is R, W, C, and F. What are the effective rights in this subdirectory?

3 · This directory is a subdirectory of the one from scenario #2. The effective rights from scenario #2 then become the inherited rights for this scenario. In addition, the IRM is set to R, W, and M. What are your effective rights?

4 · As a user, you inherit the R, W, E, and M privileges from the parent directory. In addition, the IRM has been set to W, C, M, and A. What are your effective rights?

_____

_____

5 · As a member of the group ADMIN, you inherit the R, W, C, M, and F rights from the directory above. The IRM, though, blocks these rights and only allows the S, E, and A. What are your effective rights?

_____

_____

6 · As a member of the group EVERYONE, you are explicitly granted the R and F rights to the PUBLIC subdirectory. In addition, as a user, you are explicitly granted the additional rights of W, C, and E. What are your combined explicit assignments? The system manager has decided that he or she would like to restrict the W, E, and M rights in the PUBLIC/DOS subdirectory with an inherited rights mask of S, C, F, A. What are your effective rights in the PUBLIC/DOS subdirectory?

_____

_____

7 · As a member of the group ACCT, you are granted the explicit rights of R and F to the APPS/ACCT subdirectory. In addition, as a user, you inherit the rights W, C, M, and A from the APPS parent directory. What are your combined rights in APPS\ACCT? In addition, the system manager has set the IRM for APPS\ACCT to S, C, E, and A. What are your effective rights in APPS\ACCT?

_____

_____

CASE STUDY III: ASSIGNING SECURITY TO SNOUZER, INC.

Assigning NetWare security to a complex LAN design can be your most challenging task as the Snouzer, Inc. system manager. As we learned from this chapter, NetWare security relies on a multilayered model. This multilayered model calls for login password security, login restrictions, access rights, and attribute security. In addition, NetWare provides a facility for creating special user accounts and distributed system managers. In this case study, we will build on the existing Snouzer, Inc. directory structure and design appropriate security at each of the different layers of the NetWare security model. In addition, we will explore the use of work group managers, user account managers and supervisor equivalents as distributed system managers.

Let's take a look at Snouzer, Inc.'s security needs. Being in the doggy fashion business, Snouzer, Inc.'s most valuable assets are their ideas. These ideas are stored in designs on the NetWare shared disk. Snouzer, Inc. is extremely sensitive to security—both inside and outside the company. Sophy has asked you to create a distributed security management force which follows the responsibilities of the organizational chart. Frank should be a work group manager over all the users in design and production. In addition, Hal should be a user account manager over his two special designers, Rene and Bob. The Snouzer, Inc. managers are organized into three NetWare groups: Admin, Design, and Production. Here is a list of the groups and their corresponding users:

ADMIN: Sophy, Frank, Mary

DESIGN: Hal, Rene, Bob

PRODUCTION: George, Mary, Frank

These three functional groups allow you to effectively manage Snouzer, Inc's security without having to maintain it individually. The Snouzer, Inc. managers are particularly concerned about outside competition gaining access to their valuable designs. They have heard of a new hacker program that can access a five-character password in less than 30 minutes. For this reason, they would like you to require passwords for all users in excess of five characters. In addition, they would like you to have each user change their password to something unique every three months. Frank is particularly concerned about the people within his work group, and would like a facility to be able to track their login and logouts. Hal is concerned about his special designers and their use of shared disk space. Rene and Bob have been very liberal and somewhat lazy about their use of directory space for the designs—they haven't been cleaning up their old ones. For that reason, Hal would like you to limit their disk space to 50MB each.

Sophy's a little concerned about Mary because she thinks that Mary works entirely too hard. Mary has a tendency to stay around until 9:00 or 10:00 at night and Sophy is concerned about burn-out. For this reason, she would like you to restrict Mary—log her out at 7:00 each evening, and not allow her to login until 8:00 a.m. the next morning. Sophy would also like you to make sure that nobody can log into the network on the weekends because Snouzer's seven managers—who like to work hard and play hard—never work on the weekends.

That completes the requirements for general Snouzer, Inc. restrictions. Now let's take a look at access rights security. Snouzer, Inc. believes in empowering their employees. For that reason, they don't feel that it's necessary to restrict rights in the PUBLIC subdirectory. They would, however, like you to refrain from using the SAM access rights in any directories unless it is absolutely necessary. Incidentally, the SAM access rights are user rights which are rarely assigned. They are:

- **S** for supervisory
- **A** for access control
- **M** for modify

All users should have all rights except SAM to the shared data subdirectory as well. In keeping with their trend to empower the people, Snouzer, Inc. believes in granting all user rights to each user in his or her own subdirectory. The same goes for groups and group directories.

In addition, there are a few special circumstances within the user and group subdirectories. Hal and George, who are the non-Admin vice presidents, need a drop box to the ADMIN subdirectory where they can drop reports and employee evaluations. A drop box is a subdirectory where users can store files but not read, retrieve, or delete them. Production also needs a drop box to DESIGN so they can inform the designers of deadlines and production schedules. Bob and Rene need to see each other's stuff but should not have access to delete, erase, or write any files within the other user's subdirectory. Mary and Sophy have the same relationship.

The application security is extremely important to Snouzer, Inc. They feel very strongly about the type of data which is stored here and they're worried about non-authorized users having access to applications. For this reason, all users on the LAN are given read and file scan rights to the APPS subdirectory and all applications within it. The DESIGN group has all rights except supervisory and access control to the design application. All other users have only read and file scan. The production group has all rights to the accounting program except they cannot rename files, change their rights, or do anything supervisory there. In addition, the production group has rights to the 123 subdirectory except that they cannot erase any files, rename files, change their access rights, or have supervisory access there.

Finally, nobody should be allowed to erase any files from the GL data subdirectory under APPS and the A/P subdirectory under APPS except Admin. Admin should have all rights to all applications and data subdirectories within applications. Once you have established the access right security, you should augment it with attribute security making all application data files sharable and WP and DBASE applications sharable-read only.

That completes the NetWare security requirements of Snouzer, Inc. Use the user security and directory security worksheets from Appendix C to create an effective and efficient Snouzer, Inc. security design. Once you have completed this design, you can move onto implementing it through NetWare's built-in security management tools:

SYSCON—which allows system managers to assign login password security, login restrictions and user access rights

FILER—which provides the facility for implementing inherited rights mask and attribute level security

In combination, SYSCON and FILER should provide you with all the functionality you need to implement Snouzer, Inc.'s NetWare security model. Let's take a closer look at these two utilities and which screens are used to implement the different layers of NetWare security.

SYSCON

The SYSCON menu utility allows system managers to implement login/password security, login restrictions, and the first half of access rights. In addition, SYSCON provides menus for assigning special user accounts. Before we begin using SYSCON to implement Snouzer, Inc. security, we need to create the Snouzer, Inc. users and groups.

I · To create Snouzer, Inc. users, enter the SYSCON utility.

    A · Type **SYSCON** and press Enter.

    B · From the available topics menu, choose User Information and press Enter. The user names window will appear.

    C · At the user name window, press Insert and the user name input box appears.

    D · Type in **SOPHY** and press Enter. The system will ask for a path to create the user's home directory.

    E · Backspace to the SYS: and type **USERS\SOPHY** and press Enter. The system will ask you to verify the creation of a new directory.

    F · Highlight YES and press Enter.

Sophy has now been created. In order to customize Sophy's user account, you can press Enter at the user's name window and the user information window appears. This screen provides 16 different options for customizing NetWare user accounts. We will use this screen later for implementing certain aspects of Snouzer, Inc. security model. For now, press Escape and return to the user name window. Now create the other Snouzer, Inc. managers.

2 · To create Snouzer, Inc.'s three groups, press Escape to return to the available topics menu.

    A · Choose Group Information and press Enter. The Group Names box appears. This is exactly the same type of format as the user name box.

    B · Press Insert and the New Group Name input box appears.

    C · Type **ADMIN** and press Enter. The group name ADMIN has now been created.

Using the same procedure, create the other two groups: PROD and DESIGN. Once the Snouzer, Inc. users have been created, we can use these new user accounts to implement the four different aspects of Snouzer, Inc. security. Let's begin with assigning special user accounts.

SPECIAL USER ACCOUNTS

I · Sophy has decided that she does not want to use the supervisor account and wants to be supervisor equivalent. To assign supervisor equivalence to Sophy, highlight User Information from the available topics menu and press Enter.

    A · Highlight Sophy from the user name window and press Enter. You'll get Sophy's user information box.

    B · Move down to Security Equivalences and press Enter. The security equivalences list will appear with the group EVERYONE. These are all the users and groups which Sophy is equivalent to. By default, every user has the security equivalence to the group EVERYONE.

    C · Press Insert for a list of other users and groups.

    D · Highlight Supervisor and press Enter. At this point, Sophy has been made security equivalent to the user supervisor. She can now perform all operations and have access to all security rights that the user supervisor has.

E · Press Escape to return to Sophy's user information screen.

2 · Frank needs to be a workgroup manager. In order to create a workgroup manager, you must be supervisor or supervisor equivalent. Press Escape to move to the available topics window.

    A · Once there, highlight Supervisor Options and press Enter. The final choice under Supervisor Options is Workgroup Managers.

    B · Highlight Work Group Managers and press Enter. A list of workgroup managers will appear. If the list is blank, don't be concerned—it means there are no work group managers.

    C · Press Insert and other users and groups will appear.

    D · To make Frank a work group manager, highlight the FRANK user and press Enter. Frank's name will now appear under the work group manager's list. This is only part one. In order to assign users and groups to Frank as work group managers, you must go to Frank's user information menu.

    E · Press Escape twice to move to available topics.

    F · Highlight user information and press Enter.

    G · Highlight FRANK and press Enter. Frank's user information window will appear.

    H · Highlight Managed Users and Groups and press Enter. This is a list of all the users and groups which Frank has been made a work group manager over. Currently the list is empty.

    I · Press Insert and other users and groups will appear.

    J · Use F5 to highlight both the DESIGN group and the PROD group.

    K · Once they are highlighted, press Enter. The DESIGN and PROD groups now appear under Managed Users and Groups. This means Frank has been made a work group manager over these two groups.

3 · In order to make Hal a user account manager over Rene and Bob, we must move to Hal's user information window.

    A · Press Escape a few times to exit to the user names window and highlight HAL and press Enter.

    B · At Hal's user information window, perform the same operation as you did with Frank except this time adding Rene and Bob to Managed Users and Groups for Hal. Since we did not insert Hal as a work group manager under Supervisor Options, Hal by default becomes a user account manager over these users.

Refer to the text in this chapter for a description of the difference between work group managers and user account managers.

LOGIN/PASSWORD

The next layer of Snouzer, Inc. security model is login/password security. In this particular section, Snouzer, Inc. is concerned about password length, frequency of changing the passwords and their uniqueness.

I · To change the login/password restrictions for all users in the system, you must have set these login restrictions before you created the users. Remember, the default account balance/restriction option in Supervisor Options only applies to users who are created beyond this point. Since we have already created the users, we are stuck—or so it seems. Earlier in the chapter we discussed a little trick—F5 lets you highlight specific users and change only their configurations.

    A · In order to do this, use F5 to highlight all users from the user name window and press Enter. A Set User Information box appears with the following four choices:

> ▸ Account Balance
> ▸ Account Restrictions
> ▸ Station Restrictions
> ▸ Time Restrictions

B · To change the login/password security for these users, highlight Account Restrictions and press Enter. The Set Marked Users Account Restrictions screen appears.

C · Change the appropriate settings and press Escape. Once you press Escape, the system will ask you if you want to change all marked users restrictions to these settings.

D · Highlight YES and press Enter.

Don't you just love it when a plan comes together?

LOGIN RESTRICTIONS

Login restrictions are the gates which separate the Snouzer lobby and its main office. These restrictions allow the system manager to apply a final layer of security blocking users from accessing the system at specific times or using certain amounts of disk space. Within this area of security, Snouzer, Inc. has the requirements of limiting disk space for Rene and Bob, limiting time restrictions for Mary, no weekends for anybody and Frank would like to track his people. Limit disk space can be performed under the user information options for Rene and Bob. The same with Mary's time restrictions. In order for Frank to track his people's login and logouts, he must activate NetWare accounting. This is performed by highlighting Accounting from the available topics menu and pressing Enter. Finally, in order to restrict all users from not logging in from the weekend, you must highlight Time Restrictions from the Set User Information option we talked about above.

ACCESS RIGHTS

Access rights are broken into two parts:

▸ User Trustee Assignments

▸ Directory Inherited Rights Mask

User trustee assignments are granted within the User Information and Group Information menus of SYSCON. The inherited rights mask is assigned within the subdirectory information option of FILER. In this exercise, we will describe the steps for assigning one set of rights and then you can use this model to continue the application of Snouzer, Inc. access requirements. Let's begin by assigning the group EVERYONE all rights to the shared data subdirectory.

1 · In order to assign the group EVERYONE as a trustee of the shared data subdirectory, you must highlight Group Information from the available topics menu. Press Enter.

A · At the Group Names menu, choose EVERYONE and press Enter. The Group Information Box appears.

B · One of the choices in the Group Information Box is Trustee Directory Assignments. Press Enter. The Trustee Directory Assignment list appears. This list shows all directories to which the EVERYONE group is a trustee. It also shows all the rights. On the left side is a list of all directories to whom the group EVERYONE is a trustee and on the right side all the rights.

C · To add a directory, press Insert and the system responds with Directory In Which Trustee Should Be Added.

D · Type **SYS:DATA** and press Enter. The system will automatically add the DATA directory to the trustee directory assignments list. By default, all new directories are assigned read and file scan rights.

E · In order to add more rights, highlight DATA and press Enter. The trustee rights granted list appears with File Scan and Read.

F · Press Insert and the system responds with Trustee Rights Not Granted.

G · In order to grant all rights, use F5 to mark Access control, Create, Erase, Modify, Supervisory and Write and Press Enter. All the rights are now moved over to the Trustee Rights Granted window.

H · Press Escape and notice that all rights are added to the rights list for the DATA subdirectory.

I · Press Escape three more times to return to the available topics window.

Use this same procedure to assign your user- and group-specific trustee assignments from the appropriate worksheets in Appendix D.

2 · In order to assign the inherited rights mask for the GL subdirectory, we will use the FILER utility. Escape SYSCON and return to the PUBLIC subdirectory and type FILER.

FILER

Filer provides a facility for managing NetWare directories, files and volumes. In this exercise, we will use FILER to manage the inherited rights mask and attribute levels of Snouzer, Inc. security model.

I · At the available topics menu of FILER, highlight Select Current Directory and press Enter. The system will respond with the current directory path menu. At this point we will input the directory we are customizing.

A · Backspace over PUBLIC and type **APPS\ACCT\GL**. NetWare will move you back to the available topics menu. Notice that in the header of the FILER utility, the default directory has now been moved to APPS\ACCT\GL.

B · To view current information about this directory, highlight Current Directory Information and press Enter. Among many other choices, the system responds with the inherited rights mask. By default, the inherited rights mask for all new subdirectories is *all rights*.

C · Highlight Inherited Rights Mask and press Enter. The system will respond with a list of available inherited rights.

D · Highlight the Erase Directory File right and press Delete. The system will respond with a question: Would you like to revoke the right?

E · Highlight YES and press Enter. Now the Erase right has been removed as an option in this subdirectory.

F · Press Escape and notice that the inherited rights mask now includes all rights except the Erase privilege.

G · Perform the same procedure to restrict the Erase right from the inherited rights mask of the AP subdirectory of Accounting.

3 · The next level of FILER functionality is attribute security. In attribute security, we will modify the attributes of WP and DBASE subdirectories of APPS.

A · To move to the WP subdirectory of the current directory, choose Select Current Directory from the available topics menu and press Enter.

B · Backspace over ACCT\GL and input **APPS\WP**. Notice that the current subdirectory changes in the FILER available topics menu. Now that we have moved to the APPS\WP subdirectory, we can alter its attribute security. At this point, we are not altering the directory information, we are altering the information of the files underneath.

C · In order to access information about files in a particular directory, highlight directory contents from available topics and press Enter. The system will respond with a directory contents window including all files in the subdirectory. In addition, it displays double dot (..) which is the parent directory and backslash (\) which is the root directory.

D · Use F5 to mark all the files and press Enter. The multiple operations window appears. One of the choices in this window is Set Attributes.

E · Highlight Set Attributes and press Enter. The file attributes window appears and it should be empty, which means all these files have been set to the default Sharable-Read/Write attribute. Press Insert to get a list of available attributes.

F · From the other file attributes option, highlight Sharable and Read Only. Press Enter. The system will add Sharable, Read Only, Delete Inhibit, and Rename Inhibit to the file attributes screen. Rename Inhibit and Delete Inhibit are implied with the Read Only attribute because Read Only files cannot be renamed or deleted.

G · Press Escape and the system asks you if you would like to set marked files to the specified attribute. Highlight YES and press Enter.

Now you have completed the attribute level of security for the Snouzer, Inc. model. Use the same procedure to apply sharable read only attributes to the DBASE subdirectory.

That's it for the implementation of Snouzer, Inc.'s security model. In this exercise, we have explored the multiple layers of NetWare security and used SYSCON and FILER to implement special user accounts, login password security, login restrictions, access rights, and attribute security. Once the security model has been created and put into place, the system manager must focus on general network management. As far as Snouzer, Inc. is concerned, we will create and implement login scripts and user interface. Let's begin with login scripts.

NetWare 3.12 Utilities

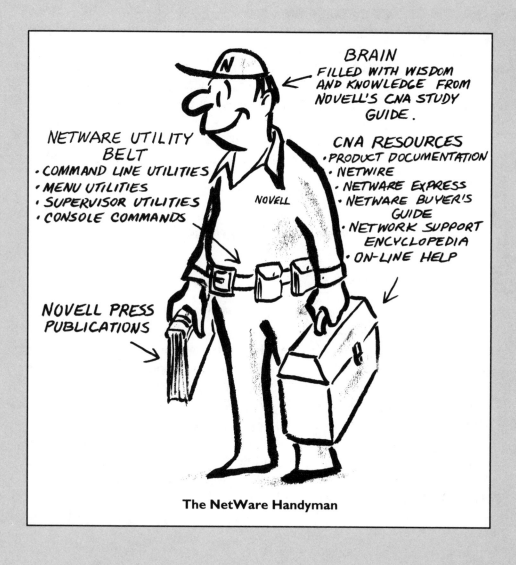

The NetWare Handyman

Everybody loves a handyman. The handyman is capable of feats beyond those of mere mortals. He is faster than a speeding torque wrench, able to leap tall ladders in a single bound. He will come to the rescue whenever you are in trouble. He's also the unheralded hero of our Park Place Hotel. As the NetWare system manager, you are the handyman of the LAN. It is your responsibility to maintain existing LAN hardware and fine-tune network software. The NetWare handyman comes to the rescue of all users in their most dire need: fixing printers, replacing NICs, adjusting monitors, and performing the impossible.

> A handyman is capable of feats beyond those of mere mortals. As the NetWare system manager, you are the handyman of the LAN.

The NetWare handyman relies on a variety of CNA resources, including product documentation, NetWire, NetWare Express, the NetWare Buyer's Guide, Network Support Encyclopedia, on-line help and valuable Novell Press publications. But by far the most important handyman tool is the NetWare utility belt—Batman's toolbox.

QUOTE

What the world calls originality is only an unaccustomed method of tickling it.

George Bernard Shaw

The NetWare utility belt is comprised of a variety of different tools—command line utilities (CLUs), menu utilities, supervisor utilities, and console commands. Command line utilities are productive management tools which provide NetWare customization from the workstation command line. CLUs are the mainstay of the NetWare arsenal. These utilities are primarily designed for system managers, but there are a few tools which appeal to NetWare users as well. Menu utilities provide the same functionality as CLUs, but with a friendly menu interface. In addition, some menu utilities provide extended functionality beyond what the CLUs offer. Menu utilities are more popular than CLUs and comprise 85% of most system manager utility belts. Supervisor utilities are specialized CLUs and menu tools which have been designed for supervisor use only.

Most supervisor utility tools come equipped with a warning label—"WARNING: This tool contains explicit supervisor functionality. Keep out of the reach of children and NetWare users." Finally, console commands are NetWare tools which provide NetWare customization at the file server. Console commands are advanced utilities and must be executed at the file server console. These tools can be very hazardous if not handled correctly.

In the Park Place Hotel, many of the guests and staff don't recognize the contributions of the handyman. The handyman is always there when you need him, but never around to be thanked. Without the hotel handyman, all of the luxurious furniture and equipment would break down and melt into a useless heap. The handyman performs emergency repairs when the ice machine goes down. Besides fixing elevators when they get stuck, adjusting air-conditioning in the guests' rooms, and fixing the shower nozzle when the water doesn't come out just right, the handyman is also responsible for fine-tuning hotel electrical systems, phone systems and plumbing. In many cases, a skilled handyman can be the difference between a hotel's success and its failure. So, never underestimate the value of the hotel handyman.

In the same way, a good NetWare utility belt can be the difference between success and failure for the NetWare handyman. In Chapters 1 and 2, we started our NetWare utility belt with a holster of microcomputer DOS fundamentals and NetWare basics. In this chapter, we will fill the holster with valuable NetWare tools: menu utilities, supervisor utilities, and console commands. In addition, we will examine practical applications for these tools and practice using them with lab exercises and NetWare simulations. Let's begin with NetWare menu utilities.

KNOWLEDGE

In this chapter, you may have noticed that the command line utilities are missing. Since there are so many CLUs and they represent the mainstay of your utility belt, we have opted to cover them in detail throughout the chapters as they apply to CNA objectives. This is a much more effective strategy for learning the many CLUs and gaining practical experience using them in a "real world" environment.

Menu Utilities

Menu utilities are the most productive and friendly of the NetWare system management tools. NetWare menu utilities provide all of the same functionality as command line utilities plus some additional features all wrapped up in a friendly user interface. NetWare provides a variety of menu utilities which perform a variety of different tasks. These tools can be broken down into two basic categories: user menus and supervisor menus. Some user menus double as supervisor menus. This allows supervisors to perform additional administrative tasks—including user creation, directory maintenance, security, and login/password configurations.

> Menu utilities are the most productive and friendly of the NetWare system management tools.

In this section, we will discuss the two most popular NetWare menu utilities: SYSCON and FILER. These utilities are for users and system managers. The next section focuses on supervisor-only menu utilities. But before we begin our discussion of NetWare's two most popular menus, let's take a moment to discuss the look-and-feel of NetWare menu utilities.

LOOK-AND-FEEL

NetWare menu utilities are a progression of screens which provide additive levels in an easy-to-use format. Each menu screen consists of a border—either single-lined or double-lined. The single-lined border denotes an information only box which means that the contents of this box cannot be edited—it is for viewing only. A double-lined border denotes an editable box which contains information that can either be viewed or edited. All NetWare menu utilities are displayed in a blue and gold color format which is the default color palette.

TIP

The color palette for NetWare's menu utilities are configurable using the COLORPAL menu utility. The default menu colors are defined as Palette 0.

Learning to use a menu is not something I think you'll have a lot of trouble with. These menus are designed to be simple, straightforward, and provide basic system management facilities—all within an easy-to-use framework. Most of the menu functions are self explanatory, but there are a few keys which you should be aware of to help you navigate through NetWare's menu utilities:

RETURN key or ENTER moves you to the next level

ESCAPE key returns to the previous level

INSERT adds an entry in a particular double-bordered box

DELETE will remove an entry

F1 provides help

F1 F1 (press F1 two times) identifies the function keys which we are talking about now

The last three function keys are NetWare-specific keys which provide specialized functionality solely within NetWare menu utilities.

F3 modifies the highlighted choice and allows you, for example, to rename users and directories as well as modify security rights

F5 marks multiple options. It is a toggle switch. If you press F5 again, it is de-highlighted. Marking multiple options with F5 is particularly useful in environments where you are configuring multiple options

Alt-F10 quickly exits a NetWare menu utility without saving. Alt-F10 is very useful if you want to jump out of a menu from within multiple nested screens without saving any of the work you've accomplished.

KNOWLEDGE

When you come across a list screen with a double border, NetWare allows you to highlight particular options within that list and continue. If the double-bordered list is empty, it is a perfect opportunity for using the INSERT key—to insert a choice into the list. This is particularly evident when assigning rights and user names.

In addition to the main menu utility interface, the NetWare 3.12 includes two graphical-based utilities: NetWare User Tools and Electro Text. These two utilities provide basic user and documentation functionality in an easy-to-use MS Windows interface. See Figure 10.1.

NetWare menu utility navigation is a little quirky at first but you'll soon get the hang of it and find yourself buzzing through windows like a pro. Now we will move onto the two most popular NetWare menu utilities in a little more detail: SYSCON and FILER. Let's start with SYSCON which is the most popular administrative utility within NetWare.

▶ · ◀

F I G U R E   10.1

The ElectroText Interface

And the manuals are still here.

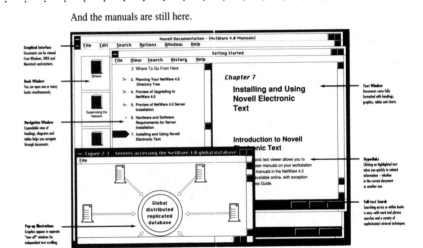

SYSCON

SYSCON is the mother of all utilities. SYSCON stands for SYStem CONfiguration and it is used for most of the system management tasks. It is used to configure trustees, trustee assignments, account restrictions, login restrictions, accounting, login scripts, users and group information. During our discussion of menu utilities, we will focus on both the command line utilities

▶ · · · · · · · · · · · · · · ◀

SYSCON is the mother of all utilities. SYSCON stands for SYStem CONfiguration and it is used for most of the system management tasks.

which are integrated into the menu utility and the extended functionality that the menu utility provides.

The SYSCON menu and its submenus can be viewed in Figure 10.2. Notice in the figure, the standard NetWare menu utility format of having the name of the menu utility across the top header with the date and time. The next line provides

F I G U R E 10.2

The SYSCON Menu Utility

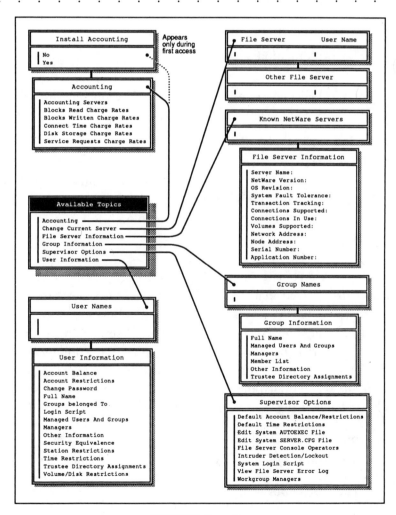

SYSCON Overview

user information and the filer server that you are currently attached to. The available topics menu in SYSCON contains six choices:

- ▶ Accounting

- ▶ Change Current Server

- ▶ File Server Information

- ▶ Group Information

- ▶ Supervisor Options

- ▶ User Information

Below is a detailed description of these six SYSCON options. Study them carefully, because SYSCON will be your friend.

General Functions

Of the six available topic choices in SYSCON, three of them fall into the category of general functions. These three include Accounting, Change Current Server and File Server Information. Let's explore these general SYSCON functions in more detail.

Accounting The Accounting submenu of SYSCON is where the system manager installs and manages NetWare accounting. NetWare accounting is a feature which allows system managers to monitor and charge customers for access to specific file server resources. Another strategy for using NetWare accounting is to track network usage and resource utilization by charging specific prices for particular network resources such as disk blocks read, disk blocks written, file server attach time and processor utilization. Accounting, including an elaborate reporting system, is built into NetWare 3.12.

QUOTE

Nine-tenths of wisdom consists in being wise in time.

Theodore Roosevelt

To install accounting, simply highlight the accounting option from the available topics menu in SYSCON and press Enter. The system will respond with a prompt asking **Would like to install accounting?** Highlight Yes and it will install accounting on the default server. It is possible to install accounting on multiple servers from this SYSCON menu by inserting multiple file servers in the Accounting Servers window.

The accounting submenu provides six choices: Accounting Servers and the five different resource accounting features (blocks read, blocks written, connect time, disk storage, and service requests). Network accounting supports two other command line utilities which provide reporting functionality: ATOTAL (which provides a summary of weekly accounting charges) and PAUDIT (which provides a detailed tracking of all user logins, logouts and accounting charges). These utilities rely on two NetWare system files for accounting data: NET$ACCT.DAT and NET$REC.DAT. NET$ACCT.DAT is a binary file in the SYS:SYSTEM directory which stores all user login and logout activity. NET$REC.DAT provides a translation table for the PAUDIT reporting utility.

Change Current Server   Change Current Server simply allows the user or the system administrator to change the server upon which they are using SYSCON. This changes the default server from the current server to any one which is currently attached to the internetwork. Change Current Server displays a menu with the current default file servers on the left-hand side, and the user names that are used to login on the right-hand side. To add a server to this list, attach to another server, or change current servers, press the INSERT key at the Change Current Server menu screen. The system responds with a list of available servers. Highlight a server from the Other File Server screen and the system will ask for a user name and password. Keep in mind you are attaching to another file server so it is important that you follow the same login security levels as you would if you were logging in.

KNOWLEDGE

The only difference between attaching and logging in is that when you attach, you do not execute the login scripts. NetWare 3.12 allows you to attach to 8 file servers at one time.

File Server Information   The File Server Information screen is a single-bordered box which displays relevant details about the current default server. These details include server name, NetWare version, operating system revision, level of system fault tolerance, network address, serial number, and the number of connections supported and in use.

TIP

A connection is not a user but a physical workstation connection to the server. A connection is also a print server, or a router, or any other device which requires communication with the NetWare file server. If, for example, you buy a 100-user version of NetWare, you are actually buying 100 connections for this particular operating system server. Since you are buying a 100-connection license and the print servers and routers cut into these connections, NetWare supports 16 additional connections beyond the 100 to support print servers and routers. If you have more than 16 print servers and routers, you will start to lose user connections. The moral of the story is a 100-connection version of NetWare will support 116 connections but only 100 user connections because NetWare does discern between user connections and print server and router connections.

The Supervisor Options Menu in SYS-CON is the most productive system administration facility. The supervisor will spend most of his/her time here.

Supervisor Options

The next option in the available topics menu of SYSCON is Supervisor Options. This is where the system manager spends most of his/her time. It is the submenu which provides the most system administrative functionality. In NetWare 3.12, the Supervisor Options menu provides eight different choices which can only be accessed by a Supervisor or supervisor equivalent:

Default Account Balance Restrictions allows the system manager to set global default accounting balances and login restrictions for users who are created beyond this point

Default Time Restrictions allows the same functionality for time restrictions

Edit the System AUTOEXEC File provides the functionality of editing the AUTOEXEC.NCF file server boot file from within SYSCON. This is particularly useful because the only other option would be to access the file server console itself

File Server Console Operators creates console operators who can access the FCONSOLE utility

Intruder Detection/Lockout activates this login tracking feature and allows the system manager to set global parameters

System Login Script is the most valuable login script. It executes for all users. By the way, the Supervisor is the only person who can edit the system login script

View File Server Error Log gives the Supervisor the ability to access all system errors which have occurred since the error log was last cleared

Workgroup Managers assigns workgroup manager status to distributed supervisors.

We'll explore these choices in greater depth in Chapter 11—Network Management. The NetWare system manager will be much better off if he/she can spend most of his/her time in the Supervisor Options screen—and stay away from customizing user and group information.

User/Group Information

The User Information option in SYSCON is the largest and most useful of the SYSCON submenus. In NetWare 3.12, the User Information submenu provides 14 different options including full name, password, login script, security equivalences, time restrictions, trustee directory assignments and volume disk restrictions. Refer to Figure 10.2 for a complete list. The User Information window is preceded by a list of users in the Users List screen. At this point, users can be deleted, inserted or highlighted.

TIP

NetWare provides a hidden facility for configuring small, select groups of users. The system manager can use F5 to mark multiple users in the User Names window of SYSCON. Pressing Enter provides a limited configuration window for setting specific parameters for the marked users. The window is called Set User Information and it consists of four choices: Account Balance, Account Restrictions, Station Restrictions, and Time Restrictions. This is as close as you are going to get to configuring global login restrictions.

The User Information submenu is used to specifically configure security and environmental variables. The system manager can use the User Information submenu of SYSCON to focus group-wide and system-wide security down to the user level. This is done through the user login script, user-specific passwords, trustee assignments, and account restrictions. The less time system managers spend in the user information screen, the better off they are. The assumption is that each time a change is made in the user information screen, it must be performed for all other users as well. This can be quite overwhelming in an environment where 500 or 1,000 users exist on one server.

KNOWLEDGE

The User Information submenu in SYSCON can also be used by users to customize their own environment, to change their login scripts, passwords, or full name. The user information screen will appear with all 14 options for a specific user as long as he/she is accessing their own user information options. An abbreviated version of this User Information menu will appear if a user tries to access the configurations of any other user. The User Information menu will appear for other users except it will have two options: full name and groups belonged to. The idea here is to provide information about users to anyone in the LAN without allowing just anybody to come

along and change other user configurations. The supervisor will gain full access to the User Information for all users.

The Group Information submenu provides information and configuration options for NetWare groups. The Group Information submenu is similar to the user information submenu in functionality, but provides only the following:

- ▸ Full name
- ▸ Managed users and groups
- ▸ Managers
- ▸ User list
- ▸ Other information
- ▸ Trustee directory assignments
- ▸ Trustee file assignments

But before you can enter the Group Information screen, you must identify which group you would like to view. This is done with an intermediate menu called the Group Names menu—which is a double-bordered box. At this point, you are allowed to either insert, delete or choose a specific NetWare group. The Group Information box in SYSCON is particularly useful for assigning group specific or group-wide security options. Trustee assignments can be made for large groups of users by using the group information window. This is a very effective strategy for curing baldness in system managers who worry too much about user-specific security.

QUOTE

Worry gives a small thing a big shadow.

Swedish Proverb

Assigning Managers

The system manager's job can become overwhelming as more and more users are added to the LAN. User demands and daily management tasks can take their toll on even the most robust NetWare handyman. This is why NetWare provides the facility for distributed network management. NetWare allows the system manager to create a variety of distributed managers and operators. As you remember from our discussion in Chapter 9, these different managers and operators have unique privileges which allow them to oversee small groups of users. SYSCON provides the facility for assigning four of the six distributed network managers. They are: supervisor equivalent, workgroup manager, user account manager, and console operator.

The supervisor equivalent is assigned under the user information option from SYSCON. Supervisor equivalents are assigned by accessing a specific user's information window and choosing Security Equivalences. At the security equivalences window, the system manager presses INSERT and highlights the supervisor as a security equivalent for this user.

TIP

Be careful; the supervisor equivalent can perform all functions of the supervisor including downing the server and editing the system login script.

The workgroup manager is the next level below supervisor equivalent. The workgroup manager can create, delete and manage workgroups of NetWare users. The workgroup managers can be assigned by only the supervisor and must be assigned in the supervisor options window in SYSCON. To insert a workgroup manager, simply choose the workgroup managers choice from supervisor options and press Insert to add the user's name. Once the workgroup manager has been created, the system manager must go to that user's user information window and assign a group of users to be managed.

User account managers are distributed managers who have less functionality than workgroup managers but provide the same facility. User account managers can be created by other user account managers, workgroup managers, or supervisor equivalents. The user account managers cannot delete other users and have limited functionality over their particular workgroup. User account managers are created in the user information window in SYSCON by going into Managed Users or Groups and inserting a group of users. Once these users have been inserted, they will become a workgroup for this user account manager.

Finally, console operators are created through the supervisor options window in SYSCON. Console operators can access all the facilities of FCONSOLE except downing the server or clearing connections. Keep in mind that assigning distributed managers in a NetWare environment is a very good idea because it provides stress relief for the NetWare handyman and keeps the workload manageable.

Related Commands

SYSCON incorporates 8 command line utilities that we've introduced so far:

- ▸ GRANT

- ▸ REMOVE

- ▸ REVOKE

- ▸ RIGHTS

- ▸ SETPASS

- ▸ SLIST

- ▸ TLIST

As you can see, the SYSCON menu utility is quite extensive and provides a great deal of functionality for NetWare system managers. It is very important that you become well aware of the many features of the SYSCON menu utility and become familiar with its use. The next menu utility is as broad in scope, but it doesn't affect users and groups—it helps manage the NetWare directory structure.

> FILER is just as extensive as SYSCON, but instead of configuring users and groups, FILER specifically configures files, directories, volumes, and subdirectories.

FILER

The FILER NetWare menu utility is designed to control volume, directory, file, and subdirectory information. FILER is just as extensive as SYSCON in its approach but instead of configuring users and groups, FILER specifically configures files, directories, volumes, and subdirectories. The FILER menu utility is extremely refreshing for users who are restricted by the DOS interface. FILER provides exceptional functionality beyond what DOS does by allowing you to rename directories, delete entire branches of the tree, and change file security. These features are very similar to some of the third-party DOS utilities such as Norton Utilities and XTree.

The FILER Available Topics menu (Figure 10.3) includes these five choices:

- ▸ Current Directory Information
- ▸ Directory Contents
- ▸ Select Current Directory
- ▸ Set FILER options
- ▸ Volume Information

FILER provides a consistent interface with SYSCON and the other menu utilities in that it uses double-bordered and single-bordered boxes. It uses the same blue and gold format and the same header across the top. The header in FILER's case, instead of describing the user and the file server you're attached to, describes your current default directory. While FILER can be used by both users and system administrators, it does limit the functionality to directories and files where users have rights. The system administrator has full functionality within the FILER utility. Let's take a moment to explore the five submenus under the FILER available topics window.

Volume Tasks

Volume information is similar to SYSCON's file server information in that it is a single-bordered box which provides information only about the default volume. Volume Information includes the file server name, the volume name, the type of volume, the total size, the kilobytes available, and information about directory entries.

FIGURE 10.3

The FILER Menu Utility

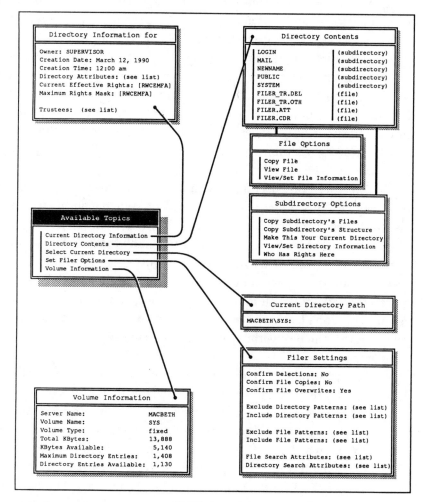

FILER Overview

Directory/File Tasks

The next available topics menu choice is Directory Contents. The Directory Contents menu provides a listing of all files and directories within and underneath the current default directory. The directory contents menu is where the system administrator can perform file and subdirectory creation, deletions, pruning, and general maintenance. Besides subdirectories and files, the directory contents menu includes two other components: the double dot (..)—which represents the parent directory—and the backslash (\)—which represents the root directory.

System managers and users can highlight subdirectories/files and press Enter to receive a third submenu which provides additional functionality—subdirectory options and file options. The subdirectory options screen includes functionality for copying subdirectories, making this your current directory, viewing directory information, or getting a list of who has rights to this subdirectory. The file options submenu provides information about copying, moving, and viewing files. You can also get information about viewing and editing file information and again, who has rights to this file.

The Directory Contents option within FILER is probably one of the most versatile menu utilities provided by NetWare. The system manager can insert or create directories at this point by pressing INSERT, or delete directories by using DELETE. Another interesting feature provided by the directory contents screen is pruning. When the system manager highlights a directory and presses DEL, the system responds with two choices: delete only a subdirectory's files, or delete the entire subdirectory structure. In the latter case, you would prune the directory tree at the branch level. This is a very effective way to delete entire portions of the directory structure without having to delete each of the files and subdirectories alone.

The Select Current Directory option simply allows you to move throughout the directory structure and change your default directory. This is useful when moving back and forth between current directory information and the Select Current Directory options box. The Set FILER Options choice allows you to set the parameters which are currently used by the FILER utility for accessing, editing, and viewing NetWare directories/files. Numerous parameters can be configured in the Set FILER Options, including confirm deletions, confirm file copies, preserve file attributes, include and exclude patterns, and search attributes. The last choice is specifically useful when searching for hidden files and those which are not normally displayed in the directory contents box of FILER.

Security Tasks

Current Directory Information provides detailed information about the current default directory. It provides information such as the owner, the creation date and time, the directory attributes, and other security information. Some of the most valuable information in the current directory information box is security related. It provides a detailed list of directory and file attributes, inherited rights mask, trustees and their trustee assignments, including effective rights. This is the only menu utility which provides calculated effective rights because it incorporates both trustee assignments and the inherited rights mask.

TIP

The trustee assignments and inherited rights mask boxes within the directory information screen of FILER are double-bordered which means this information can be edited by the system manager—or anyone with access control rights in this directory. This FILER screen provides an effective strategy for calculating and managing NetWare security at the directory level.

Related Commands

The associated command line utilities which are incorporated into the FILER menu utility are:

- ▸ FLAG
- ▸ LISTDIR
- ▸ NCOPY
- ▸ NDIR
- ▸ RENDIR
- ▸ DOS XCOPY command

SYSCON and FILER comprise 95% of the system manager's utility needs. They are both extensive in functionality and easy to use. An additional utility—SESSION—provides an abbreviated list of user functions—including drive mappings, user lists, and so on. The SESSION menu utility is extremely useful from the user's standpoint in that it provides a single central point for accessing NetWare's user-specific configurations and features. The SESSION menu controls file servers, default drive mappings, search drive mappings, messages, and lists of users and groups. There are four associated command line utilities that work in conjunction with the SESSION menu utility. They include:

> SYSCON and FILER comprise 95% of the system manager's utility needs. They are both extensive in functionality and easy to use.

- ▸ MAP
- ▸ SEND
- ▸ USERLIST
- ▸ WHOAMI

That completes our discussion of NetWare menu utilities from the system manager point of view. The next set of NetWare tools is Supervisor Utilities. These utilities are designed specifically for the supervisor and should not be shared with NetWare users.

QUOTE
Everything comes to him who hustles while he waits.

Thomas A. Edison

Supervisor Utilities

Supervisor Utilities are Batman tools designed especially for NetWare system managers. They allow you to customize and configure dangerous NetWare environments. Supervisor utilities come in two flavors—command line utilities and menu utilities. Some of the most hazardous supervisor utilities are tucked away in the SYS:SYSTEM directory, while the harmless user utilities reside in PUBLIC. By placing supervisor utilities in the SYSTEM subdirectory, NetWare is restricting access to only those users with rights to SYSTEM. By default, nobody has rights to SYSTEM except the Supervisor and supervisor equivalents. This effectively limits the use of supervisor utilities to only system managers and users with appropriate rights.

> Supervisor Utilities are Batman tools designed especially for NetWare system managers. They allow you to customize and configure dangerous NetWare environments.

In this section we will discuss the most popular supervisor command line utilities and the most effective supervisor menu utilities. Once we have a firm grasp on the purpose and functionality of supervisor utilities, we will move on to the console commands which provide customization at the file server console.

SUPERVISOR COMMAND LINE UTILITIES

As the system manager, it is important that you get a firm grasp on the use of these utilities. They will provide a very specialized and powerful set of tools for your NetWare utility belt. Here's a detailed look.

BINDFIX

BINDFIX is an extremely dangerous supervisor utility which allows for corruption recovery and restoration of the NetWare bindery. The NetWare bindery is the most important system file within NetWare besides the operating system file itself—SERVER.EXE. The NetWare bindery keeps track of users, groups, file servers, print servers, routers, and anything else with a name. It stores their rights, connections, configurations, and so on. All objects which use the network, all properties, and all values

> All objects which use the network, all properties, and all values which define the NetWare LAN are tracked in the NetWare bindery which consists of three files: NET$OBJ.SYS, NET$PROP.SYS, and NET$VAL.SYS.

which define the NetWare LAN are tracked in the NetWare bindery. The Net-Ware 3.12 bindery consists of three files: NET$OBJ.SYS, NET$PROP.SYS, and NET$VAL.SYS.

The system manager can run BINDFIX from the SYSTEM subdirectory in cases where he/she suspects foul play—somehow the bindery has been corrupted or objects and values are not tracking correctly. BINDFIX can run consistency checks on the bindery and track relationships between objects, properties, and values. If an error is found, BINDFIX will restore the error and de-corrupt the bindery. Two other functionalities which are built into BINDFIX include deleting rights and trustees for users who no longer exist, and deleting MAIL\userid subdirectories for users who no longer exist. BINDFIX, while fixing the bindery, creates a backup of the original bindery in the names of NET$OBJ.OLD, NET$PROP.OLD, and NET$VAL.OLD. These .OLD files are text files which can be copied from the network and kept on a diskette.

TIP

It is always a good idea to run a BINDFIX on a new network so that the pristine bindery can be saved as .OLD files on a diskette—just in case corruption occurs and BINDFIX does not solve the problem in the future. Also, run BINDFIX twice before making backups—once for de-corruption and once to backup the repaired bindery.

BINDREST

BINDREST is a related utility which restores .OLD files from a BINDFIX session. BINDREST can also be used to restore old copies of the bindery which were backed up onto a floppy diskette from earlier bindery sessions. Using BINDFIX and BINDREST on a routine basis, such as once a month, can help you save thousands of hours of work in creating users over again and reconfiguring NetWare security. Remember, when running BINDFIX and creating a backup copy of the bindery, it's a good idea to run BINDFIX twice. The reason for this is the first run will fix any problems and the second run will create a valid set of .OLD files.

SECURITY

The SECURITY supervisor utility is an excellent utility for identifying weaknesses in file server security. The SECURITY command, when entered at the command line from the SYSTEM subdirectory, will analyze the NetWare bindery and report any instances of security weakness or violation. NetWare identifies a variety of different security conditions as violations including passwords which are fewer than five characters, users who have security equivalents to supervisor, who have been assigned as workgroup managers, who are not required to enter a password, who have no full name attached, and so on. The security report is very long, so consider redirecting it to a file or printer.

WSUPDATE

The WSUPDATE supervisor utility can be used to update workstation shells and configuration files from one central location. The WSUPDATE utility compares the date and time of all destination workstation configuration files with a central source file and will copy or replace existing workstation shell files with the source file if the source file is found to be newer than the workstation originals. The WSUPDATE utility is not limited to NetWare shell files. This utility can update any file including application and program files. The command syntax for WSUPDATE is **WSUPDATE [source file name] [destination file name] /[switch]**.

There are a variety of different switches in WSUPDATE, most notably:

/F=[file name]—allows the system manager to set a variety of different WSUPDATE files in one text file and then specify that text file for reading in source and destination information

/I—forces the utility to prompt you for an action each times it finds an outdated file (this is the default option)

/C—automatically copies a new file over an existing file without prompting

/R—copies the new file over the old file and renames the old file with a .OLD extension

/S—instructs the utility to search beyond the destination path and include all subdirectories.

/L=[path and file name]—creates a detailed log of all activity, all searches, all finds, and all copies

/O—copies over and updates Read/Only files. Since many of the NetWare shell files on the workstation are flagged Read/Only for protection, the /o parameter is required to update Read/Only files. This parameter will instruct the utility to change the attribute of the file to Read/Write, copy over it, update it, and then change the attribute back to Read/Only.

That completes our discussion of supervisor command line utilities. As you can see, they provide you with a variety of different system manager tasks and tools. Now we will focus on supervisor menu utilities which will further enhance the NetWare Batman utility belt.

SUPERVISOR MENU UTILITIES

While the supervisor CLUs provide direct functionality from the command line, the supervisor menu utilities provide greater functionality within a friendly user interface. Some of the supervisor menu utilities are also stored in the SYS:SYSTEM subdirectory and their use is restricted to the Supervisor, supervisor equivalents, or users with Read and File Scan rights to SYSTEM. These 10 menu utilities provide a variety of features—from printing and disk management to user setup and even downing the server. The following is a detailed description of each of the 10 different supervisor menu utilities and the features they provide for the NetWare system manager.

DSPACE

DSPACE provides the same functionality as the disk restriction option in SYS-CON except here you can choose users and volumes from a central location. The available options menu of DSPACE includes three choices: change file server, user restrictions, and directory restrictions (see Figure 10.4). While in

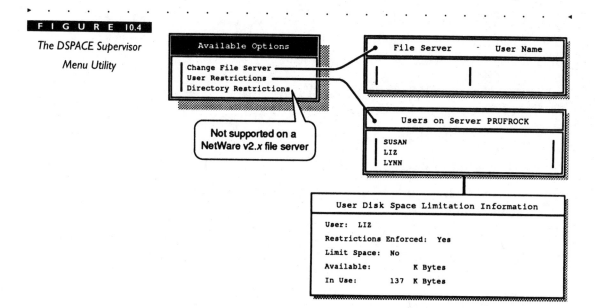

FIGURE 10.4

The DSPACE Supervisor
Menu Utility

NetWare 3.12, DSPACE allows system managers to limit users' disk space within directories—NetWare 2.2 does not support this feature. The user disk space limitation information screen provides the system manager with a central place to specify the user, the amount of space to restrict and the amount of space which is available for this each user. The DSPACE utility is one of the rare supervisor menu utilities which is placed in the PUBLIC directory during installation.

MAKEUSER

The MAKEUSER menu utility provides the ability to design large user scripts which can be used to create or delete multiple users. The MAKEUSER functionality is based on a text script file with the extension .USR. This is used by the MAKEUSER program to create and delete large numbers of users, set security, establish groups, and define home directories and login scripts.

The MAKEUSER syntax is similar to login scripts in that it requires specific key commands and syntax. Below is a list of the 19 MAKEUSER key words. Each command must be preceded by a pound (#) sign:

ACCOUNT_EXPIRATION followed by the month, the day, and the year when the account expires

ACCOUNTING followed by a balance and a low limit

CLEAR/RESET clears the processing of the script from this point on

CONNECTIONS specifies the maximum number of concurrent connections

CREATE followed by a user name and a variety of different options. This command creates users with specific full names, passwords, group membership, and directory rights

DELETE followed by user name

GROUPS followed by a group name. This assigns users to specific groups

HOME_DIRECTORY followed by a path which creates a home directory for this user

NO_HOME_DIRECTORY which overrides the creation of a default home directory

LOGIN_SCRIPT followed by a path which points to a specific text file written in login script syntax

MAX_DISK_SPACE and a number which establishes a maximum disk space for this user

PASSWORD_LENGTH specifies a minimum password length between 1 and 20

PASSWORD_PERIOD followed by days specifies the number of days before the password will expire

PASSWORD_REQUIRED

PURGE_USER_DIRECTORY will delete subdirectories owned by the user when the user is deleted

REM (for Remark) for documentation

RESTRICTED_TIME day, start, and end specifies which days and hours the users cannot login in

STATIONS followed by the network number and the station address for station restrictions for this user

UNIQUE_PASSWORD requires new passwords that are unique.

That completes the MAKEUSER key words. Keep in mind that once a MAKEUSER script has been created, it can be used over and over again to establish new or existing user environments. This is particularly useful in situations where a system is recreated every semester in school environments or where there's been a failed disk and you need to restore the user bindery information.

SALVAGE

The SALVAGE utility is used to recover or purge files that have been erased from the network. SALVAGE recovers data from its original directory. If the directory was also deleted, SALVAGE stores these files in a special directory called DELETED.SAV—which is a hidden system directory off the root of each volume. The SALVAGE main menu (Figure 10.5) consists of four options:

Salvage from Deleted Directories provides the system manager or user with the ability to salvage files which have been deleted from directories that have been deleted and this facility works from the DELETED.SAV directory.

Select Current Directory provides the facility for changing the default directory.

View/Recover Deleted Files allows users or system managers to go in and get a list of all deleted files in the current directory. At this point you can choose whether or not to restore them.

FIGURE 10.5

The SALVAGE

Supervisor Utility

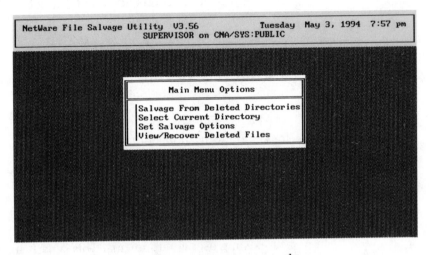

```
NetWare File Salvage Utility  V3.56          Tuesday  May 3, 1994  7:57 pm
                 SUPERVISOR on CNA/SYS:PUBLIC
```

```
          Main Menu Options

Salvage From Deleted Directories
Select Current Directory
Set Salvage Options
View/Recover Deleted Files
```

Set Salvage Options allows the user or system manager to set the default parameters such as sort list by deletion date, file size, file name, or owner.

TIP

Deleted files are only salvageable between file server downs, or when the system has enough space. If the system runs out of space, it will begin to write over salvageable files. If the file server is downed, all salvageable files are lost.

USERDEF

USERDEF provides the same functionality as MAKEUSER in that it allows you to create large numbers of users from one simple menu utility. The difference between USERDEF and MAKEUSER is that MAKEUSER uses a script format and allows the supervisor to create *and* delete users. While USERDEF is a template format which only allows the supervisor to create users. The USERDEF template (Figure 10.6) provides a more user friendly, graphic environment for the system manager to customize user parameters. However, it doesn't provide nearly the

F I G U R E 10.6

The USERDEF Template

```
┌─────────────────────────────────────────────────┐
│          Parameters for Template CLERK            │
├─────────────────────────────────────────────────┤
│ Default Directory:  SYS:                          │
│ Copy PrintCon From: (see list)                    │
│ Groups Belonged To: (see list)                    │
│ Account Balance:                      1000        │
│ Limit Account Balance:                No          │
│     Low Limit:                                    │
│ Limit Concurrent Connections:         No          │
│     Maximum Connections:                          │
│                                                   │
│ Require Password:                     Yes         │
│     Minimum Password Length:          5           │
│ Force Periodic Password Changes:      Yes         │
│     Days Between Forced Changes:      90          │
│ Require Unique Passwords:             Yes         │
└─────────────────────────────────────────────────┘
```

flexibility or versatility that MAKEUSER does. The USERDEF template includes user parameters such as default directory, groups belonged to, account balance, concurrent connections, require password, password changes, and unique passwords. Refer to Figure 10.7 for an illustration of the USERDEF menus.

USERDEF limits the system manager to creating large groups of files using one template at a time which means the system manager can only create similar groups of users at the same time. MAKEUSER, on the other hand, provides the facility for changing configurations in mid-stream and creating all users from one script.

F I G U R E 10.7

The USERDEF Supervisor
Menu Utility

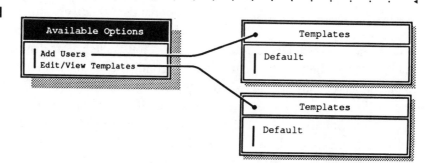

Console Commands

At the beginning of the chapter, we defined console commands as advanced NetWare tools which provide customization of the NetWare operating system. Console commands are advanced utilities which must be executed at the file server console. These tools can be very hazardous if not handled correctly—so please make sure to keep them out of the reach of children or NetWare users.

QUOTE

The most thoroughly wasted of all days is that on which one has not laughed.

Chamfort

Console commands allow the handyman to perform a variety of administrative tasks including controlling file servers, printers, and disk drives, sending messages, setting the server clock, and performing general LAN maintenance. Some of the more popular console commands include LOAD, BROADCAST, CLS, EXIT, MOUNT, BIND, and of course DOWN. These console commands can be quite dangerous if not used properly. The syntax of console commands is relatively straightforward. The command itself is entered at the console prompt—which is a colon (:)—and various switches are displayed. Keep in mind that anybody can execute a console command as long as they have access to the file server console. This is a very good reason to limit access to the file server console and possibly keep the file server itself under lock and key.

> Console commands allow the handyman to perform a variety of administrative tasks including controlling file servers, printers, and disk drives, sending messages, setting the server clock, and performing general LAN maintenance.

Console commands have a direct line to the operating system so they can perform customization of the SERVER.EXE code. In addition, NetWare 3.12 provides remote access to the server console through the RCONSOLE supervisor utility. For this reason and the inherent lack of security, console commands are the most dangerous supervisor utilities. Let's begin with a detailed discussion of the 22 most popular NetWare 3.12 console commands.

SCREEN

NetWare 3.12 provides the facility for screen console commands. These console commands build on 2.2 by providing the NetWare handyman with the ability to broadcast or send messages, clear the screen or exit from the file server console. Keep in mind that the screen console commands only affect what is on the screen.

BROADCAST

BROADCAST is a console command which is used to send a message of 40 characters or fewer to all users who are currently logged in or attached to the file server. The BROADCAST console command syntax is **BROADCAST [message]**.

The messages users receive with the BROADCAST command are exactly the same as messages users receive with the SEND command. That message is 40 characters at the bottom of the screen with the prompt **Press Control-Enter to Clear**. These messages will lock up the workstation until the user intervenes. Only users who are actually logged into the system will receive the BROADCAST command. Any user who is simply attached to the file server's LOGIN directory will not receive that server's BROADCAST message. Again, BROADCAST is used to send a simple message to all users in the network simultaneously.

TIP

All these console commands are internal operating system commands that are very similar to DOS's internal commands. They are built into the network operating system—SERVER.EXE. Earlier we talked about the menu utilities, command line utilities, and supervisor utilities that were stored in either SYSTEM or PUBLIC. The console commands are not stored in either of these directories; they are inherent to the operating system and therefore can only be executed at the console prompt.

SEND

The SEND console commands focuses on the broadcast command by providing the facility to send a file server console message to either all users who are logged in, or to a list of specific users—or connection numbers. The SEND message can be up to 55 characters and you can send a list to either a username or a connection number. SEND also supports the AND delimiter which provides the facility for sending a message to a group of users or connection numbers. The syntax for SEND is SEND ["message in quotes"] TO [user names or connection numbers].

TIP

The down side of the SEND command is that it locks up the destination computer until the combination Control-Enter is input. This can have very harmful effects in situations where a particular process is running on a computer—for example, the computer is unattended and a message is sent to that computer. The process will halt and the message will not be cleared until a user comes up to that machine and presses Control-Enter. To avoid messages locking up unattended machines or to avoid having messages broadcast on your particular machine, there are two command line utilities: CASTOFF (which will block) and CASTON (which will reopen the line for these messages).

EXIT

The EXIT command allows the system manager to return to DOS at the file server console once this file server has been brought down. The EXIT command is useful in that it allows you to access the DOS partition and rerun the SERVER.EXE file with new parameters.

TIP

The EXIT command can be used in conjunction with the REMOVE DOS console command to reboot the file server.

CLS

The CLS, or Clear Screen console command, is a new NetWare 3.12 command which allows the system manager to clear the file server console. This is particularly useful when the file server console becomes cluttered with binding LAN drivers, loading disk drivers, and other console commands. In addition, this can be useful for troubleshooting if the system manager suspects that there are other people accessing the file server console. The system manager simply issues a **CLS** and comes back later to see if the screen has been accessed.

INSTALLATION

The installation console commands are new to NetWare 3.12 and provide the NetWare handyman with the necessary tools for installing a NetWare 3.12 server. Keep in mind, the NetWare 3.12 installation is not menu driven as in 2.2. NetWare 3.12 installation consists of a simple group of tasks which must be executed in order from the file server console. These tasks, include LOAD, BIND, and MOUNT.

LOAD

The LOAD console command is used to load and unload NetWare Loadable Modules—Lego pieces. Later in the chapter we will discuss the four different types of NetWare Loadable Modules and their functionality. For now, it is important to note that NetWare Loadable Modules are the Lego pieces which bind together to add functionality to the file server operating system core. As you recall, NetWare 3.12 architecture consists of an NLM software bus and loadable modules. The NLMs add incremental functionality to SERVER.EXE. The LOAD console command is used to load these file server modules into memory and bind them to the software NLM bus. Some of the most common NetWare Loadable Modules are LAN drivers and disk drivers. The LAN driver is loaded during NetWare 3.12 installation to initialize the file server network interface card. The disk driver is loaded during installation to initialize and open communications between the operating system and internal shared hard disk. The syntax for the LOAD command is **LOAD [module name]**.

BIND

The BIND console command is used to link LAN drivers to a specific communication protocol for this server. Once a LAN driver has been loaded, the communications protocol must be bound to the LAN board so that it can start to receive packets. If the LOAD command is issued but the BIND command is not, the file server NIC will not be able to receive network packets. The default communication protocol for file server binding is IPX. The syntax of BIND is BIND IPX TO [name of LAN driver].

> NetWare 3.12 architecture consists of an NLM software bus and loadable modules. The NLMs add incremental functionality to SERVER.EXE. The LOAD console command is used to load these file server modules into memory and bind them to the software NLM bus.

MOUNT

The MOUNT console command is used to activate internal file server volumes. The MOUNT command makes volumes available to users and can be used either to mount or dismount several volumes while the file server is running. The MOUNT command must be issued in order for a volume to be active. If MOUNT is not issued, the file server volume is not available to the users and they cannot access or distribute NetWare files.

TIP

Mounting and dismounting of volumes can be used as a security feature for volumes which are rarely accessed. Mount them during access hours and dismount them when they are not being used. This is a particularly useful security strategy because no matter what security a user has, he/she cannot access a dismounted volume.

KNOWLEDGE

The term MOUNT comes from the mainframe world where it was typical for computer operators to have to mount a reel of tape in order for users to access data. While the NetWare mounting process is not nearly as complex, it does follow the same general rule.

MAINTENANCE

Maintenance console commands are used by the NetWare handyman for general file server maintenance. These console commands are extremely useful in daily operations and can be used to proactively address possible problems before they occur. The maintenance console commands can be used for operations such as clearing workstation connections which are not being used, removing DOS from the background of server memory, downing the server and enabling or disabling logins. Let's take a closer look.

CLEAR STATION

The CLEAR STATION console command is a dramatic utility which allows the system manager or anyone from the file server console to abruptly clear a workstation's connection. This command removes all file server resources from the workstation and can cause file corruption or data loss if executed while the workstation is processing transactions. This command is only useful in environments where workstations have crashed or users have turned off their machines without logging out. In each of these particular instances, the connection would stay open even though the files are not currently being used. The syntax for the CLEAR STATION command is **CLEAR STATION [number]**.

The connection number for a specific workstation can be viewed from either the MONITOR NLM or FCONSOLE. This number is incrementally allocated as workstations attach and is not the same from one session to another.

DISABLE LOGIN

The DISABLE LOGIN command provides a feature for the NetWare system manager to use when troubleshooting or maintaining critical NetWare components such as the bindery or volumes. DISABLE LOGIN prevents anyone from logging into the system until login is re-enabled. DISABLE LOGIN is particularly useful when system managers are working on the bindery, backing up files, loading software or dismounting or repairing volumes. Keep in mind that DISABLE LOGIN does not affect users who are currently logged in. This command should only be used in situations where it's absolutely necessary.

ENABLE LOGIN

The ENABLE LOGIN command enables file server logins. It also provides one other facility: the supervisor account can be reactivated in the case where intruder detection/lockout has locked it. ENABLE LOGIN only works on the Supervisor account.

DOWN

The DOWN command is the most dramatic and potentially harmful NetWare console command. It completely shuts down the file server activity and closes all open files. Although the FCONSOLE supervisor utility provides its own internal downing feature, DOWN performs a variety of different activities before it shuts down the operating system. First it clears all the cache buffers and writes them to disk, then it closes all open files. It proceeds to update the appropriate directory and file allocation tables with the particular files which have been written to disk. It dismounts all volumes, clears all connections and finally shuts down the operating system. Once DOWN has been entered at the file server console prompt, the system responds with a message to type EXIT to return to DOS.

> The DOWN command is the most dramatic and harmful NetWare console command. It completely shuts down file server activity and closes all open files.

KNOWLEDGE

DOWN is potentially harmful because of its effects on maintenance background statistics. **MONITOR NLM** relies heavily on background information and averages for providing information about statistics and fine-tuning performance. **Once the system is down, all of these statistics are flushed and brought back to a default state. Obviously, the statistics are more meaningful the longer they are being measured.**

QUOTE

Do not take life too seriously; you will never get out of it alive.

Elbert Hubbard

REMOVE DOS

The REMOVE DOS command is particularly useful because it removes COM-MAND.COM from file server memory. This is useful because the memory that was used for DOS is returned to the operating system for file caching. This is particularly important in environments where file server memory is low and users need the additional memory. REMOVE DOS can also be used to increase file server security. When DOS is removed, loadable modules cannot be loaded from the file server's DOS drives because they do not exist. Also, users cannot issue a DOWN and EXIT command at the console and return to the DOS partition. If this particular instance occurs while DOS is removed, the file server will issue an automatic reboot—weird, huh?! Once this command is issued, the file server cannot access DOS afterwards without downing the server, exiting and rebooting.

UNBIND

The NetWare handyman uses UNBIND to remove communication protocol from a LAN driver after it has been bound (using the BIND command). UNBIND disables communications for this internal network interface card. Once the UN-BIND command has been used, the network interface card cannot receive communications or packets from the network. This is an effective strategy for disconnecting a particular LAN network from the file server. The syntax for UN-BIND is **UNBIND [protocol] FROM [LAN driver]**.

You can replace [protocol] with IPX, for example, which is NetWare's native default protocol. The UNBIND command is also a particularly useful strategy for removing communications from network interface cards which are disrupting the LAN—or sending incomplete packets which are conflicting with other external or internal routers. Incidentally, the BIND and UNBIND commands include a variety of different parameters which must be used to customize the network interface card environment. The most notable of these parameters is the network address parameter which tells the network what the unique address will be of a particular network interface card. If the network address parameter is not used with BIND or UNBIND, then the system will ask for it. These parameters are also useful because multiple cards can exist in the file server with the same LAN driver. For example, if there are two or three NE2000 network interface cards in the file server, the system would bind each of these with a different interrupt and different network address. The UNBIND command must specify which network interface card is to be unbound and therefore would have to indicate the interrupt and the network address of the card which is being unbound.

UNLOAD

The UNLOAD command is used to unload a loadable module which has been previously loaded using the LOAD command. When the module is unloaded, all resources are returned to the operating system memory for file caching. The syntax for UNLOAD is UNLOAD [loadable module].

The UNLOAD command is particularly useful in environments where the file server is running out of RAM, or where internal loadable modules are causing intermittent problems. When the system manager unloads the LAN driver, the driver is automatically unbound from all communication protocols and removed from all network boards. Once the LAN driver is unloaded, logged-in users will receive the message Error receiving from network; abort, retry. This is an indication that the file server communications have been terminated. Also before unloading name space modules, you must make sure to dismount all volumes that are using the module. Finally, when a disk driver is unloaded, all volumes on the system are dismounted and data is no longer available to be shared.

TIP

When loading and unloading NLMs that rely on other NLMs, the order they're unloaded must be the reverse of the order in which they were loaded. For example, to use remote management, the system depends on two NLMs: RSPX and REMOTE. The REMOTE NLM is loaded first and RSPX is loaded second. So, if the system manager tried to unload REMOTE without unloading RSPX, the system would respond Unable to unload module remote—Error 2 **which indicates that REMOTE was relying on other NLMs which had not yet been unloaded.**

CONFIGURATION

The configuration console commands are handyman tools which allow the system manager to configure, maintain, and monitor the file server operating system. While most of the configuration console commands are information only, some of them provide the facility for optimizing the NetWare environment. Let's take a closer look.

CONFIG

The CONFIG console command is used to display the operating system's hardware information for all known internal components. CONFIG is useful not only for the NetWare file server but also for external dedicated routers. The type of information displayed using the CONFIG command includes the file server or router name, the number of service processes which have been defined, LAN network interface card configuration information and disk channel configuration. The network interface card information includes the network address, the card's hardware type, the version of the shell, and the configuration settings (IRQ, I/O and memory address). The disk channel information includes the hardware type with the shell version information and the hardware settings including the I/O and the interrupt.

NAME

The NAME console command simply displays the name of the file server. It uses an underscore (_) to represent a space in the name. Remember, space is not a valid character. The file server name may range from 2 to 45 characters.

VOLUMES

The VOLUMES console command is used to view a list of all volumes which are currently mounted on the file server. The VOLUMES command can be useful in determining which volumes are mounted and which volumes are dismounted. As you remember from our earlier discussion, the MOUNT console command can be a security feature which allows the system manager to restrict volumes at times when they are not needed.

UPS STATUS

The UPS STATUS command is used to indicate the status of a connected uninterruptible power supply. This utility does not provide any functionality for editing the parameters of the UPS, it simply displays the status. Other uninterruptible power supply manufacturers provide software which works in conjunction with NetWare to provide what is called UPS monitoring. UPS monitoring sends a message to the file server when power falls below a particular threshold. The file server responds by sending a message to users, closing all open files and downing the file server. This is done to avoid data corruption which occurs when the file server's power is abruptly turned off or lost.

That's it for NetWare console commands. These console commands are part of the NetWare operating system and they provide functionality for configuring or customizing the internal workings of NetWare—SERVER.EXE. Since console commands are entered at the file server console with no security, they can therefore be quite dangerous. The only security against console commands is locking up the file server.

NetWare Loadable Modules

NetWare Loadable Modules are the Lego pieces of our LAN. As you remember from our discussion of NetWare 3.12 architecture, the operating system core consists of SERVER.EXE. All other functionality is made possible through the attachment of modular Legos. The modular functionality available from these loadable modules provides the operating system with communications, file sharing, security, monitoring, and configuration. NLMs are made possible because of NetWare 3.12's 32-bit architecture. The 32-bit modularity provides a great deal of flexibility for NetWare system managers in loading and unloading certain modules. NLMs are valuable for a variety of different reasons.

> NetWare Loadable Modules are the Lego pieces of our LAN. The NetWare 3.12 operating system core consists of SERVER.EXE. All other functionality is made possible through the attachment of modular Legos.

First, there is their versatility. Second is the ability to unload and load them without disrupting the LAN. This is particularly useful in optimizing file server memory. Third is the ability to configure the system and customize it for whatever needs the users have at that time. Finally, NLMs are valuable because they provide a facility for independent programmers to develop applications that can run on the NetWare server without having to disrupt the operating system core.

NLMs are broken into four different categories: disk drivers, LAN drivers, name space, and management NLMs. Disk drivers are primarily responsible for the interface between the NetWare operating system and internal hard disks. LAN drivers are responsible for initiating communications with the internal server NIC. Name space modules provide support for non-DOS naming schemes. Management NLMs are used for monitoring, maintenance and configuration of the NetWare environment. By default, all NetWare Loadable Modules are loaded into the SYSTEM subdirectory and are accessible solely by the NetWare supervisor. Let's take a closer look at these four different types of loadable modules.

DISK DRIVERS

As mentioned earlier, disk drivers control communications between the NetWare operating system and the internal shared disk. You can load and unload disk drivers as needed. The loadable module must be loaded in order for the disk to be shared or accessed by users. Disk drivers have a .DSK extension and are stored in the SYSTEM subdirectory. During the installation procedure, the first task for the NetWare system manager is to load the .DSK driver. Some common .DSK drivers include ISA.DSK, IDE.DSK, SCSI.DSK, and DCB.DSK for disk coprocessor boards.

LAN DRIVERS

LAN drivers control communication between the NetWare operating system and the internal network interface cards. You can load and unload these drivers as needed to make communications available to all users on the LAN. Keep in mind that when a LAN driver is loaded, the system manager must specify the configuration options which are being used by this card. These include interrupt, memory address, I/O port, and DMA. LAN drivers have the .LAN extension and are also stored in the SYSTEM subdirectory. Some popular LAN drivers which are available from Novell are TRXNET for ArcNet, NE2000, NE3200 for Ethernet, and TOKEN.LAN for token ring NICs.

NAME SPACE

Name Space modules allow non-DOS naming conventions to be stored on the server directory and file system. Name space is important so that Macintosh, UNIX and OS/2 names can be supported in cooperation with the DOS environment. Name space modules have the .NAM extension and they are stored in the SYSTEM subdirectory. Some common name space modules include MAC.NAM for Macintosh and OS/2.NAM for OS/2. Once a name space module has been loaded, the system manager must execute the **ADD NAME SPACE** console command to activate the name space on each particular volume. Name spaces provide support for access from simultaneously different workstation platforms. There are only a few special backup systems which recognize NetWare's additional name space. NBACKUP recognizes only DOS and Macintosh name space whereas SBACKUP, a NetWare server backup utility, recognizes DOS, Macintosh, OS/2 and UNIX name spaces.

MANAGEMENT NLMs

Management NLMs provide the functionality for configuration, maintenance and monitoring of the file server environment. These NLMs do not allow for the customization or optimization of the file server core because they are only additional Lego pieces which are attached to the core. In order to optimize SERVER.EXE, the system manager must use the SET console parameters. We will discuss these in depth in Chapter 13.

Management NLMs all have the .NLM extension and they are typically stored in the SYSTEM subdirectory. These NLMs range in function from installation to monitoring to system fault tolerance. Three of the most common NLM management utilities are INSTALL, MONITOR and UPS. The INSTALL NLM (Figure 10.8) is a menu-driven program which provides the last 25% of the install procedure. INSTALL allows system managers to:

▸ Mirror hard disks

The INSTALL NLM

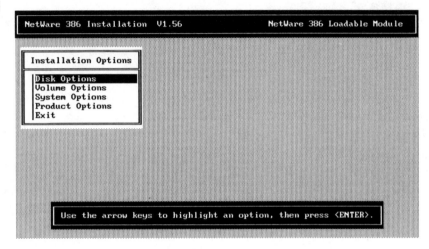

```
NetWare 386 Installation   V1.56              NetWare 386 Loadable Module

    ┌─ Installation Options ─┐
    │ Disk Options           │
    │ Volume Options         │
    │ System Options         │
    │ Product Options        │
    │ Exit                   │
    └────────────────────────┘




    Use the arrow keys to highlight an option, then press <ENTER>.
```

▸ Create NetWare partitions

▸ Create volumes

▸ Create or modify NetWare boot files

▸ Copy the SYSTEM and PUBLIC files onto the file server

▸ Load the 3.12 diskettes

▸ Install and configure additional products on the file server including Macintosh or UNIX support.

The MONITOR NLM utility (Figure 10.9) is the most useful file server management tool from the standpoint that it provides a plethora of information about key memory and communication processes. The different types of resources which can be tracked using the MONITOR include file connections, memory, disk information, users, file lock activity and processor utilization. In Chapter 13, we will learn how to use the MONITOR NLM to answer all of your tough NetWare handyman questions.

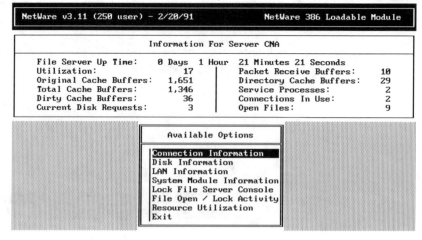

F I G U R E 10.9

The MONITOR

Main Screen

QUOTE

Man will not live without answers to his questions.

Hans J. Morgenthau

System fault tolerance support is available through the UPS NLM which allows the system manager to install the UPS monitoring functionality. UPS monitoring provides a connection between the file server through a serial port and the uninterruptible power supply. The monitoring will determine when the uninterruptible power supply is low on battery and instigate automatic UPS shutdown. UPS shutdown procedures on the file server include sending a message to all users and downing and exiting the server console. Finally, there are other management NLMs which provide capability for multiple protocols, source routing in a token ring environment and remote booting for diskless workstations.

That completes our discussion of the roles and responsibilities of the NetWare handyman. At the beginning of this chapter, we described the NetWare handyman as a true hero in proactively maintaining the health of the NetWare LAN. In this chapter, we have explored the role of the NetWare handyman and pro-vided a large variety of tools for your NetWare utility belt. These tools have included many utilities including supervisor utilities and console commands as well as NetWare Loadable Modules. NetWare 3.12 provides a large, diverse collection of tools for the NetWare handyman. As the system manager, it is your responsibility to learn these tools as best you can, so that in times of need you can put on your red cape and save the day.

In the next chapter, we will explore network management in greater detail, discussing the specific tasks which the system manager must perform in fine tuning and optimizing the user environment. We will shift roles from the NetWare handyman to the hotel manager who is responsible for overseeing the smooth operations of the hotel. Park Place, being a luxury hotel, relies heavily on the hotel manager to optimize the hotel's image and motivate the staff. The goal is for all guests to be treated as kings and queens. As the NetWare hotel manager, you will be responsible for understanding login scripts, user interface, application software, menus, multi-protocol support, system backup and the remote management facility. In order to wrap all these functions up into a nice package, we will begin our discussion of network management with an exploration of the different management strategies. This should be fun.

> NetWare 3.12 provides a large, diverse collection of tools for the NetWare handyman. As the system manager, it is your responsibility to learn these tools as best you can, so that in times of need you can put on your red cape and save the day.

NetWare 3.12 Network Management

The key to Park Place's success is the hotel manager. He/she oversees the resort's daily hustle and bustle and projects long-term strategies for growth and success. The hotel manager has a variety of responsibilities, which include:

► Overseeing registration

► Making sure the guests have a mint on their pillow

► Marketing and public relations

► Staff management

► Convention organization

► Coddling VIPs

► Contingency plans

Registration is extremely important to the success of a hotel because this is where the clients check in and check out. In addition, the registration desk establishes the initial client environment by making the guests feel comfortable and at home. A nice touch is providing the guests with a welcome pack including a mint on their pillow.

> The key to Park Place's success is the hotel manager. He/she oversees the resort's daily hustle and bustle and projects long-term strategies for growth and success.

Marketing is another extremely important responsibility of the hotel manager. This facet of his/her job provides an avenue for displaying the resort's many benefits through the local and national media. Public relations helps to develop an image of the hotel which is both appealing and non-threatening. In addition to marketing and public relations, the hotel manager must oversee the hotel staff and work very closely with the interior decorator to create an ideal resort environment.

Besides the ordinary guests who frequent Park Place on a daily basis, the hotel manager must be involved in the organization of conventions and the creation of competitive convention packages. In addition, when VIPs visit Park Place, the hotel manager must make them feel special and make sure that their every need has been satisfied. VIPs must also be able to find their way to the Park Place suites.

Finally, the hotel manager is responsible for making sure that all staff and guests are aware of emergency plans. He/she must develop and implement emergency strategies in the case of natural or unnatural disasters. Unfortunately, this facet of the hotel manager's responsibility is often overlooked. Until, of course, there's a major emergency. In order to perform his/her duties, the hotel manager must be fair, congenial, firm, and well-organized—all at the same time. Most successful hotel managers have a strategy they employ for approaching these responsibilities. A hotel management plan is almost required.

As the manager of your NetWare hotel, you will have many of the same responsibilities as our friend at Park Place.

▸ Your registration duties will consist of the development and maintenance of login scripts. Login scripts create an environment for users when they first login to the system.

▸ Your marketing and public relations duties will involve the creation of a productive and friendly user interface. In addition, as you oversee your user staff, components such as menu software, application systems, and E-mail will help keep them organized.

▸ The conventions and VIPs of your LAN are the non-DOS workstations. NetWare employs a multi-protocol management model called Open Data-link Interface (ODI)—which allows for the integration of DOS, Macintosh, OS/2, and UNIX workstations. It is your responsibility to implement ODI for the non-routine guests.

▸ Your final NetWare system manager responsibility is NetWare backup. NetWare backup consists of a new powerful system called storage management services (SMS). You will never fully appreciate the importance of backup until all of your data is lost.

In general, as the NetWare system manager, you will breathe life into an otherwise limp and lifeless LAN. The network designer and installation team have left you with wires, workstations, a file server, and some barely functional software.

It is your responsibility to connect the staff and hotel amenities in creating a productive integrated NetWare environment.

During your stint as the NetWare system manager, you will be taking an empty frame and filling it with users, groups, applications, menu systems, security, login scripts, and System Fault Tolerance (SFT). Network management is the most challenging, exciting, and rewarding aspect of the NetWare hotel. In this chapter, we will explore the responsibilities of the NetWare system manager by discovering login scripts, user interface, multiprotocol management, and NetWare back-up. In addition, we will learn about remote management facilities—NetWare support for management from a remote site. But before we begin our trek into the challenging world of network management, we need to take a moment to explore some general management strategies and develop an approach to your daily network management duties. Roll up your sleeves because this is going to be a very fun chapter!

QUOTE

Experience shows that success is due less to ability than to zeal. The winner is he who gives himself to his work, body and soul.

Charles Buxton

Management Strategies

Just like the Park Place manager, you must have an approach to NetWare system management. A management plan will help you integrate the many diverse facets of your job. The plan can act as a reminder for daily maintenance duties or user setup procedures. In addition, the management plan can act as a guideline for backup managers who need to follow your previous configurations. NetWare provides a large variety of tools to aid the NetWare system manager in the creation of a management plan.

- ▸ NetWare 3.12 worksheets
- ▸ Command line utilities for tracking network information

- ▸ Custom configuration files
- ▸ Advance management utilities
- ▸ This book
- ▸ Shell update procedures
- ▸ Documentation
- ▸ The foundation of a NetWare log book

These tools in combination can create a very effective strategy for approaching NetWare system management. In this section, we will take a brief look at these system management tools and learn how to use them to construct an effective NetWare management plan. Use this plan to help implement the four different areas of NetWare management:

- ▸ Login scripts
- ▸ User interface
- ▸ Multiprotocol management
- ▸ NetWare backup

Let's start with the NetWare 3.12 worksheets.

NETWARE 3.12 WORKSHEETS

Novell provides a variety of different worksheets which can be used by the system manager to detail hardware and software LAN configurations. These system management worksheets form the beginning of the NetWare log book. Refer to Appendix C for a copy of all the NetWare 3.12 worksheets. They detail, among other things:

> Novell provides a variety of different worksheets which can be used by the system manager to detail hardware and software LAN configurations.

- ▸ File server hardware information

- ▶ Workstation hardware information

- ▶ Configuration of boot files

- ▶ NetWare directories

- ▶ Users and group information

- ▶ Default login restrictions

- ▶ Trustee assignments

- ▶ Login scripts

The NetWare system manager should keep these worksheets by his/her side at all times. They can provide the facility for documenting updates and initial configurations. Let's take a look at the eight NetWare worksheets.

File Server Worksheet

The file server worksheet provides information about the file server name, the make and model of the machine, and the system manager who installed it. The file server worksheet is primarily hardware-oriented. It provides detailed information about the network board, internal network number, floppy disk drives and internal hard disks. In addition, the file server worksheet allows the system manager to document all of the LAN driver and network interface card configurations. Additional information the system manager can add to the file server worksheet could include details about the make and model of the NetWare operating system.

Workstation Configuration Worksheet

The workstation configuration worksheet details hardware and software information about each workstation. The worksheet includes a list of details about the user who uses this particular workstation, the serial number of the machine, who installed it, the type of workstation it is, and node address information about the internal network interface cards. In addition, the workstation configuration worksheet details memory, internal hard disk types and configurations for network interface cards, I/O, interrupt, and memory address.

The workstation configuration worksheet also includes software information including a list of details about how the machine is booted, whether or not it boots from a remote boot PROM, the DOS version it is using and the files which are needed to attach to the network. Each workstation should have its own detailed configuration worksheet.

Directories Worksheet

The directories worksheet is a matrix of directory structure and internal security. On the left side it provides a list of volumes, directories, and subdirectories including names and a description of host files. In addition to directory organization information, the directories worksheet includes a list of detailed file attributes, directory attributes, and each directory's inherited rights mask. This information can prove to be quite valuable when the NetWare system manager is developing access rights security.

Users Worksheet

The users worksheet provides a detailed list of all user names, full names, and the groups they belong to. In addition, the users worksheet documents the applications that users use, what their access rights are, and any restrictions. Finally, the user worksheet can be used as a central source for tracking special user accounts.

Group Worksheet

The group worksheet is similar to the users worksheet in that it provides a detailed list of group names and access to directories. In addition, the group worksheet provides a list of all users who are currently members of this group— in alphabetical order. Finally, the group worksheet details trustee directory assignments, access to files, and trustee file assignments. Group worksheets can be used in conjunction with user worksheets to provide a central location of all information about NetWare user/group configurations.

User Defaults

The user defaults worksheet documents the global login restrictions. These defaults are set in the supervisor option screen of SYSCON and control login restriction configurations for all users that are created beyond this point. The user defaults worksheet is extremely important because it can be used to track which users were created using which login restriction defaults. The user defaults worksheet provides information about account restrictions, intruder detection lockout, password restrictions, accounting and time restrictions. The user defaults worksheet should be kept with the file server worksheet.

Trustee Directory Security Worksheet

The trustee directory security worksheet is an extremely useful tool for NetWare system management. It provides a central document outlining all trustees of all directories and what their corresponding rights are. This worksheet can become quite large but it is very important that the NetWare system manager use it during the creation of access rights security. The trustee directory security worksheet can be included in the NetWare log so that current and future system managers have a place to reference NetWare security. The structure of the trustee directory security worksheet is a matrix. On the left-hand side, it provides a list of all directories in the system. Across the top is a list of the trustees of that directory and in the corresponding box an inventory of their rights. The trustee directory security worksheet should be catalogued with the users and group worksheets in the NetWare log.

Login Scripts Worksheet

The login script worksheet is an extremely useful tool for creating system and user login scripts. The worksheet includes a grouping of corresponding dialog boxes with suggested login script topics. These topics include:

- Preliminary commands
- Greetings
- Displayed login messages
- Attach to other file servers

- Utility mappings

- DOS directory mappings

- Application directory mappings

- Miscellaneous search drives

- Preliminary commands

- Username mappings

- Work directory mappings

- Default printer mappings

- Exit to a program

The login script worksheet provides a tool for the system manager to create effective, efficient, and comprehensive system and user login scripts. The login script worksheet also provides documentation for updates and future modifications. The system manager should keep the login script worksheets with the file server and user default worksheets in the NetWare log.

The above management worksheets can be very effective tools in tracking network management activities.

QUOTE

Business is like riding a bicycle—either you keep moving or you fall down.

Anonymous

TRACKING NETWORK INFORMATION

There are two other network management tools which can be effective for tracking network type information: NDIR and LISTDIR. NDIR provides file and directory searching facilities along with control functions for shared disk space. Using NDIR, supervisors can track the amount of disk space used by each user, see the date that the network was last accessed, and search for specific types of files. NDIR has an extensive list of supported switches. LISTDIR, on the other hand, provides a graphical tree of directories and subdirectories. For each subdirectory, system managers can view associated information such as the inherited rights mask, effective rights and creation date. Both NDIR and LISTDIR are described in detail in Chapter 8.

CUSTOM CONFIGURATION FILES

Tracking network information can be important for system managers to keep on top of disk space utilization and directory structure formats. In addition, system managers can use this information to monitor shared resources and make decisions about future upgrades. NetWare relies heavily on configuration files for the establishment of user environments. These configuration files define both local and NetWare parameters. NetWare supports two different types of configuration files: workstation boot files and file server boot files.

> NetWare relies heavily on configuration files to establish user environments and define both local and NetWare parameters.

Workstation boot files define DOS-specific environments for loading COMMAND.COM and workstation shells. The file server boot files are required for the proper loading and configuring of the NetWare operating system. Let's take a closer look.

Workstation Boot Files

The system manager uses workstation boot files to customize the workstation environment. These boot files include:

► AUTOEXEC.BAT

► CONFIG.SYS

► SHELL.CFG

► NET.CFG

AUTOEXEC.BAT is a DOS configuration file which is automatically loaded during initial workstation startup. In Chapter 1, we learned that AUTOEXEC.BAT can be used to customize and define workstation specific parameters. These parameters include PATH statements, SET parameters, and the PROMPT command. In addition, the DOS Requester workstation installation adds the following line to the top of the AUTOEXEC.BAT.

@CALL C:\NWCLIENT\STARTNET.BAT

The STARTNET.BAT file provides support for ODI implementation and VLMs (Virtual Loadable Modules). It looks like this:

```
C:
CD\NWCLIENT—default Requester directory
LSL.COM
NE2000.COM
IPXODI.COM
VLM.EXE—NetWare DOS Requester files
F:—first network drive
LOGIN username
```

The CONFIG.SYS workstation boot file is similar to AUTOEXEC.BAT except that it loads drivers and defines critical workstation environments. During the NetWare DOS Requester installation, the following line is added to the CONFIG.SYS file:

LASTDRIVE=Z

This command is necessary for the NetWare DOS Requester to operate properly because it shares drive table information with DOS. If C is the last local drive, D becomes the first network drive.

KNOWLEDGE

The LASTDRIVE=Z command is required for the NetWare DOS Requester, but it plays havoc with old IPX and NETx workstation files. If this command is used in NetWare 2.2 or 3.11, no network drives will be available.

SHELL.CFG is a NetWare specific configuration file which is loaded from the workstation. SHELL.CFG defines parameters for the loading of IPX and NETx. The SHELL.CFG file can be customized by the NetWare system manager to provide the facility for Windows support, COMSPEC, file handles, workstation buffers and SPX connections. A recent enhancement to the SHELL.CFG file has been made in the form of the NET.CFG file. NET.CFG configuration files support all of the same parameters as SHELL.CFG plus some additional parameters for ODI workstations and the NetWare DOS Requester. ODI drivers rely on the NET.CFG file for the configuration of link support layer, link drivers, and protocol. The NetWare DOS Requester uses it for preferred server and defining the first network drive. We'll discuss the role of NET.CFG and the ODI drivers later in this chapter.

File Server Boot Files

File server boot files allow the system manager to customize the startup of NetWare file servers. As you recall, the NetWare 3.12 file server actually boots from DOS. It then loads SERVER.EXE to become a NetWare server. The file server boot files provide the facility for customizing both the loading of DOS on the file server and the execution of SERVER.EXE. File server boot files include AUTOEXEC.BAT, STARTUP.NCF and AUTOEXEC.NCF. The file server AUTO-EXEC.BAT simply has one line: server. It allows the file server to transparently move from booting DOS into the SERVER.EXE program. Once the SERVER.EXE operating system file is loaded, STARTUP.NCF and AUTOEXEC.NCF take over. STARTUP.NCF is loaded first. This file server boot file contains commands to load disk drivers and name space support. It is generated automatically by the INSTALL program and can be maintained afterwards using INSTALL.NLM. AUTOEXEC.NCF loads after STARTUP.NCF. This server boot file performs all other customization including the file server name, IPX internal network number, loading LAN drivers, binding IPX, and mounting volumes. All of these custom configuration files provide a facility for the system manager to manage workstations and file servers.

ADVANCED MANAGEMENT UTILITIES

In addition to the utilities we have learned so far, NetWare provides some advanced management utilities which offer specialized functionality. They include:

- ▸ Security

- ▸ Secure console

- ▸ Search

- ▸ Modules

- ▸ Memory

The SECURITY management utility is the system manager's best friend. It discreetly reports holes in NetWare security which can cause possible violations. By issuing the security command from the SYSTEM subdirectory, the supervisor can be notified of possible file server security violations including no password, secure password, supervisor equivalency, root directory privileges, no user login script, and excessive rights.

> The SECURITY management utility discreetly reports holes in NetWare security which can cause possible violations.

TIP

The **SECURITY** command can save a system manager's job by pointing out possible security risks which would have otherwise gone unnoticed. But remember, the **SECURITY** command does not correct violations; it only reports them.

QUOTE

As machines get to be more and more like men, men will come to be more like machines.

Anonymous

SECURE CONSOLE is another security-oriented management utility which provides a facility for securing the file server console. SECURE CONSOLE does not prohibit access to the file server console, it only limits the functions users can perform there. When activated, SECURE CONSOLE restricts loading of NLMs from anywhere but SYSTEM, restricts the copying of files into SYSTEM, prevents anyone except the console operator from changing the date and time and removes DOS from the server. Earlier we mentioned that once COMMAND.COM is removed from the file server, any user downing and exiting the file server will cause the server to reboot. This is a security feature which prohibits user access to the DOS partition of the file server.

The SEARCH console command allows the system manager to build a search list at the console level for the system to search NLM and NCF batch files. By default, the system will search only the SYSTEM subdirectory for these files. MODULES is a command which displays the following information about NLMs that are currently loaded in the server:

- ► Long module name and description string

- ► Short name used to load the module

- ► Version number for disk and LAN driver

Finally, the MEMORY command is used to display the total amount of installed memory that the operating system can address. NetWare 3.12 automatically addresses memory above 16MB for EISA computers. For Micro channel and ISA computers, the system manager must use the REGISTER MEMORY command for the operating system to enable memory above 16MB.

NOVELL PRESS PUBLICATIONS

In addition to these five advanced management utilities, NetWare provides myriad tools for your NetWare utility belt. One of the best ways to become proficient at using these tools is to visit your local Novell Press library. Novell Press is dedicated to providing publications which augment NetWare education. These publications are designed to provide insight into specialized areas of NetWare where most people don't get a chance to go. Novell Press publications are written by internal Novell employees or specialists in the industry. Some of the most exciting books include *Novell's Guide to Network LAN Analysis, Novell's Guide to*

NetWare 4.0 Networks, Novell's Guide to NetWare 3.12 Networks, and, of course, *Novell's CNA Study Guide*, all from SYBEX.

QUOTE

Some books are to be tasted; others swallowed; and some few to be chewed and digested.

Francis Bacon

DOCUMENTATION

In addition to Novell Press publications, Novell provides a full set of documentation when purchasing NetWare products. The NetWare 3.12 reference set consists of 20 electronic, on-line books, including:

- ▶ Installation

- ▶ System Messages

- ▶ Utilities Reference

- ▶ System Administration

- ▶ Concepts

- ▶ Installation Supplements

- ▶ Print Server

The NetWare 3.12 Installation documentation includes site preparation, upgrade, file server and workstation installation, and a detailed cookbook method for network setup. System Messages is a fully indexed catalog of command line, operating system, NLM, printing, and shell messages. The Utilities Reference is an encyclopedia-oriented alphabetic reference of all utilities and complete instructions on syntax and execution. The System Administration book includes a more detailed reference of file server utilities, remote console, and some troubleshooting items. Concepts is an extended glossary of NetWare terms in alphabetic order. The Installation supplements provide detailed information concerning the installation of specialized networking hardware. Finally, print server documentation runs the system manager through the process of designing, installing, and configuring NetWare printing services.

THE NETWARE LOG BOOK

The final NetWare system management strategy is the pièce de résistance. The NetWare Log Book is the most important tool a system manager can have. It is a detailed step-by-step log of all activity from the point of LAN conception to the present. The NetWare Log Book includes worksheets, floor plans, receipts, restrictions, a list of all NetWare files on the shared disk, pictures of the hardware, pictures of the system manager's mother, cabling layouts, application installation information, and various random notes.

It is extremely important that the system manager take the log book seriously. He/she must start the log book before the network is installed and diligently maintain it as long as management duties continue. The log book should be tab-indexed with an easy-to-follow table of contents and written on acid-free paper. If nothing else, the NetWare Log Book can be used by the system manager to justify his or her existence.

That's it for NetWare management strategies. Keep in mind, this is an extremely important facet of the system manager's role and should be approached with caution and excitement. In this chapter, we will explore the four different areas of NetWare system management. As the hotel manager, it is your responsibility to make everybody happy, run the registration desk, plan conventions, and establish contingency plans. This is where the fun begins!

Login Scripts

Welcome to NetWare Registration!

Once users have been authenticated with a valid username and password, the system greets them with login scripts. These are the mints on the user's pillow. NetWare provides a variety of different login scripts for system-wide and user-specific configurations. In addition, login scripts can establish important session-specific environments such as drive mappings. If you think back for a moment to our discussion of drive mappings, you remember that they are temporary user mappings which point to specific areas of the shared disk. Drive mappings are activated each time a user logs in and must be defined by the user each time. Login scripts allow the system to establish and define custom user configurations—transparent to the user.

Login scripts are batch files for the network. As the NetWare system manager, it is your responsibility to create login scripts which are both productive and easy to maintain. NetWare provides

> NetWare provides a variety of different login scripts (batch files for the network) for system-wide and user-specific configurations.

three different types of login scripts—the system login script, the user login script, and the default login script. The system login script provides user configurations and system-wide drive mappings for everybody who logs into the network. The user login script is a user-specific script which provides user-customized configurations—each user executes his/her own script. The default login script executes in cases where there is no user script. The default login script contains minimum drive mappings and system configurations.

TIP

It is important to note that while login scripts are not required, they are a luxury. A well-designed and well-written login script can save the system manager literally hours of individual configuration. It is highly recommended that you make use of this particular NetWare tool for decreasing your maintenance load and increasing your general quality of life.

In this section, we will explore the details of these three different login script types. In addition, we will bolster our NetWare holster with a comprehensive understanding of NetWare login script commands and their syntax.

LOGIN SCRIPT TYPES

Above, we learned that there are three different types of NetWare login scripts—the system login script, user login script, and default login script. All of these scripts work in coordination to provide system-wide drive mappings and user-specific customization. Let's take a closer look.

System Login Script

The system login script provides a facility for system-wide drive mappings. The system login script is executed by all users as soon as they log in. This script can only be created and edited by the supervisor (under the supervisor options menu of SYSCON). The system login script is a special text file—NET$LOG.DAT. It is stored in the SYS:PUBLIC directory so all users can have access to it. The system login script file must consist of valid login script commands and be organized according to NetWare login script syntax and conventions.

User Login Script

The user login script is a user-specific script. It provides customization at the user level. The supervisor can use this script to further customize user parameters beyond the system login script. The user login script typically contains user-definable drive mappings and commands that are customized for particular individuals. While the user script is a nice feature, it can quickly become a maintenance nightmare—imagine hundreds and hundreds of user login scripts to constantly maintain. The user login script is the text file LOGIN in each user's unique SYS:MAIL\userid directory. If you remember back to our discussion of directory structures, we talked about a system-generated series of user directories under SYS:MAIL. This subdirectory is used to store user-specific configuration files such as the user login script.

TIP

The intelligent system manager can create an effective system login script which makes user login scripts obsolete. This is ideal because it provides the flexibility of user-customization while retaining the ease of maintenance and centralization of one system script. Try as hard as you can to fit all of your login script commands into one system login script.

Default Login Script

The default login script is activated only when a user login script doesn't exist. The default login script contains some basic mappings for the system and a COMSPEC command which points to the appropriate network DOS directory. The default login script cannot be edited because it exists as part of the LOGIN.EXE system file. The default login script was created and is maintained by the NetWare system and therefore cannot be edited, modified, or deleted. Earlier you learned that the ideal scenario is to have a system login script with no user login script. In this case, the default login script would execute after the system login script. The downside to this is that the default login script contains specific system-wide mappings which stomp all over the already-created system login script mappings. This is not good.

There are a variety of different strategies towards remedying this situation. One of these is to create a user login script with just one line. While this is an effective strategy, it doesn't make sense because it defeats the purpose of having one centrally located login script. The best strategy is to employ the EXIT command and bypass the default login script. We will discuss this option a little later.

Login Script Execution

It is important to have a firm understanding of how the different login scripts relate to one another and how they are executed. The system script executes first and contains system-wide configurations. If a user login script exists, it will execute after the system login script. Once the user login script has been executed, the system will return to the NetWare prompt—at which point the user has control of the system. If a user login script does not exist, the system will automatically execute the default login script (part of the LOGIN.EXE file). The default login script will also execute in situations where no system or user login script exists. This is typically the case when the system is first created.

Again, the ideal scenario is one system login script, and no user or default script. We'll talk about how to do this in a moment.

QUOTE

Consider the postage stamp, my son. It secures success through its ability to stick to one thing till it gets there.

Josh Billings

LOGIN SCRIPT COMMANDS

Login scripts consist of commands and identifiers just like any other program or batch file. A NetWare login script—whether it's a system, user, or default script—must be composed of valid login script commands and recognizable identifier variables. In addition, the script must follow valid syntax and conventions. The syntax for login script programming is quite simple—each line begins with a login script command and must contain either an identifier variable or a fixed value. For example, consider the following line:

MAP F:=SYS:\USERS\%LOGIN_NAME

This follows login script syntax because it contains the login script command MAP and the login script identifier variable %LOGIN_NAME. Identifier variables are extremely useful login script components which provide diverse customization. The idea is to establish one login script command which serves a variety of different users. For example, the %LOGIN_NAME identifier variable will return the value of each user's login name depending on who logs in. This is

> A NetWare login script—whether it's a system, user, or default script—must be composed of valid login script commands and recognizable identifier variables.

particularly useful for mapping user directories in a system login script. Remember, the ideal scenario is to have one login script which customizes both system-wide and user-specific environment variables. This is made possible through the use of identifier variables. Some of the more useful login script identifier variables are:

▸ MEMBER OF "GROUP"

▸ DAY

- ▸ DAY_OF_WEEK

- ▸ YEAR

- ▸ GREETING_TIME

- ▸ FULL_NAME

- ▸ LOGIN_NAME

- ▸ USER_ID

- ▸ MACHINE

- ▸ OS

- ▸ OS_VERSION

Identifier variables (Figure 11.1) are preceded by a % sign and must be capitalized. In order to be an effective system manager and create productive NetWare login scripts, you must have a firm understanding of all of the login script commands and how they are used in system, and of user and default login scripts. In the remainder of this section we will focus on the 14 most recognizable NetWare 3.12 login script commands. In addition, we will discuss how they are used to optimize the system and user environment. Remember, our focus in this section is to create one system login script which can satisfy both our system-wide and user-specific needs.

COMSPEC

COMSPEC (COMmand SPECifier) is a very, very important login script command. It redirects the DOS COMMAND.COM file to the appropriate NetWare DOS directory. This is required because as applications load into workstation memory, they have a tendency to knock the COMMAND.COM file out of RAM. If an application loads itself and unloads the COMMAND.COM file, the system has to know where to go to find the COMMAND.COM file. That's where COMSPEC comes in—it tells NetWare where to find COMMAND.COM. Without it, users will receive the message **Invalid COMMAND.COM**, or **COMMAND.COM cannot be found**, or **Insert boot disk in drive A**. This can be quite disruptive to users in a network environment.

FIGURE II.I

NetWare 3.12
Identifier Variables

Identifier variable	Function
CONDITIONAL	
ACCESS_SERVER	Returns TRUE if Access Server is Functional, otherwise FALSE
ERROR_LEVEL	An Error Number, 0=No Errors
MEMBER OF *"group"*	Returns TRUE if member of group, otherwise FALSE
DATE	
DAY	Day number (01-31)
DAY_OF_WEEK	Day of week (Monday, Tuesday, etc.)
MONTH	Month number (01-12)
MONTH_NAME	Month name (January, June, etc.)
NDAY_OF_WEEK	Weekday number (1-7, Sunday=1)
SHORT_YEAR	Year in short format (88, 89, etc.)
YEAR	Year in full format (1988, 1989)
DOS ENVIRONMENT	
< >	Use any DOS environment variable as a string
NETWORK	
NETWORK_ADDRESS	Network number of the cabling system (8 hex digits)
FILE_SERVER	Name of the filer server
TIME	
AM_PM	Day or night (am or pm)
GREETING_TIME	Morning, afternoon, or evening
HOUR	Hour of day or night (1-12)
HOUR24	Hour (00-23, midnight = 00)
MINUTE	Minute (00-59)
SECOND	Second (00-59)
USER	
FULL_NAME	User's full name (from SYSCON files)
LOGIN_NAME	User's unique login name
USER_ID	Number assigned to each user
WORKSTATION	
MACHINE	The machine the shell was written for, e.g., IBMPC
OS	The workstation's operating system, e.g., MSDOS
OS_VERSION	The version of the workstation's DOS
P_STATION	Station number or node address (12 hex digits)
SHELL_TYPE	The workstation's shell version
SMACHINE	Short machine name, e.g., IBM
STATION	Connection number

COMSPEC is important because it tells the system where to look for the appropriate COMMAND.COM. Keep in mind that each version of DOS on each of your workstations supports a different type of COMMAND.COM. You must use the DOS directory structure we discussed earlier to store the different COMMAND.COM files. In addition, use a drive mapping—typically S2—to make them easier to find. There are three identifier variables which allow us to map the appropriate search drive to the appropriate DOS subdirectory based on which machine was used. This is a very effective strategy when used in combination with the COMSPEC command. We will talk about these identifier variables and mapping DOS directories later when we get to the MAP command. At this point, it is important to note that COMSPEC is an important login script command which provides support for COMMAND.COM redirection. The syntax for COMSPEC is **COMSPEC S2:COMMAND.COM**. Remember, it must follow the appropriate MAP S2 command. Refer to the MAP command later in this section for a discussion of S2, COMSPEC, and DOS.

DISPLAY/FDISPLAY

The DISPLAY and FDISPLAY login script commands allow the system manager to display a text file as soon as users reach a certain point in the login process. The text file is displayed on the screen in its most simple format, without any control codes or formatting characters. If a text file contains control codes and formatting characters, the DISPLAY command will display those characters as ASCII bullets. This can be quite distracting for users who see garbage all over the screen. The FDISPLAY command will filter these types of text files and won't display control codes—the characters are filtered out and only the text is displayed. The syntax of DISPLAY and FDISPLAY are identical: **DISPLAY textfile**.

When the login script execution comes to this particular line, it goes out and finds the selected text file. Then it displays it on the screen. This particular command is useful when used in combination with the PAUSE command—which allows the system to pause execution until a key is pressed. Without the PAUSE command, the text display will go by on the screen very quickly.

DRIVE

The DRIVE command is a useful login script command which allows the system manager to specify where NetWare should leave the user once login script execution has finished. By default, the system will leave the user at the first available network drive—typically F:. In some cases, this can be confusing because F is typically mapped to LOGIN and the users will think, "Wow, I've already logged in. Why am I back here?" The DRIVE command is an effective strategy for system managers who want to leave users in their own home area—this is accomplished with DRIVE U:. Again, this strategy assumes that you've set up a home directory for each user and it specifies the U: drive.

DRIVE can also be useful if you are going to use the EXIT command to exit to a menu program at the end of login script execution. The menu program typically will be stored either in a public place—Z:—or in each user's own subdirectory—U:. The DRIVE command can be used preceding the EXIT command. This will dump the user in the directory where the menu command is to be executed.

EXIT

The EXIT command is a very useful login script command which provides a number of functions. EXIT terminates the login script and executes a specific network program. The network program can be any .EXE, .COM or .BAT file and must reside in the default drive. When used in combination with the DRIVE command, EXIT can be an effective strategy for creating a transparent turnkey system whereby users log in

> When used in combination with the DRIVE command, EXIT can be an effective strategy for creating a transparent turnkey system whereby users log in and are left within a menu system.

and are left within a menu system. The syntax for the EXIT command is relatively simple: EXIT [name of program file].

TIP

It is important to note that the program inside the quotes can only be a maximum of 14 characters long. Some system managers find this a harsh limitation because they might want to execute a particular

program name with many switches. To remedy this situation, you can create a batch file to perform the appropriate program commands and switches.

KNOWLEDGE

The EXIT command is that it will skip all other login script execution. So, if the EXIT command is included in the system login script, it will skip the user and default login script. Earlier you learned that the ideal circumstance is to have one system login script with no user login scripts to maintain. Also, I suggested skipping the execution of the default login script. The EXIT command allows you to do this by exiting the system login script to a menu program—thereby jumping over the user and default scripts. While this is an effective strategy, it is also very dangerous. Keep in mind that the EXIT statement in the system login script will bypass any user login scripts which have been created—past, present, or future.

FIRE PHASERS

FIRE PHASERS is a fun command which emits an ear-piercing, Star Trek-like phaser sound from the workstation. FIRE PHASERS is useful in cases where text is displayed on screen and you want to draw users' attention to it. FIRE PHASERS can also be used in cases where you feel there is a breach in security. The syntax for FIRE PHASERS is simply FIRE [number].

The maximum number of phasers which can be fired in one command is 9—a 1-digit number limitation. If you would like to fire phasers more than 9 times, you can simply nest multiple fire commands one after another. There is no limit to the number of FIRE PHASERS commands you can have in a row, although it can get quite annoying.

IF ... THEN ... ELSE

The IF ... THEN command is probably the most versatile login script command—it provides for script programming logic. IF ... THEN checks a given condition and executes your command only if the condition is met. Otherwise, the IF ... THEN skips the conditional command. For example, if you would like the system to display a message and fire phasers on each person's birthday, you can use the date identifier variables and the IF ... THEN command to search for a specific date. This is also useful in displaying text messages on Fridays or Tuesdays, whenever there are staff meetings, or if a report is due at the end of the week.

IF ... THEN is also useful in customizing group login scripts. Since there is no facility for group login scripts, the IF ... THEN command can be used with the MEMBER_OF_GROUP identifier variable to configure specific drive mappings and configurations for groups of users. The IF ... THEN command in combination with all of the many different identifier variables makes it possible for the intelligent system manager to create one system login script which satisfies all user-specific customization needs.

QUOTE
Experience is a comb that life gives you after you lose your hair.

Judith Stern

If multiple activities are dependent upon a condition, NetWare allows you to use the BEGIN and END commands in conjunction with IF ... THEN. This allows the system manager to create groups of conditional commands. For example:

```
IF DAY_OF_WEEK = "FRIDAY" THEN BEGIN
    WRITE "Welcome to Friday. Glad you could make it"
    DISPLAY Friday.txt
    MAP R:=SYS:DATA\REPORTS
END
```

TIP
NetWare 3.12 supports nested IF ... THEN statements to 10 levels.

INCLUDE
The INCLUDE login script command is provided for cases where one login script isn't enough. The INCLUDE statement branches to a DOS text file which is written using proper login script conventions. INCLUDE will execute the text

file as if it were a login script. Once the INCLUDE statement is finished, the original login script continues from the point of the INCLUDE statement. This is useful when used in combination with IF ... to provide customization for specific users and groups.

MAP

MAP is the most widely used user-specific configuration. Mapping is a very important part of NetWare navigation and provides a facility for representing large directory paths as drive letters. The problem with mapping is that it's both session-specific (meaning drive pointers disappear when users logout) and user-specific (meaning they're unique for each user). The temporary nature of drive mappings makes them particularly annoying—the complex map commands must be entered each time a user logs in. Fortunately, NetWare provides a facility for mapping automation—the system login script.

MAP commands are entered at the very top of the system login. Also, network mappings are typically activated before search drive mappings—search mappings are a lot more friendly in their acquisition of drive letters. All MAP commands work in login scripts except the MAP NEXT command, which can only be used at the NetWare prompt. The default login script includes two MAP commands:

```
MAP S1:=SYS:PUBLIC
MAP S2:=SYS:PUBLIC\%MACHINE\%OS\%OS_VERSION
```

Earlier we mentioned the importance of having different DOS versions in the network directory structure. This is to provide workstation access to the appropriate COMMAND.COM. The MAP S2 command, in conjunction with three identifier variables, allows us to intelligently MAP the appropriate DOS directory for the appropriate version of workstation DOS. The above S2 command uses three different identifier variables:

- %MACHINE—identifies the machine type—IBM_PC for example

- %OS—identifies the operating system—MS-DOS for example

- %OS_VERSION—identifies the DOS version—v5.00 for example

This one command satisfies the COMSPEC requirement for all users on all workstations using all versions of DOS. Remember to put the correct COM-MAND.COM file in each %OS_VERSION directory. Also, be very precise about the directory structure which you created—it must match the parameters exactly.

PAUSE

The PAUSE command pauses execution of the login script at a certain point and asks the workstation user to **Press a key to continue**. This is particularly useful when combined with the DISPLAY and FDISPLAY commands to display large messages one screenful at a time.

REMARK

REMARK allows comments and documentation to be placed in the login script without generating an error. Besides the word REMARK, NetWare 3.12 supports three other uses of the REMARK command—REM, an asterisk (*), and a semi-colon (;). Any text preceded by REMARK is ignored by the system. This is an effective strategy for tracking script editing when you have multiple supervisors maintaining the system login script. This is also a useful strategy for documenting large login scripts for system managers who follow you.

TIP

When these system login scripts get quite large and complex, it is very hard to follow exactly what is going on. Novell, for example, in their international headquarters, has a login script which supports the whole organization—it exceeds 17 pages. This system login script must be highly documented so that people can follow exactly what's going on and how it's being implemented.

WRITE

The WRITE command is probably the most versatile login script command because it allows you to display any message on the screen. Any comment enclosed in quotes following the WRITE command is displayed at the appropriate point in login script execution. WRITE can display information not only in a text nature but can also display identifier variable type information. For example, WRITE can display:

```
WRITE "Your username is %LOGIN_NAME"
WRITE "Your workstation number is %STATION"
WRITE "You DOS version is %OS_VERSION"
WRITE "Today is %DAY_OF_WEEK"
```

KNOWLEDGE

Another interesting identifier variable which is used with WRITE is GREETING_TIME. GREETING_TIME will return a value of Morning, Afternoon, **or** Evening **depending on the time of day.** WRITE "Good %GREETING_TIME, %LOGIN_NAME" **provides a nice greeting to all users.**

(DOS Executable)

The DOS executable (#) command is extremely detrimental in *any* login script. It has been included by Novell in a last-ditch effort to support other commands outside of the login script—but it can cause more harm than good. Any non-login script command preceded by the # can be executed from within a login script. The problem is that while the command is running, the entire login script is stored in workstation RAM. Once the # command is finished, NetWare reloads the login script from memory. The problem is many workstations do not completely free up the workstation RAM which was occupied by the login script temporarily. In many cases, as much as 70 to 100K of workstation RAM can be lost when using the #.

A more effective way to execute non-login script commands is the EXIT command. It is a good idea to use the EXIT command to execute a batch file at the end of the login script. This will remove the login script from memory and execute any list of non-login script commands from within a batch file.

> The DOS executable (#) command is extremely detrimental in *any* login script. Any non-login script command preceded by the # can be executed from within a login script. The problem is that while the command is running, the entire login script is stored in workstation RAM.

TIP

The CAPTURE command is a critical component in NetWare printing and needs to be executed at start-up. This command can be launched from a system batch file upon exiting the system login script.

REQUIRED COMPONENTS

At the beginning of this section, we described login scripts as a luxury. While most of these login script commands are optional, there are three required components in NetWare system login script. They are:

▸ A search drive mapping to PUBLIC

▸ A search drive mapping to DOS

▸ COMSPEC to the DOS mapping

The search drive mapping to PUBLIC directory can be established by using the following command: **MAP S1:=SYS:PUBLIC**. This should be the first search drive mapping and provide the facility for user and system manager access to common NetWare utilities.

The second required component is a search drive to the DOS directories. As you recall, the system manager should create an intelligent structure of DOS sub directories. Each of these DOS sub directories will have the appropriate version of COMMAND.COM for each of the workstation DOS types. The required drive mapping would read as follows:

MAP S2:=SYS:PUBLIC\%MACHINE\%OS\%OS_VERSION.

This mapping statement would provide a facility for users to find their appropriate COMMAND.COM upon the exit of a network application.

The final required login script component is COMSPEC, which ensures that each workstation will reload the appropriate COMMAND.COM at the appropriate time. The syntax for COMSPEC is **COMSPEC=S2:COMMAND.COM**. These three required components will load whether or not a system or user login script exists because they make up the fundamental components of the default login script.

That completes our discussion of NetWare login scripts. Keep in mind that login scripts are very effective tools for customizing user workstation environments and providing system-wide drive mappings. A well-designed system login script can save hours of maintenance for the NetWare system manager. Once you have established an effective strategy for NetWare registration and created a comfortable and productive environment for your users, it is time to move on to user interface. User interface represents the marketing components of the system manager's job. A well-designed user interface can make or break the productivity of a LAN. There's nothing worse than grumbling users.

QUOTE

When down in the mouth, remember Jonah. He came out all right.

Thomas Edison

User Interface

The marketing world would have you believe that "image is everything!" Well, they're not far off. The media onslaught of the late twentieth century has opened our eyes and emptied our pocket books. The goal of marketing is to associate products with positive feelings: a car with the open road, sneakers with athletic ability, a soft drink with beauty.

As the NetWare system manager, you must market the LAN to your users. Help them to associate their workstation with productivity and general peace-of-mind. The trick is to make your users WANT to be on the LAN. User interface is the key. It involves workstation software, application software, menu systems, and E-mail. A well-designed user

> As the NetWare system manager, you must market the LAN to your users. Help them to associate their workstation with productivity and general peace-of-mind.

interface can make your users feel comfortable with the network. There is nothing worse than users who are apprehensive, intimidated, and threatened by the idea of logging in to a large network.

There has been a lot of hyperactivity lately surrounding the Big Brother syndrome and many people are becoming LANphobic. They feel that becoming part of a larger electronic system will cause them to lose their individuality. One of the most important cures for LANphobia is to provide user customization and individuality for each user. Even though they are part of a larger whole, they can feel as if they are a very important part of the system alone.

Another important aspect of user interface is productivity. It is the system manager's responsibility to set up a productive software environment for each user. Then they can perform their tasks in synergy with the other LAN users while at the same time maintaining some unique job specialization. This strategy is accomplished by intelligently loading application software that is both shared by everyone on the LAN, yet customized for each specific user's needs.

In this section, we will explore the user interface responsibilities of the NetWare system manager by focusing on the intelligent installation of application software for specific user productivity and the alleviation of LANphobia by installing an intelligent and friendly custom menu environment. In addition, we will teach users how to communicate using simple electronic mail. But before we begin, let's take a look at workstation software and the many different shells that connect the user with the NetWare LAN. Keep your eyes open for LAN marketeers.

WORKSTATION SOFTWARE

NetWare 3.12 prides itself on its ability to transparently support a multitude of different workstation environments. NetWare 3.12 currently supports workstations running DOS, OS/2, Macintosh, and UNIX. Although NetWare was primarily designed to support the DOS workstation, it does allow transparent access from these other environments as well. DOS workstations can store DOS-like files on the NetWare shared disk without any problem. Other workstation platforms must use name space modules to support non-DOS naming schemes. OS/2, for example, supports 255 characters and extended attributes in its naming scheme.

Since most of its customers are using DOS workstations, Novell has concentrated its workstation efforts on DOS-oriented shells. These shells use one of two different strategies: IPX/NETx or ODI/VLM. The IPX/NETx strategy has been around since NetWare was first invented and utilizes two files: IPX.COM and NETx.EXE for both protocol and requester communications. The second strategy: ODI/VLM, employs a more modern modular approach towards protocols and requester facilities. ODI drivers and VLMs are much more flexible and allow for easy management and configuration.

KNOWLEDGE

NetWare is moving towards full ODI compliance with NetWare 4.0 and 3.12 shells. They use what are called VLMs or Virtual Loadable Modules. VLMs are part of the DOS requester, which provides fully modular loading of workstation components.

Now we'll take a closer look at how the system manager can use IPX/NETx and ODI/VLM to configure DOS workstations. In addition, we will explore NetWare support for non-DOS platforms.

IPX/NETx

IPX is the protocol utility which controls communications between NETx.EXE and the internal network interface card. IPX is generated using the WSGEN utility and requires approximately 32K of workstation RAM. NETx.EXE is the NetWare shell which handles the communications between DOS and the IPX.COM protocol. NetWare provides three versions of the NETx shell which accommodate different workstation environments:

NETx.EXE—the basic NETx shell which loads in conventional memory. It supports any version of DOS from v2.1 to v6.00.

EMSNETx.EXE—the EMS (Expanded Memory Specification) version of NETx. EMSNETx.EXE runs in expanded memory and frees approximately 34K of conventional RAM. On the downside, EMSNETx.EXE is very slow.

XMSNETx.EXE—the XMS (Extended Memory Specification) version of NETx. XMSNETx.EXE runs in extended memory and also frees approximately 34K of conventional RAM. On the downside, XMSNETx.EXE occupies the same 64K high memory as DOS v5.00 and v6.00. Therefore, DOS HIGH and XMSNETx can't operate together—the user must choose one or the other.

Figure 11.2 provides an illustration of NetWare shells and workstation RAM.

KNOWLEDGE

The workstation memory requirements for NetWare 3.12 differ depending on the user activities. Normal workstations require 512K of RAM, while workstations running WSGEN require the maximum conventional RAM of 640K.

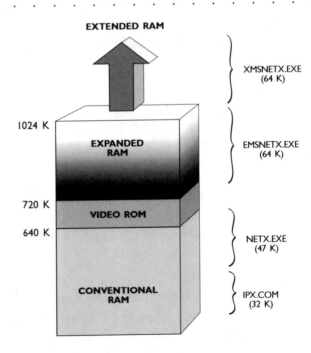

F I G U R E 11.2

*Shells and
Workstation RAM*

ODI/VLM

ODI drivers and VLMs are a relatively new addition to the NetWare puzzle. They are modular-oriented subcomponents which combine to enhance the functions of IPX.COM and NETx.EXE. There are four different components that define the ODI/VLM environment. They are:

- ► LSL
- ► LAN driver (NE2000.COM, for example)
- ► Protocol stack (IPXODI.COM)
- ► VLM (the NetWare DOS Requester)

These four components combine together to initialize the workstation network interface card and open communications between the workstation and the NetWare server. Refer to Figure 11.3 for a comparison of this architecture and the IPX/NETx solution. Once ODI drivers have been initialized, the VLMs can be loaded to control communications between the workstation operating system and the protocol. LSL.COM defines the link support layer. It enables the workstation to communicate over several protocols. The LAN driver component or NE2000.COM, for example, communicates directly between LSL and the internal network interface card. Most common network interface card manufacturers provide ODI compliant LAN drivers for their specific network interface card. Finally, the protocol stack file, such as IPXODI.COM, manages protocol communications between the

> ODI drivers and VLMs are modular-oriented subcomponents which combine to enhance the functions of IPX.COM and NETx.EXE. They initialize the workstation network interface card and open communications between the workstation and the NetWare server.

workstation and the server. Another example of a protocol stack file would be TCPIP.EXE which provides support for communications over TCP/IP protocol LANs.

The key to ODI drivers is the NET.CFG file. The NET.CFG file provides a facility for configuring these different components. It contains information about the link support layer, network interface card driver configurations, interrupt memory address, and details about the protocol which is being bound. We will discuss support for multiple protocols in the next section.

The NetWare DOS Requester (VLM) is the connection point between the local operating system (DOS) and network services. The DOS Requester consists of one management file (VLM.EXE) and many supporting Virtual Loadable Modules (*.VLM). NetWare 3.12 supports VLMs for packet signing, printing, communications, and even NETx emulation. These VLMs are advantageous because they can be loaded and unloaded, they reduce workstation overhead, and provide third-party developers with a platform for new ideas. When VLM.EXE is executed, it loads all VLMs found in the current directory (C:\NWCLIENT, by default). You can specify other VLMs or a different directory in the NET.CFG file. VLM.EXE supports the following options:

VLM /C=path loads the DOS Requester using VLMs found in another directory.

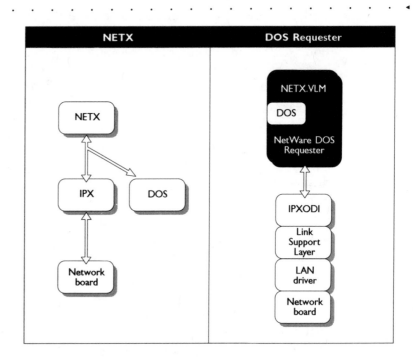

Comparison of NETx and NetWare DOS Requester architectures

VLM /mc   loads the DOS Requester in conventional memory.

VLM /me   loads the DOS Requester in expanded memory.

VLM /mx   loads the DOS Requester in extended memory.

TIP

The NetWare DOS Requester can be used with NetWare 3.11 workstations, but remember: you must change the CONFIG.SYS file to support LASTDRIVE=Z, because the Requester and DOS share drive table information.

TIP

If you are moving to the NetWare DOS Requester, your users will find that F: is no longer the first network drive. In many cases it will be changed to D:. To force it back to F:, add FIRST NETWORK DRIVE = F to each NET.CFG file.

Non-DOS Workstations

NetWare provides a variety of other solutions for non-DOS workstations. These products work in conjunction with NetWare at the Server and with the native OS at the workstation.

OS/2—the OS/2 Requester which comes with NetWare 3.12. It loads on the OS/2 workstation and controls communications between the workstation operating system and NetWare. The OS/2 Requester also provides Named Pipes support for native OS/2 communications.

Macintosh—the NetWare for Macintosh product contains two components—NLM and DA. The NetWare for Macintosh NLM loads on the NetWare 3.12 server and provides translation tables between NetWare and AppleTalk—the Macintosh protocol. The NetWare for Macintosh DA is a group of Desk Accessories which load on the Macintosh workstation and provide elementary NetWare tools in the native Macintosh interface.

UNIX—NetWare 3.12 supports UNIX workstations through NetWare NFS. This product loads as a collection of NLMs on the file server. It provides support for native NFS communications between NetWare volumes and UNIX workstations. With NetWare NFS, users can share files between DOS and UNIX workstations.

It is important to choose the correct NetWare workstation software. Keep in mind, the workstation is the user's link to the LAN. In many cases, it can make or break user productivity.

APPLICATION SOFTWARE

As you learned earlier, one of the most important responsibilities of the Net-Ware hotel manager is the development of a productive user environment—that is, a balance between custom user needs and global application synergy. This is accomplished through a 7-step approach of installing application software. In this section, we will explore this 7-step approach and learn how it optimizes application software in a NetWare environment. It is important to note that this is a general discussion. Most application software involves specific instructions for network installation and shared configurations. For the most part, these 7 steps will help in creating a synergy between user productivity and shared application software.

QUOTE

To be absolutely certain about something, one must know everything or nothing about it.

Olin Miller

Step 1: NetWare Compatibility

It is important to determine whether the application software is NetWare compatible before you buy it. There are approximately 4,000 software packages which are compatible and registered with Novell. This compatibility information is important because NetWare makes demands on application software which in some cases can cause it to corrupt data or, at the very least, provide a non-productive work environment. NetWare compatibility information can be accessed on Netwire (Novell's electronic bulletin board) or from your local Novell sales and operations center. In addition, you can contact the software vendor for NetWare compatibility information.

> It is important to determine whether the application software is NetWare-compatible before you buy it. There are approximately 4,000 software packages which are compatible and registered with Novell.

Step 2: Multi-User

For the best results and best user productivity in a NetWare environment, it is critical that the application software support multiple users simultaneously. A large number of application software programs are not multi-user and are designed to be used by one user—one at a time in a stand-alone environment. Most of your large software manufacturers are creating multi-user versions of their popular software which provide file sharing and multi-user access. Again, it is important to determine multi-user compatibility with the software before you purchase it so that you can be assured of the most productive user environment.

TIP

Single-user software works in a NetWare environment. NetWare supports any DOS application, but these applications aren't very effective because they don't provide data-sharing/application-sharing capabilities.

Step 3: Directory Structure

Before you can install the software or configure any of its components, it is extremely important to have an intelligent organization directory structure which supports not only the application software but the data it will generate as well. Each application program should have a specific subdirectory under the directory heading of APPS to avoid cluttering the root directory. This also organizes application software for easy and efficient security design. Some software applications will create their own directory structure during the installation process. Unfortunately, this directory structure is typically created off of the root directory. While this works fine in a local hard-disk environment, it does not work in a NetWare shared environment. Remember, we have many more people accessing the shared disk. In order to fool the system into installing its directory structure in the appropriate place, you can map root the F: drive to SYS:APPS. The system will then think that the APPS subdirectory is in fact the root and it will create its directory structure under APPS instead of under the real NetWare root.

Step 4: Installation

The installation process is typically left up to the application itself. Most applications require that you run a setup or install program. The install program performs two functions: customization of network configurations, and file decompression. It is not a good idea to just copy the programs off of the install disks. Instead, use the INSTALL program. If you must copy the disks to the NetWare drive, make sure to use NCOPY—not the DOS copy command—because it both retains security and is a much more efficient command line utility for file copying.

Once the network software has been installed, there are three more steps which define special configurations.

Step 5: File Attributes

It is very important that application software have the correct file attributes so they can be shared without being destroyed. Application files are normally flagged Sharable-Read Only, whereas data files are typically flagged Sharable-Read/Write. Most multi-user and NetWare compatible application software will provide some information about specific file attributes and the flagging of files for their particular application's needs.

Step 6: User Rights

The second software configuration is User Rights. It is very important to grant user access to network applications. By default, users have no rights to the new directory structure you've created. If you were to install the application software and walk away, the users would have no access to the applications and would not be able to run them.

Typically, if everyone is going to use all of the same applications, you can use the group EVERYONE to assign the access rights and assign them to the APPS directory. As you recall, access rights flow down to all subdirectories of the parent directory. Typically, the RF (Read and File Scan) rights are sufficient for all files in an applications directory. In addition, all rights except supervisory, modify, and access control are needed in data directories. Application data can be stored in a variety of different places depending on the type of data. User-specific data should be stored in the user's own home directory. Group-specific data should be stored in a group subdirectory off of the root. Globally-shared data should be stored in a data directory from the root.

Step 7: Workstation Configuration

Many programs require special DOS configurations at the workstation for them to run properly. The most notable is CONFIG.SYS (which we talked about in Chapter 1), which customizes the DOS environment. For example, there are device drivers which must be loaded for programs that use a mouse. There is also an environment space variable for large programs which use lots of workstation RAM. Environment space can be increased using the SHELL command. The syntax is SHELL = C:\COMMAND.COM /p /e:1024.

This command provides enough environment space for local DOS applications and NetWare drive mappings—1024 bytes (the default is 256). See Chapter 1 for a more detailed description of the DOS configuration files.

Once the application software has been installed and users have proper access rights, a friendly menu environment should be created to guide users from one application to another. In addition to making it easy for users to access network applications, a menu friendly environment also helps alleviate LANphobia. Let's take a look.

MENU SOFTWARE

NetWare has a built-in menu system which provides custom NetWare-looking menus. This system uses a very simple script file for system managers to create a batch-file menu system. The execution of this custom menu environment is versatile to the point that large groups can share the same menu file or each user can have his/her own specific file. In addition, NetWare supports a customized color palette which allows each menu or submenu to have different colors and different characteristics—so it can be distinguished from previous menus.

> NetWare has a built-in menu system which provides custom NetWare-looking menus.

The most appealing thing about NetWare's menu system is that it uses exactly the same function keys and the same look-and-feel as all other menus, including SYSCON, FILER, SESSION, and so on. This makes it very easy for users and system managers to understand and maintain. NetWare's menu facility has specific syntax and rules for execution. Before we review those, let's take a moment to talk about how custom menus can be used to enhance transparent connectivity—it's called a turnkey system.

Custom Menu Environment

A turnkey custom menu environment provides transparent user access from the point of turning on the computer to the point of bringing up applications. The idea is to perform as many of the configuration functions and access activities as possible in the background so that the entire system is transparent to the user. The term "turnkey" comes from the notion that you can turn the key and everything takes care of itself. While this is a very nice environment and simple to use, it is somewhat complex for the system manager to set up and maintain. A turnkey system consists of four components:

▶ **The workstation boot disk** should contain the hidden system files, COMMAND.COM, an IPX file for accessing the NetWare protocol, and a NETx file for attaching to the server. Finally, the workstation boot disk should include an AUTOEXEC.BAT batch file which not only loads IPX and NETx but also moves to the F: prompt and logs in the user.

▶ **The system login script and user login script** should be maintained so they include an EXIT command which exits the user to a specific menu format. Whether the menu is user-specific or system-wide is not as important as the fact that the login script itself executes the menu.

▶ **The menu** must be easily executed and customized to the user's needs. The menu can be executed either from a user-specific directory where a customized menu resides or from a shared directory where all users are accessing the same menu file.

▶ The fourth component of a turnkey system is the menu execution options from within the menu itself. It is important that the users have access to all of the applications, functions, and utilities they need. They should all originate from within one central menu program.

Menu Syntax

Novell has revamped their menu system in NetWare 3.12—with a little help from Saber, Inc. The new menu structure is a "run-time," partial version of the successful Saber menu system. It follows the same simple Saber syntax, and produces familiar NetWare-looking Blue and Gold menus (GO CAL BEARS!). NetWare 3.12 menu syntax is based on two simple command types: *organizational* and *control*. Organizational commands provide the menu's look and feel, while control commands process internal menu instructions. Let's take a closer look.

TIP

If you are still using NetWare 3.11, refer to the NetWare 2.2 menu section of this book. The menu syntax and execution are identical.

Organizational Commands Organizational menu commands determine what the menu will look like. The two NetWare 3.12 organizational menu commands are:

▶ MENU—identifies the beginning of each menu screen.

▶ ITEM—defines the options which appear on the screen.

KNOWLEDGE

The NetWare 3.12 menu system is only a partial version of Saber's own product. Therefore, NetWare menus cannot be fully customized. For example, system managers cannot specify the location of menus on the screen, nor avoid the default color pallette—BLUE AND GOLD. In addition, NetWare's menu system is limited to 11 cascaded screens—one main menu and 10 submenus.

The MENU command is left-justified and followed by a number. A single Net-Ware 3.12 menu file can support 254 different menus—1 through 255. The menu number is followed by a comma and the title of the menu. Refer to the sample below for exact syntax. Options are listed under the menu command with the ITEM command. Each option is granted a letter (A-Z) and will appear in the exact order in which it is written. If you would like to force a different letter for a particular option, simply precede the text with a carat (^) and the desired letter—refer to the menu below. ITEMs can be customized using one of four built-in options:

  ▶ {BATCH}—shells the menu to disk and saves 32 KB of workstation RAM

  ▶ {CHDIR}—returns the user to the default directory upon completion of the item

  ▶ {PAUSE}—temporarily stops menu execution and displays the message "Strike any key to continue"

  ▶ {SHOW}—displays DOS commands in the upper-left corner—only if they are executed

KNOWLEDGE

If you use the caret (^) for one option, you must use it for all ITEMs under a given MENU.

Control Commands   Control commands execute menu instructions. They are the workhorses of NetWare 3.12 menu commands. The six control commands are:

- ▸ EXEC—executes any internal or external program
- ▸ SHOW—branches to another menu within this menu file
- ▸ LOAD—branches to a different menu file
- ▸ GETO—optional user input
- ▸ GETR—required user input
- ▸ GETP—assigns user input to a DOS variable

TIP

While GET commands add power and flexibility to the NetWare 3.12 menu system, they are difficult to program and extremely finicky. Be careful.

The EXEC command causes particular internal and external commands to be executed. The command can be either an .EXE file, a .COM file, a DOS command, or any of the following internal commands: EXEC EXIT to exit the menu and return to the NetWare prompt, EXEC DOS to return to the NetWare prompt temporarily, and EXEC LOGOUT, which exits the menu and logs users out of the network. The SHOW and LOAD commands provide the same services from a slightly different angle. SHOW branches menu execution to a menu within the current menu file, while LOAD branches menu execution to a completely different menu file. Refer to the sample menu below for an illustration of the SHOW and LOAD syntax.

The final three control commands allow for user input. This feature was previously not available in NetWare menus. GETO, GETR, and GETP are powerful commands, but their syntax is a little tricky. The format for these commands is:

GETx *instruction {prepend} length,prefill,SECURE {append}*

Instruction is replaced by the message you want to display to the user, *prepend* attaches data to the front of the answer string, *length* is the maximum input window size, *prefill* provides a default response, *SECURE* displays asterisks in the user window, and *append* attaches data to the end of the answer string. Some rules to follow for GETx commands are:

- ► commands must be entered in uppercase

- ► a maximum of 100 GETx commands per ITEM

- ► limit one prompt per line

- ► you can display 10 prompts per dialog box— use a carat (^) to force one prompt per box

KNOWLEDGE
When using GETx commands, the ENTER key accepts the input but doesn't execute the command. To activate the corresponding EXEC command, the user must press <F10>.

The GETO command receives optional input from the user. The GETR command, on the other hand, requires input from the user. If the user does not respond, the menu will patiently wait until he/she does. The user can, however, press Esc to return to the previous menu. Both the GETO and GETR commands can only handle one piece of information at a time. The GETP command can handle many pieces of information at once. In addition, the GETP command stores user input as DOS variables—%1, %2, %3, %4, and so on. These variables can be used by other menu commands to further customize user menus.

Refer to the following sample .SRC file for a head-start on NetWare 3.12 menu syntax:

```
MENU 01,TOM'S MAIN MENU
    ITEM ^AApplications
        SHOW 05
    ITEM ^UUtilities
        SHOW 10
    ITEM ^JJERRY's Main Menu
```

```
            LOAD U:\USERS\JERRY\JERRY.DAT
        ITEM ^DDOS Prompt
            EXEC DOS
        ITEM ^LLogout
            EXEC LOGOUT

    MENU 05,Applications Submenu
        ITEM Word Processing
            EXEC wp
        ITEM Spreadsheet
            EXEC ss
        ITEM Windows
            EXEC win :

    MENU 10,Utilities Submenu
        ITEM ^1NetWare Menu Utilities
            SHOW 12
        ITEM ^2NetWare Command Line Utilities
            SHOW 14

    MENU 12,NetWare Menu Utilities
        ITEM System Configuration {BATCH}
            EXEC syscon
        ITEM FILER {BATCH}
            EXEC filer
        ITEM Network User Tools {BATCH}
            EXEC session

    MENU 14,NetWare Command Line Utilities
        ITEM List Servers {SHOW}
            GETO Enter Server Name and Option: { } 25,, {}
            EXEC SLIST
        ITEM Copy a File {PAUSE}
            GETP Enter Source {} 25,, {}
            GETP Enter Destination {} 25,, {}
            EXEC NCOPY %1 %2
        ITEM Display a MAP listing {SHOW CHDIR PAUSE}
            EXEC MAP
```

Menu Execution

NetWare 3.12 menu source files are created using any text editor—with the .SRC extension. These files are then complied using MENUMAKE.EXE into a .DAT file. The smaller, more flexible DAT file is then executed using NMENU.BAT. In addition, NetWare 3.11 menu files (.MNU) can be converted into 3.12 source files (.SRC) using the MENUCNVT.EXE utility. See Figure 11.4.

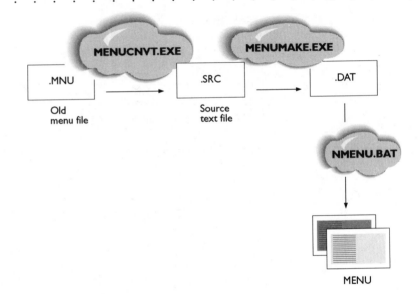

FIGURE 11.4

NetWare 3.12 Menu Execution

QUOTE

Spoken language is merely a series of squeaks.

Alfred North Whitehead

The NMENU.BAT program is stored in the PUBLIC directory so it can be accessed from anywhere by any NetWare user. In addition, there are some security concerns which affect the execution of NetWare menus, specifically:

▶ Users must have the Read and File Scan rights to the directory that holds the .DAT file—which is typically their own directory or a shared directory like PUBLIC.

▸ Users must have Write and Create rights in the directory in which they are currently logged when they execute the menu command. This is because the menu command creates temporary batch files in the current directory. You should have users accessing or running menus from their own directory whether or not they are executing a menu file which exists there.

▸ If a menu file is going to be used by multiple users, it should be flagged as sharable.

E-MAIL

NetWare 3.12 includes a sophisticated messaging system called Basic MHS— Basic Message Handling Service. Basic MHS provides electronic message delivery on a single server. Another product, Global MHS, provides a more far-reaching E-mail solution. Both Basic and Global MHS are messaging engines—they aren't E-mail packages. Messages are created in an electronic mail application and delivered by Basic MHS. The E-mail package must comply with the Novell interface standard—SMF, Standard Message Format.

Novell has included Basic MHS with NetWare 3.12 in an attempt to provide a comprehensive network solution. Messaging has recently become one of the most productive features of local area networking. Novell has also included an entry-level E-mail application called First Mail. First Mail is a simple, MHS-compliant application which provides straightforward E-mail on a single server.

Basic MHS

Basic MHS consists of an NLM at the server and an ADMIN utility at the workstation. To install Basic MHS, follow these simple steps:

1 · Load INSTALL at the server and choose Product Options.

2 · Add Basic MHS to the Currently Installed Products screen and enter the path to the Basic MHS files.

3 · Enter a workgroup name and confirm SYS:MHS as the destination directory.

4 · Let the system use your current bindery information to build a list of mail users. Also, choose "login names" instead of full names.

5 · Let the installation program change your system login script and AUTOEXEC.NCF files. It will simply set "MV=" environment variables.

TIP

Create all of your users before installing Basic MHS. This way you can let the system create your mail users from the bindery. Otherwise, you have to create them manually using ADMIN.EXE.

Once Basic MHS has been installed, you can administer the system through the ADMIN.EXE utility in MHS\EXE. It allows you to create new users, modify and delete existing accounts, manage distribution lists, register E-mail applications, and modify the Basic MHS system configuration. In order to run ADMIN.EXE at your workstation, you must first load the Btrieve Requester (BREQUEST.EXE).

First Mail

Basic MHS provides the background service of managing user accounts and mail directories, but it doesn't provide a user interface for creating, sending, receiving, or deleting mail. Any E-mail package that uses SMF can use Basic MHS. One such application is First Mail—which is included with NetWare 3.12. First Mail provides basic messaging capabilities for a single server. It is a comprehensive E-mail application and supports both DOS and Macintosh clients. First Mail is installed automatically when you install Basic MHS, and it resides in the SYS:PUBLIC subdirectory as MAIL.EXE.

That completes our discussion of E-mail and user interface in general. Keep in mind that menus, application programs, and user configurations can provide a very useful strategy for warding off LANphobia. But I have found that the most effective strategy is a warm touch and a kind heart.

Multi-Protocol Management

Life would be so easy if NetWare only supported one type of user and one type of workstation. The NetWare system manager could focus his/her energy on DOS workstations and DOS shells. This would be analogous to having only one type of guest at the Park Place resort: regular, well-behaved, and high-tipping. The hotel manager wouldn't have to deal with the huge variety of personalities, the conventions, the VIPs, and the complaints. Unfortunately, though, this is not a perfect world. And besides, where would the fun be? It's been said many times that "variety is the spice of life." Well, NetWare has embraced variety with three arms: OS/2, UNIX, and Macintosh. In addition, NetWare 3.12 supports a variety of different protocols: FTAM for OSI, AppleTalk for Macintosh, and TCP/IP for UNIX-type machines.

One of the hotel manager's most challenging responsibilities is the planning and organization of unique events such as VIP visits, press conferences, and weekly or monthly conventions. While unique visits create stress in the hotel manager's life, they also provide an entertaining source of variety. In the same way, the NetWare system manager is responsible for supporting unique workstations. Unique workstations include different types of protocols, other operating systems, and connections to larger host machines.

Multiprotocol management is supported through the ODI architecture model. ODI stands for Open Data-link Interface. Open Data-link Interface is an industry standard for supporting and sharing multiple protocols over one LAN medium. In addition, ODI compliant network interface cards can simultaneously support both IPX, TCP/IP, and AppleTalk protocols. This level of transparent workstation access does not come without a price. ODI architecture is complex and difficult to install. In addition, multiprotocol management is a relatively new and misunderstood art. The system manager must be well aware of his or her responsibilities in supporting non-DOS workstations. The good news is information and tools are growing rapidly in this arena.

> The NetWare system manager is responsible for supporting unique workstations such as different types of protocols, other operating systems, and connections to larger host machines.

Let's take a brief look at the architecture of Novell's ODI model and explore the implementation of ODI at the workstation, file server, and non-DOS platforms.

THE ODI ARCHITECTURE MODEL

The ODI architecture model was developed jointly by Novell and Apple in 1989. It defines a set of standards at the datalink layer of the OSI model. The ODI architecture model (Figure 11.5) consists of three different layers: the open data-link interface layer (ODI), protocol stack layer, and NetWare services layer. The ODI layer includes the LAN adapter, MLID (Multiple Link Interface Driver), LAN driver, and LSL link support layer. These three components work together to provide simultaneous support for a variety of different types of protocols.

The protocol stack layer works in conjunction with NetWare STREAMS to provide specific services to IPX, TCP/IP, OSI, or AppleTalk protocols. The protocol stack layer communicates directly with NetWare services to provide the same type of file and print services to all four different protocols. This model is ideal where TCP/IP and IPX packets can be interpreted by the file server network interface card. They communicate with the appropriate protocol stack layer and have access to the same NetWare file services. This is how UNIX workstations share files with DOS and OS/2 workstations.

▶ . . . . ◀

FIGURE II.5

The ODI Architecture Model

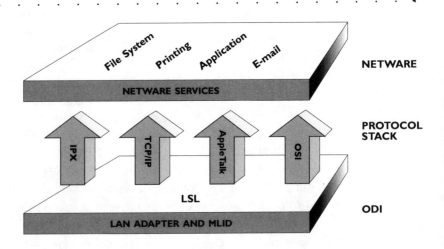

When orchestrated well, the ODI model provides a variety of benefits including:

- ▸ Communication with a variety of workstations, file servers, and mainframe computers via different protocol stacks

- ▸ Communication through any LAN adapter written to ODI specifications simultaneously

- ▸ Few hardware components to support

- ▸ Flexible configurations through the use of NET.CFG files.

Let's take a closer look at the key components of the ODI architecture model.

LAN Adapter and MLID

The bottom layer of the ODI model consists of the physical LAN adapter and custom MLID driver. The LAN adapter is the physical component which communicates directly with the LAN media and provides connectivity between workstations and file servers. The MLID driver, or multiple link interface driver, is a special type of network interface card driver which supports any type of packet. MLID packet support includes IPX packets, AppleTalk packets, or TCP/IP packets. Special network interface cards with MLID supported drivers can simultaneously speak a variety of different languages.

TIP

MLID drivers are provided by the NIC manufacturer and must be ODI-compliant. Incidentally, the MLID driver is typically executed as a .COM file with the file name of NE2000, NE1000, TOKEN, and so on. The file name of the MLID driver corresponds with the type of network interface card it is supporting.

LSL

The link support layer is the next layer in the ODI architecture model. It acts as a type of switchboard to route packets between the LAN adapter and protocol stacks. The LSL is responsible for identifying the type of packet it receives. It then passes the packet to the appropriate protocol in the protocol stack layer. LSL functionality is provided by a NetWare-specific .COM file called LSL.COM. This file is the first ODI workstation file to be loaded.

Protocol Stack

The protocol stack layer contains protocol stacks such as IPX, AppleTalk, and TCP/IP. A stack is a protocol-specific group of files which are used to translate and negotiate specific protocols. Once a packet arrives at the specified protocol stack, it either passes through and communicates with NetWare 3.12, or is sent back down to the LSL layer. Once packets are sent down to the LSL layer, they are shuffled off through the MLID and network interface card to another network. The protocol stack layer provides routing services for NetWare file servers. Routing involves two steps: interrogating NetWare packets and deciding whether to keep the packet or send it to the next LAN. Protocol stack functionality is provided at the file server through an internal set of applications called NetWare STREAMS. Protocol stack support at the workstation is provided through a .COM or .EXE file which specifies the type of protocol. The IPX file is IPXODI.COM. The TCP/IP implementation consists of TCP/IP.EXE. The protocol stack file is loaded after the MLID driver, which is loaded after the LSL driver at the workstation.

KNOWLEDGE

There really isn't any reason not to use ODI drivers. ODI is flexible, reliable, and fast. In addition, NetWare currently updates ODI drivers and protocol stacks several times a year. Support for IPX and NETx files have been less aggressive. The current versions of IPX, ODI, and LAN drivers work extremely well with Windows and are fully supported by all NetWare applications. In addition, the ODI model is the future of LAN communications.

QUOTE

Ah, but a man's reach should exceed his grasp, Or what's a heaven for?

Robert Browning

Now that we understand the structure and value of NetWare ODI, let's take a look at how ODI is implemented in a variety of different situations.

ODI IMPLEMENTATION

ODI implementation differs for workstations, file servers, and non-DOS platforms. Novell has put a great deal of effort into simplifying the process of ODI Implementation. It is safe to say that ODI implementation is reliable, flexible, and straightforward. In this section, we will focus on the implementation of the ODI model at the workstation and at the file server. In addition, we will discuss the steps involved in implementing ODI for Macintosh, OS/2, and UNIX environments. NetWare, by default, supports IPX protocols from DOS and OS/2 workstations. Customization of the multiprotocol environment is only required for TCP/IP or AppleTalk communications from UNIX or Macintosh workstations. Let's start by exploring ODI implementation at the NetWare workstation.

> ODI implementation differs for workstations, file servers, and non-DOS platforms. Customization of the multiprotocol environment is only required for TCP/IP or AppleTalk communications from UNIX or Macintosh workstations.

Workstation

ODI implementation at the workstation is simple and straightforward. It involves loading three separate files, each with the .COM extension. For DOS ODI, using an NE2000 network interface card and IPX protocol stack, the following three components must be loaded in the following order:

1 · LSL

2 · NE2000

3 · IPXODI

Once the three ODI components have been loaded, NETx can be loaded to finish the implementation of workstation shells. Further customization of ODI implementation can be added by changing the name of the LAN driver or protocol stack file. The system manager can provide support for both TCP/IP and IPX protocol stacks by issuing the TCP/IP.EXE command instead of the IPXODI protocol stack. In either case, the LAN driver NE2000 will remain the same.

The configuration of the network interface card through NE2000 and IPXODI is implemented by the NET.CFG file. NET.CFG is a text file which exists in the same directory as the ODI driver files. This text file contains three separate ODI references:

 ▶ LINK SUPPORT

 ▶ PROTOCOL

 ▶ LINK DRIVER

The link support options in NET.CFG provide configuration for the LSL.COM file. If you remember, the LSL.COM file is a switchboard which handles communications between the NE2000 driver and the corresponding protocol stack. The link support line in NET.CFG supports two commands: buffers and mempool. The buffers option configures the number and size of receive buffers that will be maintained by LSL. The IPX protocol stack does not use LSL communication buffers. TCP/IP protocol stack requires at least two buffers. The default is set to 0.

The protocol configuration choice in NET.CFG allows the system manager to bind the IPXODI protocol to a specific LAN driver. By default, NetWare will bind the IPXODI protocol to the first network board it finds. Using the PROTOCOL *name* line, and underneath it BIND *name* allows the system manager to specify which network interface card the protocol will be bound to.

Both link support and protocol are optional in NET.CFG. The only command which is required is the LINK DRIVER command. Link driver allows the system manager to define specific hardware configurations on the internal workstation NIC. The syntax is:

```
LINKDRIVER NE2000
    INT 3
    PORT 300
    MEM D0000
    FRAME Ethernet_802.3
```

By default, IPXODI will use the network interface card's original factory settings. If the workstation is using IPXODI and default factory settings, the system manager does not have to configure a NET.CFG file.

TIP

Workstation ODI drivers can be unloaded. This feature is not available from the earlier IPX.COM implementation. To unload ODI drivers, simply type the name followed by a /u. Note: the drivers must be unloaded in reverse order.

File Server

ODI implementation at the file server is a bit more complex. The NetWare operating system inherently supports ODI workstations using the IPX protocol stack. Other workstation platforms using other protocols require additional software. NetWare 3.12 ships with two main multiple protocol management tools. They are:

▸ PROTOCOL console command

▸ STREAMS.NLM

The PROTOCOL console command is used to view the protocols registered on the file server. IPX is automatically registered with the operating system. Other protocol stacks also register themselves, including TCP/IP and AppleTalk. The PROTOCOL console command is an extremely useful tool in troubleshooting and managing multiple protocol environments.

The STREAMS.NLM is the beginning of a group of NLMs which work together to provide multiple protocol capability. The STREAMS suite, as it is called, is a common interface between NetWare and other transport protocols. These transport protocols are used to shuffle requests between protocol stacks and the NetWare file services. NetWare

> The NetWare operating system inherently supports ODI workstations using the IPX protocol stack. Other workstation platforms using other protocols require additional software.

STREAMS makes the transport protocol transparent, thus allowing the same set of services to be provided no matter which protocol is being used. Without STREAMS, NetWare would only support IPX protocols. The STREAMS suite is implemented as a series of four NLMs loaded at the file server. These NLMS are loaded in the following order:

1 · STREAMS

2 · CLIB

3 · TLI

4 · IPXS

STREAMS is the controlling interface NLM. CLIB is a library of routines and functions that the other loadable modules use. TLI stands for Transport Level Interface, and it is a communications service that sits between streams and user applications. IPXS is the IPX protocol stack NLM. The STREAMS suite supports DOS-based services over non-IPX protocols. To support other non-DOS platforms, the server must load a group of NLMs specific to that platform. Novell provides optional products for the file server and workstation to support Macintosh, OS/2, and UNIX. Let's take a look.

Macintosh

Macintosh connectivity is provided through a product known as NetWare for Macintosh. NetWare for Macintosh is an add-on product that has a group of NLMs and a workstation DA (or desk accessory). The Macintosh server component provides a group of multiprotocol NLMs that support the AppleTalk filing protocol—or AFP. The NetWare for Macintosh product provides NetWare file, print, and routing services to Macintosh computers through AFP NLMs. Macintosh workstations load the NetWare desk accessory to provide common user tools through the native Macintosh interface. NetWare for Macintosh is an effective strategy for integrating DOS and Macintosh workstations on a NetWare 3.12 LAN.

OS/2

OS/2 connectivity is provided through the NetWare requester for OS/2. The requester runs on the OS/2 workstation and is included with the NetWare 3.12 operating system. File server support for OS/2 is provided through NetWare's inherent IPX protocol stack. The workstation uses OS/2's high performance file system to replace the file allocation table used by DOS. OS/2's HPFS supports long names and extended attributes. NetWare support for long names and extended attributes is provided through the OS/2 name space. Name space runs on the NetWare file server while the OS/2 workstations communicate using IPX protocol.

In addition, the NetWare requester for OS/2 supports Named Pipes and NETBIOS so that OS/2 workstations can communicate directly with each other—without interfering with the IPX protocol stack on the NetWare server. The best thing about the NetWare requester for OS/2 is that it's free.

UNIX

UNIX connectivity is the most complex. NetWare supports UNIX connectivity in three different ways:

- ▸ TCP/IP routing

- ▸ NFS filings on the NetWare server

- ▸ NetWare workstation connectivity to UNIX hosts

TCP/IP Routing   The TCP/IP (Transmission Control Protocol/Internet Protocol) was developed specifically to permit different types of computers to communicate over large internetworks. TCP/IP routing refers to NetWare's ability to aid in the communications between two UNIX workstations over a TCP/IP network. NetWare servers can coexist on TCP/IP internetworks while still speaking IPX with their workstations.

If the system manager loads the native TCP/IP NLMs in NetWare 3.12, the file server can communicate packets from one UNIX workstation to another but cannot process those packets. This option does not provide NetWare services to UNIX workstations. This means that the protocol stack will accept the TCP/IP packet and then send it back down the protocol stack—off to another TCP/IP node. The NetWare 3.12 TCP/IP NLMs are stored in the SYS:SYSTEM directory when NetWare is installed. In addition, the ETC root directory is created to store additional database files which are needed for TCP/IP routing. If the system manager wishes to process TCP/IP packets and provide NetWare services to UNIX clients, an additional product is required. That product is NetWare NFS.

QUOTE

Necessity is the mother of invention.

Jonathan Swift

NFS Support on the NetWare Server   NetWare NFS (Network File System) allows NetWare file servers to process TCP/IP packets from UNIX clients. It is the de facto industry standard for UNIX files. With NetWare NFS, NetWare file systems can be accessed using NFS and NetWare print queues can be used to view the UNIX line printer commands. NetWare NFS allows UNIX workstations to share files and print services with DOS clients.

NetWare Workstations Attached to UNIX Hosts   The final approach towards UNIX connectivity is NetWare workstations attaching themselves to UNIX hosts. NetWare workstations running ODI drivers can attach directly to UNIX hosts using an optional product called LAN Workplace for DOS. LAN workplace for DOS loads a series of drivers and commands on the NetWare workstation to allow it to emulate a UNIX client. The NetWare workstation can then communicate directly to the UNIX host using UNIX commands and proper syntax. LAN Workplace for DOS does not provide the facility for sharing files between DOS and UNIX. NetWare workstations must use the UNIX conventions.

TIP

Novell provides two other interfaces for LAN WorkPlace: LAN Workplace for Windows and LAN Workplace for OS/2.

That's it for multiprotocol management. As you can tell, it's not easy to incorporate a variety of different workstations into one cohesive LAN. While NetWare provides the facility for transparent multiple protocols, it takes some massaging in order for it to work smoothly. While multiprotocol management can be frustrating at times, it is extremely rewarding when all things come together and users become one big happy family. Speaking of happiness, one sure way of maintaining a happy family is to be prepared for emergencies. In the next section, we will discuss the hotel manager's contingency plan for natural and unnatural disasters. As they say, "Preparedness is the first step toward wisdom."

KNOWLEDGE

It wasn't raining when Noah built the Ark.

NetWare Backup

As the old adage goes, "You never miss anything until it's gone." This holds especially true for NetWare data. NetWare backup is often overlooked because it is not needed on a day-to-day basis. As soon as the data is lost, NetWare backup is the first responsibility which the NetWare manager is reminded of. In many cases, NetWare backup can be the difference between a successful and prosperous career as a NetWare system manager and the unemployment line. Make sure *never* to neglect your Net-Ware backup duties.

NetWare backup is not quite as simple as inserting a diskette and copying files. This complicated process in-

> As the old adage goes, "You never miss anything until it's gone." This holds especially true for NetWare data.

volves the bindery, NetWare compatibility, reliability of backed up data, maintenance, and efficient restore procedures. In this section, we will briefly discuss the NetWare backup considerations and spend some time with NetWare 3.12's new Storage Management Services (SMS).

NETWARE BACKUP CONSIDERATIONS

In a stand-alone environment, a backup consists primarily of the data and directories. In a network environment, the backup consists of not only data and directories but also security, file attributes, the NetWare bindery, and users and groups. That is why one of the most important considerations of a NetWare backup system is NetWare compatibility. Many backup systems say that they work well with NetWare or that they are NetWare comfortable, but that doesn't mean that they're NetWare compatible. The key component in NetWare compatibility is whether the system can recognize the bindery. Backing up the bindery is a very serious task because it requires that the bindery be closed and re-opened—you cannot back up a file which is currently open.

Few backup systems know how to access the NetWare bindery. They can't close and open it without bringing down the network. Most large name brands are, however, NetWare compatible and provide facilities for backing up the NetWare bindery. Another important consideration is user interface—how easy is it to use. Another consideration is *who* performs the backup. In order to do a full NetWare backup including the bindery, the user must be Supervisor or supervisor equivalent. It's a good idea to perform the back up when no other users are logged into the system. This is because the closing and opening of the bindery can cause very serious problems for users who are accessing the bindery at that moment. Also, it's very difficult to back up data which is open. If users are currently logged in using data files or application programs, those files will not be backed up.

This brings up another consideration: unattended backup. It seems contrary to want to log in as a supervisor and yet have an unattended backup because that leaves the system susceptible and vulnerable during non-working hours. The best strategy is to create a supervisor equivalent who logs in at a particular time and whose time restrictions lock the account after, let's say, 3:00 a.m.—so that the system only stays logged in for a limited period of time.

TIP

Some of the newest backup systems include a facility which logs the user in, performs the backup, and logs the user out—automatically.

The final NetWare backup consideration is reliability. It is very important to implement an intelligent schedule which provides complete data security, while at the same time not producing 365 tapes per year. The grandfather method, for example, utilizes 24 tapes and provides at least 4 or 5 years' worth of data integrity. It calls for recycling tapes every day, week, month, and year. Reliability is maintained by performing periodic restores to non-active disks so that you can verify that the backup is truly good and that the restore functionality of the back-up system works. One of the biggest problems with backup systems these days is that you spend your days, weeks, months, and years backing up data—and never actually restore it. It could be very disconcerting to find out that the system does not restore properly after you have years' worth of backup tapes.

NetWare 3.12 provides a sophisticated NetWare-compatible backup engine called Storage Management Services (SMS). Let's take a closer look.

STORAGE MANAGEMENT SERVICES

Storage Management Services (SMS) comprises a combination of related services that allow data to be stored and retrieved from a variety of different targets—Target Service Agents (TSAs). SMS is a backup engine which operates independently from the front-end (application) and back-end (devices). Many manufacturers are currently developing products which support NetWare 3.12's SMS engine. Figure 11.6 shows how five different TSAs can be backed up to three different backup devices.

NetWare 3.12 includes a rudimentary SMS application called SBACKUP. SBACKUP, an NLM which operates at the file server, is efficient because data files travel directly from the server to the attached backup device—hence, no network traffic. In addition, security and performance are enhanced. Finally, SBACKUP supports multiple protocols, internetworking, and four different name spaces. Let's take a closer look at the features and backup/restore rules of SBACKUP and Storage Management Services.

TIP

Novell's NetWare backup strategy has evolved rapidly. NetWare 2.2 supports only NBACKUP—a limited workstation product. Net-Ware 3.11 supports both NBACKUP and SBACKUP—but not Storage Management Services. NetWare 3.12 and NetWare 4.0 support only SBACKUP and the new SMS implementation. For NBACKUP details, refer to Chapter 6, "NetWare 2.2 Network Management."

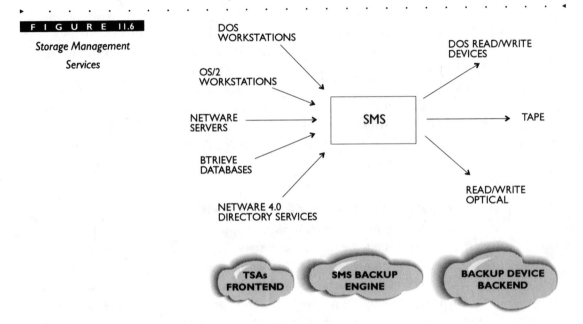

FIGURE 11.6

Storage Management
Services

Features

SBACKUP provides three main features beyond those of its NBACKUP cousin. First of all, it can support non-DOS name spaces including DOS, Macintosh, OS/2, and UNIX. Secondly, NetWare 3.12 SBACKUP can be used to back up other NetWare 3.12 servers. SBACKUP relies on the concept of a host file server and target file server. The host file server runs the SBACKUP NLMs and has the tape backup drive attached. The target NetWare 3.12 file server loads target service agents (TSA) which provide the capabilities for a centralized backup of multiple remote file servers. SBACKUP, like all other facilities, supports multiple file server connections at one time. And, finally, SBACKUP has enhanced performance because it does not cause additional load on the network. The tape unit is connected directly to the file server and SBACKUP communicates directly with the internal shared disk.

In addition, SBACKUP supports a wider variety of backup devices in the form of independent .DSK device drivers. Hardware manufacturers can provide these drivers for any NetWare compatible backup device. SBACKUP supports three different backup strategies (see Table 11.1):

FULL Completing a full backup each time is the most thorough option. It is, however, not very practical. In Table 11.1, the "Clear Modify Bit" option is set to Yes and all other default SBACKUP options are chosen.

INCREMENTAL The second option backs up only the files which have changed since the last backup. While this choice offers a quick backup, restoring can be a nightmare—you restore one full and every incremental since the last backup. In Table 11.1, the "Clear Modify Bit" option is set to Yes and "Exclude files that have not changed" is set to Yes.

DIFFERENTIAL The final, and most effective, strategy employs a combination of the first two. The differential strategy backs up only the files which have changed since the last FULL backup. This makes for quick backups and easy restores—you restore one full and the latest differential. In Table 11.1, the "Exclude files that have changed" option is set to Yes and all other SBACKUP defaults are used—including "Clear Modify Bit" at No.

TABLE 11.1 *Comparing Three SMS Backup Strategies*			
BACKUP STRATEGY	**BACKUP**	**RESTORE**	**MODIFY BIT**
FULL	SLOW	EASY	CLEARED
INCREMENTAL	QUICK	HARD	CLEARED
DIFFERENTIAL	QUICK	EASY	NOT CLEARED

Rules

As mentioned earlier, SBACKUP relies on the host-target architecture. The SBACKUP host runs the SBACKUP NLM and communications software. The target software runs target service agent NLMs. Host software includes SBACK-UP.NLM, SIDR.NLM, and the corresponding tape device NLM. SBACKUP.NLM contains the backup interface. It reads and translates requests, determines the type of session being started and decides which modules to activate. SIDR.NLM is Novell's data requester. It passes data requests to and from the host and target service agent components. The SIDR.NLM uses Novell's built-in SMSP (storage management services protocol). The third component of host software is the tape device driver NLM. This can be any of the .DSK drivers provided by the device manufacturer.

The target service agent NLMs consist of two components: TSA.NLM and TSA312.NLM. TSA.NLM is the link between the data requester, SIDR, and the target-specific module—such as TSA312. TSA312.NLM is the target-specific part of server backup for file servers running NetWare 3.12. It processes data using the target's data structure.

KNOWLEDGE

SMS supports target service agents for other types of NetWare servers including workstations.

In addition to the required NLMs, SBACKUP has a few other usage considerations:

- ► Never mix SBACKUP and NBACKUP data formats. They are not compatible. Data backed up using NBACKUP must be restored with NBACKUP.

- ► You *must* run SBACKUP.NLM from the file server. This is a requirement. The backup device which you are using must also be attached to the file server.

- ► SBACKUP supports many non-DOS name spaces but the interface still supports only DOS-type file names. When entering a file name that has a different format, use the DOS equivalent. For example, NOS2 file with 32 characters or 40 characters would have to be entered as its 8-character DOS equivalent.

- ► Finally, never mount or dismount a volume during a backup or restore session. It could cause irreparable damage to the volume and NetWare bindery.

- ► Know the passwords assigned to servers and workstations.

TIP

Exit SBACKUP before unloading the support NLMs. Otherwise the server could ABEND—Abnormal End.

Backup Steps

SBACKUP backup tasks are more complex than NBACKUP back up tasks. This is because of the server requirements and support for target service agents. Here's a brief outline of what's involved:

1 · **Loading the required NLMs.** Before using SBACKUP, you must load the required NLMs. Load the TSA modules on the target file server by typing **LOAD TSA** at the file server console prompt. The program will automatically load the applicable modules and files. At the host server, the system manager must load the SBACKUP NLM. Even if the host server is the only server being backed up, the TSA module must be loaded as well. Loading SBACKUP at the host server is accomplished by typing **LOAD SBACKUP.** The system will respond with a username and password. This is to ensure data integrity and valid NetWare security. Users accessing the SBACKUP facility can only back up files which they have sufficient rights to.

2 · **Select a target for backup.** After you enter the username and password, a preliminary prompt appears asking you to choose the available device driver. After you select the driver, the main menu appears and you can select a target for backup or restore. From the list of available target service agents, choose the file server you wish to backup. If it is different from the host server, you will be asked for your username and password on the target file server as well.

3 · **File server backup menu.** The file server backup menu provides four choices. First, select working directory. The working directory defines a place where the SBACKUP facility can store session-specific log and error files. Next, the system manager must choose backup selected target. The backup selected target option provides access to a detailed configuration menu.

4 · **At the proceed with backup prompt, select YES.** The system will respond with a complex media ID. Write the media set ID on the tape cartridge to identify it for restore sessions. Incidentally, the media set ID consists of the media label, the cartridge number, and date and time of backup.

5 · **At the start backup menu prompt, select one of two choices.** Select now to back up now, or later to defer backup to a future date and time. The system manager will be asked to input the unattended backup time in the start backup timer window. The final two choices from the backup menu allow the system manager to view the backup log and error log.

QUOTE

I like work; it fascinates me. I can sit and look at it for hours.

Jerome K. Jerome

TIP

When backing up, be aware of rights security. To back up files, you must have Read and File Scan rights. This means you must have [RF] rights to SYS:SYSTEM to back up the NetWare 3.12 bindery files.

Restore Steps

Before restoring data to the target file server, make sure the server has enough free disk space. The file server must have approximately 20% free disk space above the amount needed to restore. This space is needed to store temporary files and additional name space information. Below is a brief outline of the SBACKUP restore steps.

I · **Load the TSA and SBACKUP NLMs.** Before using the SBACKUP restore function, the system manager must load the same NLMs he/she loaded during the SBACKUP backup session. These include the SBACKUP NLM and TSA target service agent NLMs on all target file servers. In addition, the system manager will be asked for his or her username and password.

2 · The target for restore. The system manager will then be provided with a list of available target service agents for SBACKUP restore. Select the appropriate target service agent and enter the username and password.

3 · The restore menu. The SBACKUP restore menu has five choices: select working directory, restore session, restore without session files, view backup log, and view error log. The system manager can use the backup log to determine which data to restore and identify the media ID for this set. In this step, the system manager can choose the select working directory option and input the same working directory that he/she used for the backup session. The system manager will then choose either restore session or restore without session files. The restore without session files option checks sequentially through backup entries on a tape to find a session to restore.

4 · At the proceed with restore prompts, select YES.

5 · At the start restore prompt, select YES. Insert the media when prompted and the mounting media message is displayed. Just as for backup when the restore session begins, the status window appears showing what data is being restored, what data has been restored, and how much time has elapsed in the restore window. To stop a restore session, press Escape and then press Enter to confirm. The session stops as soon as the current data set is restored.

That completes our discussion of NetWare backup and network management in general. Keep in mind that network management is an extremely volatile part of your job. The many different activities and different responsibilities of the NetWare manager are quite a puzzle. But once you get all of the puzzle pieces in place, the Novell picture is quite beautiful.

Remote Management Facility

Now that you've learned about all the many roles and responsibilities of the NetWare system manager, it's time to take a vacation to Bali. Bali can be quite beautiful this time of year—clear aqua oceans, sparkling sunshine, and incredibly exotic drinks with little umbrellas. Two days into your vacation, your cellular phone rings. It's the poor guy you left in charge of the LAN while you were gone. It seems as though he's having a horrible time getting the print server NLM to load on the server. In addition, he says that there are some memory problems with loading Macintosh name space. So what do you do? Well, you have two choices:

▶ Hop on a plane and fly back to the office, cutting your vacation short and fixing the problem in person.

▶ Implement NetWare's built-in RMF (remote management facility). It allows you to hook up your notebook modem to the cellular phone and dial up the network from Bali.

In addition, NetWare's remote management facility allows you to access the file server console from a remote workstation. Let's take a closer look at how you would implement RMF to fix the network problem—before your drink gets warm.

RMF COMPONENTS

The remote management capability of NetWare allows you to manage all your NetWare file servers from one location. Hence, a workstation can act as a file server console. This is particularly useful because file server security states that the file server should be locked away in a cabinet with no monitor and no keyboard. This can be troublesome when you need to load and unload NLMs or use the MONITOR facility for routine network monitoring.

> The remote management capability of NetWare allows you to manage all your NetWare file servers from one location. Hence, a workstation can act as a file server console.

Remote management supports both access from a workstation or access from a modem. The remote management facility consists of two main components:

- The RMF NLMs
- The RMF console program

The remote management facility NLMs are broken into two parts: the REMOTE.NLM and CONNECTION.NLM. The REMOTE.NLM manages the information exchange to and from the workstation and the server. REMOTE.NLM provides the facility for using RMF and defining an RMF password. The CONNECTION NLM provides communication support for remote workstations and the REMOTE.NLM.

When the system manager is accessing REMOTE.NLM from a modem, the connection NLM is RS232.NLM. In the other scenario, where the system manager is accessing REMOTE.NLM from a workstation on the LAN, the CONNECTION.NLM is RSPX.NLM. In either case, the remote NLM must be loaded before the CONNECTION.NLM.

TIP

The REMOTE.NLM provides the facility for creating a user password by typing LOAD REMOTE password. **In many cases, this creates a security risk because the system manager is tempted·to put the** LOAD REMOTE [password] **command in the AUTOEXEC.NCF. The AUTOEXEC.NCF is a text file which can be viewed by any user on the LAN who has access to the SYSTEM subdirectory. NetWare solves this problem by making the supervisor's password a default password for remote management. The system manager can simply load REMOTE without a password, in which case the supervisor's password would be the remote management password.**

The second major component of remote management is the remote management program file. This program utility provides the capabilities to:

- Perform all tasks available at the file server console
- Scan directories

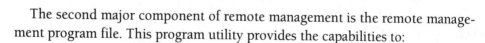

▸ Copy files to but not from directories on the server.

In the first scenario, where the system manager is accessing the remote console from a modem, the remote program utility is ACONSOLE.EXE. In the second scenario, where the REMOTE.NLM is being accessed from a workstation on the LAN, the remote management utility is RCONSOLE.EXE. In either case, RCONSOLE or ACONSOLE is executed from a remote workstation. Let's take a closer look at how RCONSOLE and ACONSOLE work in the remote management environment.

RCONSOLE

RCONSOLE provides the ability for system managers to remotely access the file server console from a workstation attached to the same LAN. The RCONSOLE utility is a supervisor utility, which means it only resides in the SYSTEM subdirectory. Once the system manager executes RCONSOLE.EXE, the preliminary remote management menu appears. This menu shows a list of all available file servers. Each server on the internetwork which is available to this workstation and has the REMOTE NLM and RSPX.NLM loaded will appear on the list. The system manager simply chooses the file server and enters the appropriate password. Once the correct password has been entered, the system will automatically jump to the file server console screen.

The console screen will appear as it was left. This could be in a variety of different states. That is to say, the MONITOR NLM could be running with the worm screensaver, the console prompt could appear with the colon (:), or the TRACK ON or TRACK OFF facility could be activated, in which case it would be a list of file server routing activity. In any case, the system manager now has direct access to the file server console and can exercise any command at the console that could otherwise be entered had the system manager actually been at the file server.

An additional list of available options can be activated by pressing the asterisk key (*) on the number pad. This brings up the available options menu for RCONSOLE (Figure 11.7), which has the following six options:

▸ Select a screen to view

▸ Directory scan

FIGURE II.7

The Available Topics Menu
of RCONSOLE

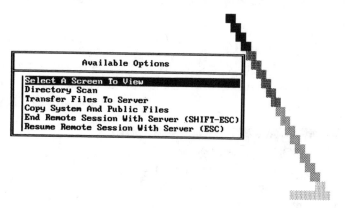

```
                  Available Options
 ┌──────────────────────────────────────────────┐
 │ Select A Screen To View                        │
 │ Directory Scan                                 │
 │ Transfer Files To Server                       │
 │ Copy System And Public Files                   │
 │ End Remote Session With Server (SHIFT-ESC)     │
 │ Resume Remote Session With Server (ESC)        │
 └──────────────────────────────────────────────┘
```

- ▸ Transfer files to server

- ▸ Copy SYSTEM and PUBLIC files

- ▸ End remote session with server

- ▸ Resume remote session with server

The select a screen choice allows the system manager to move from one file server screen to another. The directory scan provides the facility for a scan of file server directories. Transfer files to server allows the system manager to transfer files from the local workstation to the file server hard disk. Copy SYSTEM and PUBLIC files is a similar function which allows the supervisor to copy the SYSTEM and PUBLIC files from the diskettes located at the remote workstation. This choice would be used when the supervisor is using a remote workstation to install NetWare on an existing server. Shift-Escape will end the remote session with the server and the Escape key will return to the file server console.

TIP

Whenever a remote session is granted to either RCONSOLE or ACONSOLE, the file server broadcasts a message to the error log and console prompt. This indicates that a remote session was attempted at a particular node address and that it was, in fact, granted

at a particular node address. This is particularly useful for system
managers who are tracking who is trying to have access to the file
server console using the remote management facility.

ACONSOLE

ACONSOLE is particularly interesting because it allows the system manager
to access the file server console from a remote, remote, remote, remote workstation—like Bali. This remote workstation
is attached to the file server by modem.
The modem must be attached directly
to the file server and does not provide
any facility beyond access to the file
server console. This is not an option for
system managers who are interested in
providing remote access to the LAN for
their users. Remote access for users
would have to go through a communications gateway providing login security,
and so on.

> ACONSOLE is particularly interesting
> because it allows the system manager to
> access the file server console from a remote,
> remote, remote, remote workstation—
> like Bali.

KNOWLEDGE
**Novell provides a gateway called the NetWare Access Server, which
provides simultaneous login sessions from a single communications
gateway.**

ACONSOLE allows a remote workstation with a modem to attach directly to
the file server console and perform the same activities over modem lines. ACON-
SOLE relies on the REMOTE.NLM and the RS232 communications NLM. The
ACONSOLE.EXE file also exists in the SYSTEM subdirectory, but it must be
copied to a diskette or to the hard drive of the remote machine. The ACONSOLE
main menu has two choices:

▶ Connect to remote location

▶ Configure modem

The configure modem option allows the system manager to configure the modem at the remote workstation and establish parameters such as speed, parity, and so on. Configuration of the file server modem is performed using the RS232 NLM. Once the modem is configured, the system manager can use the Connect to remote location option from the main menu to gain access to the server console. At this point, the system manager must provide a phone number and appropriate communications protocols. Incidentally, the ACONSOLE connect to remote location facility provides a built-in database for multiple locations and multiple phone numbers.

Once an ACONSOLE session has been activated, the system manager can use the asterisk key on the number pad to bring up the same remote console menu. Refer to Figure 11.6. One interesting problem presents itself when upgrading or installing file servers from remote locations. The copying of the SYSTEM and PUBLIC files can be quite cumbersome. The 15 to 20 megabytes worth of diskette files can take days if copied from a remote asynchronous connection. If the system manager is installing NetWare using the ACONSOLE facility, he/she must ship the SYSTEM and PUBLIC diskettes to the remote location and have somebody at that location insert the diskettes at the appropriate times at the physical file server. This will help expedite the remote installation procedures.

Let's review your trip to Bali. Well, you pulled up your ACONSOLE utility from your notebook, attached it to the cellular modem and called up the office

> Well, that's it for hotel network management. We learned about registration, marketing, conventions, and emergency plans. It's certainly an exciting life!

file server console. You activated the print server utility and loaded the appropriate name space modules for Macintosh. You performed all this simple network management from Bali and did it before your exotic drink got warm. Let this be a lesson to all of you that all work and no play makes Johnny and Jane dull kids!

QUOTE

Great minds have purposes, others have wishes.

Washington Irving

Well, that's it for hotel network management. You learned about registration, marketing, conventions, and emergency plans. In addition, you gained some valuable expertise on network management from Bali. The most important part of NetWare network management is to develop a management plan and stick to it like glue. This management plan can help you remain consistent and comprehensive in your management duties. In addition, the NetWare management plan can help bail you out of some sticky network situations.

The next place to visit is the Park Place restaurants where we'll learn all about how the chef prepares gourmet meals and monitors room service. As the NetWare chef, you will develop an effective and efficient printing philosophy. There is an art to NetWare printing just as there's an art to preparing fine cuisine. No cookbooks here!

EXERCISE 11.1: DEBUGGING LOGIN SCRIPT COMMANDS

Locate and correct the errors in the following login script:

1. TURN MAP DISPLAY OFF

2. MAP S1:SYS: PUBLIC

3. MAP SEARCH 2:+PUBLIC\%MACHINE\%OS|%OS VERSION

4. COMPEC S2:COMMAND .COM

5. MAP 1;=SYS;USERS\LOGIN NAME

6. MAP 2: =SYS:USERS\LOGIN NAME\REPORTS

7. MAP S3: =SYS:APPLIC\WP

8. MAP S4: =SYS:APPLIC\DATABASE

9. WRITE: "GOOD GREETING TIME, %LOGIN NAME

10. WRITE "THE TIME IS"

11. WRITE "TODAY IS% DAYOFWEEK, %MONTHNAME % DAY

12. If %2 ="DATABASE" THEN BEGIN

13. MAP 3; SYS\DBDATA

14. END

15. DISPLAY SYS:SUPERVISOR\MESSAGE.TXT

16. TURN MAP DISPLAY ON

17. MAP

See Appendix D to check your answers.

CASE STUDY III: WRITING LOGIN SCRIPTS FOR SNOUZER, INC.

The first of two procedures for implementing Snouzer, Inc. network management is login scripts. Login scripts allow the system manager to customize system-wide and user-specific configurations. While Snouzer, Inc. doesn't care how you implement these customizations, they would like them to be as user-specific as possible. If you refer to the login script section of this chapter, you will see that the system manager's responsibility is to create one system login script that satisfies all user needs. In this exercise, we will focus on designing a system login script for Snouzer, Inc. which satisfies their needs while maintaining a single point of network management.

Sophy has made some straightforward requests with respect to the NetWare system login script. Following is a detailed list of the components as they should appear in the Snouzer, Inc. system login script. Use the login script worksheet in Appendix D to design their script on paper. Then use the SYSCON menu utility to implement the Snouzer, Inc. login script. Incidentally, the system login script choice is under Supervisor Options of SYSCON.

- ▶ A system greeting which includes user name and date

- ▶ Regular drive mappings as designed in Case Study 8.3.

- ▶ Search drive mappings as designed in Case Study 8.3. Keep in mind that some of the regular drive mappings are group specific, which means in order to implement these in the system login script, you must use the IF...THEN login script commands.

- ▶ A COMSPEC to search drive 2.

- ▶ Sophy would like you to fire phasers and write a message stating that it's Friday whenever the day of the week equals Friday.

- ▶ Also, Sophy would like to display a large text file called PAY.TXT on the 20th of every month which will display the information that today is payroll day and that employees should turn in all payroll information.

- ▶ You should input a PAUSE command after the FDISPLAY so that it will show on the screen.

‣ Sophy would like all users to jump directly into a user-specific menu from the login script. The user-specific menu will be defined in Case Study 11.2.

Once the system login script has been created according to Snouzer, Inc. specification, you can focus on the user interface. User interface requirements consists of a batch file for executing from the login script and a user-specific menu. Let's move onto Case Study IV, Building a Menu System for SNOUZER, INC.

<table>
<tr><td>**CASE STUDY IV: BUILDING A MENU SYSTEM**</td></tr>
</table>

The second component in Snouzer, Inc. network management is the development of a transparent user interface. A transparent and friendly user interface is the most important component in defeating LANphobia. Snouzer, Inc.'s managers have very little experience using networks and would appreciate a simple user interface. In order to develop a simple user interface, you must first have the login script execute a user specific menu. In addition, you must establish CAPTURE commands and other user-specific configurations before executing the menu. In order to accomplish all of these, you will exit the system login script to a batch file called START.BAT. START.BAT will reside in each user's subdirectory and consist of:

- ▸ CAPTURE commands
- ▸ User specific configurations
- ▸ A menu command

The menu command will specify a user-specific menu which resides in each user's subdirectory. This menu will be based on a system-wide menu but have minor modifications for each user. In this exercise, we will concentrate on developing a system-wide template for the user menu and then you can customize it as needed.

The Snouzer, Inc. menu consists of some straightforward applications and a logout command. The title of the Snouzer, Inc. menu is SNOUZER, INC. The four main title options are:

- ▸ Applications
- ▸ User Utilities
- ▸ File Management
- ▸ Logout

The Applications option will consist of a submenu which we'll talk about in just a moment. The user utilities option consists of a branch to the SESSION

NetWare user utility. File management option consists of a branching to the FILER user network utility. And, finally, the logout option will exit the menu and log the user out.

The Applications submenu lists all five of Snouzer, Inc.'s main applications. Three of these aplications are particularly memory-intensive—DBASE, WP, and 123. The five application options under Applications are:

- ▸ ACCT
- ▸ DBASE
- ▸ WP
- ▸ 123
- ▸ DESIGN

Furthermore, the ACCT option consists of another submenu with the following options:

- ▸ AP
- ▸ GL
- ▸ AR

The Snouzer, Inc. menu should be friendly, easy, and productive. In addition, Sophy is concerned about users being confused when they exit the menu and appear at the NetWare command line. To solve this problem, you will create a secure menu system which prevents users from escaping by using Esc. Refer to the answers in Appendix D for a discussion of this unique strategy.

Good luck and happy menu making!

NetWare 3.12 Printing

"See! The problem was with the cable, not the printer."

Here's a surefire recipe for success:

- ▸ 2 cups of technology
- ▸ 1 bushel of wisdom
- ▸ 7 ounces of creativity
- ▸ 1 liter of common sense
- ▸ 1 dollop of patience

Mix the technology and the wisdom into a large bowl. Beat vigorously. Stir in common sense and let the mixture sit at room temperature for an hour. Add creativity and bake at an extremely high temperature for 3 hours. Remove from the oven and sprinkle with a little ability and patience. Now you have something.

> Mix two cups of technology and a bushel of wisdom into a large bowl. Beat vigorously. Stir in 1 liter of common sense and let it sit at room temperature for an hour. Add 7 ounces of creativity and bake at an extremely high temperature for 3 hours.

Park Place owes a great deal of its success to its 5-star restaurants. They are renowned throughout the world for providing the most interesting and exciting culinary treats. The Park Place chef is a master of his/her trade, responsible for shopping, prep work, baking and presentation. As the restaurant shopper, the chef must ensure the best quality foods without sacrificing price or freshness. Once the raw ingredients have been purchased, the chef prepares them for baking, broiling or cooking. Prep work involves cutting vegetables, peeling potatoes, and so on. Once the ingredients have been prepared, baking, broiling and cooking transforms the raw ingredients into delectable treats. Finally, the chef must use his/her creativity to present the meal so that it's appetizing and pleasing to the eye. This is where the chef gets to show off his/her ability in creating little animals out of rutabagas.

QUOTE

It is better to create than to be learned, creating is the true essence of life.

Barthold Georg Niebuhr

In addition to his/her main responsibilities, the chef must develop interesting restaurant menus and keep on top of the latest in food technology. After all, what would a 5-star restaurant be without a robomixer?

As the master of the NetWare cafe, it is your responsibility to set up and maintain a productive printing environment. A well-designed printing system can be almost as exciting as visiting a 5-star restaurant. The NetWare chef is responsible for printing setup (shopping), performance optimization (prep work), printing maintenance (baking) and overseeing user printing operations (presentation).

In this chapter we will learn about the fundamentals of NetWare printing and explore the four roles and responsibilities of the NetWare chef. In addition, we will discover a few strategies for approaching printing troubleshooting. Let's begin with a discussion of printing fundamentals and the NetWare Cafe.

> A well-designed printing system can be almost as exciting as visiting a 5-star restaurant.

The Fundamentals of NetWare Printing

One of the most important shared resources in the LAN is the network printer. Printers produce quality hard-copy output for brochures, reports, memos, and general bureaucratic paperwork. Network printing is one of the most productive and useful functions of a NetWare LAN.

On the surface, NetWare printing may appear to be easy, but don't be fooled—it is probably the most troublesome and mysterious management issue in the NetWare LAN. The fundamentals of NetWare printing are relatively straightforward but it is the demands of the users which can quickly frazzle the system manager. NetWare 3.12 printing is designed around three different components:

- ▸ The Print Queue

- ▸ The Print Server

- ▸ The Printer

The NetWare print queue is a shared area on the file server which stores print jobs in the order in which they are received. The print queue lines up the print jobs and sends them to the printer in an organized and efficient manner. The print server is responsible for directing the print jobs as they move from the queue to the network printer. The printer is the output device in a NetWare printing system (Figure 12.1) and it typically receives the jobs and prints them appropriately.

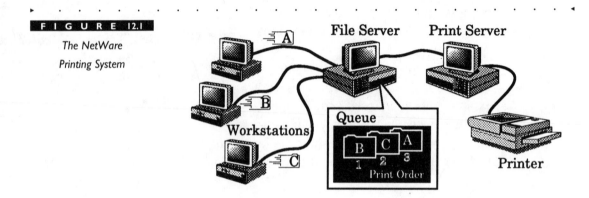

In a transparent NetWare printing environment, users print directly from their network applications and the output magically appears in the printer down the hall. This type of sophistication, while it might seem trivial to the user, is a source of great effort for the system manager. Figure 12.1 shows the structure of the NetWare's printing system and points out the relationships between print queues, print servers and network printers.

In this section, we will discuss these three different printing components in detail and provide an in-depth study of how they affect the NetWare printing system. The system manager must keep on top of these components and have a firm understanding of how they relate to each other. Let's start with print queues.

PRINT QUEUES

The word *queue* means "to stand in line." Typically, British citizens are found queuing-up, waiting for tickets to cricket matches. In a printing environment, the queue analogy holds firm; that is, print jobs stand in line and wait to be sent off to the network printer. Since print jobs are simply data which is being trans-lated by the printer, print queues must exist as directories on the NetWare file server. Print queues are stored as sub-directories under the SYS:SYSTEM directory and are given random, 8-digit hexadecimal names. As print jobs are sent from network workstations to the print queue, they are stored in the cor-responding directory as files on the disk. The files are ordered by the print server and tracked on their way from the file server to the network printer.

> In a printing environment, the queue analogy holds firm; that is, print jobs stand in line and wait to be sent off to the net-work printer.

TIP

The print server never stores the print job information, it only directs and controls it.

Print jobs are sent directly to print queues in one of two ways: CAPTURE or network application printing. The CAPTURE command is a NetWare 3.12 com-mand which literally captures the local workstation's parallel port and redirects print jobs off to a NetWare queue. Printing from NetWare applications, on the other hand, is a little more sophisticated because those applications recognize NetWare print queues and print directly to them. In either case, the workstation NETx shell formats the print job so that the network can recognize it and place it in the correct queue.

When print queues are created, the system assigns print queue operators and print queue users. These are special NetWare managers who control and use Net-Ware print queues. The print queue operator has the ability to add, delete, or reorder the print jobs in a given print queue. By default, the user Supervisor is assigned as the print queue operator on all NetWare print queues. Print queue users have the ability to insert print jobs into NetWare queues. By default, the group EVERYONE is assigned as a queue user for all new print queues.

PRINT SERVERS

The NetWare print server is not so much a physical device as a logical process. The print server can exist as a dedicated workstation or as a process running on top of a NetWare file server. As a dedicated workstation, the print server process runs through a file called PSERVER.EXE which is included with NetWare 3.12.

As a non-dedicated process running on top of a NetWare file server, the print server exists as PSERVER.NLM—a NetWare Loadable Module.

> The NetWare print server is not so much a physical device as a logical process. The print server can exist as a dedicated workstation or as a process running on top of a NetWare file server.

In either case, the print server's purpose is to control and redirect print jobs as they travel from NetWare workstations to file server print queues, and ultimately to network printers. The print server constantly monitors the print queues and network printers and makes logical attachments from one to the other. When a job is inserted into the print queue, it works its way to the top of the line. At that point, the print server redirects it to the appropriate network printer. In addition, print servers monitor printers to make sure they are not out of paper, off-line, or jammed. If any of these situations occur, the print server will notify the print server operator or Supervisor.

There are certain specifications which restrict the functionality of the NetWare print server. The print server itself can only have up to 5 printers attached directly to it: LPT1, LPT2, LPT3, COM1, and COM2. The print server can service print jobs from print queues on up to 8 different file servers. In addition, NetWare has provided an auxiliary functionality which expands the 5-printer limitation. It's called remote printing. Remote printing allows workstations with local printers to designate those printers as network devices. In NetWare 3.12, the print server supports a total of 16 printers.

Print servers in NetWare 3.12 can be installed on two different devices: dedicated workstations or the file server. The creation of a dedicated print server on a workstation is made possible through the PSERVER.EXE file. In this particular case, the system manager must create a special NET.CFG file on the workstation which defines the command SPX CONNECTIONS = 60. This command is required so that communications can be maintained with multiple users, queues, and file servers.

The non-dedicated or internal print server is defined as PSERVER.NLM. It runs on a NetWare 3.12 file server. The NetWare Loadable Module runs in parallel to the operating system. While NLMs do take up considerable file server resources, they are well designed and coexist peacefully with the operating system functions. In addition to NetWare's print server functionality, there are some third party products which provide more tasks and detailed print job accounting. One of the most popular is Bitstream's Mosaic print server software.

Each of these two different print server strategies has its own advantages and disadvantages. The advantage of running PSERVER.NLM on a file server is that it does not require additional hardware. The disadvantage is that it partially taxes the server's internal resources—CPU and RAM. On the other hand, the main advantage of the workstation print server is that it is a dedicated device that doesn't share processes with any other server facility. The disadvantage to having a dedicated workstation print server, however, is that it requires additional hardware. Typically, the minimum configuration for a NetWare 3.12 print server is an 8088 with a 20MB hard disk and 1MB RAM. Incidentally, this configuration has now been adopted as the industry doorstop. Let's take a closer look at these two different NetWare 3.12 print servers.

File Server

As mentioned above, running the print server process on a NetWare file server requires a NetWare Loadable Module. The NLM runs in parallel to the network operating system and shares the same 386-based server processor and RAM. PSERVER.NLM operates from the SYS:SYSTEM subdirectory. The system manager can activate an NLM print server by typing **PSERVER** print server. Before the print server can be activated, it must be created and configured in the PCONSOLE utility. We will discuss this part of the NetWare print server setup process later in the chapter.

Workstation

The process of installing the print server on a dedicated workstation is much more simple. The dedicated print server file exists as PSERVER.EXE. This file runs as any other application program and completely takes over the processor and memory of the workstation. Before PSERVER.EXE can be run, the system manager must attach the workstation to the network cabling. This is accomplished by running IPX and NETx. The system manager does not have to login this workstation in order for the dedicated print server facility to operate. The facility only requires an attachment—so the system manager could run IPX, NETx, and PSERVER.EXE followed by a name for the print server.

QUOTE

Nothing is really work unless you would rather be doing something else.

James Matthew Barrie

PSERVER.EXE is not a large file and it can be stored in the root directory of the workstation or on a diskette. Keep in mind that if you are going to run PSER-VER.EXE on a dedicated workstation, you must include the SHELL.CFG file with one line: SPX CONNECTION = 60. This will open up enough connections so that the print server can communicate with multiple users, print servers, and file servers.

PRINTERS

The real star of this show is the network printer—the shared device that provides hard copy output to multiple NetWare users. Shared printers can be either attached to the print server, attached to the file server, or attached to local workstations using the remote printing facility. Printers attached directly to the file server use NetWare 3.12's internal printing functionality—PSERVER.NLM.

Printers attached directly to print servers are controlled by a dedicated print server and can service users on up to 8 different file servers. Printers attached directly to local workstations and shared as network devices must use the remote printing facility. Remote printing is made possible through a terminate-stay-resident (TSR) program called RPRINTER.EXE—which runs in workstation

> The real star of this show is the network printer.

RAM. RPRINTER communicates directly with the print server and makes the printer available through the workstation NetWare shell.

In addition to these traditional printing configurations, the industry is providing some new, exciting, intelligent printers which are capable of communicating directly with the print server. Intelligent printers have internal network interface cards which allow them to attach directly to the LAN trunk. These printers act as workstations with remote printers attached. Some examples of intelligent printers include the new Hewlett-Packard Laserjet IIIci and the Laserjet IV.

Print jobs find their way to network printers through print queues and print servers. The NetWare printing model provides a variety of different configurations including one queue per printer, multiple queues per printer, and multiple printers per queue. The system manager must be well versed on NetWare's many printing management issues so he/she can optimize the printing environment. Printing management is a difficult and rewarding proposition.

PRINTING MANAGEMENT

Printing management is at the heart of what the NetWare chef does. Printing management defines the roles for printing setup, optimization, and maintenance. In addition, printing management can define certain strategies for approaching printing troubleshooting. Printing setup involves the procedures for creating print queues, print servers and defining NetWare printers. In addition, during the setup procedure, the system manager must assign queues to printers. Performance optimization involves the organization of printing components so that speed and reliability are optimized. Printing maintenance allows the system manager to control queues, print servers, and printers on a daily basis. The development of a good printing maintenance strategy will increase the quality of user output.

Let's take a brief look at the four different components responsible for NetWare printing management.

Setup
Printing setup is defined by four steps:

▶ Creating print queues

- ▸ Creating print servers

- ▸ Defining printers

- ▸ Assigning queues to printers

The NetWare system manager can implement NetWare printing through the use of one utility: PCONSOLE, which creates and manages certain aspects of print queues and print servers. In addition, PCONSOLE provides the facility for activating print job configurations. The above four steps provide a good framework for vanilla LANs—networks with less sophisticated printing needs. More sophisticated LANs require additional setup considerations. These considerations include remote printing, multiple file servers, queue design and custom printer parameters. We will discuss printing setup in depth later in the chapter.

Performance Optimization

Optimization of the printing environment can make the difference between a 2-star and a 5-star LAN. The NetWare system manager must be aware of a variety of performance issues including printing capacity, queue priority, multiple queues per printer, and multiple printers per queue. In addition, the system manager must be well versed in the detailed steps of the printing process. These steps define the print job's path from workstation to queue to print server and finally to printer.

Maintenance

Printing maintenance monopolizes the NetWare chef's day. Printing maintenance involves the daily routine of controlling and managing print queues, print servers and NetWare printers. Queue maintenance is performed using the PCONSOLE utility. PCONSOLE provides a print job configuration window which can be used to view and prioritize current print jobs. Print server control involves access to the print server itself—through PCONSOLE or the PSC command line utility. The PSC printing maintenance tool provides a wide range of maintenance options. We will discuss printing maintenance and the use of PSC later in the chapter.

Troubleshooting

Unfortunately, since things don't always go as planned in the NetWare kitchen, the system manager must be light on his/her feet in case things start falling apart. The good news is NetWare has a built-in resiliency against printing disasters. The system manager has a variety of tools available to him/her for battling print jobs which don't print properly or print servers which don't load properly. Later in the chapter we will discuss some of the most common printing troubleshooting problems and provide suggested courses of action. I guess this particular section would fall under the category of "if you can't stand the heat, get out of the kitchen."

PRINTING

So what does this all mean? The real goal in NetWare printing is to magically transform electronic data into a beautiful combination of ink and paper. NetWare provides three different ways to do this:

- ▸ NetWare-aware applications

- ▸ CAPTURE

- ▸ PCONSOLE/NPRINT

NetWare-aware applications communicate directly with file server queues. These applications are intelligent enough to understand the sophistication of NetWare printing. NetWare-aware applications, such as Windows and WordPerfect, print directly to NetWare queues and require no intervention from the system manager. Applications which aren't aware of NetWare queues require a printing facility known as CAPTURE. CAPTURE literally hijacks the local workstation port and redirects print jobs to NetWare queues.

Finally, the user or system manager has the choice of inserting a job directly into a NetWare queue through the use of the PCONSOLE menu utility or NPRINT command line utility. PCONSOLE allows users to choose print job files

> So what does this all mean? The real goal in NetWare printing is to magically transform electronic data into a beautiful combination of ink and paper.

and insert them into valid NetWare queues. The NPRINT command performs the same function from the command line. When print jobs finally reach the NetWare printer, they contain a variety of customized configurations. These print job configurations can be defined by the NetWare system manager using the PRINTCON menu utility. We will discuss the actual process of printing towards the end of the chapter.

QUOTE

As machines get to be more and more like men, men will come to be more like machines.

Joseph Wood Krutch

As you can see, NetWare printing is a sophisticated and complex system. NetWare provides a variety of different components for reliably moving print jobs from workstation A to printer B. In this chapter, we will explore the four major components of NetWare printing—printing setup, printing performance optimization, printing maintenance, and general user printing. In addition, we will learn of some common printing problems and suggest possible courses of action. Let's start with printing setup.

Printing Setup

The first step for the NetWare chef is shopping. At this point, the system manager must get printing started by collecting all the necessary resources. Printing setup involves the acquisition of printers, the setup of print servers and the definition of the NetWare printing environment.

Printing setup is a relatively straightforward task involving four simple steps:

1 · Create print queues

2 · Create print servers

3 · Define printers

4 · Assign queues to printers

During step 1, the system manager creates the print queues on the system and assigns print queue operators and users. During step 2, the system manager creates the print server and gives the print server a unique name and password. In step 3, the system manager continues with print server definition by defining the printers, assigning names to the printers, and configuring their internal parameters. These parameters include, among other things, port type, interrupt and serial configurations. The final step in print server setup is assigning the queues to printers. This step is required so that print jobs can find their way from specific queues to appropriate printers.

> Printing setup involves the acquisition of printers, the setup of print servers and the definition of the NetWare printing environment.

As discussed earlier, these four steps provide adequate functionality for most vanilla LANs. Unfortunately, some NetWare cafes insist on pushing the envelope of NetWare printing. For these LANs, NetWare provides some additional setup configurations. In this section, we will explore these considerations including multiple file servers, queue design and custom printer parameters. Let's begin by exploring the four standard setup steps in some depth.

STEP 1: CREATING PRINT QUEUES

Print queues are the central component of NetWare printing because they provide the link between NetWare workstations and shared printers. Print queues are created using the PCONSOLE menu utility which is stored in the PUBLIC directory (Figure 12.2).

To create a print queue in PCONSOLE, simply choose Print Queue Information from the available topics menu of PCONSOLE and press Insert at the Queue Name box. Next, type in a queue name up to 47 characters and press Enter. At this point, the print queue name will appear in the queue names box.

Once a print queue has been created, the system will assign it an 8-digit hexadecimal number and a subdirectory under the SYSTEM root directory. Using

F I G U R E 12.2

Step 1: Creating

Print Queues

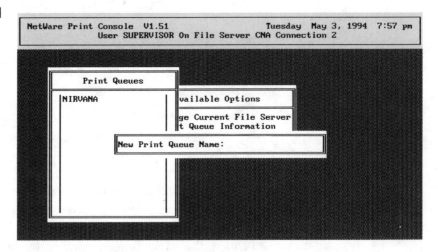

PCONSOLE, the system manager can define other print queue parameters including:

> **The Current Print Job Entries** screen provides a list of all print jobs which are currently held in this queue. This screen is a central point for queue management and job reordering.

> **Current Queue Status** displays the status of the queue with respect to the number of entries in the queue, and the number of servers being serviced by this queue and operator flags.

> **Currently Attached Servers** is a list of print servers that can service this queue. Those print servers keep track of which network printers are also servicing this queue.

> **Print Queue ID** is the 8-digit random number which is assigned to this particular print queue and it matches the subdirectory under SYSTEM.

> **Queue Operators** is a list of users who have been assigned queue operator status. By default, the Supervisor is the only queue operator.

> **Queue Servers** is a list of print servers which can service this queue. It does not mean they are currently attached. The system manager can add or delete print servers from this list.

Queue Users includes a list of all users who can add jobs to this queue. By default, the group EVERYONE is assigned as a queue user for all new print queues. Once the print queue has been created, the system manager can move onto defining and creating the print server and attaching a link between the two.

Figure 12.3 illustrates the Print Queue Information screen in PCONSOLE.

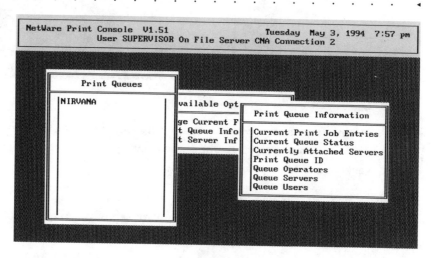

FIGURE 12.3

Print Queue Information in PCONSOLE

STEP 2: CREATING PRINT SERVERS

Print server creation consists of two steps: setup and installation. The setup step involves creating a print server in PCONSOLE. The print server installation step involves choosing a print server type and activating appropriate print server files—for a print server on the file server the file is PSERVER.NLM; and for a print server on a dedicated workstation it's PSERVER.EXE.

Print server setup is accomplished through the PCONSOLE utility using the printer server information menu from available options (Figure 12.4). The system manager simply presses Insert at the print server's menu screen and enters a print server name.

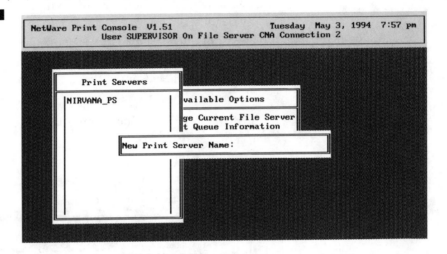

FIGURE 12.4

Step 2: Creating

Print Servers

TIP

It is recommended that the system manager use the file server name followed by _PS to show the relationship between print servers and file servers they service.

Once a print server has been created, the system manager can customize the print server configurations through the print server information screen (Figure 12.5). This screen includes the following information:

- ▶ Change Password
- ▶ Full Name
- ▶ Print Server Configuration
- ▶ Print Server ID
- ▶ Print Server Operators
- ▶ Print Server Users

The Change Password option allows the system manager to assign a password to the print server so that not just anybody can activate it. The Full Name provides more information about this particular print server and what queues

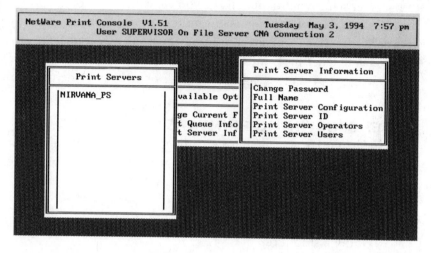

Print Server Information in
PCONSOLE

and file servers it services. Print Server Configuration is used for steps 3 and 4 in print server installation. Print Server ID defines the object ID of the print server. This is not particularly useful information because it is not used by any other NetWare configuration. Print Server Operator displays the list of the users and groups who have been assigned as operators for the print server. Print Server Users is a list of users or groups who can send print jobs to printers which are defined using this print server. By default, the Supervisor is assigned as a print server operator and the group EVERYONE is defined as print server users for all newly-created print servers.

Once the print server has been defined, the system manager must activate it. Print server activation consists of simply typing **PSERVER** followed by the name of the server:

> File Server—LOAD PSERVER print server
> Workstation—PSERVER print server

TIP

Before the print server can be properly activated, you must complete setup steps 3 and 4.

Once the print server has been configured and activated, a seventh choice will appear in the print server information menu—print server status/control. The print server status/control option lets you view the status of the print server and provides valuable information about print servers which are currently running. This particular choice will not be available to system managers if the print server is not activated. Once the print server has been created and before the print server is activated, the system manager must move on to step 3—defining printers.

STEP 3: DEFINING PRINTERS

Printer definition is accomplished through the PCONSOLE utility under Print Server Information. The print server configuration menu provides a list of four choices which involve printer definition:

- ▸ File Servers to be Serviced
- ▸ Notify List for Printer
- ▸ Printer Configuration
- ▸ Queues Served by Printer

The printer definition choice is Printer Configuration. This option allows the system manager to define up to 16 printers for this print server and customize their ports and configurations. By default, the 16 print server printers are assigned numbers 0 through 15, in order. The system manager also has the flexibility of assigning a name to printers. This is so they can be tracked for management and queue assignment.

To define a NetWare printer, choose the printer number from the top of the list (which is typically 0 for the first printer) and press enter. The printer 0 configuration option appears which gives a variety of different options for defining, naming and configuring NetWare printers (Figure 12.6). The first option is Name. The printer name will again define it for printing management and queue assignment. The Type parameter is particularly useful in that it allows the system manager to define not only serial or parallel but whether or not this printer is going to be attached to a remote workstation. The printer types option appears with 19 different choices. The first seven are parallel and are used by printers which are attached directly to the print server: LPT1, LPT2, LPT3, COM1, COM2, COM3, and COM4.

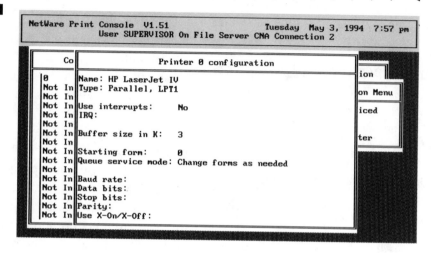

Step 3: Defining Printers

The next seven type options are assigned to printers which are attached to local workstations running remote printing. These include remote parallel and remote serial. The final two are other *unknown which* and *defined elsewhere*. Other unknown is used by intelligent printers with internal NICs. Defined elsewhere is for printers which are being serviced by other print servers on other file servers. We will discuss this option in more depth in a few minutes.

Once the printer type parameter has been set, the system manager can choose interrupts for parallel printing or BAUD rate, data bit, stop bits, parity, and XON/XOFF for serial printing.

STEP 4: ASSIGNING QUEUES TO PRINTERS

Assigning queues to printers is important because it provides a path from the NetWare file server queue to the appropriate printer. If the system manager forgets this step, then users become quite miffed. The symptom is that print jobs are sent off to the NetWare queue and they sit there forever waiting to be serviced by the print server. It is typical for up to 100 or so print jobs to gather in the print queue without one of them being serviced by the printer. If this is the case, the first place to check would be the assignment from queue to printer.

Queue assignments are accomplished using the print server configuration menu and the queues serviced by printer option. Simply choose this option and the system responds with a list of defined printers. Choose the printer which is going to be serviced and press Enter. The system responds with the queue list. If this is the first queue which is to be assigned to this printer, the queue list will be empty. The system manager presses Insert and the system responds with a list of available queues. Choose the appropriate queue and assign a priority number which establishes the queue assignments with the printer (Figure 12.7).

> Once the print queues have been created, the printers have been defined, and the queue has been assigned to the printer, users are ready to print. While print servers at first glance seem very complex, they really aren't—they're just sophisticated!

Once a print queue has been assigned to the appropriate printer and all other steps have been accomplished, users can now print directly to the queue and their jobs will be forwarded to the appropriate printer.

That's it for the printing setup process. Once the print queues have been created, the printers have been defined, and the queue has been assigned to the printer, users are ready to print. While print servers at first glance seem very complex, they really aren't—they're just sophisticated!

FIGURE 12.7

Step 4: Assigning Queues to Printers

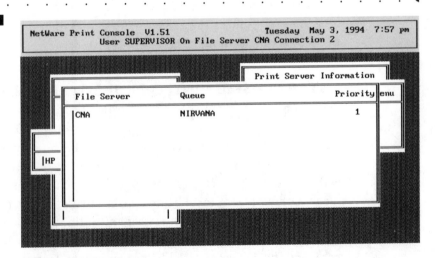

QUOTE

The light at the end of the tunnel has a train attached.

Anonymous

The standard printing setup we described here will work well with most vanilla LANs. But vanilla is boring. Most NetWare cafes strive for more—more variety, more customization, more sophistication. NetWare 3.12 provides additional facilities for supporting non-vanilla LANs. Let's explore some of its unique printing setup features.

ADDITIONAL SETUP CONSIDERATIONS

NetWare's built-in printing facility is quite sophisticated. It supports a multitude of different print types and user requirements. In addition, NetWare's printing setup design has been incorporated as a standard for network type applications. Besides the above four setup steps, NetWare provides additional setup considerations. These considerations help to support remote printing, multiple file servers, unique queue design, and customized printer parameters. In this section, we will expand on NetWare's standard printing setup by exploring the additional setup considerations. Let's begin with remote printing.

Remote Printing

Remote printing allows system managers to distribute network printers throughout the layout of the LAN. Remote printing defines local workstation printers as shared network devices. The RPRINTER command is the workstation utility which provides the remote printing facility. RPRINTER is a terminate-stay-resident program which runs in workstation RAM and controls the movement of print jobs from queues to the local workstation. The RPRINTER syntax includes

Remote printing allows system managers to distribute network printers throughout the layout of the LAN. Remote printing defines local workstation printers as shared network devices.

RPRINTER—brings up the RPRINTER menu.

or

RPRINTER PS=[print server] P=[printer number]

The second command in the AUTOEXEC.BAT file will activate the RPRINTER facility. Keep in mind, RPRINTER does take up some workstation RAM and communicates directly with local printer ports. RPRINTER can be unloaded using the -r switch, which removes it from memory.

TIP

There are two commands which can prevent local printers from operating as shared network devices: NET.CFG and PSC. The NET.CFG file can be configured to include the LOCAL PRINTERS = 0 command. This will block communications between workstations and attached printers. The PSC command can be used with the /PRI switch to activate PRIVATE mode. The PRIVATE printer mode switches the local printer's function from shared to private. This condition may be reversed by using the /sh switch (shared).

KNOWLEDGE

RPRINTER does not require that the user actually be logged into the network—but simply attached. An RPRINTER attachment can be accomplished by issuing an IPX and NETx. Once the workstation has been attached to the network, RPRINTER can be issued.

Multiple File Servers

Earlier we mentioned that NetWare 3.12 supports print queues on up to eight different file servers. Since the print server is a separate process from the file server, one print server can support multiple file servers. It is required, however, that the file servers upon which the different queues reside must be connected on an internetwork. To support queues on multiple file servers, the system manager must specify which file servers the print server will service. This is done as part of the print server installation, step 2 above. The multiple file servers setup process allows users on multiple different file servers to print to the same printer. This requires a few additional setup steps:

1 · The system manager must define an identically-named print server on each of the file servers that will be serviced by this print server. In other words, give it exactly the same name.

2 · The system manager must go to Step 3, defining printers, and configure printers with exactly the same numbers and names on the new print servers. The difference is these printers will be defined in the type field as Defined Elsewhere instead of LPT1. This type tells the phony print server that the real printers are defined on another file server. The system is intelligent enough to know which file server it needs to go to for the printer definitions.

3 · Assign each of the defined printers to a print queue located on the host file server.

4 · Finally, the system manager must go to the print server configuration of the real print server and highlight file servers to be serviced from the print server configuration screen. The system manager will press Insert and a list of available file servers will appear. Highlight and press Enter on each of the file servers which have phony print servers defined on them and they will be sharing the services of this one print server.

Here's an example. The system manager creates a print server called Print Server A. In Print Server A, the system manager defines all of the printers and the appropriate assignments from queues to printers. The system manager has a few users and a queue on File Server B which needs to access printers on Print Server A. The system manager goes to File Server B and defines a phony Print Server A on File Server B with identical printers and Defined Elsewhere in the type field. Next, the system manager assigns each of the phony printers to real queues on File Server B. The last step is to insert File Server B as a file server to be serviced on the real print server A.

Queue Design

The NetWare system manager can optimize printing performance by planning efficient queues. To achieve an efficient queue design, the system manager can rearrange work groups, set queue priorities, add or delete queues, assign queue operators, or remove print servers. The supervisor is automatically assigned as a queue operator during print server setup. This gives the supervisor the ability to efficiently design and maintain NetWare print queues. Print queues are subdirectories residing on file servers so they cannot easily be moved.

> The NetWare system manager can optimize printing performance by planning efficient queues.

When creating queues, remember that you can only assign queues to printers which have already been created. The current queue status option in PCONSOLE can be used to view the number of entries in a queue and the number of print servers attached to the queue. The system manager can monitor current print queue status to track queues which are being overloaded and queues which are not being used. In addition, the system manager can use queue priorities to rearrange the printing order of various queues.

The simplest design defines one print queue per printer. While this is ideal in most circumstances, some LANs require multiple queues per printer. In these cases, make sure to pay close attention to the different queue priorities.

TIP

Novell provides an additional utility for monitoring queue efficiencies. The program called QueueScan. It provides detailed information about print queues and how they are being utilized by appropriate print servers. QueueScan is currently available on Netwire.

Printer Parameters

Most of our discussion so far has focused on the optimization and development of efficient print servers and print queues. Let's not forget that the real workhorse of network printing is the printer itself. NetWare provides the facility for configuring custom printer parameters. These parameters fall into three categories: forms, notifications, and queue servicing.

Forms are printing definitions which detail the width and length of the printer's current paper. NetWare allows the system manager to define up to 256 different forms. The default form (Form 0) calls for an 8.5x11 piece of white paper. The system manager can use the PRINTDEF utility to define other forms and mount them as needed. Notification is extremely important in the printing environment because it allows NetWare managers to configure alerts for job completion or problem notification.

Job completion notification is a print job configuration which the user can define during the job customization process. Problem notification is defined by the system manager during the setup process. The notify list for problem alerts is created under the print server configuration menu of PCONSOLE. By default, the Supervisor, as a print server operator, is added to the problem notification list.

Finally, queue servicing defines how the printer will react to mounting multiple different forms. By default, the printer will call for various forms as they are needed. The NetWare system manager can configure queue servicing so that the printer services only the mounted form or minimizes form changes across or within queues. Minimizing form changes is a more efficient approach which instructs the printer to ask for form changes across all queues, or within queues only when all jobs using the current form have been completed.

Printing setup can be as simple or complex as you like. NetWare provides a wide range of facilities for satisfying your every printing need. The standard four steps of printing setup accommodate 95% of NetWare printing needs. For those LANs with unique printing needs, NetWare provides additional setup considerations and facilities. Once printing setup has been established and the users are actively involved in NetWare printing, the system manager can shift his/her attention to optimizing the existing process. Printing performance optimization involves a detailed understanding of the printing process and issues which affect it.

In the next section we will take a closer look at the detailed events of the printing process and how these events can be optimized.

Printing Performance Optimization

Imagine how difficult it would be to create a gourmet meal if the chef and his/her assistants did not prepare the food beforehand. Printing performance optimization is the process of preparing the printing components so that the actual process of printing can operate smoothly. This is where the NetWare chef peels the potatoes and chops up the vegetables. But before you can dive into printing optimization issues, you must first have a detailed understanding of the events involved in the printing process. Let's take a quick look at the process of printing from Workstation A to Printer B and then we will move on to the more pressing issues of performance optimization.

> Printing performance optimization is the process of preparing the printing components so that the actual process of printing operates smoothly. This is where the NetWare chef peels the potatoes and chops up the vegetables.

THE PRINTING PROCESS

Fortunately, NetWare printing is transparent to the user. It's hard to imagine the chaos that would result if users truly understood what was going on as print jobs were moving from their workstation off to the network printer. As the system manager you do not have the luxury of closing your eyes to these details. The details for the NetWare printing process are illustrated in Figure 12.8 which shows four main components: the workstation shell, print queue, print server, and NetWare printer.

QUOTE

One machine can do the work of fifty ordinary men. No machine can do the work of one extraordinary man.

Elbert Hubbard

Let's take a close look at the steps as the print job is sent from a non-network aware application to a central shared printer.

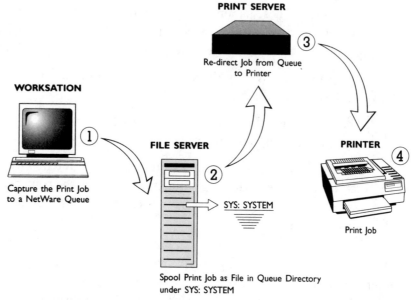

FIGURE 12.8

The Printing Process

PRINT SERVER

③ Re-direct Job from Queue to Printer

WORKSATION

① Capture the Print Job to a NetWare Queue

FILE SERVER

② SYS: SYSTEM

PRINTER ④

Print Job

Spool Print Job as File in Queue Directory under SYS: SYSTEM

1 · The CAPTURE command activates the printing components of the NetWare shell and tells the system to redirect any jobs destined for the local LPT1 port off to a NetWare queue.

2 · The shell places the CAPTURE parameters into a buffer in NETx.

3 · The user uses the non-network aware application to print a job to the local LPT1 port. The system recognizes the job as destined for the LPT1 port and redirects it to a NetWare queue. The shell adds the printer specific information to the print header and print tail.

4 · The print job is sent off to the file server as a NetWare file.

5 · The file server accepts the file and recognizes that it is indeed a print job. It reads the print header information and redirects it to the appropriate queue subdirectory on the shared hard disk.

6 · When the print job is redirected during step 3, the print job finds its way to the correct queue, and the shell appends the parameters to the SYS file in the queue. The .SRV file holds print server information.

7 · The print job is affected by a variety of performance optimization parameters. These parameters include the printing capacity of the printer, the queue priority, whether or not there are multiple queues per printer, or whether there are multiple printers for this queue.

8 · The print job moves up the queue priority ladder and is eventually serviced by the print server.

9 · The print server then routes the print job file from the NetWare queue and off to the appropriate printer.

10 · Finally, the print job is printed at the NetWare printer. Once the print server recognizes that the printing is completed, the print server will issue a command to the file server to delete the print job file from the shared queue directory.

As you can see, there's a lot going on when the user sends a print job to the printer down the hall. The user thinks it is all magic because he or she presses the print button and a few seconds later their job begins printing out of a shared printer. Somewhere in the middle of all this, the print queue is subject to a variety of optimization issues. These issues affect the print job's ability to move up the priority ladder.

PERFORMANCE ISSUES

Let's take a closer look at some of the more dominant performance issues. The print job's ability to be serviced by the print server can be affected by a variety of different events. These events include issues controlling the capacity of the printer, the priority of the queue and the number of types of queues per printer. The system manager should have a firm grasp on how these performance issues are balanced in his/her printing system. If the system manager monitors a particular performance problem, he/she can alter the printer or queue's ability to get the job done.

Printing Capacity

Printing capacity defines the number and size of jobs that each printer can handle. If jobs overlap in the queue, print time is affected. Printing performance is not only affected by a printer's capacity but also by the size of the jobs ahead of a particular print job in the queue. For example, if a one-page memo is sitting behind a 500-page manuscript, this will have a dramatic effect on the writer of the memo. It is important to monitor printing load. If large documents are printed on a regular basis, the system manager can explore alternatives such as using temporary printers, deferring printing to later at night, or changing priorities for specific jobs.

Queue Priority

One option for alleviating printing loads is changing the queue priority. Each queue has a priority which is established during the printing setup phase. A queue's priority defines when its jobs are serviced by the print server. A queue with priority 1, for example, will have the highest priority in sending jobs to a queue printer. A print job in a queue with priority 2 will not be serviced until all jobs in the priority 1 queue have been completed. This is effective for differentiating the priority of work groups throughout the LAN. For example, month end reports should not be sent to queues with a lower priority than administrative faxes or memos. Queue priority also provides a strategy for isolating key users and providing them with the best printing performance.

Multiple Queues Per Printer

The number and types of queues per printer will also affect printing performance. The simplest setup is one queue per printer. However, for complex printing environments, printers often have more than one queue assigned to them. When multiple queues are serviced by one printer, the print server determines order according to criteria. First, the queue priority. If the print server comes across two queues with the same priority, it will use the first come, first served criteria. Sometimes queues become quite overloaded. In these cases, the system manager can consider having multiple printers per queue.

Multiple Printers Per Queue

This type of printing flexibility is ideal for high load environments such as typing pools. All printers should be grouped in one area. In addition, all the printers serviced by one queue should be identical in all configurations—type, memory capacity, and so on.

TIP

If you are going to utilize multiple printers per queue, you must manually assign the one queue to each of the NetWare printers. Having multiple printers per queue can dramatically increase printing performance in high load environments.

As you can see, printing performance optimization is not a simple proposition. It involves a variety of different components and their interrelationships. The relationships of queues to printers and print server priorities play a strong role in how quickly user print jobs are processed. The NetWare chef should periodically monitor the printing environment to determine which is the best course of action. After all, NetWare printing is like a 10-course meal.

Printing Maintenance

Once printing setup and optimization procedures have been accomplished, the NetWare chef can concentrate on the daily operations of the NetWare Cafe— printing maintenance. Printing maintenance is the periodic monitoring and management of NetWare print queues, print servers and printers. Printing maintenance tasks include:

- ▸ Print job customization

- ▸ Print job prioritization

- ▸ General queue maintenance

- ▸ Checking the printer's status

- ▸ Mounting forms
- ▸ Monitoring printer definitions

Printing maintenance is accomplished using two NetWare printing utilities: PCONSOLE and PSC. PCONSOLE is the mother of all printing utilities. It provides the facility for management and maintenance of print queues, print servers and NetWare printers. As you recall, PCONSOLE allowed the system manager to access real time printing information.

> Printing maintenance is the periodic monitoring and management of NetWare print queues, print servers, and printers.

The PSC (Print Server Command) command is used to issue instructions directly to printers and print servers from the NetWare command line. The NetWare chef can use these two utilities to enhance the presentation of the printing meal. In many cases, printing maintenance determines the daily reliability of the printing operation.

QUOTE

Those who work most for the world's advancement are the ones who demand least.

Henry Doherty

In this section, we will learn how to implement NetWare printing maintenance through the use of PCONSOLE and PSC. In addition, we will discover some routine maintenance tasks which can proactively eliminate possible printing problems. Let's begin with a discussion of queue control.

QUEUE CONTROL

The first line of attack for NetWare printing maintenance is queue management. Queue management involves the monitoring of print jobs and changing of their print job parameters. This information is detailed in the current print job entry screen of PCONSOLE. Figure 12.9 show an illustration of the print queue entry information window in PCONSOLE.

FIGURE 12.9

Print Queue Entry

Information in PCONSOLE

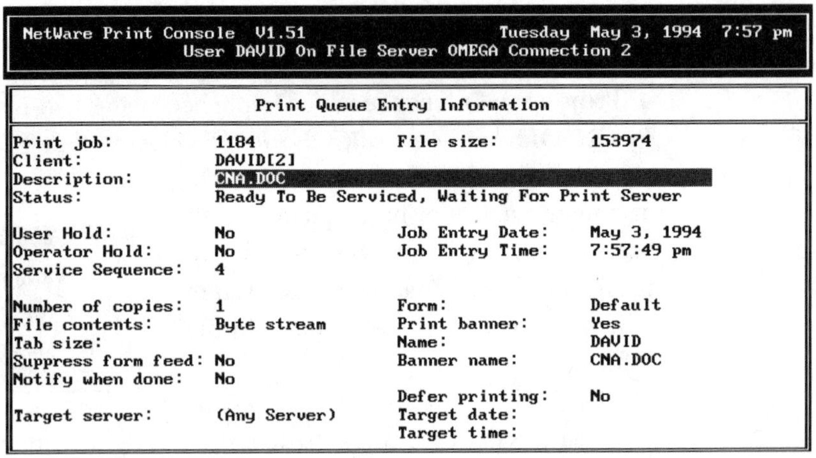

```
NetWare Print Console  V1.51                    Tuesday  May 3, 1994  7:57 pm
              User DAVID On File Server OMEGA Connection 2

                        Print Queue Entry Information

Print job:          1184            File size:         153974
Client:             DAVID[2]
Description:        CNA.DOC
Status:             Ready To Be Serviced, Waiting For Print Server

User Hold:          No              Job Entry Date:    May 3, 1994
Operator Hold:      No              Job Entry Time:    7:57:49 pm
Service Sequence:   4

Number of copies:   1               Form:              Default
File contents:      Byte stream     Print banner:      Yes
Tab size:                           Name:              DAVID
Suppress form feed: No              Banner name:       CNA.DOC
Notify when done:   No
                                    Defer printing:    No
Target server:      (Any Server)    Target date:
                                    Target time:
```

This queue management screen provides a variety of different parameters which can be monitored and maintained by the NetWare system manager. An explanation of some of the more interesting parameters follows:

Print job—a random number assigned by NetWare for each print job which enters the queue. The print job number is used to track print jobs as they move up the priority ladder and off to NetWare printers.

File size—an indication of the size of the file as its exists in the print queue. This is listed in bytes.

Description—an identification string detailing the type of file it is. An LPT1 catch shows it was a CAPTURE command redirected from the workstation's local LPT1 port.

Status—an indication of the current status of this particular print job. Status indicates that the print job is ready and waiting to be serviced by the print server, or that it's being added to the queue, or currently being printed.

User hold and operator hold—two facilities for putting a hold on the print job. Print jobs on hold will be paused in the print queue until the hold flag is removed. A user hold can be set by a user or a print queue operator and can be removed by either. An operator hold can only be set by a print queue operator and cannot be removed by the user.

Service sequence—an indication of where the particular job currently resides in the queue priority list. A service sequence of 1 means that the job is currently at the top of the ladder and waiting to be serviced by the print server.

File contents—specifies which mode the printer should use in processing tabs and control characters. Text mode replaces all tabs with spaces while byte stream allows an application to use formatting commands to print the document. Byte stream is the default and works for most print jobs adequately.

Form—an indication of the form number which this job needs to be printed.

Notify when done—allows the user to change the flags so that the system notifies them when the print job has been completed. Print job completion notifications are broadcast as one line commands at the bottom of the workstation screen.

Print banner—a one-page title screen which appears at the beginning of each print job. The banner lists the name of the user and a descriptive banner name string.

Deferred printing—allows system managers and users to delay jobs to be printed until a later date. The target date and target time parameters allow the system manager or print queue operator to schedule unattended printing. Only the operator can defer someone else's print job. The default listing for deferred printing is 2:00 AM the following morning. The assumption is that jobs which are deferred are typically large and should be printed during off hours.

TIP

The current print job entry screen can be accessed by highlighting a print job from the particular queue and pressing Enter. Once

changes have been made to the entry information window, the system manager or user can insert the job back into the queue by pressing Escape. It will retain its appropriate place in the ladder.

In addition to queue management, NetWare provides the PSC command to control and maintain NetWare print servers. The print server's primary function is the routing of information from appropriate queues to appropriate printers. In addition to the PSC command, the system manager can use the PCONSOLE utility to view the current status of printers and print servers.

PRINT SERVER AND PRINTER CONTROL

The PSC command is a very useful printer and print server control utility. System managers use it to manage and maintain NetWare print servers. PSC provides similar functionality to PCONSOLE except it performs its operations from the command line and issues commands directly to the printer or print server. You can perform the following PCONSOLE tasks with PSC:

- View the Status of Printers
- Pause the Printer Temporarily
- Stop Printing the Current Job
- Start the Printer
- Mark the Top of Form
- Advance Printer to Top of Next Page
- Mount a New Form

The syntax for PSC is **PSC PS=[printserver] P=[printer]**.

TIP
You can use the DOS SET command to set a default print server and printer number for PSC so that you do not have to specify this information at the command line every time.

The NetWare chef is responsible for a variety of different print server and printer maintenance tasks. The following is a brief list of these tasks along with some insight into how they can be executed using the PCONSOLE or PSC utilities.

View the Status of Printers. The system manager can check printer status in PCONSOLE by accessing the print server status and control option from print server information. This type of information can also be viewed from the command line using the **STAT** flag with PSC.

Stop Jobs. The system manager or print server operator can stop the current job using PCONSOLE or PSC. PCONSOLE provides this option from the status of printer box. The system manager can highlight Printer Control in the Status of Printer box and select Abort Print Job. This action will stop the current print job and continue to the next job in the queue. The system manager can also choose the Stop Printer choice which will abort the current job but not continue to the next print job in the queue until the system manager chooses to resume printing, using the Start Printer option.

Similar functions can be used from the command line using PSC. The system manager can abort print jobs using the **AB** flag or stop the printer using the **STO** flag. In addition, the system manager will have to use the **STAR** or start flag to restart the printer if the stop flag switch is utilized.

TIP

When print jobs are stopped or aborted, NetWare automatically deletes their corresponding files from the queue directory. If the system manager would not like the print job to be deleted, he/she can issue the K flag which will keep the job and resubmit it at the top of the queue.

Mount Forms. The system manager can mount forms for printers using PCONSOLE or PSC. The PCONSOLE utility provides the mounted form option under printer status and control. The system manager can simply type in the form number as assigned with the

PRINTDEF utility. Mounting forms with PSC is performed using the MO F=[number] flag. The number parameter indicates the form number as defined by PRINTDEF.

Change to Private Setting. Print server operators or system managers can prevent other network users from accessing remote printers by issuing the PRI private flag with PSC. This will break communications between the print server and the local workstation printer. Remote printers can be reinstigated as shared printers by issuing the SHAR or share flag.

Cancel Down. NetWare provides two facilities for downing the NetWare print server. Both of these choices are accessed from the print server status control option in PCONSOLE. The two choices are Going Down After Current Jobs or DOWN. If the system manager chooses Going Down After Current Jobs, the system will pause the queue and continue finishing all active print jobs. New print jobs added to the queue will continue to line up but will not be printed. The system manager has the capability to cancel the down command if they choose Going Down After Current Jobs. This is because a lag occurs between the time the down command is issued and the time the printer actually comes down. The cancel down command can only be issued using the PSC utility and the CD flag. The other option for downing a print server is to select DOWN from the Print Server Status/Control menu. Issuing DOWN will immediately down the print server and the system manager will not have the capability of canceling the down.

TIP

Downing the print server does not delete any jobs from the queue, it simply stops the print server from servicing queues and printers.

Rewind Printer. Since NetWare print jobs are files in the queue directory, NetWare provides the facility for rewinding print jobs if an error occurs. If the printer jams in the middle of a 100-page job, the system manager can pause the job and fix the printer. Once the printer has been fixed, the system manager can use PCONSOLE to rewind the print job back a few pages and start on page 70, for example, instead of on page 1. The Rewind Printer facility is available in the Print Server Status/Control menu.

Other print server or printer maintenance options which can be implemented using PCONSOLE or PSC include:

▸ Form Feed

▸ Mark Top of Form

▸ Pause Printer

It is important for the NetWare chef to pay very close attention to printing maintenance. He/she should routinely check these different components weekly or monthly. Routine maintenance of the print queue, print server, and printer can dramatically improve printing quality, performance, and reliability. Speaking of reliability, the next topic of discussion is troubleshooting.

Printing Troubleshooting

No matter how many precautions the NetWare chef takes, he's going to burn some toast sooner or later. It is not a perfect world—yet. NetWare 3.12 printing is riddled with LAN mines and pitfalls. The best way to avoid them is to be prepared and take a proactive stance towards printing maintenance. But once in a while some simple little problem is going to fall through the cracks. In that case, we have a few suggestions for you:

> No matter how many precautions the NetWare chef takes, he's going to burn some toast sooner or later. It is not a perfect world—yet! NetWare 3.12 printing is riddled with LAN mines and pitfalls.

▸ Make sure to check network interface cards and printing cables before you go too far.

Many printing problems are the results of conflicting interrupts or faulty hardware.

▶ Use PCONSOLE to review the setup of print queues, print servers and printers. In addition, interrogate the printer configurations used in the third stage defined printers.

▶ If the user is using CAPTURE to redirect print jobs from local ports to NetWare queues, make sure that the CAPTURE command is in fact activated. Also check the parameters which the CAPTURE command is using.

▶ Finally, check the print queue itself. Make sure the queue is reliable and has not been corrupted. If all else fails, delete and recreate the print queues and print servers.

While this advice provides some general guidance in printing troubleshooting, most NetWare printing problems fall into one of four categories. In this section, we will explore these four categories and provide some suggested avenues of action. Let's begin with print jobs that go to the queue but not to the printer.

PRINT JOBS THAT GO TO QUEUE BUT NOT TO PRINTER

The system manager checks the print queue information box in PCONSOLE and finds that print jobs are piling up in line waiting to be serviced by the print server. If this is the case, there is a variety of causes and solutions. As you recall, the print server is responsible for routing print jobs from queues to printers. The main area to focus on for this particular problem is the print server itself. Let's take a look at the three possible causes and solutions.

Printer Definition

The first cause could be that the printer definition is not established correctly for this printer. The system manager can check the print server information screen in PCONSOLE and make sure that the configuration for this printer does in fact match its location. That is to say, if it is a remote printer, is it defined as a remote printer. If it is a printer attached directly to the print server, is it in fact defined as an LPT or COM1 printer.

Also, the printer could be offline, jammed, or out of paper. In this particular case, print jobs would wait and queue up in the print queue because the print server would recognize the printer as not being capable of processing them.

QUOTE

Give us the fortitude to endure the things which cannot be changed, and the courage to change the things which should be changed, and the wisdom to know one from the other.

Oliver J. Hartp

NET.CFG

The NET.CFG or SHELL.CFG file could have the line Local Printers = 0. This is particularly serious if the local printer is attached to a workstation which is running RPRINTER. RPRINTER allows the local workstation printer to act as a shared network device. If the **Local Printers = 0** command has been issued at the NET.CFG for this workstation, the system will not recognize the local printer as a network device.

Private

The final possible cause is the use of the **PSC** private flag. The private flag breaks communications between remote printers and the print server. To solve this problem, the system manager must issue the **PSC /SHAR** command flag to re-establish the local printer as a shared device.

KNOWLEDGE

The best indication that the print server is performing normally is the Waiting for Job Message at the print server screen. Each printer which is defined and currently waiting for a job should have this message displayed at the print server screen.

PRINT JOBS THAT DON'T PRINT PROPERLY

The next printing problem is that print jobs go to the printer but do not print properly. One possible cause is a mismatch between the printing configuration and the current printer status. For example, postscript jobs being sent to a non-postscript printer will print garbled characters. In addition, a byte stream print job sent in text mode will also cause the same effect.

A more common problem is with interrupt mismatch. The printer definition screen defines hardware interrupts for shared network printers. If the interrupt listed in the print server setup screen is different from the interrupt that the printer is using, printing will be slow and erratic.

Finally, one culprit for common printing problems is the RPRINTER remote printing facility. RPRINTER has been known to interact unfavorably with complex memory workstations or enhanced Windows setups. The best course of action in this particular case is to move the remote printer to another workstation and try RPRINTER there. Also, upload the newest RPRINTER fix from Novell's Netwire bulletin board.

PRINTER IS OUT OF PAPER OR OFFLINE

One of the most common printing error notifications is that the printer is out of paper or offline. In this case, you can't always believe your eyes. Many cases when the print server indicates that the printer is out of paper or offline, the printer is in fact not attached to any port or the correct port on the print server. A more accurate message would be that the printer is *out of printer,* not out of paper.

If you receive the message that the printer is out of paper or offline, the first thing to check is the printer definition screen. Check which port the printer has been defined for and make sure that the suspect printer is in fact attached to that port. If the printer is in the correct location, check the hardware interrupts that have been defined. One way to isolate an interrupt problem is to create a

> Many cases when the print server indicates that the printer is out of paper or offline, the printer is in fact not attached to any port or the correct port on the print server. A more accurate message would be that the printer is *out of printer,* not out of paper.

dummy print server and queue and define the local printer as no interrupts. If this works fine, then the problem is certainly interrupt oriented.

PRINT SERVER PASSWORD PROMPT APPEARS

One of the most annoying printing problems is the print server password prompt. In many cases, the print server will prompt you for a password even when no password exists. This can delay the automatic loading of the PSERVER.NLM from AUTOEXEC.NCF. There is a variety of reasons this could happen. Let's explore some of those causes now.

PSERVER

PSERVER.NLM or PSERVER.EXE may have been loaded without specifying a print server name. In this case, the system will try to load without a name. A print server without a name will be prompted for a password. Another possibility is that when PSERVER was loaded, the print server name was typed incorrectly. To test this theory, simply unload the print server and try again.

Bindery

It is possible that the bindery at some point became slightly corrupted and lost track of the print server name information. This is actually the most common cause of the password error. To solve bindery problems, simply decorrupt the bindery by running BINDFIX from the SYSTEM subdirectory. Incidentally, the BINDFIX command line utility can be used to solve many NetWare bindery-oriented errors.

New File Server

Finally, the print server password prompt will erroneously appear if a new file server has been added but a print server was not defined on it. In this case, the print server looks to all attached file servers for print queue information and notices a new file server with an attached queue. The attached queue is mapped to this print server but the print server itself has not been defined on the new file server. In this case, the print server will load but assume an erroneous name. This is the same type of situation as loading PSERVER without specifying a name.

While NetWare printing can be troublesome and mysterious, a good proactive maintenance strategy will solve many of these problems. In addition, a few notes in the NetWare log book can help present and future NetWare system managers troubleshoot common printing problems. Remember, even the best chefs in the world drop a souffle once in a while.

Printing

Now that the preparation is over, it's time for the big event. The chef has gone out and purchased all the raw materials, prepared the vegetables and slaved over a hot stove. The plate has been garnished and it's time to serve the meal.

THREE WAYS TO PRINT

The ultimate goal of all of this setup, optimization, and maintenance is the movement of a print job from Workstation A to Printer B. NetWare provides three different ways to do this:

- ▶ Printing from NetWare-aware applications
- ▶ Using CAPTURE to redirect local ports
- ▶ PCONSOLE/NPRINT to insert print jobs directly into NetWare queues.

Users can use one or many of these three different approaches towards NetWare printing. The bottom line is that the user presses the print button and the job magically appears in the printer down the hall. If the system manager has done his/her job correctly, NetWare printing is completely transparent to the user. But don't be fooled—this level of printing transparency is difficult to install and a bear to maintain. In the end, it's worth the effort when the system manager sees the smile on his/her user's

The ultimate goal of all this setup, optimization, and maintenance is the movement of a print job from Workstation A to Printer B. NetWare provides three different ways to do this: NetWare-aware applications, CAPTURE, and NPRINT.

face. We can only imagine it is the same feeling a chef enjoys when a guest raves about the restaurant's meal.

QUOTE

Every action of our lives touches on some chord that will vibrate in eternity.

Edwin Hubbel Chapin

Let's take a look at the three different ways to print in a NetWare printing system.

NetWare-Aware Applications

A few special applications exist which fully understand NetWare printing. These applications are aware of NetWare queues and can print directly from workstations to centralized queues and shared printers. Two of the most popular NetWare-aware applications are WordPerfect and Microsoft Windows. The WordPerfect word processing program prints directly to NetWare queues through the printer edit facility. The system manager can define the NetWare queue name as an auxiliary printing device. Microsoft Windows works in much the same way except it relies on its own internal print manager. The Windows print manager is aware of local ports as well as NetWare queues. Printing directly from any Windows application to a NetWare queue is seamless and transparent.

These two NetWare-aware applications and their printing sophistication have created a groundswell around NetWare printing intelligence. More and more applications are exploring the concept of printing directly to NetWare queues, thus solving some common problems with local port redirection. Most of your non-NetWare-aware applications currently pose difficulties for system managers. These applications can be obtrusive and uncooperative in redirecting from local ports to NetWare queues. Unfortunately, most other NetWare applications aren't aware of NetWare queues. These non-NetWare-aware applications print directly to local ports as if a local workstation is attached.

CAPTURE

The CAPTURE command is a printing utility which provides flexibility for the workstation so that printing can be done from non-NetWare applications. CAPTURE literally hijacks the local printer port and redirects all print jobs destined for that port off to a NetWare queue. The syntax is **CAPTURE QUEUE=[name of queue] /[switch]**.

There is a huge variety of additional parameters which can be used with the CAPTURE command to customize the way that print jobs are printed. Some of the more interesting CAPTURE parameters include:

/b for banner name

/c for copies

/ff for form feed

/j for job (which is a PRINTCON utility)

/l=[number] for the local port which needs to be CAPTUREd by default. Without the /l=[number] CAPTURE will capture the LPT1 parallel port.

/nff for no form feed

/nt for no tabs

/sh for show which will display the current status of the CAPTURE command

/t for tabs=[number] to replace all tab characters with spaces if you specify

/ti for timeout which is a timeout feature that is important for certain misbehaving non-network applications

Here's a sample CAPTURE command that is useful in most environments: **CAPTURE QUEUE=[queuename] /nb /nt /ti=10 /nff**. Once CAPTURE has been loaded into memory, it cannot be unloaded or stopped unless you issue an ENDCAP command. ENDCAP is particularly useful because it allows the flexibility to capture to specific queues for specific applications and then end that capture session and recapture for another queue in another application. Incidentally, all of this can be accomplished using batch files.

PCONSOLE/NPRINT

NetWare provides a third method for access to shared printers. This method involves one menu utility and one command line utility. The menu utility PCONSOLE provides the facility for inserting print jobs directly into NetWare queues. The system manager can highlight the pre-queue information screen for PCONSOLE and highlight an appropriate queue. The system manager can then move into the current job entry screen and press the Insert key. Pressing Insert at the current job entry screen displays an input box into which the system manager puts a NetWare file. This file will be inserted directly into the queue using the default print job configurations. This is an effective strategy for system managers who need to quickly print text files directly from the shared disk. This is not a good strategy for printing files with complex control codes and application-specific formatting.

NPRINT is a workstation command line utility which sends a text file directly to a NetWare queue. NPRINT's syntax is **NPRINT [queue name]** and it uses the same parameters as CAPTURE. In this case, instead of capturing from a local port, NPRINT prints a text file from the command line directly to a NetWare queue. There's no port involved.

PRINT JOB CUSTOMIZATION

PRINTCON is an advanced NetWare system management printing utility which is used to customize print job configurations. Using PRINTCON, the system manager can define a specific set of configurations for a user and then attach those configurations to a print job using the CAPTURE /j parameter. The print job parameters are identical to the switches from CAPTURE except PRINTCON provides a facility for permanently storing these parameters in a menu format.

TIP

PRINTCON configurations are user-specific. They exist as the file PRINTCON.DAT in the user's SYS:MAIL\userid subdirectory. The system manager must define these parameters for each user.

PRINTCON offers the facility to copy printing configurations from one user to another.

Wow, wasn't that fun!? In this chapter, we explored the NetWare Cafe from the system manager's printing point of view. We learned about the fundamentals of NetWare printing and explored the relationships between printer servers and printers. We went through the four steps of setting up vanilla printing systems and then moved on to setup considerations for unique printing systems. We learned about how to optimize printing performance through printing capacity, queue priority and multiple queues and printers. Printing maintenance focused on the print queue, the print server, and the printer using PCONSOLE and the PSC command line utility. We explored some serious printing problems and discovered possible courses of action and finally we defined the three different ways that NetWare users can send print jobs from their workstation to shared NetWare printers.

I wish there was a cookbook you could follow in setting up the most reliable and efficient NetWare printing system. Unfortunately, NetWare printing seems to be more trial by fire. The good news is you have a good printing education under your belt and some Novell resources to rely on. Much more than Betty Crocker ever had.

> I wish there was a cookbook you could follow in setting up the most reliable and efficient NetWare printing system. Unfortunately, NetWare printing seems to be more trial by fire.

NetWare 3.12
Performance Management

**On the planet Zenon,
system managers improve file server
and communication performance by constant vigilance.**

What would a luxury hotel be without interior decorating? How appealing would it be without fancy drapes and interior fountains, beautiful paintings and ice sculptures?

The interior decorator is responsible for the subtle nuances that make the difference between ultimate comfort and just a place to stay. The Park Place decorator spends hours each day walking the halls and examining the interior luxuries of the hotel. He/she inspects the rooms, examines the restaurants and monitors the interior artwork. When the decorator finds any small discrepancy which could be improved upon, he/she acts very quickly. Interior decorating at a luxury resort is a 24-hour-a-day job.

As the NetWare system manager you are the interior decorator of your LAN. You are responsible for examining the LAN's furnishings and making improvements wherever possible. The goal of NetWare interior decorating is performance optimization. The system manager must be 100% committed to optimizing file server and communication performance.

> As the NetWare system manager you are the interior decorator of your LAN. You are responsible for examining the LAN's furnishings and making improvements wherever possible.

Performance revolves around two key functions: monitoring and optimization. NetWare monitoring involves the examination of key file server resources and determination of possible discrepancies. File server optimization is the continuation of NetWare decorating. This function involves correcting the discrepancies found in the monitoring stage. Diligent monitoring and effective optimization can make the difference between LAN success and failure.

As the NetWare interior decorator, the system manager focuses his/her performance management efforts on a variety of different components. These components affect shared disk usage, file server communications, memory, security access, and processor utilization. In this chapter, we will explore the file server performance management components and gain an understanding of their role in monitoring and optimization. We will explore the file server memory pools in depth and learn how they combine to provide an efficient and effective memory management strategy.

Once we have gained an understanding of performance management components and file server memory pools, we will move on to monitoring and optimization. File server monitoring is performed using the MONITOR.NLM utility. We will explore its variety of features. File server optimization is performed using the SET CONSOLE command and we will explore its nine different optimization categories.

Performance management is as important to your NetWare LAN as water fountains and ice sculptures are to Park Place. It is one of your most important responsibilities and as we mentioned earlier, it can determine the success or failure of your LAN.

QUOTE

Science does not know its debt to imagination.

Ralph Waldo Emerson

Performance Management Components

Performance management components determine how NetWare file servers interact with shared resources. They control communications, shared disk access and memory management. NetWare incorporates two main performance management components: tables and allocation units. Tables control shared disk organization and hold properties of NetWare files and directories. Allocation units define logical groups of data as they reside in memory and on the disk. In addition, NetWare employs a performance optimization strategy called *caching* which increases file server disk access by an amazing 10,000%. Caching is explained in detail below. Tables and allocation units are analogous to the art work and fabric which the Park Place interior decorator uses to improve the quality of the hotel rooms and lobby.

> NetWare incorporates two main performance-management components: tables and allocation units. Tables control shared disk organization and hold properties of NetWare files and directories. Allocation units define logical groups of data as they reside in memory and on the disk.

In this section, we will explore tables, caching, and allocation units. We will discover their responsibilities and relationship to memory management and optimization. Let's begin with NetWare drive tables.

TABLES

NetWare drive tables are the phone books of the LAN. They record information about where files are located and what kind of information resides in shared NetWare files. There are two different types of NetWare drive tables: the directory entry table (DET) and file allocation table (FAT). The directory entry table maintains information about file names, trustees, security and ownership. The file allocation table in NetWare performs the same function as it does in DOS; that is, to provide a master index of file names and physical locations on the shared disk. Directory entry tables and file allocation tables work together to provide an organized and efficient method of indexing, retrieving, and storing shared network data.

Directory Entry Table

The directory entry table is unique to NetWare—it doesn't even exist in DOS. The directory entry table contains information which would otherwise not be necessary in a stand-alone environment. The network specific type data includes ownership, rights, attributes and shared name space. NetWare's directory entry table maintains a basic list of directory entries. Directory entries include files and directories. The directory entry table stores valuable information about directory entries such as:

- ► Name of files
- ► Ownership
- ► Date of last update
- ► The first block of the network hard disk in which the file is stored
- ► Trustees of files and trustees of directories
- ► A pointer to the file allocation table.

The file allocation table contains the actual physical address of each block of a shared network file.

TIP

The file server does not cache the entire directory entry table. It only caches directory blocks that are being used or areas of the directory entry table which are in use. This differs from earlier versions of NetWare which did, in fact, cache the entire directory entry table. Directory entry tables are stored for each volume on the disk.

File Allocation Table

The file allocation table (FAT) in NetWare performs exactly the same function as it does in DOS. It maintains a list of all files on the shared disk and their physical track, sector and cylinder addresses. The FAT works very closely with the DET to provide files to NetWare clients. When a user requests a particular file from the central shared disk, the directory entry table matches that user's trustee assignments against the properties of the file. If the two match, a pointer is sent off to the file allocation table. The system then searches the file allocation table for all corresponding addresses for this file and returns the values to the disk controller. The disk controller then returns the data to the network interface card where it is sent off to the user. Unlike directory entry tables, the entire file allocation table is cached in file server memory.

TIP

NetWare provides a facility for more efficient and faster access to very large files. Files which exceed 64 blocks or 64 file allocation table entries are turbo-indexed. Turbo FAT indexing provides a facility for grouping these blocks together in the FAT. This makes access of large files much more efficient and lightning fast.

KNOWLEDGE

NetWare file allocation tables theoretically support 536,870,912 file allocation table entries and 2,097,152 directory entry table entries.

NetWare stores DETs, FATs, and files on the shared internal disk. As we learned from Chapter 1, disk storage is much slower than memory storage. Temporary RAM storage can be used to increase the performance of accessing and retrieving shared data through caching.

CACHING

Caching means storing frequently-used files and tables in memory rather than on the disk. NetWare 3.12 provides three built-in performance features that relate to caching:

▶ Directory caching

▶ Directory hashing

▶ File caching

Directory caching is the process of copying the directory entry table and file allocation table into file server RAM and accessing them from there. Accessing these tables from memory instead of disk is 100 times faster. Directory caching substantially increases file server performance because the DET and FAT tables are accessed every time a user requests a file. As mentioned earlier, NetWare 3.12 only copies the most recently used DET portions into file server RAM.

Directory hashing indexes the memory stored DET. This process in effect alphabetizes the NetWare phone book. Searches of indexed DETs are performed 30% faster than non-hashed directory entry tables.

QUOTE

No brain is stronger than its weakest think.

Thomas L. Masson

Finally, file caching is the automatic process of storing frequently-used files in server RAM. When a file is first requested by a user, it is accessed from disk and a copy is stored in RAM. Subsequent requests from users are then accessed from RAM 100 times faster than they would be from disk. NetWare 3.12 uses all available memory beyond the operating system and other resources for file caching.

TIP

**The more file caching memory available, the faster file server perfor-
mance. One of the most important strategies for performance
management is increasing the amount of memory available for file
caching.**

ALLOCATION UNITS

Allocation units are the most important performance management components. Allocation units define areas of file server storage which are reserved for
files and tables. NetWare defines two
different types of allocation units:
blocks and buffers. Blocks are data
storage areas on the hard disk. Buffers
are data storage areas in file server
memory. Blocks and buffers have a
dramatic impact on file server performance. They determine the speed and
efficiency of the file server disk's read
and write operations. In addition, buf-
fers control directory and file caching. Let's take a closer look at NetWare's performance management allocation units.

> Allocation units are the most important
> performance management components. Al-
> location units define areas of file server
> storage which are reserved for files and
> tables. NetWare defines two different types
> of allocation units: blocks and buffers.

Blocks

Blocks are data storage areas on the disk. NetWare divides the file server disk
into small allocation units called blocks. Typically the default block size in Net-
Ware is 4K. This means that a 100MB hard disk is allocated into 25,000 blocks.
These blocks are organized into two different types: disk allocation blocks and
directory entry blocks.

Disk Allocation Blocks Disk Allocation blocks store NetWare data. Net-
Ware divides each volume into several disk allocation blocks which provide the
smallest common denominator for storing network data. These allocation
blocks can be configured in 4, 8, 16, 32, or 64K increments. The default size is

4K. As files are stored on the NetWare disk, they are broken down into multiple blocks. Since a file can consist of more than one block, it is important that the file allocation table link these blocks together. Files which contain more than 64 blocks are turbo FAT indexed, meaning that NetWare has a built-in algorithm for faster access of these types of files.

The advantage of having large block sizes is that they provide more efficient disk access because the read/write head doesn't have to work as hard to access the data. The disadvantage of large block size is that they waste a lot of disk space. For example, a 4K file would use an entire 64K block if the block size had been set to 64K.

KNOWLEDGE

If the block size is set to 64K, it's possible to run out of disk space on an 80MB file server disk by loading just the SYSTEM and PUBLIC files. The reason for this is that many of the files are much less than 64K and the block size is wasted.

The advantage of small block sizes is that they are more efficient about the way that they store files. Thus, less disk space is wasted. The disadvantage to small block size is that they require a great deal more read/write head activity and can cause wear and tear on the disk. In addition, volumes with small block sizes have worse performance with respect to file access time.

Directory Entry Blocks   Directory entry blocks store NetWare DETs. Directory entry blocks are special allocation units which are reserved for storing the directory entry table. Directory entry blocks are a default 4K in size and cannot be changed. Each DET is divided into one or more directory blocks which store directory entries. By default, NetWare reserves six directory entry blocks to store the early DETs. This number will rise as needed and can reach as many as 65,536 blocks.

Each volume has its own DET and therefore reserves its own directory entry blocks. A directory entry block can accommodate thirty-two 128-byte entries. Keeping in mind the maximum number of directory blocks, that gives us a total number of directory entries of 2,097,152. Keep in mind, the main difference between directory entry blocks and disk allocation blocks is that directory entry blocks are always 4K. Disk allocation blocks can be made larger or smaller, as needed.

Buffers

The next allocation unit type is buffers. Buffers are storage areas in file server RAM. Buffers are important to file server performance because they are the areas where directory entries and files are cached. Each buffer corresponds with a particular type of block on the disk. For example, disk allocation blocks are stored in file cache buffers whereas directory entry blocks are stored in directory cache buffers. The third type of buffer, packet receive buffers, defines communication holding cells for user requests (Figure 13.1).

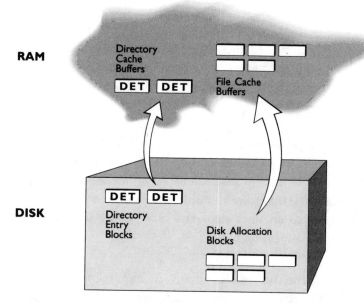

File Cache Buffers   File cache buffers are the most important buffer with respect to file server performance. File cache buffers are buffers in RAM which temporarily store disk allocation blocks. Since these buffers store blocks, they are sometimes referred to as cache blocks—an extremely confusing term. Figure 13.1 shows how the disk allocation blocks are stored on disk. These disk allocation blocks then correspond to file cache buffers. The file cache buffers can also be configured for differing sizes, but they have a smaller range. 4K is the default, but they can be configured for 4K, 8K, or 16K sizes.

Earlier we mentioned that file caching improves disk performance by 10,000%. Since file caching is such an important component in performance management, cache buffers then become an extremely important component in increasing server performance. File cache buffers and disk allocation blocks have a 1:1 relationship (as illustrated in Figure 13.1). That is, each disk allocation block is cached in memory in one file cache buffer. This becomes important in understanding the relationship between disk allocation block size and cache buffer size. If, for example, the cache buffer size exceeds the block size, this would create an environment of inefficiency and waste server RAM. If, for example, the cache buffer size was 8K and the disk allocation block size was 4K, each 4K block would take 8K of memory. This is bad.

> File cache buffers are the most important buffer with respect to file server performance. File cache buffers are buffers in RAM which temporarily store disk allocation blocks.

TIP

If the cache buffer size is larger than the smallest disk allocation block size on all volumes, then the file server will not mount the volume. This is because the cache buffer services all blocks on all volumes. If there are multiple volumes on the server with different disk allocation block sizes, the cache buffer size must match the smallest allocation block size.

Directory Cache Buffers Directory cache buffers are areas of server RAM which hold the DET blocks. Figure 13.1 shows the 1:1 relationship between directory entry blocks and directory cache buffers. By default, the directory cache buffer size matches the directory entry block size, which is 4K. NetWare allocates directory cache buffers as needed for caching the most frequently used portions of the DET. As more directory entries are added to the system, directory entry blocks increase and the system allocates file cache buffer area for directory cache buffers. As the number of directory cache buffers increases, file cache buffers decrease. This can make it tough to balance performance versus storage organization. Later in this chapter, we will learn how to monitor the number of directory cache buffers and use SET parameters to optimize server performance.

Packet Receive Buffers　The final server buffer type has nothing to do with disk storage. Packet receive buffers describe an area in server memory which is set aside or reserved to temporarily hold user requests while they are waiting to be serviced by NetWare. These user requests arrive at the file server as packets. Packets are communication components which include, among other things, user requests for data or processing information. These packet requests are handled by file service processes. File service processes (FSPs) are built-in subroutines which respond to incoming user requests. NetWare treats FSPs and PRBs in much the same way a bank treats its clients.

In Figure 13.2, you can see that the file service processes are like bank's tellers. These tellers service clients one at a time as they come in for requests to withdraw or deposit money. Clients who are waiting to be serviced by the tellers wait in the bank lobby—large enough to hold 50 to 100 important clients. The bank lobby is analogous to the packet receive buffer. Packets wait in the buffer until an FSP becomes available. Once an FSP becomes available, they are serviced accordingly and their request is acknowledged.

If there are not enough tellers to service all of the clients, the lobby can become quite full. And if it overflows, clients are forced to wait outside. Much the same thing happens in the NetWare environment if the number of file server processes is not enough to service all of the packets waiting in the buffer. If a client or a packet user request is forced out of the packet receive buffer, the user will receive an error sending on the network and the packet will be lost.

Efficient network performance then becomes a balance between having a large number of file service processes and the right size packet receive buffer. Both the FSP and PRB components can be optimized using MONITOR and SET parameters.

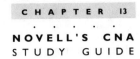
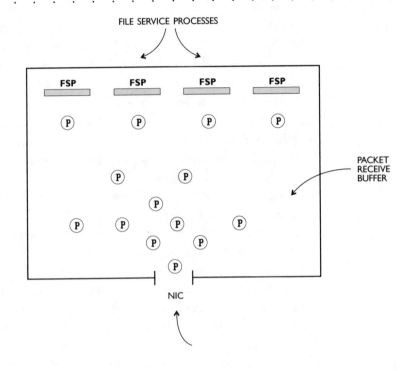

F I G U R E 13.2

The NetWare Bank

FILE SERVICE PROCESSES

PACKET
RECEIVE
BUFFER

QUOTE

Nothing is impossible for the man who doesn't have to do it himself.

A. H. Weiler

That completes our discussion of performance management components. In this section we have described the directory entry table and file allocation table, focusing on their function in organizing network data. We then discussed the caching features which provide efficient and high performance access to network data. Finally, we explored allocation units which provide areas of disk and server memory for storage of directory entry tables and user data.

In the next section we will discuss server memory management and how Net-Ware allocates particular areas of RAM for performance management components, resources and operating system requests.

Server Memory Management

NetWare 3.12 uses memory for many different functions. The minimum memory of 4MB is required for the operating system to barely function. NetWare supports (addresses) memory up to 4GB. The dynamic configuration of NetWare 3.12 and its 32-bit processing capabilities allow the server to allocate memory according to need and availability. The many different resources, components, and functions which require server RAM can be served efficiently and dynamically.

> NetWare 3.12 uses memory for many different functions. The dynamic configuration of NetWare 3.12 and its 32-bit processing capabilities allow the server to allocate memory according to need and availability.

MEMORY POOLS

In order for NetWare to dynamically service all of the many different resources which need server RAM, memory has been allocated into logical pools. These pools do not actually physically exist within the NetWare RAM, but are used as logical pointers to areas of available RAM. Figure 13.3 shows a graphic of all available server RAM. The graphic shows most RAM occupied by one large pool called file cache buffers. Earlier we mentioned that NetWare makes all available

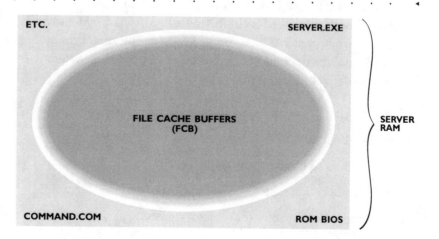

FIGURE 13.3

Server RAM in NetWare 3.12

ETC.

SERVER.EXE

FILE CACHE BUFFERS
(FCB)

SERVER
RAM

COMMAND.COM

ROM BIOS

RAM available for file caching. Memory not available for file caching is reserved for operating system requirements such as the SERVER.EXE operating system file, COMMAND.COM which is running in the background, the ROM BIOS and so on.

QUOTE

Memory is the cabinet of imagination, the treasury of reason, the registry of conscience, and the council chamber of thought.

Saint Basil

The file cache buffer pool serves all of the server's file caching needs. In addition, this pool services the other five memory pools which provide allocated areas of RAM for specific file server resources and functions. Some of the most common functions for memory pooling include NLM loading, DET and FAT tables, turbo FAT, drive mappings, packet receive buffers, disk and LAN drivers and so on. In this section, we will discuss the file cache buffer pool and the other five pools which provide logical extensions of server RAM. In addition, we will learn how to optimize server memory by controlling the size and dynamic allocation of these pools.

Let's begin with file cache buffers.

File Cache Buffers

NetWare uses file cache buffers to speed access to shared disk storage. When the server boots, it loads SERVER.EXE, COMMAND.COM and a few other files which eat into server RAM. All other available file server memory is automatically added to one pool: file cache buffers. The operating system uses cache buffers for a variety of different functions including:

- ▶ Caching frequently used files

- ▶ Loading NLMs

- ▶ Caching of the directory entry table

- ▶ File allocation table

- ▶ Building hash tables for directory hashing

▸ Turbo FAT indexing

▸ Servicing other memory pools

As the five other memory pools draw from file cache buffers, the user's ability to cache frequently-used files decreases. Keep in mind that all other memory pools draw originally from file cache buffers. Two of these pools reside directly in the file cache buffer area—they are the cache non-movable and cache movable subpools.

> When the server boots, it loads SERVER.EXE, COMMAND.COM, and a few other files which eat into server RAM. All other available file server memory is automatically added to one pool: file cache buffers.

Cache Non-Movable

The cache non-movable memory pool resides directly in the cache buffer area. In Figure 13.4, this pool is shown as a door. The cache non-movable memory pool can be thought of as a door to file cache buffers—it provides a port for NLMs to load into server RAM. Cache non-movable is so named non-movable because, as a port, it cannot move its location in RAM.

FIGURE 13.4

The Cache Non-Movable Memory Pool

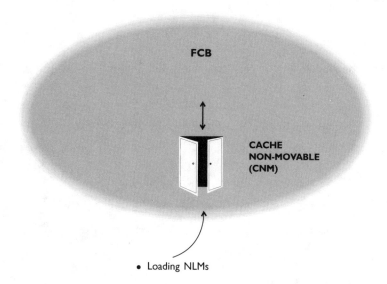

FCB

CACHE
NON-MOVABLE
(CNM)

• Loading NLMs

KNOWLEDGE

This analogy holds true, because most doors would be fairly useless if they were able to move their locations randomly. It would be funny, though.

The cache non-movable door borrows memory temporarily from file cache buffers and returns it when not needed. This is indicated by the double arrow which resides above the door. Once NLMs enter the cache non-movable door, they continue on through server memory and grab RAM from other pools.

Cache Movable

The second subpool which resides directly in the file cache buffer area is cache movable. Cache movable pool is so named because it contains components which are flexible enough to move their address throughout RAM. This is done to optimize memory usage and avoid fragmentation of the file cache buffer pool. This pool is used by system tables that grow dynamically, such as directory entry tables and file allocation tables. Directory hashing is also performed within the cache movable pool. Figure 13.5 shows the cache movable pool with wings to illustrate that it can move throughout the file cache buffer area. The double arrows above cache movable show that this pool works the same as cache non-movable—it returns memory to file cache buffers when it is finished.

F I G U R E 13.5

*The Cache-Movable
Memory Pool*

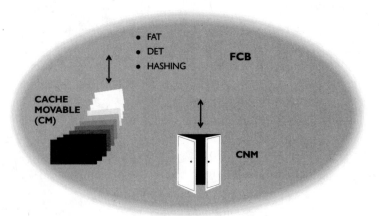

Permanent

Another subpool which draws from file cache buffer is the permanent memory pool. The permanent memory pool is not as cooperative in its returning of memory as cache movable and cache non-movable. As a matter of fact, as you can tell from Figure 13.6, there is a one-way arrow which indicates that the permanent memory pool draws memory from file cache buffers and does not return it. This attitude on behalf of permanent memory can cause the pool to grow quite large, diminishing the amount of memory available for file caching.

The permanent memory pool is used by NetWare for long-term memory needs and permanent resources. These resources include permanent tables and packet receive buffers. If you return to our analogy of the packet receive buffers being the lobby of a bank, it is quite difficult for that lobby to grow dynamically once it has been established in concrete. The process of changing the size of the packet receive buffer, for example, involves the downing and re-initializing of the server. This is serious.

Because of their permanent nature, permanent memory pools do not provide memory to loadable modules. NetWare loadable modules can be loaded and unloaded and therefore change dynamically. Permanent memory, once it is allocated, cannot be changed.

F I G U R E 13.6

The Permanent
Memory Pool

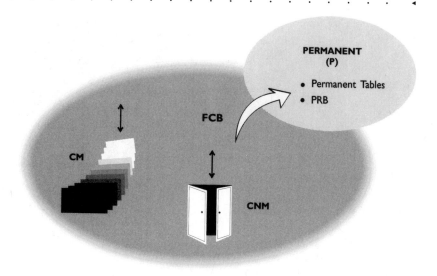

Semi-Permanent

There are, however, a few types of loadable modules which are semi-permanent in their function. That is to say they are loaded and rarely unloaded. These loadable modules are serviced from a subpool of permanent memory called the semi-permanent memory pool. Semi-permanent memory is a subpool of permanent memory. This pool draws from permanent memory as needed and returns unused RAM. It is used for small amounts of memory that the loadable module uses for a long period of time.

Two common types of NetWare loadable modules which are semi-permanent in nature are LAN drivers and disk drivers. LAN drivers are NLMs which are loaded at the server to initialize communications between NetWare and the NIC. Disk drivers are similar loadable modules which control communications between the shared disk and the NetWare operating system. See Figure 13.7 for an illustration of the semi-permanent memory pool as an amoeba with a double-lined arrow. The graphic illustrates that the semi-permanent memory pool can in fact change in size and does migrate throughout the permanent pool.

The Semi-Permanent
Memory Pool

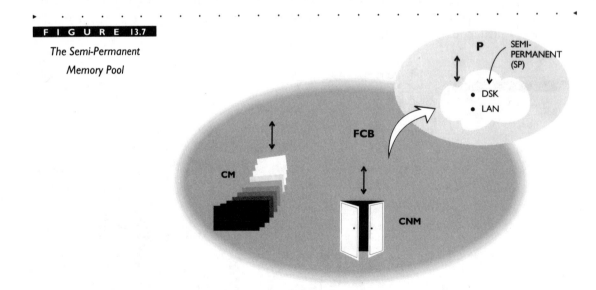

Alloc Short Term

Earlier we mentioned that NetWare loadable modules enter through the cache non-movable memory door and spread their wings throughout server RAM. File cache buffers themselves do not service NetWare loadable modules. Neither do permanent memory pools. So where do loadable modules go? There is one last memory pool which feeds off of permanent memory called alloc short term memory.

Alloc short term memory is used for short term memory requests and loadable module menus. Figure 13.8 demonstrates that the alloc short term memory pool indeed feeds off of permanent memory in the same way that permanent memory feeds off file cache buffers. That is to say, a one-way arrow which means memory is not returned once it is unused. This can become quite a problem because alloc short term memory can

> NetWare loadable modules enter through the cache non-movable memory door and spread their wings throughout server RAM.

FIGURE 13.8

The Alloc Short-Term Memory Pool

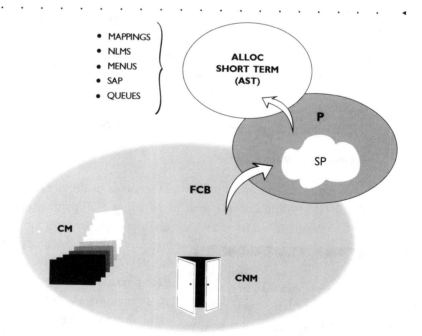

- MAPPINGS
- NLMS
- MENUS
- SAP
- QUEUES

ALLOC SHORT TERM (AST)

P

SP

FCB

CM

CNM

grow quite large in size as multiple NLMs are loaded. Once the NLMs are un-loaded, the alloc short term memory pool retains its size even though it is not using 100% of the memory.

Besides NetWare loadable modules, other short-term resources and functions include drive mappings, menu programs, service advertising packets and queue manager tables. One of the best examples of the use of alloc short term memory is pop-up windows in NetWare loadable modules. MONITOR, for example, has pop-up windows which provide a facility for navigating from one menu to another. As users move through the MONITOR utility, the previous menu information is stored in alloc short term memory until the user returns, then it is released. As the system manager moves through the MONITOR utility—popping up more and more windows—alloc short term memory grows larger and larger. Once the NLM is unloaded, all of this memory becomes unused—but it is NOT returned to permanent memory.

In Figure 13.9, you can see an illustration of how on the top, when the NLM is loaded, alloc short term memory and permanent memory grow larger and larger. It takes memory away from file cache buffers and when the NLM is un-loaded, the pool itself stays large while its usage shrinks—the lower picture. This is an efficiency problem because it decreases the amount of memory available for file cache buffers. If you remember from our earlier discussions, file caching is one of the most important performance optimization tools available in NetWare.

QUOTE

The willingness to take risks is our grasp of faith.

George E. Woodberry

The system manager can monitor inefficiencies in memory pools—using the MONITOR NLM—and control their sizes using SET parameters. Later in the chapter, we will discuss how we can monitor these memory pools using MONITOR and control their sizes using SET parameters. The only way to return these memory pools to their default state is to down the server, turn off the file

> The system manager can monitor inefficiencies in memory pools—using the MONITOR NLM—and control their sizes using SET parameters.

• ◄

FIGURE 13.9

*The Memory Effects
of Loading and
Unloading NLMs*

NLMS
use max
RAM

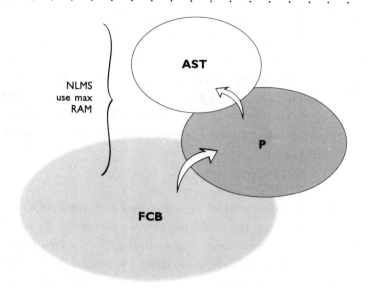

WITH NLMS LOADED

Used RAM
shrinks, but
Pools stay
large

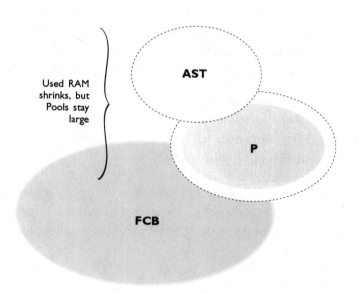

AS NLMS ARE UNLOADED

server machine and reboot the NetWare operating system. This will return all memory pools to their default.

TIP

While downing the server might seem like a good idea for memory efficiency, it is a bad idea for a lot of other reasons—including error tracking, communications reliability, and so on. You should only down the server when all other courses of action have been exhausted.

KNOWLEDGE

Try to think of NetWare memory inefficiencies as milking a cow. In the analogy, the cow would be file cache buffers and the pail is alloc short term memory. The farmer milks the cow into the pail until the pail is full. Let's say we're using a medium-sized pail and one morning Betsy decides to give it her all. Suddenly, the pail is not large enough for all the milk. So the farmer goes out and buys a larger pail. Well, the next day, the cow Betsy has a bad day and only half the pail is full. Well, the farmer cannot take the pail back and is therefore forced to use the larger pail for the rest of his life, whether or not Betsy ever fills it again. In NetWare, the alloc short term memory pail will grow large and never shrink in size.

Now you can see how memory pools play a very important role in NetWare performance management. These pools can provide a dynamic link for file caching and other performance features, but at the same time create large inefficiencies through alloc short term memory pools.

In the next section, we will learn how to use the MONITOR NLM to track these memory pools and use SET parameters to optimize their use. But before we move on to the MONITOR NLM, we need to take a moment to explore the different memory requirements of NetWare and learn how to calculate minimum memory needs.

MEMORY REQUIREMENTS

Many of the different resources and functions of the operating system are granted memory as needed from various different pools. While NetWare is dynamic and effective in its allocation of memory, it is important to consider the minimum memory requirements when using this operating system. Some of the following resources to consider when calculating minimum memory include:

- ▸ Minimum memory to run NetWare, which is 4MB

- ▸ Memory required by NLMs

- ▸ Memory required by drivers

- ▸ Memory required by communication products

- ▸ Memory required by hard disk and volume for directory caching

- ▸ Block size, which affects the buffer size

- ▸ Directory entry tables, file allocation tables and finally memory needed for file caching.

While certainly file caching is the most important memory requirement, all of the previous operating system functions must be considered as well. The following is a simple formula which can be used to balance all of these resources in determining how much memory is required.

- ▸ For a DOS volume, the memory requirement calculation is memory = .023 x the volume size in megabytes, divided by the block size. The requirement for each volume is calculated and then added together. The minimum to run NetWare, which is 4MB, is added to the number so the total memory calculation then becomes memory for all volumes plus 4MB rounded to the highest number.
    Suppose, for example, you have a file server disk with two volumes. Volume I is 80MB and Volume II is 100MB. The memory requirement for Volume I is .023 x 80 divided by 4 (the default block size). This gives us a value of .46MB. The memory requirement for Volume II is

.023 x 100 divided by 4 which is .575. Adding these two together gives us a value of 1.045. Add 1.045 to the 4MB NetWare 3.12 minimum and round to next whole number—6MB.

▶ Another calculation is required for volumes which have name space added. Name space is the facility built into NetWare which allows for files using name conventions other than DOS. These file name conventions can include OS/2, Unix, and Macintosh. Volumes which require name space use the formula .032 x volume size in megabytes divided by block size. Incidentally, notice that the .032 and .023 are simple reversals of each other.

Volumes with name space are treated exactly the same as DOS volumes. The following is a sample calculation. We have a file server with three volumes: one DOS volume, one UNIX volume, and one Macintosh volume. The DOS volume is 80MB, the UNIX volume is 300MB and the Macintosh volume is 100MB. The memory requirement for this server would consist of the following calculations: the DOS volume would be .023 x 80 divided by 4, which gives us .46MB. The Unix volume calculation would be .032 x 300 divided by 4, which gives us 2.4MB. The Macintosh volume calculation would consist of .032 x 100 divided by 4 or .8MB. Therefore, the final memory requirement for this server would consist of .46 plus 2.4 plus .8 and then plus 4 rounded to the higher value, or a memory requirement of 8MB.

TIP

Memory requirements are the absolute minimum for supporting the disk space as well as the name space and block sizes. The optimal environment would consist of double this number making more file server RAM available for file caching. Remember the old rule: the more you can cache, the better off you are.

That's it for server memory management. We discussed the different memory pools and how they allocate server RAM to NetWare resources and operating system functions. Then we discussed the memory requirements and how to calculate minimum memory for given situations.

Now the rest of this chapter will be dedicated to monitoring these different components and memory pools, and to using SET parameters to optimize the balance. Keep in mind that as the NetWare interior decorator, it is your responsibility to balance resources and components to create the most beautiful and most effective and productive environment for your users. The moral of the story is that you better watch out where you hang that painting.

Monitoring Server Performance with MONITOR

So far we have learned about the resources which are available to the hotel interior decorator. He/she must be concerned with a variety of different components when optimizing the design and layout of Park Place. The interior decorator is responsible for:

- Hanging paintings

- Arranging flowers

- Dressing windows

- Buying furniture

- Choosing fabric

- Designing color schemes

- Overseeing the general maintenance of hotel amenities.

The NetWare interior decorator is also responsible for the optimization of LAN resources. The focus of your interior decorating efforts and LAN optimization is at the file server. The file server houses all shared resources including disk, printing, memory, and communications. As the NetWare interior decorator, you are responsible for:

- Hanging hard disks

- Arranging memory pools

▸ Designing internal NICs

▸ Buying more memory

▸ Picking NLMs

▸ Designing server configurations

▸ Overseeing the general maintenance of LAN amenities

The NetWare interior decorator has two tools available for his/her use: MONITOR and SET. The MONITOR server NLM is used for monitoring the server components while the SET parameters allow for proactive configuration of optimal settings. In this section we will learn about monitoring server performance with the MONITOR.NLM utility and move on to optimizing server performance with SET in the next section. Let's begin with the main screen of MONITOR.

> The MONITOR server NLM is used for monitoring the server components while the SET parameters allow for proactive configuration of optimal settings.

MAIN SCREEN

MONITOR.NLM is the major tool used by NetWare to view information on memory and resource utilization. The main screen in MONITOR (Figure 13.10) provides a snapshot of current resource settings. This screen is dynamic so that it changes as NetWare services user requests.

The available options menu in MONITOR provides nine choices, which can be broken up into four different categories. They are:

Resource utilization which provides information on tracking resources and server memory statistics

Processor utilization which is a histogram of internal file server processes

Information screens which provide information only windows for connection, disks, LAN and system module information

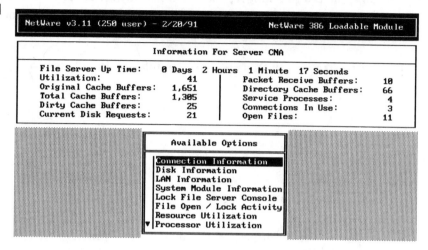

```
┌──────────────────────────────────────────────────────────────────────┐
│ NetWare v3.11 (250 user) - 2/20/91          NetWare 386 Loadable Module│
├──────────────────────────────────────────────────────────────────────┤
│                    Information For Server CNA                          │
│                                                                        │
│  File Server Up Time:    0 Days  2 Hours  1 Minute  17 Seconds         │
│  Utilization:               41  │ Packet Receive Buffers:      10      │
│  Original Cache Buffers:  1,651 │ Directory Cache Buffers:     66      │
│  Total Cache Buffers:     1,305 │ Service Processes:            4      │
│  Dirty Cache Buffers:        25 │ Connections In Use:           3      │
│  Current Disk Requests:      21 │ Open Files:                  11      │
└──────────────────────────────────────────────────────────────────────┘

                         ┌─────────────────────────┐
                         │     Available Options    │
                         ├─────────────────────────┤
                         │ Connection Information   │
                         │ Disk Information         │
                         │ LAN Information          │
                         │ System Module Information│
                         │ Lock File Server Console │
                         │ File Open / Lock Activity│
                         │ Resource Utilization     │
                       ▼ │ Processor Utilization    │
                         └─────────────────────────┘
```

Other available options which include facilities for locking the file server console, viewing file lock activity, and exiting the system.

MONITOR.NLM is loaded from the file server console prompt by typing LOAD MONITOR. The three different switches which can be used following the MONITOR command are:

ns—loads MONITOR without issuing the screen save worm

nh—does not load MONITOR help, which saves approximately 10 to 15K of file server RAM

p—loads MONITOR with the processor utilization menu choice available.

TIP

Once MONITOR loads, it has a built-in screen saver which has a dual function. Affectionately known as the *worm,* **the screen saver consists of a box which travels around the screen in a random pattern with a tail following it around. While it's amusing to look at, the tail actually has a performance utilization function; i.e, the length of the tail indicates utilization. So, for example, as utilization rises above 25% or**

30%, the tail gets longer, and the worm moves around the screen faster. This is a very quick way of monitoring file server performance without having to dive into any detailed menus.

The main screen in MONITOR provides information on the following four categories:

- ▸ Utilization

- ▸ Buffers

- ▸ Service processes

- ▸ Other information

In addition to this information, the main screen provides the server name and an indication of file server up time detailing the days, hours, minutes and seconds this particular file server has been active. Let's take a quick look at the four different types of information provided by the MONITOR main screen.

Once MONITOR loads, it has a built-in screen saver which has a dual function. Affectionately known as the *worm*, the screen saver consists of a box which travels around the screen in a random pattern with a processor utilization tail.

Utilization

Utilization is a measurement of how busy or active the file server processor is. The utilization percentage from 0 to 100 indicates the percentage of time the processor is busy. As user requests are stored in the packet receive buffer and file service processes continue to process these requests, utilization will climb. Typically utilization will jump from 4% or 5% to 20% or 30% rather quickly and then back down to 5%. The processor is rarely utilized above 25% for an extended period of time.

Buffers

As you recall, buffers are storage areas in file server RAM. In our discussion of performance management components, we learned about three different types of buffers: file cache, directory cache, and packet receive. The main screen in

MONITOR provides valuable information about the status of these buffers in addition to original cache buffers and dirty cache buffers.

QUOTE

People are very open-minded about new things--as long as they're exactly like the old ones.

Charles F. Kettering

Original Cache Buffers   Original cache buffers indicate the number of cache buffers available when the file server is first booted. This is the number of blocks installed as memory in your server minus the operating system components such as SERVER.EXE, COMMAND.COM and so on. The default buffer size again is 4K so the actual memory is calculated as 4 times the number of original cache buffers. In Figure 13.10, you'll see 1651 times 4 or 6,604,000 bytes. This file server has 8MB of memory so roughly 1.5MB is required by the operating system components.

Total Cache Buffers   Total cache buffers is an indication of the number of buffers currently available for file caching. The difference between original cache buffers and total cache buffers is the memory allocated to permanent, semi-permanent and alloc short term memory pools.

Total cache buffers decreases as other server modules are added and memory pools draw from the central cache pool. Total cache buffers are extremely important for memory and performance because they provide the number one file access feature in NetWare: file caching. You should, as the system manager, constantly monitor the availability of total cache buffers and track other pools as they are drawing from this central pool. An alarm clock should go off in your head as soon as the total cache buffers

> Total cache buffers decreases as other server modules are added and memory pools draw from the central cache pool.

reach half the original number. At this point, only 50% of your original cache memory is available for file caching. If this occurs, then you should move to the server memory statistic screen where you can get a more accurate description of the percentage of total cache buffers available. If the percentage in the server memory statistics window drops to 20%, you have a real crisis situation.

During a memory caching emergency, the system manager has two courses of action:

▸ You can either add more memory immediately or

▸ Down the file server and reboot the file server machine to regain inefficiencies from permanent and alloc memory pools.

The bottom line is if total cache buffers reaches 20%, action must be taken immediately.

Dirty Cache Buffers   Dirty cache buffers are an interesting anomaly. They are areas of cache memory which contain files that have not yet been written to disk. If you remember from our discussion of file caching, file caching stores frequently used files in memory so users can perform read and write operations much more quickly. If a user saves a file which is frequently used, it will be stored in cache before it is written to disk. If the hard disk is busy or the processor is busy, this information will be stored in cache temporarily waiting to be written to disk. The problem with dirty cache buffers is that if a lot of changes are made and this information is kept in memory before it is written to disk and the power goes out, the users will lose all of their edits or changes.

The ideal situation is for dirty cache buffers to be at or near zero. If the number of dirty cache buffers rises and reaches 70% of the total number of cache buffers, this is a very serious situation. What this means is that 70% of your total cache memory has not yet been written to disk and is vulnerable in the case of a power outage. The percentage of dirty cache buffers can be calculated by dividing the number of total cache buffers into the number of dirty cache buffers.

A possible cause for an increase in dirty cache buffers is a slow hard disk or busy processor. The action the system manager should take in increasing the speed of writes from dirty cache buffers is the maximum concurrent disk cache write set parameter. Increasing the value of this particular SET parameter will improve the performance of writing from cache memory to the hard disk. Incidentally, increasing the concurrent disk cache write parameter will hurt the performance of disk cache reading. Refer to the optimization section under the SET parameter for a discussion of the maximum concurrent disk cache write parameter.

Packet Receive Buffers Packet receive buffers are the lobby of our NetWare bank. They are a holding cell for user requests which are waiting to be serviced by file service processes. The packet receive buffers item in the main screen of MONITOR provides an indication of how many buffers are currently reserved for incoming user requests. The minimum default value is 10 and this number will not change in most docile networks. As user requests increase and the need for a larger lobby occurs, NetWare will automatically assign packet receive buffers from the permanent memory pool. Keep in mind that the packet receive buffers memory draws from cache RAM.

Packet receive buffers and file service processes are closely linked. They rely on each other for optimal performance of the NetWare server. As packet receive buffers increase, the need for file service processes decreases because more requests can wait in RAM. On the other hand, as file service processes become more busy, a need for large packet receive buffers can be decreased by adding file service processes. Both of these parameters are setable using SET parameters and can be dynamically increased and decreased as needed by NetWare.

If the number of packet receive buffers approaches 100, this is an indication that there are not enough file service processes to service all of the user requests. It could also be the case that user requests are coming in faster than the packet receive buffers can keep up. By default, the largest number of packet receive buffers available is 100. If the number reaches 100 and cannot go any further, this puts dramatic pressure on the file service processes. If both the packet receive buffers and file service processes are maxed out, the system will begin to drop packets and eventually crash. The system manager can increase the maximum number of packet receive buffers allowed using the SET parameter discussed in the next section.

Directory Cache Buffers Directory cache buffers cache commonly-used portions of the directory entry table. The default minimum number of directory cache buffers is 20 which is typically enough to store 640 directory entries. This is only a start. Most busy servers with large numbers of files and directories will quickly reach 100 directory cache buffers. One hundred directory cache buffers can cache 3,200 directory entries. But remember that the entire directory entry table is not cached.

The maximum number of directory cache buffers available is 500 but Novell suggests that if the number of directory cache buffers exceeds 100, the minimum number should be increased to 200 or 300. Increasing the minimum number of directory cache buffers will increase directory searches because the system does not have to dynamically allocate directory cache buffers as users need them. Reserving a large number of cache buffers will make that memory immediately available and increase the speed of directory searches. The SET parameters relating to directory cache buffers will be discussed in the next section.

That completes our discussion of buffer tracking. Now let's take a look at some of the other related parameters from the main screen of MONITOR.

Service Processes

Service processes are the tellers of our NetWare bank. They are task handlers which are internal subroutines that service user requests. NetWare dynamically allocates service processes as needed for incoming packets. As we mentioned earlier, service processes are dynamically linked to the packet receive buffers which are the lobby of our NetWare bank.

In Figure 13.10 you'll see service processes at four and the packet receive buffers at a minimum of ten. Although this system has 41% utilization, there are only three connections in use and it is not very busy at all. A very busy network with 50 or so users and 70 to 80 percent utilization will max out packet receive buffers at 100 and max out service processes at 20. The service processes maximum can be increased up to 40 using the SET parameter. Incidentally, it is suggested that you increase the maximum service processes parameter by increments of five.

> Service processes are the tellers of our NetWare bank. They are task handlers which are internal subroutines that service user requests.

Also, increasing the number of service processes does take up a dramatic amount of server RAM. If file cache buffers are low or memory caching is a concern, service processes should be increased cautiously. Refer to the optimization section for a more thorough discussion of the relationship between packet receive buffers and service processes.

Other Information

The final information options available from the main screen of MONITOR include general type system information. The current disk request option shows the number of disk requests that are waiting in a line to be serviced by the NetWare server. These are dirty cache buffers which have been sent to the disk. The connections in use option is an indication of how many stations are currently attached to the file server. The available options menu provides further choices for viewing details about these two connections. Finally, open files is the number of files currently being accessed by the server which are open on network workstations. The available options menu also provides a choice for viewing detailed information about currently opened files.

The main screen in MONITOR provides a snapshot of valuable statistics concerning performance management components. It is a very good place to start for the system manager to track and identify components which need further attention. The available options menu in MONITOR provides a great deal more detail in analyzing the sources and destination of server memory and resource utilization. Let's take a closer look at some of the more useful available topics options. We'll start with resource utilization.

RESOURCE UTILIZATION

Resource utilization is the most important performance monitoring menu. It provides a detailed log of server memory pool utilization. In addition, resource utilization provides a method for tracking resources and discovering how server resources are utilizing internal memory pools. The system manager should routinely use the resource utilization option for viewing detailed information about memory pools and tracking suspect NLMs and internal resources.

> The system manager should routinely use the resource utilization option for viewing detailed information about memory pools and tracking suspect NLMs and internal resources.

Discoveries made here can go a long way toward optimizing file service performance using SET parameters.

The resource utilization menu provides two different types of information: server memory statistics and tracked resources. Server memory statistics is a summary screen which provides detailed information and percentages for the five main NetWare 3.12 memory pools. Tracked resources information is a detailed navigation of screens which allows the system manager to zero in on NLMs and internal routines which are utilizing various pools of server RAM.

QUOTE

Vision: the art of seeing things invisible.

Jonathan Swift

Let's take a closer look at server memory statistics and tracked resources.

Server Memory Statistics

The server memory statistics screen in resource utilization can be viewed in Figure 13.11. This menu lists the five main memory pools on the left and their current size in bytes on the right. In addition, server memory statistics provides the percentage of total server work memory each pool is occupying. In the cases

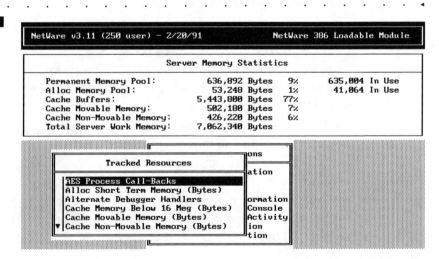

F I G U R E 13.11

Server Memory Statistics and Tracked Resources in MONITOR.NLM

NetWare v3.11 (250 user) – 2/20/91			NetWare 386 Loadable Module

Server Memory Statistics			
Permanent Memory Pool:	636,892 Bytes	9%	635,004 In Use
Alloc Memory Pool:	53,248 Bytes	1%	41,064 In Use
Cache Buffers:	5,443,800 Bytes	77%	
Cache Movable Memory:	502,180 Bytes	7%	
Cache Non-Movable Memory:	426,220 Bytes	6%	
Total Server Work Memory:	7,062,340 Bytes		

```
                    Tracked Resources              ons
                                                   ation
   AES Process Call-Backs
   Alloc Short Term Memory (Bytes)
   Alternate Debugger Handlers                     ormation
   Cache Memory Below 16 Meg (Bytes)               Console
   Cache Movable Memory (Bytes)                    Activity
 ▼ Cache Non-Movable Memory (Bytes)                ion
                                                   tion
```

of permanent and alloc memory pools, it provides an indication of how much of their maximum size is currently being used.

Total server work memory is an indication of how much memory is currently available to file cache buffers and the other pools. Total server work memory is the total amount of memory installed minus SERVER.EXE, DOS and ROM BIOS. This number should closely match the number calculated for original cache buffers. The small discrepancy between the two can be attributed to auxiliary operating system memory requirements. In this case, the number 7,062,340 bytes is 400,000 or so more than the original cache buffers. That means that 400K has been reserved by auxiliary operating system routines. They are available as server work memory but not available for caching.

Notice in Figure 13.11 that permanent memory pool and alloc memory pool show a value of memory in use. If you remember from our earlier discussion of memory pools, these two memory pools draw memory from file cache buffers but do not return this value. If you refer to Figure 13.9, you'll see the dotted line as indicating the actual growth size of these pools but the shaded area is considerably less. The shaded area would be represented by the in-use value of the server memory statistics screen.

Cache buffers should always be the largest percentage of total server work memory. In this case, 77% is a good healthy number for file caching. Cache movable and cache non-movable should roughly match permanent memory pool and in this case they do. Alloc memory is typically a lot smaller. Remember from our earlier discussions, cache non-movable is the door through which NLMs enter the file cache buffers and then move on to alloc short term memory. Keep in mind that most of the memory requirements made by NLMs are provided from cache non-movable memory.

Tracked Resources

Detailed information about which resources are using the memory pool can be viewed through the tracked resources menu. MONITOR's tracked resources facility provides a list of operating system components which make demands for server RAM. Figure 13.11 shows the alphabetic listing of tracked resources starting with AES process call-backs and continuing on.

The system manager can use this menu to track resources and gain valuable information about how they are using server RAM. By highlighting a resource, alloc short term memory for example, and pressing Enter, the system will return a list of resource tags. Resources tags are NLMs which are associated with this particular resource. The NLMs or server applications are using this resource to access server memory. For example, highlighting the alloc short term memory resource and pressing Enter provides a list of resource tags. These tags include INSTALL.NLM, MONITOR.NLM, REMOTE.NLM, SERVER.NLM, and so on.

By highlighting the MONITOR.NLM resource tag, we gain valuable information about how much alloc short term memory MONITOR is using. Figure 13.12 shows the resulting screen from highlighting the MONITOR.NLM resource tag. This graphic tells us that of the 46,080 bytes of memory currently being used in alloc short term, 15,960 are being used by MONITOR.NLM.

This strategy is particularly useful if certain NLMs or resources are monopolizing file server RAM. The server memory statistics screen which shows an abnormally high amount of permanent or alloc memory, and the system manager could use resource tracking to identify the greedy NLM culprit.

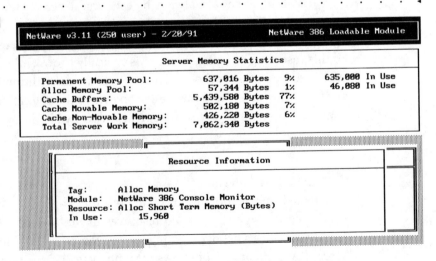

F I G U R E 13.12

Monitoring NetWare 3.12 Resources

```
NetWare v3.11 (250 user) - 2/20/91              NetWare 386 Loadable Module

                        Server Memory Statistics

     Permanent Memory Pool:      637,016 Bytes    9%    635,000 In Use
     Alloc Memory Pool:           57,344 Bytes    1%     46,080 In Use
     Cache Buffers:            5,439,580 Bytes   77%
     Cache Movable Memory:       502,180 Bytes    7%
     Cache Non-Movable Memory:   426,220 Bytes    6%
     Total Server Work Memory: 7,062,340 Bytes

                         Resource Information

     Tag:      Alloc Memory
     Module:   NetWare 386 Console Monitor
     Resource: Alloc Short Term Memory (Bytes)
     In Use:       15,960
```

INFORMATION SCREENS

Beyond resource utilization, there are other information screens provided through MONITOR available options which the system manager can use to gain valuable information about shared server resources. These information screens include connection information, disk information, LAN information, and system module information.

> In addition to resource utilization, MONITOR provides four other server monitoring screens: connection information, disk information, LAN information, and system module information.

Connection Information

The connection information screen in MONITOR provides valuable information about active connections. The system manager can view connection-oriented details including:

- Connection time
- Network node address
- Number of requests made by this connection
- Kilobytes written
- Kilobytes read
- Logical record locks
- Status

The status field provides one of three options: normal (logged in and functioning), waiting (an indication that the connection is waiting for a file to be unlocked) or not logged in (the connection is attached to the file server but not currently logged in). In addition to connection-oriented details, the connection information screen provides a list of all open files which are currently in use by this connection. This is particularly useful for system managers who are tracking shared files, databases, record locking and user performance. The initial connection information screen lists all active connections with their connection number and user login name. This is also useful because it provides a facility not only for connection oriented but login name oriented details.

Disk Information

The disk information option in MONITOR (Figure 13.13) provides details about the internal shared hard disk. It provides a summary list of valuable disk statistics. Some of the more interesting statistics are in:

► The driver name

► Disk size

► Mirror status

► Data blocks

► Redirection blocks

The redirection blocks show how many blocks have been reserved for hot fix internal dynamic bad block remapping or hot fix. The redirected blocks show how many blocks have been used. It is a good idea for the system manager to track the number of redirected blocks to see if the redirection area is being utilized. If the hot fix redirection area is being filled up quickly, this is an indication that the server disk is about to fail and any number exceeding 50% is a point for concern. In disk emergencies where the redirected blocks exceed 50% of the

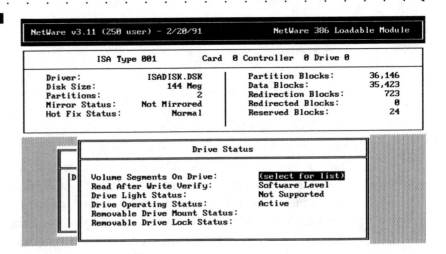

FIGURE 13.13

Disk Information in MONITOR.NLM

reserved redirection blocks, the system manager should either replace the hard disk or reformat it and reinstall NetWare.

The disk information option also provides a supplementary window called drive status which provides information about read after write verification, the drive operating status and volume segments that have been assigned to this drive.

LAN Information

The LAN information option in MONITOR provides details about internal server network interface cards. The initial LAN driver information screen provides a list of all internal NICs and their configuration including port, interrupt and frame type. The system manager can highlight the appropriate network interface card or press enter to view a much more detailed list of custom NIC statistics. These statistics include node address, protocols that are bound to this network interface card, the network address, and generic communication statistics. Figure 13.14 illustrates the generic statistics for the GES386AT network interface card. These statistics include total packets sent and

> The LAN information option in MONITOR is a valuable tool for isolating and troubleshooting network communication problems.

FIGURE 13.14

LAN Information in MONITOR.NLM

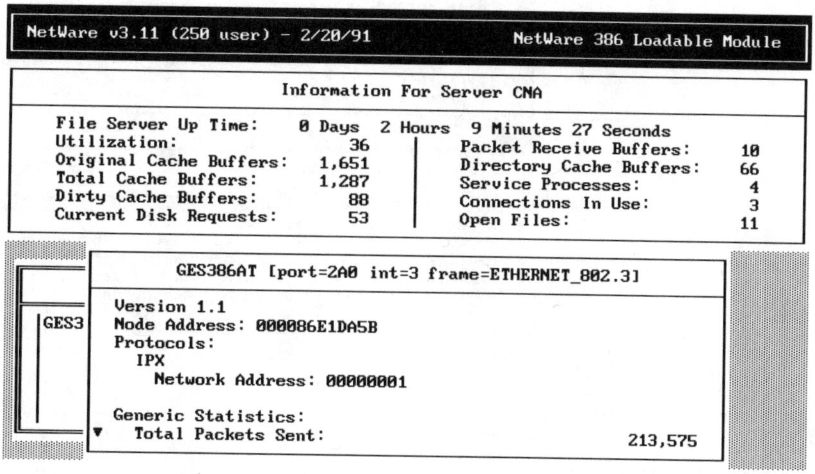

```
NetWare v3.11 (250 user) - 2/20/91          NetWare 386 Loadable Module

                     Information For Server CNA

   File Server Up Time:    0 Days  2 Hours  9 Minutes 27 Seconds
   Utilization:              36       Packet Receive Buffers:    10
   Original Cache Buffers: 1,651      Directory Cache Buffers:   66
   Total Cache Buffers:    1,287      Service Processes:          4
   Dirty Cache Buffers:       88      Connections In Use:         3
   Current Disk Requests:     53      Open Files:                11

              GES386AT [port=2A0 int=3 frame=ETHERNET_802.3]

   GES3    Version 1.1
           Node Address: 000086E1DA5B
           Protocols:
              IPX
                 Network Address: 00000001
           Generic Statistics:
             Total Packets Sent:                           213,575
```

total packets received. In addition, the system manager can view information about collisions and possible lost packets.

The LAN information option in MONITOR is a valuable tool for isolating and troubleshooting network communication problems.

System Module Information

The system module information option in MONITOR provides a detailed listing of internal operating system modules and their corresponding resource tags. This menu provides the same type of information as resource utilization except that it is module specific instead of resource specific.

Highlighting the appropriate system module and pressing Enter provides a window of resource tags. The system manager can then get a feel for what type of resource a particular module is using and how much of what type of memory is currently being used. Figure 13.15 shows an illustration of the type of details for the SERVER.NLM module. SERVER.NLM is the operating system itself as it resides in module form. Keep in mind there is no such thing as SERVER.NLM—this is SERVER.EXE but as a module it appears to the system as an NLM.

FIGURE 13.15

System Module Information
in MONITOR.NLM

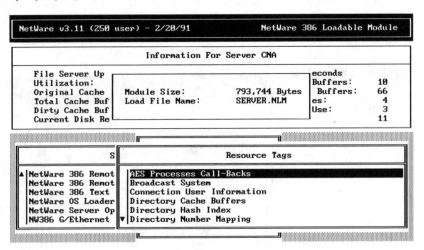

QUOTE

Get your facts first, then you can distort them as you please.

Mark Twain

Highlighting the NetWare operating system provides a supplemental menu of the resource tags which SERVER.NLM is using. As you can see from Figure 13.15, SERVER.NLM is using almost 800K of memory. The system manager can view more detailed information about how SERVER.NLM is using resources such as directory cache buffers, connection user information, directory entry tables, disk cache buffers, extended attributes, file locks, IPX protocol stacks, sockets, semi-permanent memory, NCP tables, print queues, routing information, transactional tracking and user disk space restrictions.

It is evident that the system module information facility is quite detailed in scope and provides a great deal of information for tracking problematic NetWare modules.

PROCESSOR UTILIZATION

The final MONITOR tool available to NetWare interior decorators is processor utilization. The processor utilization menu choice becomes available if the system manager loads MONITOR with the /p switch. Processor utilization provides a histogram of internal NetWare processes and the type of load they are putting on the server CPU. The transitional utilization screen provides a list of available processes and interrupts. These processes and interrupts are competing for CPU resources. The system manager can use F5 to highlight all the processes

> The processor utilization menu choice becomes available if the system manager loads MONITOR with the /p switch. Processor utilization provides a histogram of internal NetWare processes and the type of load they are putting on the server CPU.

he/she is willing to track, and press Enter. The system will respond with a histogram similar to the one in Figure 13.16. This illustration shows all of the processes available minus the interrupt choices.

The processor utilization histogram provides three different types of information: time, count and load. The time parameter shows the amount of time the

FIGURE 13.16

The Processor Utilization Histogram in MONITOR.NLM

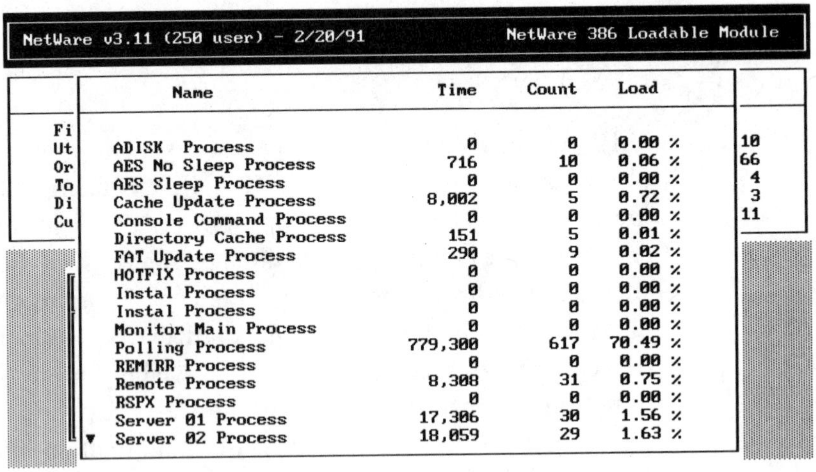

NetWare v3.11 (250 user) - 2/20/91   NetWare 386 Loadable Module

Name	Time	Count	Load
ADISK Process	0	0	0.00 %
AES No Sleep Process	716	10	0.06 %
AES Sleep Process	0	0	0.00 %
Cache Update Process	8,002	5	0.72 %
Console Command Process	0	0	0.00 %
Directory Cache Process	151	5	0.01 %
FAT Update Process	290	9	0.02 %
HOTFIX Process	0	0	0.00 %
Instal Process	0	0	0.00 %
Instal Process	0	0	0.00 %
Monitor Main Process	0	0	0.00 %
Polling Process	779,300	617	70.49 %
REMIRR Process	0	0	0.00 %
Remote Process	8,308	31	0.75 %
RSPX Process	0	0	0.00 %
Server 01 Process	17,306	30	1.56 %
Server 02 Process	18,059	29	1.63 %

CPU has spent working on this particular process. The count is the number of times the process ran during the sample period. The load is the most important statistic of all. It indicates the percentage of processor use per second. Notice from Figure 13.16 that the majority of the processor's time is spent in the polling process. This is the processor waiting idly by for processes to come by and bother it. The most aggressive process in this particular graphic is the remote process and the cache update process.

The processor utilization histogram can be used by system managers to monitor and track how active the file server processor truly is. If server responses tend to be a bit sluggish, the system manager can open this screen and monitor how different processes are accessing the CPU. A detailed help screen is available within processor utilization by pressing F1.

That completes our discussion of performance monitoring using the built-in NetWare MONITOR.NLM utility. As you can see from this discussion, MONITOR.NLM is a highly extensive facility with a great deal of detailed information for the system manager. It is a good idea for the system manager to set up a schedule of daily or weekly visits to MONITOR, focusing on specific areas. Some of the most common areas are server memory statistics in resource utilization, the main menu and disk, and LAN statistics. So far in this chapter we have focused on what to look for and how to look for it. Now that we have learned the different strategies the NetWare interior decorator can use for performance management, it is time to roll up our sleeves and focus on exactly what kind of actions can be taken when problems are found.

Optimizing Server Performance with SET

The SET console command provides the facility for customizing the SERVER.EXE program and optimizing the variety of different parameters. The SET command defines nine different areas of customization and they are:

- ▶ Communications

- ▶ Memory

- ▶ File caching

- ▶ Directory caching

- ▶ Miscellaneous

- ▶ File system

- ▶ Locks

- ▶ Transaction tracking

- ▶ Disk

NetWare 3.12 provides almost 100 different SET parameters for proactive performance optimization. In this section, we will discuss the 20 most effective SET parameters. Let's begin with communications.

The SET parameters are customizing the SERVER.EXE program while the server is running. This is like trying to tune a moving car. It is extremely important that you realize that a lot of damage can be done by setting the wrong parameters. Be very cautious in using the SET parameters. Also, focus on where the SET parameters need to be set. Some parameters which relate to communications, caching, and disk, for example, must be set in the STARTUP.NCF and will not take effect until the server is down and brought back up. All other SET parameters can be set at the console prompt or in the AUTOEXEC.NCF file. There are only six SET parameters which must be set in the STARTUP.NCF and they are:

▶ Auto register memory above 16MB

▶ Auto TTS backout flag

▶ Cache buffer size

▶ Maximum physical receive packet size

▶ Maximum subdirectory tree depth

▶ Minimum packet receive buffers

Keep in mind that any parameters installed in the AUTOEXEC.NCF or STARTUP.NCF files will not take effect until the file server is down and rebooted.

The SET parameters are customizing the SERVER.EXE program while the server is running. This is like trying to tune a moving car. Be very cautious in using the SET parameters.

Current SET parameter values can be viewed by typing **SET** at the console prompt and pressing Enter. The system will respond with a list of the nine different categories, numbered 1 through 9. The system manager will then press a number and the system will ask if you would like to see advanced settings. Advanced settings are SET parameters which configure detailed and advanced operating system parameters. If the system manager chooses Yes, the system will respond with all SET parameters and values for that particular group. In order to configure a specific SET parameter, the system manager must type **SET** and the name of the parameter followed by an equal (=) sign and a value. For example, to change the subdirectory tree depth, the system manager would type **SET MAXIMUM SUBDIRECTORY TREE DEPTH = 25**.

Throughout the chapter we have discussed the need for SET parameters and optimizing file server performance. Earlier we talked about the different components which affect file server performance and in the last section we used the MONITOR.NLM to track resources utilization and performance management components. In the remaining sections of this chapter, we will discuss the 20 most popular set parameters and how they are used to implement maximum file server performance. Let's begin with the communications parameters.

COMMUNICATIONS

The communications SET parameters control communications between the server, network interface card, and incoming and outgoing packets. Communication SET parameters focus on two different areas of server communications: packet receive buffers and watchdog packets. Packet receive buffers are the waiting area in server RAM where user requests are held until file service processes are available. In our earlier analogy, these are the lobby of our NetWare bank. Watchdog packets, on the other hand, are NetWare sentries which patrol the LAN cabling for inactive workstations. The watchdog packet will disconnect or drop a connection for a workstation which does not respond after a specific number of tries. Let's take a closer look at these two different types of communication SET parameters.

> The communications SET parameters control communications between the server, network interface card, and incoming and outgoing packets.

Packet Receive Buffers

As we discussed earlier, packet receive buffers are the holding cell for user requests. Packet receive buffers are closely linked to file service processes in that they provide a waiting area for incoming packets. If NetWare does not allocate enough file service processes, the packet receive buffer can become quite full. In addition, very busy file servers require large packet receive buffers as well. NetWare provides two different SET parameters which configure or customize the packet receive buffers: maximum and minimum settings. Another communication parameter which relates to packet receive buffers is maximum physical packet size. The packet receive buffers are 4K by default and contain four 1K packets per buffer. If the LAN communications protocol can support larger or smaller packets, the system manager must configure this setting to accommodate. In our earlier analogy, the maximum physical packet size would represent the size of the people waiting in line. Obviously, the larger the number of people, the larger the lobby needs to be. Let's take a closer look at the packet receive buffer settings.

Maximum Packet Receive Buffers   The maximum packet receive buffers parameter determines the maximum number of packet receive buffers the operating system can allocate. The default setting is 100. This setting is much too low for busy, busy servers. As we mentioned earlier, the system will dynamically allocate packet receive buffers as needed. If the number reaches 100 and this is not adequate, packets will get lost and the system will eventually crash. A setting between 300 and 500 is ideal for busy servers.

Minimum Packet Receive Buffers   The minimum packet receive buffers parameter determines the minimum number of packet receive buffers the operating system can allocate. The default is 10. The minimum setting is important because the operating system will reserve this many buffers as soon as the server boots. This is a much faster scenario for allocating packet receive buffers then waiting for the dynamic allocation. Dynamic allocation of packet receive buffers decreases system performance. If your LAN is extremely busy and you find communications a little sluggish, it is a good idea to increase the minimum packet receive buffers in intervals of 10. NetWare supports up to 1,000 minimum packet receive buffers.

TIP
The minimum packet receive buffers parameter can only be changed in the STARTUP.NCF file. This is because the minimum number must be set when the file server is booted. Therefore, the minimum packet receive buffers set parameter cannot be issued at the console prompt.

QUOTE
Our life is frittered away by detail. Simplicity, simplicity, simplicity!

Henry David Thoreau

Maximum Physical Packet Size

Maximum physical receive packet size determines the maximum size of packets that can be transmitted on any of the file server's networks. The default is 1K including the packet header. The default setting is ideal for most token ring or Ethernet LANs. If you have high end token ring NICs which are capable of transmitting 4K packets, increasing the maximum physical receive packet size will increase communications performance. Keep in mind that increasing the maximum physical receive packet size will dramatically affect the performance of packet receive buffers. The system manager will have to increase the minimum and maximum number of packet receive buffers if the maximum physical receive packet size is increased.

TIP

This parameter must be set and can only be set in the START-UP.NCF file. This is because it defines the communications tolerance of the internal NIC. Maximum physical receive packet size parameters cannot be set at the console prompt.

Watchdog

The next type of communication SET parameter is watchdog. Watchdog is a built-in NetWare facility for patrolling active connections. If a workstation is occupying a valid connection from the file server and not responding to routine watchdog packets, the system will disconnect the workstation. This is a built-in efficiency feature which is designed to drop inactive connections. There are two watchdog SET parameters which specifically affect the performance of NetWare communications:

- ► The number
- ► The delay

Let's take a closer look.

Number of Watchdog Packets   The number of watchdog packets parameter defines how many packets the server will send without receiving a reply from a workstation. The default is 10. This means that NetWare will send out 10 watchdog packets to all workstations. If a particular workstation does not respond after the 10th packet, that connection will be dropped.

Delay between Watchdog Packets   The delay between watchdog packets is a related parameter which defines how long the server waits between sending watchdog packets. The default is 4 minutes and 56.6 seconds. The range is 1 second to a maximum of 10 minutes and 26.2 seconds. A system manager who is concerned about inactive connections can set the number of watchdog packets to 5 and the delay between watchdog packets to 10 or 12 seconds. This means that the system will drop workstations who don't respond after a minute's worth of polling.

MEMORY

The next type of SET parameter is associated with memory. Memory SET parameters control the size of the dynamic memory pools, block sizes of cache buffers and the automatic registering of memory on EISA bus computers. These parameters do not specifically apply to file or directory caching—those parameters have their own particular groupings.

> Memory SET parameters control the size of the dynamic memory pools, block sizes of cache buffers and the automatic registering of memory on EISA bus computers.

The system manager should focus his/her memory SET parameters on the following three factors that are associated with performance management:

- ▶ Maximum alloc short term memory

- ▶ Auto register memory above 16MB

- ▶ Cache buffer size

Let's take a quick look.

Maximum Alloc Short Term Memory

Maximum alloc short term memory parameter controls how much memory the operating system will allocate to alloc short term memory. The default is 8MB and NetWare supports a value of up to 32MB. The smallest maximum setting is 50K. If you remember from our earlier discussions, the alloc memory pool grows in size and does not return memory to file caching. The maximum alloc short term memory parameter can be used to limit the actual size that alloc short term memory can grow. Keep in mind, though, that if the alloc short term memory pool reaches its default maximum of 8MB, the system will not allow the loading of NLMs or additional drive mappings.

This scenario could also have a dramatic effect on user connections, queue management, and the opening of locked files. If the system manager is not concerned about the growth of alloc short term memory, he/she can increase the maximum in increments of 1,000,000 bytes.

KNOWLEDGE

Many NetWare 3.12 features draw heavily on alloc short-term memory, including GUI utilities, disk drivers, and drive mappings.

Auto Register Memory Above 16 Megabytes

The auto register memory above 16MB parameter is used to automatically register memory in excess of 16MB. This parameter only works for EISA computers. If you remember from our earlier discussion of console commands, NetWare does not automatically register memory above 16MB for ISA or microchannel machines. It does, however, automatically register memory for EISA computers. This is only the case if the auto register memory above 16MB SET parameter is set to ON (the default setting).

TIP

This particular parameter must be set and can only be set in the STARTUP.NCF file because it defines the operating system configuration and identification of internal RAM.

TIP

It's a good idea to set the auto register memory above 16MB parameter to OFF if you installed a network board or disk adapter that uses online DMA. This is because these boards use 24 bit address lines and can only address 16MB of memory without crashing.

Cache Buffers Size

The cache buffers size parameter controls the block size of the cache buffer. By default, all cache buffers are 4K. As mentioned earlier, NetWare provides the facility for having 4, 8 or 16K buffer size. This parameter is directly linked to the disk allocation block size (which is 4K by default). If disk allocation block sizes are larger on all volumes, the cache buffer size can be increased. This increases file service performance and the efficiency of file cache buffer RAM. Remember, if you increase the cache buffer size parameter without increasing the disk allocation block size, the system will recognize this as a huge inefficiency. NetWare takes action against people with buffer sizes larger than their smallest block size, and will not mount any volumes in which this is the case.

TIP

The cache buffers size parameter can only be set in the STARTUP.NCF file because it defines the smallest allocation unit of server RAM.

QUOTE

Common sense is instinct, and enough of it is genius.

Josh Billings

FILE CACHING

Two of the most important functions of file server memory are file caching and directory caching. File caching increases the server's disk performance by up to 10,000%. Directory caching caches most commonly used portions of the directory entry table. NetWare provides three different SET parameters for both file caching and directory caching which dramatically improve server performance.

The file caching parameters are:

- ▸ Minimum file cache buffers

- ▸ Minimum file cache buffer report threshold

- ▸ Maximum concurrent disk cache writes

> NetWare provides three different SET parameters for both file caching and directory caching which dramatically improve server performance.

The system manager is responsible for balancing these settings with cache buffer size and other directory caching parameters. Settings here will impact the system manager's ability to react in cases where caching is becoming a problem.

Minimum File Cache Buffers

The minimum file cache buffers parameter sets the minimum number of cache buffers the operating system can allow for file caching. This is the minimum level the system manager is willing to accept. As you recall from our earlier discussions, all memory not allocated for operating system processes are given to file caching. As memory is requested from other pools, it is drawn from the file cache buffer pool. The default setting of 20 buffers is equivalent to 80K of file cache RAM. A number this low is almost inconsequential because the file server will probably lock up or crash before it reaches as low as 20 file cache buffers.

The range is 20 to 1,000. That is to say, the maximum number of file cache buffers the system will support is 1,000. If the system manager sets the minimum file cache buffers setting too high, let's say to 1,000, then the other five supplemental memory pools will have difficulty acquiring needed RAM. In the case where the minimum file cache buffer size is set to 1,000, most NLMs will not be able to load. This is because alloc short term memory and cache non-movable is restricted and cannot allocate memory to NLMs for loading. The key to the minimum file cache buffer is balance. A setting too small will not allow the system to protect itself against losing all of its file cache buffers, whereas a setting too large will reserve too many file cache buffers and not allow for the allocation of memory to supplemental pools.

Minimum File Cache Buffer Report Threshold

The minimum file cache buffer report threshold is an advanced parameter which sets a threshold for notifying the system manager when file cache buffers are getting too low. The threshold specifies a range in excess of the minimum. The default is 20 so if all defaults are set, the system will display a console message when file cache buffers reach within 20 of the minimum (which is 40). So if all but 40 cache buffers have been allocated, the system will respond with **Number of cache buffers is getting too low**. Again, even 40 file cache buffers is not enough to operate NetWare on an effective basis.

Regardless of where the threshold is set, the system will respond when file cache buffers fall below the minimum. The following console message will be displayed: **Cache memory allocator exceeded minimum cache buffer left limit**. Keep in mind that the system manager will probably see some auxiliary symptoms of low cache limits before he/she ever sees the console message.

Maximum Concurrent Disk Cache Writes

The maximum concurrent disk cache writes parameter sways the balance of disk performance to favor writing. This advance parameter determines how many write requests from dirty cache are put in the elevator before the disk head begins a sweep across the disk. The default is 50. This means that 50 requests are sent to the disk all at one time. If the number of dirty cache buffers on the main screen of MONITOR is over 50% or 70% of the total cache buffers, this parameter must be increased. Increasing the maximum concurrent disk cache writes will increase the number of requests which can be taken from the dirty cache buffers and sent to the disk simultaneously. The maximum value for this setting is 100.

TIP

Increasing the number of concurrent disk cache writes decreases the performance of reading. This is because the system spends more time and more effort writing and buffering write requests and does not prioritize the access of reads. The good news is this particular setting is transparent to most users.

DIRECTORY CACHING

Directory caching allows fast access to frequently used directories. The directory cache buffer holds directory entries in it as long as they are being accessed frequently. The default is every 33 seconds. When a particular directory entry is not being accessed every 33 seconds, it can be overwritten by a more frequently accessed SET entry.

There are three SET parameters which directly relate to directory caching:

▸ Maximum directory cache buffers

▸ Minimum directory cache buffers

▸ Maximum concurrent directory cache writes

Directory cache buffers are permanent reserved areas of memory which are allocated by the permanent memory pool. As directory cache buffers increase, file cache buffers decrease thus creating a tradeoff between directory caching and file caching. Let's take a closer look at the three directory caching SET parameters.

Maximum Directory Cache Buffers

Maximum directory cache buffers sets the maximum number of cache buffers used for directory entries. The default is 400 and the system will tolerate values from 20 to 4,000. Allocation of directory cache buffers is dynamic and NetWare assigns them as needed. If the server disk is populated by a very large amount of file and directory entries, the DET and directory cache buffers can increase quite rapidly. Once all these files are deleted, the permanent memory pool maintains its size and the directory cache buffers remain high. Keep in mind that directory cache buffers, once allocated, do not go away until the file server is rebooted.

When the maximum number of directory cache buffers is reached, directory entries will be dropped from memory and accessed from disk. This will increase the situation. Users will begin to notice that directory and file searches become quite sluggish. The system manager can increase the maximum directory cache buffer size if the file server is responding slowly to directory searches. Keep in mind, though, that as the maximum is increased and directory cache buffers are allocated, the permanent memory pool continues to grow and draw from file caching.

QUOTE

For people who like peace and quiet: a phoneless cord.

Anonymous

Minimum Directory Cache Buffers

The minimum directory cache buffer parameter determines the number of cache buffers that the operating system will allocate immediately for directory caching (the default is 20, but it can be set as high as 2,000). When the minimum number of directory cache buffers has been allocated and another one is needed, the operating system will wait a specified amount of time (the default is 1.1 seconds) before allocating another buffer. This means that users will see noticeable decreases in directory and file search performances as new directory cache buffers are allocated. Increasing the minimum directory cache buffer setting automatically sets a reserved number of buffers at file server bootup. This means that user file and directory searches are performed much quicker. On the down side, a high level of minimum directory cache buffers causes the permanent memory pool to grow—whether or not the unneeded portions are used.

Maximum Concurrent Directory Cache Writes

The maximum concurrent directory cache writes parameter is identical in function to the maximum concurrent disk cache writes. This advanced parameter determines how many write requests the directory cache buffers can put in the elevator before the disk head begins a sweep across the disk. The default is 10 and the range is from 5 to 50. If you increase the maximum concurrent directory cache writes, the system will favor writing directory entries from directory cache buffers to the disk. If you decrease the number, the system will favor reading directory entry tables from the disk and allocating them to directory cache buffers.

KNOWLEDGE

NetWare does not provide a facility for viewing the number of dirty directory cache buffers.

MISCELLANEOUS

The miscellaneous grouping of SET parameters describes two different areas the system manager should be concerned with:

▸ Maximum service processes

▸ Alerts

The maximum service processes parameter is used to define the number of tellers in the NetWare bank. There is a variety of alerts parameters which can be used to broadcast system messages in cases of minor emergency. Let's take a look at some of these valuable miscellaneous parameters.

Maximum Service Processes

The maximum service processes parameter determines the maximum number of service processes that the operating system will use. The default is 20 and the range is from 5 to 40. If you remember from our earlier analogy, the file service processes are task handlers or tellers which service user requests. File service processes are linked very closely with packet receive buffers which are the lobby where the user requests wait. If the packet receive buffer lobby is too small, the number of file service processes needs to be increased so user requests can be processed more quickly.

The number of file service processes currently available can be viewed in the main screen of MONITOR. If this number approaches 20, the maximum should be increased in increments of 5. Increasing the maximum number of file service processes makes more tellers available to process user requests. Increasing this number decreases the amount of available file cache buffers. Incidentally, Net-Ware dynamically allocates file service processes as needed. It starts at 1 or 2 and increases to the maximum.

Alerts

Alert parameters control the broadcast of messages on the server console when particular conditions or emergencies occur. The system manager can use the alert SET parameters to control which alerts are broadcast and which aren't. Here's a brief list of the four file console alerts and their default values.

Display Spurious Interrupt Alerts	ON
Display Lost Interrupt Alerts	ON
Display Disk Device Alerts	OFF
Display Relinquish Control Alerts	OFF

Each of these alerts can be used to notify the NetWare system manager when serious operating system problems are evident. Incidentally, most of these alerts are not fatal and the system will continue although it will make lots and lots of noise.

That completes our discussion of the performance management SET parameters and a variety of different strategies for optimizing file server performance. SET parameters are serious operating system tools and should be used extremely cautiously. There are a few SET parameters left which don't directly apply to file server performance but do affect the ability of the file server to perform its duties. These other SET parameters fall into four categories:

▸ File system

▸ Locks

▸ Transaction tracking

▸ Disk

OTHER SET PARAMETERS

In the remainder of this section, we will take a brief look at these four different groups and some possible SET parameters which can increase the system manager's quality of life. Think of these as the little details which provide that extra touch beyond what ordinary interior decorators would do.

File System Parameters

File system parameters control how NetWare interfaces with the shared file system. There are three file system parameters which control warnings about volumes, four parameters controlling file purging, and one advanced parameter that controls the reuse of turbo FATs. Of these eight parameters, three jump out at you as useful NetWare tools:

- ▸ Volume low warning threshold

- ▸ Maximum percent of volume used by directory

- ▸ Maximum subdirectory tree depth

Let's take a quick look at these file system SET parameters.

Volume Low Warning Threshold   The volume low warning threshold controls how little free disk space can remain on a volume before the operating system issues a console warning. The default is 256 blocks. The supported values are 0 to 100,000 blocks. Using the default values, this means that NetWare will send a broadcast message as soon as the available disk space on the volume falls below 1MB. If you increase the disk allocation unit or block size on each volume, this particular threshold will change accordingly. For example, a volume with a 64K block size will issue this warning once available disk space falls below 16MB.

KNOWLEDGE

The volume low warning threshold also is sent to each workstation as a broadcast console message.

Maximum Percent of Volume Used by Directory   The maximum percent of volume used by directory parameter limits the portion which may be used as directory space. By default, 13% of the volume space can be used for directory entries. This number becomes important when working with small server disks and many, many directory entries. Incidentally, in earlier versions of NetWare, this number was not a setable parameter. It was a complex calculation of volume space and directory entries. If the system manager has a small disk with multiple volumes, he/she can increase the maximum percentage of volume space used by a directory in which case the system will not lock out the creation of additional directories.

Maximum Subdirectory Tree Depth   The maximum subdirectory tree depth parameter determines how many levels of subdirectories the operating system will support. The default value is 25 and it goes as high as 100. This means that by default NetWare's file system supports 25 subdirectories underneath each other from the root.

TIP

Maximum subdirectory tree depth parameter must be set in the STARTUP.NCF file and will not take effect until the file server is rebooted. This is because the parameter redefines the structure of the file system at bootup time.

QUOTE

Periods of tranquility are seldom prolific of creative achievement. Mankind has to be stirred up.

Alfred North Whitehead

Locks

Lock parameters control how many open files each station can have and how many total open files the operating system will handle. They also control how many record locks each connection can have and how many total record locks the operating system will handle. These parameters control three different types of locks: file, physical, and logical.

> Lock parameters control how many open files each station can have and how many total open files the operating system will handle.

A file lock secures the entire file and prevents other stations from accessing it. A physical record lock controls data access by multiple users. It prevents other users from accessing or changing a range of bytes or a record in a file. A logical record lock also controls data access by multiple users except that in this case it relies on the application to assign the range of bytes or record. NetWare provides four different SET parameters for customizing record lock activity.

Transaction Tracking

The transaction tracking parameters control NetWare's internal transaction tracking system. TTS provides a guarantee that a transaction will either be written to disk in its complete form or backed out in case of a fault. This ensures database integrity and provides general peace of mind to users of large database files. NetWare provides five different SET parameters which control its internal TTS function.

Disk

The disk SET parameters control one facet of the shared NetWare environment—hot fix redirection. There is one disk parameter which controls read after write verification. It is enable disk read after write verify. By default, read after write verification is set ON. The system manager has the flexibility to set read after write verification to OFF. The OFF parameter is only useful in cases where disks are mirrored and the speed of disk writes are a problem. Turning read after write verification ON will almost double the speed of disk writes in cases where mirroring and duplexing has been activated.

Disabling read after write verification does not disable hot fixing but it does decrease its effectiveness. With read after write verification turned off, hot fixing relies on write redirection and read redirection during actual reading and writing operations. This is less reliable than utilizing hot fix redirection.

That completes our discussion of the NetWare optimization using SET parameters. This particular section provided a proactive strategy for acknowledging MONITOR problems and fixing them. In this chapter, we have explored the many different performance management components and learned how their interrelationships affect file server management. In addition, we used the MONITOR.NLM to track resources and their effect on memory pools. We gained valuable information about disks, LAN, network interface cards and file server memory.

The SET parameters allowed us to configure and optimize the operating system in areas such as communications, memory, file caching, directory caching and service processes. We learned about a large variety of different parameters, components and MONITOR statistics and how to correct situations with SET parameters. Table 13.1 provides a review of these actions and the different SET parameters which need to be set to solve the problems. Keep in mind that NetWare interior decorating is not an exact science. It requires diligence, patience, and creativity, not to mention some NetWare taste.

As the NetWare interior decorator, you can see it's extremely important to create a comfortable environment for the users that is both productive and pleasant to use. Performance management is one of the most important NetWare system

T A B L E 13.1 *Summary Actions*	MONITOR	SET
File Cache Buffers	Check that total cache buffers does fall below 20% of original cache buffers. If that is the case, then …	Add more memory or unload NLMs.
Dirty Cache Buffers	Make sure they don't reach 70% of total cache buffers. If so …	Set maximum concurrent disk cache writes = 100.
Directory Cache Buffers	If directory cache buffers reach 100, then …	Minimum directory cache buffers = 200 and maximum directory cache buffers = 500.
Packet Receive Buffers	If packet receive buffers grow beyond 20, then …	Set the minimum packet receive buffers parameter to 50 and the maximum packet receive buffers to 500.
File Service Processes	Check the file service processes in MONITOR and if they are approaching 20, …	Increase the number to 25 or 30 in increments of 5.

	MONITOR	SET
Alloc Short Term Memory	If alloc short term memory approaches 8,000,000 bytes, …	Set maximum alloc short term memory = 9,000,000, increasing in 1,000,000 increments.
Packet Size	Under LAN information, you're using a network interface card capable of larger packet sizes, …	Increase the physical receive packet size to 4202 and increase the minimum packet receive buffer to 200 and the maximum packet receive buffer to 1,000.

management responsibilities and should be taken very seriously. As a CNA, it is your duty to continually monitor file server performance using the MONITOR and SET parameters, and at intervals optimize the settings we talked about in this chapter. The performance management duties are the final responsibilities of the NetWare system manager. As the interior decorator, you need to follow up on the other responsibilities before you.

That's it for NetWare 3.12 and the many hats of the NetWare CNA. In this program, we have learned what it's like to be the NetWare architect, house detective, handyman, hotel manager, painter, and interior decorator. The analogy of Park Place has helped us understand the varying responsibilities that fill up a day in the life of the NetWare CNA. If you take these responsibilities to heart and treat the network as a valuable resource for your users, you will live a long and prosperous life as a successful NetWare CNA. I trust this book will be the beginning of your journey and I wish you the best of luck in attaining your life's goal. Live long and prosper!

> ▶ · · · · · · · · · · · ◀
>
> Performance management is one of the most important NetWare system management responsibilities and should be taken very seriously. As a CNA, it is your duty to continually monitor file server performance using the MONITOR and SET parameters, and at intervals optimize the settings we talked about in this chapter.

EXERCISE 13.1: PERFORMANCE MANAGEMENT COMPONENTS

1. FAT

A. Can be configured in 4K, 8K, 16K, 32K or 64K sizes

2. DET

B. This table is only partially cached in NetWare 3.12

3. Directory caching

C. Increases disk I/O 100 times

4. Directory hashing

D. Stores the directory entry tables in memory

5. File caching

E. The lobby of the NetWare bank

6. Disk allocation blocks

F. Speeds file access by caching DET and FAT

7. Directory entry blocks

G. Must match disk allocation block size in order for volume to mount

8. File cache buffers

H. Special reserved area which stores DETs on disk

9. Directory cache buffers

I. Keeps track of physical locations of files on disk

10. Packet receive buffers

J. Increases disk performance by 30%

1. Total server memory

2. File cache buffers

3. Cache non-movable memory

4. Cache movable memory

5. Permanent memory

6. Semi-permanent memory

7. Alloc short term memory

A. Used to store packet receive buffers

B. Used by loadable modules with pop-up windows

C. Acts as a door for the entrance of NLMs

D. Used by system tables that grow dynamically such as DETs and FATs

E. Cannot be used by NLMs

F. Provides memory for LAN drivers and disk drivers

G. Provides memory for both semipermanent and alloc short term memory

H. Stores information such as mappings, user connection information and temporary messages

I. Where SERVER.EXE resides

J. Used as an original source for all other memory pools

CASE STUDY V: PERFORMANCE MANAGEMENT

The final step in implementing the Snouzer, Inc. NetWare LAN is performance optimization. Sophy has come to you and voiced some concerns about intermittent problems she and her managers are having on the LAN. Of course, it has nothing to do with how you set up the LAN—it's just a manifestation of daily operations. She has asked if you wouldn't mind monitoring these problem areas and fixing them if you can. Of course, from what you've learned in this chapter, you know that your monitoring duties will be performed using MONITOR.NLM and optimization will be performed using the SET parameters. Here are some of Sophy's performance concerns:

▶ File access has been slow

▶ The message **Error sending on network** has appeared for some users

▶ The server is slow to respond when it is rebooted

▶ Directory searches are sluggish

▶ Certain NLMs won't load

As Snouzer, Inc. system manager, it is your responsibility to address each of these issues and suggest some possible courses of action. Let's take a closer look.

1 · File access has been slow. The users have been experiencing slow file access and sluggish applications.

▸ What MONITOR statistics would you check?

_____

_____

▸ How would you remedy the situation?

_____

_____

2 · Some users are experiencing the message **Error sending on network** and loosing their connection. This occurs at random intervals when trying to access the file server.

▸ What MONITOR statistics would you check?

_____

_____

▸ How would you remedy the situation?

_____

_____

3 · The server is slow to respond when it is rebooted. Whenever Sophy turns on the server, it takes a great deal of time for it to come back up. This has caused some concern in that the system is vulnerable and down during that time period.

▸ What MONITOR statistic would you check?

_____

_____

▸ How would you remedy the situation?

_____

_____

4 · Directory searches are sluggish. Users are experiencing very sluggish directory searches. In addition, some users are losing their connection during directory searches.

▸ What MONITOR statistic would you check?

_____

_____

▸ How would you remedy the situation?

_____

_____

5 · NLMs won't load. Sophy has been trying to load some network management NLMs at the server and has found that NLMs which require pop-up menus will not load. She receives an error message to the effect that the appropriate memory pool is out of space.

▸ Which MONITOR statistic would you check?

_____

_____

▸ How you remedy the situation?

_____

_____

Once you have completed your performance management design and suggested some possible courses of action, you can use SET parameters and other tools to implement Snouzer, Inc.'s performance optimization. Once you have done so, the network is completed.

Congratulations! You have designed, installed, and managed a NetWare LAN for Snouzer, Inc. You have completed directory structures, drive mapping, security, login scripts, user interface, and performance management. You took a barely functioning system and breathed life into it. As a NetWare system manager and CNA, you should be very proud of your efforts and use this experience to gain momentum in your next project. Good luck and happy LANning!

Part III—NetWare 3.12

ACROSS

4 The mother of all NetWare utilities

5 To backup OS/2 and UNIX files

6 Swimming with DETs and FATs

8 Default directory for loading NLMs

9 The extension of disk driver NLMs

12 The Ultimate LAN hotel

16 Swimming with NLMs and mappings

18 The user login script file

21 Provides split seeking enhancement

26 Protect your files from SALVAGE

27 Tool of choice for console operators

28 Fool users with pseudo roots

DOWN

1 Spice up user menus with color

2 The default NetWare attributes

3 Allocation units of RAM

6 The goal!

7 Attaches protocol to server NIC

8 The ultimate NetWare 3.12 right

10 The NetWare 3.12 legos

11 Unlocking the Supervisor's account

13 The CNA's chief directory tool

14 The extension of name space NLMs

15 Blocks inherited rights

17 Tool for optimizing memory pools

ACROSS

29 Tool for tracking memory pools

DOWN

19 Taboo for NetWare drive mappings

20 Keeping track of user accounting

22 The NetWare 3.12 OS core

23 Rights granted to trustees

24 Swimming with PRBs

25 Activating server NLMs

See Appendix D for answers.

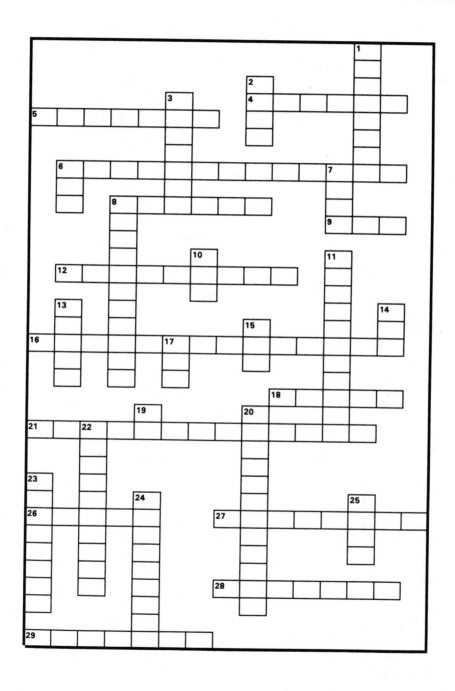

Appendices

"CNA's face an obstacle course
of connectivity problems,
user complaints,
and security violations."

Overview of Novell's Education Strategy

Novell is dedicated to serving all LANkind. At the onset, managers set goals to support NetWare on all major LAN platforms. Unfortunately, they didn't expect to be supporting 3,000,000 LANs in 10 years. The challenge facing Novell today is to provide customer support while maintaining quality control and corporate image. In order to successfully overcome this challenge, Novell works with a series of organizations and certified professionals to distribute the responsibility of supporting the millions of NetWare users worldwide. At the heart of Novell's distributed support strategy is Novell Education and the Certified NetWare Administrator/Engineer programs.

To make training available to as many NetWare users as possible, Novell has developed a worldwide network of more than 900 Novell Authorized Education Centers (NAECs) and Novell Education Academic Partners (NEAPs) including colleges and universities. Only organizations that meet Novell's stringent educational standards are authorized to teach Novell-developed courses. These courses must be taught by Certified NetWare Instructors (CNIs) who are qualified through an extensive training program conducted by Novell. Novell-authorized courses are intended to train and certify consultants, independent service organizations, technicians, support professionals, LAN administrators, and end-users.

The goal of Novell education is to provide high quality NetWare education to potential NetWare support engineers. Currently, over 26,000 Certified NetWare professionals support 3,000,000 NetWare LANs. That's roughly 150 LANs per professional—plenty of work!

In this Appendix, we'll take a thorough look at Novell's education strategy by exploring the many different certification programs and adaptive testing offered by NAECs. In addition, we will briefly discuss the variety of NetWare courses and alternative education methods. Let's begin with Novell's education philosophy.

Novell's Education Philosophy

Novell's mission is "to accelerate the growth of network computing." In order to achieve this goal, Novell puts a great deal of effort into the education of support professionals. According to Novell, market leadership is perpetuated through product diversification and education. After all, it is difficult to implement and support a product nobody understands. More than anything else, this could be seen as one of the reasons for the downfall of OS/2.

Novell Education is the leading training provider in the network computing industry. Just last year, Novell Education trained 210,000 students—45,000 more than the previous year. And over the years, Novell Education has provided NetWare-oriented training to almost 1,000,000 users. Novell Education is designed to help industry professionals develop network design, installation, and management skills. Novell courses provide comprehensive training in network performance, enhanced network functionality, and boosting user productivity.

To make the training available to as many NetWare users as possible, Novell has developed a worldwide network of more than 900 authorized education partners. These partners can be categorized into two different groups: NAECs and NEAPs. NAECs (Novell Authorized Education Centers) are private independent training organizations which meet Novell's strict quality standards. NEAPs (Novell Education Academic Partners) are colleges or universities which meet the same strict guidelines. NEAPs also provide Novell-authorized courses in a normal semester- or quarter-length format.

NAECs and NEAPs offer over 30 different NetWare-oriented courses. Students can simply drop in for one or two courses or complete one of the four different certification programs: CNA, CNE, ECNE, and CNI. The CNA (Certified NetWare Administrator) program is designed for users or managers who are responsible for the day-to-day operation of the LAN. The CNE (Certified NetWare Engineer) program certifies service technicians or consultants to provide quality support for NetWare networks including system design, installation, and maintenance. The ECNE (Enterprise Certified NetWare Engineer) program is designed to give CNEs an opportunity to achieve a higher level of certification, focusing on the support of enterprise wide networks or UNIX connectivity. Finally, the CNI (Certified NetWare Instructor) program is a comprehensive training program for those who want to teach Novell courses. CNI candidates are required to attend courses, pass very high-level tests, and perform satisfactorily at a rigorous instructor performance evaluation course.

Candidates who are interested in attaining any of these certifications must pass comprehensive exams. These exams are designed to provide the most accurate and efficient measurement of a candidate's skill level. Novell currently uses a form of testing called adaptive testing. Adaptive testing tailors itself to your ability. The test molds itself as the candidate answers questions correctly and incorrectly. The two main advantages of adaptive testing over traditional testing are accuracy and efficiency. Adaptive testing minimizes the number of questions by focusing on the candidate's true level of expertise. Novell testing is provided through Drake Authorized Testing Centers.

Novell Education currently offers over 30 different courses in three different categories: Core courses, operating system courses, and elective courses. Novell Education's core courses focus on fundamental and advanced issues in NetWare LAN management. Topics include Microcomputer/DOS basics, networking technologies, and service and support. Operating system courses highlight the roles, responsibilities, and tools available to NetWare managers in any of the three different product lines—NetWare 2.2, NetWare 3.12, and NetWare 4.01. Elective courses are designed to add specialized functionality to the basic core and operating system courses. Elective courses supplement NetWare products by providing detailed information on key issues. Topics include product information for authorized resellers, NetWare 4.0 design and implementation, NetWare internetworking products, and NetWare programming: basic services. Elective courses also provide in-depth training on new and proven Novell products. Topics include NetWare NFS, NetWare for Macintosh connectivity, UnixWare, NetWare for SAA installation and troubleshooting, BTRIEVE: an Overview, and many more.

In addition to these instructor-led courses, Novell offers a variety of educational alternatives including self-study workbooks, computer-based training, and video-based training. These self-study materials have been provided to diversify the delivery method of Novell-based education. Because these products are self-paced, you can focus on information you are unfamiliar with and reduce training time. You can also review course materials as often as necessary and refer to them as needed to learn specific skills. Additional education alternatives include Novell Press books, users groups, conferences, and free seminars—routinely provided by the CNE professional association.

As you can tell, Novell's education philosophy is quite comprehensive. Whether you are interested in becoming a NetWare expert or just want to learn the basics, you can count on Novell Education to meet your training needs.

Now let's explore each of Novell's education strategies and provide detailed information about how you can benefit from Novell Education. It really is an excellent way of learning the ins and outs of NetWare.

Education Centers

More than 900 NAECs and NEAPs worldwide offer instructor-led courses and self-study education products to give you convenient access to a Novell education. You can count on the classes to be topnotch. Only organizations that meet Novell's rigorous standards are authorized to teach Novell courses. Furthermore, Novell guarantees complete customer satisfaction for all its courses. NAECs and NEAPs are required to meet four strict education guidelines:

- ▸ The facility must use Novell-developed course materials.

- ▸ The course must be taught within a recommended time frame or in the case of NEAPs, a time frame that exceeds the recommended number of hours.

- ▸ The facility must be Novell authorized. Authorization is based on a strict set of standards for equipment and student comfort.

- ▸ Courses must be offered by a Certified NetWare Instructor who is certified to teach the specific course.

To ensure training quality, Novell routinely inspects education partner facilities. In addition, students are provided with an opportunity to evaluate the course material, the instructor, and the facility at the end of each course. These evaluation forms are forwarded immediately to Novell for review. Facilities that do not live up to these strict standards are removed from the program.

Let's take a quick look at NAECs and NEAPs.

NAEC

NAECs (Novell Authorized Education Centers) are private training organizations which provide Novell courses. Many NAECs are solely in the business of training. The advantage of attending a NAEC is that these organizations typically have a great deal of experience in technology training and are driven to provide quality education. You can be assured that since the success of the NAEC is dependent on the quality of the training, all courses are accurate, timely, and comprehensive. In order to become an NAEC, the private training organization must submit an extensive application to Novell Education. It also pays an initiation fee and annual licensing fees. In addition, NAECs are required to offer a variety of different courses in a consistent and timely manner. For a list of NAECs in your area and the courses they are authorized to teach, call 1-800-233-3382 in the US and Canada. In all other areas, call 1-801-429-5508 or contact the nearest Novell office. Look for the NAEC logo.

NEAP

The NEAP (Novell Education Academic Partner) program was recently created to provide quality Novell education through accredited colleges and universities. NEAP implementation was driven by students who wanted to participate in Novell courses in a traditional education format. This implementation was also driven by colleges and universities that saw the value of NetWare-oriented training. NEAPs must follow the same strict guidelines as NAECs and provide Novell courses as part of their standard curriculum. There's currently a very limited number of colleges and universities authorized to teach NEAP courses—but the number is quickly growing. For a list of participating schools, call 1-800-233-3382 in the US and Canada. In all other areas, call 1-801-429-5508 or contact the nearest Novell office.

Certification Programs

Novell Education uses a two-pronged approach to NetWare-oriented training. On one hand, each course is designed to offer self-contained education on a specific topic, is clearly outlined, and can be completed in a 1- to 5-day format.

On the other hand, Novell Education courses can be combined to provide a comprehensive certification. Novell Education's certification programs are designed to develop a high level of expertise in the management implementation of NetWare-oriented products. To ensure the availability of quality NetWare administrative and technical support professionals, Novell has developed the following certification programs:

- Certified NetWare Administrator (CNA) program

- Certified NetWare Engineer (CNE) program

- Enterprise Certified NetWare Engineer (ECNE) program

- Certified NetWare Instructor (CNI) program

Let's take a brief look at the four different certification programs.

CNA

The CNA program is designed for users who are responsible for the day-to-day operation of a network. NetWare administrators typically perform tasks such as adding and deleting users, backing up the server, loading applications, and maintaining security. CNA candidates may currently choose to specialize in NetWare 2.2, 3.12, or the new NetWare 4.0 operating system. CNAs are certified by passing one CNA test for each operating system. It is possible then to become a CNA by passing one test and to specialize in one of the three operating systems.

Successful completion of the certification test serves as a valuable credential in the networking industry. CNA program objectives are covered in the operating system courses for NetWare 2.2, NetWare 3.12, and NetWare 4.0. These objectives are identical to the CNE objectives in most areas. The only difference is that some of the advanced CNE objectives have been removed and are not required for CNA certification. This book, for example, covers all of the CNA program objectives and some additional CNE objectives. The candidate who passes the CNA test will receive a certificate from Novell identifying him or her as a Certified NetWare Administrator. If a NetWare 2.2 CNA decides to go on to become a CNE, the knowledge gained in the courses will be useful, but the CNA certification is completely independent from the CNE.

The NetWare 3.12 and NetWare 4.0 CNA programs are a little different. These program objectives are identical to the objectives covered in the *NetWare 3.12 Administration* and *NetWare 4.0 Administration* courses. Candidates who pass these tests can, in fact, apply the credits towards a future CNE credential.

CNA Requirements

The CNA requirements are designed to teach the fundamentals of NetWare 2.2, 3.12, or 4.0 system management. Attendance in the following courses is not required. Candidates must simply pass a single CNA exam covering some of the system management course objectives. *Novell's CNA Study Guide* provides all of the objectives for passing NetWare 2.2 and 3.12 CNA exams. It also provides most of the CNE system management objectives. Following is a complete list of Novell's CNA courses and corresponding exams.

NetWare 2 CNA

Course No.	Course Name	Credits	Test No.
501	NetWare 2.2: System Manager	3	50-115
502	NetWare 2.2: Advanced System Manager	2	50-115

NetWare 3.1x CNA

Course No.	Course Name	Credits	Test No.
508	NetWare 3.12 Administration	3	50-390

NetWare 4 CNA

Course No.	Course Name	Credits	Test No.
520	NetWare 4.0 Administration	3	50-391

In addition to the CNA program objectives which are covered in the system manager and advanced system manager courses, CNA candidates should gain the prerequisite knowledge from the Microcompter/DOS workbooks. The objectives in these workbooks, however, are not tested for the CNA certification. If you have any more questions about Novell's CNA program, contact Novell Education at 1-800-233-3382 in the US and Canada. In all other locations, contact your local Novell office or call 1-801-429-5508.

CNE

The CNE program certifies service technicians and consultants to provide quality support for NetWare networks. This support includes system design, installation, and maintenance. Once certification requirements are met, Novell stands behind its CNEs with technical support and up-to-date product profiles. To earn a CNE certification, candidates must demonstrate mastery of networking concepts by passing a series of tests. CNE certification consists of 19 credits, each roughly equivalent to one day at a NAEC. There are three requirements for CNE certification:

- Core Requirements

- Operating System Requirements

- CNE Elective Requirements

Core Requirements—10 credits

The CNE core requirements are designed to provide the candidate with the fundamentals of networking technology, service, and support and microcomputer/DOS basics. In addition, Novell Education requires a signed CNE agreement after the candidate completes his/her first test. Candidates can obtain CNE agreements by calling 1-800-NETWARE. The core requirements provide 10 credits towards the 19 needed for a CNE. Note: credits are earned by passing exams, not by attending courses. The four Core Requirement courses and tests are as follows:

Course No.	Course Name	Credits	Test No.
1100	DOS for NetWare Users	2	50-15
1101	Microcomputer Concepts	2	50-15
200	Networking Technologies	3	50-80
801	NetWare Service and Support	5	50-118

It is important to note that these core courses are not intended to be completed first. The DOS/Microcomputer course provides a good general overview. *Networking Technologies* and *NetWare Service and Support*, however, are highly advanced courses. These two courses are designed to be completed after the candidate satisfies the operating system certification requirements.

Operating System Requirements—5 credits

The CNE operating system requirements are designed to make sure that Certified NetWare Engineers understand the details of one of the three NetWare operating systems. CNE candidates can choose any of the three tracks: NetWare 2.2, NetWare 3.12, and NetWare 4.0. The operating system requirements provide 5 credits of the 19 towards the CNE credential. Below are the courses and tests that satisfy the operating system requirements in each of the three operating system tracks.

NetWare 2.2 Track

Course No.	Course Name	Credits	Test No.
501	NetWare 2.2: System Manager	3	50-20

Course No.	Course Name	Credits	Test No.
502	NetWare 2.2: Advanced System Manager	2	50-44

NetWare 3.12 Track

Course No.	Course Name	Credits	Test No.
508	NetWare 3.12 Administration (also applies toward CNA)	3	50-130
518	NetWare 3.12 Advanced Administration	2	50-131

NetWare 4.0 Track

Course No.	Course Name	Credits	Test No.
520	NetWare 4.0: Administration (also applies toward CNA)	3	50-122
525	NetWare 4.0: Advanced Administration	2	50-123

CNE Elective Requirements—4 Credits

CNE elective requirements are designed to provide candidates with a specialization or NetWare-oriented expertise. Candidates must pass two tests covering any of the instructor-led courses. These courses are detailed later in this section. In addition, CNA candidates can choose to apply alternative operating system tracks towards their elective credits. For example, candidates who choose NetWare 3.12 as an operating system track can pass the 2.2 tests and apply the credits towards CNE elective requirements. Candidates cannot, however, apply *NetWare 3.11 to 3.12 Update* towards elective credits if they chose the 3.12 track. Similarly, candidates who choose the 4.0 track cannot apply the *NetWare 3.11 to 4.0 Update* credits towards the CNE elective requirements.

Novell Education is exploring alternatives for providing NetWare-oriented training to a larger variety of individuals. This book, for example, is an illustration of Novell's continuing commitment to improving the delivery of training materials. It covers all objectives for the CNA and 95% of the operating system requirements for the CNE/CNI.

ECNE

The ECNE (Enterprise Certified NetWare Engineer) program is designed to give CNEs an opportunity to achieve a higher level of certification, focusing on the support of Enterprise-wide networks. ECNE candidates must demonstrate proficiency in specialized networking technologies. At the very least, ECNE candidates must have a CNE certification. ECNE candidates are also required to complete up to an additional 19 certification credits.

The ECNE program is viewed by many as the advanced degree of NetWare certification. As with the CNE program, ECNE candidates must complete electives in three different groups: Core Requirements, Operating System Requirements, and ECNE Elective Requirements.

Core Requirement—CNE

The only Core Requirement for ECNE certification is that the candidate already be certified as a CNE. There is no additional agreement for becoming an Enterprise CNE.

Operating System Requirements—7 or 10 credits

The ECNE Operating System Requirements are designed to ensure that ECNE professionals have an in-depth understanding of both NetWare 3.12 and 4.0 operating systems. The assumption is that it's difficult to support advanced networking technologies if the ECNE professional does not understand the fundamentals of the NetWare operating system. The ECNE can choose one of two tracks for satisfying his or her operating system requirements: NetWare 3.12 or NetWare 4.0.

NetWare 3.12 Track

Course No.	Course Name	Credits	Test No.
508	NetWare 3.12 Administration	3	50-130
518	NetWare 3.12 Advanced Administration	2	50-131
526	NetWare 3.11 to 4.0 Update	2	50-124

These three tests equate to 7 operating system credits. An additional 12 elective credits are required for the ECNE certification.

Course No.	Course Name	Credits	Test No.
508	NetWare 3.12 Administration	3	50-130
518	NetWare 3.12 Advanced Administration	2	50-131
520	NetWare 4.0: Administration	3	50-122
525	NetWare 4.0: Advanced Administration	3	50-123

These four tests provide 10 operating system credits. An additional 9 elective credits are required for the ECNE certification. The ECNE candidate can choose one of these two 3.12 tracks.

NetWare 4.0 Track

Course No.	Course Name	Credits	Test No.
520	NetWare 4.0: Administration	3	50-122
525	NetWare 4.0: Advanced Administration	2	50-123

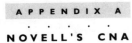
Course No.	Course Name	Credits	Test No.
506	NetWare 3.11: OS Features Review	2	50-45

These three tests equate to 7 operating system credits. An additional 12 elective credits are required for the ECNE certification.

Course No.	Course Name	Credits	Test No.
520	NetWare 4.0: Administration	3	50-122
525	NetWare 4.0: Advanced Administration	2	50-123
508	NetWare 3.12 Administration	3	50-130
518	NetWare 3.12 Advanced Administration	2	50-131

These four tests provide 10 operating system credits. An additional 9 elective credits are required for the ECNE certification. The ECNE candidate can choose one of these two 4.0 tracks.

ECNE Elective Requirements—9 or 12 credits

ECNE Elective Requirements are included to provide a variety of specialization areas for Enterprise CNE candidates. Candidates have the freedom to choose from a variety of electives but are encouraged to specialize in a given networking area. Some areas to consider for specialization are UNIX connectivity, internetworking products, NetWare programming, NetWare 4.0, and UnixWare. The same electives apply as the CNE elective chart and these are included in the next section.

CNI

The Certified NetWare Instructor program is a comprehensive training program for people who want to teach Novell courses. Candidates who have been accepted into the program are required to attend courses, pass tests, and satisfy a rigorous instructor-performance evaluation. Novell Education recognizes that CNIs are the heart of their education philosophy. CNIs are the delivery mechanism for NetWare-oriented training and Novell courses. Good CNIs help the program shine and not-so-good CNIs can cause irreparable damage. Novell Education views the CNI's role as a partnership with the NAEC and NEAP. Novell feels that CNIs share a common mission—"to broaden the availability of quality Novell product training in the marketplace."

CNI responsibilities include:

▸ Staying up to date on current technology and communicating this knowledge to students.

▸ Teaching Novell courses at NAEC or NEAP facilities.

▸ Making sure Novell course objectives are met, using original Novell course materials, completing required update training, and passing required competency tests. In addition, they must ensure that student course evaluations are completed after each Novell class and that everybody has a good time while learning NetWare-oriented topics.

To become a CNI, you must meet four fundamental requirements:

1 · Application approval.

2 · Attend courses which you want to teach.

3 · Complete the tests.

4 · Satisfactorily pass an Instructor Performance Evaluation (IPE).

Let's take a moment to review these four steps.

Step 1: Application Approval

The first step is to obtain and submit a CNI application to your local Novell Technology Institute (NTI) Manager. To contact your local NTI Manager, call 1-800-233-3382. When you submit your application, make sure to complete it in full. You will be required to submit a copy of your resume, highlighting your education, work experience in the network computing industry, and professional teaching experience. You will also be asked to provide three references. The application form will be accompanied by a signed CNI agreement which outlines your future roles and responsibilities.

In addition to the CNI application, you must submit an order form for an IPE instructor kit and a check or money order for your first instructor performance evaluation. As part of the application process, you must identify your intended area of specialization:

- Core/OS products

- Advanced products

- Development products

You must also indicate the first course you want to teach.

After you submit your application, your NTI Manager will arrange an interview with you. This interview will focus on your background, experience and qualifications. Your application will be evaluated on the basis of your qualifications and the CNI program prerequisites listed earlier. Once your application has been approved by your NTI Manager, you will be considered a CNI candidate and will be sent additional information along with an instructor kit for your target course.

Step 2: Course Attendance

You must attend a standard presentation of each course you want to teach. You must attend standard courses at an NAEC. CNI candidates who attend courses at NEAP sites will be authorized only to teach at NEAP sites.

Attending a standard Novell course gives you an opportunity to become familiar with the flow of the course. It also provides firsthand experience at being a student and ensures that the quality of Novell instruction will continue improving.

After you attend a course, you must send or fax a copy of your course certificate to CNI Administration. The fax number is 1-801-429-3900.

Step 3: Testing

In addition to attending a course, you must pass the test for courses you wish to teach. When registering for a test, you must specify that you will be taking the CNI version of the test. CNI tests are nearly identical to CNE tests except that candidates are required to pass the test at a higher proficiency level. A list of CNI test numbers can be obtained by calling 1-800-233-3382. Note: candidates who pass the CNI tests may apply those credits towards the CNE certification.

In addition to passing the tests for the courses you wish to teach, CNI candidates are required to pass a group of prerequisite tests for each of the three different areas. Here's a list of those tests:

Core/OS products

CNI DOS/Microcomputer Concepts for NetWare Users—Test No. 50-15

Advanced products

CNI DOS/Microcomputer Concepts for NetWare Users—Test No. 50-15

CNI NetWare 3.12 Administration—Test No. 50-230

CNI NetWare 4.0 Administration—Test No. 50-222

CNI Networking Technologies—Test No. 50-81

Development products

CNI DOS/Microcomputer Concepts for NetWare Users—Test No. 50-15

CNI NetWare 3.12 Administration—Test No. 50-230

CNI NetWare 4.0 Administration—Test No. 50-222

CNI candidates can register for a test through Drake Training & Technologies. The number for test registration is 1-800-RED-EXAM. One important note is that while most CNI proficiency tests are adaptive, some are form tests. Form tests can contain approximately 60 to 75 questions and have time limits which range from 60 to 90 minutes.

Step 4: Instructor Performance Evaluation (IPE)

To certify to teach Novell courses, you must attend and pass a two-day instructor performance evaluation at a Novell Technology Institute. You are required to pass one IPE for each course area you want to certify in. If, for example, you're interested in certifying for two of the three areas, you must pass two IPEs. The IPE process is designed to ensure that a CNI's instructional skills and level of technical knowledge meet Novell's standards.

You can register for an instructor performance evaluation only after you have met all the other certification requirements. During a two-day IPE, you'll be required to set up a classroom or lab and then teach a 45- to 60-minute section of your target course. Though you'll be sent an instructor kit for your target course and information about evaluation criteria before attending the IPE, you will not know which section of the course you will be asked to teach until the day before your presentation.

During the presentation, you'll be evaluated on your technical knowledge, your ability to communicate that knowledge to the audience, and your presentation skills. After you have met all certification requirements including passing your IPE, you will be sent a letter of certification and a "welcome aboard" kit containing CNI tools and resources. You will also be assigned a CNI identification number used by CNI administration for tracking certified instructors.

Adaptive Testing

In November, 1991, the Novell testing program began using computerized adaptive testing technology which is now used to deliver many Novell certification tests. Although adaptive testing has been used by various government agencies, professional organizations, and school districts for more than a decade, it is still an unfamiliar concept to most people.

Traditional paper and pencil or computerized tests deliver the same set of questions to every examinee regardless of his/her level of knowledge or proficiency. Your score on a traditional test depends on the number of questions you answer correctly. Nevertheless, a traditional test is not the most efficient way to measure a candidate's knowledge or proficiency. Adaptive testing, on the other hand, works more like a conversation. It begins by giving you a question of moderate difficulty. After you respond, the test scores your response and estimates your level of ability. It then looks for a question whose difficulty matches your presumed ability. It presents that question, and when you respond, the program scores your response and revises its estimate of your ability on the basis of the *two* questions given thus far. This process continues with the program revising its estimate of your ability following each response.

As you can imagine, the estimate becomes more and more accurate with each question. The test concludes when

A · Your ability is estimated with sufficient accuracy

B · The program is at least 95% confident that your ability score lies somewhere above the passing score

C · The maximum number of questions is given.

Because an adaptive test tailors itself to your ability, it is not a good idea to base your score on the number of correct answers. Adaptive testing scores are based on the difficulty of the questions you answer correctly and incorrectly. In other words, the score is based on your *ability* rather than simply the number of items you get right. Novell Education has adopted an ability score scale that has a minimum value of 200 and a maximum value of 800. For each test, a passing score will be established somewhere on the scale. You will pass the test if your ability is equal to or greater than the passing score. The two main advantages of adaptive testing over traditional testing are accuracy and efficiency. Questions that are too easy or too difficult provide little information about your true ability. By minimizing the number of such questions, adaptive testing can accurately measure your ability with fewer questions—saving you valuable time. Adaptive tests can also save you from the boredom or intimidation of questions that are too easy or too hard. You should find that most of the items you receive are moderately challenging, helping to make the testing sessions more interesting and less stressful; that is, if you can imagine an unstressful test.

Novell provides adaptive testing for certification through Drake Authorized Testing Centers—or DATCs. Drake is a third-party organization which has been licensed to provide testing to Novell candidates. Drake Authorized Testing

Centers are located worldwide. To register for a test, candidates must call 1-800-RED-EXAM. Candidates are required to provide two forms of ID to take a Novell test.

While each test is different, most of them follow a common format. They range from 10 to 20 questions in some cases, and 15 to 25 in others. Regardless of the range, Novell provides 30 minutes for completing adaptive tests. Candidates can retake tests as many times as necessary (as long as they pay each time). The CNE program requires that candidates complete all 7 tests within a one-year period starting from the time they pass the first test. ECNE and CNI certification, on the other hand, do not have a time limit. For a complete list of Novell courses and the corresponding test numbers for CNEs, ECNEs, and CNAs, please refer to the list in the following section. In addition, a vast collection of sample CNA test questions has been included with this book. Please avail yourself of this valuable opportunity!

Testing is tricky business and while nobody enjoys taking a test, it is safe to say that Novell has tried to make the experience quick, painless, and accurate.

Instructor-Led Courses

Novell Education's goal is to deliver well-designed courses with technically accurate information from talented CNIs in a superior and comfortable facility. Novell courses are recognized as the best in the technical training industry. Feedback from the new NetWare 4.0 courses shows that the introduction of new concepts and techniques makes the education materials even more productive. As mentioned earlier, Novell Education offers over 30 different instructor-led courses. These courses are organized into three different groups:

- ▶ Core Courses
- ▶ Operating System Courses
- ▶ Elective Courses

In this section, you will find a list of all of Novell's courses and how they fall into each of these different categories. In addition, you will find the course number, number of credits, and testing number. Let's begin with the core courses.

CORE COURSES

Novell Education's core courses are designed to provide students with fundamental networking technology education. There are currently two instructor-led core courses which provide hands-on experience as well as detailed information about the general networking technologies industry.

Course No.	Course Name	Credits	Test No.
200	Networking Technologies	3	50-80
801	NetWare Service and Support	5	50-118

Again, it is important to note that these courses are designed to be taken AFTER the operating system requirements have been met.

OPERATING SYSTEM COURSES

Novell Education operating system courses are designed to provide detailed information about system design, installation, and maintenance of NetWare 2.2, NetWare 3.12, and NetWare 4.0. In addition, the operating system courses provide a great deal of hands-on practical knowledge in using and implementing these products. Currently the operating system courses are the foundation of Novell's education philosophy.

Course No.	Course Name	Credits	Test No.
501	NetWare 2.2: System Manager	3	50-20
502	NetWare 2.2: Advanced System Manager	2	50-44
508	NetWare 3.12 Administration	3	50-130
506	NetWare 3.11: OS Features Review	2	50-45
507	NetWare 3.11 to 3.12 Update	1	N/A

Course No.	Course Name	Credits	Test No.
518	NetWare 3.12 Advanced Administration	2	50-131
520	NetWare 4.0: Administration	3	50-122
525	NetWare 4.0: Advanced Administration	2	50-123
526	NetWare 3.11 to 4.0 Update	2	50-124

ELECTIVE COURSES

Novell Education provides a variety of courses designed to enhance the system manager or consultant's ability to provide networking services. These courses focus on a variety of general topics including internetworking, design and implementation, programming, and product information.

Course No.	Course Name	Credits	Test No.
205	Fundamentals of Internetwork and Management Design	2	50-106
220	UNIX OS Fundamentals for NetWare Users	2	50-107
305	Product Information for Gold Authorized Resellers	2	50-19
530	NetWare 4.0: Design and Implementation	3	50-125
535	Printing with NetWare	2	50-137
550	NetWare Navigator	2	50-138
601	LAN Workplace for DOS 4.1 Administration	2	50-104
605	NetWare TCP/IP Transport	2	50-86

Course No.	Course Name	Credits	Test No.
610	NetWare NFS	2	50-87
615	NetWare for Macintosh Connectivity	2	50-93
625	NetWare NFS Gateway	1	50-119
678	UnixWare Installation and Configuration	1	N/A
680	UnixWare System Adminstration	3	50-134
685	UnixWare Advanced System Adminstration	2	50-135
708	LANtern Services Manager	3	50-89
715	NetWare Dial In/Dial Out Connectivity	2	50-112
718	NetWare Connect	2	50-114
720	NetWare for SAA: Installation and Troubleshooting	3	50-141
730	NetWare Management System for MS Windows	2	50-128
740	NetWare Internetworking Products	2	50-142
750	NetWare Global MHS	2	50-108
804	NetWare 4.0: Installation and Configuration Workshop	2	50-126
851	UnixWare Service and Support	3	50-136
904	BTRIEVE: An Overview	1	50-127

Course No.	Course Name	Credits	Test No.
905	Programming with BTRIEVE v2.0	2	50-129
911	NetWare Database Adminstrator	2	N/A
912	Programming with NetWare SQL	2	N/A
930	NetWare programming: NLM Development	3	N/A
940	NetWare Programming: Basic Services	3	N/A

Keep in mind that Novell is constantly upgrading and evolving its courses. So check with your local Novell office to verify course numbers, test numbers, and credit values.

In addition to the obvious value of gaining knowledge and advancing toward Novell certification, Novell instructor-led courses are recognized by the International Association for Continuing Education and Training. Anyone who completes a standard Novell course may apply for continuing education units (CEUs) by sending in the CEU application card provided by the NAEC. As required by the Association, Novell will maintain permanent records of students requesting CEUs for Novell course completion and will be prepared to issue a transcript of record at the request of the participant.

Education Alternatives

In addition to the instructor-led courses, Novell provides a variety of alternatives, which include workbooks, computer-based training, video, and Novell Press publications. Educational alternatives have been included so that professionals can become trained at their own pace in a more convenient manner.

Alternative education materials can be purchased through authorized NAECs. Below is a brief discussion of the most popular Novell Education alternatives.

WORKBOOKS

Self-study workbooks are designed to supplement existing instructor-led courses or provide additional details in areas of specialty that do not warrant an instructor-led course. Novell authorized workbooks are intended to be completed at the student's own pace. Each section within the workbook includes objectives, a list of terms, and review questions. Here's a list of currently available Novell Education workbooks:

- DOS for NetWare Users

- Microcomputer Concepts for NetWare Users

- NetWare Lite

- LANalyzer for NetWare

- NetWare Management MAP for OS/2

- Using LAN Workplace for DOS 4.1

- Administering SNAD for NetWare Global MHS

- Administering SMTP for NetWare Global MHS

COMPUTER-BASED TRAINING

A sophisticated series of computer-based training courses has been included to augment the existing Novell Education materials. These courses are fully graphical and interactive. They are based on the Microsoft Windows interface and use a run-time version of ToolBook. In addition to providing the technical information in an easy-to-understand format, the computer-based training courses include mastery tests and review questions. There are seven existing computer-based training courses:

- NetWare User Basics

- Introduction to Networking

- ▸ Networking Technologies
- ▸ NetWare 3.12 Adminstration
- ▸ NetWare 3.12 Advanced Administration
- ▸ NetWare 4.0: Administration
- ▸ NetWare 4.0: Advanced Administration

Novell Education provides a collection of CBT samplers, free of charge, to candidates. Make sure to take a look at this wonderful, interactive, graphical format. Once you start one, you won't be able to quit!

VIDEO

In addition to self-paced workbooks and computer-based training, Novell Education offers video-based training for candidates who learn best through the graphical representation of technical topics. Video training has only recently become available. Currently Novell Education offers the following video series:

- ▸ NetWare 3.12 Administration
- ▸ LANalyzer for NetWare

COMPANIONS

In addition to Novell Education, there is a variety of other organizations which provide supporting materials for NetWare-oriented training. These organizations are primarily concerned with the development and distribution of accurate technical information. The serious NetWare professional can dramatically improve his/her understanding of NetWare-related topics by dabbling in any of the following five educational companions:

- ▸ Novell Press
- ▸ Users groups
- ▸ Conferences
- ▸ CNEPA

▶ LAN*imation*

▶ NetWire

Let's take a closer look.

Novell Press

Novell Press was originally created to provide technically accurate and detailed supplements for Novell courses. The goal is to provide a sound basis for understanding the complex technologies that await students once they enter the work force. Novell Press, in cooperation with SYBEX, publishes technical books targeted at Novell users and the networking community at large. All books are written by experts and provide the kind of practical information that is highly prized by network administrators. This book, for example, is designed to provide supplemental discussions of key topics for Certified NetWare Administrator candidates. In addition, information in this book can be used towards the CNE, ECNE, and CNI certifications.

Users Groups

NetWare Users International (NUI) is an organization created to provide support to distributed NetWare users groups. These users groups meet monthly to discuss critical technology issues and provide short training seminars. Through NUI, users present a united voice to Novell giving vital feedback on improving products and services. In addition, NUI members learn new networking techniques, and can help plan regional NetWare users conferences held in major cities worldwide. NetWare Connection, NUI's bimonthly user focus magazine, is sent to all NUI members. For more information about joining NUI, call NUI's administrative support staff at Novell at 1-800-228-4NUI.

Conferences

The networking industry has rallied around the need for focused technical conferences. More and more of today's conferences are becoming focused on networking issues and training considerations. The NetWare users conferences, for example, provide full-day tutorials and two-hour seminars on a variety of

NetWare-oriented technologies. Professionals and engineers can attend these conferences and gain valuable information from leaders in the networking industry. In addition, national conferences such as Comdex, Network Expo, and BrainShare provide annual or biannual opportunities for networking professionals to discuss key technologies and future NetWare solutions. A great deal of value can be gained from attending such conferences.

CNEPA

The Certified NetWare Engineer Professional Association (CNEPA) supports CNE candidates and certified professionals. The CNEPA is a nonprofit professional association which provides a variety of services to its members, including a monthly newsletter, seminars, and hands-on labs at users conferences. In addition, the CNEPA sponsors vendor seminars at Novell offices, provides discounts on Novell Press materials, and even negotiates lower rates on NetWare-oriented courses. The CNEPA gives you an opportunity to interact with other CNE professionals. To receive more information on the CNEPA and request membership, call 1-800-9CNEPRO.

LANimation

LANimation is an organization of CNEs, students, authors, and professionals who have banded together to offer NetWare assistance to networking professionals and end users. In addition to LAN tips and answers, LANimation provides a FREE remote on-line network for students who do not have a LAN to practice with on their own. Students can use the remote LAN free of charge to practice laboratory exercises and explore key NetWare concepts. For more information on joining LANimation or benefiting from their services, refer to the introduction of this book.

NetWire

NetWire is Novell's on-line information service. It provides access to Novell product information, press releases, technical support, a calendar of events, forums, and downloadable files—patches, upgrades, and shareware utilities. NetWire is available 24 hours a day through the CompuServe Information

Services (CIS). It is structured into 18 forums and many software libraries. The NetWire forums provide valuable conversation and advice for NetWare and users, developers, CNEs, vendors, and Certified NeWar Instructors. The Net-Wire libraries include a myriad of downloadable files. NetWire currently serves over 100,000 network and end users and professionals.

NetWire is an invaluable resource for NetWare system managers. It requires a personal computer, modem, communications, and an account with Compu-Serve. CompuServe, Inc. is currently offering a free introductory membership to explore NetWire, including a $15 usage credit and step-by-step instructions. Contact CompuServe at (800) 848-8199 in the U.S. and Canada, or at (614) 457-0802. Ask for Representative #200.

In this appendix, we have explored Novell's education strategy and learned of the many different facets of Novell courseware and certification programs. As you can see, there's a huge variety and diversity to Novell's education approach, and it successfully accomplishes the goal to accelerate the growth of network computing. As networking technology evolves in complexity and sophistication, the need for NetWare-oriented education will grow even larger. Fortunately, there exists a wide base upon which to build the future of network computing.

NetWare 2.2 Worksheets

▶ . . . . ◀

External Hard Disk Worksheet

Controller Type: _____ Controller: _____ Drive: _____   **Ref #:**
                 Controller type: _____

Mfg. Model #/ Name: _____ Type #: _____
Removable Media: _____

ZTEST ☐ Yes ☐ No   Interleave ☐ 1   ☐ 2   ☐ Other_____
Physical size: _____ Logical size: _____ Hot Fix size: _____

Mirror Status: ☐ Primary ☐ Secondary   w/ Reference # _____
Capacity (MB):_____ **Netware partition** (MB): _____ bootable ☐   **Other** (MB): _____

Controller Type: _____ Controller: _____ Drive: _____   **Ref #:**
                 Controller type: _____

Mfg. Model #/ Name: _____ Type #: _____
Removable Media: _____

ZTEST ☐ Yes ☐ No   Interleave ☐ 1   ☐ 2   ☐ Other_____
Physical size: _____ Logical size: _____ Hot Fix size: _____

Mirror Status: ☐ Primary ☐ Secondary   w/ Reference # _____
Capacity (MB):_____ **Netware partition** (MB): _____ bootable ☐   **Other** (MB): _____

Controller Type: _____ Controller: _____ Drive: _____   **Ref #:**
                 Controller type: _____

Mfg. Model #/ Name: _____ Type #: _____
Removable Media: _____

ZTEST ☐ Yes ☐ No   Interleave ☐ 1   ☐ 2   ☐ Other_____
Physical size: _____ Logical size: _____ Hot Fix size: _____

Mirror Status: ☐ Primary ☐ Secondary   w/ Reference # _____
Capacity (MB):_____ **Netware partition** (MB): _____ bootable ☐   **Other** (MB): _____

Notes:

For use with the NetWare v2.2 Installation manual.

File Server Definition Worksheet

File server name: _____

Maximum number of open files: _____

Maximum number of open indexed files: _____

TTS backout volume: _____

Maximum number of TTS transactions: _____

Limit disk space: ❑ Yes ❑ No   If yes, number of bindery objects: _____

Install Mac VAP: ❑ Yes ❑ No

Channel 0, controller 0, drive 0 (Internal Hard Disk)   Ref #:

Mfg. Model #/ Name: _____ Type #: _____

Removable Media: _____

ZTEST   ❑ Yes ❑ No   Interleave   ❑ 1   ❑ 2   ❑ Other_____

Physical size: _____   Logical size: _____   Hot Fix size: _____

Mirror Status: ❑ Primary ❑ Secondary   w/ Reference # _____

Capacity (MB): _____   Netware partition (MB): _____ bootable ❑   Other (MB): _____

Channel 0, controller 0, drive 0 (Internal Hard Disk)   Ref #:

Mfg. Model #/ Name: _____ Type #: _____

Removable Media: _____

ZTEST   ❑ Yes ❑ No   Interleave   ❑ 1   ❑ 2   ❑ Other_____

Physical size: _____   Logical size: _____   Hot Fix size: _____

Mirror Status: ❑ Primary ❑ Secondary   w/ Reference # _____

Capacity (MB): _____   Netware partition (MB): _____ bootable ❑   Other (MB): _____

File server hardware type: _____   Installer: _____

Floppy diskette drives: **Drive A:**   **Drive B:**

❑ 5.25" 1.2MB   ❑ 5.25" 1.2MB
❑ 5.25" 360KB   ❑ 5.25" 360KB
❑ 3.5"   1.44MB   ❑ 3.5"   1.44MB
❑ 3.5"   720KB   ❑ 3.5"   720KB

For use with NetWare v2.2 Installation manual.

DOS Workstation Configuration Worksheet

Location:	Installed By:

Type of computer:

Floppy Diskette Drives:	Drive A:	Drive B:
	❑ 5.25" 1.2MB	❑ 5.25" 1.2MB
	❑ 5.25" 360KB	❑ 5.25" 360KB
	❑ 3.5" 1.44MB	❑ 3.5" 1.44MB
	❑ 3.5" 720KB	❑ 3.5" 720KB

Internal Hard Drives: Drive C: _____ MB   Drive D: _____ MB

Memory: Standard _____ KB   Expanded _____ KB   Extended _____ KB

LAN Driver:

Name	Option No.	Interrupt (IRQ)	Station Addresses	I/O Base Address	DMA Channel	RAM/ROM Addresses

Boot Information:

❑ Boot from hard disk

❑ Boot from diskette

❑ Remote boot

Additional Information for Remote Boot Workstations Only

Remote reset enabled ❑ Yes ❑ No

❑ Remote reset PROM (s)_____

Installed on LAN board _____

❑ LAN board set to configuraiton option 0

Network address _____

Node number ❑ Hex ❑ Decimal _____

Remote boot filename _____

Files contained on the Master Shell Diskette:

DOS w/ Standard Drivers _____

❑ DOS System Files   DOS version:_____

❑ IPX.COM

❑ NET4.COM or ❑ NET3.COM or ❑ NET2.COM

❑ NETBIOS.EXE and INT2F.COM

❑ EMS or ❑ XMS

❑ SHELL.CFG options (see *Using the Network*)

ODI DOS w/ ODI Drivers _____

❑ DOS System Files DOS Version:_____

❑ LSL

❑ NE2   ❑ NE2000 ❑ 3C523 ❑ 3C503
              ❑ NE1000 ❑ NE2-32 ❑ LANSUP

❑ IPXODI

❑ Net x.COM

❑ EMS or ❑ XMS

❑ SHELL.CFG options
     (see *Using the Network*)

For use with the NetWare v2.2 Installation manual.

Copy this worksheet for each workstation on your network.

Router Configuration Worksheet

Location:		Installed by:	

Type of computer: **File server name:**

Software generated from: ❑ Floppy disk —❑ 5.25"-1.2MB   ❑ 3.5"-1.44MB

                            ❑ Hard disk

                            ❑ Network drive

Memory: Standard _____ KB   Expanded_____ KB   Extended _____ KB

Operating system mode: ❑ Dedicated real mode
(routing software)

                            ❑ Dedicated protected mode

                            ❑ Nondedicated protected mode

Nondedicated network address: _____

Communication buffers: ❑ 500 (default)   ❑ _____ (specified)

Network boards:

LAN	Name	Option No.	Interrupt (IRQ)	I/O Base Address	DMA Channel	Network Addresses
A						
B						
C						
D						

Notes:

For use with the NetWare v2.2 Installation manual.

FIGURE B.5

Volume Configuration Worksheet

Volume Name	Disk Ref. No.	Size (MB)	Directory Cached?	Directory Entries(#)	Notes:
SYS					

For use with the NetWare v2.2 Installation manual.

Operating System Generation Worksheet

Operating System mode: ❏ dedicated ❏ nondedicated
Nondedicated network address: _____
Number of communication buffers: _____
Will this machine be the server? ❏ Yes ❏ No
Include core printing services? ❏ Yes ❏ No

Network boards: _____

LAN	Name	Option No.	Hardware Settings			
			Interrupt (IRQ)	I/O Base Address	DMA Channel	Network Addresses
A						
B						
C						
D						

Disk drivers: _____

Channel	Disk Driver (HBA/Controller Type)	Option No.	Hardware Settings
0			
1			
2			
3			
4			

Notes:

For use with the NetWare v2.2 Installation manual.

Printer Configuration Worksheet

Printing Option

    Core   ☐

    Print Server ☐ (see *Print Server* for setup instructions)

Serial Printers

Port	Printer No.	Printer Manufacturer/Model No.	Baud Rate	Word Size	Stop Bits	Parity	XON/XOFF	Poll	Int
COM1									4
COM2									3

Parallel Printers

Port	Printer No.	Printer Manufacturer/Model No.	Poll	Int
LPT1				7
LPT2				5
LPT3				

Notes:

For use with *NetWare v2.2 Installation*.

NetWare 3.12 Worksheets

FIGURE C.I

File Server Worksheet

File server name: _____   **Installed by:** _____

File server make/model: _____

Memory: Base: _____ Extended: _____ Total: _____   **Server boot method:**
    ❏ Diskette
Internal network number: _____   ❏ Hard disk

Non-network board information: _____

_____

_____

Network boards (Fill in columns that apply to each network board.)

Name	LAN driver	I/O port	Memory address	Interrupt (IRQ)	DMA channel	Station/Node address	Slot number	Network number

Floppy Diskette Drives: A Drive: B Drive:
                           ❏ 5.25" 1.2MB   ❏ 5.25" 1.2MB
                           ❏ 5.25" 360KB   ❏ 5.25" 360KB
                           ❏ 3.5" 1.44MB   ❏ 3.5" 1.44MB
                           ❏ 3.5" 720KB   ❏ 3.5" 720KB

Internal hard drives: C Drive: Make/Model: _____ Size: _____
                                 DOS partition size: _____ NetWare partition: _____
                                 Controller Type: _____
                D Drive: Make/Model: _____ Size: _____

Disk coprocessor boards:

Name	Disk driver	I/O port	Interrupt

Disk subsystems: Total number of devices: _____
                      Number of mirrored drives: _____

1. Drive Make/Model: _____ Size: _____ Heads: _____ Cylinders: _____ Mirrored with #: _____
2. Drive Make/Model: _____ Size: _____ Heads: _____ Cylinders: _____ Mirrored with #: _____
3. Drive Make/Model: _____ Size: _____ Heads: _____ Cylinders: _____ Mirrored with #: _____
4. Drive Make/Model: _____ Size: _____ Heads: _____ Cylinders: _____ Mirrored with #: _____
5. Drive Make/Model: _____ Size: _____ Heads: _____ Cylinders: _____ Mirrored with #: _____
6. Drive Make/Model: _____ Size: _____ Heads: _____ Cylinders: _____ Mirrored with #: _____
7. Drive Make/Model: _____ Size: _____ Heads: _____ Cylinders: _____ Mirrored with #: _____
8. Drive Make/Model: _____ Size: _____ Heads: _____ Cylinders: _____ Mirrored with #: _____
9. Drive Make/Model: _____ Size: _____ Heads: _____ Cylinders: _____ Mirrored with #: _____
10. Drive Make/Model: _____ Size: _____ Heads: _____ Cylinders: _____ Mirrored with #: _____
11. Drive Make/Model: _____ Size: _____ Heads: _____ Cylinders: _____ Mirrored with #: _____
12. Drive Make/Model: _____ Size: _____ Heads: _____ Cylinders: _____ Mirrored with #: _____

FIGURE C.2

Workstation Configuration Worksheet

Current workstation owner: _____   Serial #: _____
Network address for board A: _____   Installed by: _____
Network address for board B: _____   Type of workstation: _____

Floppy Diskette Drives:

A Drive:	B Drive:
❑ 5.25" 1.2MB	❑ 5.25" 1.2MB
❑ 5.25" 360KB	❑ 5.25" 360KB
❑ 3.5" 1.44MB	❑ 3.5" 1.44MB
❑ 3.5" 720KB	❑ 3.5" 720KB

Memory: Base: _____ Extended: _____ Expanded: _____ Total: _____
Internal hard disks: _____ Memory: _____ Driver type: _____

Network board (Fill in columns that apply to each network board.)

Name	Option number	I/O address	Memory address	Interrupt (IRQ)	DMA channel	Station/Node address	Slot number

LAN driver

LAN A						
LAN B						

Boot information:
❑ Boot from hard disk
❑ Boot from diskette
❑ Boot by Remote Reset

DOS version _____

Remote Reset checklist:
❑ Network board set to configuration option 0
❑ Remote Reset PROM(s) installed on LAN board
❑ Remote Reset enabled on network board

Remote boot filename: _____

Files needed to connect to the network:
❑ IPX.COM
❑ NET4.COM or ❑ NET3.COM or ❑ EMSNET or ❑ XMSNET
❑ NETBIOS.EXE and INT2F.COM
❑ Others_____
❑ SHELL.CFG options _____
_____
_____

Copy one page for each workstation

FIGURE C.3

Directories Worksheet for File Server

Volume:	Directory	/Subdirectory	/Subdirectory	/Subdirectory	Files (Source)	File Attributes	Inherited Rights Mask (Applies only to the contents of this directory)	Directory Attributes (None automatically flagged)
SYS	LOGIN				login files (copied in at installation)	automatically flagged	[S R W C E M F A]	
	MAIL	subdirectory for each user created automatically				automatically flagged	[S R W C E M F A]	
	SYSTEM	subdirectory for queue/print server -automatically			system files (copied in at installation)	automatically flagged	[S R W C E M F A]	
	PUBLIC				public files (copied in at installation)	automatically flagged	[S R W C E M F A]	
	HOME	user name created automatically if you use RDEF			user created	user defined	[S]	
		Machine name	Operating system MSDOS DOS Directories	DOS version	copied files from DOS diskettes	[R F]	[S R W C E M F A]	

▶ · ◀

FIGURE C.4

Users Worksheet for File Server

Full Name	Username	Application Used	Groups	Access to Directories (Specify)	Time Restrictions (If not default)	Station Restrictions (Specify network and node address)	Managed by	Operator or Manager (Specify)

Group Worksheet for File Server _____ for Workgroup _____

Group Name	Basis of Group	Access to Directories	Trustee Directory Assignments	Access to Files	Trustee File Assignments
Full Name	**Managed by**				

Usernames of Members *(NetWare utilities list names alphabetically)*

FIGURE C.6

User Defaults for File Server _____ Workgroup _____

☐ YES ☐ NO Account has expiration date?
Date account expires: _____

☐ YES ☐ NO Allow unlimited credit?
Low balance limit: _____

☐ YES ☐ NO Limit concurrent connections?
Maximum concurrent connections: _____

☐ YES ☐ NO Intruder Detection/Lockout?

Intruder Detection Threshold
(number of incorrect login attempts permitted): _____

Bad login count retention time   Days:___ Hours:___ Min:___
(how long after last incorrect login)

☐ YES ☐ NO Lock account after detection? How long? Days:___ Hours:___ Min:___

☐ YES ☐ NO Require password?
Minimum password length: _____

☐ YES ☐ NO Force periodic password changes?
Days between forced changes: _____

☐ YES ☐ NO Limit grace logins?
Grace logins allowed: _____

☐ YES ☐ NO Require unique password?

☐ YES ☐ NO Install Accounting?

Initial Account Balance: _____

Time Restrictions		
SUN		
MON		
TUE		
WED		
THU		
FRI		
SAT		

FIGURE C.7

Trustee Directory Security Worksheet for File Server

Trustee Directory Rights to Be Assigned to Groups or Individual Users
(Possible trustee rights: Supervisory, Read, Write, Create, Erase, Modify, File Scan, Access Control)

Directories (To be used in conjunction with Directories Worksheet) USER OR GROUP NAME	EVERYONE											
SYS:LOGIN	[ ]											
MAIL	automatically assigned [W C]											
SYSTEM	no rights											
PUBLIC	automatically assigned [R F]											
PUBLIC DOS Directories	[R F]											

FIGURE C.8

Trustee File Security Worksheet for File Server

Use only if you need to redefine trustee rights for individual files

Trustee File Rights to Be Assigned to Groups or Individual Users
(Possible trustee rights: Supervisory, Read, Write, Create, Erase, Modify, File Scan, Access Control)

Directory Path	Filename	EVERYONE																	
		USER OR GROUP NAME																
SYS:LOGIN		[R F]																
MAIL		automatically assigned [W C]																
SYSTEM		no rights																
PUBLIC		automatically assigned [R F]																

FIGURE C.9

Login Scripts Worksheet for File Server _____

System Login Script

rem *preliminary commands (optional)*

rem *greeting (optional)*

rem *display login messages (optional)*

rem *attach to other file servers (optional)*

rem *NetWare utilities mappings*
    MAP INS S1:=SYS:PUBLIC

rem *DOS directory mapping and COMSPEC*
    MAP INS S2: =
    COMSPEC   = S2:COMMAND.COM

rem *application directory mappings*

rem *miscellaneous search drives (optional)*

rem *supervisor mappings*

rem *preliminary commands (optional)*
    IF "%LOGIN_NAME" = "SUPERVISOR" THEN

FIGURE C.9

Continued

rem   *home or username directory mapping*

rem   *work directory mapping (optional)*

rem   *default printer mappings or printing batch files (optional)*

rem   *display directory path at prompt*
SET PROMPT = "PG"

rem   *display all current drive settings (optional)*
MAP DISPLAY ON
MAP

rem   *run miscellaneous programs*

Basic User Login Script for _____ Group _____ Workgroup _____
rem   *set environmental variables*

rem   *individual drive mappings*

Basic User Login Script for _____ Group _____ Workgroup _____
rem   *set environmental variables*

rem   *individual drive mappings*

Answers to
CNA Exercises

EXERCISE 1.1: Microcomputer Concepts

1 · E

2 · F

3 · A

4 · T

5 · P

6 · J

7 · S

8 · G

9 · N

10 · L

11 · B

12 · Q

13 · O

14 · H

15 · M

16 · C

17 · K

18 · D

19 · I

20 · R

EXERCISE 2.1: Understanding NetWare Basics

1. G
2. M
3. K
4. C
5. D
6. A
7. B
8. E
9. F
10. J
11. P
12. L
13. O
14. N
15. I
16. Q
17. H

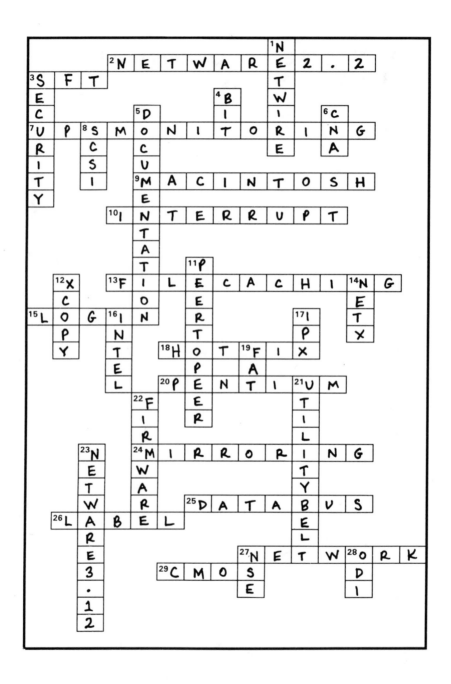

EXERCISE 2.2: Using NetWare 3.12 ElectroText

4 · 3 instances of the word CNA appear in the catalog.

6 · The word Supervisor appears 104 times in the Concepts manual and 631 times in the entire NetWare 3.12 library.

8 · The subtopic Viewer Features appears under Novell EletroText. The Quick Access Guide is not available on-line.

10 · A figure that describes the printing procedure screen appears when you double-click on the green camera icon. The book *NetWare 3.12 System Administration* appears in the outline.

EXERCISE 3.1: Using the MAP Command

1 · MAP U:=JERRY/SYS:USERS\OPUS

2 · MAP S1:=JERRY/SYS:PUBLIC

3 · MAP S16:=JERRY/SYS:PUBLIC\%MACHINE\%OS\%OS_VERSION

4 · MAP NEXT TOM/ACCT:GL\DATA

5 · MAP S16:=TOM/ACCT:AP

6 · MAP INSERT S3:=JERRY/APPS:DBASE

7 · MAP ROOT R:=JERRY/SYS:USERS\BILL\REPORTS

EXERCISE 3.2: The Effects of CD on MAP

5 · *Type MAP and press Enter. What happened and why?*
The system responds with **Bad Command or File Name** and the MAP command does not execute. This is because the **CD** command at the Z: drive remapped the PUBLIC subdirectory to the root. By doing so, the user no longer has a search mapping to the PUBLIC subdirectory and the MAP utility which resides in PUBLIC cannot be executed from this point.

7 · *Now that your Z drive has been remapped to the PUBLIC subdirectory, type MAP and press Enter. What happens and why?*
The MAP command is executed and displayed on the screen. This is because the CD command returned Z: to PUBLIC. The new search drive finds and executes the MAP utility.

13 · *Type MAP and press Enter. What happened and why?*
The system responded with **Bad Command or File Name** and the MAP command did not execute. Once again, the **CD** command remapped the Z: drive to root and the search drive 1 to PUBLIC no longer exists; it now points to the root. Therefore, when we go to the F: drive and type the **MAP** command, the system cannot find MAP.EXE.

16 · *Now type MAP and press Enter. What happened and why?*
The MAP command executes and appears on the screen. This is because the CD command was used to remap search drive 1 or the Z: drive from the root back to PUBLIC. This way, no matter where we are, even from the F: drive, the MAP command will execute because the system will use the search drive 1 to find the utility in the PUBLIC subdirectory.

22 · *Now type MAP and press Enter. What happened and why?*
The system will respond with **Bad Command or File Name** and the MAP command will not execute. This is because you have mapped a network drive to the PUBLIC subdirectory and not a search drive. Remember network drive mappings do not search through the directory tree for applications or .COM files.

24 · *Now type MAP and press Enter. What happened and why?*
The MAP command executes and appears on the screen. This is because a search drive mapping was inserted for the PUBLIC subdirectory.

EXERCISE 4.1: Calculating Effective Rights

Refer to Figure D.1 for an illustration of calculating effective rights.

1 · Effective rights = R, W, C, F.

2 · Effective rights = R and F.

3 · Effective rights = None.

4 · Combined rights = R, W, C, F.
Effective rights = R, W, F.

5 · The MRM restricts Read and File Scan. These are the default user rights. Therefore, the MRM should be set to W, C, E, M, A.

FIGURE D.1

Calculating Effective Rights
for NetWare 2.2

	R	W	C	E	M	F	A
USER RIGHTS	R	W	C			F	
MRM	R	W	C	E	M	F	A
EFFECTIVE RIGHTS	R	W	C			F	

CASE 1

	R	W	C	E	M	F	A
USER RIGHTS	R	W	C			F	
MRM	R					F	
EFFECTIVE RIGHTS	R					F	

CASE 2

	R	W	C	E	M	F	A
USER RIGHTS	R		C	E		F	
MRM		W			M		A
EFFECTIVE RIGHTS							

CASE 3

Calculating Effective Rights
for NetWare 2.2
(continued)

	R	W	C	E	M	F	A
COMBINED RIGHTS	R	W	C			F	
MRM	R	W		E		F	
EFFECTIVE RIGHTS	R	W				F	

CASE 4

	R	W	C	E	M	F	A
DEFAULT USER RIGHTS	R					F	
MRM		W	C	E	M		A
EFFECTIVE RIGHTS							

CASE 5

EXERCISE 6.1: Configuring NetWare Restrictions

7 · *Login as your supervisor equivalent account once again and change FRED's expiration date to yesterday's date. Exit SYSCON once again and attempt to login as FRED. Explain what happened.*
The system will respond with an error message saying This Account has expired or been disabled by the Supervisor. The system will not allow FRED to login. This is because FRED's expiration date has passed and the account has been locked.

9 · *Login as your supervisor equivalent account and enter FRED's account restrictions once again. Change the date the password expires to yesterday's date. Login in once again as FRED and note the changes below.*

The system allows FRED to login but displays the following message: Password for user FRED on Server CNA has expired. You have NO grace logins left to change your password. This is your last chance to change it. Enter your new password. The system freezes at the input screen asking for a new password to be entered.

13 · *Enlarge the file by typing* COPY WILMA.TXT + Z:MAIN.MENU NEW.TXT *and press Enter. Note what happens below and check the limitations in SYSCON once again for WILMA.*

During the copy procedure, the system responds with Insufficient disk space; 0 files copied and returns to the PUBLIC subdirectory. The disk space restriction in SYSCON state that the volume space limit is 4K and the volume space in use is also 4K; therefore, WILMA cannot copy or write any more files to the NetWare volume.

15 · *Enter SYSCON and choose FRED from the User Name window. In FRED's user information box, select Station Restrictions. Restrict FRED to the network number and node address that you wrote down for your workstation. Exit SYSCON and move to another workstation. Attempt to login as FRED. Make note of what happens.*

The system responds with an error message CNA/FRED:Attempting to login from an unapproved station. The supervisor has limited the stations that you are allowed to login on and the systems logs FRED out and responds with the F:\LOGIN> subdirectory.

16 · *... Make note below of what happens as the system approaches the half hour which is restricted.*

Five minutes before the half hour period, the system warns you that WILMA's account is approaching an unrestricted period. It asks that you please save your files and logout. At the half hour point, the system responds with another error message and clears the connections. The workstation receives the message Error Sending on the Network. Incidentally, this is dangerous because the system does not logout the user and close open files; it simply clears the connection.

18 · *Enter DINO's User Information window and create a password for him. Exit SYSCON and login as DINO twice, using the wrong password.*

Finally, the third time, note what happens.

Each time you login in as DINO with the incorrect password, the system responds with CNA/DINO: Access to server denied. You are attached to server CNA. The final time when you attempt to login as DINO, the system responds with the following error message: CNA/DINO: Intruder/Detection Lockout has disabled this account. At this point, DINO cannot login until the supervisor unlocks his intruder detection.

EXERCISE 6.2: Writing Login Scripts

```
REMARK **** Drive Mappings ***
MAP ROOT U:=SYS:USERS\%LOGIN_NAME
MAP G:=SYS:DATA
MAP NEXT SYS:LOGIN

MAP S1:=SYS:PUBLIC
MAP S2:=SYS:PUBLIC\%MACHINE\%OS\%OS_VERSION
MAP S3:=SYS:APPS\WP
MAP S16:=SYS:APPS\DBASE
MAP INSERT S3:=SYS:ACCT

REMARK **** COMSPEC ***
COMSPEC = S2:COMMAND.COM

REMARK **** Greetings ***
WRITE "Good %GREETING_TIME, %LOGIN_NAME!"
WRITE "Today is %DAY_OF_WEEK %MONTH_NAME %DAY. Have a
Nice Day!"

**** Informational ***
IF DAY_OF_WEEK = "Friday" THEN BEGIN
    WRITE "Congratulations, you made it through the week!
    WRITE "Welcome to your Friday."
END
```

```
IF MONTH_NAME = "May" AND DAY = "3" THEN BEGIN
    FIRE 9
    FIRE 9
    FIRE 9
    WRITE "Happy Birthday to you, happy birthday to you, you live
    in a zoo."
END

WRITE "Today is %DAY_OF_WEEK, %MONTH_NAME %DAY,
%YEAR"
WRITE "The Time is %HOUR:%MINUTE %AM_PM."
WRITE "You are running %OS %OS_VERSION."

IF MEMBER OF "Sales" THEN BEGIN
    DISPLAY SYS:GROUP\SALES\SALES.TXT
END

REMARK **** The END ***
DRIVE U:
EXIT "Start"
```

EXERCISE 6.3: Building Menus

BOB.MNU

```
%Bob's Personal Menu,12,40,1
Applications
    %Applications
Utilities
    %Utilities
System Configuration
    Z:SYSCON
File Management
    Z:FILER
Logout
    !LOGOUT
%Applications,1,1,2
Word Processing
```

```
        %Word Processing
Spreadsheet
    F:
    CD\APPS\LOTUS
    123
Windows
    F:
    CD\APPS\WINDOWS
    WIN : -- executes Windows without displaying the title screen.
Dbase
    F:
    CD\APPS\PARADOX
    PARADOX
%Word Processing,1,79,3
WordPerfect
    F:
    CD\APPS\WP51
    WP
Microsoft Word
    F:
    CD\APPS\WORD
    WORD
WordStar
    F:
    CD\APPS\WORDSTAR
    WS
%Utilities,24,79,4
Session
    Z:SESSION
Norton Utilities
    F:
    CD\APPS\UTILS
    NU
Print Management
    Z:PCONSOLE
```

Extracurricular

In order to stop users from escaping your menu, make a minor modification to your START.BAT file. Create an endless "loop" which brings users back to the menu when they try to escape. Here are the modifications:

```
ECHO OFF
CLS
CAPTURE Q=LASER /NB NFF TI=10
:TOP
MENU BOB
GOTO TOP
```

The only way to exit the menu is to press Cntrl+ Break. Note: Cntrl+Break can also be deactivated with the BREAK OFF login command.

EXERCISE 7.1: Using the CAPTURE command

1 · CAPTURE Q=REPORTS TI=7 C=4 NFF NAM=USERNAME B=FILENAME

2 · CAPTURE S=SALES Q=GRAPHICS NT NB L=2 FF

3 · CAPTURE L=3 CR=SYS:PLOTTER\FILENAME

4 · CAPTURE SH

5 · CAPTURE J=ACCOUNT

6 · CAPTURE NB NFF NT TI=10

7 · ENDCAP L=2

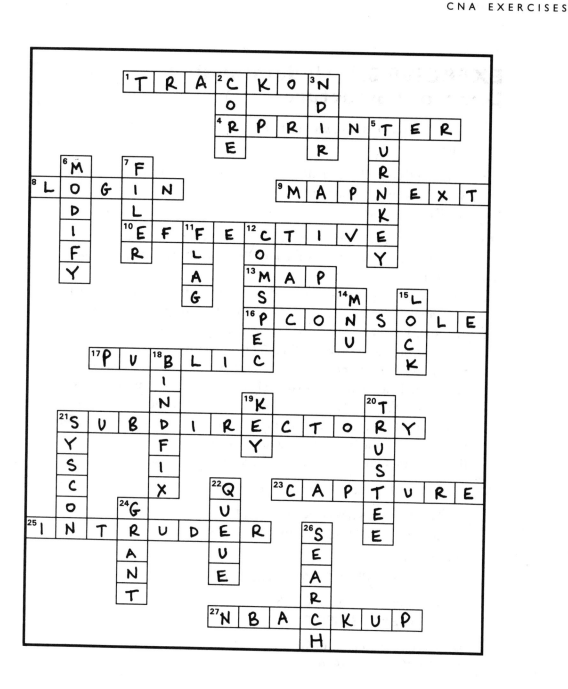

EXERCISE 8.1: Understanding Directory Structure

1 · *How many volumes have been defined in this directory structure?*
Four

2 · *Assuming that this is a NetWare 3.12 directory structure, which default system directories are missing?*
The ETC directory.

3 · *How is the volume structure organized in the accompanying graphic? What are the benefits of this structure? What are the possible pitfalls of this structure?*
The volume structure is organized according to the separation of network applications. In addition, users have been organized under their own specific USERS directory. The benefits of this structure are that users can be organized according to one directory structure and applications can be branched off into their own volume. This makes backup and fault tolerance extremely easy. The disadvantage of this structure is that the APPS volume can grow quite large and fill up independently of the available space in the SYS volume. The same goes for the ACCT volume. Keeping data in one volume then gives you the flexibility to more efficiently utilize available disk space.

4 · *Draw the path to each of the following directories:*

A · The REPORTS directory under BILL.
JERRY/SYS:USERS\BILL\REPORTS

B · MSDOS v7.00.
JERRY/SYS:PUBLIC\IBM_PC\MS-DOS\V7.00

C · The user directory for OPUS.
JERRY/SYS:USERS\OPUS

D · The data directory for GL.
TOM/ACCT:GL\DATA

5 · *How would you communicate or copy files from one subdirectory to another? Indicate the NetWare command you would use to copy a file from STIMPY's user directory to the data directory under GL.*

The easiest way to communicate between volumes and servers is to set drive mappings to destination subdirectories. To copy a file from STIMPY's user directory to the data directory under GL would be a two-step process.

I · Type **MAP NEXT TOM/ACCT:GL\DATA (G:)**

2 · From STIMPY's subdirectory, type **NCOPY filename G:**

6 · *What NetWare command would you use to view a graphical tree of the JERRY/SYS directory structure?*

From the root of the JERRY/SYS volume, type **LISTDIR /s**.

7 · *What NetWare directory command would you use to view the space available on the TOM/ACCT volume?*

From the TOM/ACCT volume root subdirectory, type **CHKVOL** for a command line listing and **VOLINFO** for a menu listing.

CASE STUDY I: Creating a Directory Structure for SNOUZER, INC.

See Figure D.2 for an illustration of the SNOUZER, INC. directory structure.

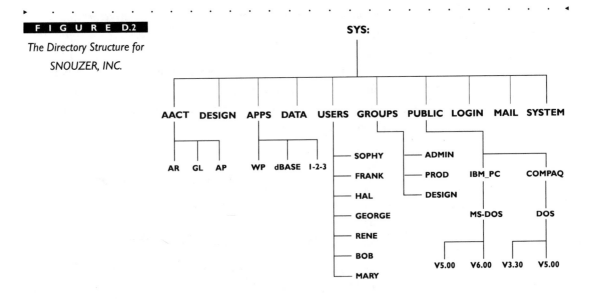

FIGURE D.2

The Directory Structure for
SNOUZER, INC.

EXERCISE 8.2: Using the MAP Command

1 · MAP ROOT G:=SYS:DATA

2 · MAP U:=SYS:USERS\JACK

3 · MAP S16:=SYS:APPS\WP
   MAP S16:=SYS:APPS\DEBASE

4 · *How does the system indicate a map root drive?*
   Within the MAP display in NetWare, the system will indicate a MAP
   ROOT by placing a backslash after the directory path.

5 · MAP DEL U:
   MAP U:=SYS:USERS\JILL

6 · MAP INSERT S3:=SYS:APPS\WINDOWS

7 · *Move to the G drive. Now type CD \ to return to the SYS volume root. What happens?*

Nothing! The system does not allow the user to move back to the volume root from the DATA subdirectory because the MAP ROOT indicates to NetWare that this is a pseudo root. Therefore, users who exist in drives which are MAP ROOTed cannot move back in the directory structure.

8 · MAP NEXT SYS:DATA

10 · *How does the system execute the MAP command from the U drive?*

The system executes the MAP command from the U: drive because MAP.EXE is a NetWare utility which exists in the PUBLIC subdirectory. By default, the PUBLIC subdirectory is defined as search drive 1 and therefore allows users to execute files from within the PUBLIC subdirectory without having to physically be located there.

14 · *Type **MAP** once again to verify your drive mappings. What happened and why?*

The system responded with the message **Bad Command or File Name** and the MAP command did not execute. This is because the search drive to PUBLIC which existed as Z: has been remapped to the root. This occurred when the user used the CD command while at the Z: drive.

16 · *Now type **MAP** and notice what happens.*

The MAP command executes and the system responds with a display of drive mappings on the screen. This occurred because the search drive 1 (Z:) was remapped to the PUBLIC subdirectory.

CASE STUDY II: Drive Mappings for Snouzer, Inc.

Regular Drive Mappings
MAP U:=SYS:USERS\[username]

MAP G:=SYS:GROUPS\[groupname]
MAP H:=SYS:DATA

Search Drive Mappings
MAP INSERT S1:=SYS:PUBLIC
MAP INSERT S2:=SYS:PUBLIC\%MACHINE\%OS\%OS_VERSION
MAP INSERT S3:=SYS:APPS\WP
MAP INSERT S4:=SYS:DESIGN
MAP INSERT S5:=SYS:ACCT
MAP INSERT S6:=SYS:APPS\dBASE
MAP INSERT S7:=SYS:APPS\123

EXERCISE 9.1: Understanding Special User Accounts

See Table D.1 for the answers to the Special User Accounts matrix.

		S	SE	WGM	UAM	CO	PQO	PSO
TABLE D.1	Grant supervisor equivalence	X	X					
Understanding Special User Accounts	Automatically acquire all rights to dir/file	X	X					
	Create other users/groups	X	X	X				
	Manage all user accounts	X	X					
	Manage special user accounts	X	X	X	X			

	S	SE	WGM	UAM	CO	PQO	PSO
Manager/operator type can be user or group	X	X	X				
Create WGM	X	X					
Assign managed users as UAMs	X	X	X	X			
Delete any user account	X	X					
Delete special user accounts	X	X	X	X			
User/supervisor functions of FCONSOLE	X	X			X		
Create print queues	X	X					
Manipulate print queues	X	X				X	
Delete print queue entries	X	X				X	
Create print servers	X	X					
Manage print server	X	X					X

EXERCISE 9.2: Calculating Effective Rights

See Figure D.3 for an illustration of calculating effective rights.

1 · Effective rights = R, W, C, F. The Explicit assignment overrides the IRM.

2 · Effective rights = S, R, W, C, E, M, F, A. The Supervisory right includes all other rights and it cannot be revoked by the IRM.

3 · Effective rights = S, R, W, C, E, M, F, A. The Supervisory right cannot be revoked by the IRM, even when it is inherited.

4 · Effective rights = W, M. The IRM only allows the W and M inherited rights to flow through.

5 · Effective rights = None. The IRM blocks all inherited rights from flowing through.

6 · Combined rights = R, W, C, E, F in SYS:PUBLIC. These rights are the combination of user and group assignments.
Effective rights = C, F in SYS:PUBLIC\DOS. The IRM only allows the C and F inherited rights to flow from the SYS:PUBLIC parent directory.

FIGURE D.3

Calculating Effective Rights for NetWare 3.12

	S	R	W	C	E	M	F	A
EXPLICIT TRUSTEE RIGHTS		R	W	C			F	
IRM	S	R					F	
EFFECTIVE RIGHTS		R	W	C			F	

CASE 1

	S	R	W	C	E	M	F	A
EXPLICIT TRUSTEE RIGHTS	S	R					F	
IRM		R	W	C			F	
EFFECTIVE RIGHTS	S	R	W	C	E	M	F	A

CASE 2

Calculating Effective Rights
for NetWare 3.12
(continued)

CASE 3

	S	R	W	C	E	M	F	A
EXPLICIT TRUSTEE ASSIGNMENTS								
INHERITED TRUSTEE ASSIGNMENTS	S	R	W	C	E	M	F	A
IRM		R	W				F	
EFFECTIVE RIGHTS	S	R	W	C	E	M	F	A

CASE 4

	S	R	W	C	E	M	F	A
EXPLICIT TRUSTEE ASSIGNMENTS								
INHERITED TRUSTEE ASSIGNMENTS		R	W		E	M		
IRM			W	C		M		A
EFFECTIVE RIGHTS			W			M		

CASE 5

	S	R	W	C	E	M	F	A
EXPLICIT TRUSTEE ASSIGNMENTS								
INHERITED TRUSTEE ASSIGNMENTS		R	W	C		M	F	
IRM	S				E			A
EFFECTIVE RIGHTS								

	S	R	W	C	E	M	F	A
EXPLICIT GROUP RIGHTS		R					F	
EXPLICIT USER RIGHTS			W	C	E			
COMBINED		R	W	C	E		F	
IRM	S			C			F	A
EFFECTIVE RIGHTS (Public\DOS)				C			F	

CASE 6

	S	R	W	C	E	M	F	A
EXPLICIT GROUP RIGHTS		R					F	
INHERITED USER RIGHTS			W	C		M		A
COMBINED		R	W	C		M	F	A
IRM	S			C	E			A
EFFECTIVE RIGHTS		R		C			F	A

CASE 7

7 · Combined rights = R, W, C, M, F, A. These rights are the combination of explicit group rights and inherited user rights. Hint: keep track of which rights are explicit and which are inherited.
Effective rights = R, C, F, A. The R and F explicit rights override the IRM. The C and A inherited rights are allowed to pass through by the IRM. The M and W inherited rights are blocked by the IRM.

EXERCISE 11.1: Debugging Login Script Commands

1 · TURN MAP should be written as MAP. TURN is not a valid login script command.

2 · An "=" sign is missing between the "S1:" and the "SYS" and there should not be a space between the colon and "PUBLIC".

3 · SEARCH 2 -- there should not be a space between "SEARCH" and "2". The "+" sign should be an "=" sign. The vertical bar after "%OS" should be a "\". There should be an underscore between "OS" and "VERSION".

4 · "COMPEC" should be "COMSPEC". There should be an "=" between "COMSPEC" and "S2" and there should be no space between "COMMAND" AND ".COM".

5 · "MAP 1" should read "MAP *1". The semicolon should be a colon both after the "1" and after the "SYS". There should be a "%" in front of "LOGIN" and there should be an underscore between "LOGIN" and "NAME".

6 · There should be an "*" in front of the "2". There should not be a space between the colon and the "=". "LOGIN NAME" again should appear as "%LOGIN_NAME".

7 · There should not be a space between the ":" and the "=".

8 · Again, there should not be a space between the ":" and the "=".

9 · There should not be a colon after the "WRITE" command. There should be a "%" before "GREETING" and there should be an underscore between "GREETING" and "TIME". There should also be an underscore between "LOGIN" and "NAME" and there should be a quote at the end of the whole LOGIN_NAME line.

10 · The WRITE command is missing the parameters for the time. It should read WRITE "The Time is %HOUR:%MINUTE %AM_PM".

11 • There should be a space between "IS" and "%". There should not be a space between the "%" and "DAY_OF_WEEK". There should be an underscore between "DAY" and "OF" and "WEEK". There should be an underscore between "MONTH" and "NAME". There should not be a space between "%" and "DAY" and it should all end with quotes.

12 • It's okay.

13 • There should be an "*" in front of "3". The semicolon should be a colon and the "SYS\" should be "SYS:".

14 • It's okay.

15 • It's okay.

16 • "TURN" should be removed. Again, TURN is not a valid login script command.

17 • It's okay.

CORRECTED VERSION:

1 • MAP DISPLAY OFF

2 • MAP S1:=SYS:PUBLIC

3 • MAP SEARCH2:=PUBLIC\%MACHINE\%OS\%OS_VERSION

4 • COMSPEC=S2:COMMAND.COM

5 • MAP *1:=SYS:USERS\%LOGIN_NAME

6 • MAP *2:=SYS:USERS\%LOGIN_NAME\REPORTS

7 • MAP S3:=SYS:APPLIC\WP

8 • MAP S4:=SYS:APPLIC\DATABASE

9 • WRITE "%GOOD GREETING_TIME, %LOGIN_NAME"

10 • WRITE "THE TIME IS %HOUR:%MINUTE %AM_PM"

11 • WRITE "TODAY IS %DAY_OF_WEEK, %MONTH_NAME %DAY"

12 · If %2 ="DATABASE" THEN BEGIN

13 · MAP *3: SYS:DBDATA

14 · END

15 · DISPLAY SYS:SUPERVISOR\MESSAGE.TXT

16 · MAP DISPLAY ON

17 · MAP

CASE STUDY III: Writing Login Scripts for SNOUZER, INC.

```
REMARK **** Greetings ***
WRITE "Welcome to SNOUZER, INC. -- The home of world famous
doggy doos!!"
WRITE "Good %GREETING_TIME, %LOGIN_NAME!"
WRITE "Today is %DAY_OF_WEEK %MONTH_NAME %DAY. Have a
Nice Day!"

REMARK **** Drive Mappings ***
MAP U:=SYS:USERS\%LOGIN_NAME
IF MEMBER OF "ADMIN" THEN MAP G:=SYS:GROUPS\ADMIN
IF MEMBER OF "PROD" THEN MAP G:=SYS:GROUPS\PROD
IF MEMBER OF "DESIGN" THEN MAP G:=SYS:GROUPS\DESIGN
MAP H:=SYS:DATA

MAP INSERT S1:=SYS:PUBLIC
MAP INSERT S2:=SYS:PUBLIC\%MACHINE\%OS\%OS_VERSION
MAP INSERT S3:=SYS:APPS\WP
MAP INSERT S4:=SYS:DESIGN
MAP INSERT S5:=SYS:ACCT
MAP INSERT S6:=SYS:APPS\dBASE
MAP INSERT S7:=SYS:APPS\123

REMARK **** COMSPEC ***
COMSPEC = S2:COMMAND.COM
```

```
REMARK **** Informational ***
IF DAY_OF_WEEK = "Friday" THEN BEGIN
    WRITE "Congratulations, you made it through the week!
    WRITE "Welcome to your Friday."
    FIRE 9
    FIRE 8
END

IF DAY = "20" THEN BEGIN
    FDISPLAY SYS:PUBLIC\PAY.TXT
    FIRE 9
    PAUSE
END

REMARK **** The END ***
DRIVE U:
EXIT "Start"
```

CASE STUDY IV: Building a Menu System for **SNOUZER, INC.**

USERNAME.SRC

(Note: USERNAME.SRC must be compiled into USERNAME.DAT using MENUMAKE.EXE)

```
MENU 1,SNOUZER, INC.
    ITEM Applications
        SHOW 2
    ITEM User Utilities
        EXEC Session
    ITEM File Management
        EXEC Filer
    ITEM Logout
        EXEC Logout

MENU 2,Applications
```

```
ITEM ACCT
   SHOW 3
ITEM DBASE {Batch}
   EXEC DBase
ITEM WP {Batch}
   EXEC WP
ITEM 123 {Batch}
   EXEC 123
ITEM DESIGN
   EXEC Design

MENU 3,ACCT
ITEM A/P
   EXEC AP
ITEM G/L
   EXEC GL
ITEM A/R
   EXEC AR
```

User the following START.BAT to create a secure menu system:

START.BAT

```
ECHO OFF
CLS
CAPTURE Q=SNOUZER /NB TI=10 NT NFF
:TOP -- creates a loop so users can't "escape" the menu
NMENU username
GOTO TOP -- points to the beginning of the loop
```

EXERCISE 13.1: Performance Management Components

1 · I

2 · B

3 · F

4 · J

5 · C

6 · A

7 · H

8 · G

9 · D

10 · E

EXERCISE 13.2: Memory Pools

1 · I

2 · J

3 · C

4 · D

5 · A, E, G

6 · F

7 · B, H

CASE STUDY V: Performance Management for SNOUZER, INC.

1 · *File access has been slow. The users have been experiencing slow file access and sluggish applications. What MONITOR statistics would you check?*

Compare the number of **Total Cache Buffers** with **Original Cache Buffers** in the Main Screen of MONITOR. Calculate the percentage of "Total Cache Buffers".

How would you remedy the situation?

File caching is the key NetWare 3.12 performance management component. If the percentage of Total Cache Buffers approaches 20%, ADD MORE MEMORY IMMEDIATELY! Ideally, it should never drop below 50%. Also, consider unloading NLMs, or downing the server to regain lost Permanent or Alloc memory.

2 · *Error sending on network. Some users are experiencing the message **Error sending on network** and loosing their connection. This occurs at random intervals when trying to access the file server. What MONITOR statistics would you check?*

Check **Packet Receive Buffers** in the Main Screen of MONITOR.

How would you remedy the situation?

Users are experiencing the problems because there are not enough packet receive buffers to store their incoming requests. If the number approaches 100, consider increasing the maximum to 500—SET Maximum Packet Receive Buffers = 500. Also, consider increasing the minimum to 50 so that PRBs become immediately allocated—SET **Minimum Packet Receive Buffers = 50.**

This parameter must be set in the STARTUP.NCF file. You will need to reboot the file server for the changes to take effect.

3 · *The server is slow to respond when it is rebooted. Whenever Sophy turns on the server, it takes a great deal of time for it to come back up. This has caused some concern in that the system is vulnerable and down during that time period.*

What MONITOR statistic would you check?

Check **Packet Receive Buffers** in the Main Screen of MONITOR.

How would you remedy the situation?

The server is slow in responding because the minimum packet receive buffers are set too low. Consider increasing the minimum to 50 so that

PRBs become immediately allocated—SET Minimum Packet Receive Buffers = 50. This parameter must be set in the STARTUP.NCF file. You will need to reboot the file server for the changes to take affect.

4 • *Directory searches are sluggish. Users are experiencing very sluggish directory searches. In addition, some users are losing their connection during directory searches.*
What MONITOR statistics would you check?
Check **Directory Cache Buffers** in the Main Screen of MONITOR.
How would you remedy the situation?
Directory cache buffers improve the performance of directory searches by caching the DET and FAT tables. If the number of Directory Cache Buffers approaches or exceeds 100, consider increasing the minimum—SET Minimum Directory Cache Buffers = 200. Also, consider increasing the maximum—SET Maximum Directory Cache Buffers =500.

5 • *NLMs won't load. Sophy has been trying to load some network management NLMs at the server and has found that NLMs which require pop-up menus will not load. She receives an error message to the effect that the appropriate memory pool is out of space.*
Which MONITOR statistic would you check?
Check **Alloc Memory Pool** in the Server Memory Statistics screen under Resource Utilization of MONITOR. Compare the "total bytes" value with the number of bytes "in use".
How do you remedy the situation?
Most NLMs, especially the programs with pop-up menus, require large amounts of Alloc Short Term memory. If the total number of bytes of Alloc Short Term memory approaches 8,000,000, NLMs do not have enough memory to load. Consider increasing the maximum value to 9 million in 1,000,000 byte increments—SET Maximum Alloc Short Term Memory = 9,000,000.

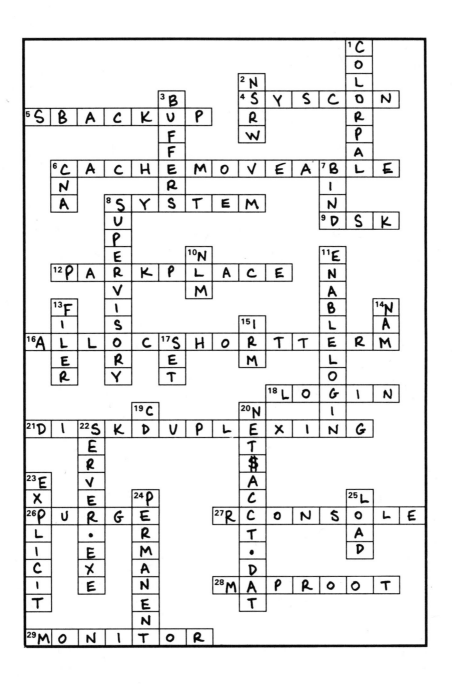

Acronyms

AFP	AppleTalk Filing Protocol
ALU	Arithmetic Logic Unit
ANSI	American National Standards Institute
ASCII	American Symbolic Code for Information Interchange
AT	Advanced Technology
AUI	Auxiliary Unit Interface
BIOS	Basic Input/Output System
BIT	Binary Digit
BNC	Bayonet Navy Connector
CBT	Computer Based Training
CD	Change Directory
CD-ROM	Compact Disk-Read Only Memory
CGA	Color Graphics Adapter
CI	Copy Inhibit
CIM	CompuServe Information Manager
CIS	CompuServe Information Service
CLS	Clear Screen
CLU	Command Line Utility
CMOS	Complementary Metal Oxide Semiconductor
CNA	Certified NetWare Administrator
CNE	Certified NetWare Engineer
CNI	Certified NetWare Instructor
COMSPEC	Command Specifier
CPU	Central Processing Unit

CRT	Cathode Ray Tube
DA	Desk Accessory
DCB	Directory Cache Buffer
DCB	Disk Coprocessor Board
DCE	Data Communications Equipment
DEB	Directory Entry Blocks
DET	Directory Entry Table
DI	Delete Inhibit
DIP	Dual In-line Package
DIX	Digit Intel Xerox
DMA	Direct Memory Access
DOS	Disk Operating System
DPI	Dots Per Inch
DRAM	Dynamic Random Access Memory
.DSK	Server Disk Driver
DTE	Data Terminal Equipment
ECNE	Enterprise Certified NetWare Engineer
EGA	Enhanced Graphics Adapter
EISA	Extended Industry Standard Architecture
EMI	Electromagnetic Interference
EMS	Expanded Memory Specification
EPROM	Erasable Programmable Read Only Memory
ESDI	Enhanced Small Device Interface
ETLA	Extended Three Letter Acronym

FAT	File Allocation Table
FCB	File Cache Buffer
FPU	Floating Point Unit
FTAM	File Transfer Access Management
GB	Gigabytes
HMA	High Memory Area
HPFS	High Performance File System
IBM	International Business Machines
IDE	Intelligent Drive Electronics
INT	Interrupt
I/O	Input/Output
IPX	Internetwork Packet Exchange
IRM	Inherited Rights Mask
IRQ	Interrupt Request Line
ISA	Industry Standard Architecture
K	Knowledge
KB	Kilobytes
KISS	Keep It Safely Shallow or Keep It Safely Secure
.LAN	LAN Disk Driver
LAN	Local Area Network
LIM	Lotus Intel Microsoft
LSL	Link Support Layer
MAN	Metropolitan Area Network
MB	Megabytes

MB/S	Megabits per Second
MCA	Micro Channel Architecture
MD	Make Directory
MFM	Modified Frequency Modulation
MHZ	Megahertz
MIPS	Million Instructions Per Second
MLID	Multiple Link Interface Driver
MRM	Maximum Rights Mask
MSAU	Multistation Access Unit
N	Normal
NAEC	Novell Authorized Education Center
.NAM	Name Space Module
NCP	NetWare Core Protocol
NEAP	Novell Education Academic Partner
NFF	No Form Feed
NFS	Network File System
NIC	Network Interface Card
NLM	NetWare Loadable Module
NOS	Network Operating System
NSE	Network Support Encyclopedia
NT	New Technology
NT	No Tabs
ODI	Open Datalink Interface
OS	Operating System

OS/2	Operating System/2
OSI	Open System Interconnection
PC	Personal Computer
PDF	Printer Definition File
PDS	Processor Direct Slot
PIXELS	Picture Elements
PRB	Packet Receive Buffer
PROM	Programmable Read Only Memory
PS/2	Personal System 2
PS	Print Server
PSC	Print Server Control
Q	Queue
Q	Quote
R	Reminder
RA	Read Audit
RAM	Random Access Memory
RD	Remove Directory
REM	Remark
RETLA	Really Extended Three Letter Acronym
RGB	Red Green Blue
RI	Rename Inhibit
RISC	Reduced Instruction Set Computing
RLL	Run Length Limited
RMF	Remote Management Facility

RO	Read-Only
ROM	Read Only Memory
RPM	Revolutions Per Minute
RSPX	Remote SPX
RW	Read-Write
S	Shareable
SCSI	Small Computer System Interface
SFT	System Fault Tolerance
SH	Shared
SH	Show
SIMMS	Single In-line Memory Modules
SMSP	Storage Management Services Protocol
SNA	System Network Architecture
SPX	Sequenced Packet Exchange
SRAM	Static Random Access Memory
SYSCON	System Configuration
T	Tip
TB	Terabytes
TCP/IP	Transmission Control Protocol/Internet Protocol
TI	Time Out
TLA	Three Letter Acronym
TLI	Transport Level Interface
TSA	Target Service Agent
TSR	Terminate-Stay Resident

TTS	Transactional Tracking System
UMB	Upper Memory Block
UPS	Uninterruptible Power Supply
VAP	Value Added Process
VGA	Video Graphics Array
VINES	Virtual Network System
VIP	Very Important People
WA	Write Audit
WAN	Wide Area Network
WORMFACE	Write Read Modify File-Scan Access-Control Create Erase
WOS	Workstation Operation System
WSGEN	Workstation Shell Generation
XMS	Extended Memory Specification

NetWare Installation
Simulations

This appendix walks you through the NetWare installation simulations found on *Novell's CNA Study Guide* Companion Disk 2. There are three simulations which cover all aspects of NetWare server, workstation, and router installation. They are:

- ▸ NetWare 2.2 Server Installation—INSTALL

- ▸ NetWare Workstation Installation—WSGEN

- ▸ NetWare Router Installation—ROUTEGEN

See Appendix G for details about the companion diskettes and instructions for installing them. Let's begin with the NetWare 2.2 Server Installation.

NetWare 2.2 Server Installation

In this exercise, you will use an education edition of the installation program. This simulation uses a modified version of the installation files. These files don't actually write to or look for a hard disk.

You will see the actual screens displayed in a real installation. Using the abbreviated worksheet on the next page, you will fill in the same information in this simulation as you would in a real installation. While you may choose any LAN driver in this simulation, the hard disk information is set. You must choose Industry Standard Architecture (ISA) for Channel 0, and Disk Coprocessor Board (DCB) for Channel 1. If you select any other disk driver, the program will still display ISA and DCB as the selected drivers. The DCB in the simulation has two embedded SCSI disk drives connected.

You will also be asked if you want to use NetWare Core Printing or not. Select Yes to this question and continue. For this simulation you MUST also answer Yes to the question **Will this be the server?** The rest of the options presented during the installation will not affect the success or failure of this simulation. You will, however, be able to see the differences in sub-options by making different choices each time you run the program.

Begin by reviewing the accompanying installation worksheet. Note: These worksheets can be found in Appendix B.

INSTALLATION WORKSHEET

1 · Operating system mode: Dedicated

2 · Network board type: NE2000

3 · Configuration of workstation network board: Option 0

4 · Configuration of file server network board: Option 0

5 · Network address: Choose from 1 to FFFFFFE

6 · File server disk channel: Channel 0

7 · File server disk driver type: ISA

8 · Configuration of file server disk driver: Option 0

9 · Number of communication buffers: 150

10 · File server name: CNA

11 · Printing services to use: Core Printing

12 · Number of open files: 300

13 · Which drives will be mirrored, and to where: None

14 · Volume names and sizes: 1st = SYS: 2nd = EMPTY:

INSTALLATION INSTRUCTIONS

Prior to a real installation, you would fill out the following worksheets; copies of them can be found in Appendix B.

- ▸ Operating System Generation Worksheet
- ▸ File Server Definition Worksheet
- ▸ Volume Configuration Worksheet
- ▸ DOS Workstation Configuration Worksheet

Use the above worksheets for this exercise.

I · Insert the SYSTEM-1 diskette or move to the CNASIMS subdirectory. Type **install** and press Enter. The Available Topics menu will appear.

2 · Select Advanced Installation. The system will respond with the welcome screen. Read it carefully, and press Enter to continue.

3 · The Operating System Generation screen appears. Refer to Figure F.1. Enter the requested information from the above worksheet. This form is larger than a single screen can show. Use the arrow keys to scroll through the different options until you complete every item.

4 · After completing the form, press F10 to save and continue. Messages that server utilities are being created will appear on the screen. The system will create custom versions of key server utilities (including COMPSURF) a disk surface analysis tool.

5 · The Z-test menu will appear. It allows system managers to test the zero boot track of internal server disks. To select and test drives, press Enter.

6 · Highlight a hard disk and press Enter.

7 · Select Yes to confirm that you wish to test the disk. You will see a screen warning you that this is a destructive test. Have no fear—this is only a simulation!

FIGURE F.1

Operating System Generation Screen of NetWare 2.2 Server Installation

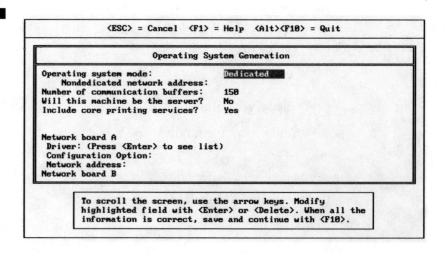

8 · The system will perform a random read/write test of all blocks in the zero boot track. After the test has finished, the results screen will appear. In the simulation you will see both Channel 0 ISA, and Channel 1 DCB.

9 · Press F10 to quit testing. The File Server Definition screen will appear. Refer to Figure F.2. Fill in the form, referring to your worksheet for the information.

10 · Press F10 to save and continue.

The system displays informational messages. The installation is now complete. At this point in a real installation you would reboot the file server with no disk in the floppy drive, and NetWare would come to life. Congratulations!

FIGURE F.2

File Server Definition Screen of NetWare 2.2 Server Installation

```
          <ESC> = Cancel   <F1> = Help   <Alt><F10> = Quit

                         File Server Definition

    File server information

        Server name:                ████████████████
        Maximum open files:         240
        Maximum open index files:   0
        TTS backout volume:         SYS
        TTS maximum transactions:   100
        Limit disk space:           No
        Install NetWare for Macintosh:  No

    Hard disk information


      To review or modify the information, use the arrow keys. Modify
      a highlighted field with <Enter>. Save and continue with <F10>.
```

NetWare Workstation Installation

The WSGEN program is very similar in operation to INSTALL. It takes just a few minutes to run. The program asks what LAN driver will be used in the workstation and how it is configured. After these selections are made, the WSGEN program creates an IPX.COM file customized for the chosen network board and its specified settings.

The configuration chosen in WSGEN must match the configuration settings made on the board installed in the workstation. Two items are selected:

- The type of Network Interface Card
- The configuration option

These options should be recorded in the NetWare Log.

INSTALLATION INSTRUCTIONS

In this exercise you will run a simulated WSGEN utility and select appropriate LAN cards with the corresponding drivers and configuration options. The result will be a virtual IPX.COM file.

Prior to running WSGEN, you should fill out the DOS Workstation Configuration Worksheet; a copy is found in Appendix B. For this exercise, you can choose whatever options you like—be creative! Fill out the worksheet accordingly, and then run WSGEN using your worksheet as a guide.

1 • Insert the WSGEN diskette or move to the CNASIMS subdirectory. Type **wsgen** and press Enter. The opening screen will appear. Note: you can use the F1 (HELP) key at every screen to become familiar with WSGEN and gain a deeper understanding of what is happening during the execution of this utility.

2 • Press Enter to continue. The LAN Drivers screen will appear. See Figure F.3.

3 • Select the appropriate network driver. Refer to your worksheet for the driver type. The Configuration Options screen will appear. Highlight the appropriate configuration and press Enter.

4 • The system will ask **Do you want to generate the NetWare workstation software with this configuration?** Select Yes and press Enter.

5 • WSGEN will generate the appropriate IPX.COM and copy it to your WSGEN diskette or WSGEN subdirectory. Press Enter to exit. The workstation software has been generated successfully.

LAN Drivers Screen for
NetWare Workstation
Installation

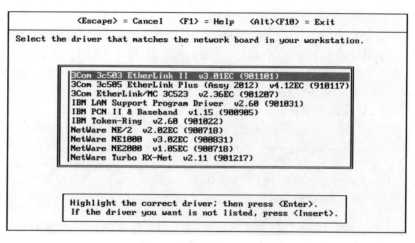

```
    <Escape> = Cancel    <F1> = Help   <Alt><F10> = Exit

Select the driver that matches the network board in your workstation.


    3Com 3c503 EtherLink II  v3.01EC (901101)
    3Com 3c505 EtherLink Plus (Assy 2012)  v4.12EC (910117)
    3Com EtherLink/MC 3C523   v2.36EC (901207)
    IBM LAN Support Program Driver  v2.60 (901031)
    IBM PCN II & Baseband  v1.15 (900905)
    IBM Token-Ring  v2.60 (901022)
    NetWare NE/2  v2.02EC (900718)
    NetWare NE1000  v3.02EC (900831)
    NetWare NE2000  v1.05EC (900718)
    NetWare Turbo RX-Net  v2.11 (901217)


    Highlight the correct driver; then press <Enter>.
    If the driver you want is not listed, press <Insert>.
```

In your own company's LAN environment, you would need to copy the result-ing IPX.COM file and the appropriate shell files to the boot device of the intended workstation. For those workstations that are using different network boards, simply re-run the WSGEN utility, choosing the options required for that worksta-tion. You can only use *one* LAN driver and *one* configuration option at a time in WSGEN.

NetWare Router Installation

ROUTEGEN.EXE creates the file to operate an external router—an intelligent data exchange device. A router performs a special function which manages the exchange of information (in the form of data packets) between different network cabling systems.

A router can connect cabling systems that use similar or different kinds of transmission media and addressing systems. It not only passes packets of data be-tween different cabling systems, but also routes the packets through the most ef-ficient path. When used to run NetWare 2.2 VAPs, a router becomes like a sub-server. In other words, it offloads some of the overhead from the file server.

The ROUTEGEN.EXE utility is similar to WSGEN.EXE. It opens with an in-formation screen explaining how to use it.

INSTALLATION INSTRUCTIONS

In this exercise, you will simulate the creation of a router (using ROUTEGEN) and select appropriate LAN cards with their appropriate drivers and configuration options. This will result in a file called ROUTER.EXE.

ROUTER.EXE would normally be copied to the boot device of the router PC. You will not be installing an actual router at this time—you will only generate the file to become familiar with how it works.

Prior to a real installation, you would fill out the Router Configuration Worksheet (copies can are found in Appendix B).

1 · Insert the ROUTEGEN diskette or move to the CNASIMS subdirectory. Type **routgen** and press Enter.

2 · After reading the opening screen, press Enter. The Router Generation screen will appear. Refer to Figure F.4.

3 · Press Enter to view the Mode options. Choose Dedicated Real Mode and press Enter. If you choose Nondedicated Protected Mode, move to the Process Address option and input any number between 1 and FFFFFFFE. Note: this number must be different from any other network address in the LAN.

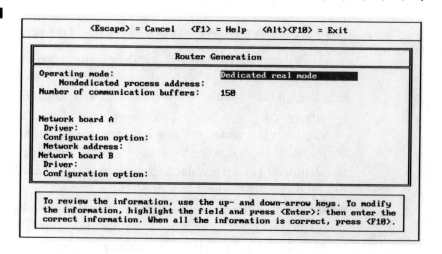

F I G U R E F.4

Router Generation Screen for NetWare Router Installation

4 · Move to Communication Buffers and notice the default is 150. Press F1 to view the HELP screen. Press Escape to exit HELP; then change the number of communication buffers to 200.

5 · Next you must decide which LAN drivers to use and what their configuration options will be. The highlight bar will automatically move to Driver under Network board A.

6 · Press Enter. The LAN Drivers screen will appear. Choose a driver and press Enter.

7 · You will be presented with a screen of options for that particular type of board. Most of the time the default option (option 0) is available and should be used—at least for the first LAN board.

8 · Next give a network address for that one NIC only. Each network address refers to the specific internal router NIC. Each network must have a unique address. The address can be any hexadecimal number between 1 and FFFFFFFE. Note: the numbers zero and FFFFFFFF are not allowed.

9 · Repeat steps 5 through 8 for Network board B. Note: if an "*" appears, it means there is an address or interrupt conflict. This allows you to determine which device should be altered to fit the needs of that individual router machine.

10 · For this exercise, select only two network boards. When the two are configured as you want them, press F10 to continue. The system will respond with some linking messages. You are finished. Congratulations!

Companion Diskette
Instructions

This appendix provides detailed information and installation instructions for the two companion diskettes to Novell's CNA Study Guide. These diskettes include three valuable CNA tools:

- ► CNA Practice Tests
- ► NetWare Buyer's Guide
- ► NetWare Installation Simulations

CNA PRACTICE TESTS

Whether you are interested in becoming a CNA/CNE or simply expanding your NetWare knowledge, these practice tests will help you evaluate your NetWare skills. The CNA practice tests will also give you an opportunity to practice answering questions in a similar format to those on the actual CNA/CNE certification exams. These tests cover all the CNA test objectives; therefore, the higher your score, the better your chances of passing the "real" exams.

The CNA practice tests are organized into two main groups: Novell's CNA Study Guide Tests and Novell's CNA Assessment Tests. The Study Guide tests are broken into 13 sections—one for each chapter. Readers are encouraged to review each chapter's test questions as they continue through the book. Novell's CNA Assessment Tests are included to provide a measure of your NetWare knowledge and preparedness for the actual CNA certification exams. The tests are broken into 15 sections—each corresponding to an appropriate section in Novell's 2.2 or 3.12 CNA program.

In both cases, at the end of each section, your numerical score will appear, enabling you to evaluate your own performance. Answers for Novell's CNA Study Guide questions are optionally provided. A review of your score should help you choose the appropriate path for your Novell-authorized education—instructor-led courses or computer-based training. Either way, these practice tests will help you achieve your ultimate goal—CNA! Let's get started!

1 · Insert Companion Disk 1 into any diskette drive.

2 · Switch to that drive (i.e. type **A:** or **B:** and ENTER).

3 · Type **CNATEST [destination]**, where destination is a valid local or network drive letter followed by a colon (i.e. **CNATEST C:**). Press ENTER. The system will copy files to your destination drive and decompress them into the CNATEST subdirectory.

4 · Switch to the destination drive (i.e. type **C:** and ENTER).

5 · Change directories to the CNATEST subdirectory. Type **CD \CNATEST** and press ENTER.

6 · To execute the tests, type **CNA** and press ENTER.

7 · Have Fun!

NETWARE BUYER'S GUIDE

The *NetWare Buyer's Guide* is a comprehensive library of Novell's strategies, product line, and services. It is a valuable CNA tool for understanding the relationship between NetWare and its support products. The guide is also important for designing sophisticated NetWare LANs. The *Buyer's Guide* is available twice a year—April and October. Until recently, it was only available in paper form. This on-line version of the guide provides instant access to critical Novell information.

The on-line *NetWare Buyer's Guide* uses a unique hyper-text retrieval program called *Folio Views*. This is the same program used in all of NetWare's help facilities. Folio provides the user with hypertext access, complex search strings, and multiple windows. In addition, the Folio View provides illustrations and technical graphics. Most of all, it's very easy to use.

The *NetWare Buyer's Guide* is broken into five sections and three appendixes. Here is a quick preview:

- ▸ Novell Corporate and Strategic Overview
- ▸ Customer Success Stories

- ▶ Novell Product Overview

- ▶ Novell Products

- ▶ Novell Support and Education Programs

- ▶ Appendix A—Novell Offices

- ▶ Appendix B—Alliances

- ▶ Appendix C—Glossary

You can also use the guide as a learning tool. Refer to it as you continue through Novell's CNA Study Guide and reference key concepts, products, and NetWare specifications. Remember—the CNA with the largest utility belt wins!

Ready to try it?

1 · Insert Companion Disk 1 into any diskette drive.

2 · Switch to that drive (i.e. type **A:** or **B:** and ENTER).

3 · Type **CNAGUIDE [destination]**, where destination is a valid local or network drive letter followed by a colon (i.e. **CNAGUIDE C:**) and press ENTER.

4 · The NetWare Buyer's Guide installation will create a CNAGUIDE subdirectory off of the root of your destination drive.

5 · The system will copy files to your destination drive and de-compress them into the CNAGUIDE subdirectory. The NetWare Buyer's Guide requires approximately 2MB of disk space.

6 · Switch to the destination drive (i.e. type **C:** and press ENTER). Change directories to the CNAGUIDE subdirectory. Type **BUYERS** and press ENTER.

7 · Have Fun!

NETWARE INSTALLATION SIMULATIONS

Understanding NetWare is one thing, installing it is another!

The installation and configuration of NetWare servers is a complex and sophisticated process. NetWare 2.2 uses a menu-driven program called INSTALL.EXE, where as NetWare 3.12 involves loading various NetWare Loadable Modules, in order. In addition to server installation, the NetWare system manager is responsible for workstation installation (WSGEN.EXE) and external routers (ROUTEGEN.EXE).

Novell's CNA Study Guide walks you through the roles and responsibilities of NetWare system management. Unfortunately, the CNA rarely has the opportunity to implement a server, workstation, or router installation. Until now! We have included three installation simulations for your enjoyment:

- ▸ NetWare 2.2 server installation—INSTALL.EXE

- ▸ NetWare workstation installation—WSGEN.EXE

- ▸ NetWare external router installation—ROUTEGEN.EXE

Note: NetWare 3.12 server installation does not lend itself well to a simulation exercise.

These simulations use the actual installation files. However, they have been modified to avoid writing to or looking for a hard disk. Instead, the simulations write to a dummy file which appears as a virtual disk. Therefore, the NetWare installation simulations can be run from diskette, local disk, or network drive. In order to achieve this level of virtual reality, we had to make a few assumptions:

Hard Disk Type:	ISA	DCB—two WNIM drives
Channel Number:	0	1

In addition, the following files have been modified:

INSTOVL.EXE	on SYSTEM-1
DSKSCTRS.EDU	on SYSTEM-1
NLINK.EXE	on SYSTEM-2
DCONFIG.EXE	on SYSTEM-2
ZTEST.EXE	on SYSTEM-2

Let's give it a try!

1 · Insert Companion Disk 2 into any diskette drive.

2 · Switch to that drive (i.e. type **A:** and press ENTER).

3 · Type **CNASIMS [destination]**, where destination is a valid local or network drive letter followed by a colon (i.e. **CNASIMS C:**). Press ENTER.

4 · The system will copy simulation files to five defined subdirectories under the CNASIMS directory of your destination drive. It will then copy INSTALL, WSGEN, and ROUTEGEN to the CNASIMS directory.

5 · To perform the simulations, follow the instructions in Appendix F.

FLOPPY DISKETTE INSTALLATION

These simulations may also be run from four high-density (1.2MB or 1.44MB) diskettes. To install the simulations on diskette, follow these simple steps:

▸ Format five high-density diskettes and label them as SYSTEM, **SYSTEM-1, SYSTEM-2, WSGEN,** and **ROUTEGEN**.

▸ Follow installation steps 1–4 above.

▸ Copy all files from each CNASIMS subdirectory to the appropriate diskettes (i.e., **COPY C:\CNASIMS\SYSTEM-1*.*** to the SYSTEM-1 diskette).

▸ Follow the instructions in Appendix F.

Index

. . . .

Note to the Reader: Page numbers in **boldface** refer to primary explanations of topics. Page numbers in *italic* refer to illustrations.

SPECIAL CHARACTERS

(pound sign)
    DOS executable command (NetWare), 262–263, **521**
    preceding a key word in MAKEUSER utility, 215, 472
$ to denote system file, 132, 332
% (percent sign)
    in menu system, 272
    preceding identifier variables in login scripts, 254, 513
* (asterisk)
    remark symbol in NetWare, 261
    wildcard in DOS, 55, 57
.. (periods) to denote parent directory, 444, 464
/ (slash)
    to identify switches in DOS commands, 56
    to separate file server name and volume in path, 136, 338
: (colon)
    as console prompt, 222, 476
    to distinguish root of volume, 136, 338
\ (backslash)
    to denote root directory, 444, 464
    to precede directory name in path, 56, 136, 338

^ (caret) preceding text to force a different MENU commandoption, 536
| (pipe symbol), 64

A

abbreviations, full versions of, 777–784
access rights, **398–414**, 435–436
    Access Control (A), 162, 273, 401
    Create (C), 162, 276, 401
    Directory level of. *See* maximum rights mask (MRM)
    Erase (E), 162, 276, 400
    File Scan (F), 162, 273, 276, 401, 409, 533
    Modify (M), 162, 273, 276, 401, 409, 425
    in NetWare 2.2, 157–158, 160–170
    in NetWare 3.12, 369–371, 395–411
    Read (R), 162, 273, 276, 401, 409
    required for common NetWare activities, *163*, 398–399
    Supervisor (S) (NetWare 3.12 only), 400, 409–411

D

E

G

H

M

information screens on, 657–661
loading, 647
main screen in, *489*, 646–653
operating system module information from, *660,* 660–661
option categories for, 646–647
performance management and monitoring with, 322, 482, 562, 631, **645–663**
processor utilization information from, 661–663
resource tracking with, *485*, 653–656
server NIC information from, 659–660
service processes information from, 652–653
utilization information from, 648
viewing workstation connection numbers with, 224, 481
watchdog parameter in, 667–668
worm screen saver in, 647–648
MONITOR.NLM, FCONSOLE facilities incorporated in, 377
MORE command (DOS), 64, 76
Motorola
as major microprocessor manufacturer, 8–9
MC68000 first chip by, 13–14
MC68020 chip by, 14
MC68030 chip by, 14–15
MC68040 chip by, 15
MC68HC000 chip by, 14
MOUNT command (NetWare), 480
mouse support in DOS, 60
MS-DOS, 50–51. *See also* DOS (disk operating system)
multiprocessing, 14–15

multi-protocol management, 543–553
multitasking, 10
multi-user compatibility, 267–268, 531

N

NAME command (NetWare), 229, 485
name space
backing up OS/2, 541
backing up UNIX, 541
memory requirements for, 644
NLMs for, 488
purpose of, 644
support of non-DOS, 544, 558
named pipes, 551
NBACKUP utility (NetWare), 276, 495, 541
features of, 541
NetWare 3.11 support of, 555
rules for using, 542
NCOPY utility (NetWare), 182–183, 268, 342, 425–426, 532
NCP Packet Signature feature, **395–397**
customizing, 396
levels of, 396, 397
process for, 395–396
NDIR command (NetWare), 138–139, 341, 343, 501–502
NETBIOS, 551
NetWare
exercise for understanding (Exercise 2.1), 115, 745
installing, **786–793**

operating system. *See* individual systems

operator accounts, 373–374, 376–378

optimization
file server, 622, 663–681
memory pool, 642
performance. *See* performance management
printing, 583–584, 598, **600–604**

organizational menu commands, 535–536

OS/2
connectivity for, 551
names for, storing, 488
NetWare support of, 114, 321, 529
ODI implementation for, 551
as operating system, 50

OS/2 Requester, 114, 266, 529, 551
OSI model, datalink layer of, 544
OSI protocols, 321, 544
output, displaying a screenful of, 64

P

packet bursting to improve server performance, 395

packets
defined, 631
maximum physical size of, 667
unique signature for, preventing hacking using, 395–397
watchdog, 667–668

parent directory, .. to denote, 444, 464

parity, setting a modem's, 48

Park Place analogy, 681
performance management compared to interior decoration in, 622–623, 645–646
print management compared to hotel chef in, 568, 576–577
security features in, 366–368
system manager's duties compared to hotel manager's duties in, 324–325, 494–496
utility tools compared to hotel handyman in, 448–449

password(s)
changing, 387
encrypting, 380
entering, 130
expiration of, 260–261, 387
of fewer than five characters, flagging, 210
forcing changes to, 221, 241–242, 387–388, 434–435
options for, 380
print queue, 207
requiring, 221, 240, 386, 434
RMF, 563–563
routine for guessing, 241
setting, 175, 419
table of, 242
tracking attempts to enter invalid, 247–248, 393
unique, requiring, 242, 387–388

PATH command (DOS), 60–61, 64, 77, 146, 503

path names, NetWare directory, 135–136, 338–339

paths in DOS, 58

PAUDIT utility (NetWare), 194, 210

PAUSE command (DOS), 59

changing configuration information of, 209
displaying configuration for, 224,
485
function of, 791
installing, 791–793, 799–800
print server on top of, 293, 304–
310
routing, internal, 96
RPRINTER utility (NetWare), 314–
315, 595–596, 613
RS232 NLM, 567
RS232 standard, 49
RSPX NLM, 484

S

Saber, Inc., 535–536
SALVAGE utility (NetWare), 229,
416, 473, 473–474
SBACKUP utility (NetWare), 495,
541
backup strategies supported by,
556–557, 557
exiting, 559
features of, 556–557
NetWare 3.11 and 3.12 support
of, 555
rules for using, 557–558
steps for backing up NetWare
with, 558–561
steps for restoring data with, 560–
561
screen
capturing data from, 138
clearing, 62, 75

displaying file contents on, 66,
138
screen console commands, 477–479
script
login. *See* login scripts
MAKEUSER, 217
programming for, 258, 517
system login. *See* system login
script
user login, 250–251, 271, 333,
509–510, 517
script files, user, 215–217
SEARCH command (NetWare), 506
search lists of directories
adding path to NetWare, 146–147
building, 58, 64, 144, 506
finding applications in, 143
maximum search drives in, 143
sequence of, 144
SECURE CONSOLE utility (Net-
Ware), 505–506
security. *See* network security
security attributes, 371
copy inhibit (C) (NetWare 3.12
only), 413–415
delete inhibit (D) (NetWare 3.12
only), 413–414
execute only (X), 171–172, 413–
414
hidden (H), 171–172, 413–414,
416
non-sharable (NS), 171, 413–
414, 416
read/only (RO), 171–172, 269,
413–414, 416, 532
read/write (RW), 171–172, 269,
413–414, 416, 532
rename inhibit (R) (NetWare
3.12 only), 413–414

T

W

X

Novell's CNA Study Guide

GET A FREE CATALOG JUST FOR EXPRESSING YOUR OPINION.

Help us improve our books and get a *FREE* full-color catalog in the bargain. Please complete this form, pull out this page and send it in today. The address is on the reverse side.

Name _____   Company _____

Address _____   City _____ State ____ Zip _____

Phone ( ) _____

1. How would you rate the overall quality of this book?

❑ Excellent
❑ Very Good
❑ Good
❑ Fair
❑ Below Average
❑ Poor

2. What were the things you liked most about the book? (Check all that apply)

❑ Pace
❑ Format
❑ Writing Style
❑ Examples
❑ Table of Contents
❑ Index
❑ Price
❑ Illustrations
❑ Type Style
❑ Cover
❑ Depth of Coverage
❑ Fast Track Notes

3. What were the things you liked *least* about the book? (Check all that apply)

❑ Pace
❑ Format
❑ Writing Style
❑ Examples
❑ Table of Contents
❑ Index
❑ Price
❑ Illustrations
❑ Type Style
❑ Cover
❑ Depth of Coverage
❑ Fast Track Notes

4. Where did you buy this book?

❑ Bookstore chain
❑ Small independent bookstore
❑ Computer store
❑ Wholesale club
❑ College bookstore
❑ Technical bookstore
❑ Other _____

5. How did you decide to buy this particular book?

❑ Recommended by friend
❑ Recommended by store personnel
❑ Author's reputation
❑ Sybex's reputation
❑ Read book review in _____
❑ Other _____

6. How did you pay for this book?

❑ Used own funds
❑ Reimbursed by company
❑ Received book as a gift

7. What is your level of experience with the subject covered in this book?

❑ Beginner
❑ Intermediate
❑ Advanced

8. How long have you been using a computer?

years _____
months _____

9. Where do you most often use your computer?

❑ Home
❑ Work

❑ Both
❑ Other _____

10. What kind of computer equipment do you have? (Check all that apply)

❑ PC Compatible Desktop Computer
❑ PC Compatible Laptop Computer
❑ Apple/Mac Computer
❑ Apple/Mac Laptop Computer
❑ CD ROM
❑ Fax Modem
❑ Data Modem
❑ Scanner
❑ Sound Card
❑ Other _____

11. What other kinds of software packages do you ordinarily use?

❑ Accounting
❑ Databases
❑ Networks
❑ Apple/Mac
❑ Desktop Publishing
❑ Spreadsheets
❑ CAD
❑ Games
❑ Word Processing
❑ Communications
❑ Money Management
❑ Other _____

12. What operating systems do you ordinarily use?

❑ DOS
❑ OS/2
❑ Windows
❑ Apple/Mac
❑ Windows NT
❑ Other _____

13. On what computer-related subject(s) would you like to see more books?

_____

_____

_____

14. Do you have any other comments about this book? (Please feel free to use a separate piece of paper if you need more room)

_____

_____

_____

_____

PLEASE FOLD, SEAL, AND MAIL TO SYBEX

SYBEX INC.
Department M
2021 Challenger Drive
Alameda, CA
94501

Disk Installation

For complete instructions on installing these disks on your computer, please refer to Appendix G of this book.

DISK CONTENTS

Companion Disk 1 contains CNA practice tests that are similar in format to actual CNA/CNE certification exams, and an electronic version of the most recent NetWare Buyer's Guide. Companion Disk 2 is a simulation of the actual NetWare installation process.

HOW CAN I GET 5¼" DISKS?

Send $5.00, plus proof of purchase, and your written request to:

 SYBEX Inc.
Customer Service Department
2021 Challenger Drive
Alameda, CA 94501
(800) 227-2346

Please include your name, complete mailing address, and the following reference number: 1139-4. Without the reference number, your request cannot be processed. Please allow six weeks for delivery.